PATRICK J. TAYLOR AND MARTIN M

GRADING FOR THE FASHION INDUSTRY

THE THEORY AND PRACTICE

SECOND EDITION
WITH CHILDREN'S AND MEN'S WEAR

LCFS
fashion media

To our wives - Maureen and Jenny

Text © Patrick J. Taylor and Martin M. Shoben 1984, 1990

All rights reserved. No part of this publication may be reproduced or transmitted in any form or by any means, electronic or mechanical, including photocopy, recording, or any information storage and retrieval system, without permission in writing from the publisher or under licence from the Copyright Licensing Agency Limited. Further details of such licences (for reprographic reproduction) may be obtained from the Copyright Licensing Agency Limited, of 90 Tottenham Court Road, London W1P 9HE.

First published in 1984 by Hutchinson Education

Second Edition published in 1990 by:
Stanley Thornes (Publishers) Ltd

Third Edition published in 2000 by LCFS Fashion Media
78 White Lion Street , Islington
London N1 9PF
Telephone: 020 7713 1991
E-mail: Learnf@shion.demon.co.uk
www.lcfsfashionmedia.com

Grading for the Fashion Industry
ISBN 0953 2395 01

British Library Cataloguing in Publication Data

Other Books by the same Author:
Pattern Cutting & Making Up the Professional Approach
ISBN 07506 0364 X

Pattern Cutting & Making Up Outerwear Fashion
ISBN 07506 21389

Art of Dress Modelling
ISBN 0953 2395 00

Printed and bound in Great Britain by Redwood Books

Contents

Acknowledgements		4
Preface		5
Introduction		7
Abbreviations		8

Part One The Theory and Principles of Grading

1	Women's sizing and surveys	11
2	Women's grading increments reference	27
3	Area commentaries	48
4	Selecting a grading system	57
5	Stands	60
6	Special areas	65
7	Computer grading	70
8	Brassiere grading	75
9	The principles of bifurcated grading	81

Part Two General Grading Techniques

10	Draft grading the basic blocks	87
11	Selecting a zero point	98
12	From draft to finished sizes	113
13	Multi-track grading	117
14	Track grading – a simplified two-dimensional system	124

Part Three Women's Style Grading

15	Introduction	135
16	Style grades 1 to 33	137

Part Four Men's Grading

17	Men's classical and fashion wear grading	241
18	Trouser grading	243
19	Jacket grading	245
20	Shirt sizing and grading	251
21	Man's waistcoat	254

Part Five Children's Wear

22	Children's grading and size charts	259
Index		287

Acknowledgements

We would like to thank Philip Kunick, Michael Thomas and our editors Brian Carvell and Tania Hackett for their help in preparing this new edition.

Preface

This book was conceived in 1982 when Patrick realised that a serious in-depth study of grading had never been attempted. Our intention was to redress this serious technical omission by writing a book that would bring together all the various principles that constitute grading, so that students and practitioners alike could have a body of knowledge to refer to. *Grading for the Fashion Industry* was first published in 1984 and has since been reprinted three times. Five years on we are very pleased to be provided with the opportunity to revise our original work.

In revising our book we have been careful to retain much of the original text and illustrations adding clarifications and selected amendments where necessary. However, the scope of this new edition has been broadened by adding children's wear and men's wear size charts, styles and grade plans. *Grading for the Fashion Industry* is now a much fuller, more comprehensive manual.

Patrick J. Taylor and Martin M. Shoben

Introduction

This book has two aims. The first is to open up the subject of grading and to reveal some of the underlying principles which govern and give rise to the many grading formulae and instructions found in varying forms within the industry. The second is to offer a practical reference manual for style grading.

This field of study is fairly complex, but can be interesting and absorbing. There is more involved than just following a set of instructions for moving a pattern piece on a sheet of paper. Unfortunately, grading is dismissed as understood once a set of instructions has been learned, and accepted with little questioning of its origin.

The pattern technician (a term which, in this book, refers to an experienced pattern cutter) should be responsible for all aspects of pattern cutting which *includes grading*. However, as the pattern technician's time is usually occupied by other concerns, grading is delegated by way of a set of instructions to an assistant, called 'the grader', who has to be highly accurate and who is responsible for the final graded production pattern. It is true to say, however, that good graders are very rare and are therefore worth looking after because, as they gain knowledge of pattern cutting, they tend to desert the grading field.

The techniques put forward in this book represent a fresh approach to grading based on firm foundations. *The details can always be argued about, particularly when dealing with statistics*, but the underlying principles are irrefutable. So it is hoped that the principles may be understood first and then the technicians are free to devise their own techniques, suitable to their circumstances. This book has been written in response to the definite demand for a work on this subject. We hope we have satisfied that demand.

Patrick J. Taylor and Martin M. Shoben

Abbreviations

CB   centre back
CF   centre front
cm   centimetres
mm   millimetres

Note
**All size chart data is in centimetres.
All grading increments on patterns are in millimetres.**

Examples
centimetres: 1.0 cm or 0.9 cm
millimetres: 10 mm or 9 mm

PART ONE

The Theory and Principles of Grading

CHAPTER 1

Women's sizing and surveys

The problem of sizing arose with the development of the production of ready-made 'off-the-peg' garments at the turn of this century. If manufacturers were to cater for public demand in this way, a detailed investigation of the range of sizes within a country was needed. It was a long time before any serious efforts were made in this direction, but in 1940 a survey was set up in the United States to measure the American female. This survey covered a sample of 10,000 women using sixty measurements. A similar survey was carried out in the United Kingdom in 1950 using a sample of 5000 adult females and thirty-seven measurements. Other surveys have been undertaken in Europe, but the main surveys have been the American and British surveys. These produced very similar results and are now the main source of data for sizing and grading systems in these two countries.

The data and results of the British survey were published in a book called *Women's Measurements and Sizes* by W. F. F. Kemsley (HMSO 1957). In this book there are comments and a number of comparisons with the American survey, and also with the Dutch and the Ministry of Food surveys. One of the main results of the survey was that it produced a set of measurements for the 'statistically average woman'.

This average figure, therefore, represents the highest percentage of the population, and radiating out from it are progressively rarer combinations. The survey team recommended the categorization of the survey sizing data in the form of several size charts. These were arrived at by taking three height and six bust categories with approximately eight hip sizes of 5.0 cm increment in each (as in Table 1), which gives a total of 126 sizes spread over sixteen categories of size charts.

Table 2 shows the sizes and percentage of population in each category, totalling 98 per cent

Table 1 126 sizes recommended by the survey to cover 98 per cent of the population

Bust girth in relation to hip girth		Short 150.0 cm	Medium 160.0 cm	Tall 170.0 cm
15.0 cm smaller than hip	Very small bust	5 sizes	6 sizes	5 sizes
10.0 cm smaller than hip	Small bust	8 sizes	8 sizes	7 sizes
5.0 cm smaller than hip	Medium bust	10 sizes	11 sizes	8 sizes
Same as hip	Full bust	10 sizes	11 sizes	8 sizes
5.0 cm larger than hip	Large bust	9 sizes	10 sizes	5 sizes
10.0 cm larger than hip	Extra large bust	—	5 sizes	—

Table 2 Sizes and percentage of the population in each category, totalling 98 per cent of the population

Bust	Short 150.0 cm	Medium 160.0 cm	Tall 170.0 cm
Very small bust	12–20 (1%)	12–22 (3%)	14–22 (2%)
Small bust	10–24 (5%)	10–24 (12%)	12–24 (5%)
Medium bust	8–26 (9%)	8–28 (20%)	10–24 (7%)
Full bust	8–26 (7%)	8–28 (14%)	10–24 (4%)
Large bust	8–24 (2%)	8–26 (5%)	10–18 (1%)
Extra large bust	—	12–20 (1%)	—

Table 3 Reduced table of sixty-three sizes covering 80 per cent of the population

	Short	Medium	Tall
Small bust	Size 10–22	Size 10–22	Size 10–22
Medium bust	Size 10–22	Size 10–22	Size 10–22
Full bust	Size 10–22	Size 10–22	Size 10–22

of the population. The other 2 per cent of the population are considered, by statistical standards, to be outside the normal range and are discarded in order not to distort the final results.

The sixteen categories can be reduced to nine and the number of sizes reduced, thereby discarding the less populated areas, as shown in Table 3.

Table 3 illustrates the reduced categories with seven sizes in each, totalling sixty-three sizes.

Table 4 shows the percentage of population per hip size and three bust categories covering all heights.

It follows that the sixty-three sizes in Table 4 cover 83 per cent of the population, and are valuable as a guide and reference to all clothing manufacturers.

For detailed information it is advisable to obtain the survey book but there is always the danger of getting lost in statistical analyses. It is for this reason that we have commented only briefly on the survey in this book, but as a subject in its own right it can be quite absorbing.

Finally it must be noted that the survey covered a wide range of ages from 18 to 65 years. The data was divided into three age categories:

1. 18 to 29 years
2. 30 to 44 years
3. 45 to 65 years

The size charts in this book are for all the age groups combined. Table 5 gives a complete list of measurements showing the statistically average figure for each age group.

BASIC SIZE CHARTS

The size charts in the survey provide vital information which enables manufacturers to select and cater for specific areas of the population. It is obvious that the whole population cannot be covered by a single manufacturer and it is even more impossible for a retailer to stock such a vast range of sizes. This must be qualified, however, by saying, first, that the type of garment will have a great influence on the number of sizes required and, second, the type of material will also affect the sizing. A loose fitting garment will not require as many sizes as a skin-tight garment, and a woven fabric will require more tolerances than a stretch fabric, and will therefore influence the number of sizes needed.

Another aspect of the situation is the number of styles needed. If only a single style is required, a manufacturer and retailer would find it economic to stock a greater range of sizes. Conversely, if many styles are required the opposite applies. This, in turn, is affected by the number of different colours and material designs used.

To narrow down options available, a manufacturer will usually select a limited area of the market and cater only for that area. Having decided on the area, the next step is to construct a basic size chart for that market. The market will be chosen by:

1. The age group
2. The figure size
3. The type of garment

The first step in constructing a size chart is to decide the increments between the sizes of the major girth which is selected to be the size indicator or code. Where there is a hip girth in the garment it is generally used as the code, otherwise the bust girth is used – except in brassiere manufacturing when the rib-cage girth is used. It is more convenient if the difference between sizes is constant.

Table 4 The percentages of population per hip size in three bust categories covering all heights

Size	10	12	14	16	18	20	22	Total
Hip cm	87.0	92.0	97.0	102.0	107.0	112.0	117.0	
Small bust %	0.9	4.0	6.4	5.4	3.2	1.5	1.0	22.4
Medium bust %	3.1	8.6	10.0	7.2	4.0	1.9	1.1	35.9
Full bust %	3.0	6.2	6.3	4.4	2.5	1.3	1.0	24.7
Total %	7.0	18.8	22.7	17.0	9.7	4.7	3.1	83.0

WOMEN'S SIZING AND SURVEYS

Table 5 Statistical averages by age

Area		Age categories 18–29	30–44	45–64
1	Height	161.0	160.0	157.5
2	Weight (pounds)	126.6	134.5	143.8
3	Hip	95.0	97.5	102.4
4	Bust	89.5	93.0	99.0
5	Waist	64.0	68.9	76.4
6	Chest	84.0	86.4	90.0
7	Top hip (11.0 cm from waist)	85.0	88.8	95.3
8	Rib cage	nil	nil	nil
9	Neck	38.0	38.5	39.0
10	Bicep	27.6	28.9	30.4
11	Elbow	nil	nil	nil
12	Wrist	nil	nil	nil
13	Thigh	nil	nil	nil
14	Knee	35.0	35.4	36.0
15	Calf	33.5	34.0	34.5
16	Ankle	nil	nil	nil
17	X-chest	31.8	32.5	33.3
18	X-back	33.3	34.0	34.7
19	Shoulder length	11.7	11.7	11.7
20	Scye width	11.4	11.9	12.4
21	Scye depth	18.4	18.8	19.2
22	Bust width	19.5	20.0	21.0
23	Nape to bust	34.8	36.0	39.0
24	Nape to waist over bust	52.0	52.0	52.0
25	Nape to waist centre back	38.2	37.8	37.0
26	Nape to hip	60.0	59.5	58.0
27	Nape to knee	95.6	95.0	93.8
28	Nape to floor	137.8	137.0	135.0
29	Sleeve length (outer)	58.4	58.0	57.7
30	Sleeve length (inner)	44.8	44.2	43.2
31	Abdominal seat diameter	24.0	25.4	27.9
32	Hip width	33.0	33.7	34.9
33	Body rise	29.0	29.7	30.9
34	Shoulder angle (degrees)	20.2	20.2	20.7

Table 6 Basic size chart hip increments

Size	10	12	14	16	18	20	22	Increment
Hip	87	92	97	102	107	112	117	5.0 cm

The sizes and increments must come within the recommended British Standards BS 3666 (see pages 21–5). The general practice in the past has been to use 2 in, but now its equivalents, 5.0 cm and 50 mm, are used. However, in some cases, in order to remain within the Standard, a 4.0 cm or a 6.0 cm increment is used for some sizes, or a mixture of all three can be used, keeping, if possible, to a constant increment, especially over a 10–22 size range.

The British Standard is very flexible. Its aim is to ensure that, for example, a size 12 shall be within a certain minimum and maximum measurement. Basically it gives a scope of 4.0 cm between the smallest and largest hip and bust within a size, which, therefore, means that a size may vary considerably. In addition, the garment's inbuilt tolerances may increase the variations within a size still further. The Standard is, therefore, fairly flexible. The main reason for this is that it must enable the manufacturer to cater for the population as a whole, which, as we have seen, consists of nine major size categories, and this is why the Standard only quotes hip, bust and height measurements. (If a tighter Standard was required, then a Standard for each of the nine categories would be needed.) Most manufacturers will, however, select the area of the market that offers the richest rewards. This area, size wise, is immediately around the statistically average figure, as can be seen by studying Tables 2 and 4. The majority of the population are either size 12, 14 or 16 in the medium height range, and this accounts for the fact that many shops only stock these sizes. It is also the reason why the state of grading in industry is so limited because, only having to operate over a range of three sizes, the crudest methods of grading can be used. It must be said that this is not the case in all sections of the industry; some areas have a very high degree of grading expertise, particularly in outerwear.

Table 6 shows the hip sizes and increments that have been chosen to form the basis of the size chart used in this book. The hip sizes have been selected because they are typical of the clothing industry. This basic chart gives a 5.0 cm constant increment and conforms to the British Standard. These hip sizes are roughly in the middle range of the Standard. A few alternative examples are given in Table 7 with non-constant increments. Table 7 also shows examples of hip sizes which conform to British Standards and illustrates the difference between the sizes, or the increments, as they are known by the grader.

HEIGHT ANALYSIS

The next factor to be considered in the basic size chart is height, i.e., which height to cater for and what height increase there should be between sizes, if any. The survey divided the population into three basic height groups:

1. Short – below 160.0 cm
2. Medium – from 160.0 – 170.0 cm
3. Tall – above 170.0 cm

The manufacturer has to choose which height group to cater for. It is not possible to cover the whole height range in one size chart and, there-

Table 7 Examples of basic size chart hip increments, which conform to BS 3666, including increments of 4.0 and 6.0 cm

	\multicolumn{7}{c}{Size}
	10	12	14	16	18	20	22
Hip	87.0	92.0	97.0	102.0	107.0	112.0	117.0
Increment	5.0	5.0	5.0	5.0	5.0	5.0	—
Hip	88.0	92.0	96.0	100.0	104.0	110.0	116.0
Increment	4.0	4.0	4.0	4.0	6.0	6.0	—
Hip	87.0	91.0	95.0	100.0	105.0	110.0	115.0
Increment	4.0	4.0	5.0	5.0	5.0	5.0	—
Hip	87.0	93.0	99.0	104.0	109.0	114.0	119.0
Increment	6.0	6.0	5.0	5.0	5.0	5.0	—
Hip	89.0	94.0	99.0	104.0	109.0	114.0	119.0
Increment	5.0	5.0	5.0	5.0	5.0	5.0	—
Hip	88.0	92.0	96.0	100.0	105.0	110.0	115.0
Increment	4.0	4.0	4.0	5.0	5.0	5.0	—
Hip	90.0	94.0	98.0	102.0	106.0	110.0	115.0
Increment	4.0	4.0	4.0	4.0	4.0	5.0	—
Hip	87.0	91.0	96.0	101.0	106.0	111.0	116.0
Increment	4.0	5.0	5.0	5.0	5.0	5.0	—

fore, most manufacturers gravitate towards the statistical average. Table 8 shows the distribution of the population according to their height, and it gives the manufacturer an idea of the numbers that can be expected in the market that has been chosen.

It should be noted that the British Standard requires an indication of height group on garment labelling; a prefix 'S' for short and 'T' for tall. No prefix is required for the medium height group.

Another consideration is whether or not to incorporate height in the size chart, that is, whether to increase height with girth. The survey indicates that height does not increase with girth and so, according to the conclusions of the survey, height should not increase with size. However, many manufacturers would argue that if the height increases with girth then the market will widen and more of the population can be served because a garment can be shortened if too long. It is more difficult to lengthen a garment unless, of course, large hems are included, but this is not always possible. These decisions must, however, be made by the individual companies.

In the early 1950s, when the survey data was first used, it seemed that the nape to waist measurement indicated in the survey was too short. In fact the average measurement given was correct but the percentage with a longer nape to waist measurement was not catered for. This led to a loss of sales because a short nape to waist is almost certain to be rejected, whereas a garment which is too long can be sold quite easily by experienced staff, either by offering to shorten the garment or by quickly introducing a blouson effect! This led manufacturers to lengthen the nape to waist measurement to around 40.0 cm for size 12 and to grade a 0.6 cm height increment per size. So it will be found that most size 12 stands and size charts are designed for this length of bodice. This brings into focus an important corner-stone of grading. It is possible to grade for:

1 Girth only
2 Height only
3 Girth and height combined

This is discussed more fully on pages 18–19.

For the purposes of this book combined height and girth grades are used on the sample styles throughout, except for one example of height only.

HEIGHT GRADE

To introduce height, the increase between sizes has to be distributed evenly over the whole figure. This is borne out by the survey. Some may argue that more must go into the leg than the torso, or vice versa. However, it has been the practice to divide the body into eight equal parts and aportion an eighth of the height increase to each. This

Table 8 Distribution of population by height

Height	Number in sample	Percentage	Population in millions
Under 145.0 cm	39	1	0.1
145.0 and 147.0 cm	273	6	1.0
150.0 and 152.0 cm	798	18	2.9
155.0 and 157.0 cm	1176	28	4.4
160.0 and 162.0 cm	1206	28	4.4
165.0 and 167.0 cm	584	13	2.2
170.0 and 172.0 cm	217	5	0.8
175.0 cm and above	56	1	0.2
Totals	4349	100	16.0

WOMEN'S SIZING AND SURVEYS

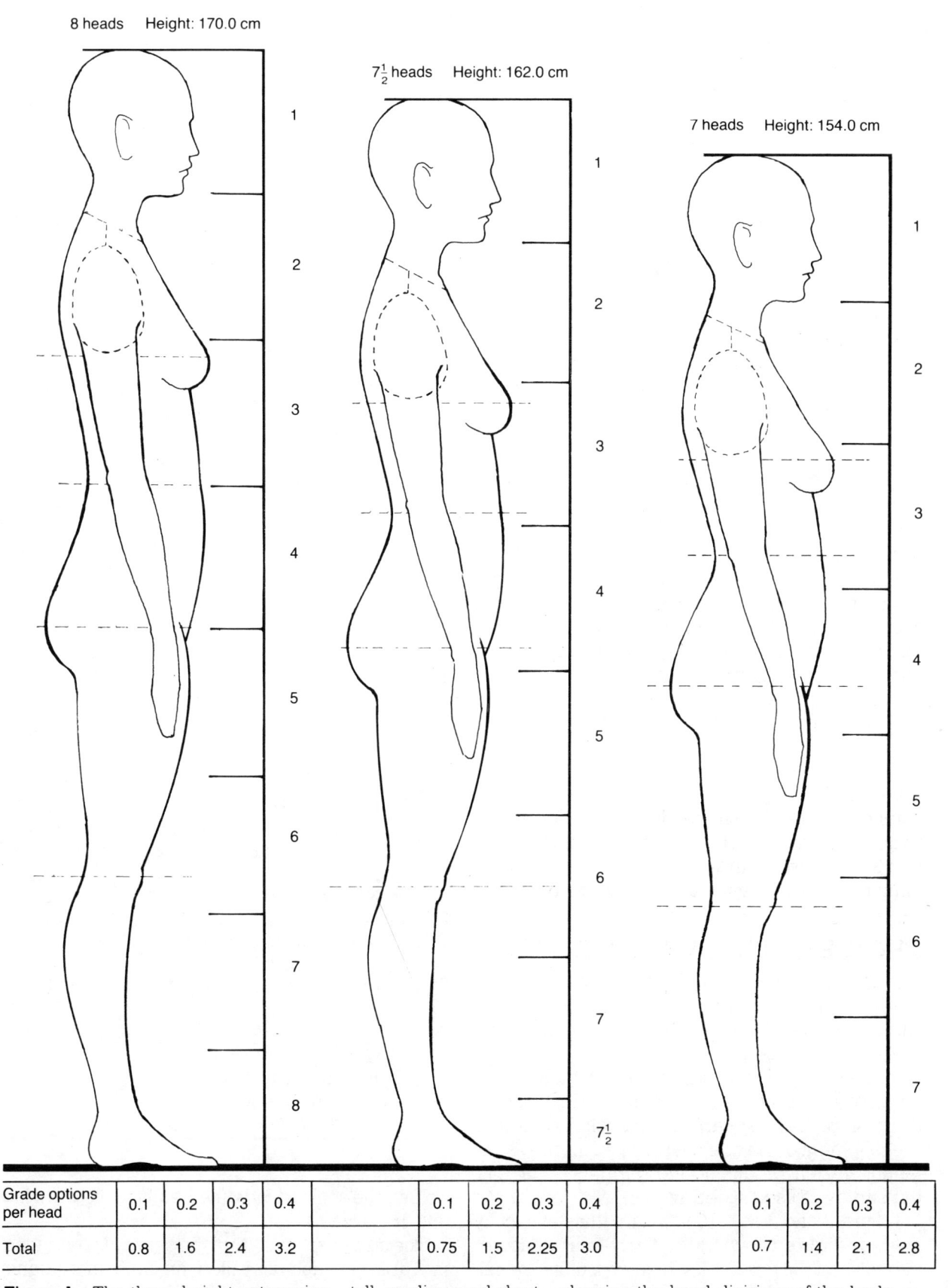

Grade options per head	0.1	0.2	0.3	0.4		0.1	0.2	0.3	0.4		0.1	0.2	0.3	0.4
Total	0.8	1.6	2.4	3.2		0.75	1.5	2.25	3.0		0.7	1.4	2.1	2.8

Figure 1 The three height categories – tall, medium and short – showing the head divisions of the body

Table 9 Basic size chart (used as the basis of the size chart for this book)

Size	10S	12	14	16	18	20T	22T	Increment
Height	159.6	162.0	164.4	166.8	169.2	171.6	173.0	2.4
Hip	87.0	92.0	97.0	102.0	107.0	112.0	117.0	5.0
Bust	82.0	87.0	92.0	97.0	102.0	107.0	112.0	5.0
Waist	60.0	65.0	70.0	75.0	80.0	85.0	90.0	5.0

practice had its origin in the imperial measurement system where an eighth of an inch was widely used and an eighth of body height roughly coincided with the size of the head, and the measurement from the top of the head to the waist was, conveniently, three-eighths of body height. As a matter of interest, the head only goes into the height eight times in the tall group where the height is above average. In Figure 1 the three height groups are illustrated to show the relationship between the head and other body proportions. Note that these drawings are to scale and that the head remains a constant size.

Height increase

Figure 1 shows three figure categories with height grade increment options. For this book the eight head figure has been selected with an overall increment of 2.4 cm per size. This amount corresponds to the 1 in increment which was widely used under the imperial system, although there is no logical reason for it to be adopted other than convention.

Note: If 2.4 cm is used, the height range will extend into the British Standard tall range in the larger sizes and short range in size 10. The total height increase is thus divided into eight equal parts of 0.3 cm for each area of the body.

CHOICE OF BUST AND WAIST SIZE

The bust used is medium, that is 5.0 cm less than the hip. There is, once again, a choice of three categories (see Table 3). The waist chosen is an average one based on the survey statistics.

Table 9 is the final basic size chart which is used for sales and retail requirements, and is used as the basis of the size chart for this book. The further development of the size chart will be for the use of technical staff producing the garments. For this, the survey is used extensively.

Figure 2 and Table 10 illustrate the statistically average figure showing the thirty-four measurements used for this book which constitute the full size chart. The drawings in Figure 2 are to scale.

Table 10 Measurements of the statistically average woman

Area		
1	Height	159.5
2	Weight (pounds)	130.5
3	Hip	98.8
4	Bust	94.2
5	Waist	70.3
6	Chest	87.0
7	Top hip (11.0 cm from waist)	90.2
8	Rib cage (under bust)	—
9	Neck	38.3
10	Bicep	29.2
11	Elbow	—
12	Wrist	—
13	Thigh	—
14	Knee	35.5
15	Calf	34.5
16	Ankle	—
17	X-chest	32.5
18	X-back	34.0
19	Shoulder length	11.7
20	Scye width	12.0
21	Scye depth	19.0
22	Bust width	20.3
23	Nape to bust	36.0
24	Nape to waist over bust	52.0
25	Nape to waist centre back	37.8
26	Nape to hip	59.5
27	Nape to knee	95.0
28	Nape to floor	137.0
29	Sleeve length (outer)	56.0
30	Sleeve length (inner)	44.0
31	Abdominal seat diameter	25.6
32	Hip width	33.4
33	Body rise	30.0
34	Shoulder angle (degrees)	20.5
	Body measurements: no tolerances added to any chart data	

To find the scale, divide the height of the drawing into 160.0 cm.

The size chart data from the survey is produced in Table 11, and is called an area increments chart.

WOMEN'S SIZING AND SURVEYS 17

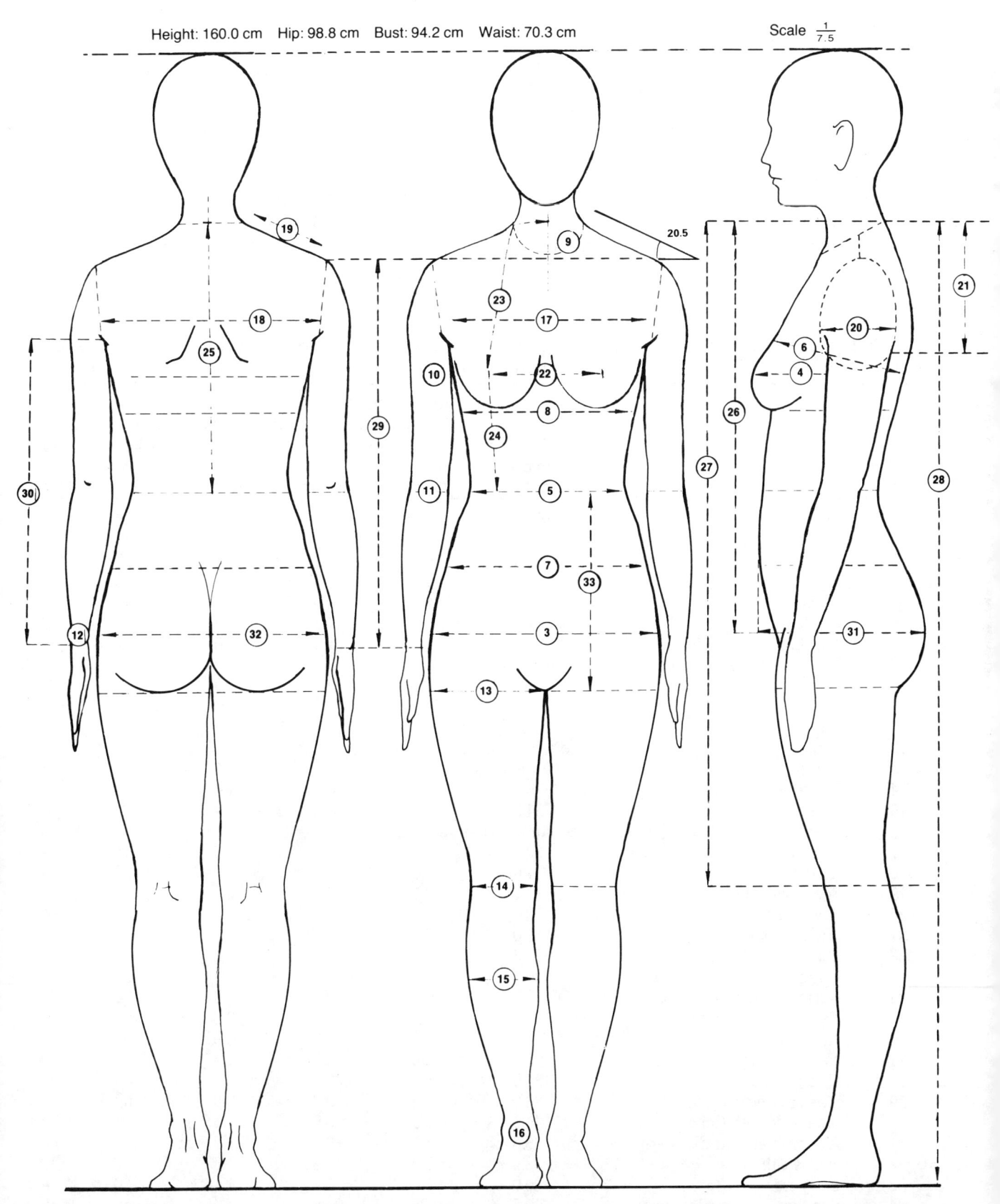

Height: 160.0 cm   Hip: 98.8 cm   Bust: 94.2 cm   Waist: 70.3 cm   Scale $\frac{1}{7.5}$

Figure 2 Scale illustration of the statistically average woman based on the British survey (see Table 10)

AREA INCREMENTS CHART

Table 11 is compiled directly from the survey data and comprises thirty-four measurements in the first column and uses the average figure data from Table 10 (which corresponds to a size 14). The second column shows increments for grading of girth only. The third column shows increments for grading of height only and the fourth column gives the sum of the previous two columns which results in increments used for grading height and girth together. The fifth and sixth columns explain how the girth and height increments are arrived at based on percentages obtained from the survey relating to hip and height. These percentages indicate the required girth and height increase for any of the thirty-four measurements in relation to the change in hip girth. As a 5.0 cm hip and 2.4 cm height has been chosen for the size chart then all the percentages will use these two figures to give the increase needed for one size.

Example: To find the neck increment
For girth only increase
14 per cent of 5.0 cm = 0.7 cm
For height only increase
8 per cent of 2.4 cm = 0.2 cm
Total for girth and height = 0.9 cm

Table 11 Area increments table based on survey data for the statistically average figure. Body measurements: increments are based on an increase of 5.0 cm girth and 2.4 cm height

Area		Statistic average figure	Increments for 5.0 cm girth and 2.4 cm height Girth	Height	Girth and height	Percentage increase related to hip and height Girth	Height
1	Height	159.5	nil	2.4	2.4	nil	100
2	Weight (pounds)	130.5	12.5	3.5	16	nil	nil
3	Hip	98.8	5.0	nil	5.0	100	nil
4	Bust	94.2	4.6	−0.2	4.4	92	−8
5	Waist	70.3	4.8	−0.5	4.3	98	−20
6	Chest	87.0	3.3	0.1	3.4	66	2
7	Top hip (11.0 cm from waist)	90.2	5.0	nil	5.0	100	nil
8	Rib cage (under bust)	no survey data					
9	Neck	38.3	0.7	0.2	0.9	14	8
10	Bicep	29.2	1.7	−0.1	1.6	34	−4
11	Elbow	no survey data					
12	Wrist	no survey data					
13	Thigh	no survey data					
14	Knee	35.5	1.2	0.2	1.4	24	8
15	Calf	34.5	1.2	0.2	1.4	24	8
16	Ankle	no survey data					
17	X-chest	32.5	0.8	0.1	0.9	16	4
18	X-back	34.0	1.0	0.1	1.1	20	4
19	Shoulder length	11.7	0.1	0.1	0.2	2	4
20	Scye width	12.0	0.7	−0.1	0.6	14	−4
21	Scye depth	19.0	0.4	0.1	0.5	8	4
22	Bust width	20.3	1.0	0.2	1.2	20	8
23	Nape to bust	36.0	1.3	0.1	1.4	28	4
24	Nape to waist over bust	52.0	0.6	0.6	1.2	12	24
25	Nape to waist centre back	37.8	nil	0.6	0.6	nil	24
26	Nape to hip	59.5	nil	0.9	0.9	nil	36
27	Nape to knee	95.0	nil	1.5	1.5	nil	60
28	Nape to floor	137.0	nil	2.1	2.1	nil	84
29	Sleeve length (outer)	56.0	nil	0.8	0.8	nil	32
30	Sleeve length (inner)	44.0	−0.3	0.6	0.3	−6	24
31	Abdominal seat diameter	25.6	1.9	−0.2	1.7	38	−8
32	Hip width	33.4	1.3	0.3	1.6	26	10
33	Body rise	30.0	1.0	0.1	1.1	20	4
34	Shoulder angle (degrees)	20.5	−0.25	0.25	0	nil	nil

WOMEN'S SIZING AND SURVEYS

Therefore, 7 mm is the size increment of the neck for a 5.0 cm hip increase on a girth only grade, and 2 mm is the size increment of the neck for a 2.4 cm increase on a height only grade. When grading for girth and height the two are added together, making 9 mm. The increments in this chart are inconvenient because they are odd quantities. For grading purposes it is better to round them off in order to make their application easier.

Table 12 is the area increments chart adapted from Table 11 by streamlining the measurements, and yet retaining the accuracy needed for an advanced system of grading.

Table 13 is the full size chart arrived at from the area increments chart for girth and height combined. This is the chart which will be used throughout this book and is a good example of a general purpose chart catering for the majority of the population. This chart is suitable for use on all types of clothing, giving body measurements which cover almost any eventuality. Note that the height goes from the top end of the short category into the lower end of the tall category. To comply with the British Standard BS 3666 an 'S' and 'T' are used to denote these categories. BS 3666 is reproduced on pages 21–5.

Table 12 Simplified area increments table. Body measurements for medium bust development: increments are based on an increase of 5.0 cm girth and 2.4 cm height

Area		Size 12	Girth only	Height only	Girth and height
1	Height	162.0	nil	2.4	2.4
2	Weight (pounds)	118.0	12.5	3.5	16.0
3	Hip	92.0	5.0	nil	5.0
4	Bust	87.0	5.0	nil	5.0
5	Waist	65.0	5.0	nil	5.0
6	Chest	82.0	3.6	nil	3.6
7	Top hip (11.0 cm from waist)	86.0	5.0	nil	5.0
8	Rib cage (under bust)	71.0	5.0	nil	5.0
9	Neck	37.0	0.8	0.2	1.0
10	Bicep	26.5	1.8	nil	1.8
11	Elbow	25.5	1.8	nil	1.8
12	Wrist	16.0	0.8	nil	0.8
13	Thigh	53.0	3.2	nil	3.2
14	Knee	34.0	1.2	0.2	1.4
15	Calf	33.0	1.2	0.2	1.4
16	Ankle	23.0	0.7	nil	0.7
17	X-chest	31.0	1.0	0.2	1.2
18	X-back	32.0	1.0	0.2	1.2
19	Shoulder length	11.5	0.1	0.1	0.2
20	Scye width	11.0	0.9	nil	0.9
21	Scye depth	18.1	0.5	0.1	0.6
22	Bust width	19.0	1.2	nil	1.2
23	Nape to bust	34.0	1.3	0.1	1.4
24	Nape to waist over bust	53.0	0.6	0.6	1.2
25	Nape to waist centre back	40.0	nil	0.6	0.6
26	Nape to hip	62.0	nil	0.9	0.9
27	Nape to knee	98.0	nil	1.5	1.5
28	Nape to floor	140.0	nil	2.1	2.1
29	Sleeve length (outer)	58.0	nil	0.9	0.9
30	Sleeve length (inner)	43.5	−0.4	0.8	0.4
31	Abdominal seat diameter	23.0	1.9	−0.2	1.7
32	Hip width	31.8	1.3	0.3	1.6
33	Body rise	29.0	1.0	0.1	1.1
34	Shoulder angle (degrees)	20.5	−0.25	0.25	nil

Table 13 Main size chart. Body measurements for medium bust development; increments are based on an increase of 5.0 cm girth and 2.4 cm height

Area		10S	12	14	16	18	20T	22T	Increment
					Size				
1	Height	159.6	162.0	164.4	166.8	169.2	171.6	173.0	2.4
2	Weight (pounds)	102	118	134	150	166	182	198	16 lb
3	Hip	87.0	92.0	97.0	102.0	107.0	112.0	117.0	5.0
4	Bust	82.0	87.0	92.0	97.0	102.0	107.0	112.0	5.0
5	Waist	60.0	65.0	70.0	75.0	80.0	85.0	90.0	5.0
6	Chest	78.4	82.0	85.6	89.2	92.8	96.4	100.0	3.6
7	Top hip (11.0 cm from waist)	81.0	86.0	91.0	96.0	101.0	106.0	111.0	5.0
8	Rib cage (under bust)	66.0	71.0	76.0	81.0	86.0	91.0	96.0	5.0
9	Neck	36.0	37.0	38.0	39.0	40.0	41.0	42.0	1.0
10	Bicep	24.7	26.5	28.3	30.1	31.9	33.7	35.5	1.8
11	Elbow	23.7	25.5	27.3	29.1	30.9	32.7	34.5	1.8
12	Wrist	15.2	16.0	16.8	17.6	18.4	19.2	20.0	0.8
13	Thigh	49.8	53.0	56.2	59.4	62.6	65.8	69.0	3.2
14	Knee	32.6	34.0	35.4	36.8	38.2	39.6	41.0	1.4
15	Calf	31.6	33.0	34.4	35.8	37.2	38.6	40.0	1.4
16	Ankle	22.3	23.0	23.7	24.4	25.1	25.8	26.5	0.7
17	X-chest	29.8	31.0	32.2	33.4	34.6	35.8	37.0	1.2
18	X-back (12.0 cm down from nape)	30.8	32.0	33.2	34.4	35.6	36.8	38.0	1.2
19	Shoulder length	11.3	11.5	11.7	11.9	12.1	12.3	12.5	0.2
20	Scye width	10.1	11.0	11.9	12.8	13.7	14.6	15.5	0.9
21	Scye depth	17.5	18.1	18.7	19.3	19.9	20.5	21.1	0.6
22	Bust width	17.8	19.0	20.2	21.4	22.6	23.8	25.0	1.2
23	Nape to bust	32.6	34.0	35.4	36.8	38.2	39.6	40.0	1.4
24	Nape to waist over bust	51.8	53.0	54.2	55.6	56.8	58.0	59.2	1.2
25	Nape to waist centre back	39.4	40.0	40.6	41.2	41.8	42.4	43.0	0.6
26	Nape to hip	61.1	62.0	62.9	63.8	64.7	65.6	66.5	0.9
27	Nape to knee	96.5	98.0	99.5	101.0	102.5	104.0	105.5	1.5
28	Nape to floor	137.9	140.0	142.1	144.2	146.3	148.4	150.5	2.1
29	Sleeve length (outer)	57.1	58.0	58.9	59.8	60.7	61.6	62.5	0.9
30	Sleeve length (inner)	43.1	43.5	43.9	44.3	44.7	45.1	45.5	0.4
31	Abdominal seat diameter	21.3	23.0	24.7	26.4	28.1	29.8	31.5	1.7
32	Hip width	30.2	31.8	33.4	35.0	36.6	38.2	39.8	1.6
33	Body rise	27.9	29.0	30.1	31.2	32.3	33.4	34.5	1.1
34	Shoulder angle (degrees)	20.5	20.5	20.5	20.5	20.5	20.5	20.5	nil

British Standard Specification for

Size designation of women's wear

0. Introduction

This British Standard is one of a series which deals essentially with the size designation of clothing, and is not directly concerned with sizing systems as such.

The primary aim of this and other British Standards in this series is the establishment of a size designation system that indicates (in a simple, direct and meaningful manner) the body size of the woman that a garment is intended to fit. Provided that the shape of her body (as indicated by the appropriate dimensions) has been accurately determined, this system will facilitate the choice of garments that fit.

The size designation system is based on body and not garment measurements. Choice of garment measurements is normally left to the designer and the manufacturer, who are concerned with style, cut and other fashion elements, and who must make due allowance for garments normally worn beneath a specific garment.

Definitions and body measurement procedure are prescribed in BS 5511 which is applicable to all categories of clothing.

1. Scope

This British Standard specifies a system of designating the size of women's outerwear and underwear garments that are classified as:

(a) covering the upper body, or

(b) covering the whole body, or

(c) covering the lower body only,

and it applies to civilian and uniform garments.*

Both the control dimensions on which the size designation system is based, and the method of indicating the size designation on a garment label, are specified.

This British Standard also contains details of a size coding scheme, which is to be included on the garment label together with the control dimensions.

2. References

The titles of the standard publications referred to in this Standard are listed on page 5.

3. Definitions

For the purposes of this British Standard, the definitions given in BS 5511 together with the following, apply.

woman. A female person whose growth in height is finished.

4. Control dimensions

4.1 Outerwear (including knitwear and swimwear). The control dimensions shall be as follows.

(a) Women's garments covering the upper or the whole body

Other than knitwear and swimwear	Knitwear	Swimwear
(1) Bust girth	Bust girth	Bust girth
(2) Hip girth		Hip girth
(3) Height		

(b) Women's garments covering the lower body only

(1) Hip girth

(2) Waist girth

(3) Outside leg length

4.2 Underwear (including nightwear, foundation garments and shirts). The control dimensions shall be as follows.

(a) Women's garments covering the upper body only

Other than foundation garments	Foundation garments
(1) Bust girth	Underbust girth
(2) —	Bust girth

(b) Women's garments covering the whole body

Other than foundation garments	Foundation garments
(1) Bust girth	Underbust girth
(2) Height	Bust girth
(3) —	Hip girth

Nightwear, 1-piece garments	Nightwear, 2-piece garments
(1) Bust girth	Bust girth
(2) Height	Hip girth
(3) —	Height

(c) Women's garments covering the lower body only

Other than foundation garments	Foundation garments
(1) Hip girth	Waist girth
(2) —	Hip girth

5. Size designation

5.1 The size designation of each garment shall comprise the control dimensions (see clause 4), in centimetres, of the intended wearer of that garment. Where practicable, the standard or the special pictogram, as given in BS 5511, should be used as a means of indicating the size designation. Where it is not practicable to use the pictogram, the control measurements shall be given, together with the descriptive

---

*Examples of garments covered by this British Standard are given in appendix A.

words such as bust girth, hip girth, etc. alongside, in the order in which they are given in clause **4**.

NOTE. The above requirements do not preclude the use, in exceptional instances of:

(a) size designations comprising only one or two of the applicable control dimensions;

(b) size designations shown as a range by stating the minimum and maximum control measurements separated by an oblique stroke or a hyphen.

5.2 Garment measurements shall not be incorporated in the size designation but, where considered of value, garment measurements may be indicated separately (see **7.3**).

6. Size code

The size code, as detailed in table 1, shall be incorporated in the garment label. Examples of how the size code number may be included in the label are given in figure 1.

Table 1. Size codes and associated body measurements

Size codes	Body measurements			
	Hips		Bust	
	from	to	from	to
	cm	cm	cm	cm
8	83	87	78	82
10	87	91	82	86
12	91	95	86	90
14	95	99	90	94
16	100	104	95	99
18	105	109	100	104
20	110	114	105	109
22	115	119	110	114
24	120	124	115	119
26	125	129	120	124
28	130	134	125	129
30	135	139	130	134
32	140	144	135	139

7. Labelling

7.1 Method. The size code and designation of each garment shall be indicated clearly, conspicuously and in a plainly legible form on a label, or on a swing ticket, or on both. Pictograms shall be large enough to ensure immediate understanding and numerals shall, in all cases, be readily discernible.

7.2 Attachment. The label or swing ticket shall be capable of being securely attached to the garment and so positioned as to be easily readable.

7.3 Additional information. Information additional to the size designation may be separately indicated on the label, or on the swing ticket, or on both, provided that it does not in any way reduce the prominence and conspicuousness of the size designation. Such additional information may include a size code number, body measurements or garment measurements considered to constitute useful information.

7.4 Examples of labels. The examples of labels given in figures 2 and 3 illustrate methods of labelling that range from the simple indication on the standard pictogram of the relevant control dimensions to more elaborate forms that provide additional information such as a garment dimension or a size code number. Figure 1 gives examples of how to incorporate the size code number into the size label.

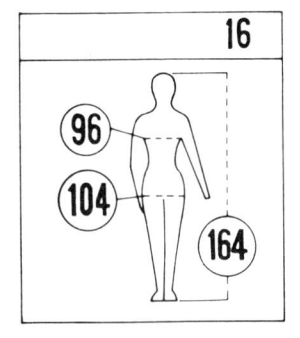

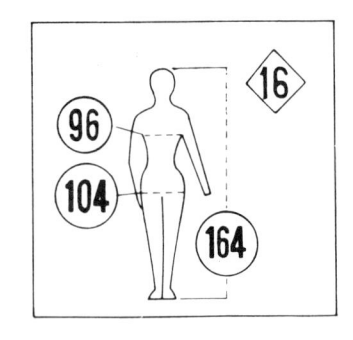

Figure 1. Examples of inclusion of size code number into label

WOMEN'S SIZING AND SURVEYS

a) Woman's jacket

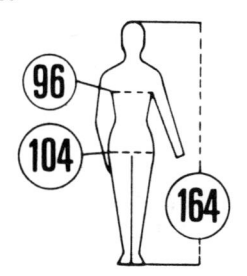

BUST GIRTH	96
HIP GIRTH	104
HEIGHT	164

b) Woman's coat or dress

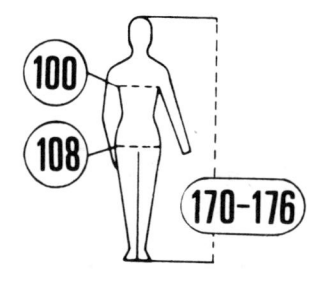

BUST GIRTH	100
HIP GIRTH	108
HEIGHT	170 – 176

c) Woman's slacks

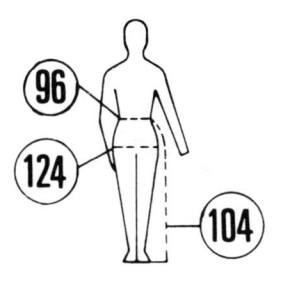

HIP GIRTH	124
WAIST GIRTH	96
OUTSIDE LEG LENGTH	104

d) Woman's cardigan

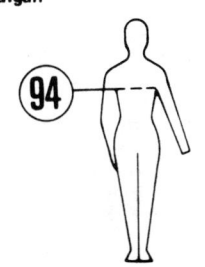

BUST GIRTH 94

e) Woman's skirt

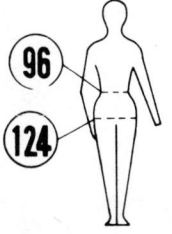

| HIP GIRTH | 124 |
| WAIST GIRTH | 96 |
| SKIRT LENGTH | 66 |*

NOTE. Examples of how to incorporate the national size code number are given in figure 1.

Figure 2. Examples of labels for women's outerwear

*Example of additional information included in accordance with 7.3.

a) Woman's brassiere

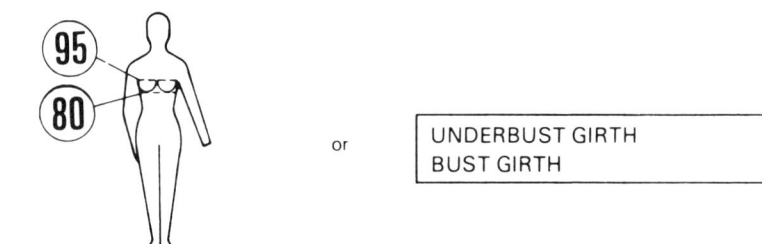

| UNDERBUST GIRTH | 80 |
| BUST GIRTH | 95 |

b) Woman's pyjamas

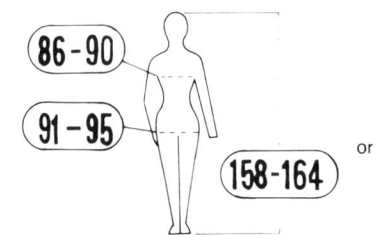

BUST GIRTH	86-90
HIP GIRTH	91-95
HEIGHT	158-164

c) Woman's girdle

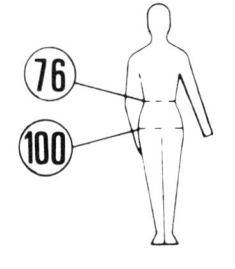

| WAIST GIRTH | 76 |
| HIP GIRTH | 100 |

d) Woman's sports shirt

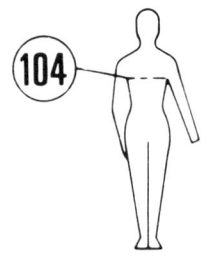

| BUST GIRTH | 104 |

NOTE. Examples of how to incorporate the national size code number are given in figure 1.

Figure 3. Examples of labels for women's underwear

Appendix A

Examples of garments

A.1 Outerwear

A.1.1 *Garments covering the upper or the whole body*
   (a) coats, topcoats, raincoats
   (b) jackets, blazers, tunics, anoraks
   (c) dresses
   (d) suits and costumes (2-and 3-piece)
   (e) dressing gowns and housecoats
   (f) overalls, dustcoats
   (g) knitwear (pullovers, cardigans, sweaters)
   (h) swimwear
   (i) catsuits.

A.1.2 *Garments covering the lower body only*
   (a) skirts
   (b) trousers, slacks, riding breeches, salopettes
   (c) shorts.

A.2 Underwear

A.2.1 *Garments covering the upper body only*
   (a) shirts, blouses
   (b) vests
   (c) foundation garments (brassieres).

A.2.2 *Garments covering the whole body*
   (a) body suits, gym suits
   (b) slips
   (c) foundation garments (corselets)
   (d) nightwear (nightdresses, sleepsuits, pyjamas).

A.2.3 *Garments covering the lower body only*
   (a) knickers, panties, briefs
   (b) half slips
   (c) foundation garments (corsets, girdles, pantie girdles).

BS 3666: 1982 is reproduced by permission of the British Standards Institution; 2 Park Street, London W1A 2BS, from whom copies can be obtained.

RELEVANT GRADING TERMINOLOGY

1. Suppression grading
2. Three-dimensional grading
3. Two-dimensional grading
4. Cardinal points
5. Balance
6. Nested (stacked) grading

SUPPRESSION GRADING
This term is applied when the amount of suppression in a pattern is increased or decreased. Suppression is, 'all forms of darts, seams, pleats and gathers which are used to control shape or contour'. It has nothing to do with styling. To suppress is to reduce a girth measurement in relation to another adjacent girth measurement.

THREE-DIMENSIONAL GRADING
This term applies to grading techniques which change suppression as well as girth and height grades.

TWO-DIMENSIONAL GRADING
When the pattern changes only in girth and height and not in shape it is termed two-dimensional. This type of grade is invariably a simplified grade and is initially easier to learn and apply.

CARDINAL POINTS
These are the points on the pattern to which grading increments are applied.

BALANCE
There are various interpretations of balance, but for the purposes of this book it refers to the relationship between the front length from nape over bust to waist and floor, and back length from nape to centre back waist to floor. It is also used as a general description, as the word suggests, for a lack of distortion.

NESTED (STACKED) GRADING
This describes the superimposing of one size on another so that the progression of increase is clearly visible.

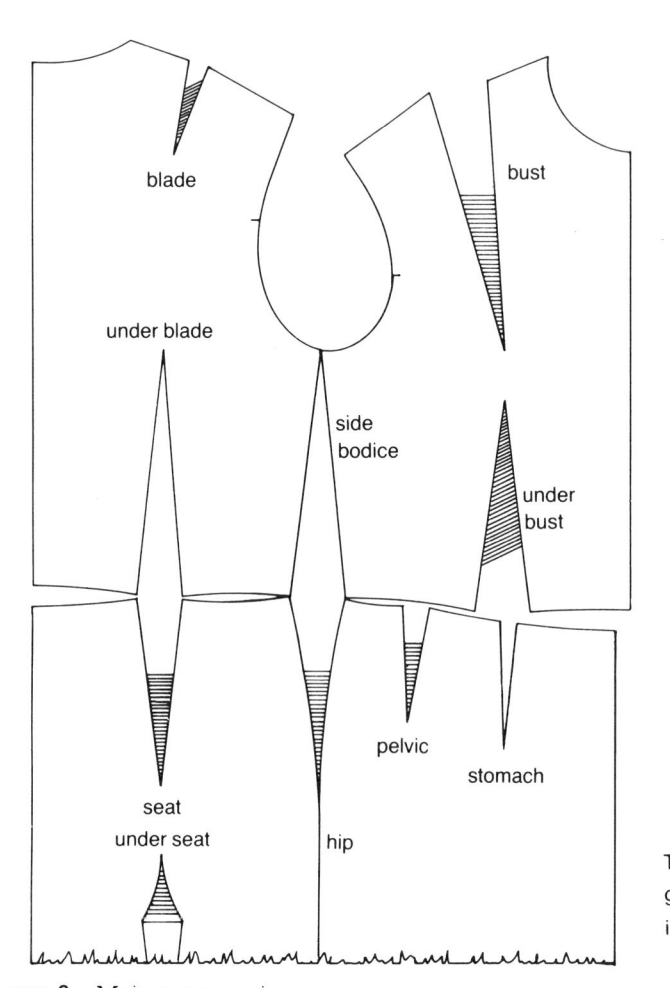

The shaded areas denote suppression changes in a grading where the three major girths (bust, waist, hip) increase at the same rate.

Figure 3 Main suppression areas

CHAPTER 2

Women's grading increments reference

This chapter is a reference for grading increments covering all types of basic block. The increments have been taken from the area distribution table (Table 12, page 19) and applied to the blocks based on the principles discussed in Chapters 3 and 5. The zero points chosen for these reference plans are purely for convenience and are explained in Chapter 11.

All the grading quantities are in millimetres throughout the book when applied to grade plans and split diagrams. When centimetres are referred to, they are expressed as, for example, 1.0 cm.

Throughout this book the difference between each size (size increment) will be 5.0 cm on the major girth (hip) and 2.4 cm on the height. This applies where a 'girth only' or a 'height only' grade is used and also on the combined grades of height and girth.

This chapter also includes a grade plan for the basic bodice and skirt, using a 4.0 cm and a 6.0 cm girth increment because these quantities may be used on their own or mixed together in a size range.

The 5.0 cm increment is used as the correct one, and the 6.0 cm and 4.0 cm increments have been calculated from the 5.0 cm as closely as possible and run reasonably accurately over the 10 to 22 size range.

The reference increment data has been presented in two forms in order to make it as clear as possible exactly where the increases take place.

The 'grade plan' is the usual way of showing increments and is based on the principle of a chosen static point on the pattern which is called the 'zero point' and the increases are registered at all the cardinal (important) points on the pattern indicating what each particular point does in relation to the zero point. The other way of expressing increases is in the form of a 'split diagram'. This indicates where the pattern must be split and opened and by how much. The combination of these two systems leaves no doubt as to the nature of a particular increase and permits the easy transference of the zero point to another location indicating the necessary calculation needed for the new grade plan. See Chapter 11.

For full explanations of the distribution of these quantities it will be necessary to combine the study of Chapter 3 with Table 12.

The two-dimensional grade instructions in Figures 7a and 7b, have been arrived at by simplifying the three-dimensional increments. These are not as efficient and must therefore only be used over a small size range because of distortion. See Chapter 4 for further discussion.

The increments for the three-dimensional skirt grades in Figures 9a and 9b, are not used very often because their application can be difficult, depending on the style, but are efficient when applicable. In general the two-dimensional grade is used and is sufficient, in most circumstances, for grading skirts.

BASIC BODICE BLOCK THREE-DIMENSIONAL GRADE

Figure 4a shows a split diagram for height only grade and Figure 4b shows a grade plan for height only grade, using 2.4 cm overall height change.

Shown in Figure 5a is a split diagram for girth only grade and in Figure 5b, a grade plan for girth only grade, using 5.0 cm hip increment.

Figure 6a shows a split diagram for girth and height combined grade. Figure 6b shows a grade plan 5.0 cm girth and 2.4 height; Figure 6c a grade plan 4.0 cm girth and 2.4 height; and Figure 6d a grade plan 6.0 cm girth and 2.4 height.

BASIC BODICE BLOCK TWO-DIMENSIONAL GRADE

A split diagram for girth and height combined grade is shown in Figure 7a, and a grade plan for girth and height combined grade based on 5.0 cm girth and 2.4 cm height is shown in Figure 7b.

28 THE THEORY AND PRINCIPLES OF GRADING

Increments for height only   Increase of 2.4 cm

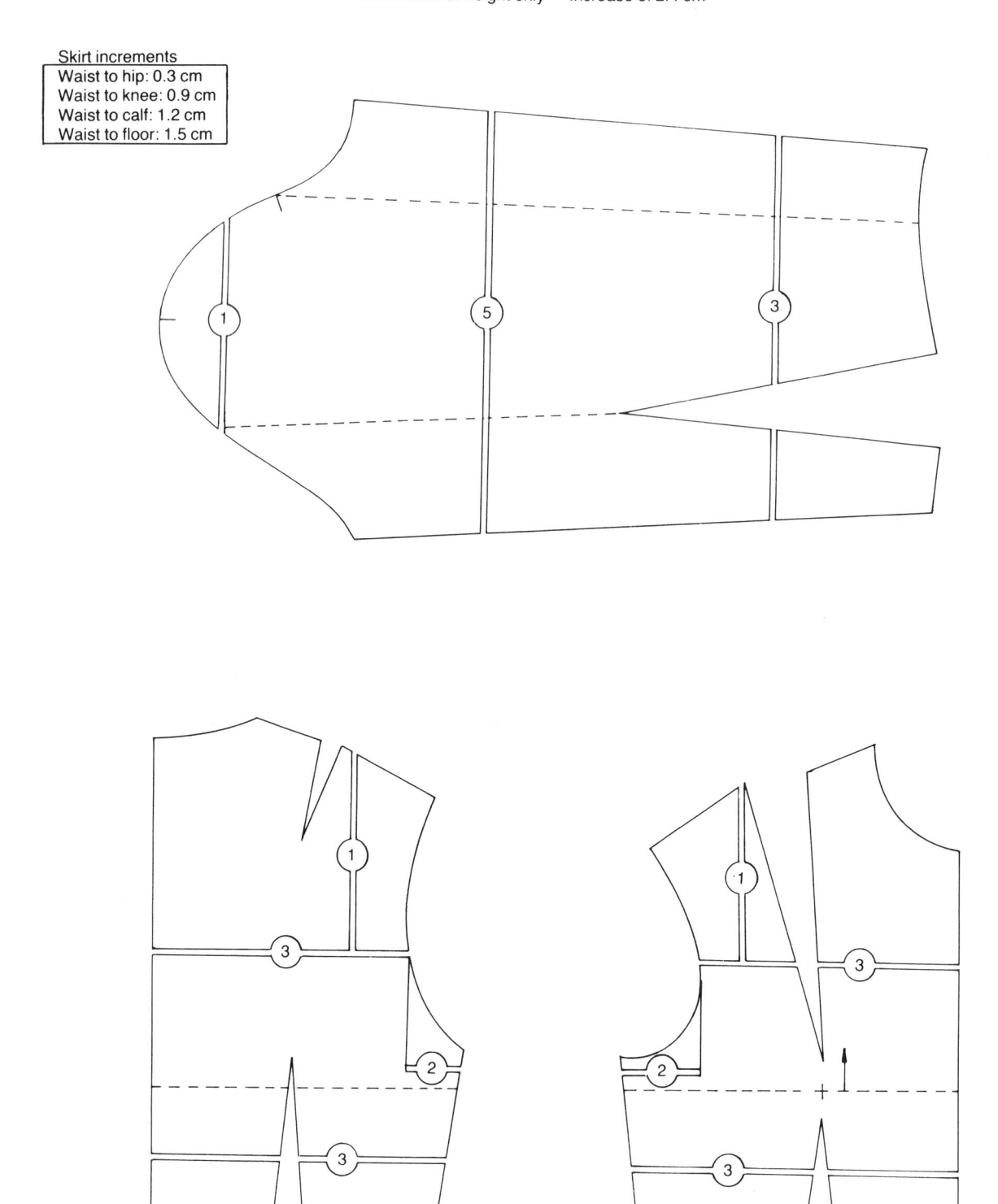

Skirt increments
Waist to hip: 0.3 cm
Waist to knee: 0.9 cm
Waist to calf: 1.2 cm
Waist to floor: 1.5 cm

Figure 4 (a) Height only bodice block split diagram

WOMEN'S GRADING INCREMENTS REFERENCE 29

Increments for height only   Increase of 2.4 cm

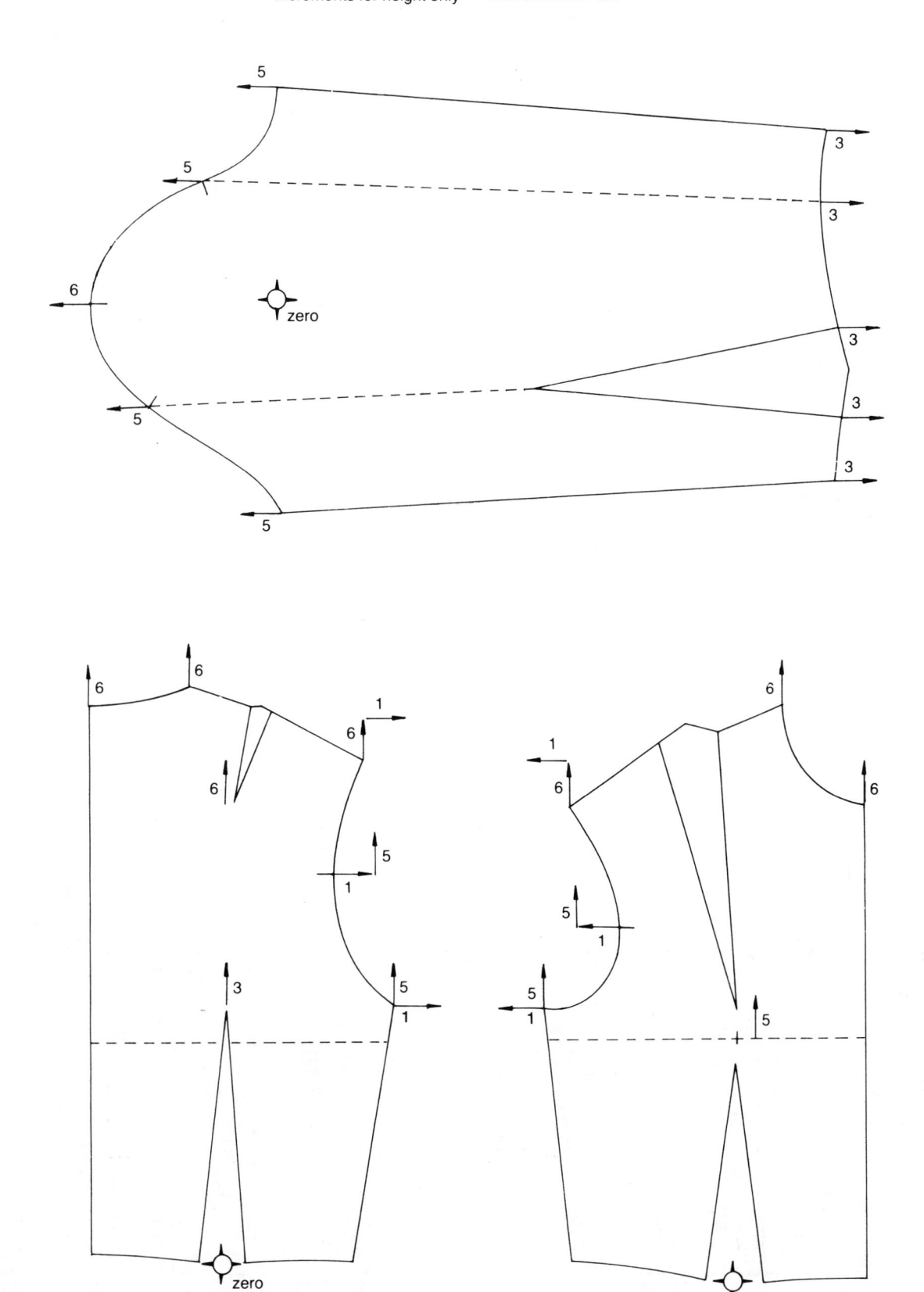

(b) Height only bodice block grade plan

Increments for girth only   Increase of 5.0 cm

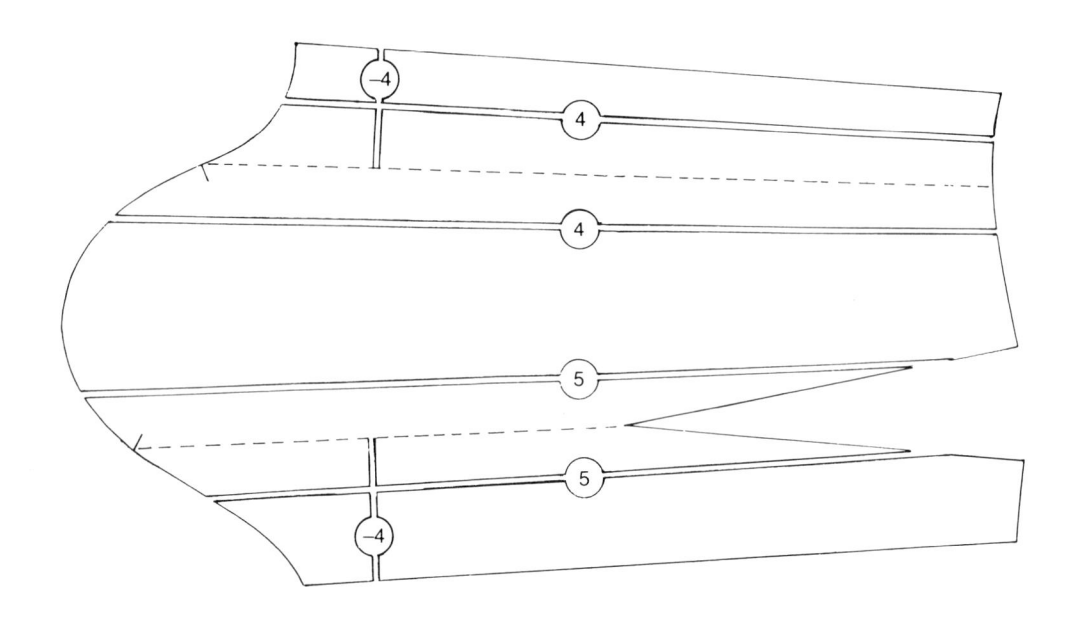

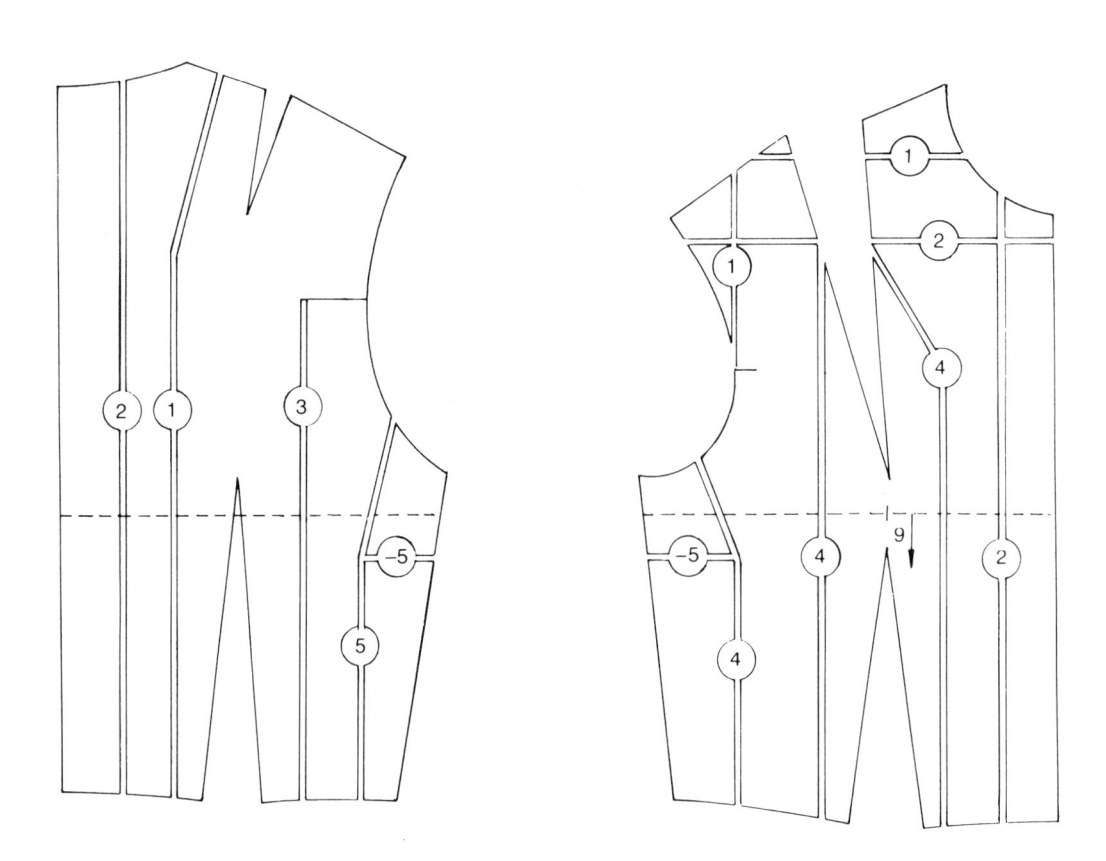

Figure 5 (a) Girth only (three-dimensional) bodice block split diagram

WOMEN'S GRADING INCREMENTS REFERENCE 31

Increments for girth only   Increase of 5.0 cm girth and 0.1 cm shoulder length

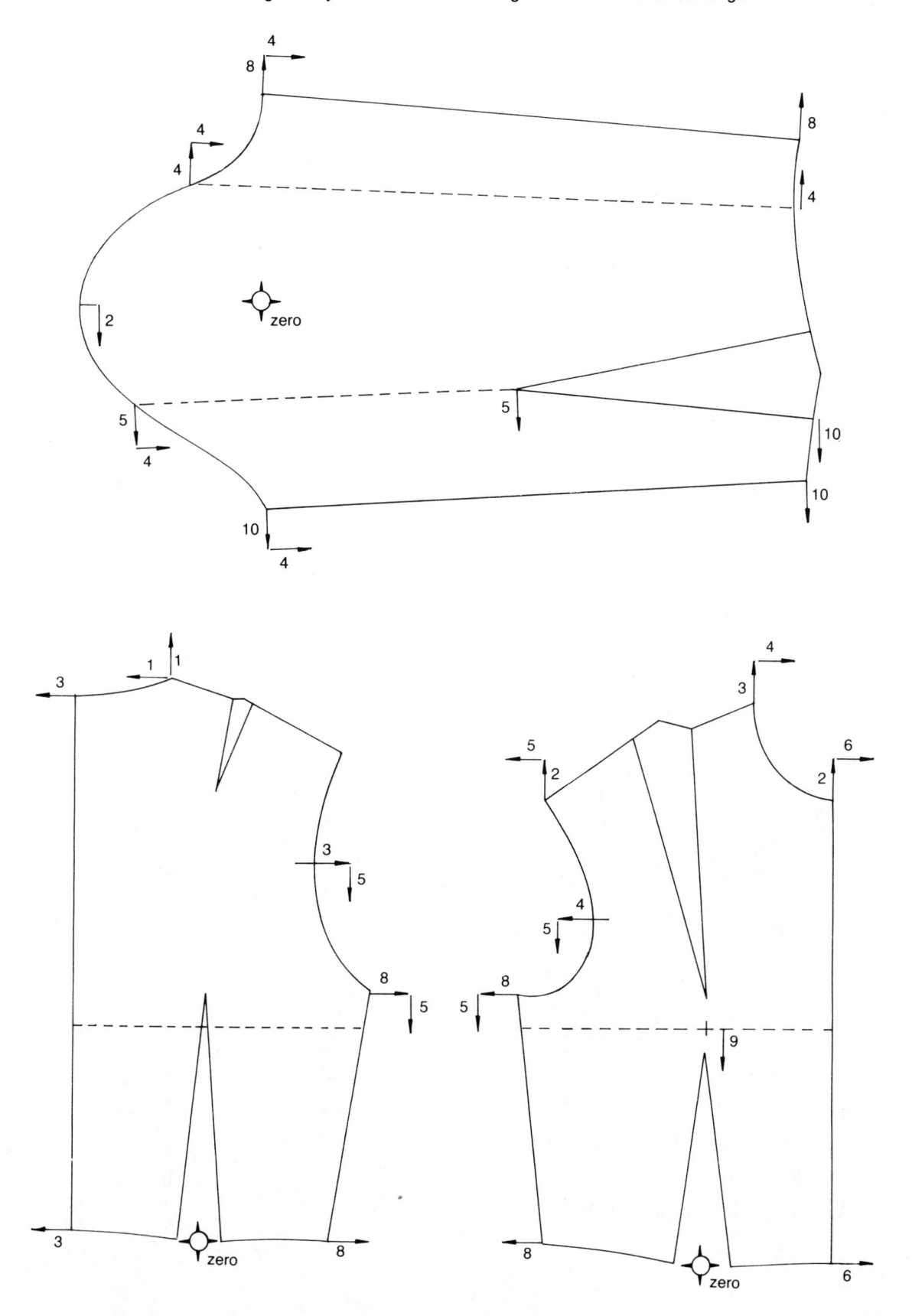

(b) Girth only (three-dimensional) bodice block grade plan

32 | THE THEORY AND PRINCIPLES OF GRADING

Increments for height of 2.4 cm and 5.0 cm girth

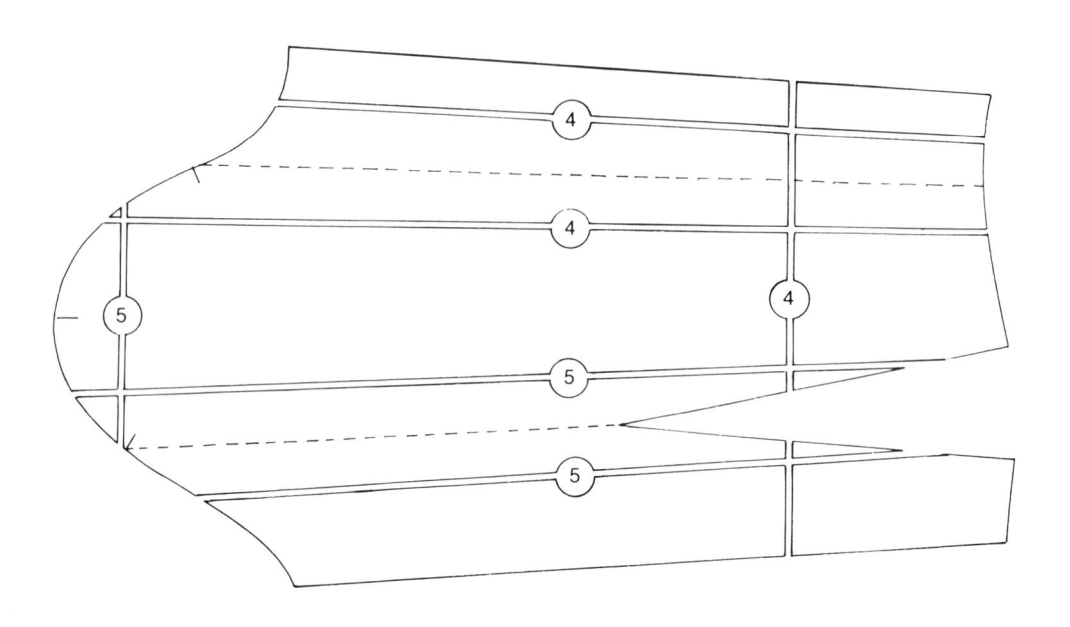

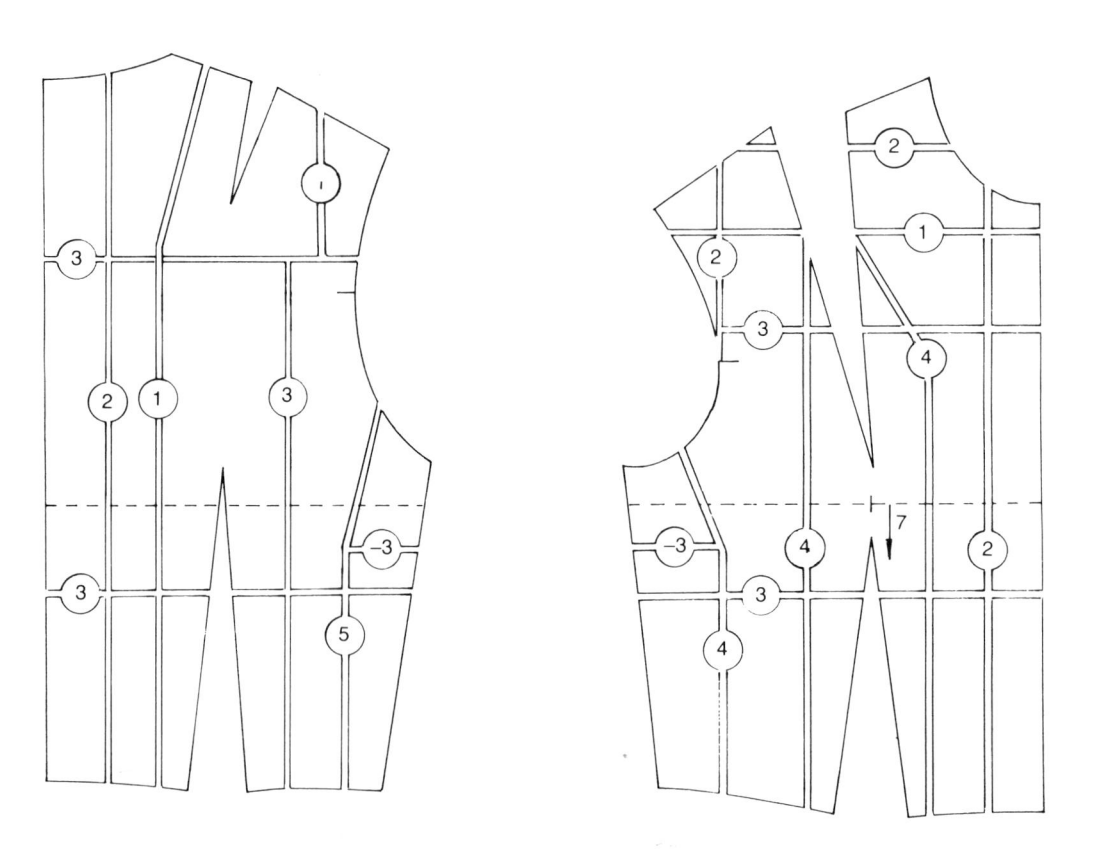

Figure 6 (a) Height and girth (three-dimensional) bodice block split diagram

WOMEN'S GRADING INCREMENTS REFERENCE 33

Increments for height of 2.4 cm and 5.0 cm girth with 0.2 cm shoulder length increase

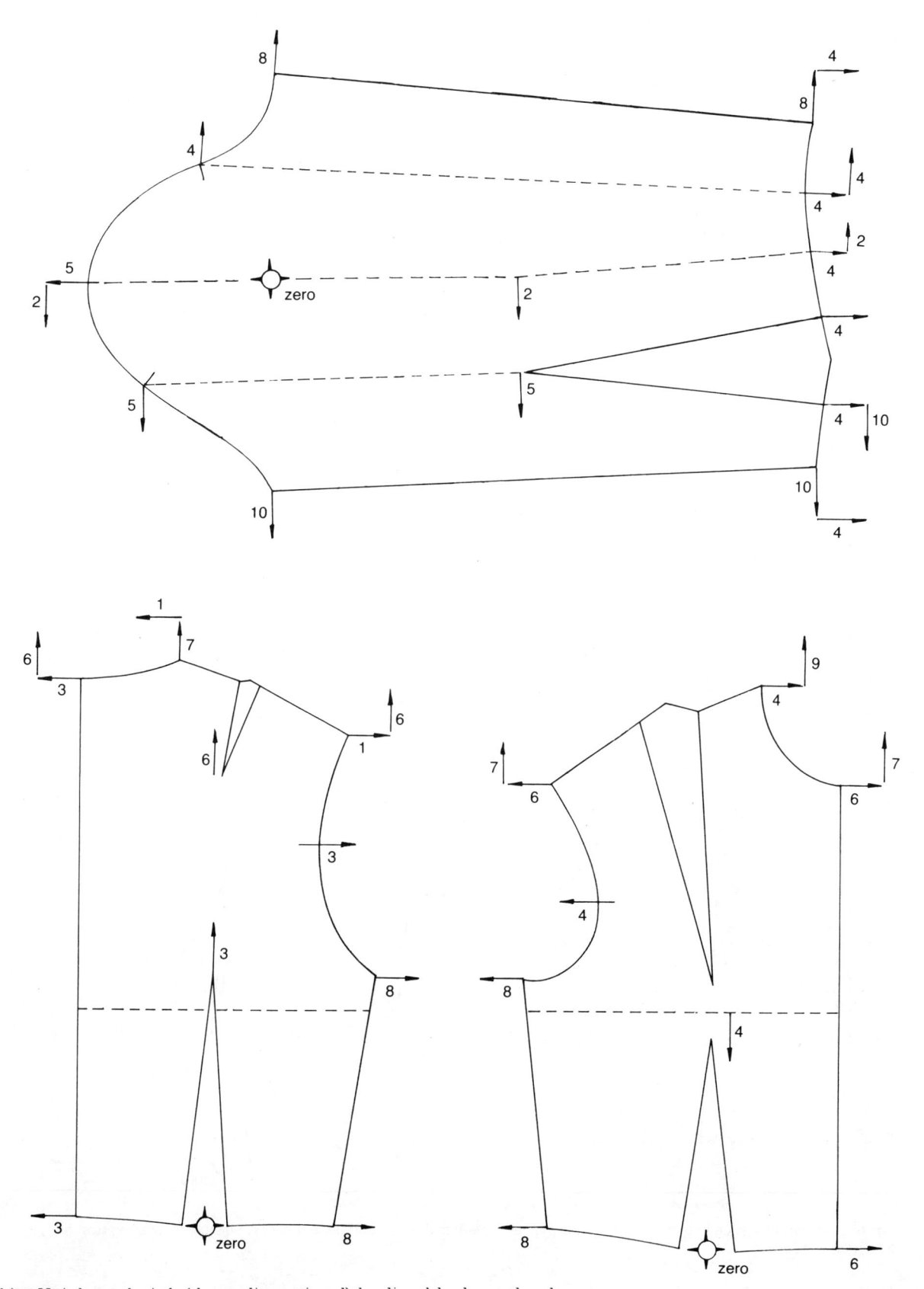

(b) Height and girth (three-dimensional) bodice block grade plan

34 THE THEORY AND PRINCIPLES OF GRADING

Increments for 2.4 cm height and 6.0 cm girth with 0.2 cm shoulder length increase

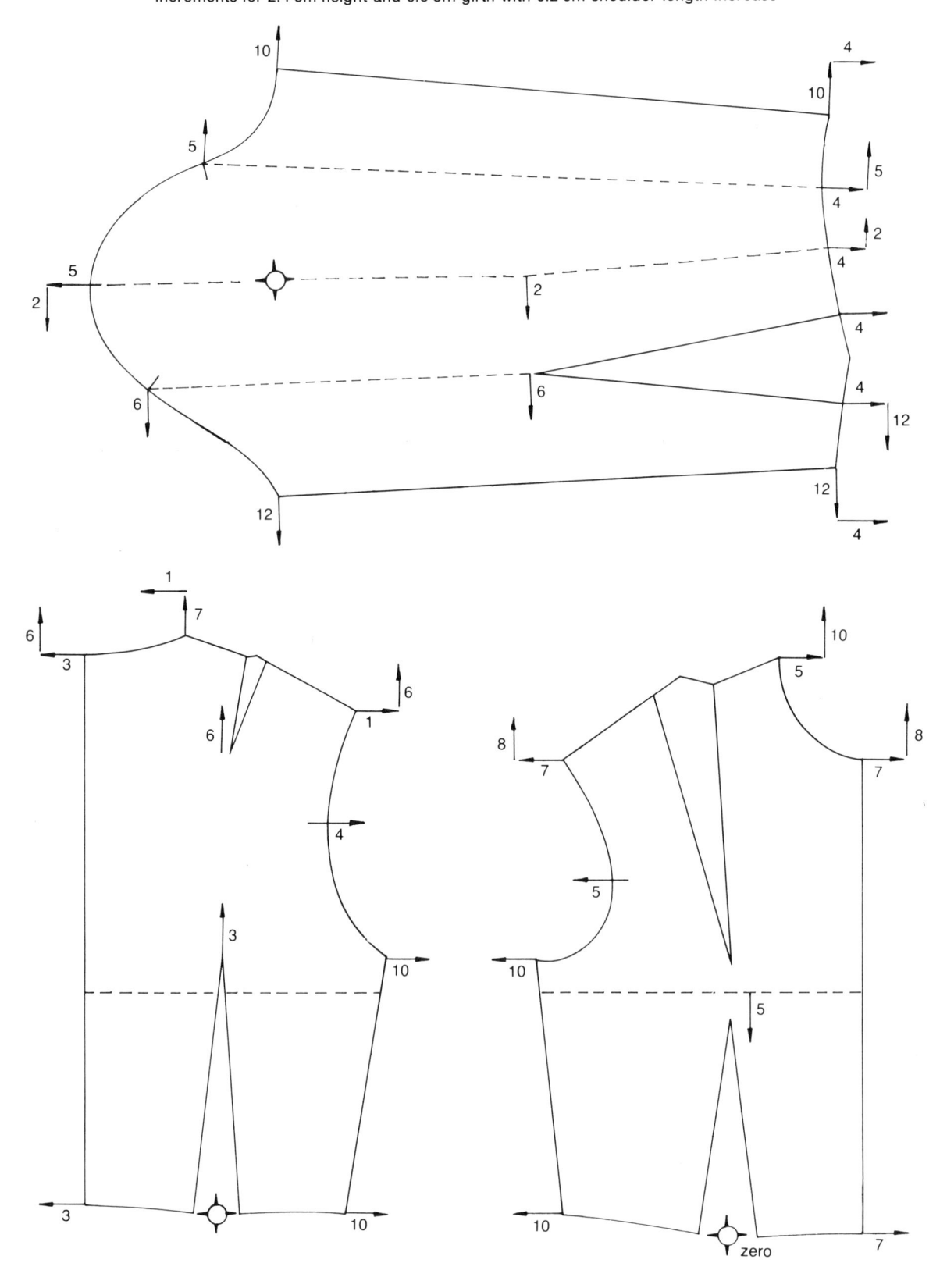

These quantities are taken from the 5.0 cm grade plan and taken to the nearest whole number. Suitable for grading over a full range of sizes.

(c) Height and girth (three-dimensional) bodice grade plan

| WOMEN'S GRADING INCREMENTS REFERENCE | 35 |

Increments for 2.4 cm height and 4.0 cm girth with 0.2 cm shoulder length increase

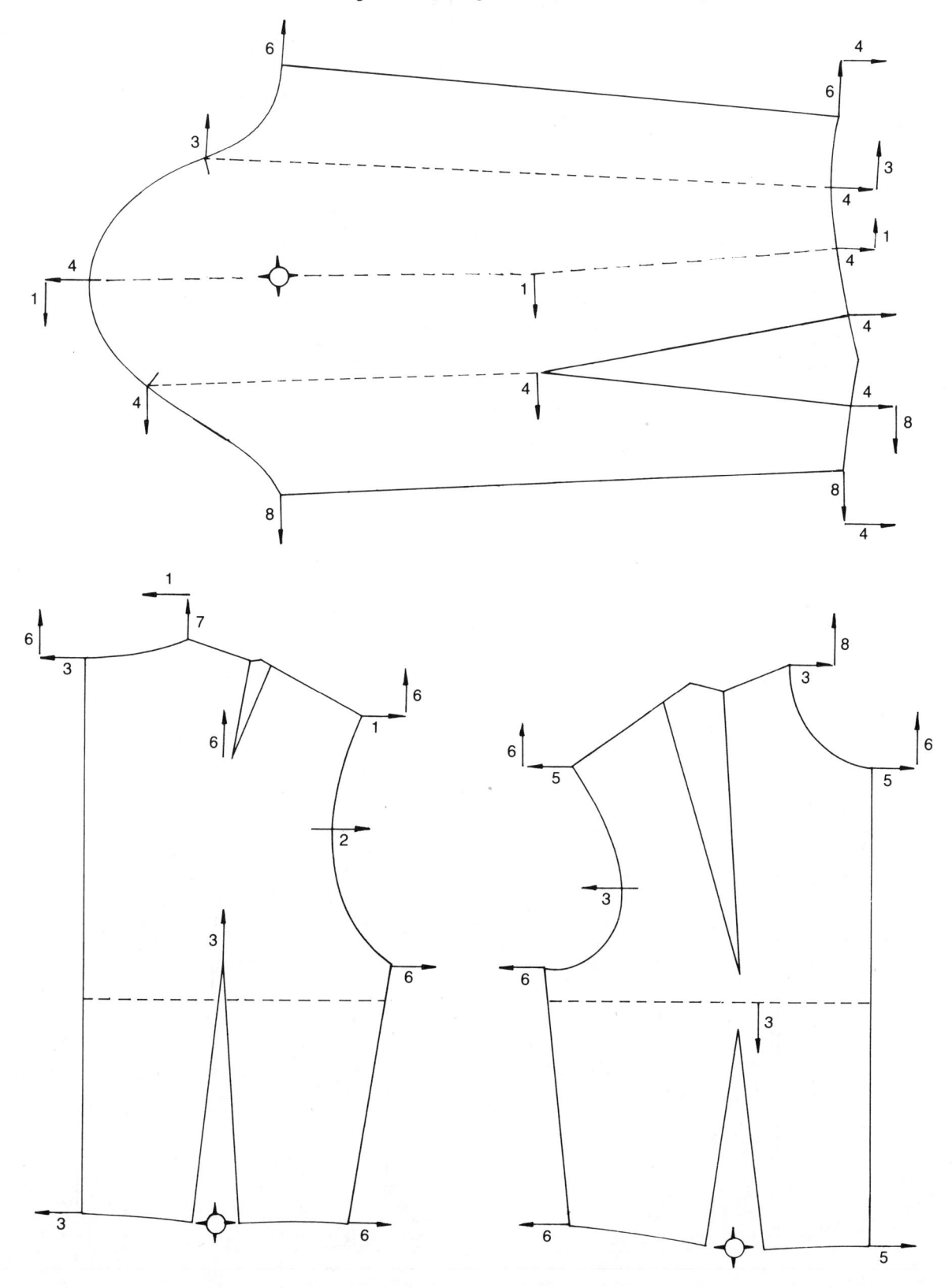

These quantities are adapted from the 5.0 cm grade plan and taken to the nearest whole number. Suitable for grading over a full range of sizes.

(d) Height and girth (three-dimensional) bodice block grade plan

Increments for height of 2.4 cm and 5.0 cm girth
Shoulder increment 0.3 cm

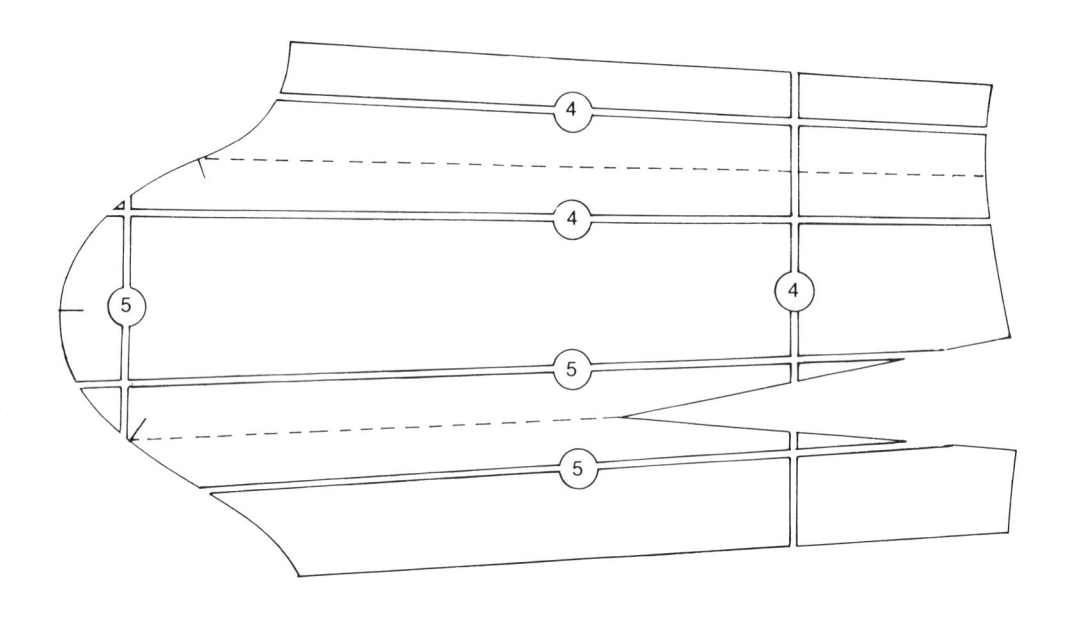

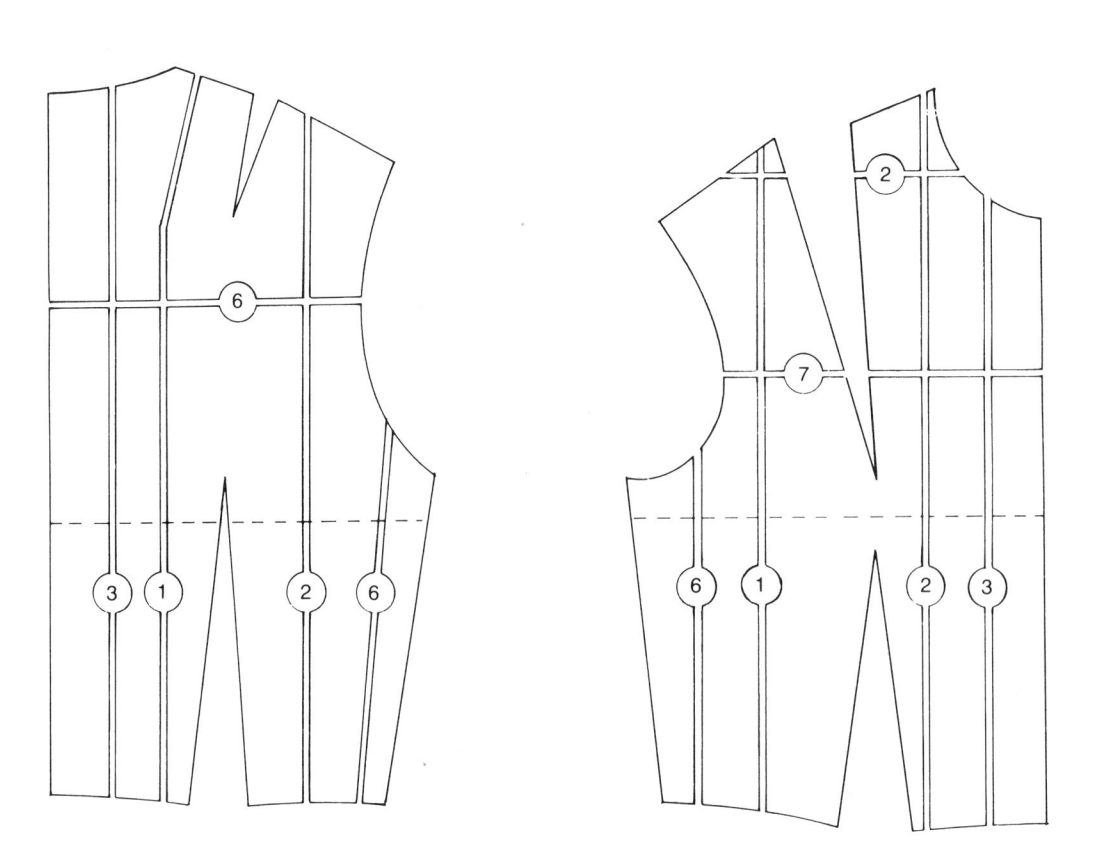

Figure 7 (a) Height and girth (two-dimensional) simplified bodice block split diagram

WOMEN'S GRADING INCREMENTS REFERENCE

Increments for height increase of 2.4 cm and 5.0 cm girth
Shoulder increment 0.3 cm

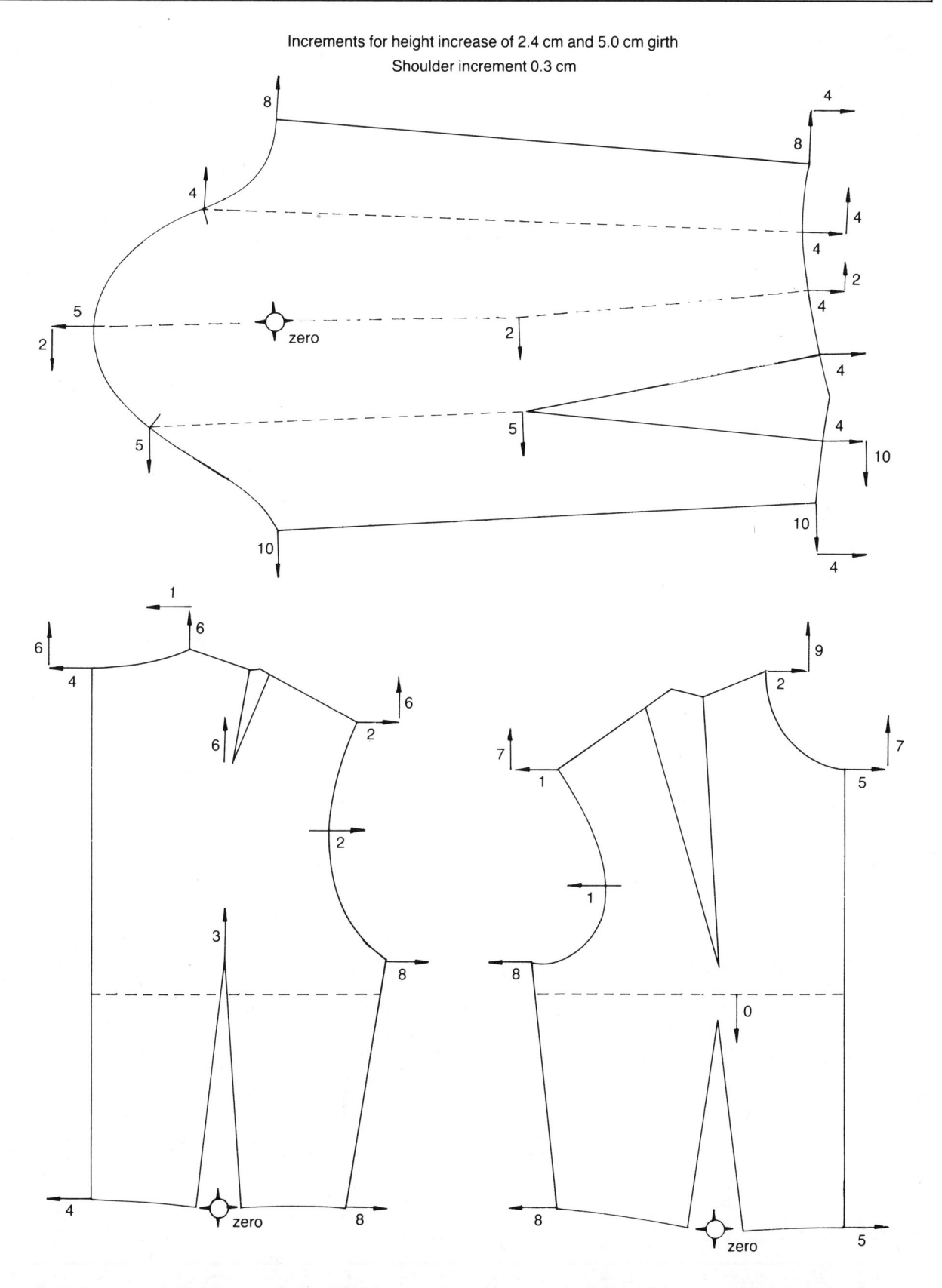

Taken from the split diagram in Figure 7a. Suitable for track grading over a small range of sizes. These quantities are offered as an average example of a simplified two-dimensional version for easy application. Many other permutations are possible depending on the degree of simplification.

(b) Height and girth (two-dimensional) simplified bodice block grade plan

BASIC SKIRT BLOCK
TWO-DIMENSIONAL GRADE

Figure 8a shows a split diagram for girth and height combined grade, and Figure 8b shows the grade plan for girth and height combined grade based on 5.0 cm girth and 2.4 cm height.

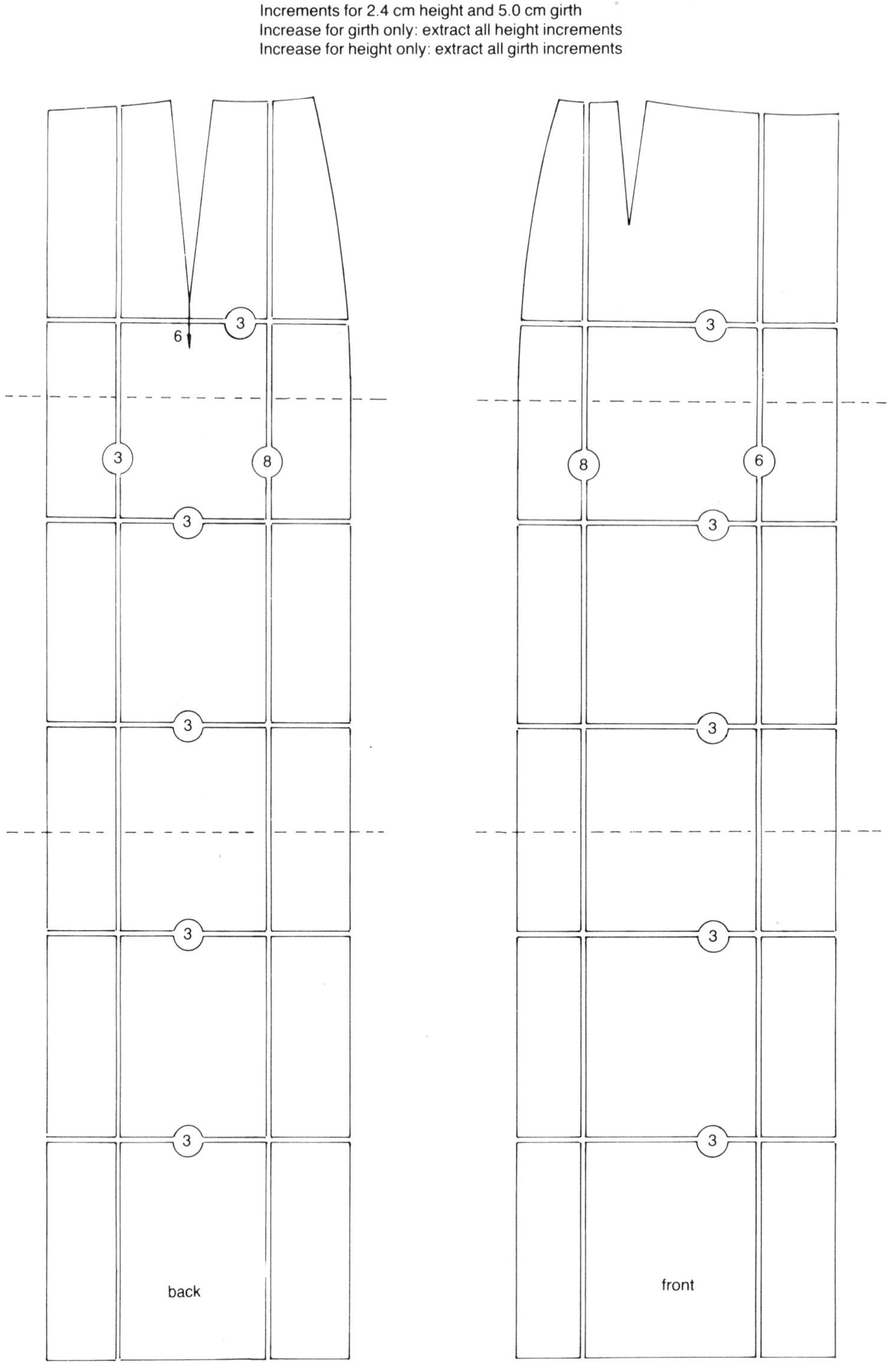

Increments for 2.4 cm height and 5.0 cm girth
Increase for girth only: extract all height increments
Increase for height only: extract all girth increments

Figure 8 (a) Two-dimensional skirt split diagram to be used with two- and three-dimensional bodice grades

WOMEN'S GRADING INCREMENTS REFERENCE

Increments for 2.4 cm height and 5.0 cm girth increase

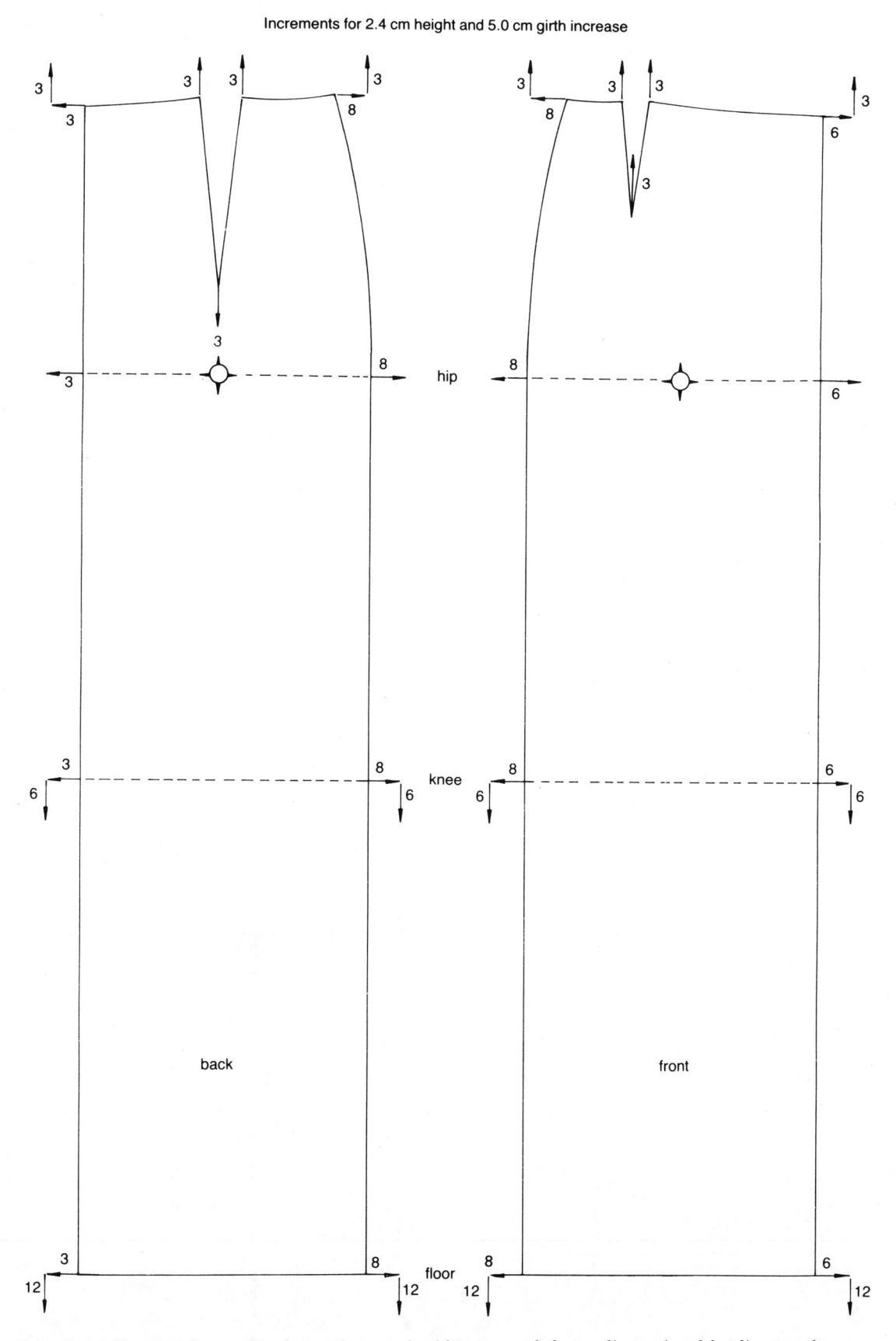

(b) Two-dimensional skirt grade plan to be used with two- and three-dimensional bodice grades

BASIC SKIRT BLOCK
THREE-DIMENSIONAL GRADE

Shown in Figure 9a is a split diagram for girth and height combined grade, and a grade plan for girth and height combined grade based on 5.0 cm girth and 2.4 cm height is shown in Figure 9b.

Increments for 2.4 cm height and 5.0 cm girth
For girth only extract all height increments
For height only extract all girth increments

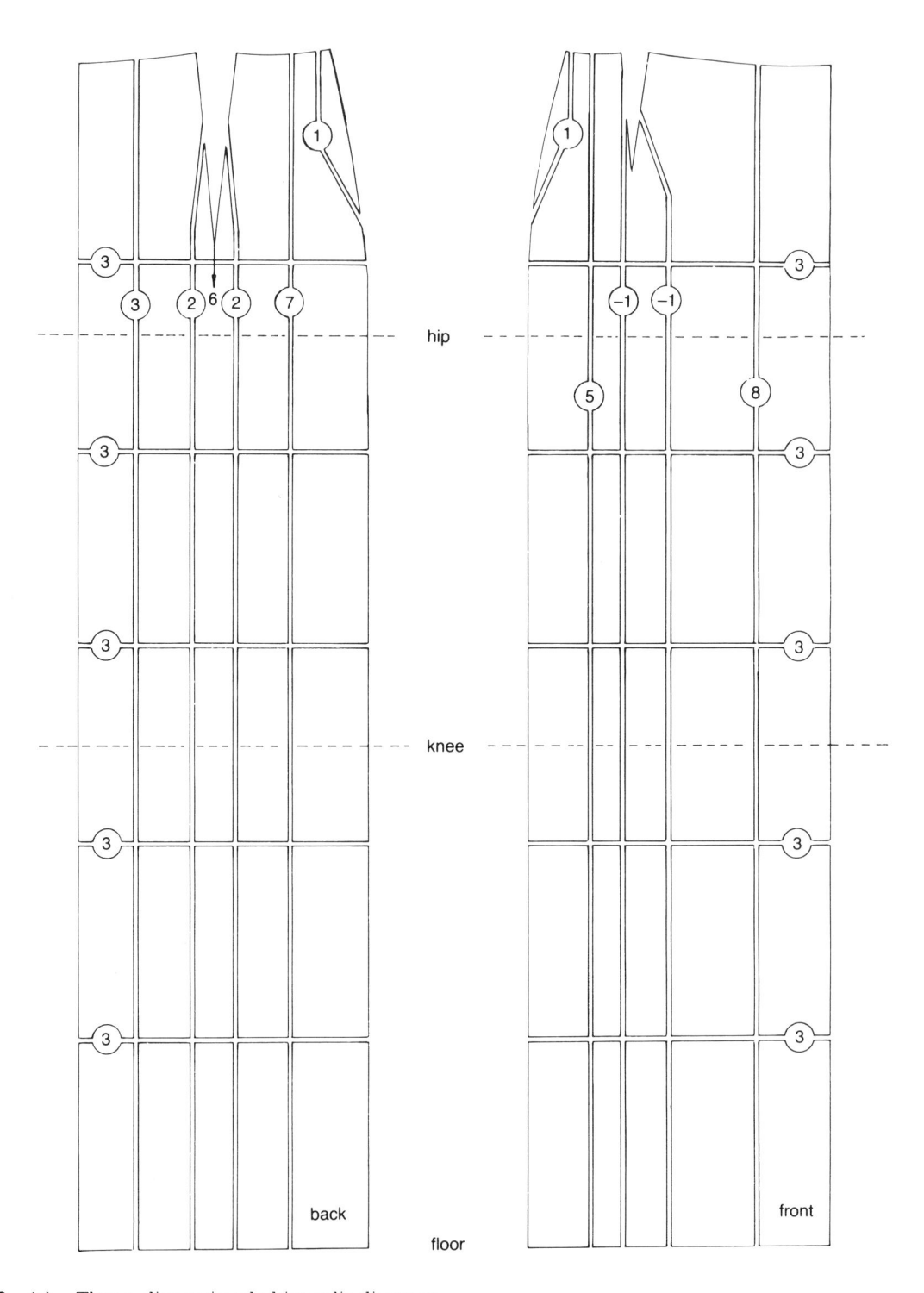

Figure 9 (a) Three-dimensional skirt split diagram

WOMEN'S GRADING INCREMENTS REFERENCE 41

Increments for 2.4 cm height and 5.0 cm girth increase

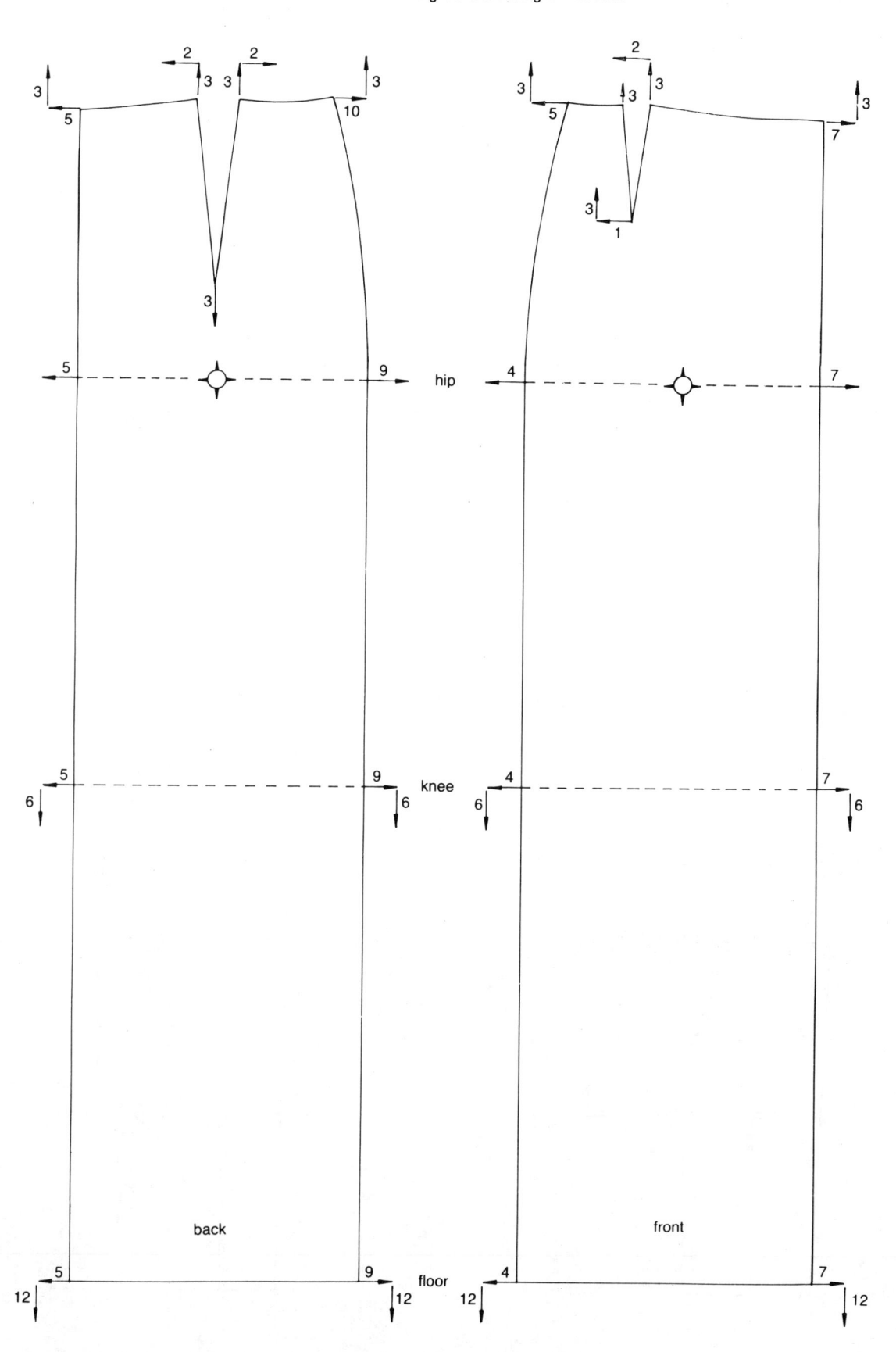

(b) Three-dimensional skirt grade plan taken from the split diagram in (a)

BASIC TROUSER BLOCK
TWO-DIMENSIONAL GRADE

Figure 10a shows a split diagram for girth and height combined grade and Figure 10b shows the grade plan for girth and height combined grade based on 5.0 cm girth and 2.4 cm height.

Increments for 2.4 cm height and 5.0 cm girth
For girth only: extract all height increments and change −8 to −10
For height only: extract all girth increments and change −8 to +2

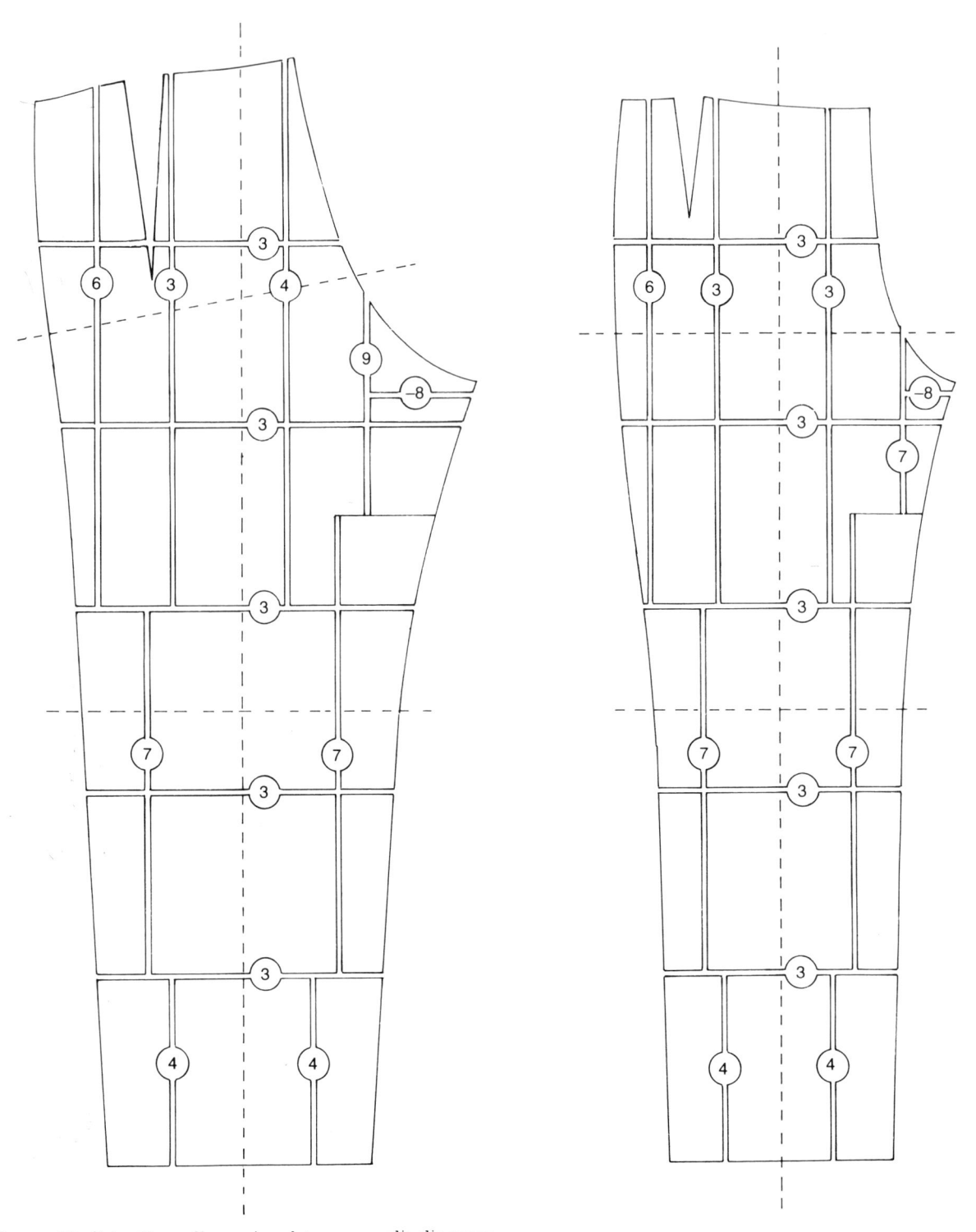

Figure 10 (a) Two-dimensional trouser split diagram

WOMEN'S GRADING INCREMENTS REFERENCE 43

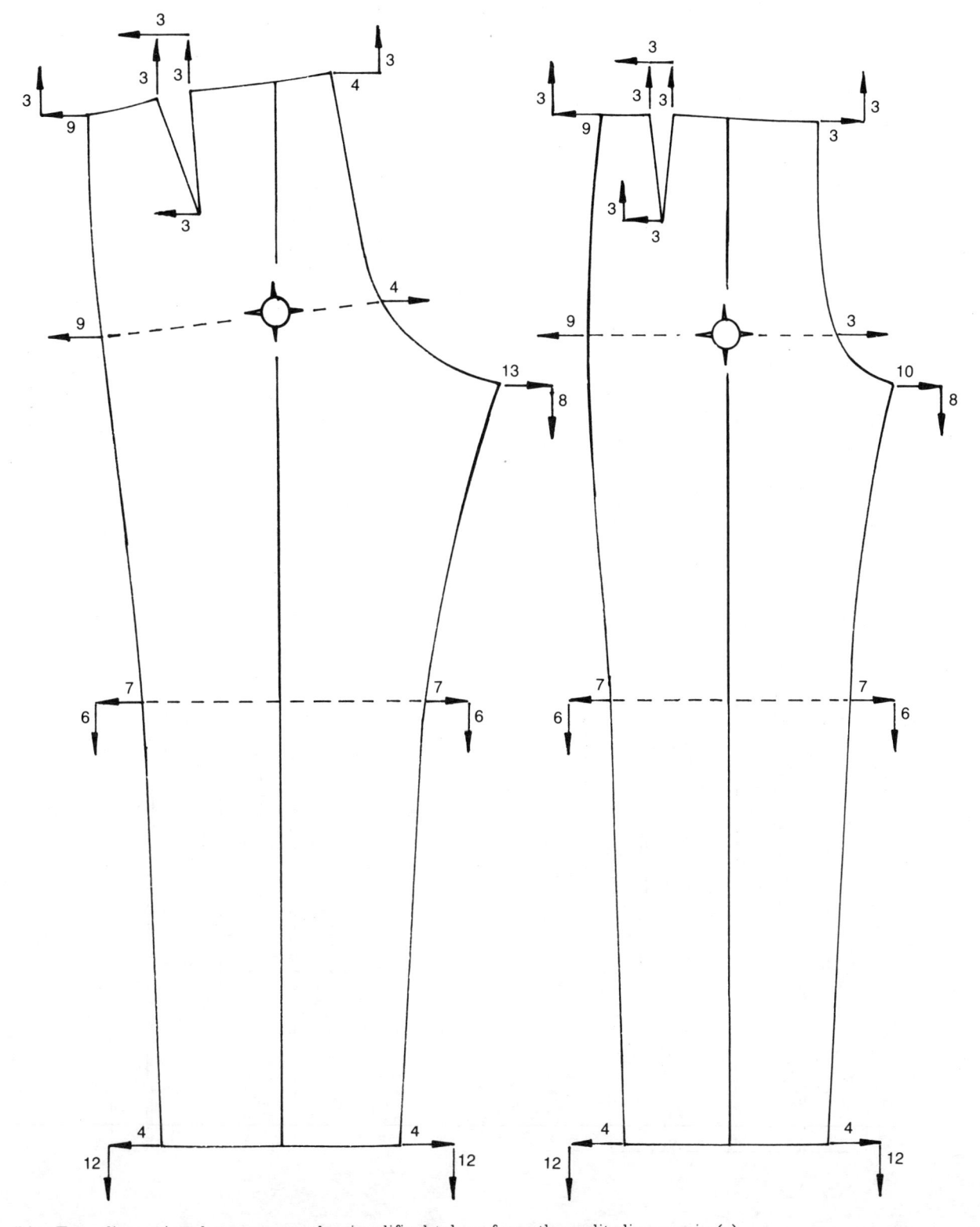

(b) Two-dimensional trouser grade simplified taken from the split diagram in (a)

BASIC TROUSER BLOCK
THREE-DIMENSIONAL GRADE

Figure 11a shows a split diagram for girth and height combined grade, and a grade plan for girth and height combined grade based on 5.0 cm girth and 2.4 cm height is shown in Figure 11b.

Increments for 2.4 cm height and 5.0 cm girth
For girth only: extract all height increments and change −8 to −10
For height only: extract all girth increments and change −8 to +2

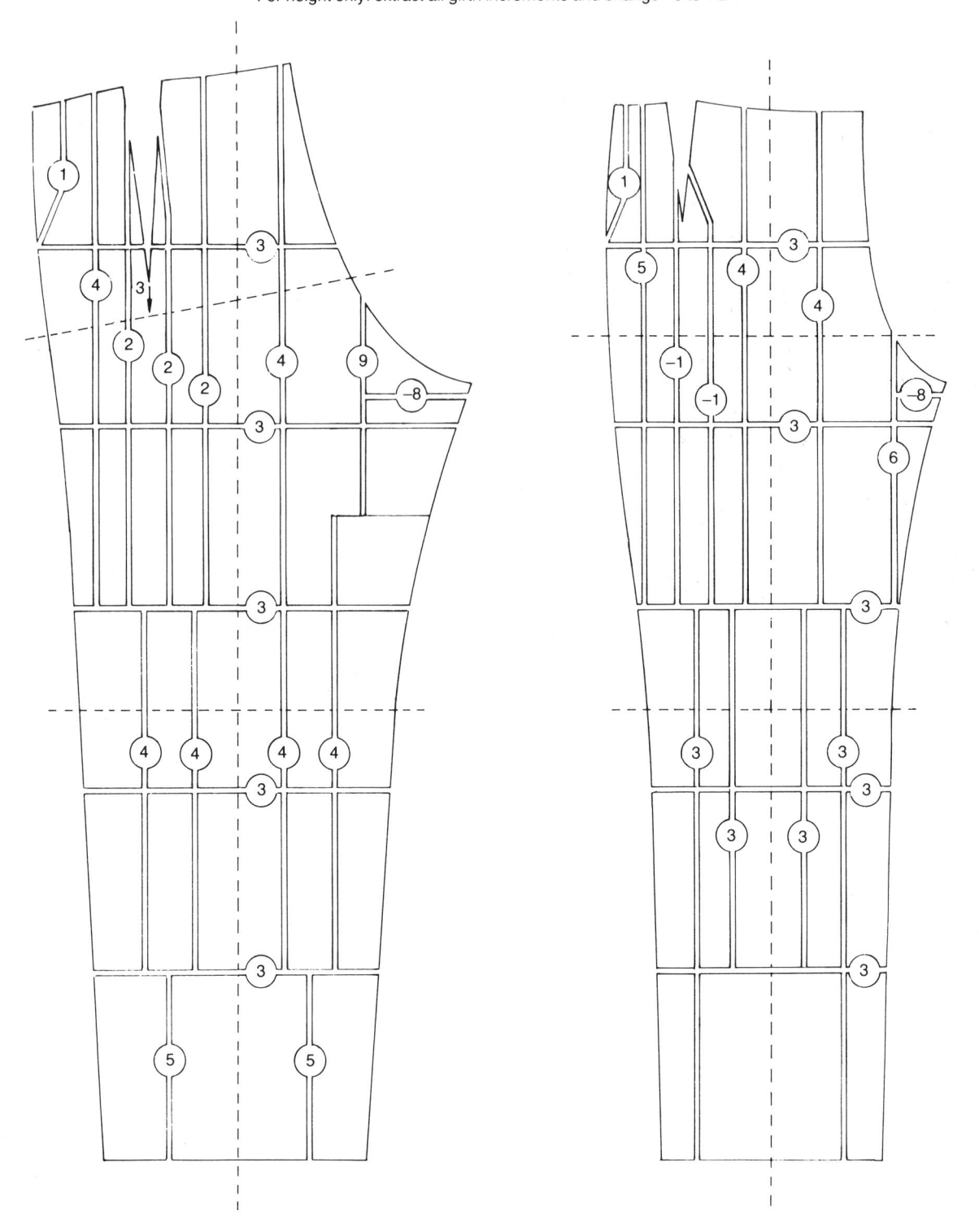

Figure 11 (a) Three-dimensional trouser split diagram

WOMEN'S GRADING INCREMENTS REFERENCE

Increments for 2.4 cm height and 5.0 cm girth
Can be used over seven sizes

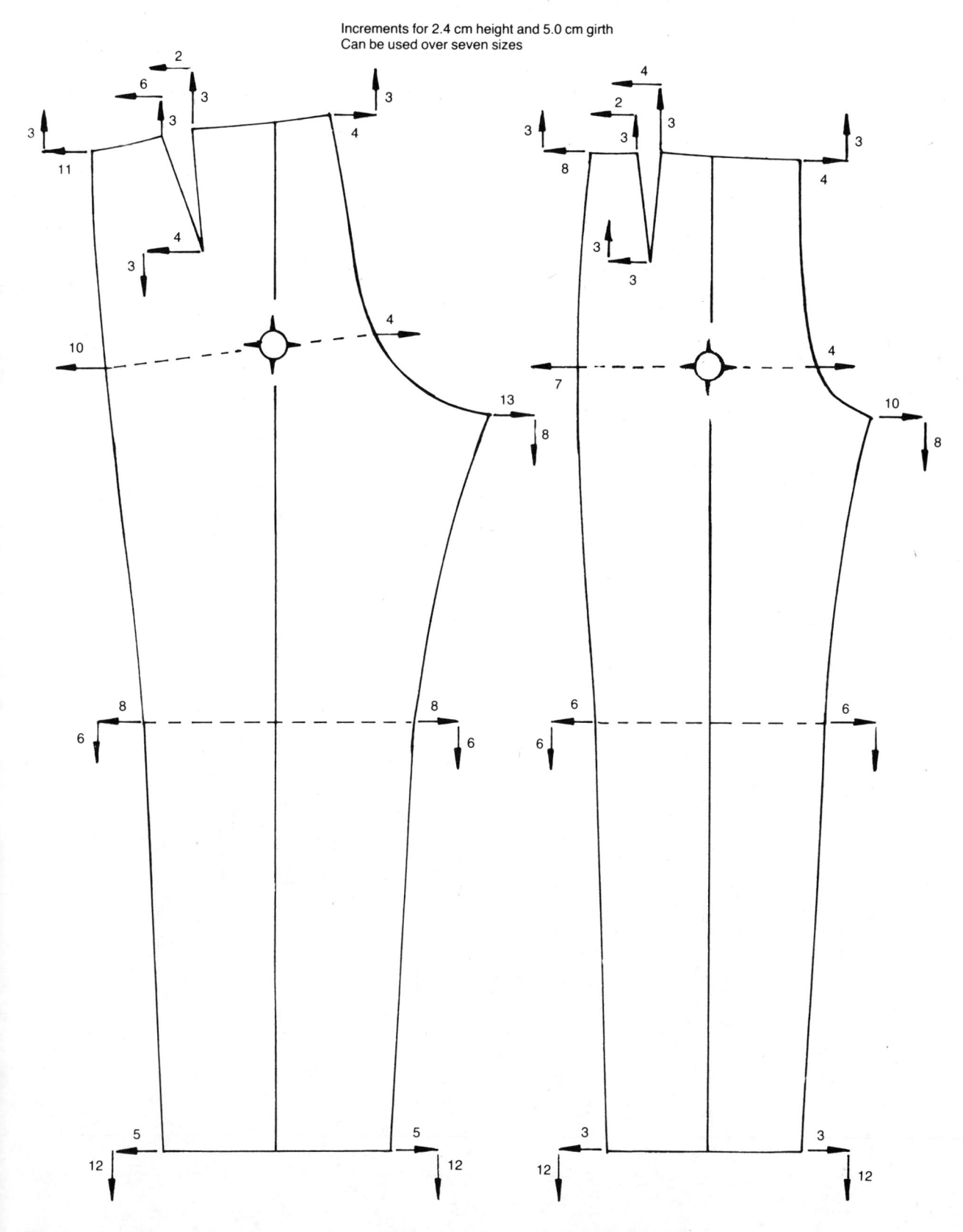

(b) Three-dimensional trouser grade plan taken from the split diagram in (a)

BASIC STRAPLESS CONTOUR BLOCK
THREE-DIMENSIONAL GRADE

Figure 12a shows a split diagram girth and height combined grade and Figure 12b shows a grade plan for girth and height combined grade based on 5.0 cm girth and 2.4 cm height.

Increments for 2.4 cm height and 5.0 cm girth

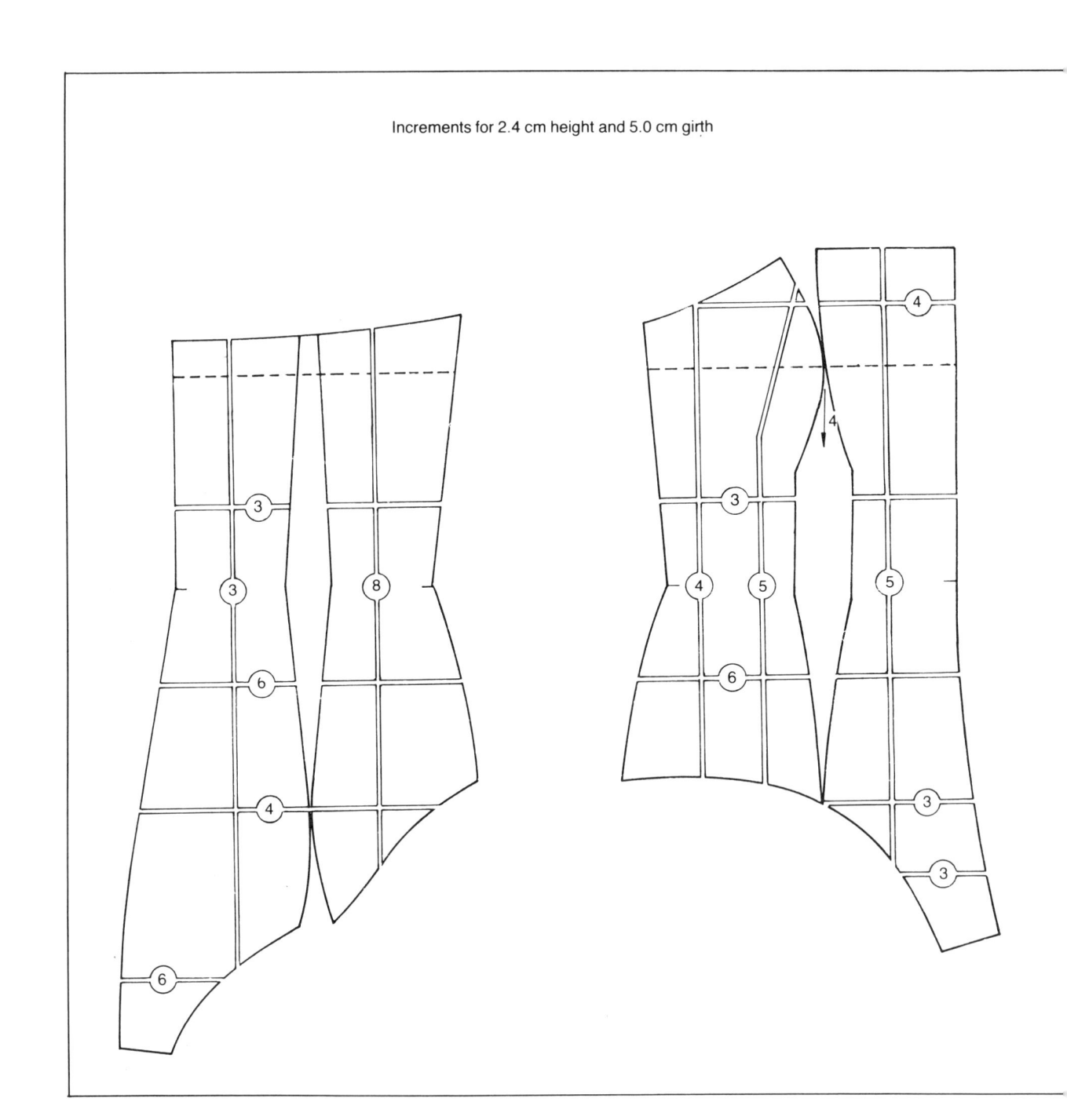

Figure 12 (a) Three-dimensional contour block split diagram

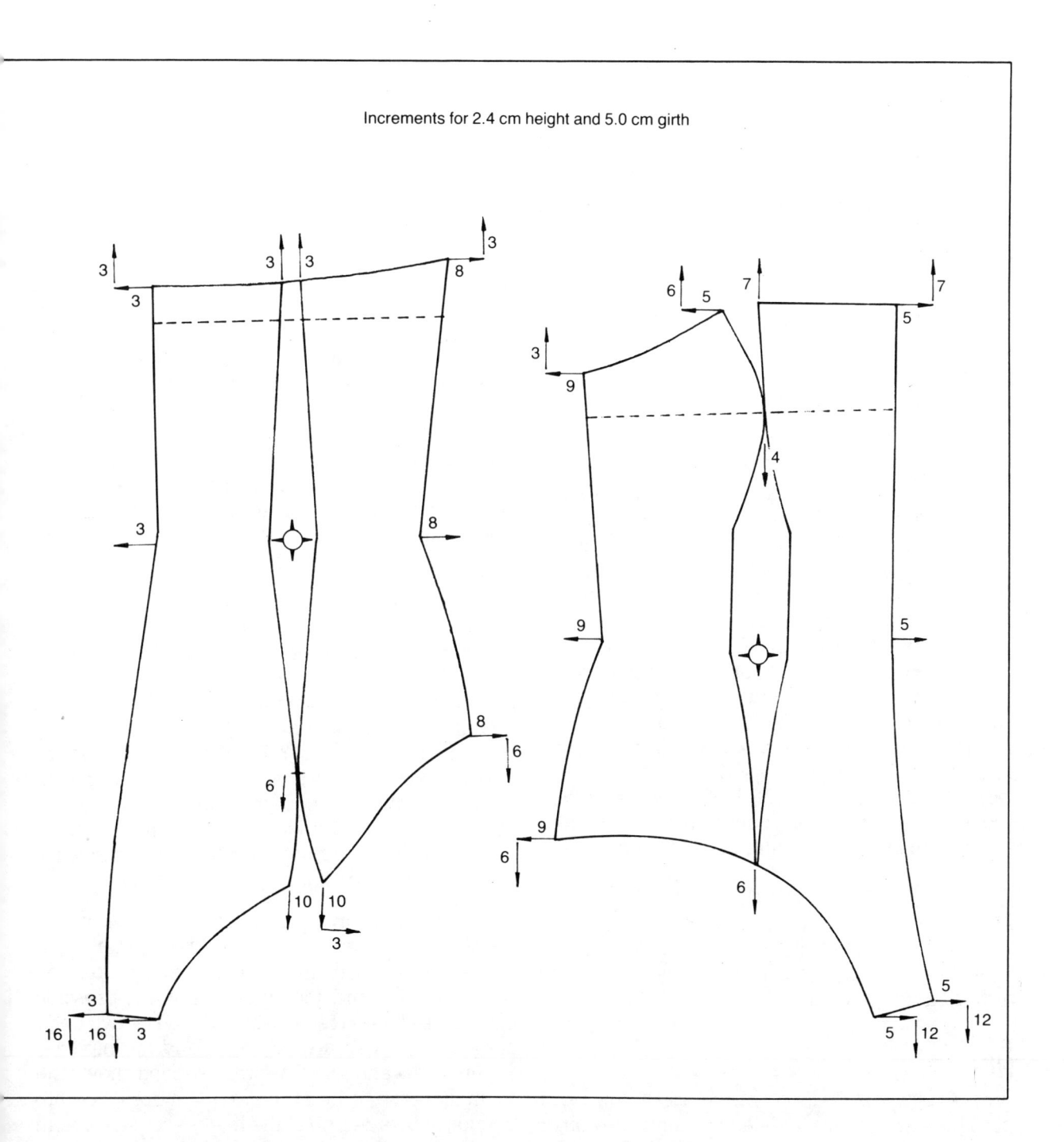

WOMEN'S GRADING INCREMENTS REFERENCE 47

Increments for 2.4 cm height and 5.0 cm girth

(b) Three-dimensional contour block grade plan

CHAPTER 3

Area commentaries

This chapter presents a part by part examination of the body increments and the problems arising in each area, taking the full size chart from area 1 to 34.

HEIGHT

Height is affected by age grouping. The survey sample covered three age groups whose average heights were:

1. 18–29 years = 161.0 cm
2. 30–44 years = 160.0 cm
3. 45–64 years = 157.6 cm

There are two factors influencing these figures. The first is that height decreases with increasing age, due to the shrinkage of the spinal discs. The second factor emerged from the survey itself, which indicated that overall height had increased within the span of two generations (a generation being taken as 25 years, i.e., the average child-bearing age). This prompted the survey team to predict a height increase for future generations, although it obviously would not go on increasing indefinitely. Their prediction has so far worked out fairly accurately. For detailed information refer to W. F. F. Kemsley's *Women's Measurements and Sizes* (HMSO 1957). These factors should be taken into account when constructing size charts and considering market areas.

WEIGHT

Weight has no direct influence on grading and is included more as a point of interest relating to girth and height data.

HIP

As previously stated, the hip is used, wherever possible, as the size indicator, being the major girth of the body. The survey data relating to the hip are:

1. Hip girth
2. Hip width (bitrochanteric width)
3. Abdominal seat diameter

For the purposes of grading two questions arise – 'By how much does the hip increase?' and 'Where?'. The survey provides the answer to 'how much' but not to 'where'.

Figure 14 outlines the problem. It illustrates a section cut through the body at the hip. Figure 14a is the section showing the measurements applicable, and Figure 14b shows two sizes superimposed.

The question is, 'With a given increase of girth how much and where does the hip section change?' The answers should be based on a properly conducted survey, as previously stated. The quantities used in this book are based on available data and observation and are as follows:

1. 8 mm at side seam, which is correct according to the hip width data supplied by the survey, assuming that the same increase is applied on the left and right hip side seams.
2. The depth of hip (abdominal diameter) is not so straightforward. How much goes on the seat and how much on the front? The quantities in Figure 14b are 12 mm on the seat and 5 mm on the front. If it is correct that the increase is greater on the seat than the front, it will indicate that an *increase of suppression is required over the seat, thus making a three-dimensional grade necessary.*

In order to follow the increases of size below the waist it is necessary to use a three-dimensional grade, because of the increase in suppression over the seat and the decrease of suppression over the pelvis and side seam areas. The two body sections involved are the waist and the hip (see Figures 14b and 18). The waist section shows the main increase to be at the front, whereas the hip section shows it to be at the back. Therefore, from grading more on to the front skirt at the waist a switch has to be made to grade more on to the seat

| AREA COMMENTARIES | 49 |

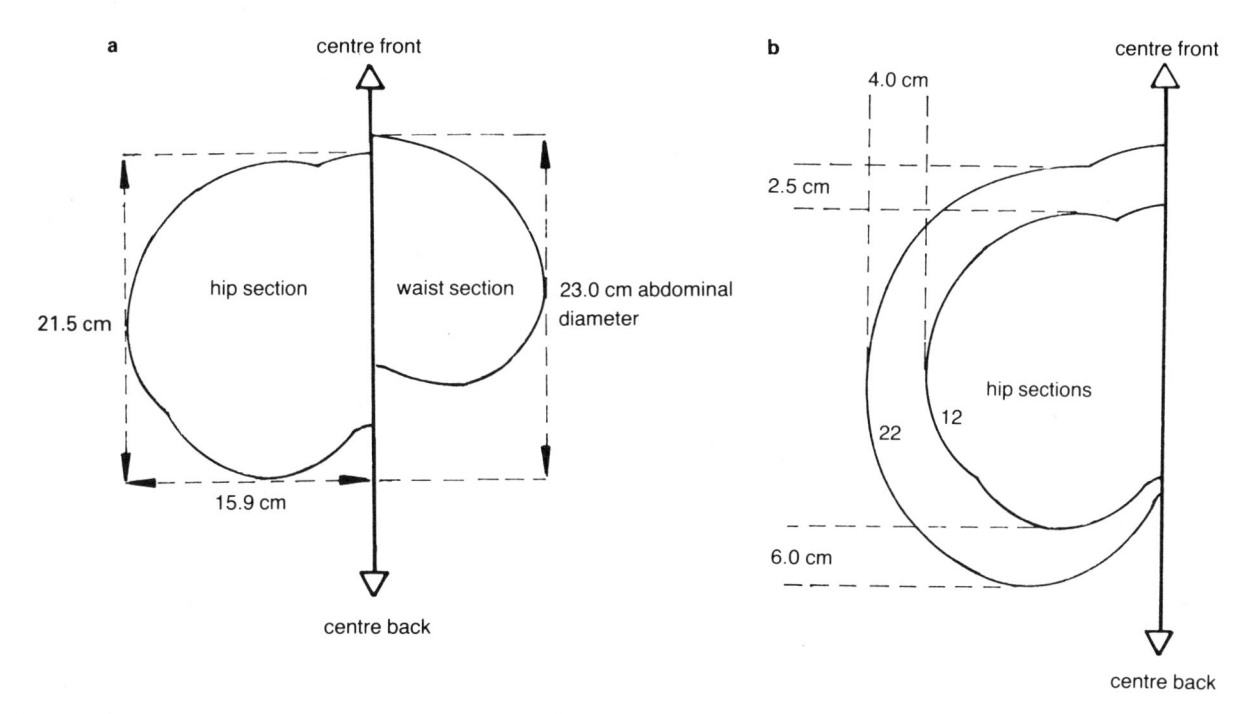

Figure 14 Hip sections
(a) Size 12 hip dimensions with waist section adjacent in true relation showing abdominal diameter
(b) Size 12 and 22 hip sections superimposed showing diameter increases. Divide these quantities by five to get single size increases

at hip level. The quantities involved here are illustrated in Chapter 2. They are applied on the half skirt at the rate of 1.4 cm on the front waist and 1.1 cm on the back waist. These quantities are reversed at the hip level to 1.4 cm on the back hip and to 1.1 cm on the front hip. In order to do this a shift of suppression is needed. The front pelvic and side suppressions are reduced and the back seat suppression is increased. Figure 15 shows a side view of the increases from 12 to 22. A–B and C–D are the largest areas of increase.

BUST

The bust development confronts the grader with perhaps the most difficult single problem in grading. First, the bust position can vary considerably, depending on the age group, the type of foundation garment worn, and where no foundation garment is worn. The bust position also depends on the girth or size of the bust. In general it can be stated that the larger the bust the lower and wider is its position. This requires the grading system to incorporate a means of lowering and widening the bust position for an increase of girth. It is the lowering factor which, if included, makes grading the front bodice more difficult. Because of this difficulty some grading systems dispense with the lowering of the bust, but this decreases the efficiency of the system if it is to be used over a wide size range. If used over a small size range then an argument can be made for omitting it. As with other body sections, the increase of bust girth is not evenly distributed and insufficient data was collected in the survey regarding depth and width of the section through the bust. Figure 16b shows a typical section through the bust, including sectional increases which are based on experience and usage, but which are not supported by survey data. Sizes 12 to 22 have been superimposed on the section and it gives the suggested sectional increases for five sizes. The diameter increase at the side seam is 3.5 cm, at the bust point 5.5 cm and at the back 1.5 cm. Figure 16a shows the side view and illustrates the through measurement increase and the bust height. This is a scale drawing representing an increase from size 12 to size 22. A–E and A–C is the increase of front balance and B–C and D–E the decrease of bust point to waist. From this it can be seen that the bust girth increase is greater at the front than at the back, and that the front balance, A–C and A–E, increase is substantial, and the back balance, A–J and A–K, increase is nil.

The grading system must incorporate factors to allow for this uneven increase of size. First, it means that extra suppression (the bust suppression) above the bust point is needed. The suppression under the bust to the waist does not increase. This is due to the even sectional increase at the rib-cage and the waist, as can be seen from the side view shown in Figure 16a. The extra bust suppression enables more girth to be added on the front bodice than on the back and permits the correct shoulder and X-chest measurements to be applied.

Second, the main factor which emerges from the study of these sections is that a greater girth increase is needed on the front than on the back, and a very small increase at the shoulder means that a substantial increase of the bust suppression is required as the simple diagram in Figure 17 shows.

WAIST

Figure 17 is the body section of the waist representing sizes 12 and 22 superimposed to show the diameter increases. It can be seen that increases are uneven, being greater at the front, less at the sides and least at centre back. See Figure 18. If full size sections are drawn the grade increments can be read off to give, in this instance, 14 mm front per size and 11 mm back. This would ensure that the side seam remained in a static position.

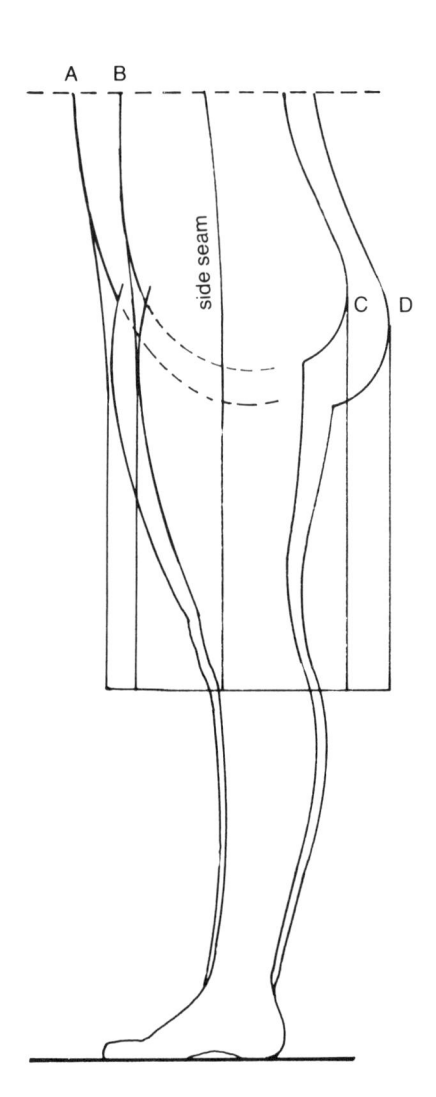

Figure 15 Skirt side view for size 12, with size 22 superimposed, showing different increases at the waist and hip giving rise to a suppression change (see hip area commentaries)

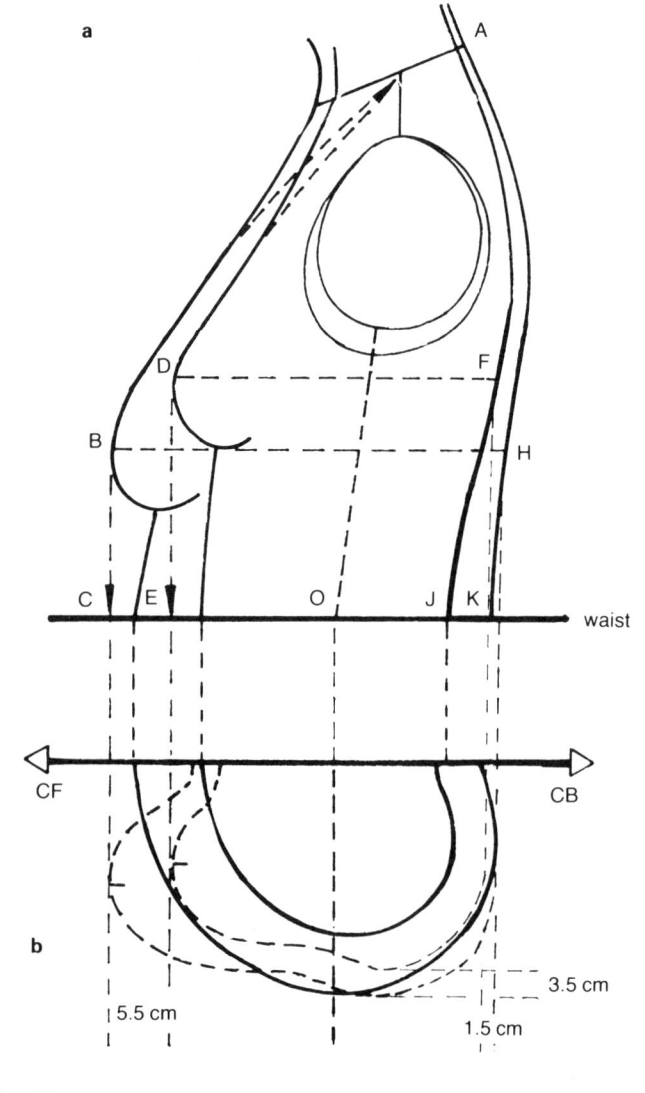

Figure 16 (a) Side view of the body from waist for sizes 12 and 22
(b) Corresponding sections of bust and waist superimposed

AREA COMMENTARIES

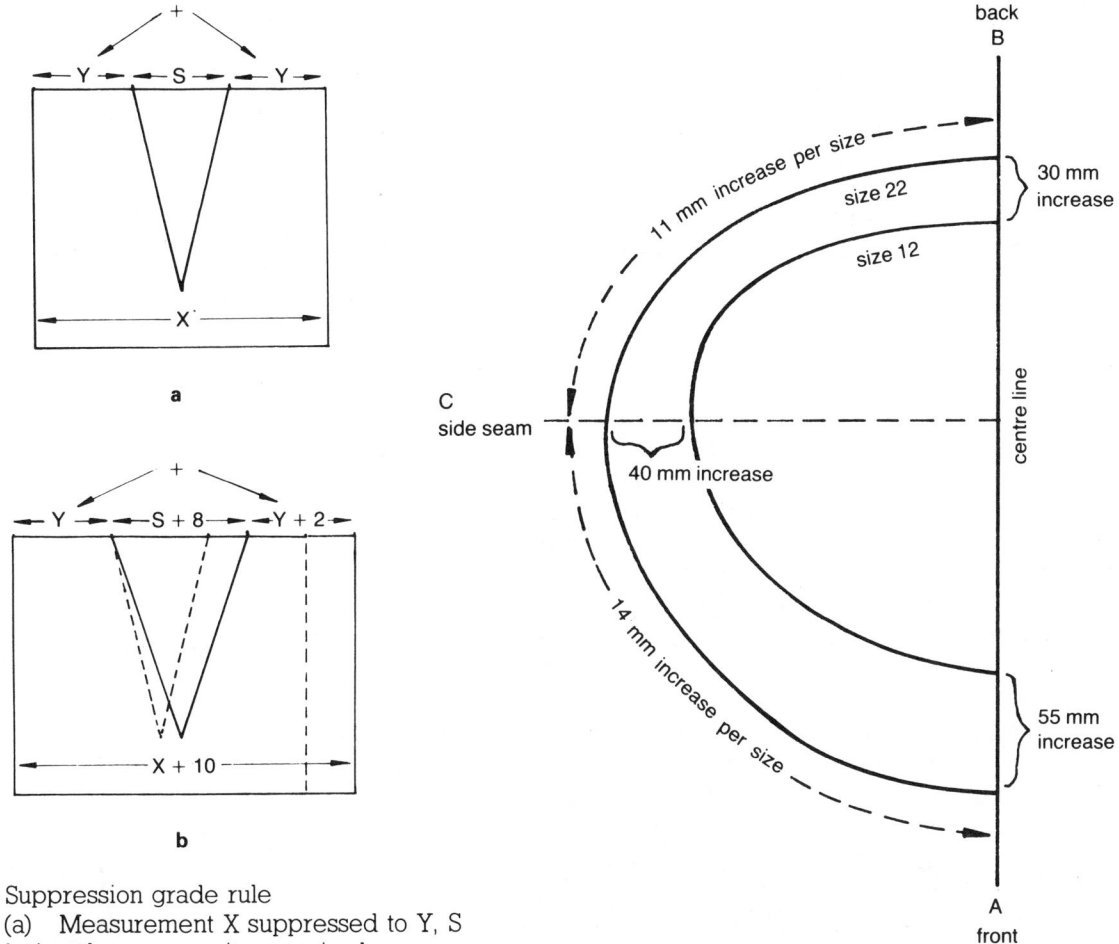

Figure 17 Suppression grade rule
(a) Measurement X suppressed to Y, S being the suppression required
(b) The British survey indicates that Y increases $\frac{1}{5}$ of the increase applied to X which results in the suppression S increasing $\frac{4}{5}$ of the increase applied to X. The shoulder–bust dimensions are very similar to this situation

Figure 18 Size 12 and 22 waist sections superimposed. This diagram shows how the waist grade increments can be calculated from the sections

CHEST

The chest girth increases by approximately 70 per cent of the bust increase. This percentage is taken from the survey and represents a statistical relationship. For a 5.0 cm increase in the bust the chest increases 3.6 cm. The statistically average figure, which is a size 14, has a bust of 92.0 cm and a chest of 85.6 cm. This is taken as a proportionate bust/chest relationship, which is a difference of 6.5 cm. If the bust is more than 6.5 cm larger than the chest for size 14 then it is a plus disproportionate bust; if it is less, it is a minus disproportionate bust.

The chest girth measurement is taken from the same point at centre back as the bust girth, but goes approximately 7.5 cm above the bust at the front.

The chest section diameter increases uniformly at the rate of 0.5 cm per size, as in Figure 19a. Figure 19b shows the sections of bust and chest superimposed. This demonstrates the geometry of the suppression of the bust girth to the chest, which is applied on the front bodice only (see *bodice contour grade*, Figure 11).

TOP HIP

Top hip girth is located half way between the hips and the waist. Its girth increases at the same rate as the hips and the waist. The diameter increase of the top hip is fairly even, unlike the waist which increases more at the front, and the hip which increases more at the back. The sectional increase will be 8 mm at the front, back and side.

RIB CAGE (under bust)

This girth measurement is taken close up under the bust. It is used in brassiere manufacture as the size indicator. For a proportionate bust development, or a 'B' cup, the difference between bust and rib-cage is 15.0 cm. The section of this area increases in diameter by the same amount as the waist; i.e., 6 mm at the back, 8 mm at the side seam and 11 mm at the front.

NECK

The survey indicates a 0.7 cm increase for a 5.0 cm hip increment for a girth only grade, and 0.2 cm for a 2.4 cm increase of height only. For a height and girth grade combined, an increase of 0.9 cm is required per size. The quantity of 0.9 cm is difficult to apply, so it is rounded up to 1.0 cm. If a large size range is to be graded care must be taken in styles where a high block neckline is used. It is recommended that no more than 1.0 cm is used. For lower neck styles or small size ranges the matter becomes less important and a larger quantity may be used, if required. The sectional diameter increases evenly, showing a 1 mm increase all round. As the shoulder seam is positioned towards the back, the front neck increases more than the back neck. Figure 20 shows the neck grade plan. These quantities add up to 0.6 cm on the half neck, but they give an increase of 0.5 cm on the half circumference which is the 1.0 cm for the whole neck.

BICEP

To maintain the sleeve balance through a large size range is difficult due mainly to the fact that the bicep increases at a greater rate at the back than at the front, whereas the back armhole tends to increase fractionally less than the front armhole. This increases the ease on the back sleeve head making insertion more difficult. For this reason the crown head notch is displaced slightly to the back on each side, which relieves the situation slightly.

There is an added difficulty for the shorter woman, because the sleeve head has to be sewn into a smaller armhole due to the shorter scye depth (see *scye width*, Figure 21, for further details).

ELBOW

There are no special notes for the elbow as it follows the bicep closely and is graded in the same way.

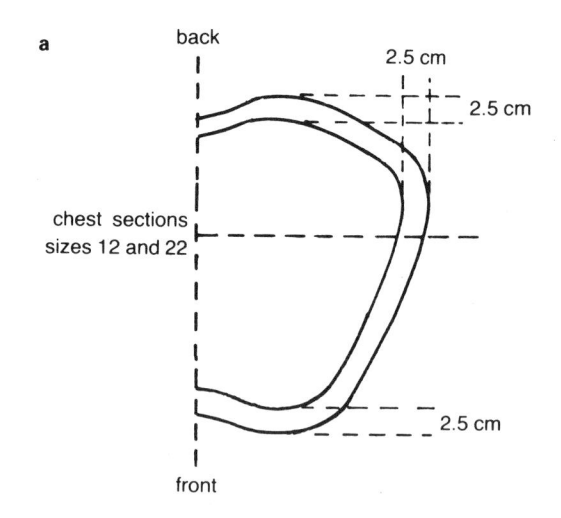

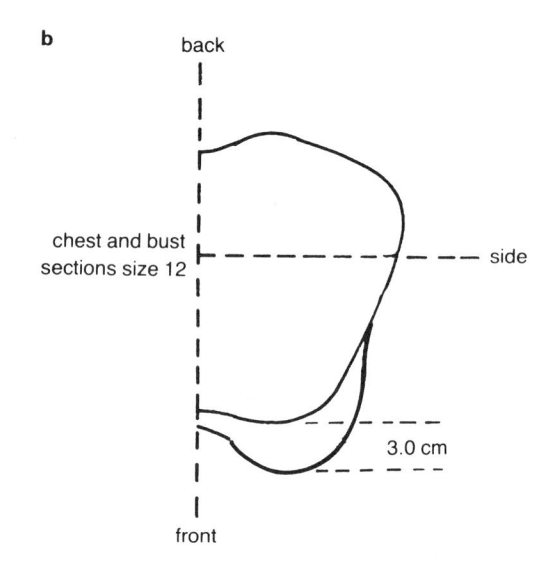

Figure 19 Chest sections

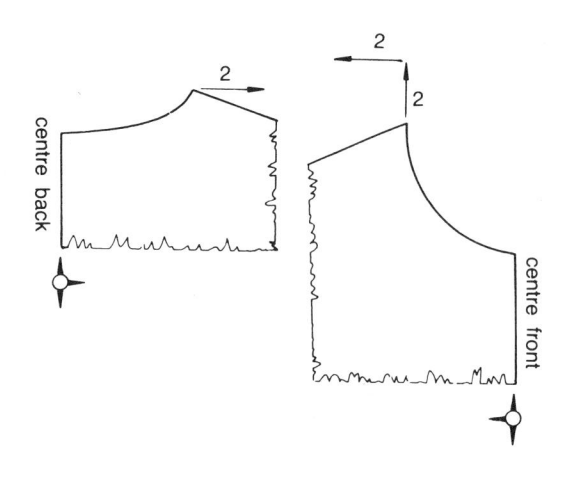

Figure 20 Neck grade plan

WRIST

The wrist girth increase for a 5.0 cm hip increment should not be more than 0.8 cm and can be as little as 0.6 cm. The increase is evenly distributed on the section. For a fitted sleeve a suppression change is required between the elbow, which increases 1.8 cm per size, and the wrist, which increases only 0.8 cm. The total wrist increase is applied only (see *block sleeve grade*, Figure 21).

THIGH

The thigh girth increases 3.2 cm for a 5.0 cm hip increment. This increase is distributed evenly on the section. The thigh measurement is taken as high as possible on the leg, underneath the buttock.

The trouser grade at the thigh area does not reflect the 0.8 cm grade at side seam and inside leg, as it is controlled by the hip increase. Thus, the grade increment on a typical trouser thigh is around 1.1 cm on the side seam and inside leg. For a close-fitting bifurcated garment, 0.8 cm would be used (see *bifurcated garments*, Chapter 9 and also Figures 10 and 13).

KNEE

The knee girth increases 1.2 cm for a 5.0 cm hip increment and 0.2 cm for a 2.4 cm height increment, giving 1.4 cm for a height and girth grade. This is applied evenly over the section giving a 0.3 cm grade at side seam and at inside leg. This is not reflected in the trouser grade where 0.7 cm is used. This is controlled by the hip. If 0.3 cm was used, the silhouette of the trouser would become distorted, becoming narrower at the knee as the size increased. Although it would still fit, the appearance would change (see also Chapter 9).

CALF

This girth increases at the same rate as the knee and the same comments apply (see Chapter 9).

ANKLE

This girth increases 0.7 cm for a 5.0 cm hip increment. Height has no influence on this increment. This gives a grade of approximately 0.2 cm on the side seam and inside leg and is used for a close-fitting garment. For loose legged styles, such as trousers, a larger amount can be used so that the silhouette of the style will not change (see Chapter 9).

X-CHEST

The X-chest increase for a girth only grade based on a 5.0 cm hip increment is between 0.8 cm and 1.0 cm, which is 0.4 cm or 0.5 cm on the half. For a height only grade of 2.4 cm the X-chest increases 0.1 cm to 0.2 cm on the half. This gives between 1.0 cm and 1.2 cm for a girth and height grade for the full X-chest. The X-chest measurement is taken at the widest point on the front scye; i.e., at the front pitch point. It should be noted that on the three-dimensional grade the X-chest increment is 2.0 cm or 1.0 cm on the half, as against a requirement of 0.6 cm on the half. The extra X-chest is absorbed by the extra suppression graded into the bust dart. It should also be noted on the two-dimensional grade that this quantity (i.e., 0.6 cm on the half) is correct. The armhole above this point has to be blended back to maintain the correct shoulder length, thus distorting the front armhole (see *special cardinal points* in Chapter 6). In general it is better to under grade the X-chest, as a surplus of material at the front scye pitch is unsightly. It will also help the insertion of the front sleeve, eliminating some of the easing.

X-BACK

X-back grade increments are the same as the X-chest; i.e., 0.6 cm on the half. This grade is applied at the back pitch point which is the widest point of the back scye box.

SHOULDER LENGTH

The length of shoulder increases very little from size to size. The survey indicates an increase of 0.1 cm per size for a 5.0 cm girth only, and 0.1 cm per 2.4 cm increase in height, totalling 0.2 cm for both. The tendency is to grade the shoulder length too much. As in other areas this length must be adhered to if a larger size range is to be catered for. If a small number of sizes are required, a larger shoulder increase can be used as it helps to maintain the front armhole shape (see *special cardinal points* and *bust suppression* in Chapter 6).

SCYE WIDTH

For a hip increment of 5.0 cm the body scye width increases 0.6 cm, but, because the bicep increases at a greater rate, a larger increment is used to maintain sleeve head insertion. An increase of at least 0.9 cm is needed to keep the balance between the scye width and the bicep increase. This is applied at the rate of 0.5 cm on the back scye width and 0.4 cm on the front scye width.

Figure 21a shows the scye box construction and the distribution of the scye grade increment between back scye width and front scye width. It shows the 0.5 cm increase on the back scye width and the 0.4 cm increase on the front scye width.

Figure 21b shows the half-sleeve increment which corresponds exactly to the scye grade increment. In a two-dimensional system this balance between the scye width and the sleeve grade is sacrificed because of the bust suppression omission involving an X-chest distortion. This increases the front scye width on the bodice (see the *two-dimensional grade plan*, Figures 7a and 7b).

SCYE DEPTH

The survey indicates a 0.45 cm increase for a girth only grade of 5.0 cm. The scye depth increases because of the build-up of flesh around the armpit area with the increase of size. The survey also indicates that, for a height increase of 2.4 cm, the scye depth only increases 0.1 cm. In other words, for a large overall increase in height, the increase in the depth of the armhole is small. This will conflict with the eight heads system of distributing the height increase because the nape to waist increase is unevenly applied, giving $\frac{5}{24}$ of the total height increase between the base of scye and waist and $\frac{1}{24}$ of the total height increase to the depth of scye. The deepening of the armhole for a girth only grade tends to be cancelled out by the height grade which is applied from the base of the scye to the waist.

Figure 21 shows the scye depth applied to the block draft, which is the nape to base of scye.

Note: the scye depth quoted in the size chart is a body measurement on to which a tolerance and seam allowance are added to arrive at the finished inset sleeve armhole depth (scye depth). The size chart scye depth can be used to indicate the under arm side seam levels for strapless type garments.

BUST WIDTH (bust point to bust point)

Very little can be said about this measurement. An increase of 0.6 cm on the half has been used for this book and is in general a practical quantity which is used widely. It is more than the survey indicates (about 0.5 cm). It is not critical as it depends largely on the type of support garment used.

NAPE TO BUST POINT AND NAPE TO WAIST OVER BUST

These two measurements can best be discussed together. The position of the bust point is influenced by the age group, and the type of foundation garment used, if any. Whether the bust is worn high or low makes no difference to the over-

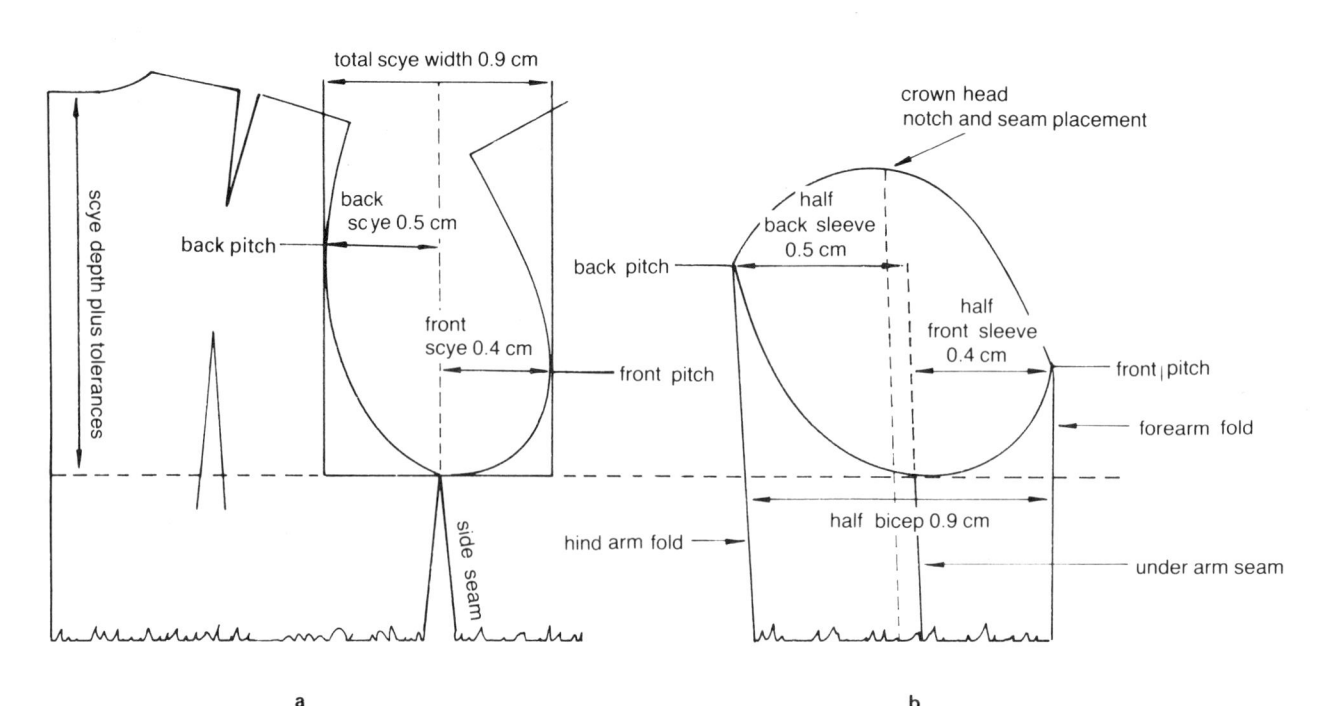

Figure 21 Scye box dimensions, grade increments, and sleeve head grade increases

AREA COMMENTARIES

all front balance. The survey indicates a difference in bust point height for the three age groups, the younger group having the highest bust point.

For an increase of size the bust point is lowered by 1.3 cm per 5.0 cm hip increase. The front balance, or nape to waist over bust, increases by 0.6 cm. This quantity consists of the back neck width increment of 0.2 cm and front balance increase of 0.4 cm. (See also *bust suppression*, Chapter 6.) Figure 16 illustrates the front balance increase.

NAPE TO WAIST (centre back)

Nape to waist increases are only necessary when grading for height. It increases at the rate of a $\frac{1}{4}$ of total height increment, based on the eight heads system.

NAPE TO HIP

This only increases when grading for height and does so at the rate of $\frac{3}{8}$ of the total height increment, based on the eight heads system.

NAPE TO KNEE

This only increases when grading for height and does so at the rate of $\frac{1}{2}$ of the total height increment, based on the eight heads system.

NAPE TO FLOOR

This increases only when grading for height and does so at the rate of $\frac{7}{8}$ of the total height increment, based on the eight heads system.

OUTER SLEEVE LENGTH

This increases only when a height increment is applied. It lengthens at the rate of $\frac{3}{8}$ of the total height increment, based on the eight heads system.

INNER SLEEVE LENGTH

This decreases with a girth grade at the same rate as the depth of scye increases. The decrease is applied at the base of the sleeve crown, not at the wrist.

When a height only grade is used the inner sleeve length increases at the rate of $\frac{9}{24}$ minus $\frac{1}{24}$ of the total height increment. For height and girth it increases at the rate of $\frac{1}{6}$ of the total height increment. As with the bodice, the girth and height grade tend to cancel each other out.

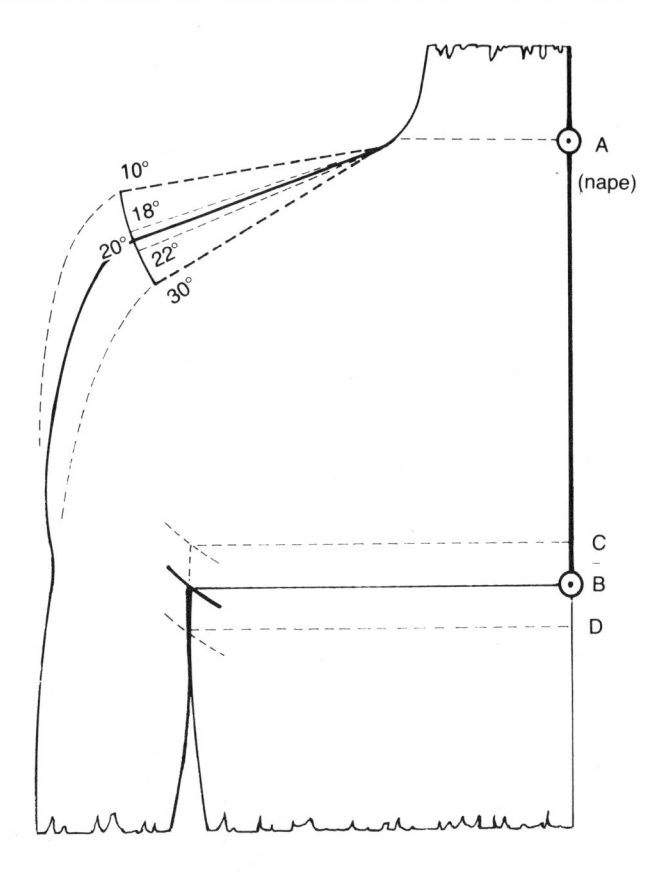

Effect of shoulder angle on scye depth.
A–B is scye depth for average 20° angle shoulder
A–C is scye depth for 10° angle shoulder
A–D is scye depth for 30° angle shoulder
18°–22° angle covers 65 per cent of the population
10° and 30° angles represent extremes measured in the survey

Figure 22 Shoulder angle

ABDOMINAL SEAT DIAMETER AND HIP WIDTH

These two areas have been discussed and explained in the hip section and will also be discussed in Chapter 9 in the section on *bifurcated garments*.

BODY RISE

The same principles apply for body rise as for the scye depth. The body rise increases because flesh is deposited in the area of the crutch at the rate of 1.0 cm per 5.0 cm girth increase. Height has very little effect on this measurement. The body rise only increases for height at the rate of 0.1 cm per 2.4 cm total height increase. This gives a total of 1.1 cm increase per size, for height and girth grades combined (See also, Chapter 9, the section on *bifurcated garments*).

SHOULDER ANGLE

The survey data indicates that for an increase of girth, there is a slight decrease of 0.15° in the shoulder angle (squarer shoulder). For height increase there is an increase of 0.14° (rounder shoulder). These amounts are minute and can be ignored. They do in fact cancel each other out for a height and girth grade.

Figure 22 shows the range of angles measured in the survey. They extend from 10° to 30°. The majority of the population are covered by the angles from 18° to 22°.

As a matter of interest, it can be noted that the shoulder angle will have an influence on the scye depth (nape to base of scye). The squarer the shoulders, the smaller the scye depth, because the whole shoulder and blade complex is carried higher, and vice versa. This is illustrated in Figure 22, which shows a scaled back view drawing of the shoulder angle and nape to base of armhole (scye depth). This measurement is 18.0 cm for a size 12 (this does not include tolerances etc.; it is a pure body measurement). This measurement can vary by as much as 1.8 cm according to the shoulder angle. It has no direct bearing on grading, but does show that the actual armhole will be the same size for all the shoulder angles for a given size, but is situated higher or lower than the standard.

Although the survey states that the average angle changes very little through the size range, it is not known how much the end of the shoulder thickens. According to certain stand manufacturers, the end thickens enough to influence the pattern angle of the shoulder. Here, a distinction must be made between the pattern angle and the actual body shoulder angle; they are not the same. In other words, if the shoulder angle on the stands is kept constant throughout the size range it is necessary to change the angle of the pattern shoulder in order to maintain the constant shoulder angle of the stand. The reason for this is that the thickness through the end of the shoulder

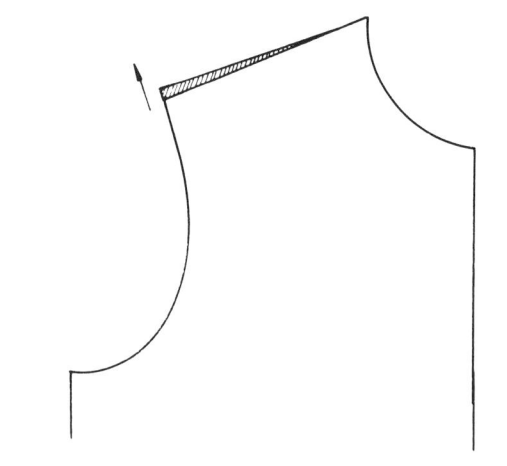

The shaded area represents extra length needed because of thickening at shoulder end. With size increase this amount at most is 3° over five sizes back and front shoulder

Figure 23 Shoulder angle

requires a greater length at the end of the shoulder on the pattern, as shown in Figure 23. Most pattern technicians maintain that the shoulder angle on the pattern should remain the same for all sizes, but the stands demand a change. Who is right? This cannot be determined because there is no survey data to throw any light on the matter. The grading data produced in this book allows for a thickening through the ends of the shoulder and thus the shoulder angle of the pattern becomes a little squarer for each size, but when assembled gives an unaltered shoulder angle.

The shoulder angle on the front bodice appears to increase (rounder shoulders) with size when a three-dimensional grade is used. In fact, the opposite is true with the quantities used in this book. When the bust dart is closed the true relationship between shoulder angles and the sizes can be seen. It is only from this position that they can be controlled or altered and then opened out again to the block form and the grade increments read off for the grade plan. (See also *special areas*, Chapter 6.)

CHAPTER 4

Selecting a grading system

It is necessary to distinguish between *grading systems* which describe the principles of body growth and *grading techniques* which are simply a means of applying these principles.

GRADING SYSTEMS

Grading can be classified into the following two broad systems:

1 *Three dimensional grading* which not only increases a pattern for size but also increases or decreases suppression in the following areas:

a bust to shoulder
b hip to waist
c elbow to wrist.

A good three dimensional system will closely follow the indications of the National Survey data on body size and figuration. If the balance and fit of the stock size garment is to be retained suppression quantities must be adjusted per size. A three dimensional system will take this increase into account.

Three dimensional grading is the optimum system and should be used whenever possible, particularly when grading close fitting or skin-tight garments and garments that progress in size from 10 to 22.

The most important garment area is the bust to shoulder suppression. This controls the shape and balance of the front bodice. Coupled with this is the movement of the bust point which has an effect on the bust to shoulder suppression quantity. The survey indicates that the bust point moves progressively closer to the waist with the increase of the girth. A technique has been devised, and is illustrated in this book, which incorporates the three dimensional bust suppression factor and the moving or non-static bust point. A good working knowledge of pattern cutting is necessary to be able to use a three dimensional grading system. The other areas of suppression change are not so important and are discussed in Chapter 3.

2 *A two dimensional grading sytem* only grades a pattern for girth and height and its application is therefore limited to loose or semi-drape type garments because it retains the stock size suppressions throughout the size range. This system is never fully recommended by the authors because fitting and balance faults will automatically occur to the graded garment range when the suppressions are not adjusted to cater for each size. However, a very loose fitting garment such as a shirt or a batwing blouse with a limited size range of say 10-12-14, may be safely graded using a two dimensional system. If, however, these garments need to be graded up to size 16 and beyond, suppressions may need to be included in the pattern and graded three dimensionally.

Criteria for selecting a grading system may be summarised as follows.

SKILLS AVAILABLE

This means the degree of knowledge of pattern construction and manipulation possessed by the technician.

TYPES OF GARMENT

There are two main categories:

1 Close fitting or skin-tight garments.
2 Loose or semi-drape garments.

The closer the garment fit, the more important it is to select a sophisticated garment grading system which adjusts the garment suppressions. The looser the garment fit the value of adjusting the garment suppressions decreases and a two dimensional system becomes more viable.

NUMBER OF SIZES

This may depend a little on whether a garment is close or loose-fitting, but it mainly refers to a situation where the company only offers a limited number of sizes. The greater the number of sizes the more complex the grading system and vice versa.

TYPES OF FABRIC

For grading purposes fabrics may be classified into two broad types, e.g. stretch and non-stretch. Stretch fabrics are more forgiving and will conform more readily to the body contours and, therefore, it could be argued that a less efficient system could be employed. A non-stretch fabric has the reverse effect and must be kept under control and in balance through the size range.

GRADING TECHNIQUES

This book illustrates in detail two techniques for applying grading increments, which are:

1. The draft or multi size (nested) grade.
2. The track or single size grade.

THE DRAFT GRADE

This term applies when the pattern is returned to its original block form or when the increment is applied to the actual pattern draft. This results in the entire size range being superimposed on top of one another and can also be described by the term 'nested' or 'stacked'. The individual pieces of pattern for each size are then spiked or traced off on to card. A draft grade can be either two or three dimensional.

The three dimensional draft grade is considered to be the ultimate method of applying grade increments. This is the system which will give the best results if it is used properly, and presupposes the use of the correct increments.

THE TRACK GRADE

This term is used when grade increments are applied to individual pieces of pattern by moving the base pattern piece along predetermined tracks, marking around the pattern section by section and thus altering its size. This system is usually two dimensional but can with difficulty be adapted to a three dimensional system.

The following sets out the advantages and disadvantages of the draft and track grading systems.

THREE DIMENSIONAL DRAFT GRADE

Advantages

1. It is the only way the front bodice suppression and the front and the bust point can be controlled.
2. Minimises mistakes in calculating grade increments, i.e. only one set of calculations is necessary.
3. Facilitates any change in suppression.
4. Permits the grading of a full size range from 10 to 22 (or more if necessary), incorporating different girth measurements if needed.
5. Eliminates the need to change to different blocks as the size increases to outsize.
6. The exact grade that is applied can be seen and any errors become apparent right away.
7. It helps the grader to become very accurate because it is a drafting situation.
8. The draft can be kept as a reference, and is thus readily available for easy style changes (based of course on the same draft).
9. Facilitates easy style proportioning of the grade because it provides an overview of the total patterning process.
10. The draft can be graded by the pattern technician, and then handed over to an assistant to be spiked off and cut out into sizes.
11. Vertical and horizontal increment application from a cardinal point has an obvious computer grading application. See Chapter 7.

Disadvantages

1. It requires a good working knowledge of pattern cutting.
2. It requires more of the pattern technician's time.

It would be wrong to give the impression that the three dimensional system is the only relevant system. In many circumstances a simplified technique may be used, e.g. the track system, which was devised because a simple and direct method was needed in order to pass the grading work onto a semi-skilled technician. The advantages and disadvantages of the track system are outlined below.

THE TRACK SYSTEM OF GRADING

Advantages

1. Requires little knowledge of pattern construction.
2. The basic instructions are easy to learn and follow.
3. The method of applying the grade increments along tracks is simple.
4. The idea behind the method is easy to understand.

Disadvantages

1. It is difficult to apply split increments to individual pattern pieces and to work out the quantities.

2. More increment calculations are involved and calculations for each size are required, thus inviting the possibility of error.
3. Mistakes can go unnoticed until the final check when all the pattern pieces are superimposed. The superimposition of the pattern pieces is in itself time-consuming.
4. By definition the system must be simplified and is therefore less efficient.
5. There is no overall view of grading for reference to proportion.
6. Proportion and other grading decisions have to be made and these are sometimes wrongly interpreted by the grader technician because of inexperience.
7. Track techniques do not lend themselves to the changing of suppression quantities. It can be done (See Chapter 6) but some styles render it almost impossible.

SUMMARY

This chapter has defined the complex set of principles behind three dimensional grading and the advantages and disadvantages behind its use. It has also defined two dimensional grading and the reasons for its application. This chapter has also described the two main grading techniques, e.g. draft and track and how they relate to a three dimensional or two dimensional application. It is hoped that the options facing the grader when selecting a grading system and application technique has now been clarified. To sum up, the choice is based on the garment style, fabric type, size range and skills available. If all these factors are taken into consideration the grader or pattern technician will be making an informed rational decision with much better results.

CHAPTER 5

Stands

The most important piece of equipment used by the manufacturer is the stand, as it plays a part in all stages of production.

It is essential to have a reliable and tested set of stand sizes which follow a natural even and progressive increase. These, unfortunately, are not so easy to find. They must increase as indicated by the survey and not just by the major girths.

If reliable stands can be acquired then it will be possible to extract the grading instructions and increments directly from them. Assuming that the stands increase evenly, it will be necessary in order to establish the increments between sizes, to make a block from the largest stand and superimpose it on the stock size, 12. Having superimposed the two sizes according to the preferences of the pattern technician, the grade quantities can be read off along tracks, parallel, and 90° to the centre back and front lines. These quantities would then be divided by the number of sizes between them, resulting in a set of single size increments.

Note: At the time of writing, the authors have not been able to acquire a set of stands which conform to an acceptable standard.

The shape of the stand is therefore paramount. It must represent the average figure shape, based on reliable survey data and, at the same time, must conform to the national standards. The stand manufacturer is, therefore, of great importance.

Stand manufacturers rely on (or should rely on) the survey data when designing suitable stands. Unfortunately, the interpretation of the incomplete data by different stand manufacturers has resulted in a wide variety of shapes which all have the correct major girth measurements. The problem lies in the fact that the surveys conducted so far have concentrated on the question 'What size?', rather than 'What size and shape?' Research in this area would benefit the industry. It may well now be possible, with the computers and electronic hardwear that are available, to devise a means of quickly measuring a complex shape, such as the human form, and process the data in order to achieve a deeper understanding of stance, posture and areas of body increase. This would require a whole new set of measurements relating to the shape of sections through the body at specific points and the relation of these sections to each other. The superimposing of different girth measurements of the same section on to each other would clearly indicate how and where the flesh or fat was being deposited, and the superimposing of different sections of the body on to each other related to a datum line would clearly show stance and posture.

If this data were collected the stand manufacturers would be in a stronger position and would be able to produce the stands appropriate for any given figure type. It would also mean they could produce a stand nearer to the average stance and posture.

The areas to be studied would fall into three groups:

1 Sectional girth increases
2 Curvature of the spine
3 Shoulder blade complex

SECTIONAL GIRTH INCREASE

An example of the through section of the waist has been taken in order to illustrate sectional girth increase and is shown in Figure 18, **page 51**. The half waist sections for sizes 12 and 22 have been superimposed. 'A' is the centre front, 'B' is the centre back and 'C' the side seam position. The position of these two sections in relation to each other is based on observations, and measurements taken from existing stands and on what is thought to be correct at the present time. Most of the increase takes place over the stomach at centre front where a 5.5 cm increase in diameter is registered. The side seam shows a 4.0 cm increase in diameter and the centre back a 3.5 cm

STANDS

61

Major body sections of size 12 and 22 superimposed on each other. Taken from Figure 25 on opposite page.
These sections are also exact scale reproductions.

(1) neck

(2) shoulder

(3) chest

(4) bust size 12 over upper bust of size 22

(5) rib cage size 12 bust size 22

(6) under bust size 22 lower rib cage size 12

front

(7) waist

(8) top hip

(9) hip

(10) thigh size 12 lower seat size 22

(11) knee

(12) calf

(13) ankle

front

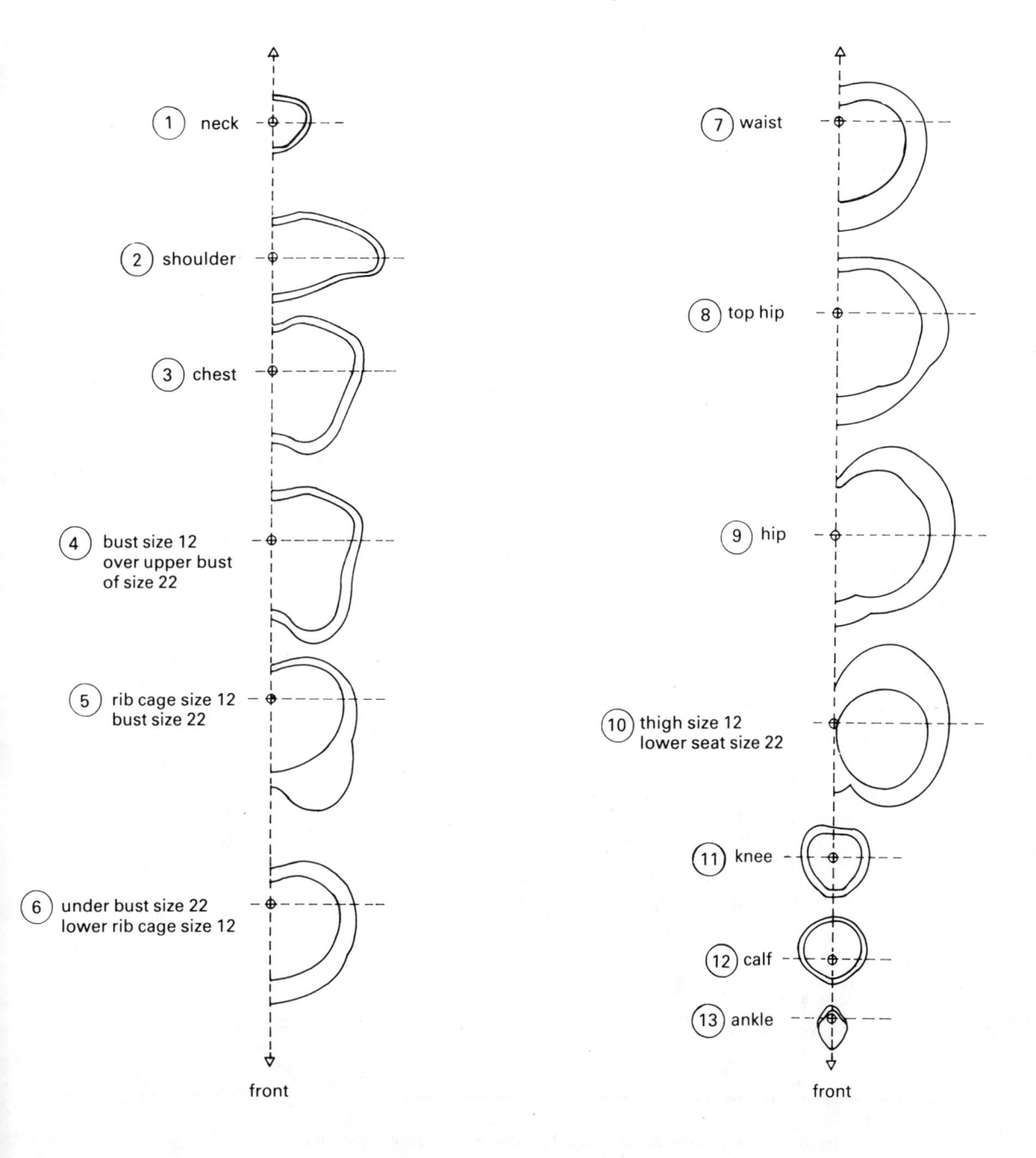

Figure 24 Major body sections of size 12 with those of size 22 superimposed on equivalent levels taken from Figure 25

62 | THE THEORY AND PRINCIPLES OF GRADING

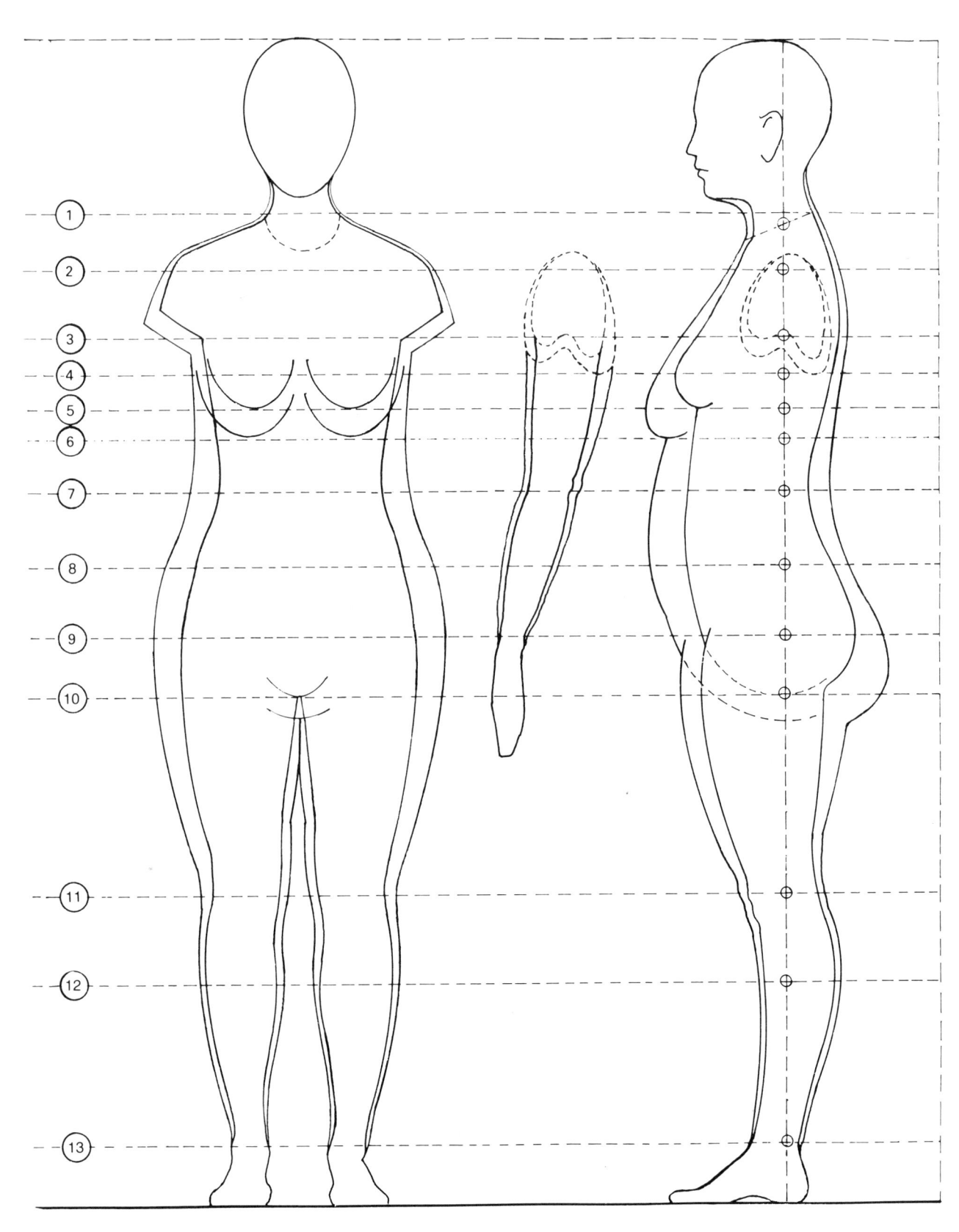

This drawing is to scale: scale = 162.0 cm divided by height of drawing

Figure 25 Body growth areas from size 12 to 22

STANDS 63

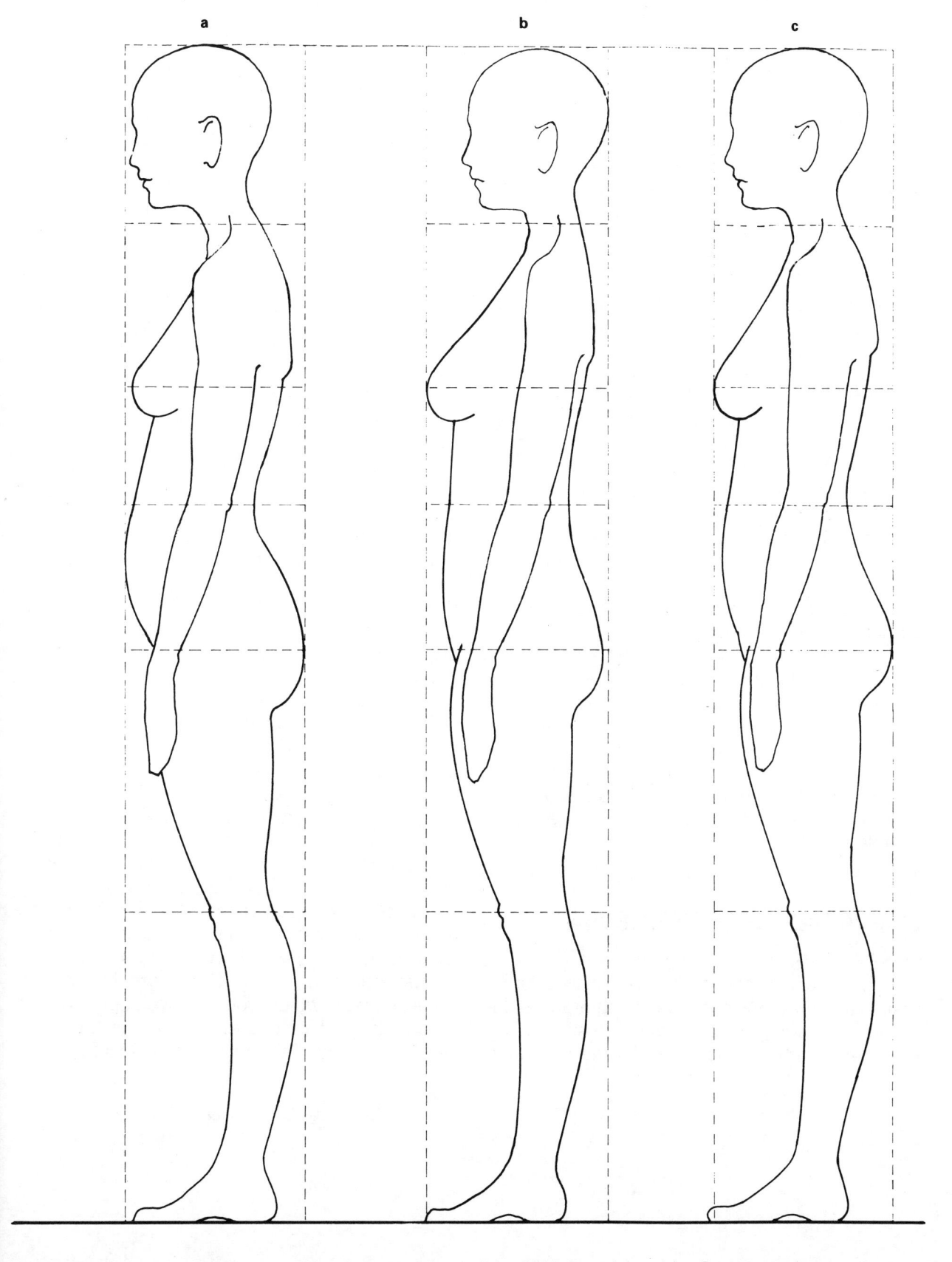

Figure 26 Basic types of stance (a) Curved spine; (b) Straight spine; (c) Average spine

increase. These quantities can be divided by five to give the increase for one size and, most important, the quarter circumferences can be measured in order to give the exact quantities for grading; that is from A to C and C to B, thus giving the grade increments for the front and back waist for the skirt and bodice.

If all the major body sections are drawn up full scale in this way, and based on accurate measurements (as illustrated in Figure 24) related to a datum line, then most of the grading increments can be determined.

Figure 24 shows all the major body sections of a size 12, with those of a size 22 superimposed. These sectional comparisons are based on the information available at the present time, and show clearly where the increases occur. All the sections have been dealt with in more detail in Chapter 3.

Figure 25 shows a size 12, which has been increased to a size 22 and superimposed. These drawings are as near to true scale as possible and can be used to produce measurements. They include a datum line to which all the sections are related and from which all the measurements are taken. The datum line has been located vertically from the heel. However, if taking measurements from a live sample, the datum line would have to be outside the body touching the most extreme part of the body. In other words the sample to be measured would stand with its back to a vertical datum line, just touching it. Each major section would then be measured in detail and its distance from the datum line and the floor recorded, in order to locate the section correctly and to establish the second and third factors, which are curvature of the spine and disposition of shoulder blade complex.

CURVATURE OF THE SPINE AND SHOULDER BLADE COMPLEX

Figure 26a and b shows two extremes of spine shape and Figure 26c shows the average spine shape. The straight spine shape results in the shoulders being pulled back and squarer, producing a flat back. This shape increases the bust suppression and decreases the blade suppression. The other extreme shows the spine rounded at the top and hollowed at the waist. This produces a pronounced stomach and protruding shoulder blades and is usually accompanied by sloping shoulders. This figure shape will require a reduction in bust suppression and an increase in blade suppression.

The shoulder blade complex is very mobile, as it is only secured to the rib-cage by muscle, although the habitual stance becomes a permanent figure shape in time.

Another characteristic of these two factors is that they alter the scye depth. In other words, the armhole or scye is carried higher on the squarer shouldered or straight figure; when the shoulder complex drops then the scye drops with it, thus increasing the measurement from nape to base of scye (see Figure 21). This is illustrated in Chapter 3.

There is one final point to discuss: should the stand include tolerances? Many pattern technicians find the inclusion of tolerances a handicap. It does, of course, depend on the type of garment being constructed. The area around the chest, neck and shoulders is usually increased and thickened on stands. This may be suitable for the construction of outer wear, but for close-fitting garments it can be very misleading and serves no purpose.

In conclusion, it can be said that the field of stand construction at the present time leaves a great deal to be desired. A lot of sales jargon comes from stand manufacturers about 'fashion shape', but there can be no such thing. The only area to be affected by fashion is the bust height and width, which is determined by the support worn, if any. This could be overcome by an inventive stand manufacturer using detachable and height adjusting bust pieces, and could be taken a stage further with an adjustable blade complex. This would be expensive but would be invaluable to pattern technicians. These are the sort of developments which would be welcomed by pattern technicians, together with a new and wider national survey of the mature female's figure.

CHAPTER 6

Special areas

CONVERTING THREE-DIMENSIONAL AND MULTI-TRACK QUANTITIES FOR TRACK AND COMPUTER GRADING

There are two problem areas which need detailed explanation:

1 The difficulty of grading the front bodice three-dimensionally using the track technique.
2 The need to convert multi-track to single track for use in a computer.

Both of these problems are resolved by recalculating the grade quantities as described below. The reason for this recalculation is that the computer only operates on two co-ordinates and, therefore, it is not possible to use multi-track quantities. It also applies to the front bodice three-dimensional grade when using a computer or track grade method. In these techniques the pattern is graded directly and not returned to its original block form before grading (see Chapter 13).

METHOD FOR RECALCULATING GRADE QUANTITIES

The first problem is that the cardinal points on the side of the front bodice, when graded three-dimensionally, move unevenly. This applies whether the bust point is dropped or not. In order to arrive at grade increments for these points it is first necessary to grade the front bodice block as usual, that is five sizes up to size 22. From this position, manipulate the darts for both size 12 and 22, putting all the suppression into the shoulder, and, second, all the suppression into the waist. These two manipulations will give the relationship of movement between the size 12 and 22; first upwards, when the darts are put into the waist, and second, downwards, when the darts are put into the shoulder. The difference can then be measured off along the two tracks and divided by five to give a single size increment. These increments will not be exact quantities. However, if a computer is being used this will not matter as it can cope with minute quantities.

Figure 27a shows the darts in the waist and typical side seam quantities for sizes 12 to 22. Figure 27b shows the same quantities when the darts are in the shoulder. These two manipulations give all that is required on the side cardinal points, i.e., three sets of grade quantities for each manipulation. These must be recorded for future use, preferably in a grade plan form. The other increments do not alter, i.e., the neck and centre front line of bodice. Figure 27a and b also shows the recorded grade quantities for these manipulations.

The second problem is the need to convert grade instructions on a multi-grade system. Figure 28 is an example.

A flared skirt is graded along its construction lines (see Chapter 13). These must be recalculated from a single track, i.e., from centre front or back.

SPECIAL CARDINAL POINTS

There are four cardinal grade points which are of special importance because they control the main balance of the garment at the shoulder. These are:

1 The front neck point at the shoulder
2 The front shoulder end
3 The back shoulder end
4 The back shoulder neck point

The front neck point controls the amount of front balance (length) on the front bodice, and is dictated by the recommendations of the survey. The front shoulder end controls the shoulder angle, bust suppression, front armhole shape and shoulder length. The back shoulder end controls the back shoulder angle, the back armhole shape, the shoulder length and the back bodice length. The back shoulder neck point controls the back balance which does not change for normal grading.

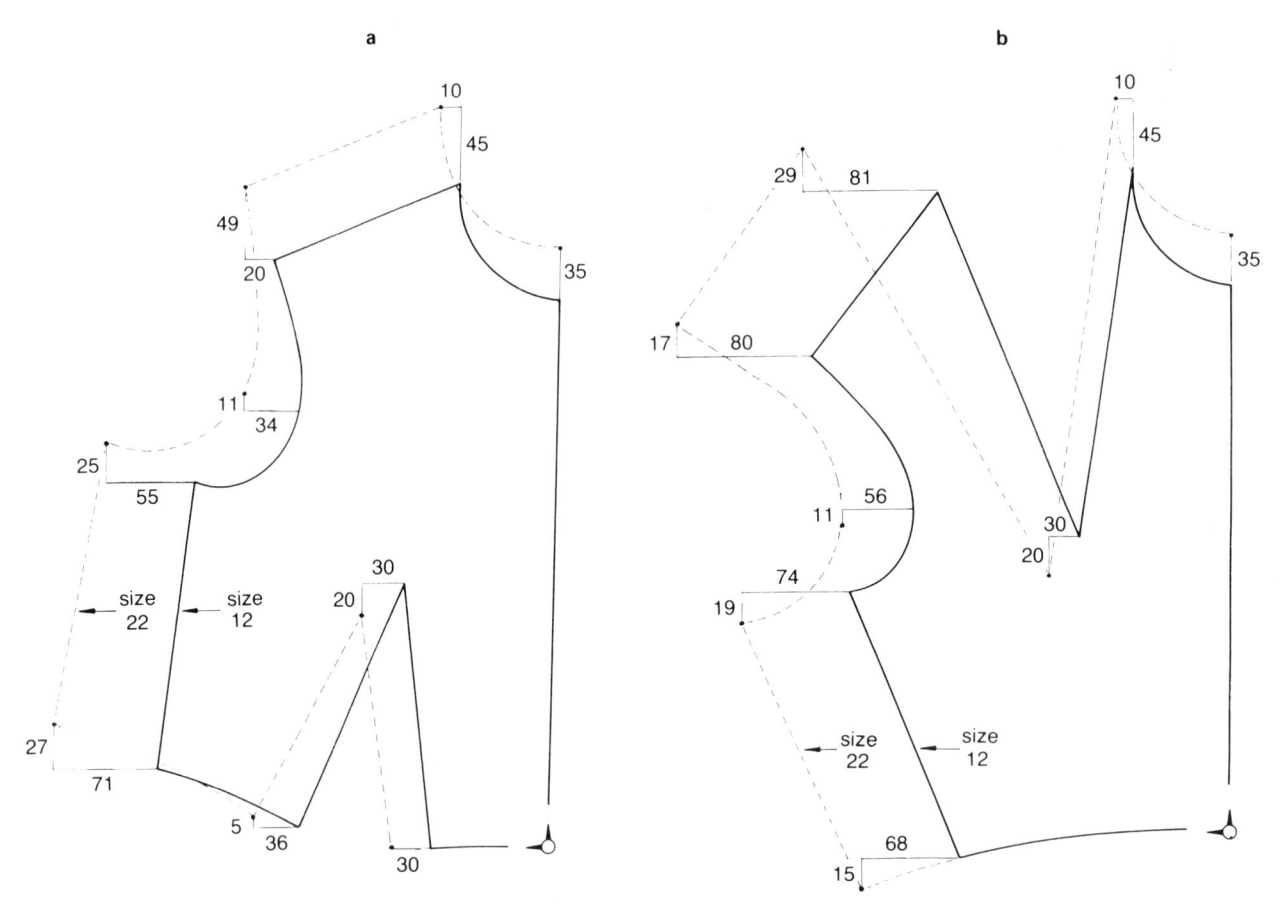

Figure 27 Front bodice single track quantities for five sizes. These increments are the results of using the three-dimensional quantities given in this book, which will give slightly different increments depending on the balance of the suppression in the blocks used

MAINTENANCE OF SHOULDER ANGLE

This is a very important factor as it controls the hang of the garment, particularly if it is loose-fitting. The general aim is to keep the shoulder angle the same for all sizes (see *shoulder angle commentaries*, Figures 22 and 27).

The need to maintain the shoulder line in a parallel position in all sizes can be best illustrated by Figure 29. (This can only be done when all darts are removed to other areas.) It shows a shoulder line from neck point A to shoulder end B, taking A as the zero point. The objectives are to grade the shoulder line upwards and outwards making the shoulder longer and to maintain the shoulder lines parallel. If it is only necessary to increase the bodice upwards or increase front balance then the increment indication upwards would be the same at both ends of the shoulder, as shown in Figure 29a. If the shoulder needs to be lengthened as well, then sideways increment indication is needed. It is at this juncture that things change at point B. In order to calculate the sideways increment at B the shoulder of the largest size must be lengthened by the required amount, as in Figure 29b, giving point M. In Figure 29c the increments needed at point B are then read off from M back along the tracks to X and from X to B. Figure 29c also shows the resultant grade indication needed at B and A. Figure 29d shows the general situation at the end of the shoulder where, for example, the shoulder may lengthen excessively to C, in which case the grade indication will be only outwards and nothing upwards, or if there is no shoulder length change then only an indication upwards is required.

SHOULDER LENGTH AND BUST SUPPRESSION

These two factors determine the amount the front shoulder should be lengthened to follow the survey indication. The shoulder length increases according to the size chart, but the bust suppression increase has to be calculated by trial and error, using a reliable stand to model from. The

SPECIAL AREAS

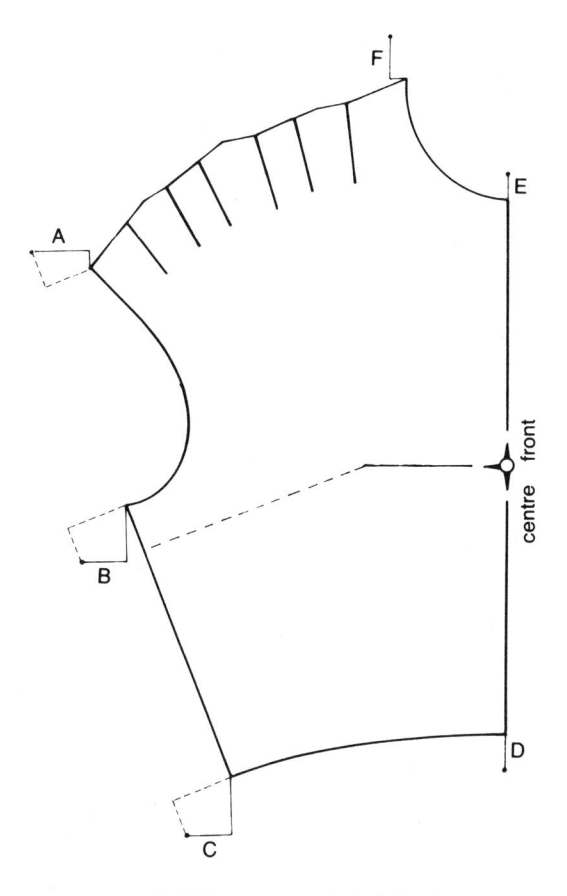

Solid lines represent single track
Dotted lines represent multi-track

Points A, B and C are requantified along the solid lines which are parallel to the original bust line track Points D, E and F are not changed, being already calculated from the original bust line

Figure 28 Converting a multi-track grading system to a single track system

extra suppression is registered by lengthening the shoulder and incorporating the extra length into the dart (see *block grading* in Chapter 10). The extra suppression works out, on average, to be 0.8 cm per 5.0 cm increase of hip (or one size). If the shoulder increases 0.2 cm per size and the bust suppression increases 0.8 cm per size then a 1.0 cm increase is needed between shoulder end and neck point. This will result in the front armhole having to be blended back slightly, but this is quite acceptable. If blending the armhole is not acceptable, the front shoulder end would need to be moved out further, although this would result in the over-suppressing of the bust which would cause tightness in the area of the front pitch point. However, this tightness would be slight and a personal choice would be made here between maintaining the exact front armhole shape, or preventing the over-suppression of the bust.

If it is required that the front armhole remain undisturbed or unblended throughout the grade, then proceed as follows (see Figure 30).

1. Mark around a size 12 front bodice block, and grade up to size 22 as usual, but omit the grade at the end of the shoulder.
2. Mark around the size 12 armhole with it displaced to the size 22 position at the front pitch point, so that the shape does not alter, except to extend side ways and upwards (as in Figure 30).
3. Close the bust dart of size 12 so that the shoulder is in its normal position B–C.
4. From point D, that is the size 22 graded neck point, draw a line parallel to B–C, making D–E 1.0 cm longer than B–C (a grade of 0.2 cm per size).
5. From the size 22 bust point S draw a line to D and, pivoting from S, using tracing paper (see page 115 for the basic technique), move the line D–E until E touches the size 22 armhole line at Y, giving E_2 and D_2 and establishing the end of the shoulder point and also the extra suppression needed for the bust (see dotted line). Note that the line E_2–D_2 is not parallel to the original size 12 shoulder line when in this position. This is because of the extra suppression in the bust dart.
6. Square off from the size 12 shoulder end along the grade tracks to Y and measure the grade increments up and out to the point E_2.

It must be repeated that this would result in an oversize bust suppression, i.e., with the armhole shape unblended. However, this method enables the technician to draw in the front armhole as he or she wishes, using a degree of blend that suits the situation. It also means that the shoulder angle need not remain parallel to the original shoulder line.

ARMHOLE SHAPING

Grading and shaping the armhole, or scye, needs special attention. It requires skill and care to arrive at a well-balanced set of nested armholes.

The general characteristic of the front scye is that it is scooped out to clear the muscle system between the chest and shoulder. This must be retained throughout the size range. The aim is to keep the general shape of the front scye unchanged except for its extension sideways and upwards.

The back scye has a different characteristic because it is not scooped out and, therefore, has a gentler shape. This must be retained as it gives back width and enables the arms to be stretched

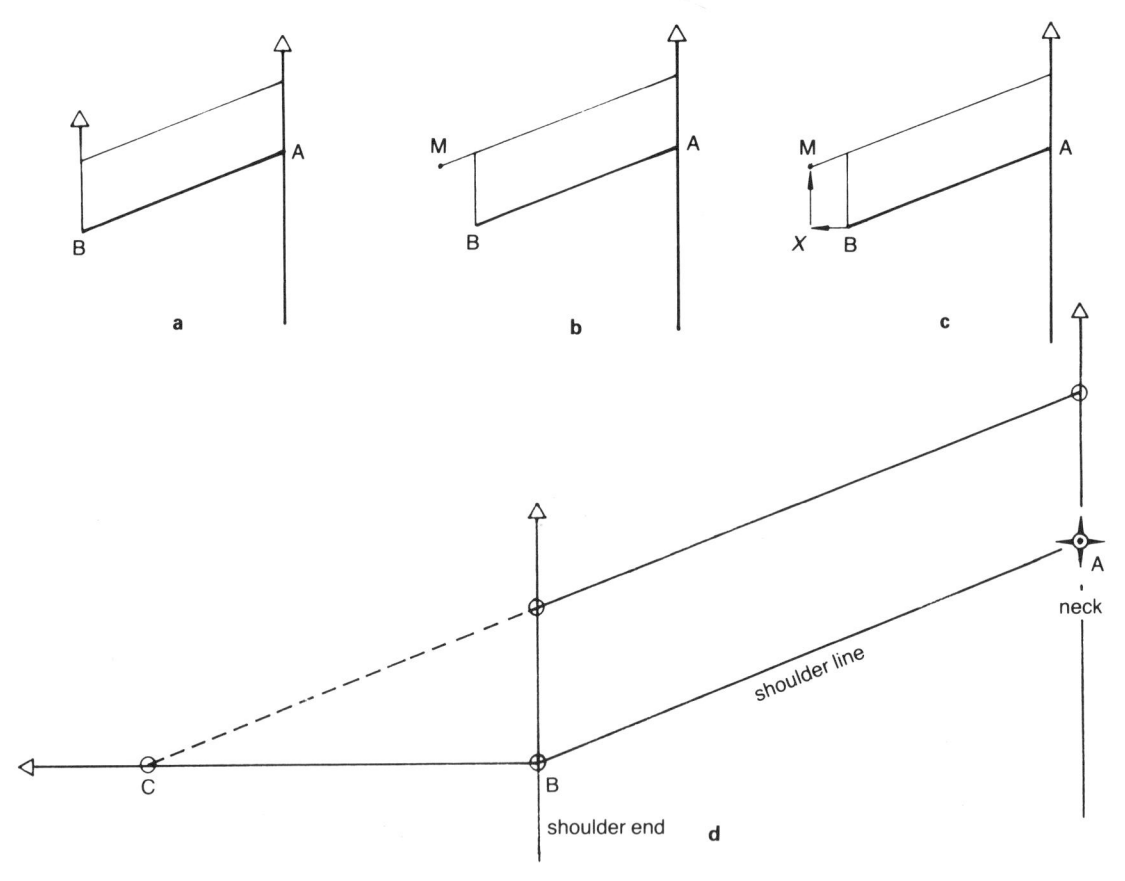

Figure 29 Basic method for establishing end of shoulder increments along a single track at 90° to centre front or back. The shoulder line need not be parallel to the original line

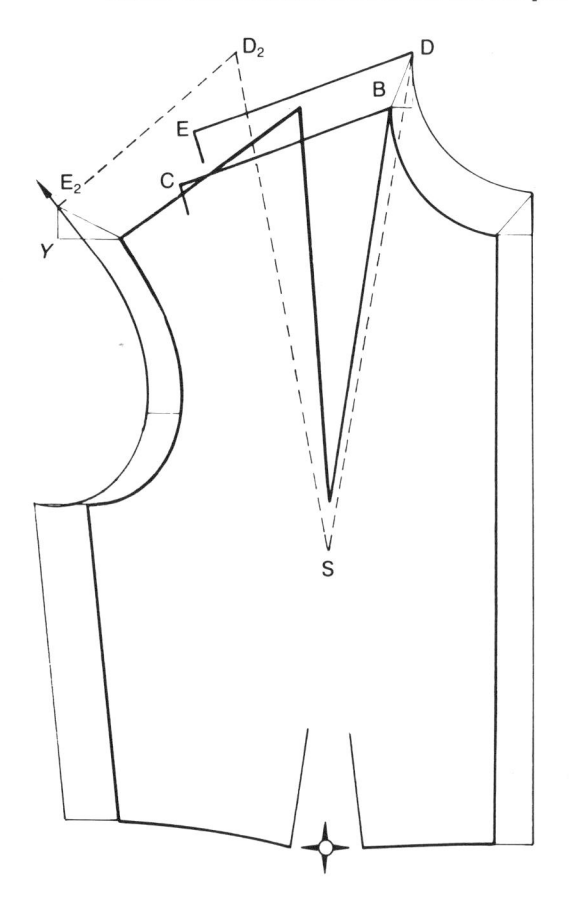

forward in comfort. If the back scye is scooped out too much it will result in the armhole splitting. The front scye shape can be maintained fairly easily if a three-dimensional system is used because the front shoulder end can be extended outwards quite considerably to allow for the extra suppression needed at the bust. If a two-dimensional system is used then the front armhole must be distorted and blended back to the shoulder end, which cannot be graded out as in the three-dimensional system. The back scye can and should be blended back to the shoulder end which is only graded out a very small amount. This is illustrated in Figure 31 which shows a three-dimensional graded scye back and front, using the front and back pitch points as the zero. It is advisable to draw up a nested set of armholes, as in Figure 31, and trace off each size to be used as a

Figure 30 Method for establishing grade increments for end of front shoulder and adjusting shoulder angle

SPECIAL AREAS   69

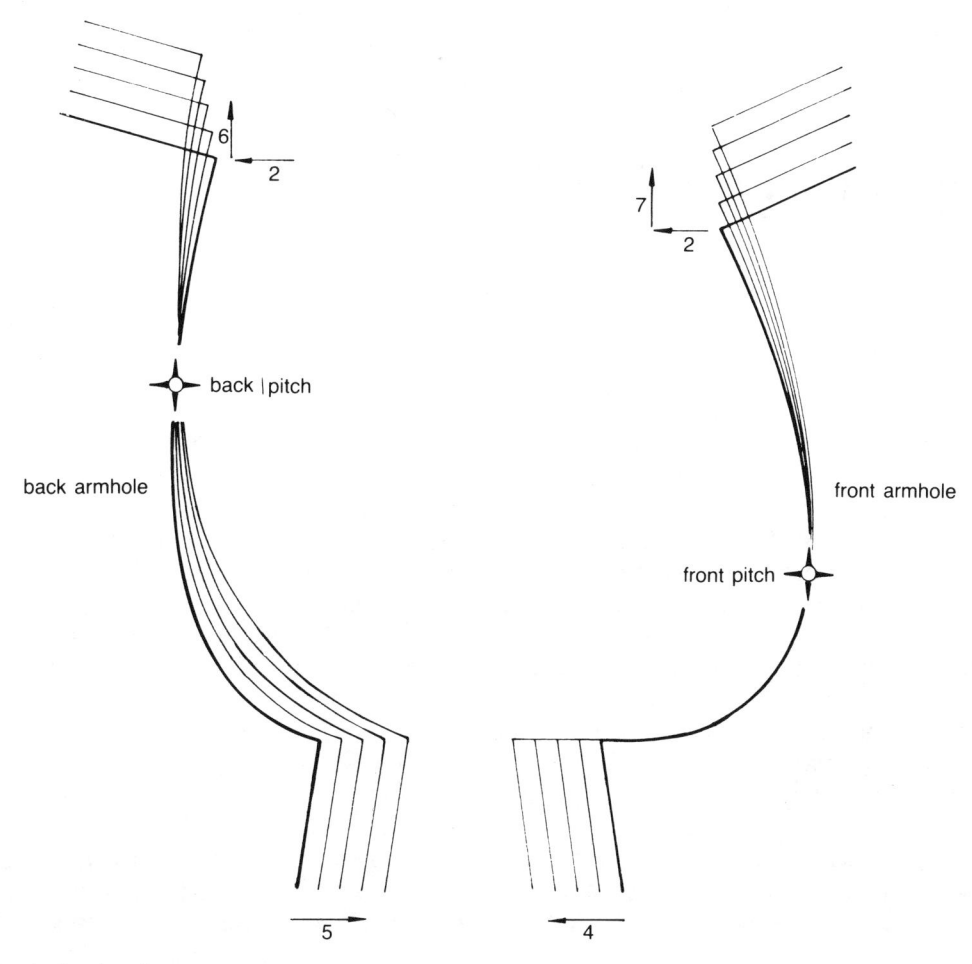

Figure 31 Armhole shaping

template to draw round when grading. This can save time because it eliminates the need to draw up the armholes each time.

It must be stressed again that the angles at the cardinal point on the pattern must remain the same on all sizes.

CHAPTER 7

Computer grading

Specific computer systems have been developed to cope with definite and limited types of function. In this case the function is related to all types of manufacturing processes involving two-dimensional shapes or patterns. These range from all types of clothing and furniture patterns to light and heavy engineering involving metal or plastic plating which are used for manufacturing anything from domestic appliances to ships. These systems come under the label of 'dedicated computers' because of their specialized area of application. They are usually main-frame computers of a modular construction, which means they can be expanded to cope with changing requirements.

The systems which have been developed for the clothing industry have a wide repertoire of functions related to two-dimensional patterns and sometimes to three-dimensional shapes – grading is just one of them. It is therefore necessary to list them all in order to give an overall view.

BASIC FUNCTIONS

1. Very large capacity disc memory and RT (real time) recall.
2. Back-up tape facility for data safe-keeping and off-line functions.
3. Two-dimensional pattern shape input, and, in some cases, a three-dimensional facility.
4. Two-dimensional pattern output, and three-dimensional representation in some cases.
5. Alpha-numeric input and output.
6. Semi-automatic grading function.
7. Marker making function.
8. Interactive facility in all areas.
9. PDS (pattern design system).
10. Cut order planning manufacture and management information.
11. Zoom capability and scale options.
12. Area and length measuring facility.
13. Off-line automatic mass production cutting.

These systems do not require computer specialists to operate them. They are designed to be used by technicians involved in the manufacturing processes outlined above. In the clothing industry this means pattern designers, graders and marker makers, and also production and cutting room managers.

A brief description of the uses of the various pieces of hardware in the computer system is given below.

DIGITISER

The digitiser comprises a large table area, adjustable for height and angle, which is used for the input of two-dimensional shapes. A digitiser has also been developed for the input of three-dimensional shapes and is used in the clothing industry for shoe design.

The table is approximately 1.5 by 1.3 metres in size. Beneath the surface there is an electrically sensitive grid which will register points up to $\frac{1}{100}$ of a centimetre apart. Any point on this surface can be fixed and related to any other point by a straight or curved line. This is done basically by registering two co-ordinates X and Y using longitude and latitude, as in navigation. A point is fixed in the computer's memory by using a free-moving cursor, which is hand operated. This includes an alpha-numeric function box. By locating the cross-wires over a point on the pattern and pressing a particular button an electrical connection is made with the table grid at that point and memorized. This is repeated round the shape until the outline is built up.

At the side of the digitiser table there is what is called 'the menu', which comprises an alpha-numeric layout. Under each number or letter is a connection which is activated by placing the cursor over it and pressing one of the buttons. This records or activates data in the memory bank, i.e., grading instructions, style numbers, etc.

I/O SYSTEMS CONSOLE (input–output)

This consists of an alpha-numeric keyboard with a

COMPUTER GRADING

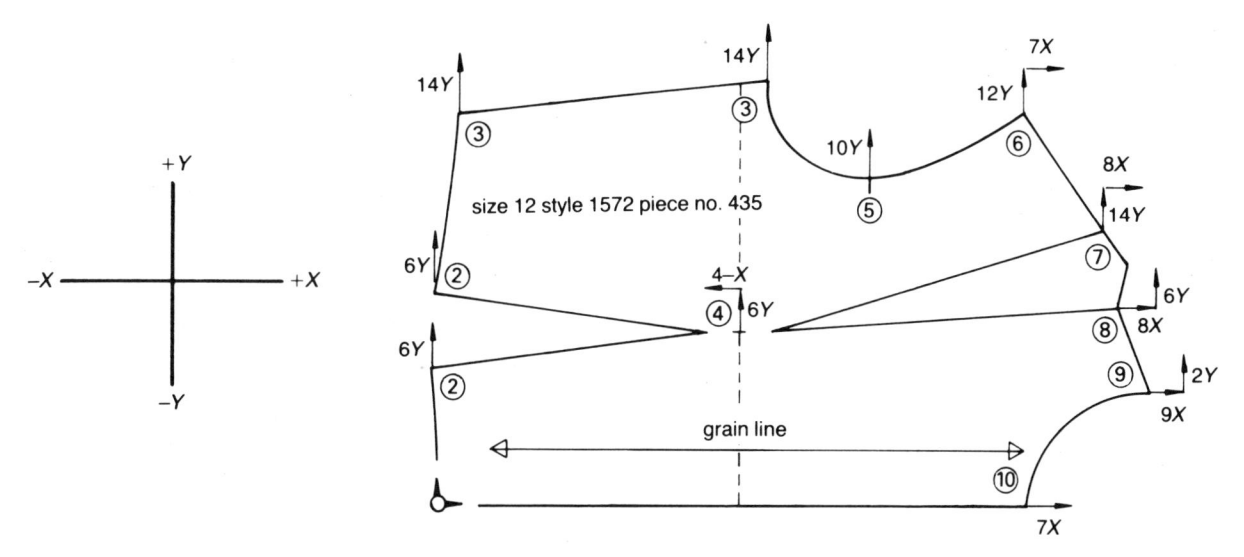

Figure 32 Pattern preparation for computer grading. Grade increments are given X and Y co-ordinates and are allocated grade rule numbers

print-out facility. It is used for entering commands and logging messages.

GRAPHIC DISPLAY
This is an ANCR (alpha-numeric cathode ray). It is used mainly for checking input and for giving on-line reports. It also handles data entry, but is not interactive.

INTERACTIVE GRAPHIC DISPLAY
This is an ANCR plus a tablet with a stylus pen. It has an input–output facility, providing a direct means of manipulating or changing pattern shapes or grade quantities already in the system, and also the ability to make markers directly on the screen and to direct permanent storage for future use.

SYSTEMS PLOTTER
The systems plotter draws full- or small-scale patterns, nested grades and markers on to paper.

CENTRAL PROCESSING UNIT (CPU)
This is a central computer which directs the system and controls and schedules the work. The system can function on all aspects at the same time so a powerful computer is required to schedule the work. If the system is being used by several operators at once, and handling many functions, the response is noticeably slower because the work has to take its place in a queue. The delay is only for a matter of seconds as opposed to almost immediate response when the load is light.

PARALLEL PROCESSORS
These calculate the data for the graphic displays.

TAPE UNIT
This is a facility for recording data for safe-keeping and to drive off-line systems such as automatic cutting machinery.

DISC DRIVE UNIT
This is a large data storage unit with real time recall. It enables the storage of patterns, styles, markers, grading instructions, softwear and firmwear programs. The disc drives are modular and can be added to when the capacity needs to be enlarged.

SYSTEMS PRINTER
This is a facility for providing hard copy reports.

PATTERN GRADING PROCEDURE

The production pattern is prepared by the pattern technician for input into the system.

The points on the pattern which require grading instructions are numbered, usually starting at the bottom left-hand corner and continuing in a clockwise direction, as in Figure 32.

Instructions for input are written on the separate pieces of pattern. Each piece has to have a style name or number and a pattern piece number. This permits the intermixing of parts of styles and facilitates the extraction of a single piece for alteration. All the usual pattern information is also written on

THE THEORY AND PRINCIPLES OF GRADING

computer will allow for this in its calculations. Having agreed on the way the pattern piece will be laid out, the grade rule for each point needing to be graded can be written on the pattern piece at the point in question. The same grade quantity may be applied to a number of points on the pattern. Each of these grading instructions is called a grade rule, and each grade rule must be entered into the computer grade library for storage under the pattern style number and piece number. Having established all the grade increments for each piece of pattern, a list must be made numbering the grade rules for input into the computer via the I/O system console. Figure 32 gives an example of a front bodice and the listed grade rules for the X and Y values for each grade point.

A zero point must be agreed upon for general use. If a different zero point is to be used then a zero point number must be established in order to identify the grade rules with a given zero because they will alter the grade if not specified.

The front bodice in Figure 32 will require a listed input sheet for the grade rules. This is called a source file and an example is shown in Figure 34. The grade can be imperial or metric. The smallest units which can be used are $\frac{1}{256}$ of an inch or $\frac{1}{100}$ of a centimetre (which is $\frac{1}{10}$ of a millimetre).

The plus sign for the X and Y co-ordinates need not be written because, if there is no prefix, the computer interprets a plus. A minus sign, when required, must always be written.

The grade rule library source file must have the following input data:

1. Name or number of style or type of garment
2. Name or number of pattern piece
3. Whether the grading is in metric or imperial
4. Base size
5. Number of sizes required
6. Number of rules for piece and style
7. Number of pieces in the style

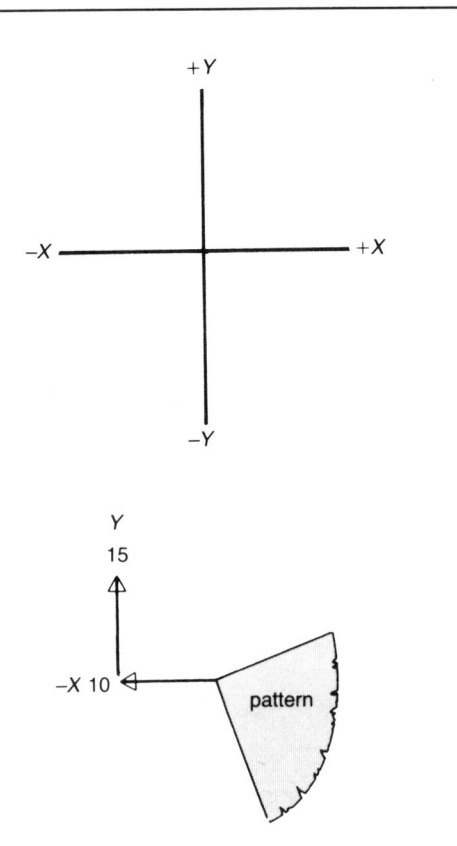

Figure 33 An example of grade instructions applied to computer co-ordinates. Ready for input as a grade rule

to the pieces; the size of base pattern, the punch holes, the grainline, and any special instructions such as stripe positions and any verbal indications required. All pieces which need to be cut twice, identical but reversed or CF and CB fold (mirrored pieces) are automatically generated by the system, and so only have to be digitised once, as are any instructions to repeat and reverse.

As previously stated, the computer establishes a pattern outline by means of data fed in on two co-ordinates. The co-ordinates correspond to the two grading tracks used in manual grading. These two tracks are represented in the computer by the X and Y axis, as in Figure 33. Each point of the pattern which needs to be graded has to be given an X and Y value corresponding to the grading quantity required for that point. It has to be agreed by all who use the computer which way the patterns will be laid on the digitiser for input: i.e., for example, CB and CF nearest with the head to the right as the operator faces the digitiser table and all points inputed in a clockwise direction starting at the bottom left-hand corner of the pattern piece. The grainline of the pattern piece does not need to be exactly parallel to the table edge because the

The source file is the stage before final input into the grade library. It can be altered and edited until a style or type of garment grade is perfected. Then it can be entered as permanent data. The rule numbers relating to specific grade increment combinations can be kept for visual reference so that when other styles become available for grading the appropriate rule numbers can be input when the pattern is being digitised, without needing a source file. It must be understood, however, that there are different options open to the operator of these computers. There are different procedures which will give the same result, so the operator has a choice of how to input and store

COMPUTER GRADING

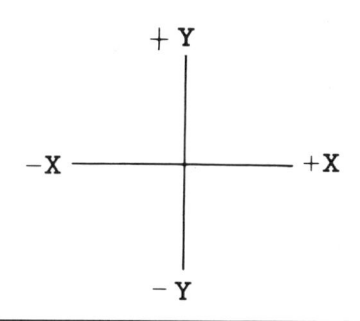

Pattern Style Number	Pattern Piece Number	Grading Increments
1572	435	1/100 cm

Base Size	Number Pieces in Style	Number Size	Number Rules
12		7	10

Size		10	12	14	16	18	20	22				
Rule Number	Axis											
1	X	0	0	0								
	Y	0	0	0								
2	X	0	0	0								
	Y	-60	0	60								
3	X	0	0	0								
	Y	-140	0	140								
4	X	40	0	-40								
	Y	-60	0	60								
5	X	0	0	0								
	Y	-100	0	100								
6	X	-70	0	70								
	Y	-120	0	120								
7	X	-80	0	80								
	Y	-40	0	40								
8	X	-80	0	80								
	Y	-60	0	60								
9	X	-90	0	90								
	Y	-20	0	20								
10	X	-70	0	70								
	Y	0	0	0								
	X											
	Y											

Figure 34 An example of a source file. The front bodice to be graded from size 12, one size down and five up, giving 7 sizes. If the size increase is constant then only one set of instructions is necessary. If there is a change then new instructions at the size of change must be added. It is always advisable to input a full range of sizes even if they are not immediately required

data and how to make it available for future use. These options will only become clear when the 'hands on' training period is in progress. It is very difficult to outline all the options in this book and to do so would only lead to confusion. In general, the training period needed in order to be able to operate one of these systems is about one month. There are four areas in which instruction is necessary: digitising, alpha-numeric input and output, marker making and off-line functions.

DIGITISING

This involves the learning of the sequence of input and the different alpha-numeric menu procedures, plus the skill of digitising curves and the frequency of input points needed to permit the computer to maintain a particular curve. For example, if not enough points are digitised round a curve then the computer will decide for itself the curve between two points and may distort the shape. On the other hand, if too many points are digitised the computer may be over-informed, and will produce a disturbed curve. It may also be necessary to create a grade point on a curve where, with manual grading, the grader would control the curve change by eye but would not actually grade that point. The computer would make its own curve which may not be correct, and so it would need instructions in that area of the curve where it changes from the base size because of the enlarging characteristics of that section.

ALPHA-NUMERIC INPUT AND OUTPUT

The input and output procedures on the keyboard have to be memorized. These alter for different makes of computer. There are also options which have to be learned and memorized. This involves learning the general working and operation of the system (this can take some time), and acquiring the necessary typing speed.

MARKER MAKING

The experienced marker maker must learn how to operate the hardware, how to use the function box and stylus pen, and how to move the pattern pieces around on the screen. This needs practice and, like everything else, it will take time to gain proficiency.

OFF-LINE FUNCTIONS

Off-line functions involve working the plotter, which can print paper markers and patterns to any scale and also nested or single grades. This piece of hardware is not very complicated, but it does require a few days training to gain proficiency.

The other main off-line hardware involves the automatic cutting of garments, either singly or in large numbers. These automated cutting machines need separate personnel to operate and supervise their running. They include laying up machinery and mobile cutting heads which are controlled by tape operated computers. The tapes are taken from the tape drive unit attached to the CPU.

CONCLUSION

The operators of these systems need to be specialists in the field of pattern design and they also have to be able to absorb the necessary disciplines of computer operations. The computers take the place of the manual work of cutting out and drawing of patterns, etc., and of laborious marker making on paper. This saves time and the accuracy achieved is considerably more than is required for this type of work. Added to this, the memory capability and storage facilities provide extremely fast and accurate recall which is beyond any human capacity.

As a matter of interest, the latest systems incorporate a PDS facility. This enables the pattern cutter and designer to store and manipulate block patterns into styles directly on and in the computer system and to change existing styles and pattern pieces already in the system. These systems eliminate the need to use pencil and paper and the usual tools for measurement, etc. In fact, French curves and shapes required as tools can be input to permanent memory for use on the screen in PDS systems. The patterns can be constructed, graded and markers made and cut out straight from the lay, without paper markers.

There is no doubt that these systems are superb tools and once used become a *must* for the pattern technician.

CHAPTER 8

Brassiere grading

This area is probably the most highly specialized in the clothing industry. Grading in this sphere has been developed to near perfection by the large manufacturers and is not a field for the amateur to dabble in. Nevertheless, it is necessary for the student to have a working understanding of the principles involved.

SIZING

Table 14 is the international brassiere size chart which is the basis of all brassiere sizing systems. It is comprised of two girths:

1. Rib-cage
2. Bust girth

The rib-cage girth is taken directly under the bust and is used as the size indicator. The bust girth is of secondary importance because of the wide variations for a given rib-cage girth. In order to cope with this situation a range of different-sized bust cups are offered with each size of rib-cage. These usually number four and are given the letters A, B, C and D (the 'A' cup is the smallest). There is a 2.0 cm bust girth difference between each cup. The 'B' cup represents the statistically average bust size where there is a difference of 15.0 cm between the rib-cage and bust girth. This corresponds to the proportionate bust size where the bust is 5.0 cm larger than the chest girth on a size 12 (see Chapter 3).

A two-tier grading system is therefore required:

1. Grading for size, i.e., rib-cage.
2. Grading the cups within that size.

SIZE GRADE

Figure 35 shows the brassiere grade plan and this is based on the contour grade shown in Figure 11. It is a three-dimensional grade where the bust suppression changes. Figure 35 shows the increments required for one size change. The width between the back and front straps increases by 0.3 cm per size on the half bodice. This has to be small or the shoulder strap will begin to approach the end of the shoulder. It corresponds closely to the shoulder grade. The bust point width increases 0.5 cm on the half and the base which the cup is set into has to increase 1.2 cm because the bust spreads in the larger sizes.

The rib-cage band, or base of the brassiere, increases 2.5 cm with the apex of the back shoulder strap changing 0.3 cm from CB. The rib-cage band also becomes deeper to cope with the extra stresses involved in the larger sizes and helps to control the increase in fat around that area. The grade quantities given here are typical but can vary quite considerably with different brassiere specifications. The upper cup has a suppression grade incorporated in it, where the strap point is graded up and in both directions, thus introducing extra suppression which is then pivoted out into the bust seam. The enlarged diagram at the bottom of Figure 35 illustrates the nested grade before closing and tracing off. When closing the extra suppression a point on the bust seam will appear which can be rounded off. The lower cup also has a suppression change which is automatically applied by the difference in the bust point grade of 0.4 cm upwards and the side cup extremes which only go up 0.2 cm.

CUP GRADE

Figure 36 shows the grade plan for the cup only grade. The rib-cage band only alters at one point; where the bust tends to spread its base as it increases in size. Therefore, the cup base increases, in this case 0.5 cm per cup size.

Figure 37 shows the section of rib-cage and bust section superimposed with the four cup sizes applied.

Figure 38 shows the side view and the four cup sizes applied.

These drawings are to scale and were used to obtain the cup increases for an increase in the bust girth of 1.0 cm on the half. An increase of 2.7 cm is required from the point A to B in Figure 37 (sections) which includes the 0.5 cm base of cup increase. Thus, for a 1.0 cm increase of bust the cup has to increase 2.2 cm from A to B. This is because the cup goes close to the body between the bust but the bust girth measurement is taken bridging the bust points, through C.

Table 14 The international brassiere and corsetry size chart

Size indicator	70		75		80		85	
	cm	in	cm	in	cm	in	cm	in
Bust girth cup sizes								
A	82–84	$32\frac{1}{4}$–33	87–89	$34\frac{1}{4}$–35	92–94	$36\frac{1}{4}$–37	97–99	$38\frac{1}{4}$–39
B	84–86	33–$33\frac{3}{4}$	89–91	35–$35\frac{3}{4}$	94–96	37–$37\frac{3}{4}$	99–101	39–$39\frac{3}{4}$
C	86–88	$33\frac{3}{4}$–$34\frac{1}{2}$	91–93	$35\frac{3}{4}$–$36\frac{1}{2}$	96–98	$37\frac{3}{4}$–$38\frac{1}{2}$	101–103	$39\frac{3}{4}$–$40\frac{1}{2}$
D	88–90	$34\frac{1}{2}$–$35\frac{1}{4}$	93–95	$36\frac{1}{2}$–$37\frac{1}{4}$	98–100	$38\frac{1}{2}$–$39\frac{1}{4}$	103–105	$40\frac{1}{2}$–$41\frac{1}{4}$
Rib cage girth directly below bust	70	$27\frac{1}{2}$	75	$29\frac{1}{2}$	80	$31\frac{1}{2}$	85	$33\frac{1}{2}$
Waist girth	60–62	$23\frac{1}{4}$–$24\frac{1}{4}$	64–68	$25\frac{1}{4}$–$26\frac{3}{4}$	70–74	$27\frac{1}{2}$–$29\frac{1}{4}$	76–80	30–$31\frac{1}{2}$
Hip girth	88–90	$34\frac{1}{2}$–$35\frac{1}{2}$	92–94	$36\frac{1}{4}$–37	96–100	$37\frac{3}{4}$–$39\frac{1}{2}$	102–106	$40\frac{1}{4}$–$41\frac{3}{4}$

Size indicator	90		95		100	
	cm	in	cm	in	cm	in
Bust girth cup sizes						
A	102–104	$40\frac{1}{4}$–41	107–109	$42\frac{1}{4}$–43	112–114	$44\frac{1}{4}$–45
B	104–106	41–$41\frac{3}{4}$	109–111	43–$43\frac{3}{4}$	114–116	45–$45\frac{3}{4}$
C	106–108	$41\frac{3}{4}$–$42\frac{1}{2}$	111–113	$43\frac{3}{4}$–$44\frac{1}{2}$	116–118	$45\frac{3}{4}$–$46\frac{1}{2}$
D	108–110	$42\frac{1}{2}$–$43\frac{1}{4}$	113–115	$44\frac{1}{2}$–$45\frac{1}{4}$	118–120	$46\frac{1}{2}$–$47\frac{1}{4}$
Rib cage girth directly below bust	90	$35\frac{1}{2}$	95	$37\frac{1}{2}$	100	$39\frac{1}{2}$
Waist girth	82–84	$32\frac{1}{4}$–33	86–90	$33\frac{3}{4}$–$35\frac{1}{2}$	92–96	$36\frac{1}{4}$–$37\frac{3}{4}$
Hip girth	108–110	$42\frac{1}{2}$–$43\frac{1}{4}$	112–116	$44\frac{1}{4}$–$45\frac{3}{4}$	118–120	$46\frac{1}{2}$–$47\frac{1}{4}$

BRASSIERE GRADING

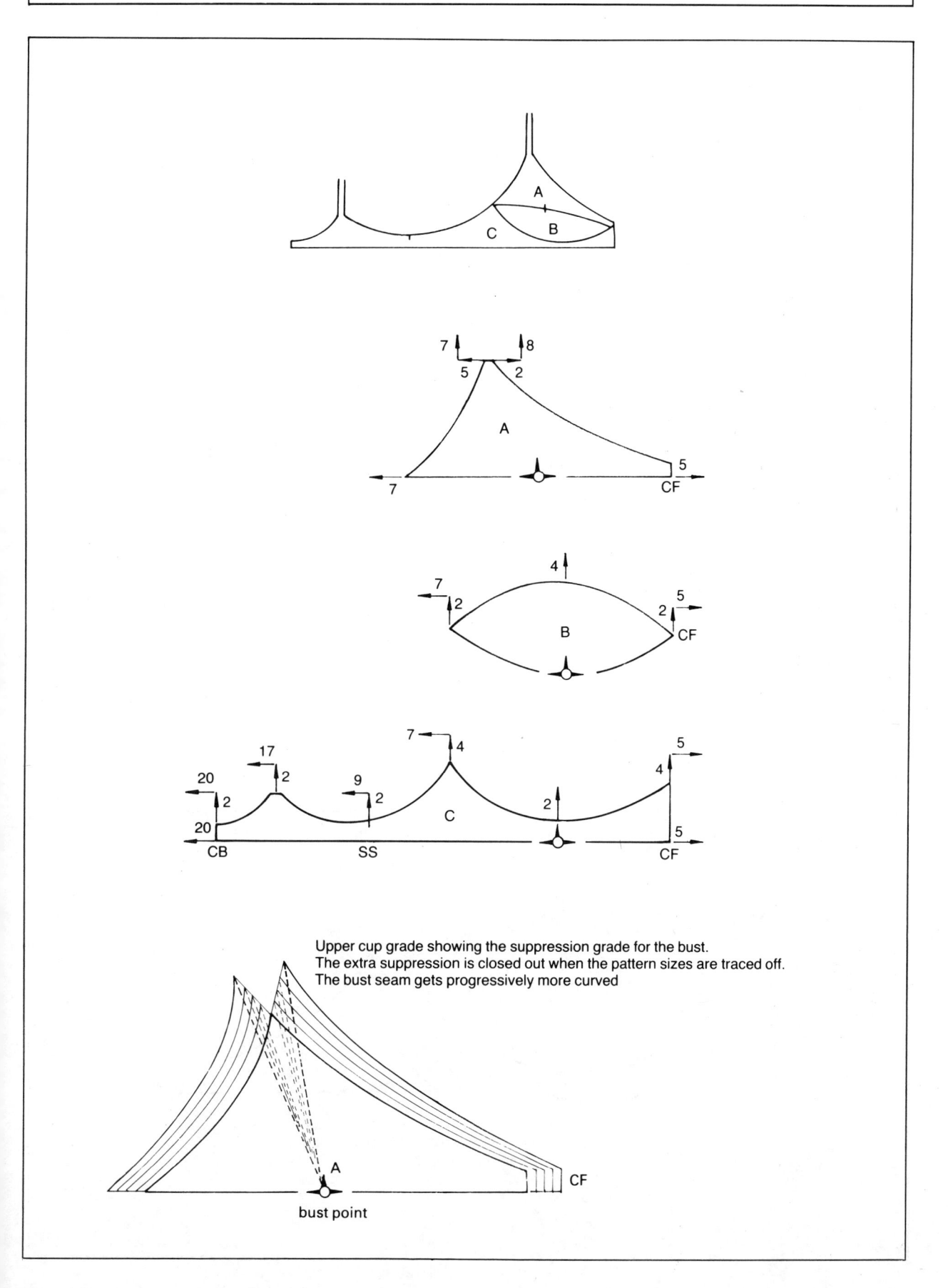

Figure 35 Brassiere size grade plan

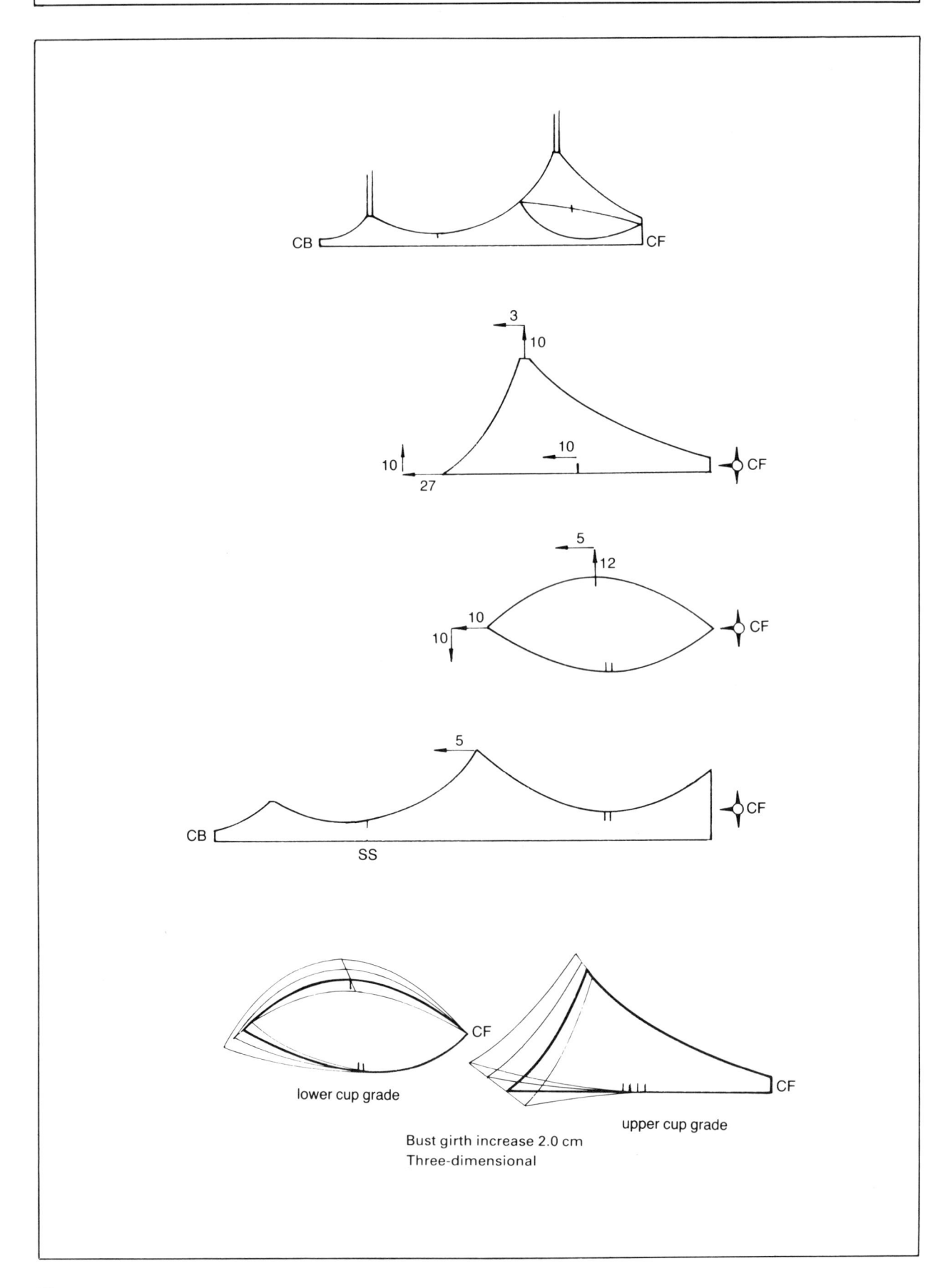

Figure 36 Brassiere cup grade

BRASSIERE GRADING

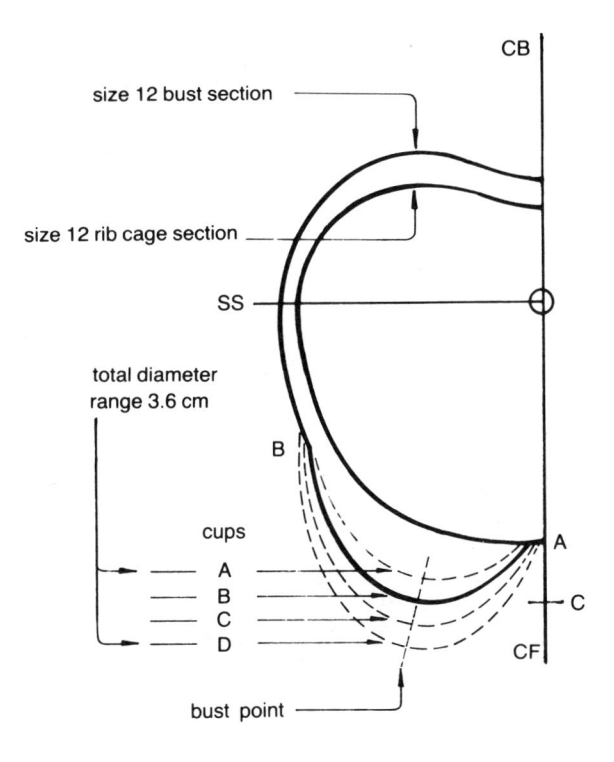

Figure 39 (side view) was used to determine the extra increase required in the cup depth, top to bottom. This shows an increase of 1.2 cm from bust point to base of bust and 1.0 cm from bust point to the front strap point. Figure 40 illustrates this and shows where and by how much the cup would have to be split open to gain the necessary extra size, excluding base increase.

This grade is, therefore, three-dimensional. The cup grade plan, unlike the size grade plan, includes the suppression grade in the size cup quantities of 2.7 cm out and 1.0 cm up on the top cup, and 1.0 cm up and 1.0 cm out on the lower cup piece. This grade is demonstrated at the bottom of the grade plan.

Figure 37 Size 12 rib-cage and bust sections

Figure 38 Size 12 side view of cup sizes

80 | THE THEORY AND PRINCIPLES OF GRADING

Dotted line illustrates the relationship between the typical natural shape bra size 12 and 22

Dotted lines indicate bust base increase of 0.5 cm per size and 2.2 cm both ways at the bust apex

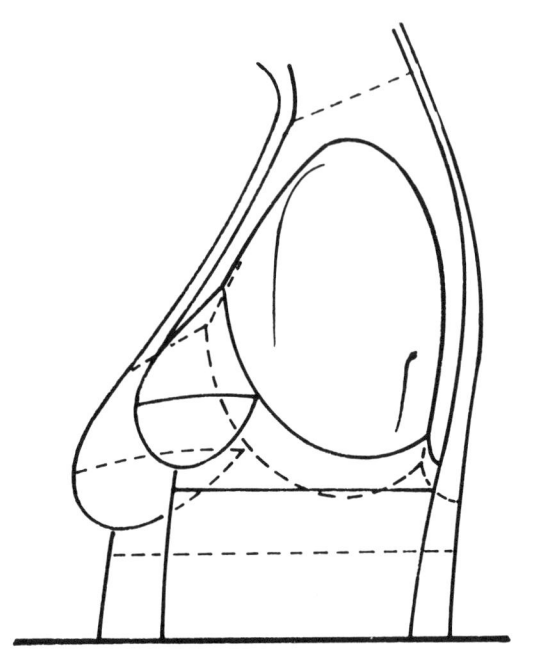

Figure 39 Size 12 side view for determining increase required in the cup depth

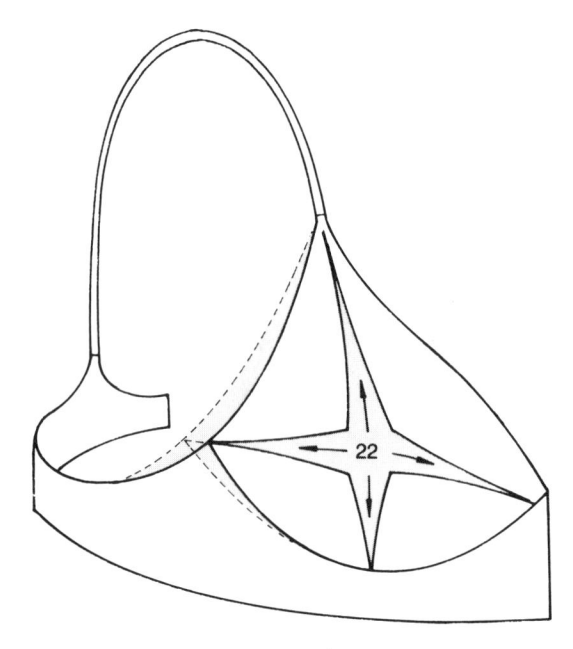

Figure 40 Brassiere cup area increases

CHAPTER 9

The principles of bifurcated grading

The grading of bifurcated garments depends mainly on three measurements. These are the abdominal diameter R–S, the body rise K–T, and the waist width O–P (see Figure 41).

The waist width increase determines the amount by which the crease line has to be displaced towards the side. The hip and thigh width also affect this, but follow from the waist, as can be seen from the section drawings in Figure 41. The crease line will move over half the width (diameter) increase of the waist. The displacement of the crease line is 0.4 cm per size; the waist width increases 0.8 cm on the half. The zero point for grading bifurcated garments is taken from a point on the crease line. In this case the hip has been selected. This means that the centre front and centre back waist seams will move out 0.4 cm from the crease line per size, and the rest of the waist girth increase will be applied at the side seam.

The abdominal diameter (maximum width through the lower body) will determine the increase of the inside leg. This increase is a total of 1.5 cm per size, and is applied at the rate of 0.6 cm at the front and 0.9 cm at the back. These quantities will be applied from the crease line, and the 0.4 cm displacement of the crease line due to the increase in the width of the waist, is added to them, giving an increase of 1.0 cm at the front inside leg and 1.3 cm at the back inside leg. The reason for a greater increase at the back than the front is made clear in Figure 41.

The final controlling measurement is the body rise. This increases at the rate of 1.0 cm per size for a girth only grade of 5.0 cm and 1.1 cm for a girth and height grade of 2.4 cm height per size. Thus, the measurement between the waist and crotch depth will increase by 1.1 cm, that is 0.3 cm up from the hip and 0.8 cm down, and 1.0 cm down from the hip for a girth only grade. This results in a total through leg measurement increase from centre front to centre back (A–B–C in Figure 41) of 2.8 cm per size – 1.2 cm on the front and 1.6 cm on the back. This increase of 2.8 cm seems incorrect at first sight because if the body rise increase is 1.1 cm and the abdominal diameter increase is 1.7 cm the total is 3.8 cm. This would be true if the crotch was square, but in reality it is curved and so takes a short cut across, thereby travelling a shorter distance. In fact it is 1.0 cm per size shorter, making 2.8 cm per size. These increases are suitable for garments that are loose-fitting at the thigh. When the garment is tight-fitting, the thigh and then the back inside leg grade is decreased to 1.0 cm, as at the front (see Figure 42). This means that the thigh diameter increase, rather than the hip diameter, is controlling the grade.

The rest of the girth grade quantities follow the three-dimensional skirt grade. The knee and ankle increments will largely depend on fashion preferences prevailing at the time.

The two-dimensional grade plan, Figure 9, is a simplified version with quantities equalized for ease of application and with no suppression changes.

Figure 42 shows a grade plan of a body measurement contour bifurcated garment with the seams and suppression placed in an ideal position for controlling the shape. They are the positions which give maximum movement of the legs, as the garment fits close up under the crotch. The pattern shape bears little resemblance to the conventional trouser style where the front and back has a centre seam and the leg pieces are all in one with the torso pattern. The conventional trouser configuration lends itself to practical considerations but is by no means the ideal solution with regard to fit and movement if a close-fitting garment is required.

82 THE THEORY AND PRINCIPLES OF GRADING

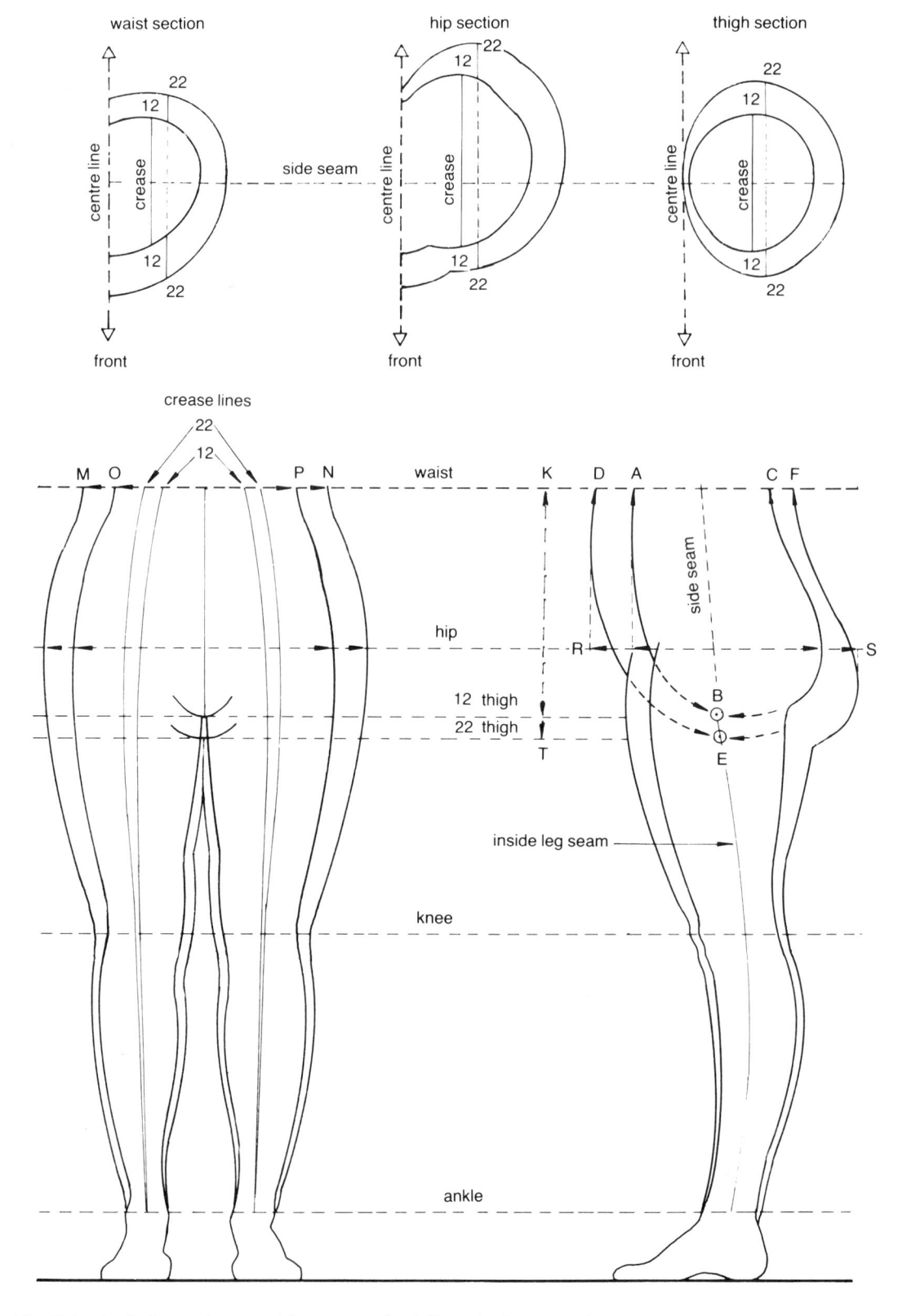

Figure 41 Principal dimensions and increases for bifurcated garments

THE PRINCIPLES OF BIFURCATED GRADING

bifurcated body contour block grade plan for 5.0 cm girth only increase

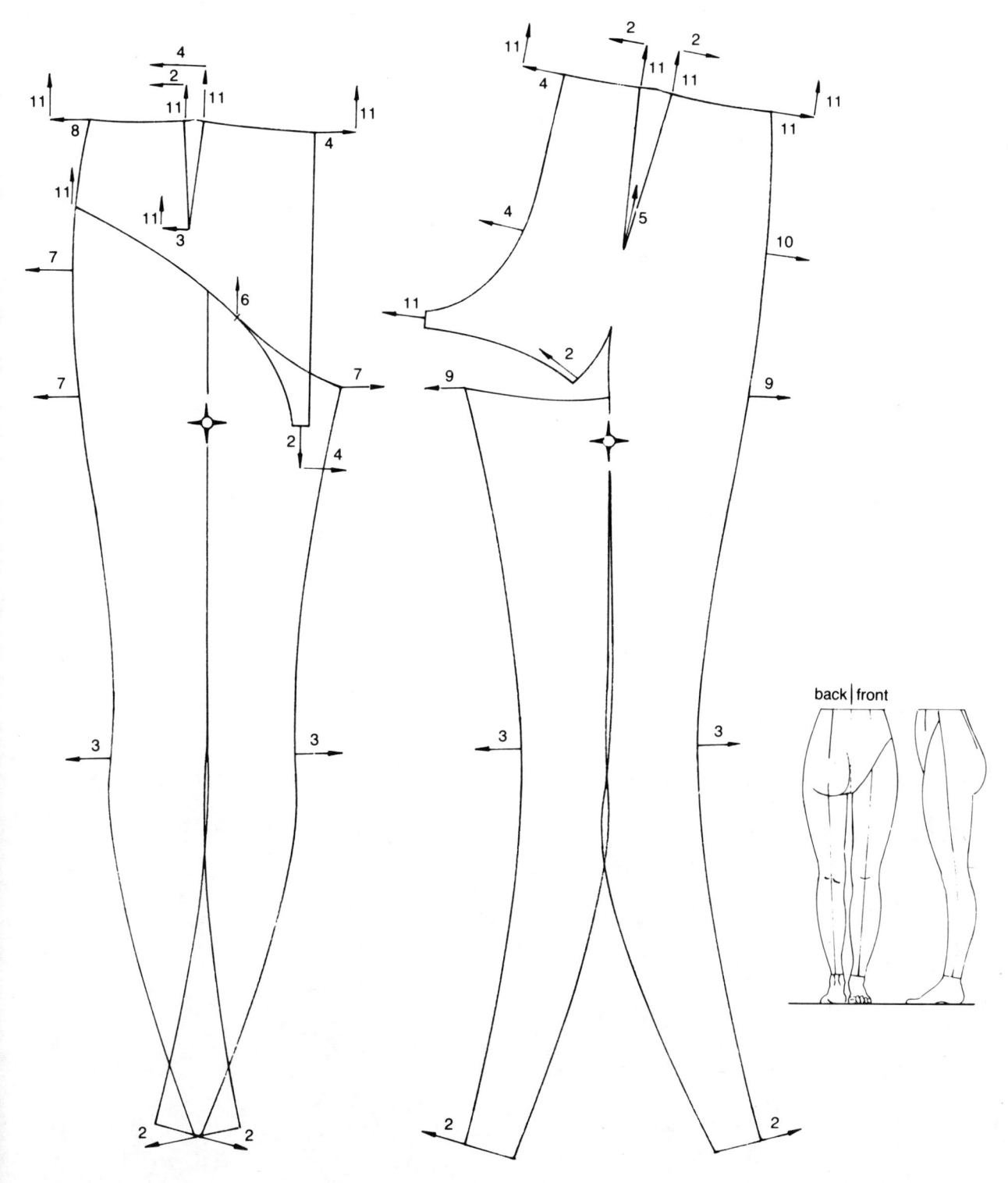

Figure 42 Bifurcated body contour block

PART TWO

General Grading Techniques

CHAPTER 10

Draft grading the basic blocks

This chapter deals with the method of draft grading the basic block bodice, sleeve and skirt and its main aim is to explain in detail the techniques of three-dimensional draft grading. Although it is not normal industrial practice to grade blocks, it is an excellent way of gaining experience of the following essential grading requirements:

1 Applying increments to cardinal points
2 Increasing and decreasing suppression
3 Drawing armholes, necklines, waistlines, etc.
4 Spiking-off sizes

It is advisable to work through all the following exercises before commencing the style grading section.

ESSENTIAL NOTES

Note 1 When using a draft grading system which incorporates the three dimensional increase of the bust suppression and the dropping bust point it is essential to return the bust suppression to the neck position before commencing the grade (see Figure 44) for the following reasons:
  a It establishes the suppression above and below the bust line which is the only position to maintain the front bodice balance throughout the size range.
  b It retains the position of the original horizontal bust line in relationship to the centre front and centre back and makes multi-track grading unnecessary. (See multi track grading, page 117.)
  c It allows the grader to adjust the bust point height according to the original block construction angle.
Note 2 Each pattern will have a zero point symbol. This will indicate grade direction.
Note 3 The main points of a pattern are called 'cardinal points'. Grading commences

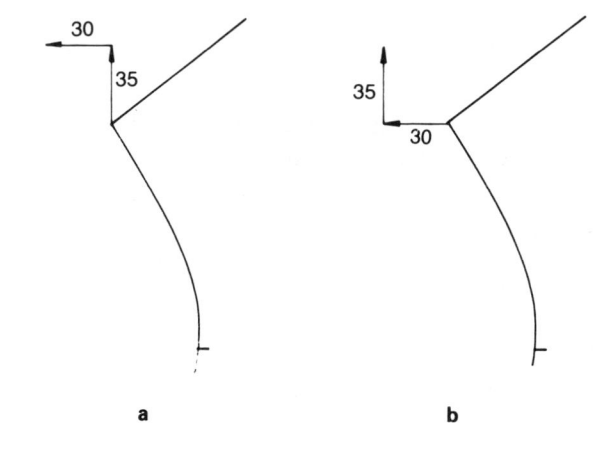

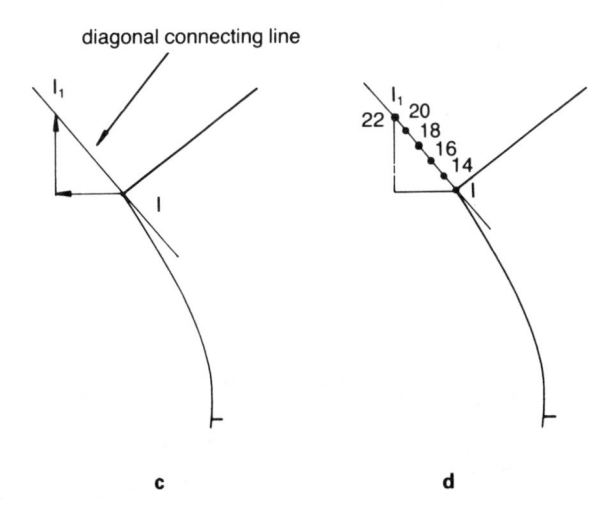

Figure 43 (a) Grade direction arrows and increments for five sizes, i.e., one size increments multiplied by five
(b) This illustration expresses the same grade increments as (a) and arrives at the same cardinal point
(c) Diagonal connecting line, joining the two graded points, for example I and I$_1$ for the size 22
(d) Divide line I–I$_1$ equally to obtain intermediate sizes

Note 4 Grade directions and the increments from each cardinal point are indicated in Figure 43a and b. *Grade directions are always vertical and horizontal to the main construction line.*

Note 5 The cardinal point on the stock size is connected to the cardinal point on the graded largest size by a 'diagonal connecting line' (see Figure 43c). Divide this line equally by the amount of sizes to obtain the intermediate sizes (see Figure 43c and d).

Note 6 All increments are expressed in millimetres.

These general notes apply to all draft grading and should be referred to frequently.

INSTRUCTIONS FOR GRADING THE BACK BODICE – HEIGHT AND GIRTH

ESTABLISHING THE LARGEST SIZE (Figures 44a and 45a)

1 Referring to Figure 44a, mark around the basic back block (size 12 in this case). Remove the basic block and then transfer the construction lines, darts and balance marks to the draft.

2 The grading specification requires the following sizes:

10 – 12 – 14 – 16 – 18 – 20 – 22

that is, five sizes up and one size down.

Therefore, multiply all the increments stated in the grade plan (Figure 44), by five to obtain the largest size. For example, Figure 44a is a grade plan and illustrates a grade of one size up, to size 14. Point A would be horizontal to the construction line 0.3 cm and vertical to the construction line 0.6 cm.

To grade five sizes up, multiply all increments by five to arrive at point A1 which will be the nape for a size 22. Points A–A1 and F–F1 in Figure 45a illustrate this procedure, which is fundamental to all draft grading. Connect points A to A1, and F to F1 with a diagonal connecting line. (See Figure 43c and d.) Continue grading around the back bodice multiplying the increments in Figure 44a by five to establish the largest size and then connect it to the stock size. Stop at point F1.

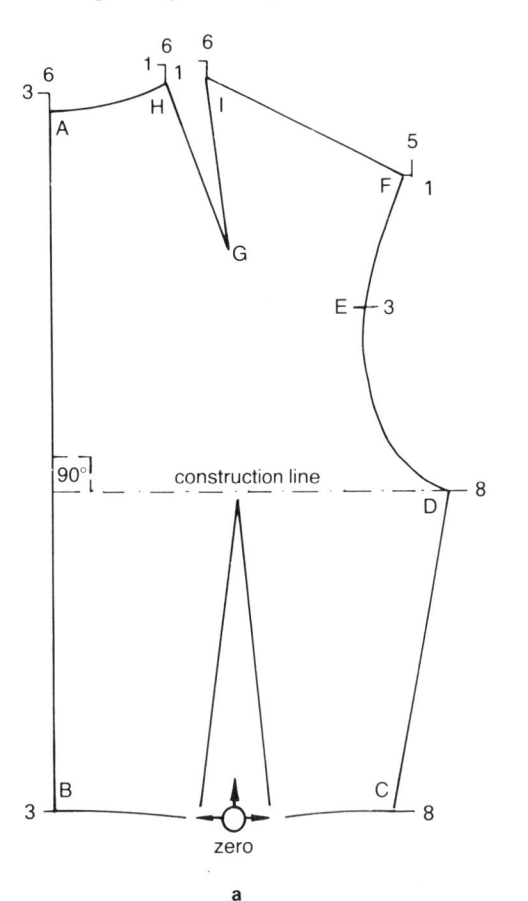

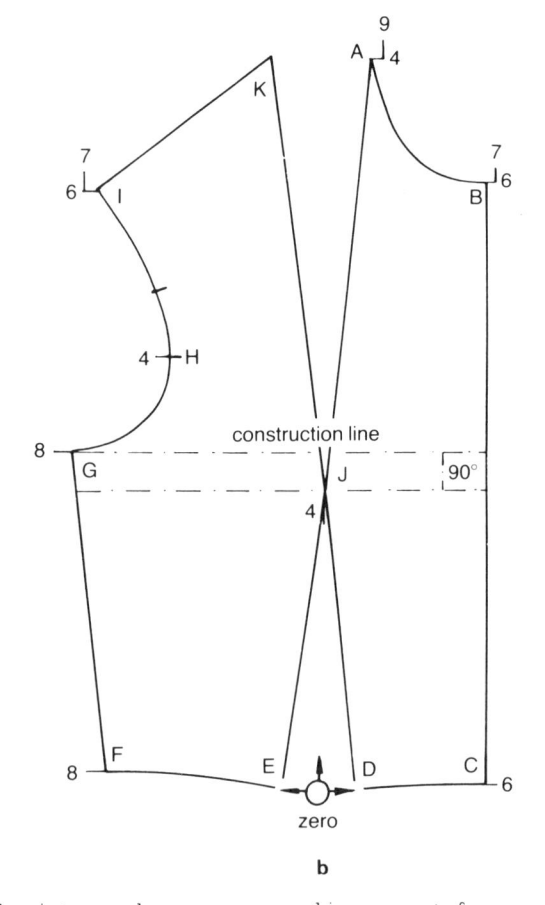

Figure 44 Grade plan indicating grade direction, cardinal points, grade sequence and increments for one size

DRAFT GRADING THE BASIC BLOCKS

THE BLADE DART (Figures 45a and 46a)

1. The blade dart quantity and the shoulder angle remain unchanged. The shoulder length increases 0.2 cm per size.
2. Grade up both sides of the dart as indicated in the grade plan, and draw the diagonal connecting lines between H–H1 and I–I1.
3. Find the centre of H–I and draw a line connecting G through J. G1 is located on line J and is 0.6 cm per size up from point G.
4. Connect I1 to F1 for shoulder size 22.
5. Connect I1 to G1 and H1 for dart size 22.

THE SIZE 22 OUTLINE

Connect up the size 22 cardinal points as shown in Figure 46a. Curves, such as the back neck and armhole, should be developed by using the original pattern as a template.

SIZE DIVISIONS AND DIAGONAL CONNECTING LINES

The lines that connect the cardinal points, for example A1–A and B1–B, must now be divided up into the amount of sizes required (in this case five sizes). Therefore divide the lines equally, as indicated in Figure 43b and c.

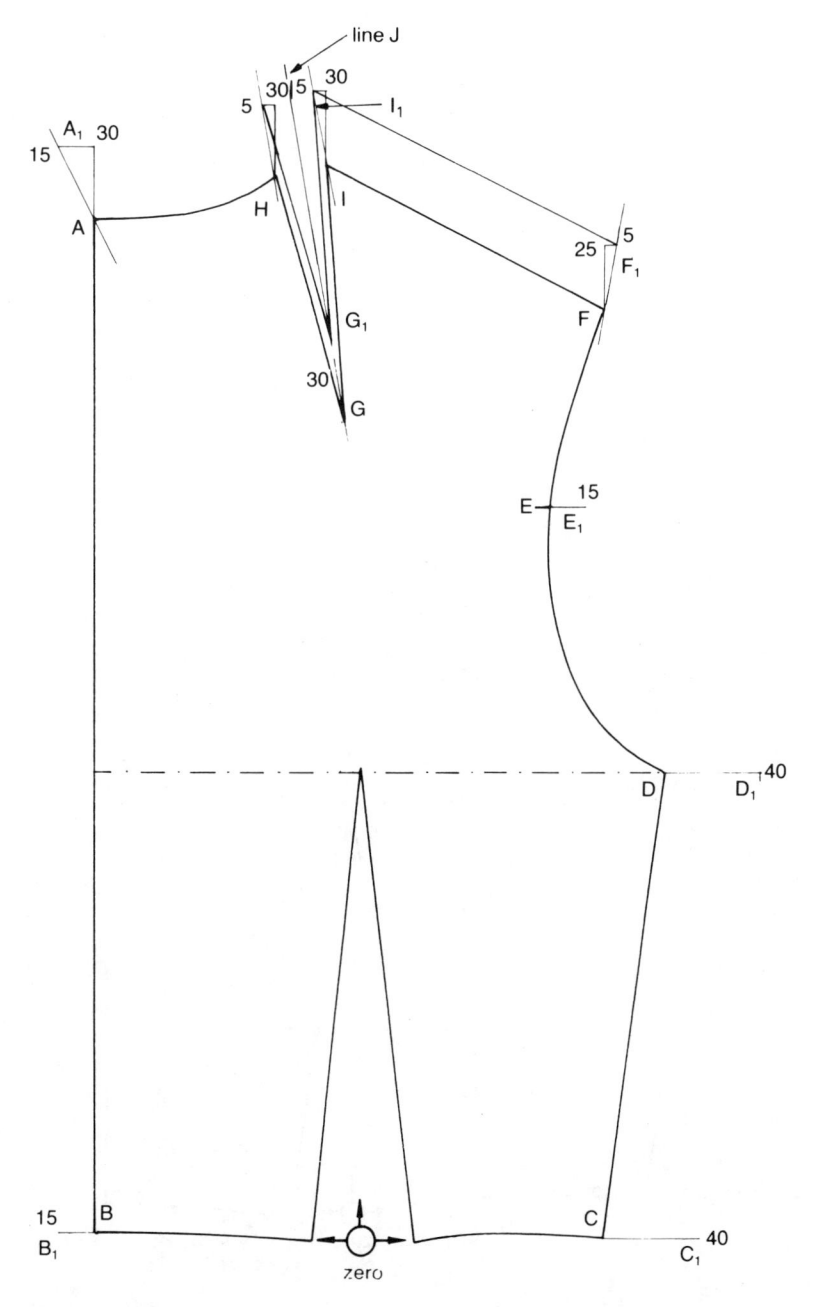

Figure 45 (a) The five size grade

90 | GENERAL GRADING TECHNIQUES

THE SIZE 10 OUTLINE
The size 10 outline is located on the extension of line A1–A, B1–B, C1–C, etc., inside the original pattern. Measure in from the size 12 outline the same increment (see Figure 46a). Use the size 12 pattern as a template.

SPIKING-OFF THE SIZES
Refer to the section on *basic techniques* in Chapter 12. Seam allowances should be added.

GRADING THE FRONT BODICE

ESTABLISHING THE LARGEST SIZE (Figures 44b and 45b)
1. Mark around the front block. Remove the basic block and transfer the bust line (the construction line), balance marks and darts to the draft.
2. As in the back grade, six sizes are required:

   10 – 12 – 14 – 16 – 18 – 20 – 22

   that is, five sizes up and one size down.

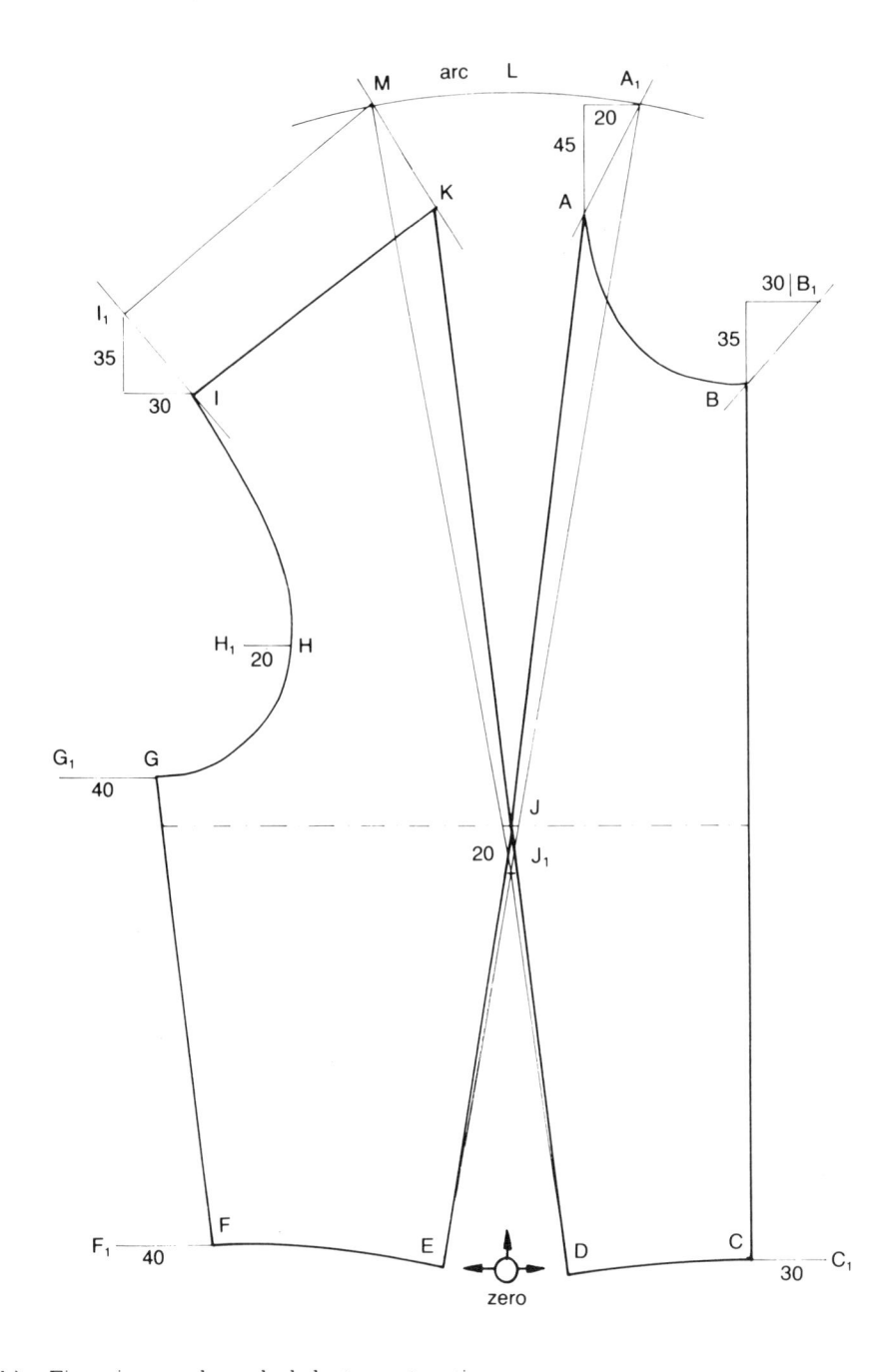

Figure 45 (b) Five sizes and graded dart construction

DRAFT GRADING THE BASIC BLOCKS

Therefore, multiply all the measurements stated in Figure 44a by five to obtain the largest size, and grade out vertically and horizontally from the original cardinal points. Establish points A–A1, B–B1, etc. around to the largest shoulder point I–I1. Connect all these points to the size 12. Stop at point I1.

THE SIZE 22 SHOULDER LENGTH AND BUST DART

The shoulder length and bust dart are established as follows (see Figure 45b):

Size 12   shoulder length = 12.5
             shoulder grade = 0.2 per size
             0.2 × 5 sizes   = 1.0 cm

The size 22 shoulder length = 12.5 + 1.0 = 13.5 cm

This measurement should be applied as follows:

1. With centre J1 swing an arc L from A1.
2. Apply 13.5 cm (i.e., the largest shoulder measurement) from I1 touching arc L. The point where it meets arc L will be the new front shoulder neck point M.

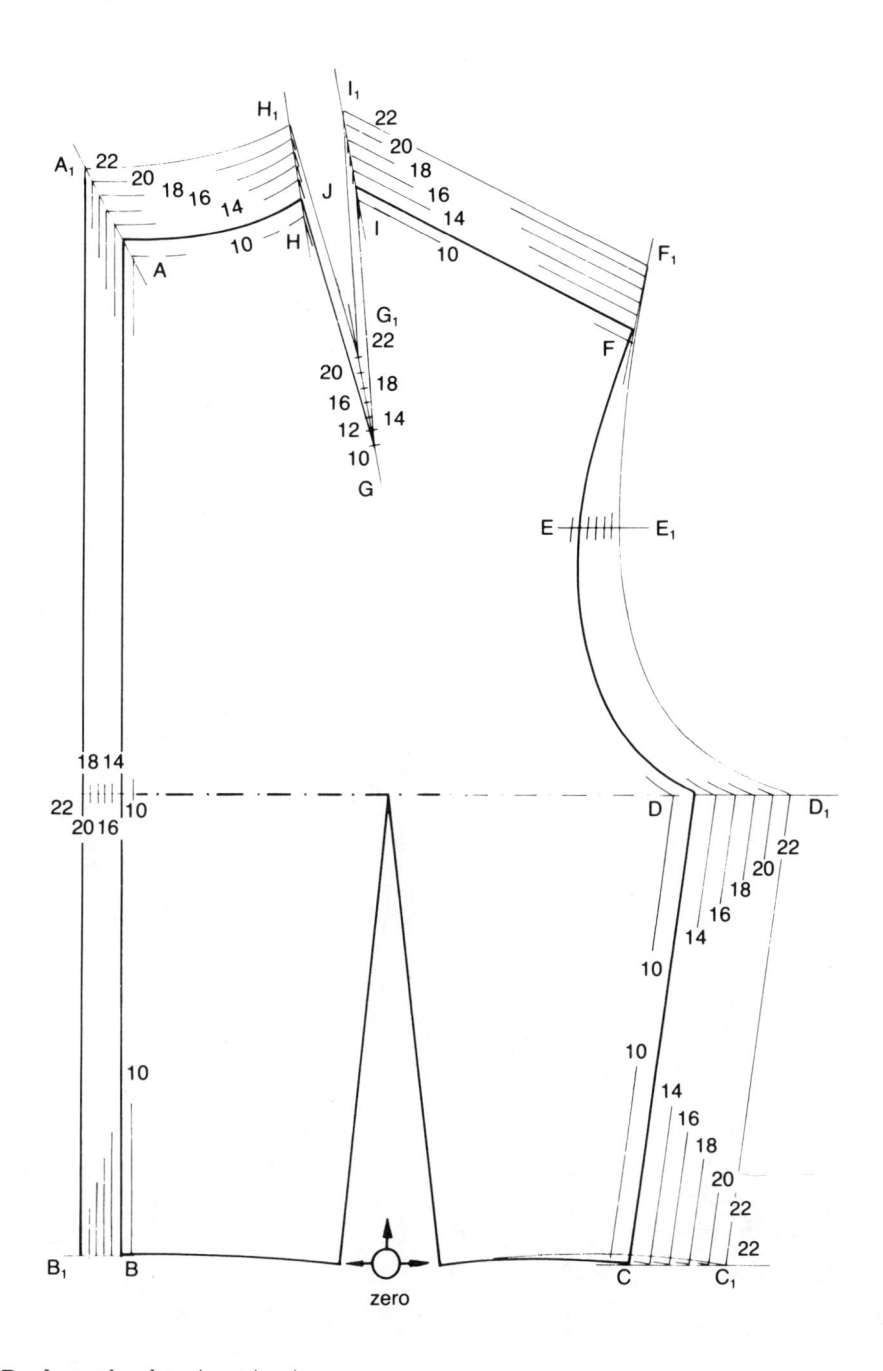

Figure 46   (a)   Draft grade showing six sizes

3 Connect J1 to A1 for front shoulder neck point.
4 Connect J1 to M for front shoulder neck point, to establish bust suppression.
5 Connect M to I1 for shoulder line.
6 Connect M to K for diagonal division line.

THE SIZE 22 OUTLINE

Continue connecting all the graded cardinal points to their original points to establish the size 22, as shown in Figure 46b.

SIZE DIVISIONS

The lines connecting the cardinal points must now be divided equally to establish the size divisions, in this case five sizes. Therefore, divide the connecting lines equally as indicated in Figure 46b. See also Note 5, Figure 43c and d. Curves such as the front neck and armhole should be developed by using the original pattern as a template. Note that when using the stock size pattern as a template, care must be taken to ensure that angles at

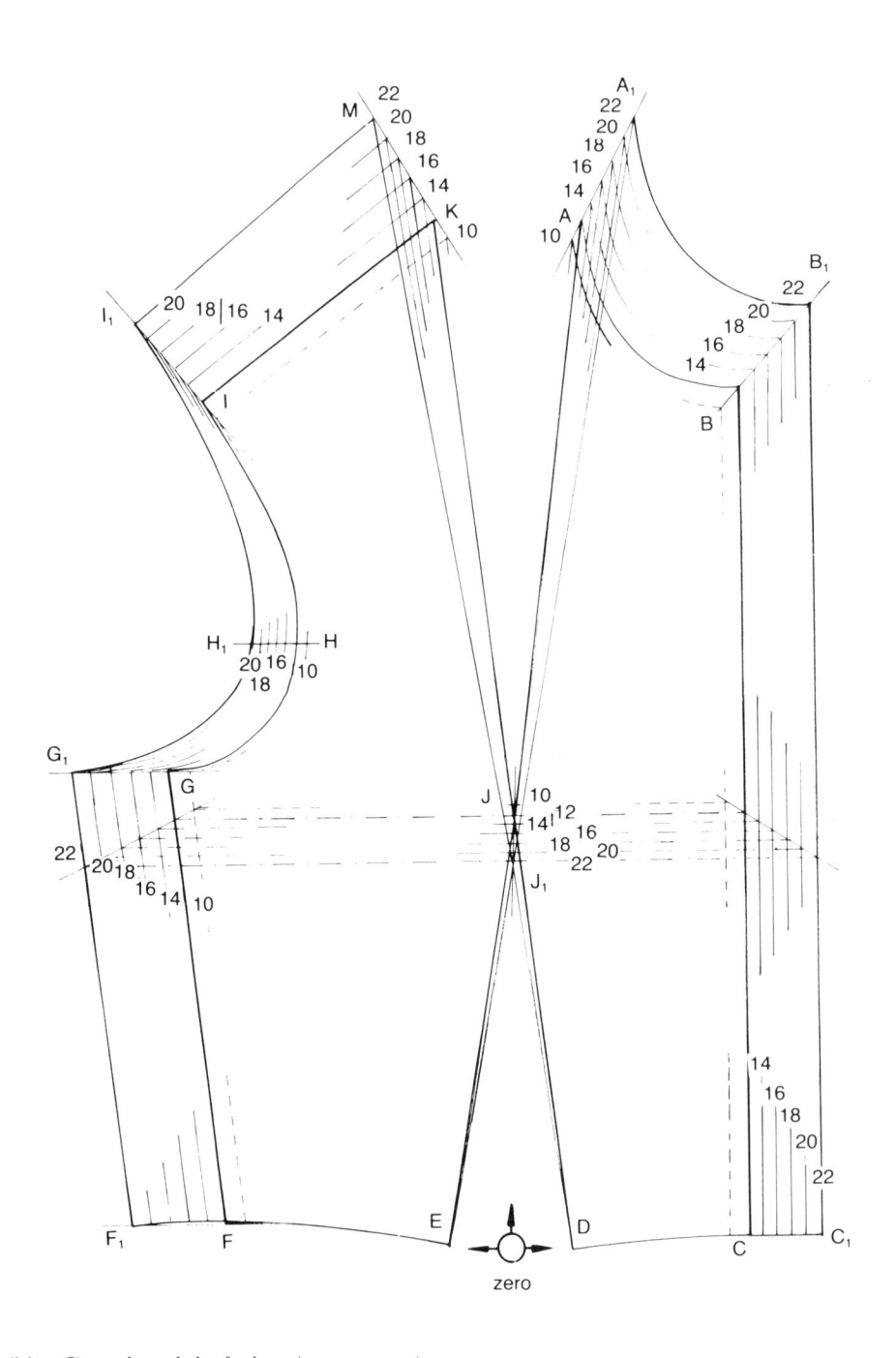

Figure 46 (b) Completed draft showing seven sizes

DRAFT GRADING THE BASIC BLOCKS

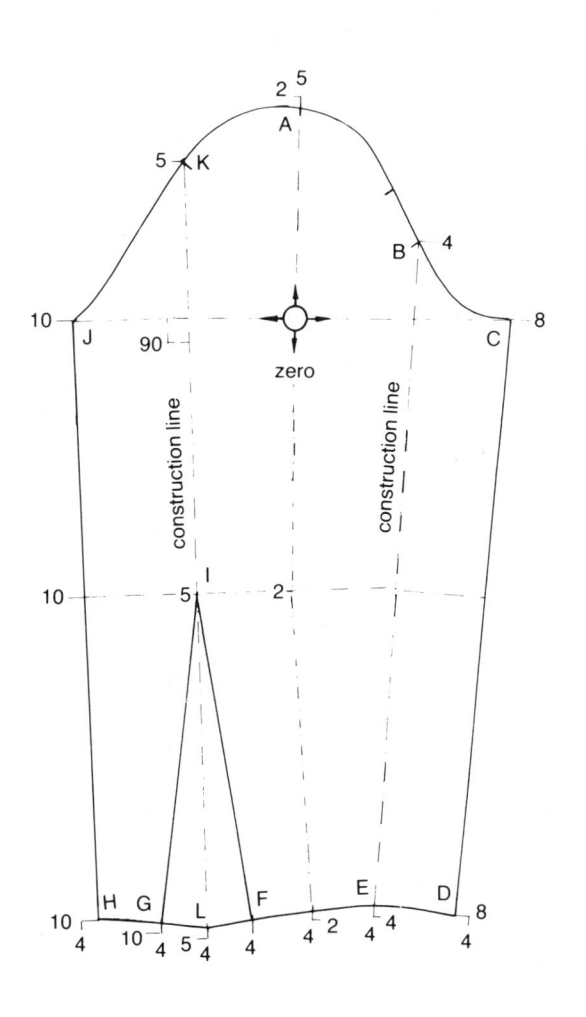

Figure 47 The fitted sleeve showing increments for one size and grade direction

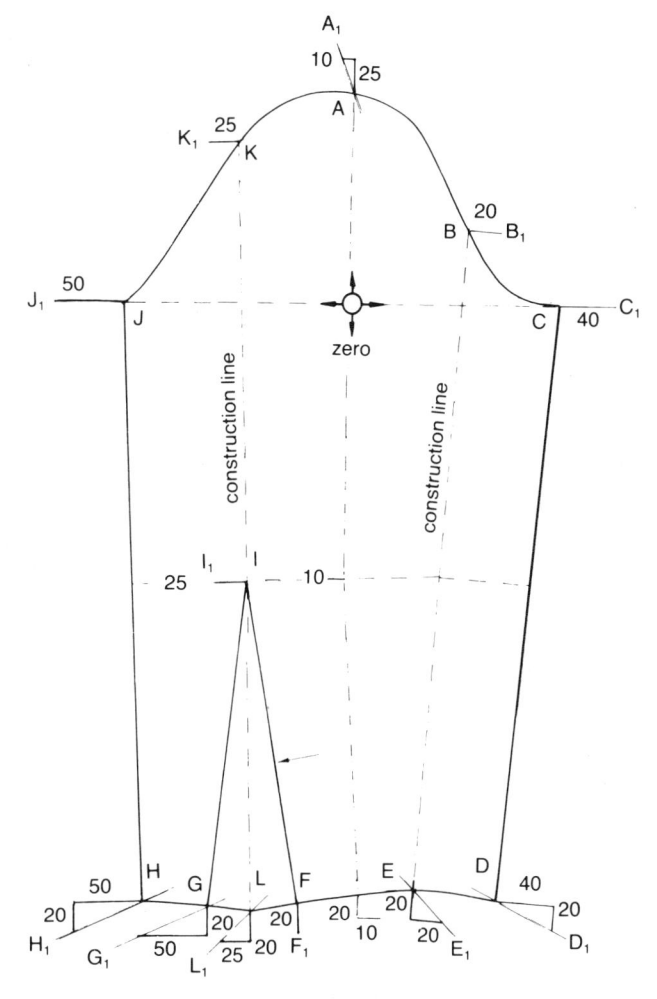

Figure 48 Establishing the size 22 cardinal points and diagonal connecting lines

underarm point and scye (to quote one example) remain constant throughout the size range. See Figure 31 for a fuller explanation.

THE SIZE 10 OUTLINE

The size 10 outline is located on the continuation of the cardinal point grade lines. See Figure 46b.

Once the size outlines have been established they can then be spiked-off.

GRADING THE SET IN SLEEVE WITH ELBOW DART

This section of the basic block is probably the most difficult to grade because of the various angles of the construction lines. Figure 47 shows these grade directions and relates them to the correct construction lines, i.e., K–L for all back grade angles and B–E for the front grade angles.

MARKING AROUND THE BLOCK (Figure 47)

1. Mark around the basic sleeve block. Transfer all construction lines and balance marks to the draft.
2. Letter all the sleeve cardinal points as shown in Figure 47. The grading directions indicated all relate to the various construction lines both vertical and horizontal.
3. The grading specification requires the following sizes:

   10 – [12] – 14 – 16 – 18 – 20 – 22

   that is, five sizes up and one size down.

ESTABLISHING THE LARGEST SIZE (Figure 48)

1. To obtain the largest size, multiply all the increments shown in Figure 47 by five and grade out to the prescribed angles. See Figure 48 to establish the size 22 cardinal points.

94   GENERAL GRADING TECHNIQUES

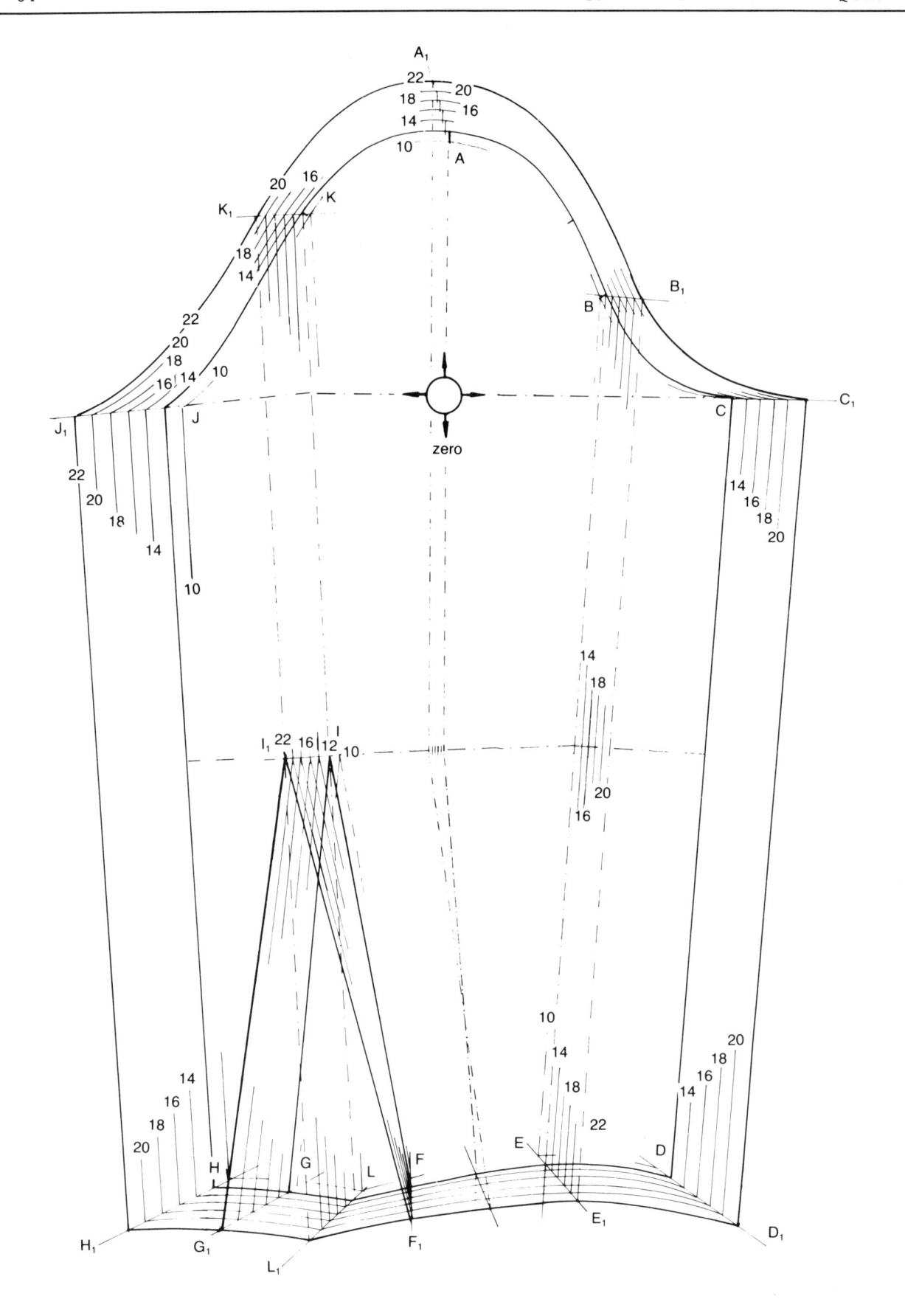

Figure 49 Fitted sleeve grade showing six sizes

DRAFT GRADING THE BASIC BLOCKS

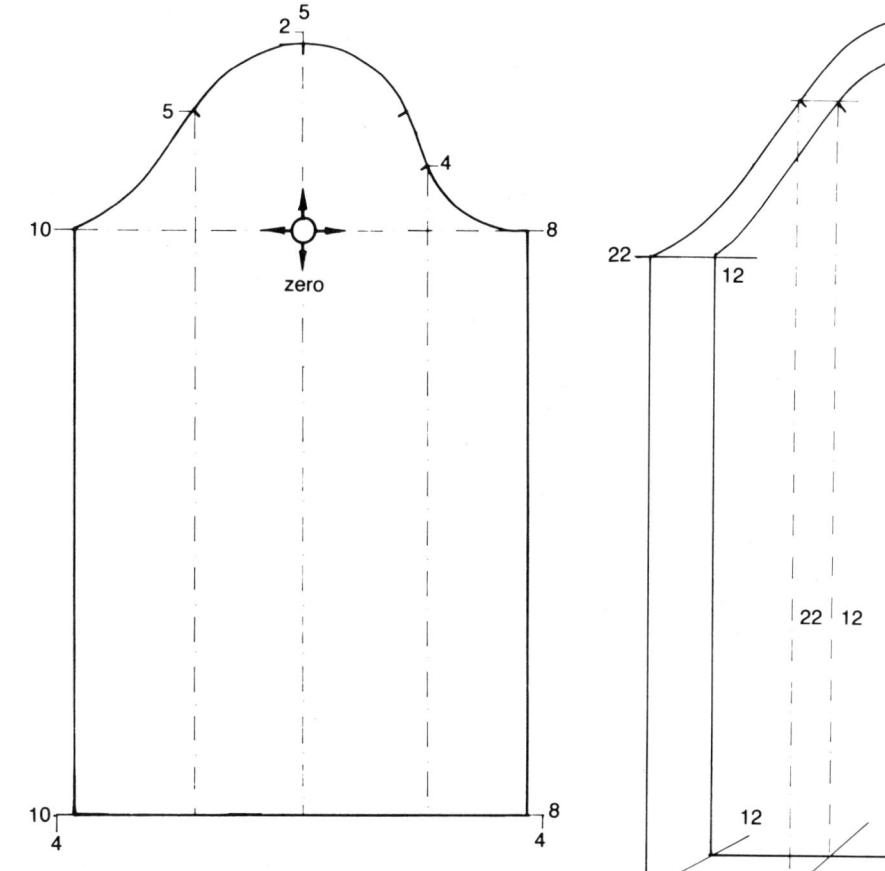

Figure 50 Straight sleeve block grade plan increments for one size

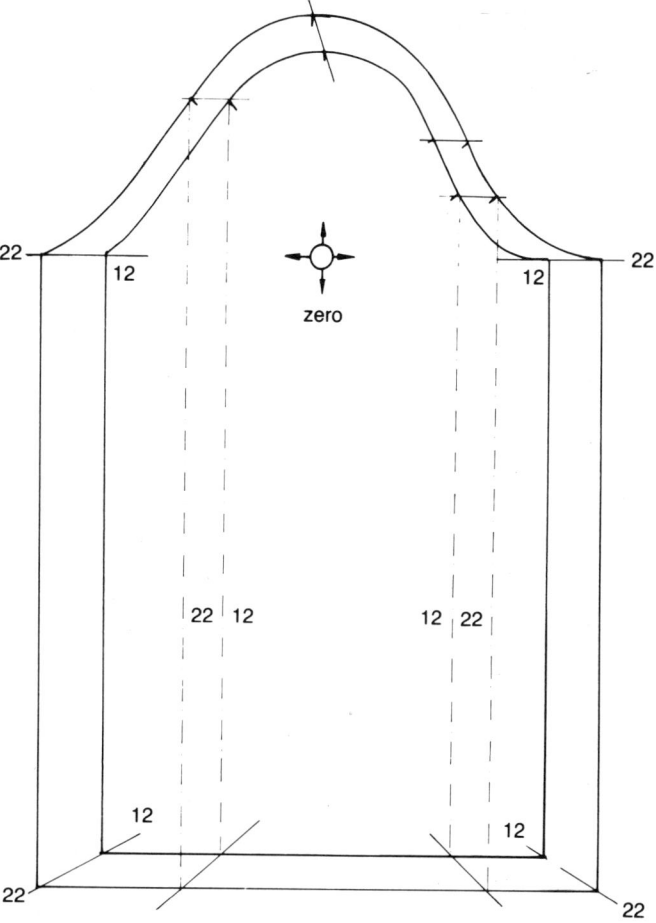

Figure 51 Straight sleeve block grade for five sizes

2 Letter these points A1–B1–C1 etc., as in Figure 48.
3 Connect A1–A, B1–B etc., all around the block.

THE SIZE 22 OUTLINE (Figure 49)
Connect all the new cardinal points as in Figure 49.

SIZE DIVISIONS
To obtain the intermediary sizes mark cardinal points on the connecting lines as indicated by dividing the line into five equal parts.

THE SIZE 10 OUTLINE
The size 10 outline is located inside the original outline. Use the block sleeve as a template to draw in the sleeve head.

The required sizes can now be spiked-off.

THE STRAIGHT SLEEVE BLOCK
This block is the basic sleeve and can be manipulated to produce a fitted sleeve block. Figure 50 shows the increments when grading from the centre bicep line. This is graded in the same way as the previous example, minus the elbow suppression. Figure 51 shows the completed grade.

THE SKIRT BLOCK

Figure 52 shows the grade plan. The plan shows all the increments necessary for a full length skirt.

Figure 53 shows the skirt grade for five sizes up and one size down. Grade as in previous examples.

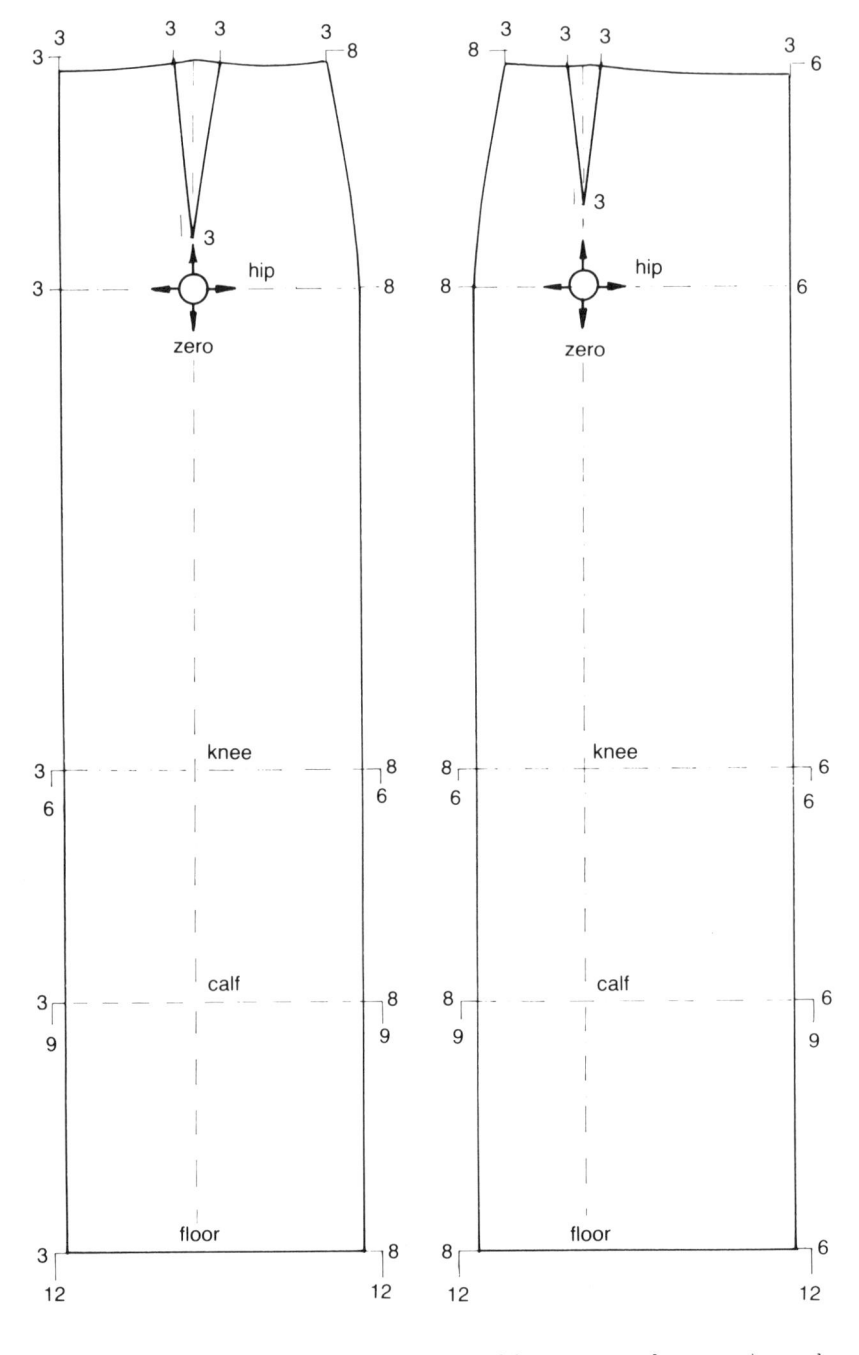

Figure 52 Skirt grade plan showing grade directions and increments for one size only

DRAFT GRADING THE BASIC BLOCKS

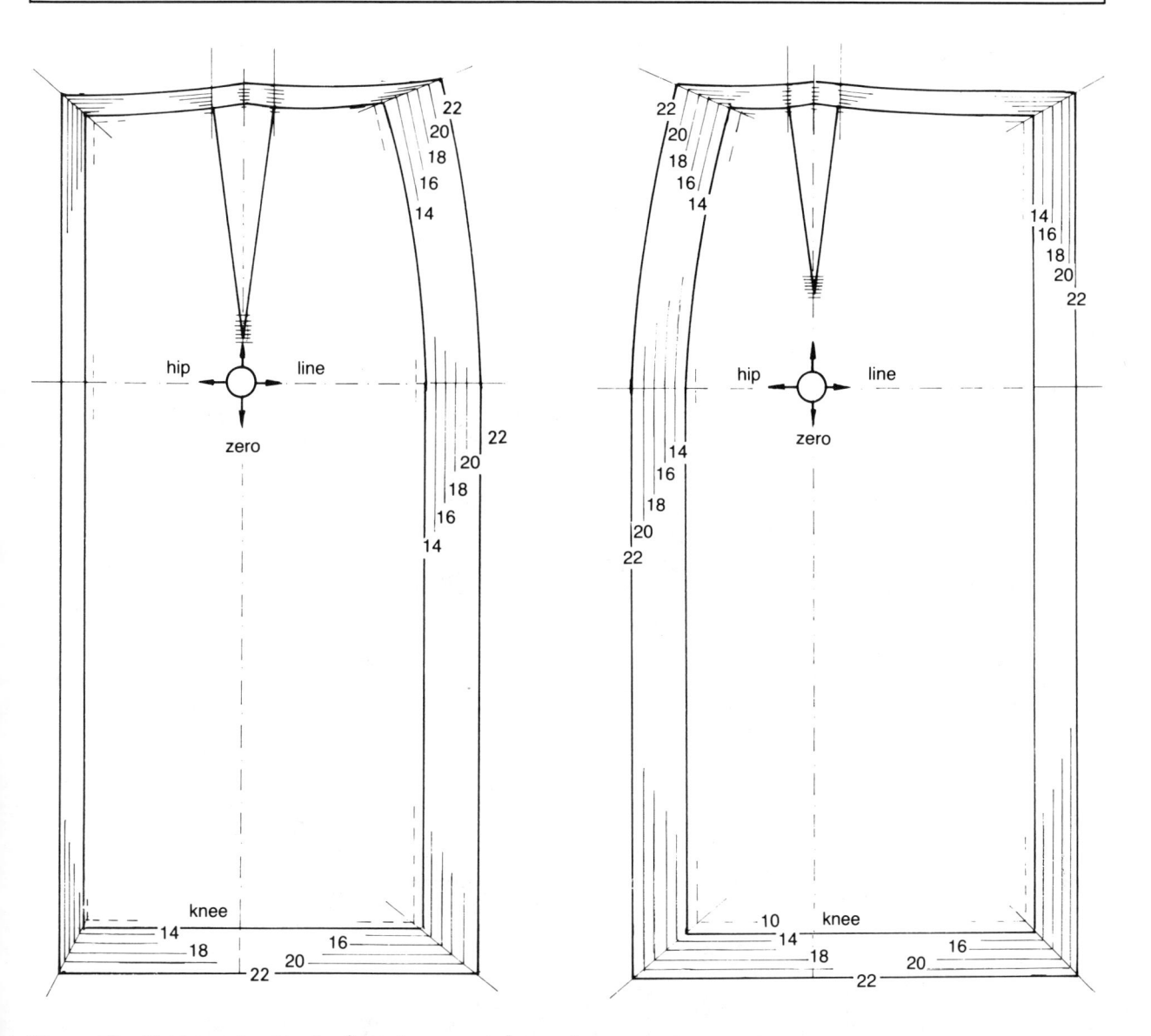

Figure 53 Skirt grade plan for five sizes up and one down

CHAPTER 11

Selecting a zero point

THE SPLIT DIAGRAMS

Split diagrams, Figure 54a and b, are a visual representation of the sectional distribution charts in Chapter 2 and illustrate the precise areas of the pattern where increments are distributed. In order to grade up or down one size, it is necessary to know these areas. These charts should be studied carefully as they provide a clear visual picture of what actually happens when a pattern has been graded, **irrespective of the grading technique or zero point chosen**.

Before implementing these increments, it is necessary *to select and establish a practical zero point.*

ZERO POINTS

Figure 55 shows the relationship between a size 12 and a size 22 front bodice when grading from

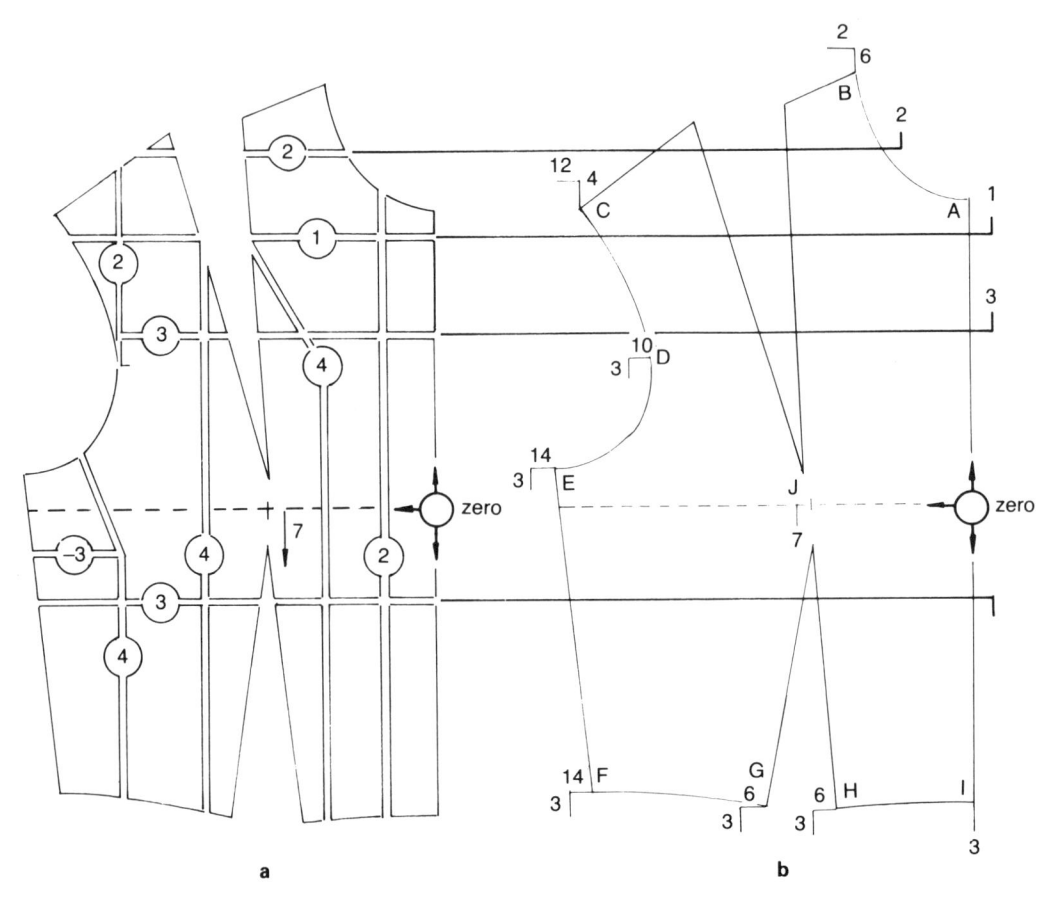

Figure 54 (a) Split diagram
(b) Grade plan using height and girth quantities

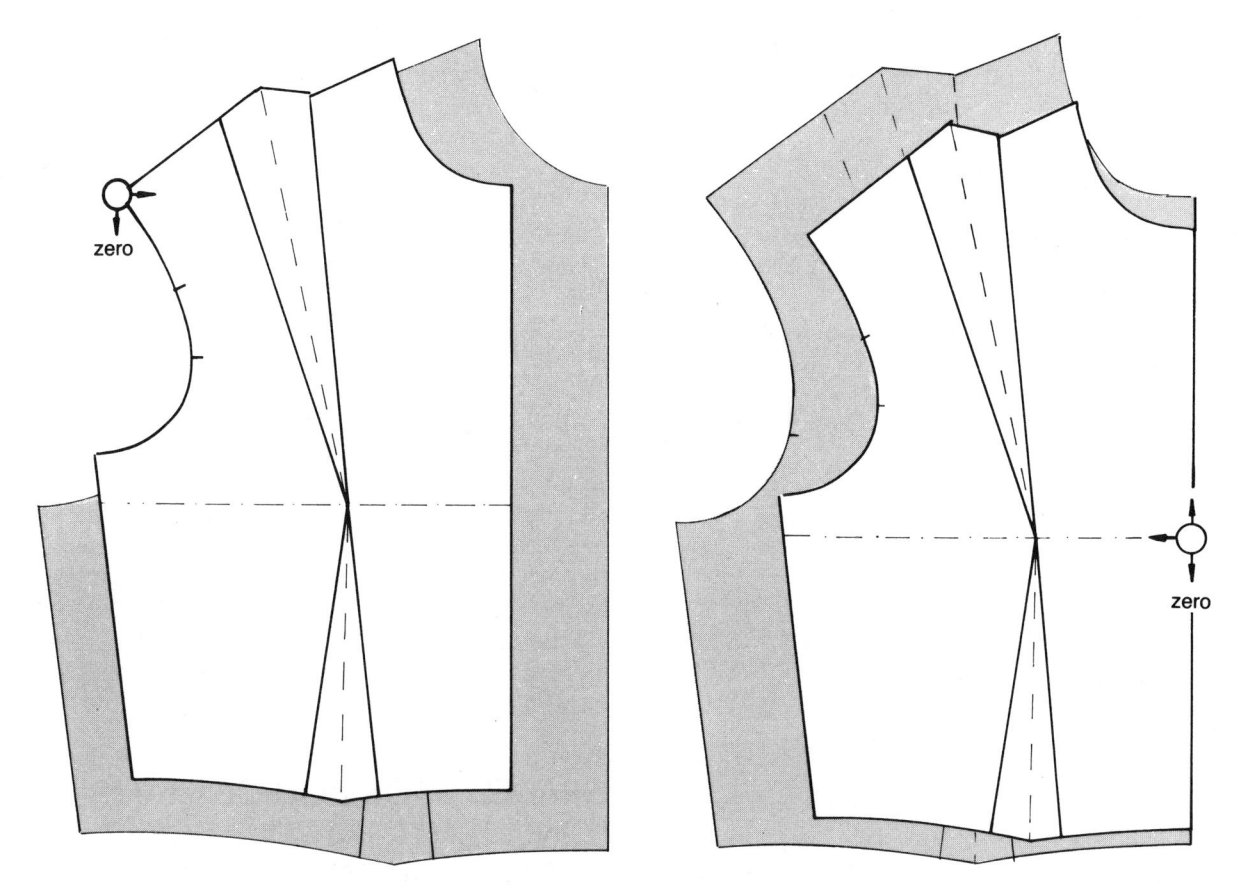

Figure 55 Illustrating the relationship between a size 12 and a size 22 front bodice when grading from different zero points

different zero points. It should be noted that the dimensions and shape of the largest size in both cases remains the same. **Only the relationship between the two sizes has changed.** The difference is that the increments calculated from the split diagram, Figure 54a, have been applied from different starting points. **The choice of starting or zero point is a crucial one, and will mainly depend on the type of style being graded.** Throughout this book there are many examples of zero points. They have been selected to illustrate the sort of options that are open to the pattern technician when planning the whole size range. The main aim of zero point selection is to attempt to keep the styling area as static as possible, thereby not interfering with the style lines of the pattern. See, for example, the raglan sleeve, Style 22.

ESTABLISHING GRADE INCREMENTS FROM ANY ZERO POINT

The ability to select a zero point and calculate incremental increases from it is one of the most essential skills of grading. The following examples, Figure 54a and b, have been selected to show the principles of these calculations.

METHOD   SELECTING A ZERO POINT
1   Select a zero point (in this case the CF bust line)
2   Locate all cardinal points (denoted by A–B–C, etc.)
3   Use the split pattern, Figure 54a, to calculate increments from each cardinal point in the following way. Total up the increments between each cardinal point and the zero (Figure 54b). Therefore:

a   between the zero and point A is a vertical increase of 4 mm to arrive at the next size
b   B will increase vertically 3 mm + 1 mm + 2 mm = 6 mm
    B will also increase horizontally from the zero by 2 mm
c   C will increase vertically from the zero by 3 mm + 1 mm = 4 mm
    C will increase horizontally from the zero by 2 mm + 4 mm + 4 mm + 2 mm = 12 mm

- d point D, i.e., the pitch point, will increase horizontally from the zero by 2 mm + 4 mm + 4 mm = 10 mm, and also vertically by 3 mm
- e E will increase horizontally from the zero by 2 mm + 4 mm + 4 mm + 4 mm = 14 mm
  E will drop vertically from the zero by 3 mm
- f F will increase horizontally from the zero by 2 mm + 4 mm + 4 mm + 4 mm = 14 mm
  F will drop vertically from the zero by 3 mm
- g G and H will both move horizontally away from zero by 4 mm + 2 mm = 6 mm
  J will move horizontally away from zero by 4 mm + 2 mm = 6 mm

These quantities should be marked on to the grade plan ready for grading (see Figure 54b).

BUST POINT HEIGHT

It is important to note that the bust point height is usually independent of the split diagram and is normally introduced after increments have been calculated. In this case J drops vertically 4 mm for the bust point + 3 mm for the bust line to waist = 7 mm.

Figure 54a and b should be used to check other zero points throughout this book. Figure 56b, c, d, e, f and g must be checked against their respective split patterns in order to understand how the zero variations are calculated.

The next stage is to look at some examples of grading from different zero points so that the importance of zero selection can be assessed. These examples will show clearly the results obtained by grading from different zero points, each of which has advantages and disadvantages. The pattern technician must evaluate these for any given style. Experience will show which zero point is the most convenient to use.

DRAFT GRADING USING DIFFERENT ZERO POINTS

The bodice is probably the most difficult pattern area to grade due to its suppression. Therefore, to illustrate how choice of zero points can affect a draft grade, Figure 56a has been selected. Figure 56b, c, d, e, f and g, show Figure 56a graded from six different zero points, all of which are practical and can be used effectively. However, it is sensible to choose the example which is the most convenient visually, and is subsequently easiest to 'spike-off' on to card.

STYLE GRADING OPTION

There is a style grading option on virtually every pattern. This means that the pattern technician is able to choose from alternative proportional effects, depending on style requirements. In Figure 56a the back yoke could remain the same depth for all sizes. The dart would, therefore, have to move up with the shoulder, or the yoke could deepen. Conversely, this would mean that the dart would lengthen. The front vertical seam width at shoulder could remain the same width (as in these examples) or it could be widened per size. The pattern technician must make the choice, between those illustrated in our six examples.

It is important to note that a back zero does not have to pair with a front zero point, but should be chosen purely on merit for each section.

GRADED BACK BODICE EXAMPLES USING DIFFERENT ZERO POINTS

Figures 57, 58 and 59 illustrate the visual variation of using different zero points for style grading. The three drafts can be evaluated to determine which zero point produces the most practical grade. Each figure has a grade plan which has been calculated from the split diagram, i.e., Figure 56b, c and d.

Figures 60, 61 and 62 illustrate the styled front bodices graded from different zero points – note the different visual effects.

It is important to note that for the purpose of calculating increments on the front bodice, the bust point is static, as in Figure 60. To accommodate figuration the bust point is dropped independently (see Chapter 3).

The zero point selected for Figure 60 is an exceptional one because it is based on the bust point which is itself dropping. **Therefore, instead of the bust point dropping towards the waist, the waist moves up towards the bust point. The bust point thus remains static, although in reality is moving downwards.**

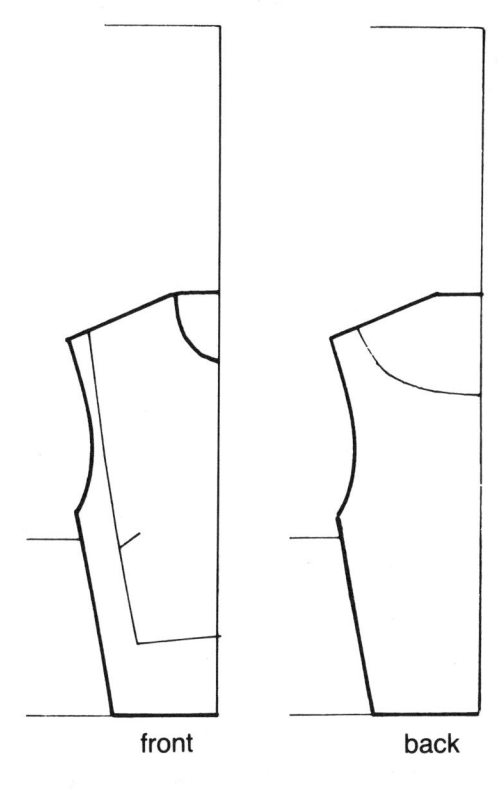

SELECTING A ZERO POINT 101

Figure 56 (a) Draft grade 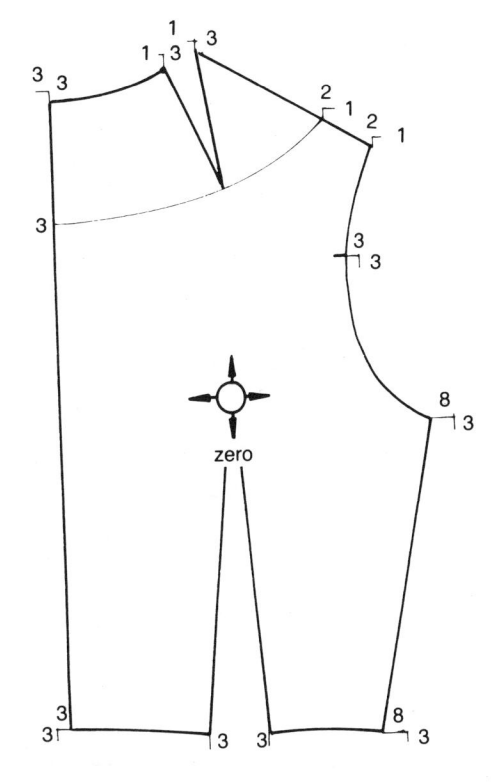   (b) Grade plan

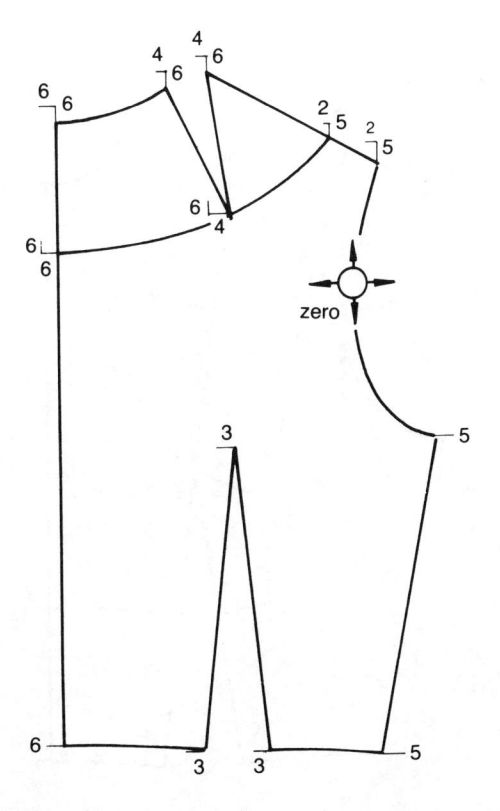

(c) Grade plan 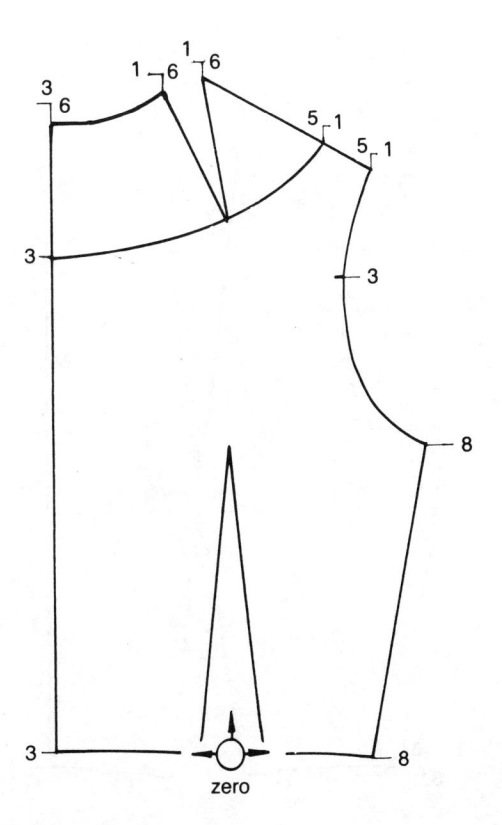   (d) Grade plan

102　　GENERAL GRADING TECHNIQUES

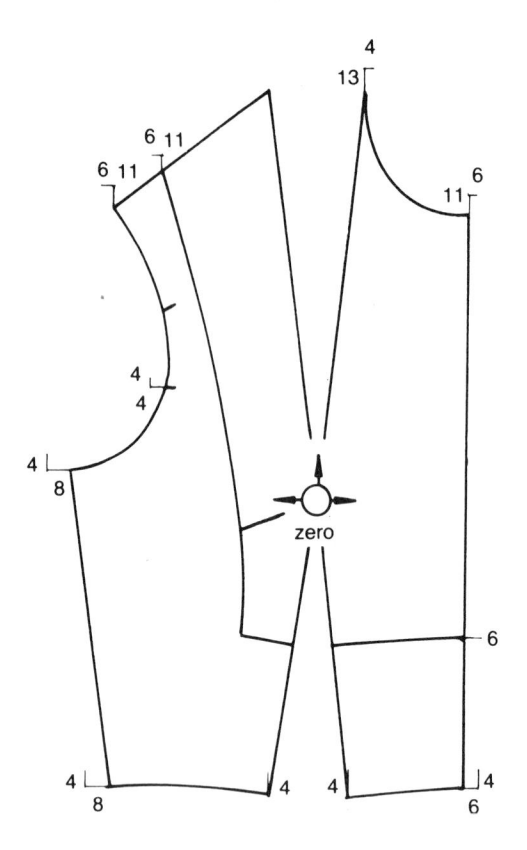

Figure 56　(e)　Grade plan

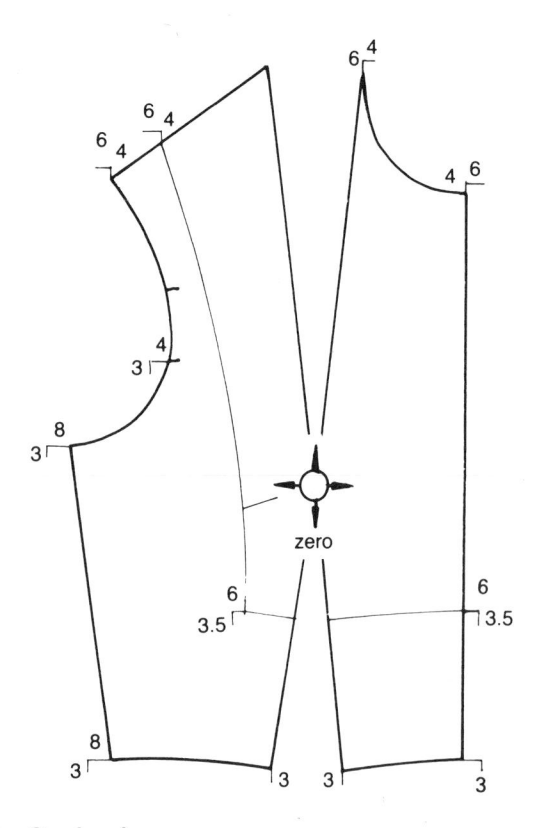

(f)　Grade plan

(g)　Grade plan

SELECTING A ZERO POINT 103

Note:
A style option. The back dart end can be lengthened to touch style line
B the panel width could be increased per size

A style option (see note below)

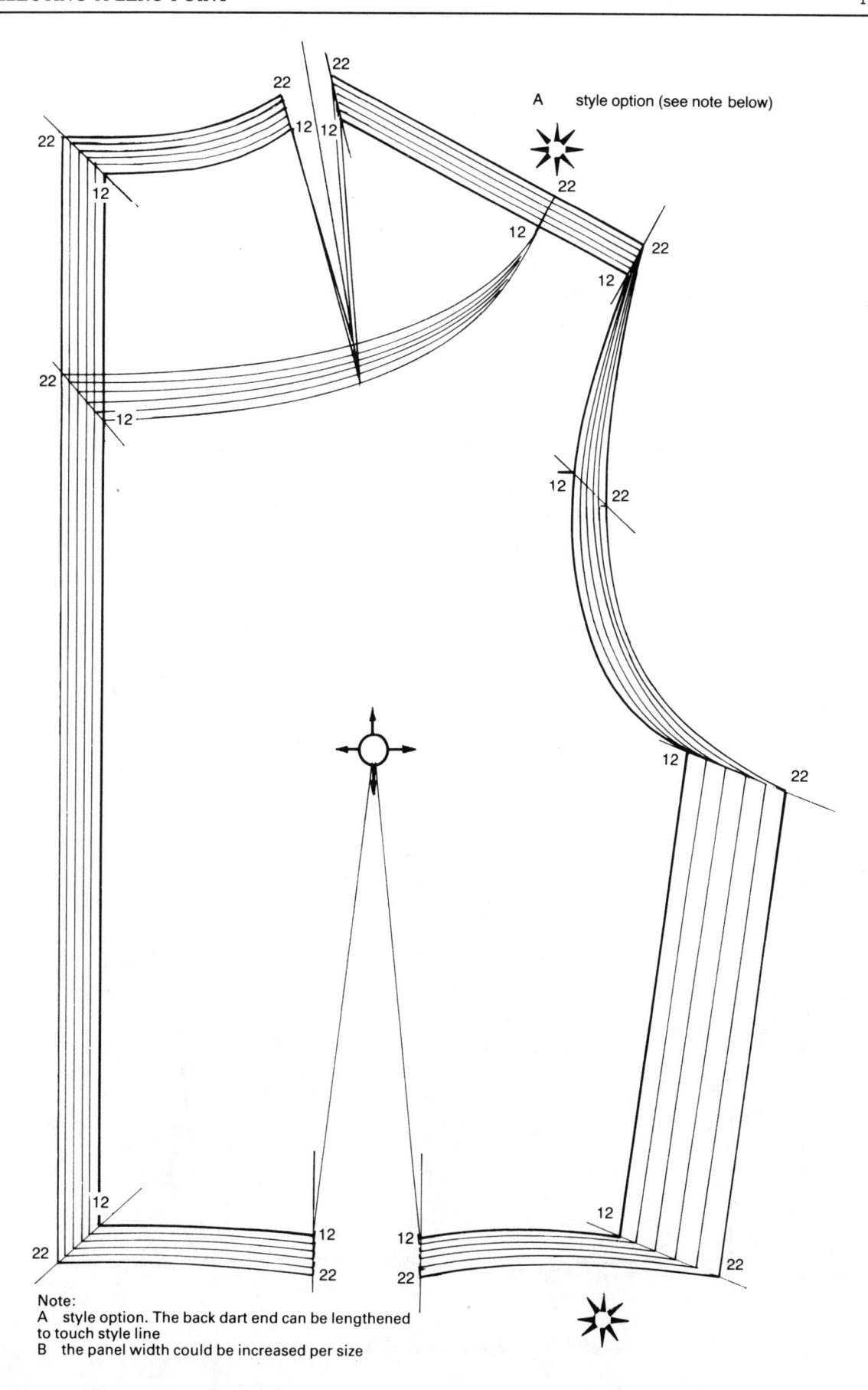

Figure 57 Draft grade five sizes up

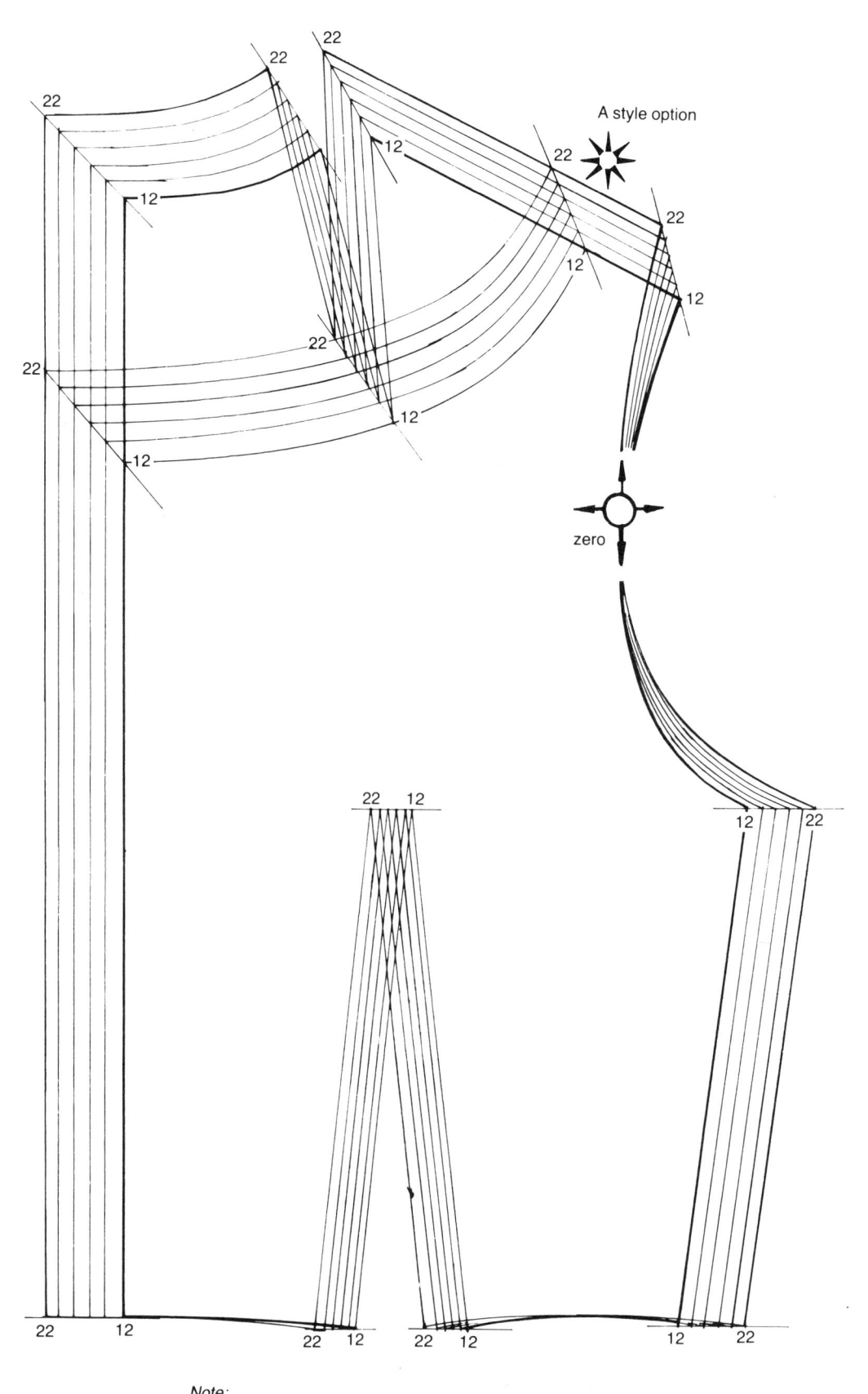

104　GENERAL GRADING TECHNIQUES

Note:
A style option. Panel width increased per size at shoulder

Figure 58　Draft grade five sizes up

SELECTING A ZERO POINT 105

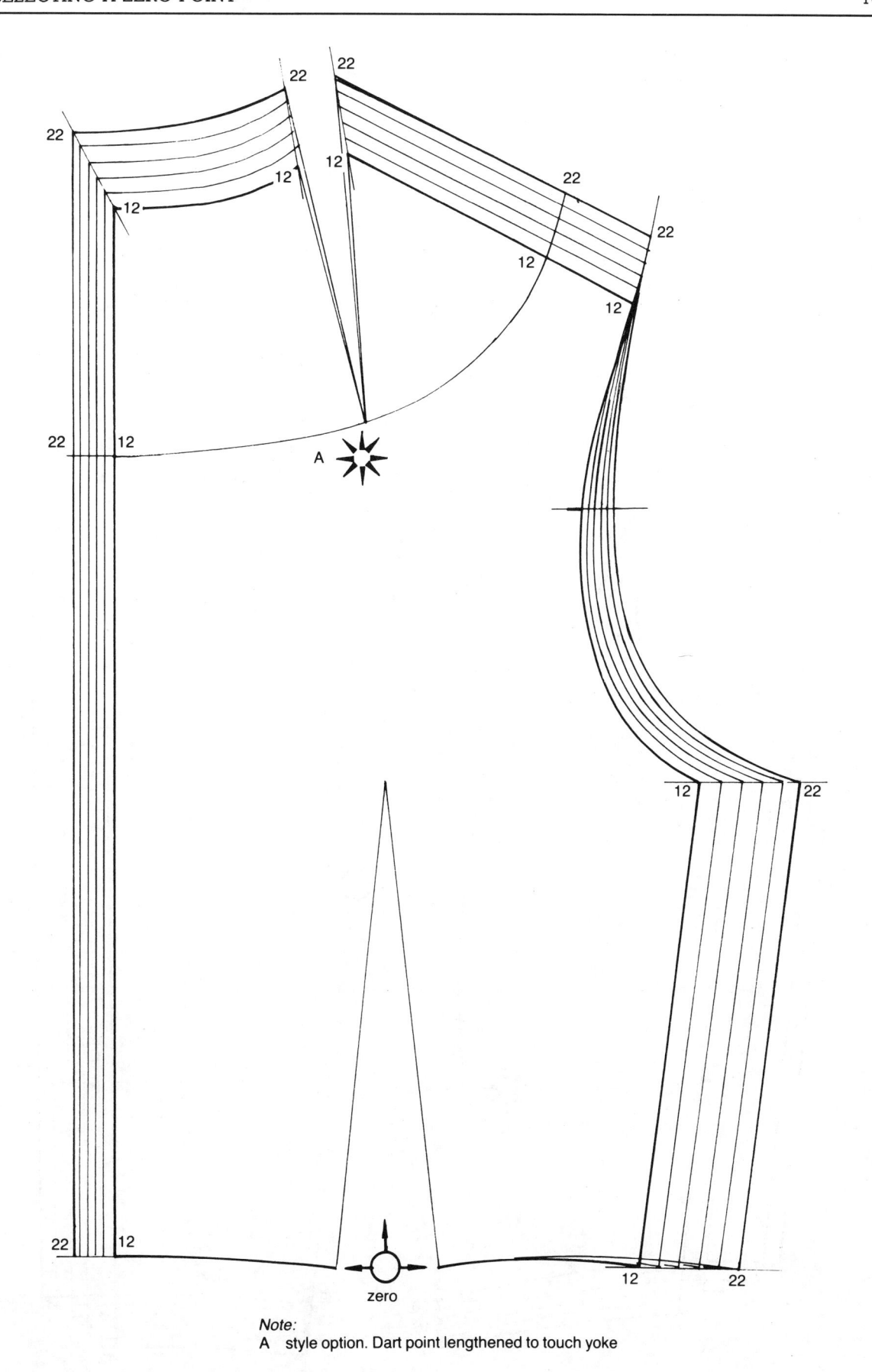

Note:
A style option. Dart point lengthened to touch yoke

Figure 59 Draft grade five sizes up

106 GENERAL GRADING TECHNIQUES

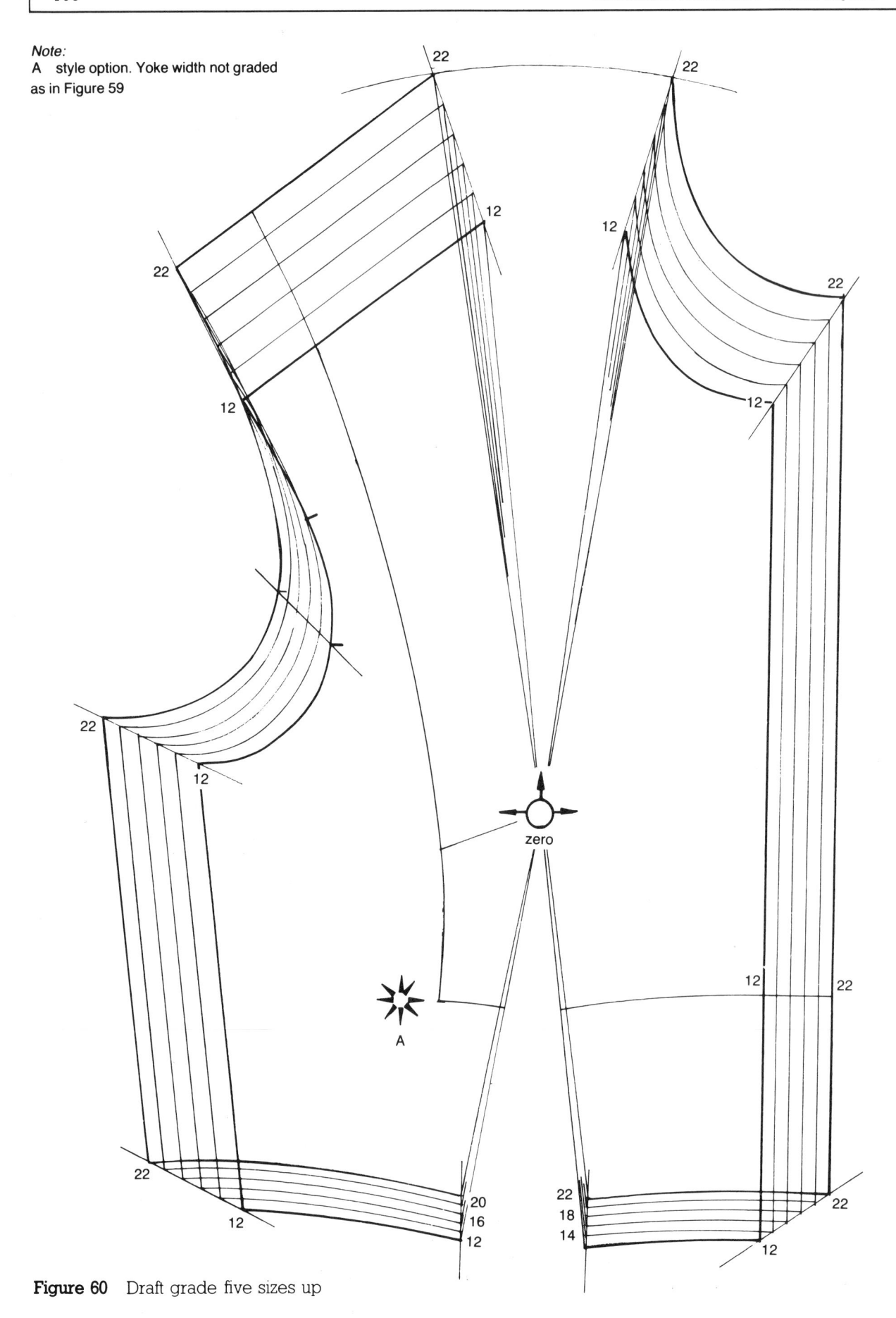

Note:
A style option. Yoke width not graded as in Figure 59

Figure 60 Draft grade five sizes up

| SELECTING A ZERO POINT | 107 |

B style option (see note below)

important – the size 12 bust point is the zero

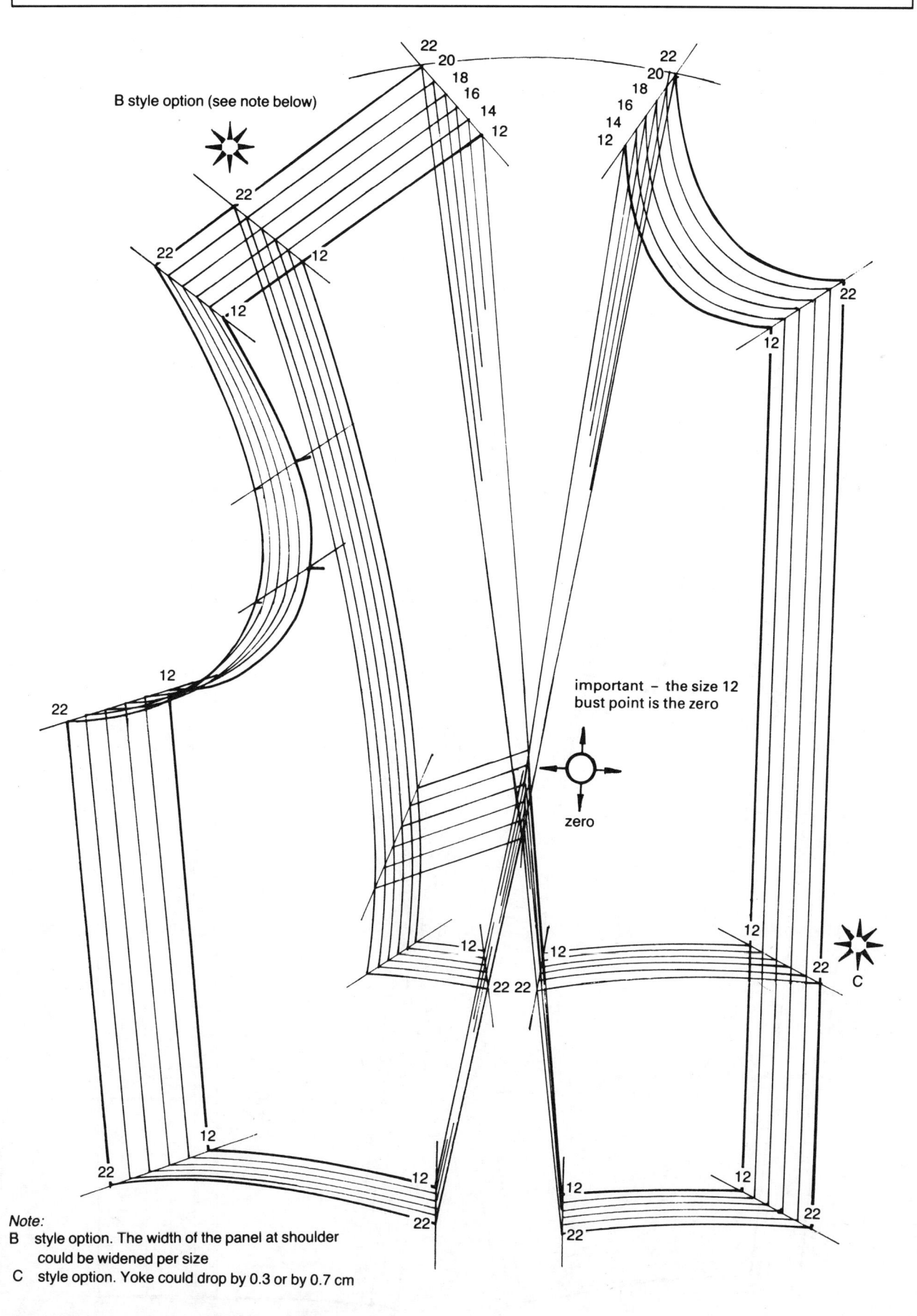

zero

Note:
B style option. The width of the panel at shoulder could be widened per size
C style option. Yoke could drop by 0.3 or by 0.7 cm

Figure 61 Draft grade five sizes up

108 GENERAL GRADING TECHNIQUES

Figure 62 Draft grade five sizes up

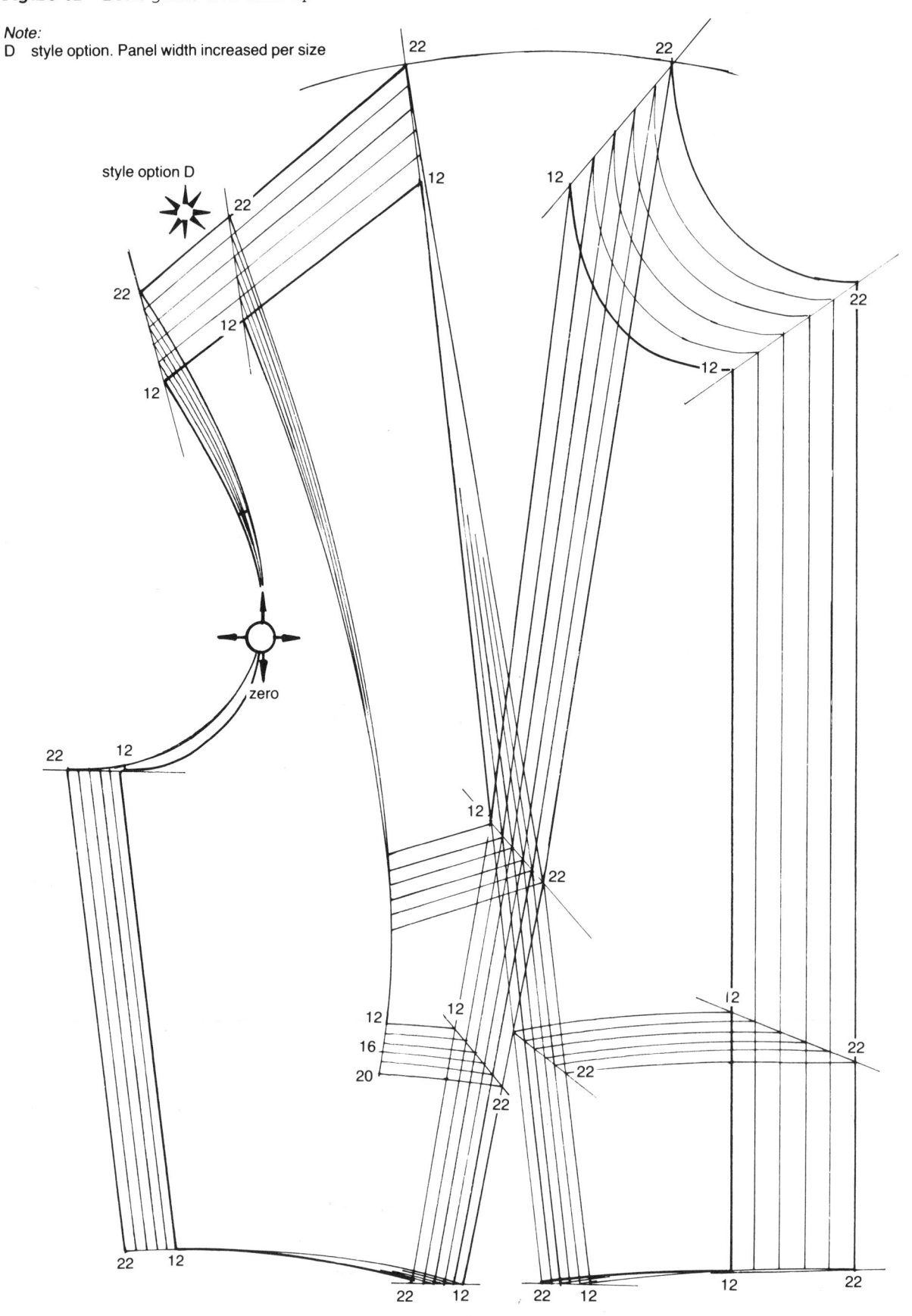

Note:
D style option. Panel width increased per size

SELECTING A ZERO POINT

All the examples given above should be studied carefully. The final choice of a zero point for any given style will depend on the complexity of the style, and the ease with which the resulting draft grade can be converted into a set of graded patterns.

SELECTING A SKIRT ZERO

The following examples of skirt zero points again illustrate the choice available to the grader.

Figure 63a is the non-graded zero diagram illustrating how the increments from the split diagram are applied when using the centre front waist point as a zero. Referring to Figure 63b, note how the darts move, thereby creating a fairly confused picture, especially if the darts are to be repositioned or re-used as other suppression forms.

Figure 64b, however, retains the dart position and is consequently an easier zero to choose for a style grade that is using the dart into any seam lines.

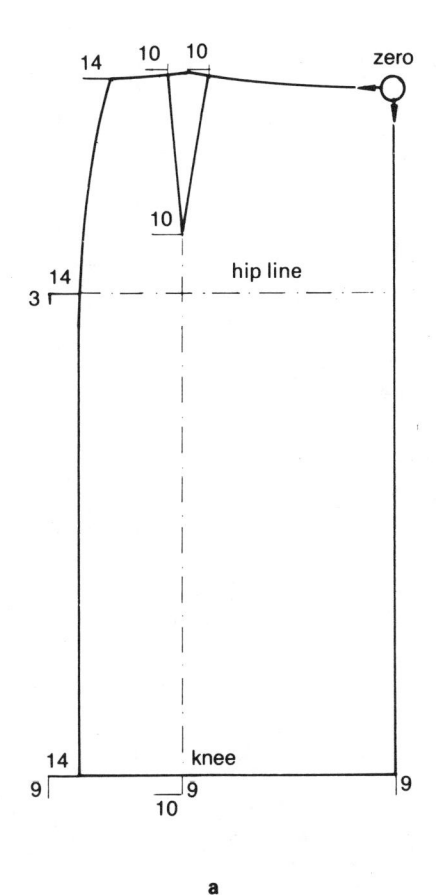

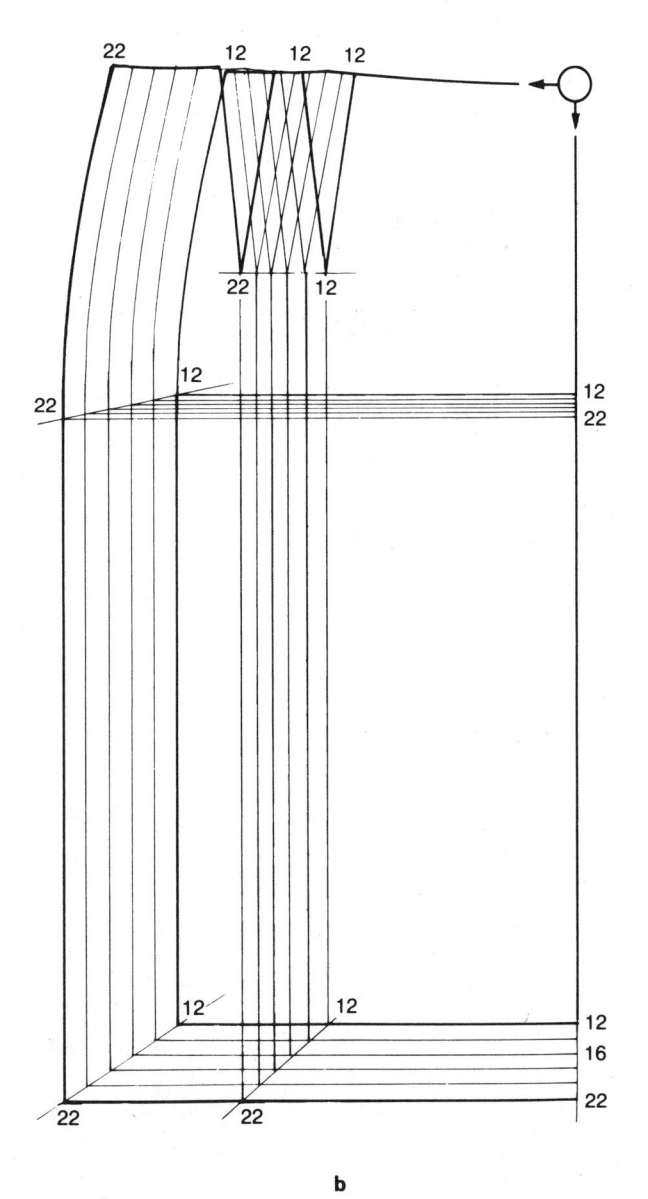

Figure 63 (a) Grade plan – one size
(b) Grade plan five sizes up

Figure 64 (a) Grade plan – one size
(b) Grade plan five sizes up

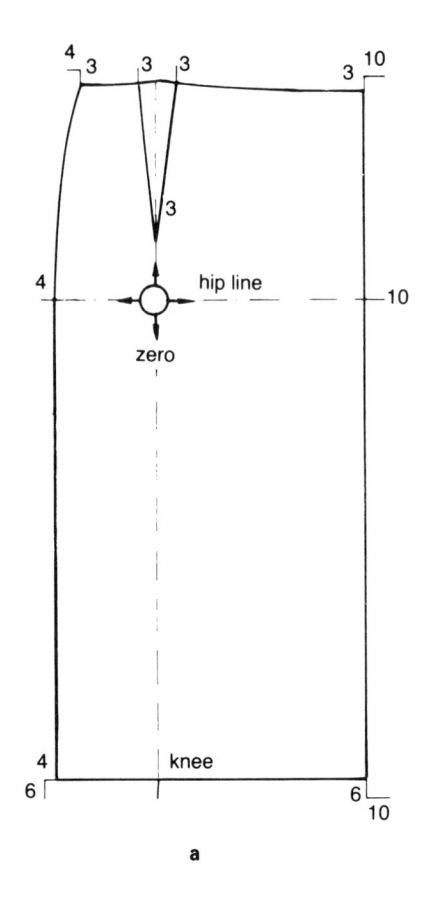

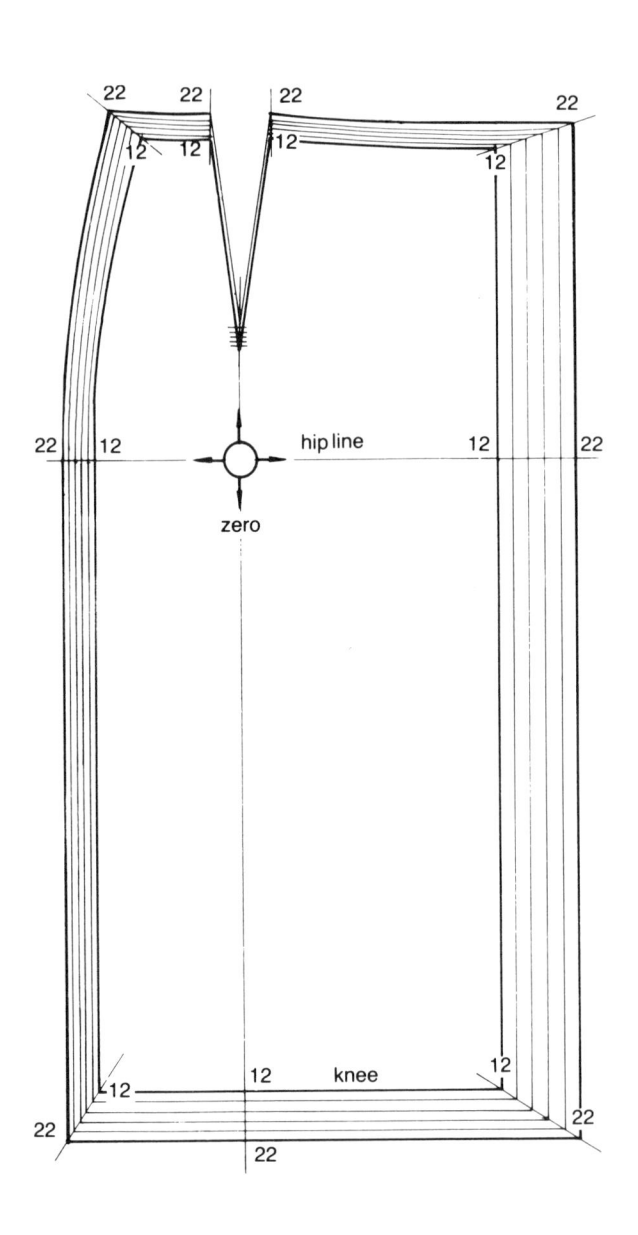

SELECTING A SLEEVE ZERO

Figures 65 and 66 show two sleeve zero points. Figure 66b is probably a better zero to choose as the largest size clearly relates to the smallest, i.e., the smaller size, particularly at the crown.

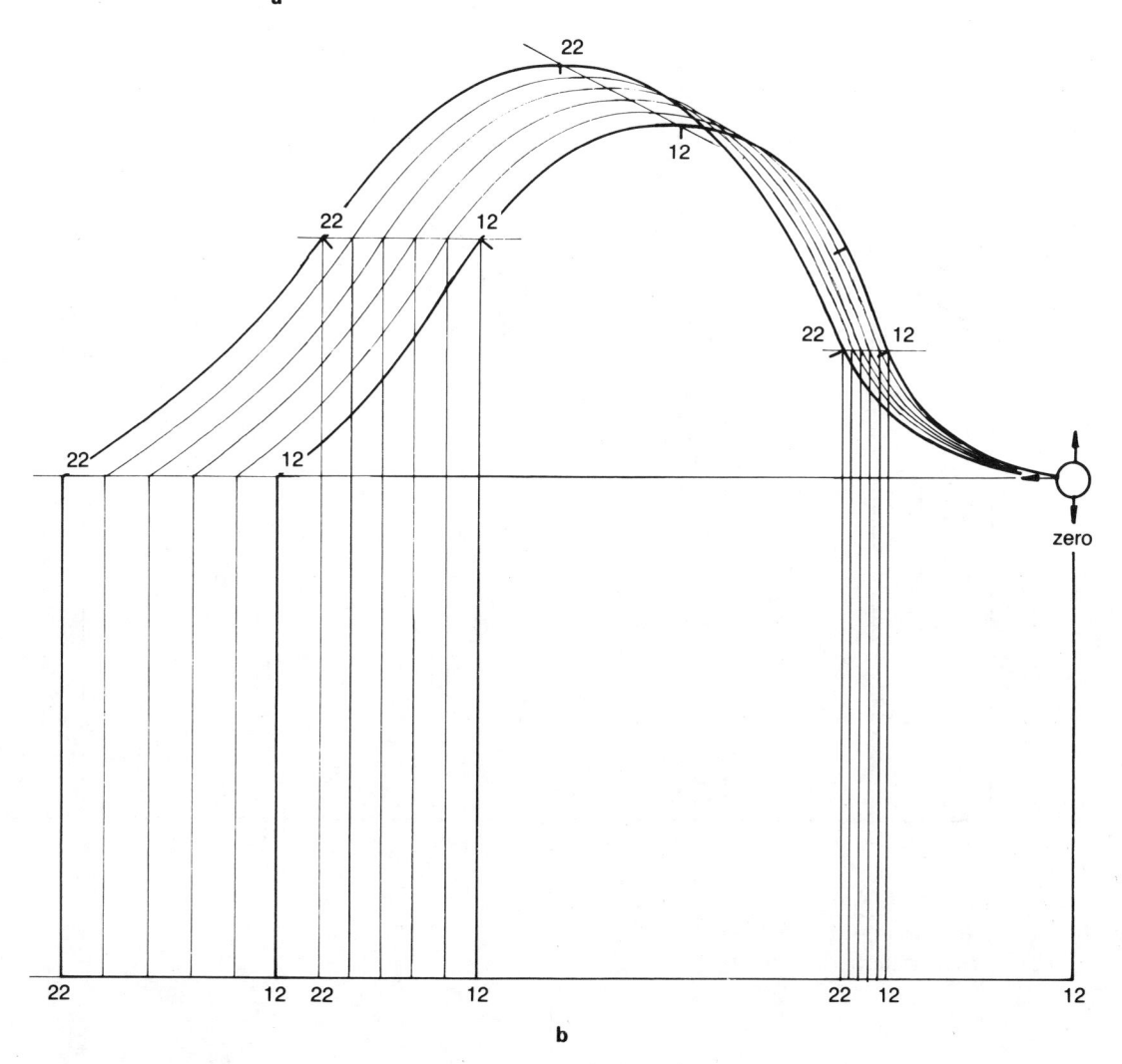

Figure 65 (a) Grade plan – one size
(b) Grade plan five sizes up

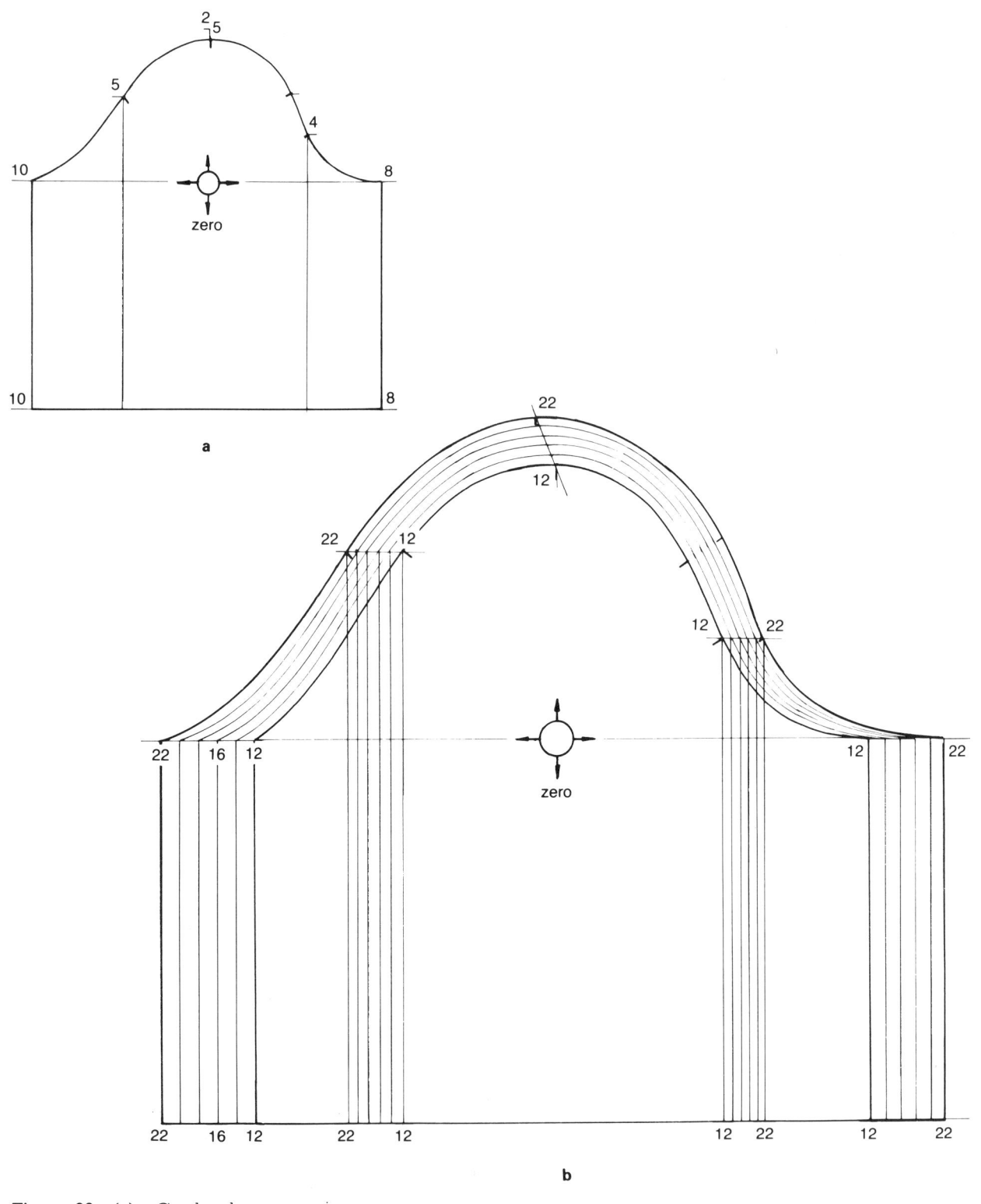

Figure 66 (a) Grade plan – one size
(b) Grade plan five sizes up

All the examples given above should be studied carefully. The final choice of a zero point for any given style will depend on the complexity of the style, and the ease with which the resulting draft grade can be converted into a set of graded patterns.

CHAPTER 12

From draft to finished sizes

SOME BASIC TECHNIQUES

TECHNIQUE 1 Spiking-off

The technique for converting a draft grade into a set of graded patterns is called 'spiking-off'.

Equipment needed – card, spike, basic patterns, weights.

Stage 1   (Figure 67)

Lay a sheet of the card under the draft. Weight or pin the draft on to it. Use a spike to point through the cardinal points of the size required.

Stage 2   (Figure 68)

Remove the draft and then connect up the points, using the original pattern as a template.

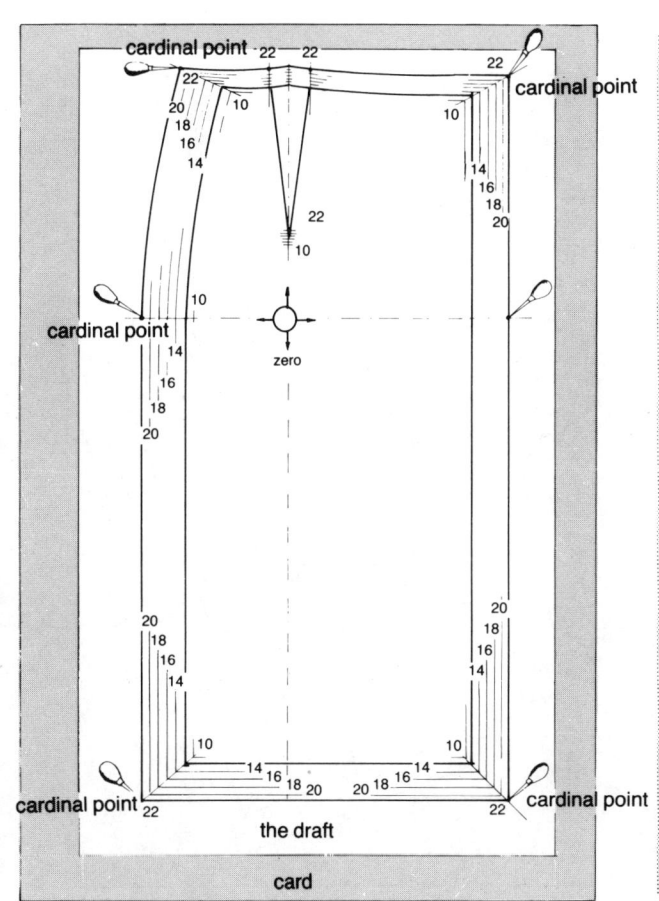

Figure 67 Stage 1 – lay card under draft and spike through cardinal points of required size

Figure 68 Stage 2 – remove the draft and connect cardinal points for outline

TECHNIQUE 2 Spiking-off
Manipulating the draft to transfer the darts.
The following technique enables the pattern technician to manipulate darts around the pattern.

Stage 1 (Figure 69)
1. Lay the draft on to a sheet of card.
2. Decide where to transfer the bust dart – in this example it will be pivoted into the waist dart.
3. Extend both sides of the dart line upwards so that they are marked on to the card – lines A–F and G–H.
4. Spike through the static points of the draft – in this example they will be points A–B–C–D–E.
5. Letter all the cardinal points as Figure 69.

Stage 2 (Figure 70)
6. Using E as a pivot, move the draft so that line G–H lies on top of line A–F, thereby closing the bust dart.
7. Spike through the points I–J–K–L–M.

Stage 3 (Figure 71)
8. Remove the draft and connect up all the cardinal points to form the size 22.

TECHNIQUE 3 Truing a style line
A feature of this drafting system is that the bust dart is returned to its original position and then graded so that it complies with size and figuration requirements. In practice this means that frequently a seamline, such as the front yoke, will have to be planned and graded **across an open dart**. The following technique should be used to deal with this situation.

Pattern drafting prior to grading
1. Figure 72 illustrates a pattern draft with the bust suppression sited at the neck point. Seamline B–C has to cross the open dart. To transfer point C across to C1 use a pivot paper (Figure 73).
2. Lay the straight edge of a sheet of transparent paper on to line B–C. Mark point C on to the paper edge (Figure 73).

Figure 69 Stage 1 – spike through static points

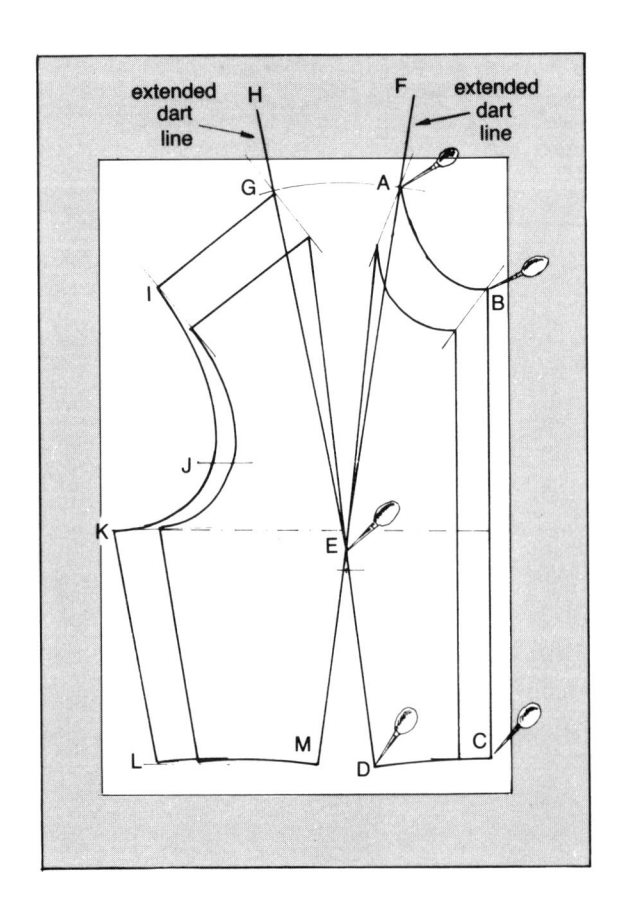

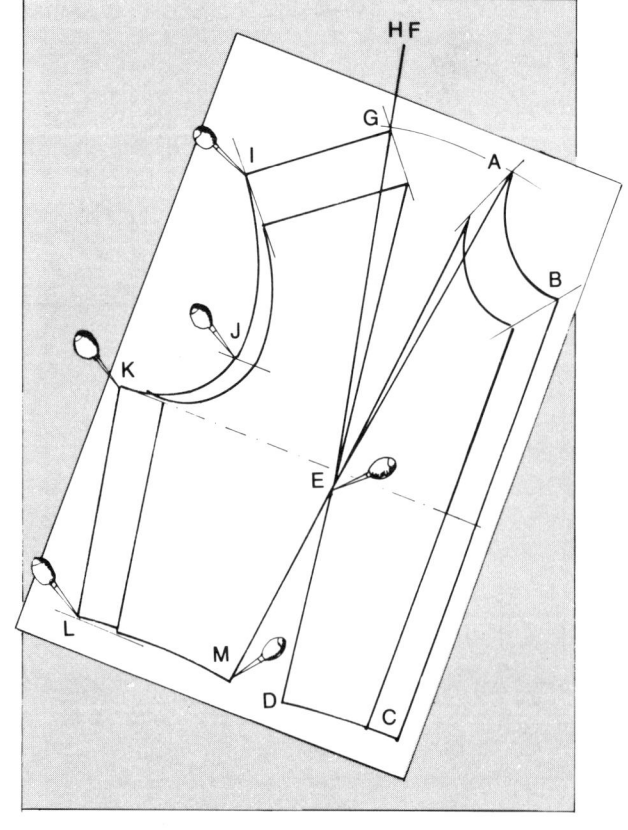

Figure 70 Stage 2 – pivot draft and spike through cardinal points

FROM DRAFT TO FINISHED SIZES

3. Using point A as a pivot, swing point C over until it touches the other side of the dart (Figure 74).
4. Draw line C1–D (Figure 74).

The same technique may be used for shaped yokes and darts etc.

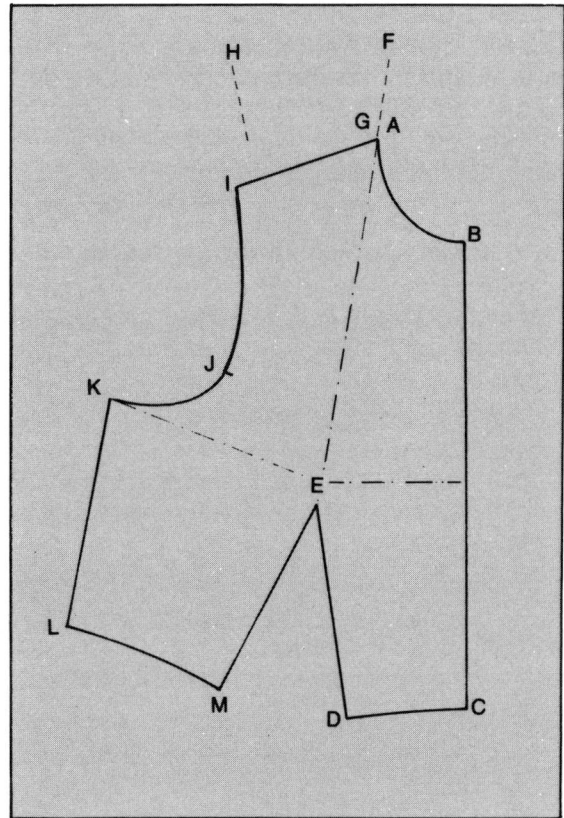

Figure 71 Stage 3 – remove draft and connect cardinal points

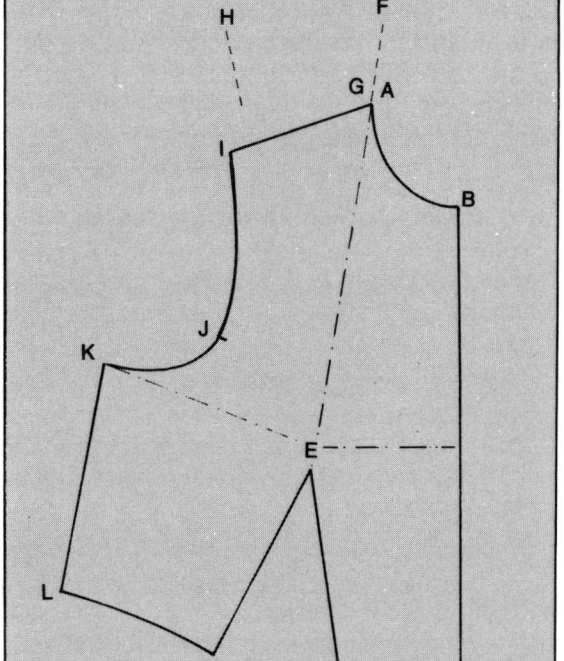

Figure 72 Planning yoke line (B–C)

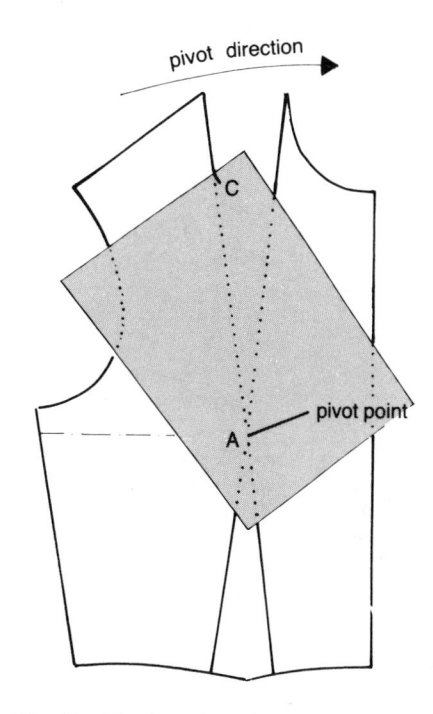

Figure 73 Positioning the pivot paper

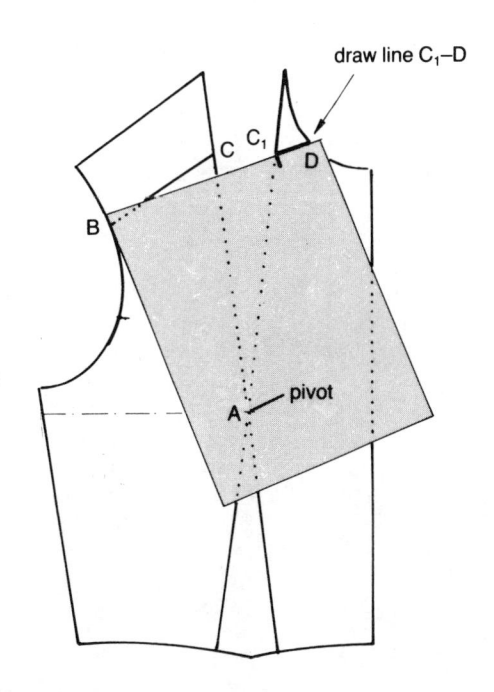

Figure 74 Draw line extension C_1–D

TRUING A GRADED STYLE LINE

In Figure 75 the line A–B–C has been planned on to the draft and transferred across the open dart by the method described in Figures 72, 73 and 74. When grading, use the following technique to establish the style runs for the largest sizes.

1. Plan line E–F.
2. Use a pivot paper to transfer F across the dart to point F1.
3. Connect up points A–E, B–F, B1–F1, C–G, with a diagonal connecting line for the intermediate sizes.

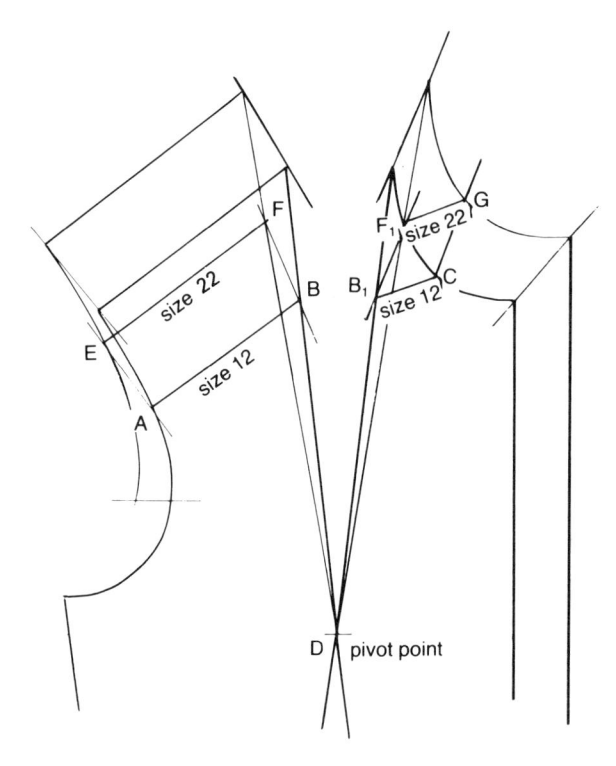

Figure 75 Using the pivot paper technique for grading

CHAPTER 13

Multi-track grading

Draft grading is the optimum system for producing accurately-sized patterns because it allows the pattern technician to plan the stock size draft and the subsequent grades as a whole, and thus provides a perfect overview of the complete size range. Ideally, this system relies on the pattern technician controlling the whole pattern cutting and grading operation. However, other situations exist and are, therefore, essential to master.

GRADING FROM A PRODUCTION PATTERN USING A DRAFT SYSTEM

The pattern technician may receive a production

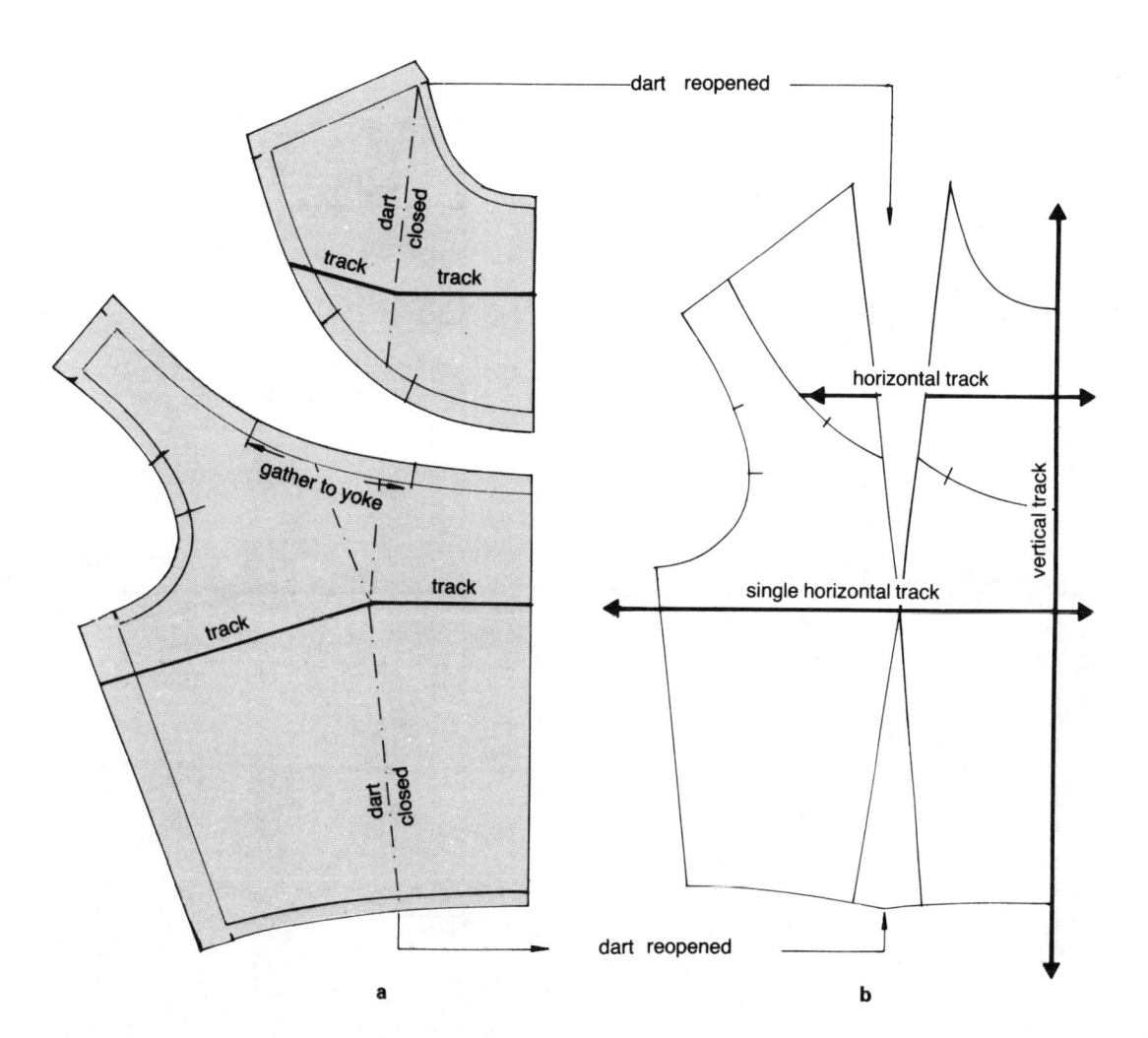

Figure 76 Draft system using basic construction lines
    (a) Multi-tracks based on centre front lines
    (b) Single tracks based on centre front lines

pattern from another technician. There are two basic ways of preparing it for a draft grade system, depending on whether a single track or multi-track system is used. This is an important factor because, as previously stated, the only method of retaining the pattern balance through a wide size range is by grading along the original construction line whether it is straight as in Figures 76b and 77a or split into multi-tracks as in Figures 76a and 77b. (see also *grading techniques* on page 58.)

SINGLE TRACK – MOVING BUST POINT
This involves returning the production pattern to its original draft form using the original suppression sites. This system is used for fitted garments where the adjusting of the bust height is important.

MULTI-TRACK – STATIC BUST POINT
This involves returning the production pattern to a draft form, but leaving the suppressions in their styled positions. This system is used for less fitted styles where the suppression is either gathers or pleats.

CONVERTING THE TRACKS OF A PRODUCTION PATTERN FROM MULTI- TO TWO SINGLE TRACKS FOR USE IN A MOVING BUST POINT SYSTEM
Figures 76a and 77b show the production pattern of a front and back bodice with yokes and gathers. The thick lines illustrate the pattern's multi-tracks which are the result of the closing of the block suppressions. These must be related to the tracks illustrated in Figures 76b and 77a. These multi-

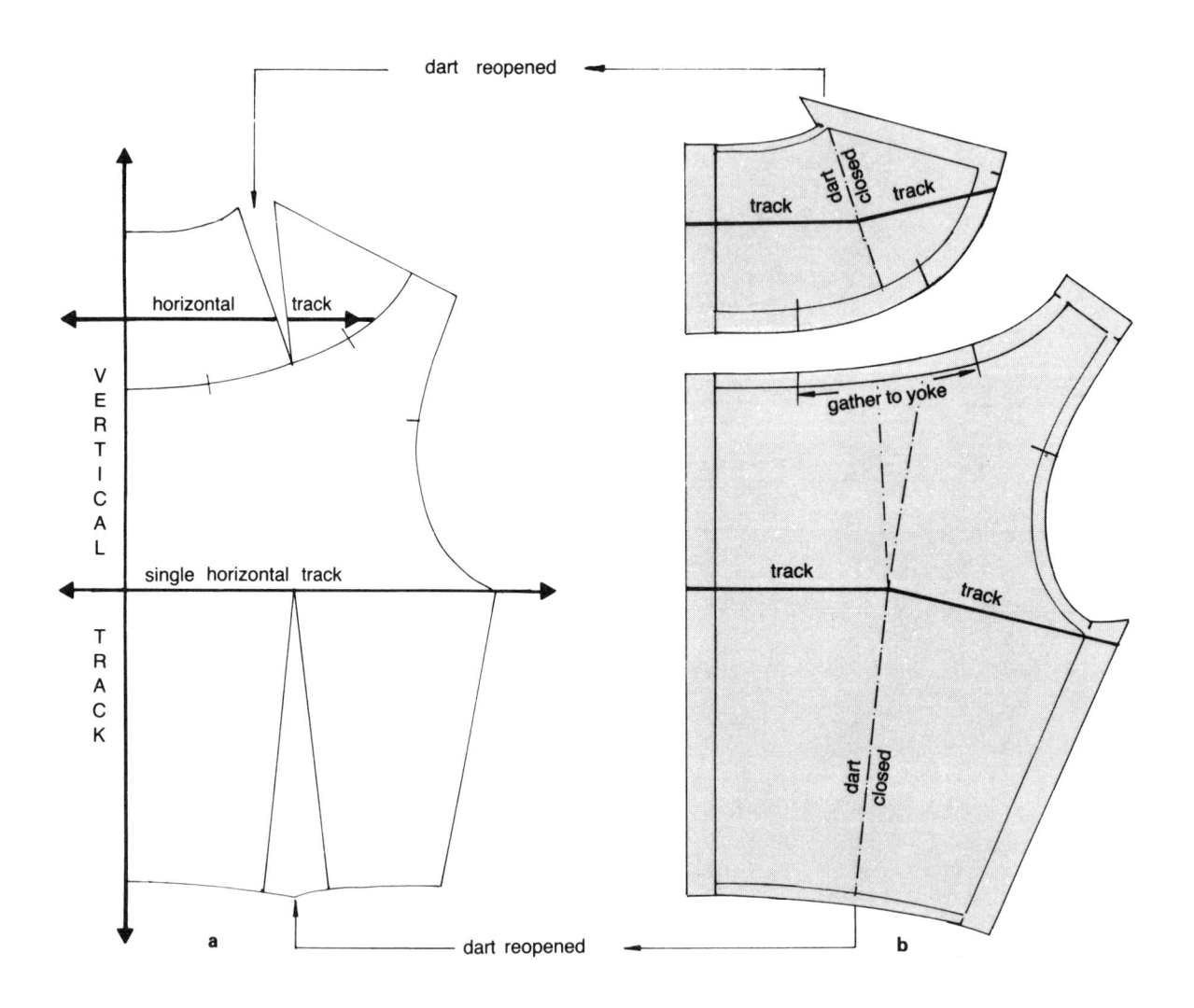

Figure 77 Draft system using basic construction lines
    (a) Single tracks based on centre back lines
    (b) Multi-tracks based on centre back lines

MULTI-TRACK GRADING

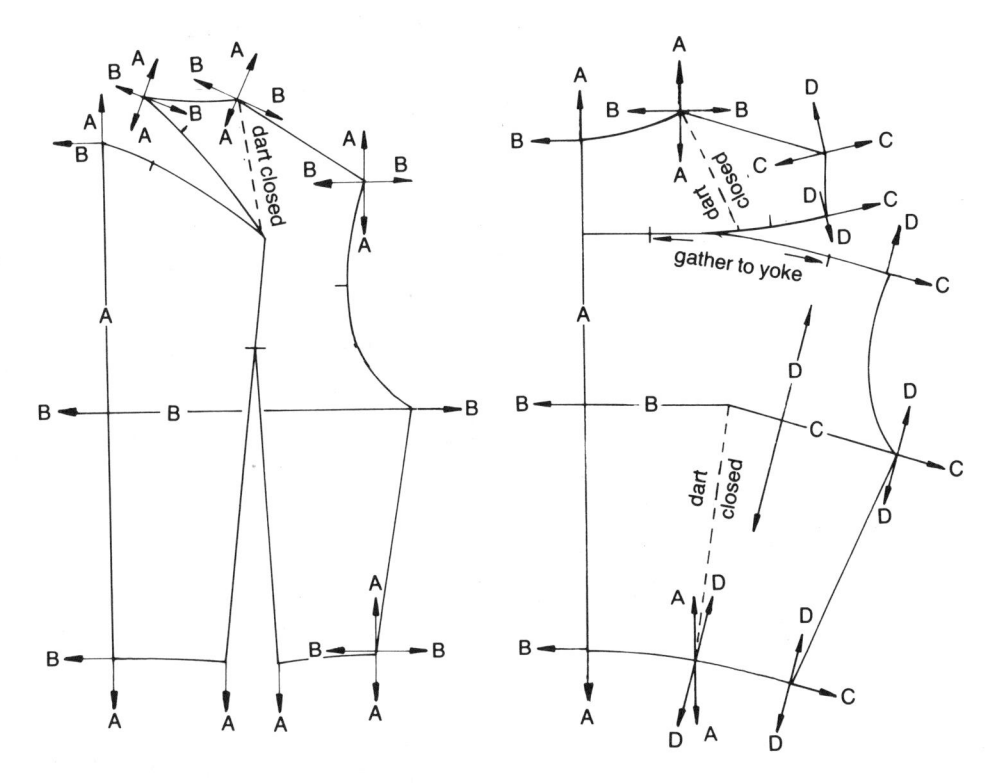

Figure 78 Grade directions – multi-tracks

tracks can be converted to a single track draft by relaying the pattern sections together as in Figures 76a and 77b, and then returning all suppressions to their basic block positions. **This emphasizes the importance of marking construction lines on to the production pattern as they provide a guide to original darts and tracks.** After returning the suppressions to their original sites *the pattern draft can now be graded using a single track bust point system*. It should be noted that the single track system is so called because it is based on the CB and CF lines and all directions are related to these lines.

STATIC BUST POINT GRADING SYSTEM USING MULTI-TRACKS

In this system of dealing with a production pattern the patterns must be laid back together on to a draft, the seamlines must overlap and the finished seamlines must be marked. Suppressions are left in their finished manipulated positions. Each cardinal point is graded according to its original construction line. See Figures 78, 79, 80 and 81, which illustrate that **'the change in direction of the basic construction lines after manipulating darts from their original position.'** This applies to all sections of the block pattern.

Note that the multi-tracks are also suitable for use in a track grading system (see Chapter 6), but this is more difficult to accomplish.

GRADING BUST SUPPRESSION

Figure 81a illustrates a pattern where the bust suppression has been transferred into the waist suppression. To grade this accurately using a 'static bust point', the following technique has been devised and is based on:

1 The change in basic construction line, i.e., multi-tracks.
2 Using the original bust suppression position to increase and decrease the styled darts.

Figure 81b, c, d, e, f and g shows the sequence to be followed.

GRADING THE FRONT BODICE USING A STATIC BUST POINT DRAFT

Figure 81a establishes the construction lines and the grade directions.

Referring to Figure 81b, select a zero point and calculate increments for the required number of sizes; in this case five.

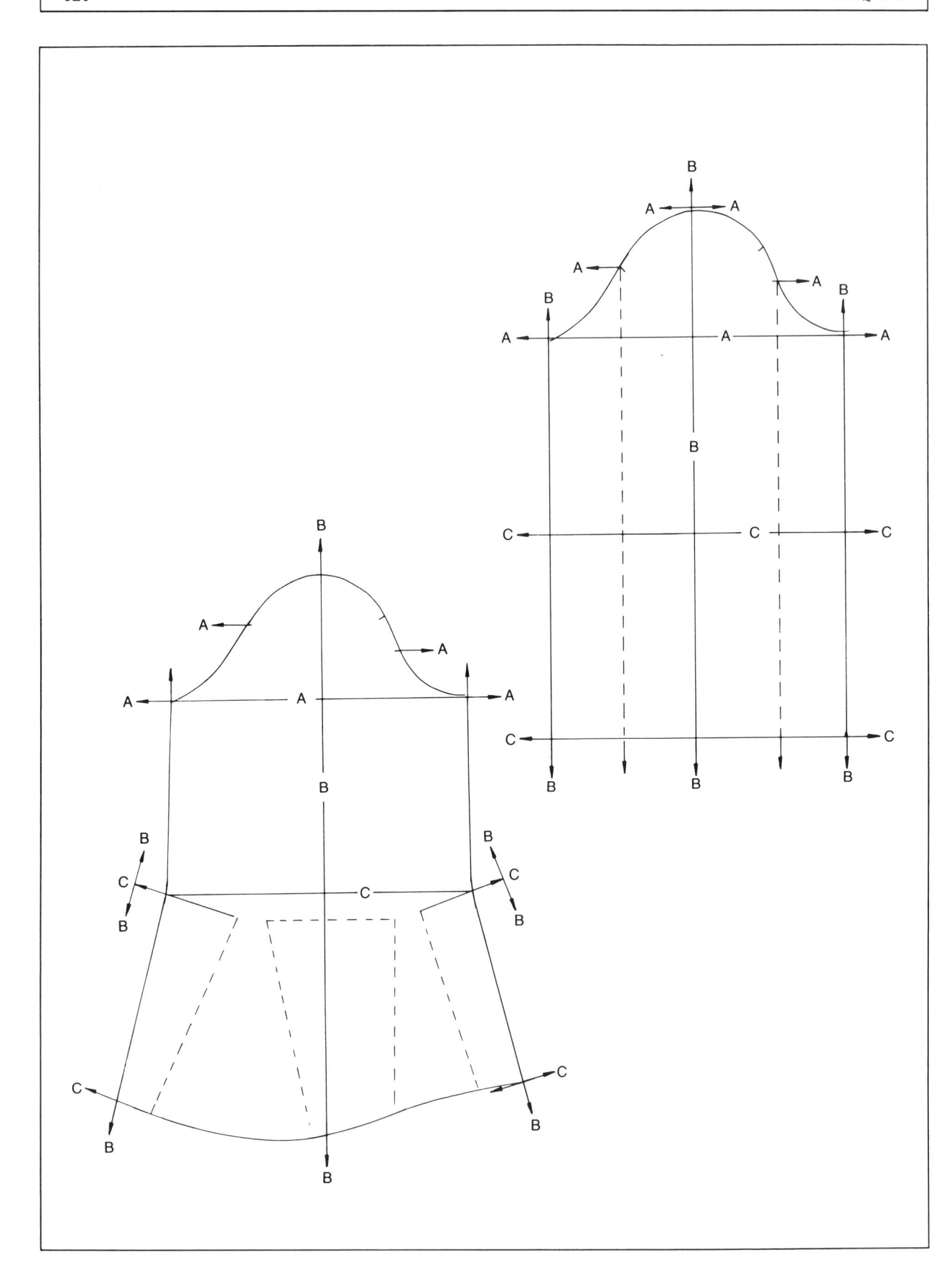

Figure 79 Straight sleeve to shirt sleeve grade directions

MULTI-TRACK GRADING 121

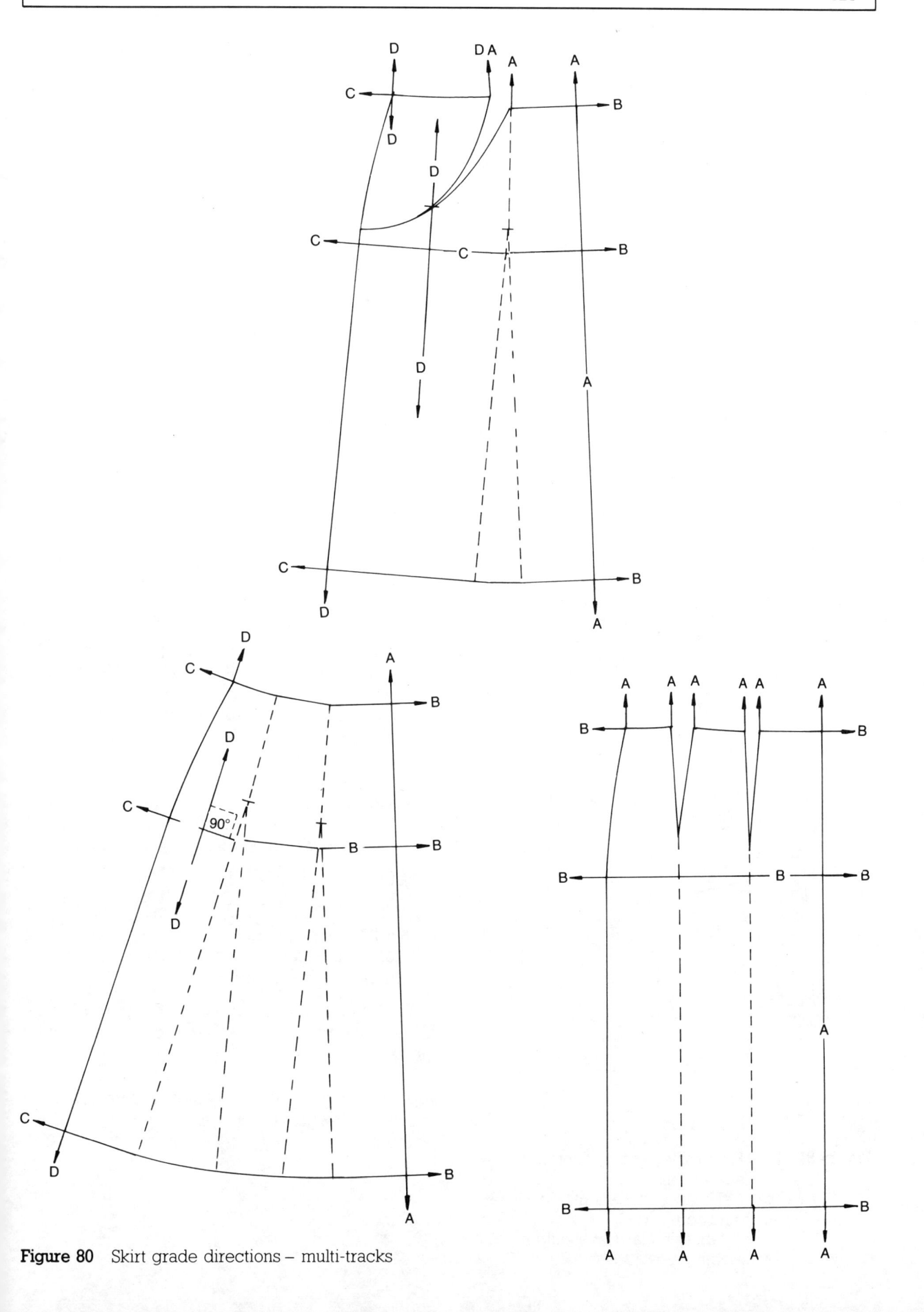

Figure 80 Skirt grade directions – multi-tracks

Referring to Figure 81c:

1. Grade from point A clockwise around to B. Line A–C is the original dart position in which extra suppression will be graded. Mark points D and E.
2. Swing arc F from bust point through point E.
3. Calculate the graded shoulder length, i.e. size 12 shoulder length plus shoulder grade. For example 12.5 + (5 × 2 mm) = 13.5 mm.
4. Swing arc G from D with a radius of 13.5 cm to disect arc F. The point where they cross is the new largest front shoulder neck point G.

Referring to Figure 81d:

1. Connect G and E to bust point for the largest suppression quantity.
2. Connect G and E to the original neck point A.
3. Connect G to C and E to C.

Divide up lines E–A and G–A in Figure 81e into five equal parts to obtain the suppression quantity for each size.

Trace off each size and pivot the extra bust suppression to its styled position. Figure 81f and g shows two examples of this.

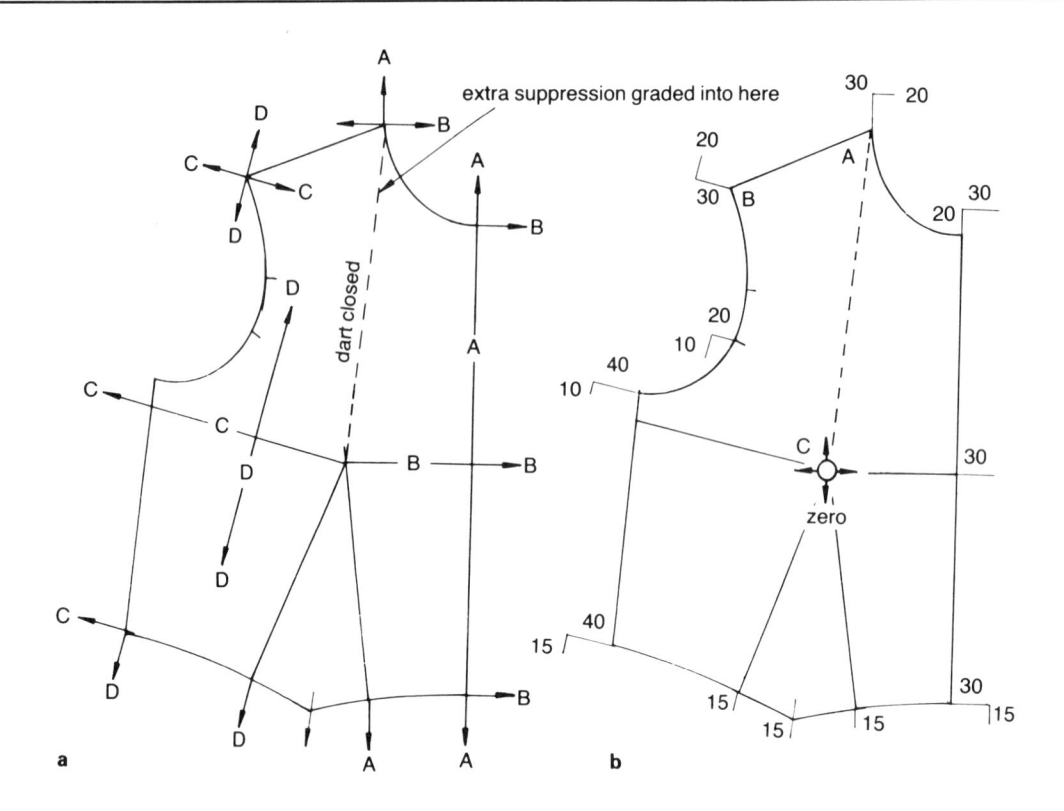

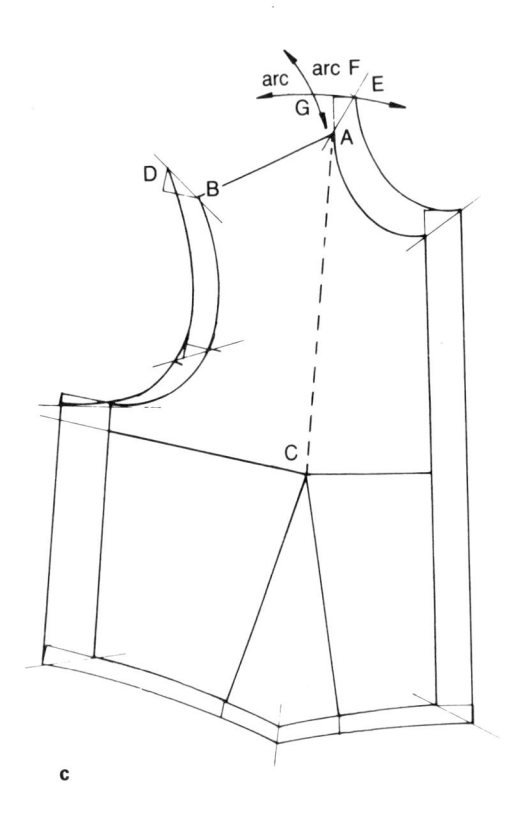

Figure 81 (a) Establishing construction lines and grade directions
(b) Calculating increments – for five sizes and zero
(c) Establishing largest shoulder point by swinging arc

MULTI-TRACK GRADING 123

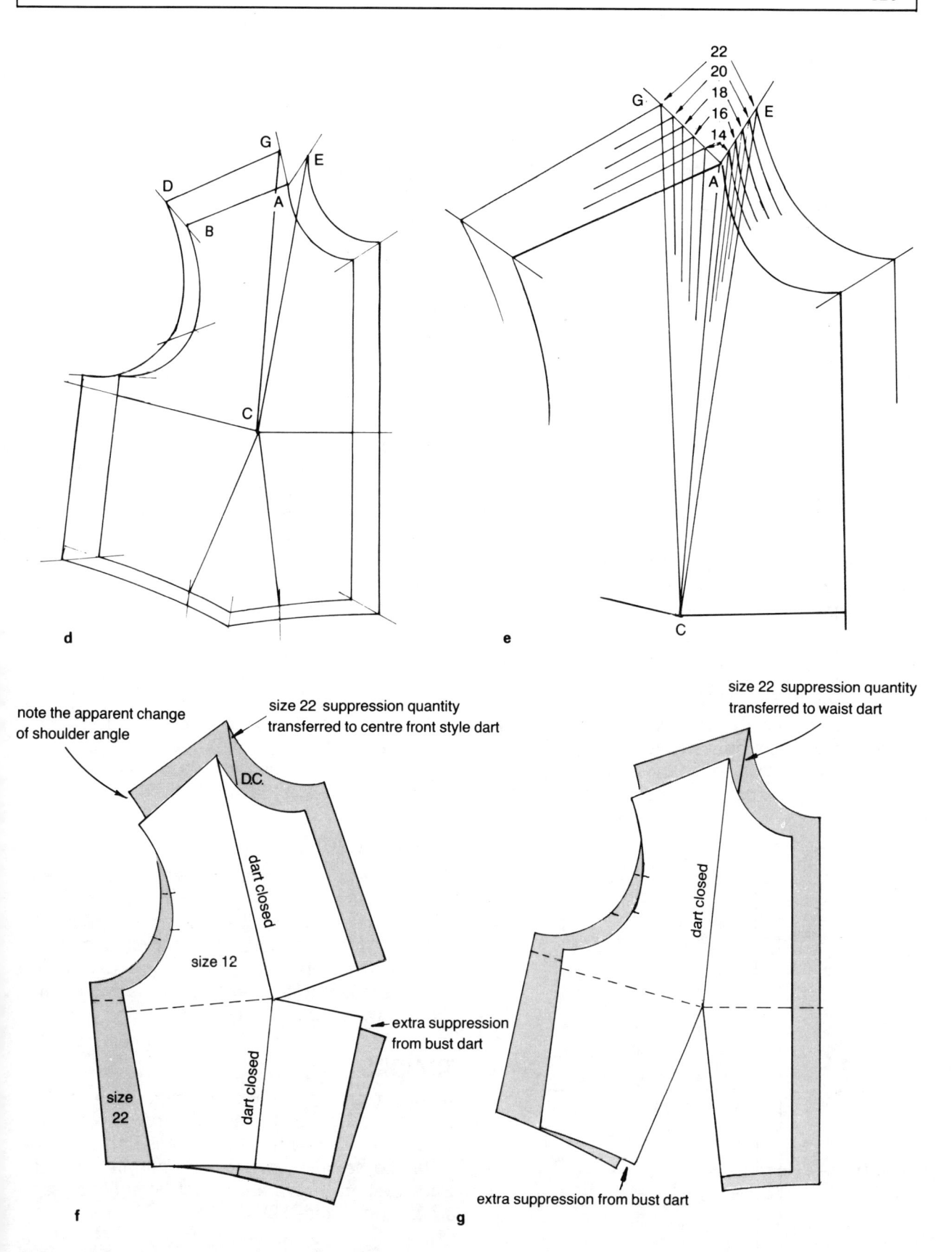

Figure 81 (d) Connecting lines to bust point
(e) Dividing up diagonal connecting lines to establish bust suppression per size
(f) Graded suppression returned to style positions
(g) Graded suppression returned to style positions

CHAPTER 14

Track grading – a simplified two-dimensional system

Track grading is accomplished by moving each individual pattern piece around a predetermined track increasing or decreasing it *one size at a time*. The track grading system described in this chapter is suitable for producing a limited size range of patterns, usually 10–12–14. For ease of application, increments are simplified to enable a grader without much detailed knowledge of pattern cutting to apply them. As with all simplifications, a certain loss of fit and suppression results. However, due to the limited size range, these imperfections are not always apparent. The following notes have been produced to explain the reasons why the split diagram (Figure 7, pages 36–7) have been developed, and will highlight the areas where the simplifications have been made.

It is important to note that *girth and height increments* are introduced *evenly throughout the pattern* and are *controlled by the overall pattern increases*, i.e., *5.0 cm girth and 2.4 cm height*. For ease of application, the *bust suppression quantity* is not adjusted; the *bust points* remain on the *static girth track*. In this simplified system, the side seam length is increased or decreased according to the bust to waist increment. This enables the grader to obtain the overall front measurement easily. *The deepening of the scye has been ignored* but it is quite easy to deepen the scye by adjusting the side seam length which could remain constant for all sizes. The neck width, back and front, has been graded slightly more than necessary. This is a simple way of preventing the shoulder lengthening too much and necks are rarely used exactly as the block pattern. Also the scye width, back and front, has been slightly overgraded. This is a simple way of obtaining the correct bust girth. The sleeve, front and back scye width grade, does not totally correspond with the armhole grade. This means that the sleeve pitch alters and becomes slightly unbalanced.

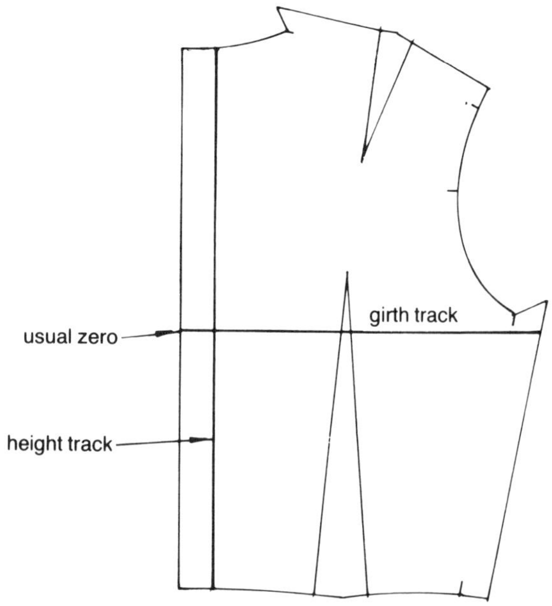

THE METHOD

Track grading is in many respects a difficult system to master, because, although the increments and sizing data is simplified for ease of application to each pattern section, the actual shifting of patterns around predetermined tracks has to be extremely accurate, particularly as increments are always stated in millimetres.

TRACKS

In order that each pattern section is graded accurately, tracks are used to serve as a grading guide. Tracks are used to increase or decrease girth and height measurements and in the single track system shown here *must be at 90° to each other* (see Figure 82).

INCREMENTS

Increments are marked on to each track and are calculated from the selected zero which is usually

Figure 82 Girth and height tracks

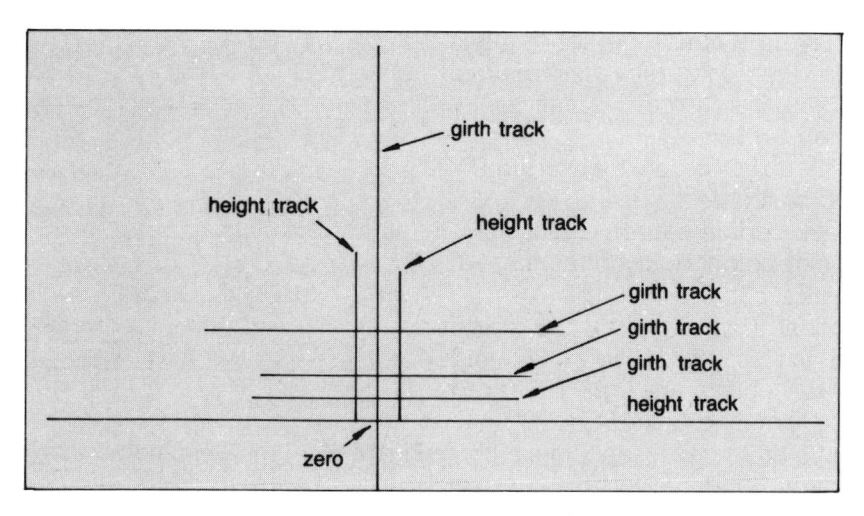

TRACK GRADING – A SIMPLIFIED TWO-DIMENSIONAL SYSTEM

Figure 83 Illustrating basic tracks marked on to card (not to scale)

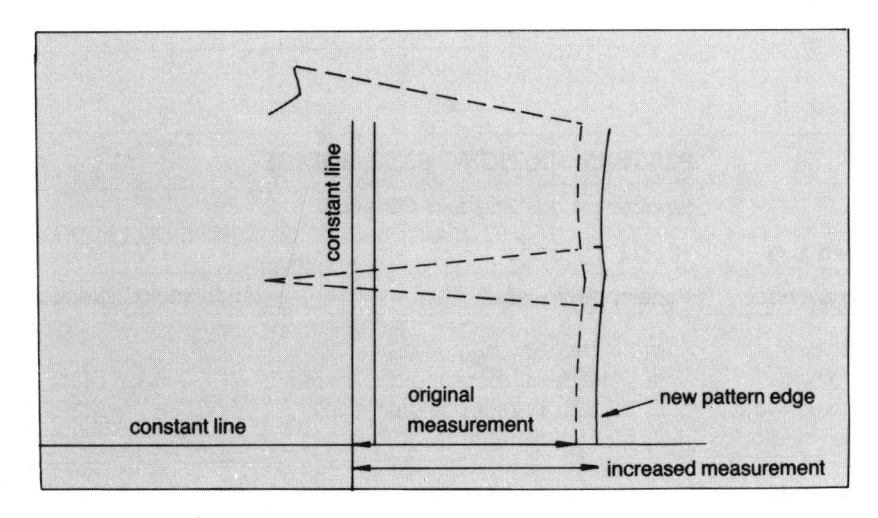

Figure 84 Pattern has shifted down. The increased length is still calculated from the constant line

at the CF or CB junction of bust line or hip line. Zero points, however, can be varied depending on style. **A symbol for the zero is not used in these diagrams and unless otherwise stated will be the junction of the two tracks** (see Figure 82). Increments are marked on to the card that is being used for the subsequent size, and are normally paralleled (see Figure 83).

CONSTANT LINES

Tracks are also 'constant lines'. Therefore, if the pattern moves vertically or horizontally from the original track, the track still remains on the new pattern, and alters the subsequent measurement (see Figure 84).

Each pattern section has been lettered to simplify grading instructions.

PREPARATION

1 Check production patterns for accuracy, etc.
2 Prepare card (Figure 85).

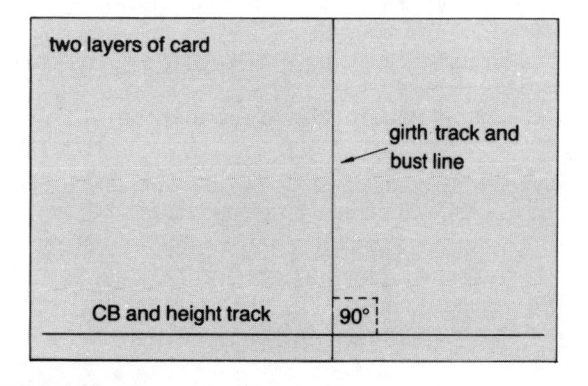

Figure 85 Preparing the card

a Staple two layers of card together. If CB is on the fold then fold the card before grading. Check that the card is sufficiently large for the new size.
b Mark height and girth tracks ensuring 90° angle at CB bust line.
3 Prepare the back bodice pattern (Figure 86).
a Mark girth and height tracks checking 90° angle at centre back.
b For the student it might help if the grade areas from the diagram (Figure 86) and lettered grade points, are lightly marked on to the pattern (see dotted lines).
4 Mark increments on to card (see Figure 87).
5 Commence grading (Figure 88).

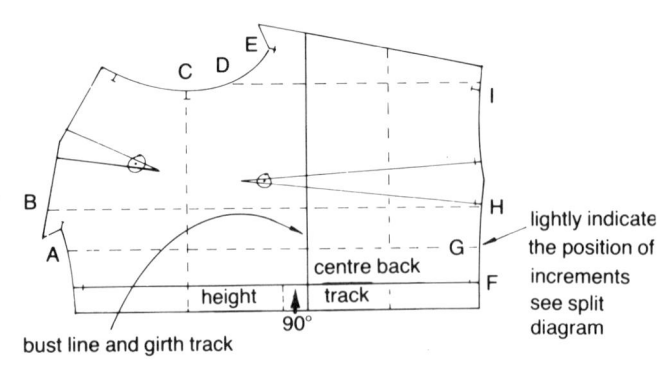

Figure 86 Preparing the pattern

BACK BODICE GRADE

Table 15

		PATTERN SECTION – BACK BODICE		
	Zero	Junction of bustline and CB seam		
	Required size	12→14 up grade		
Sequence	Pattern section	Pattern movement	Increment	Section to mark
	To increase:	*Position pattern on to tracks*		
1	Nape to scye	Shift pattern up along height track	0.3	Mark A–B
2	Back neck width	Shift pattern parallel to girth track	0.3	Mark B–C
3	Shoulder width	Shift pattern parallel to girth track	0.3	Mark C–D including dart and armhole pitch
4	Back scye depth	Shift pattern down to girth track	0.3	Mark D–E
5	Back scye width	Shift pattern out along girth track	0.6	Mark E–F
		Return to zero		
6	Scye to waist	Shift pattern down along height track	0.3	Mark G–H
7	CB to mid dart	Shift pattern parallel to girth track	0.3	Mark H–I
8	Mid dart to side mid waist	Shift pattern parallel to girth track	0.3	Mark I–J including dart
9	Back scye width	Shift pattern parallel to girth track	0.6	Mark J–K–F
		Return to zero		
10	Waist dart	Shift pattern out along girth track	0.6	Mark dart end
		Use pattern to blend all disconnected lines, i.e., armhole, waist, shoulder, etc.		
	Cut out pattern, check and mark-up			

General note: To grade down one size, i.e., from 12 to 10, reverse all the above instructions. For example, mark increments on to card as Figure 87 but in the reverse order.

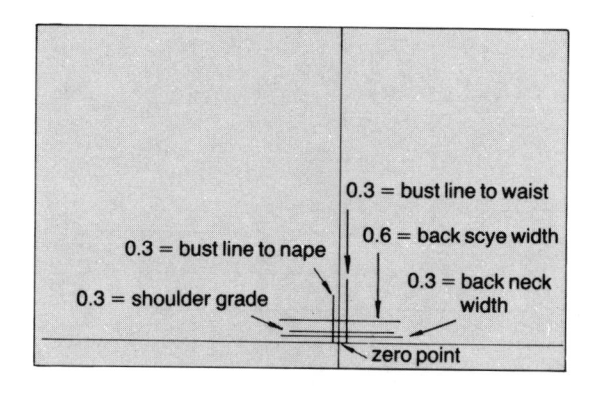

TRACK GRADING – A SIMPLIFIED TWO-DIMENSIONAL SYSTEM 127

Figure 87 Marking girth and height increments for grading up

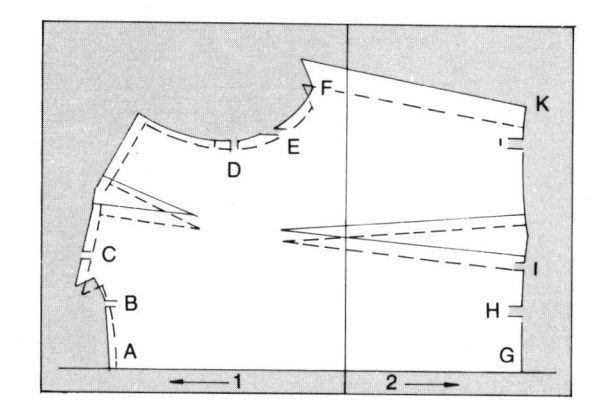

Figure 88 Commence grading up (see Table 15)

FRONT BODICE GRADE

Prepare card and pattern as shown in Figures 89, 90 and 91. Commence grading as illustrated in Figure 92, using the sequence in Table 16.

Table 16

		PATTERN SECTION – FRONT BODICE		
	Zero	Junction of bustline and CF		
	Required size	12→14 up grade		
Sequence	Pattern section	Pattern movement	Increment	Section to mark
	To increase:	*Position pattern on to tracks*		
1	Pit of neck to bust line	Shift pattern along height track	0.3	Mark A–B
2	Front neck width	Shift pattern out parallel to girth track	0.3	Mark B–C
3	Front balance	Shift pattern parallel to height track	0.3	Mark C–D–E
4		Shift pattern down parallel to height track	0.3	—
5	Front shoulder	Shift pattern out parallel to girth track	0.3	Mark E–F including dart
6	Front scye depth	Return pattern to girth track	0.3	Mark F–G Mark sleeve pitch
7	Front scye width	Shift pattern out along girth track	0.6	Mark G–H
		Return to zero		
8	Bust line to waist	Shift pattern down height track	0.3	Mark I–J
9	CF to mid dart	Shift pattern out parallel to girth track	0.3	Mark J–K
10	Mid dart to side mid waist	Shift pattern out parallel to girth track	0.3	Mark K–L including dart
11	Front scye width	Shift pattern out parallel to girth track until M meets side seam	0.6	Mark L–M–H
		Return to zero		
12	Dart ends	Shift pattern along girth track	0.6	Mark bust point and dart ends
		Use size 12 pattern to blend all unconnected lines, i.e. armhole, shoulder, waist, etc.		
	Cut out pattern, check and mark-up			

Note: To grade down one size, reverse all the above instructions.

128 GENERAL GRADING TECHNIQUES

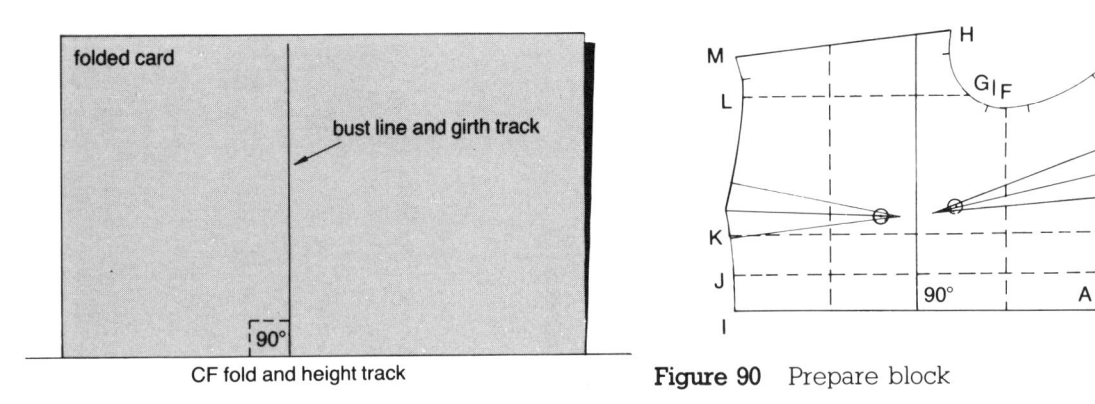

Figure 89 Folding and stapling card

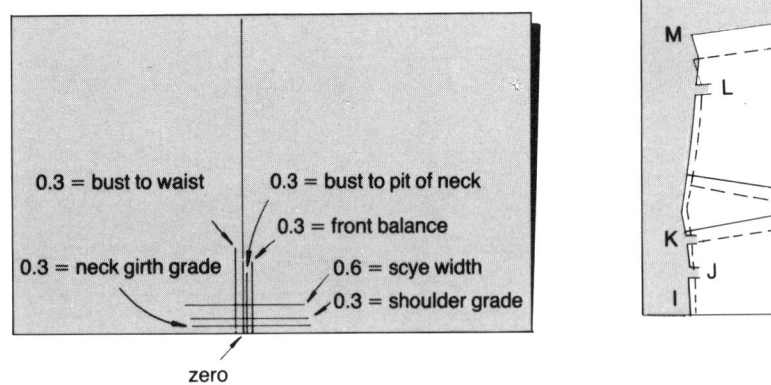

Figure 90 Prepare block

Figure 91 Marking girth and height increments

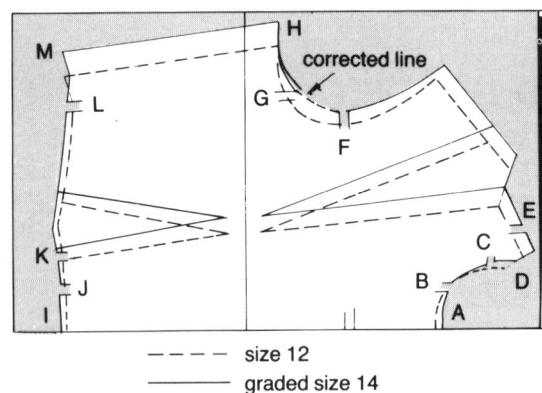

Figure 92 Commence grading up (see Table 16)

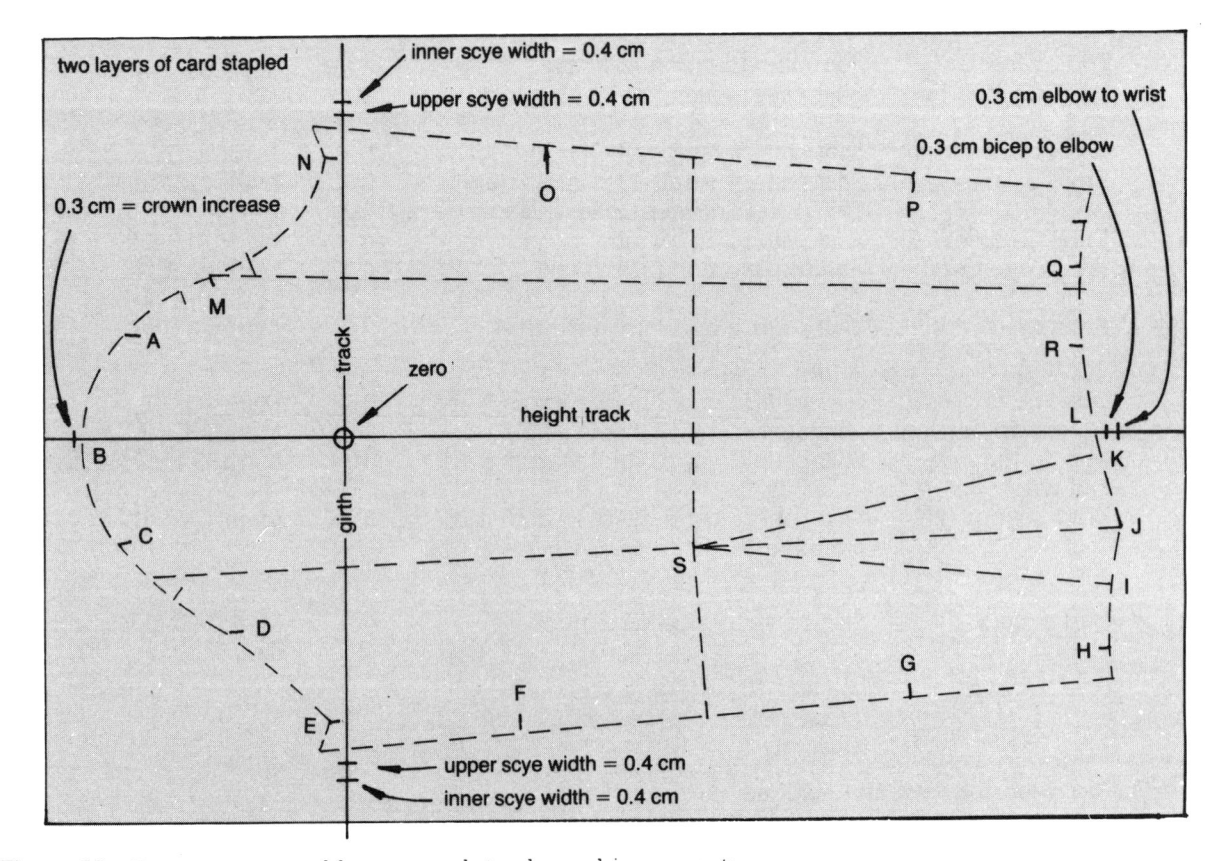

- - - - size 12
———— graded size 14

Figure 93 Prepare two card layers, mark tracks and increments

FITTED SLEEVE GRADE

PREPARATION (Figure 93)

1 Mark tracks on to two stapled layers of card as shown in Figure 93.
2 Mark height and girth tracks and increments.
3 Prepare sleeve by marking tracks:
   a *Centre* sleeve line for height track.
   b Upper arm girth line for girth track.
4 Commence grading as shown in Figure 94, using the sequence in Table 17.

Table 17

		PATTERN SECTION – SLEEVE		
	Zero	Junction of centre sleeve line and upper arm girth		
	Required size	12→14 up grade		
Sequence	Pattern section	Pattern movement	Increment	Section to mark
	To increase:	*Position pattern on to tracks*		
1	Crown height	Shift pattern up height track	0.3	A–C
2		*Return to zero*		
3	Back upper scye width	Shift pattern along girth track	0.4	C–D including balance mark
4	Back inner scye width	Shift pattern along girth track	0.4	D–E–F
5	Bicep to elbow	Shift pattern along, parallel to the height track	0.3	E–F–G and elbow notch
6	Elbow to wrist	Shift pattern along, parallel to the height track	0.3	G–H–I so that H–I remains constant
7	Wrist dart	Shift pattern in, parallel to the girth track	0.4	J, centre dart
8	Wrist dart	Shift pattern in, parallel to the girth track	0.4	K–L and dart end
9		*Return to zero*		
10	Front upper scye width	Shift pattern along girth track	0.4	A–M including sleeve notch
11	Front inner scye width	Shift pattern along girth track	0.4	M–N–O and sleeve notch
12	Bicep to elbow	Shift pattern parallel to height track	0.3	O–P including elbow line
13	Elbow to wrist	Shift pattern parallel to the height track	0.3	P–Q
14	Front inner scye width	Shift pattern in, parallel to girth track	0.4	Q–R
15	Front upper scye width	Shift pattern in, parallel to girth track	0.4	R–I
16	Elbow dart end	Point S moves down height track and along girth track	0.3	Connect R to dart ends
		Blend all unconnected lines		
	Cut out pattern, check and mark-up			

Note: To grade down one size, reverse all the above instructions.

130   GENERAL GRADING TECHNIQUES

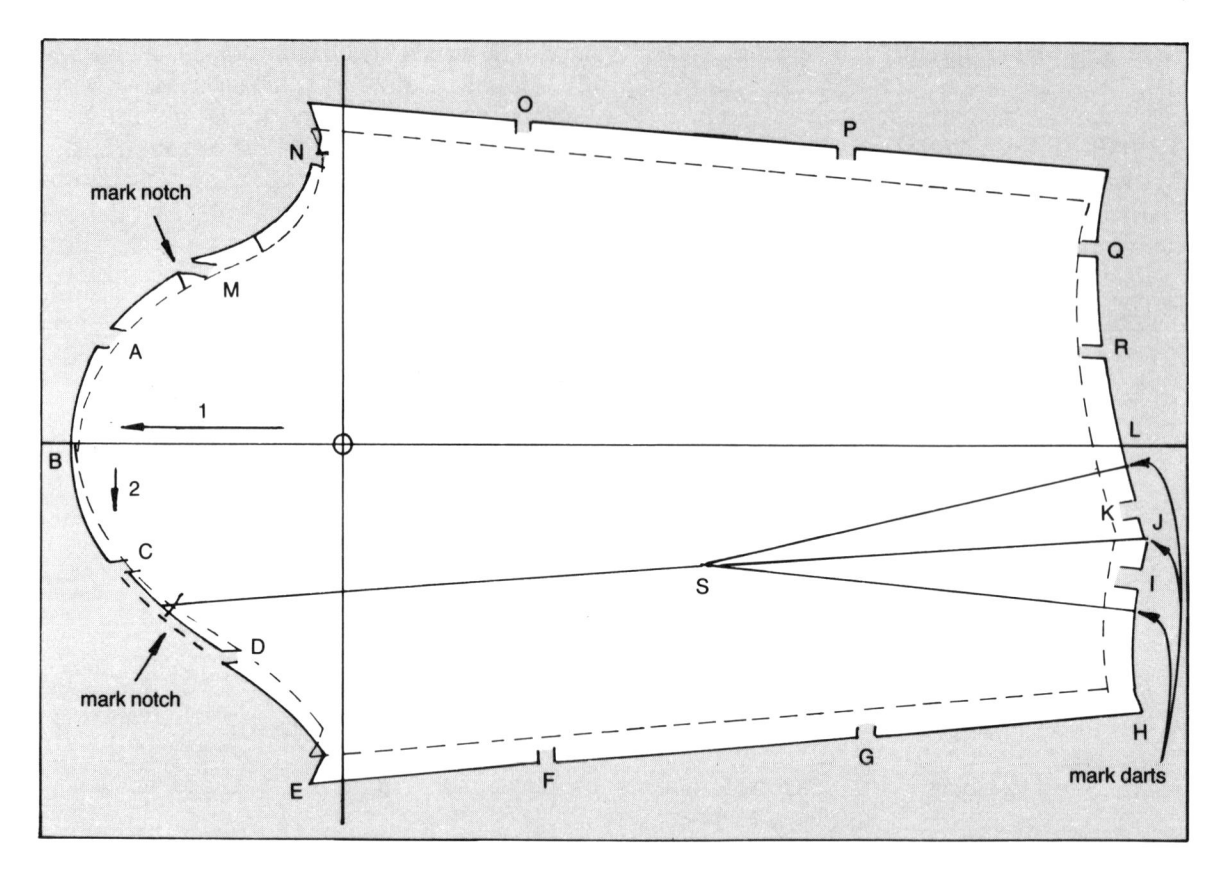

Figure 94   Graded sleeve

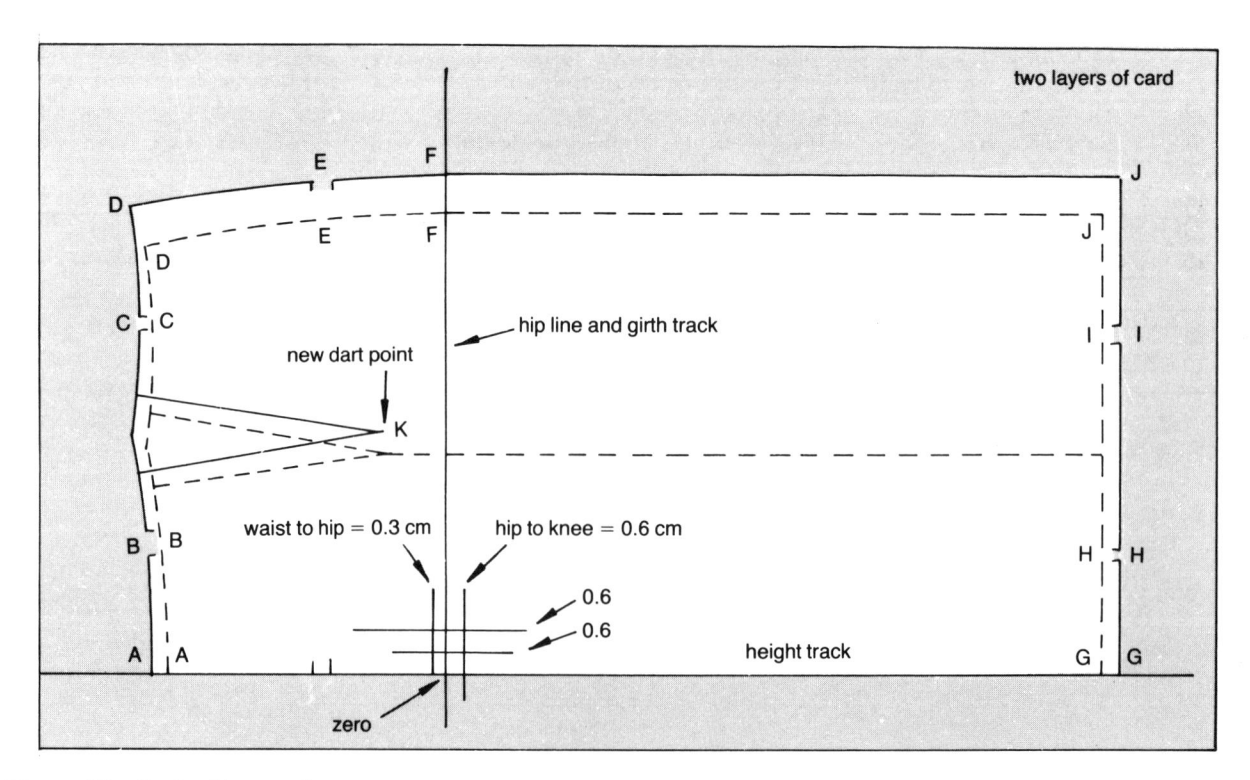

Figure 95   Back skirt grade

TRACK GRADING – A SIMPLIFIED TWO-DIMENSIONAL SYSTEM

BACK SKIRT GRADE

Prepare card and pattern, and commence grading as shown in Figure 95, using the sequence in Table 18.

FRONT SKIRT GRADE

Prepare card and pattern, and commence grading as shown in Figure 96, using the sequence in Table 19.

Table 18

		PATTERN SECTION – BACK SKIRT		
	Zero	Junction of hipline and CB seam		
	Required size	12→14 up grade		
Sequence	Pattern section	Pattern movement	Increment	Section to mark
	To increase	*Position pattern on to tracks*		
1	Hip to waist	Shift pattern up along height track	0.3	A–B
2	CB to dart	Shift pattern along parallel to girth track	0.6	B–C including dart site
3	Dart to side seam	Shift pattern along parallel to girth track	0.6	C–D–E
4	Hip to waist	Shift pattern down parallel to CB height track	0.3	E–F
		Return to zero		
5	Hip to knee	Shift pattern down height track	0.6	G–H
6	CB to dart	Shift pattern in, parallel to girth track	0.6	H–I
7	Dart to side seam	Shift pattern in, parallel to girth track	0.6	I–J–F
8	Dart end	Place pattern on to zero Shift out 0.6 Connect dart Blend lines	0.6	K
		Cut out pattern, check and mark-up		

Note: To grade down one size, reverse all the above instructions.

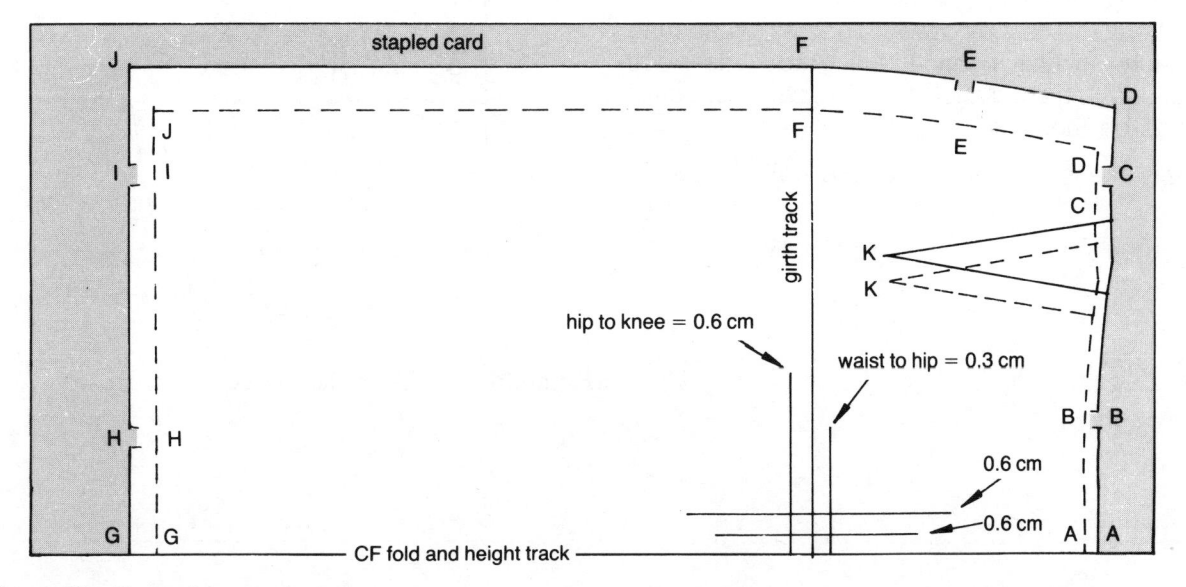

Figure 96 Front skirt grade

Table 19

		PATTERN SECTION – FRONT SKIRT		
	Zero	Junction of CF fold and girth track		
	Required size	12→14 up grade		
Sequence	Pattern section	Pattern movement	Increment	Section to mark
	To increase:	*Position pattern on to tracks*		
1	Hip to waist	Shift pattern up along height track	0.3	A–B
2	CF to dart	Shift pattern parallel to girth track	0.6	B–C including dart site
3	Dart to side seam	Shift pattern parallel to girth track	0.6	C–D–E
4	Hip to waist	Shift pattern down, parallel to height track	0.6	E–F
		Return to zero		
5	Hip to knee	Shift pattern down along height track	0.6	G–H
6	CF to dart	Shift pattern parallel to girth track	0.6	H–I
7	Dart to side seam	Shift pattern parallel to girth track	0.6	I–J
	Side seam	Connect side seam		J–F
8	Dart end	Place pattern on to zero		
		Shift out 0.6 on girth track		K
		Connect dart		
		Blend unconnected lines		
	Cut out pattern, check and mark-up.			

Note: To grade down one size, reverse all the above instructions.

CHECKING THE GRADES (Figure 97)

It is essential to check all the pattern sections that have been track graded. This can be accomplished quite simply.

1. Position size 14 on to the table.
2. Lay size 12 on top of it making sure that height and girth tracks are together.
3. Repeat this with the size 10.
4. Check the nest by drawing angles connecting each cardinal point. If the grade has been accurate the distance between cardinal points will be the same.

If a mistake is observed, trace the fault and rectify it.

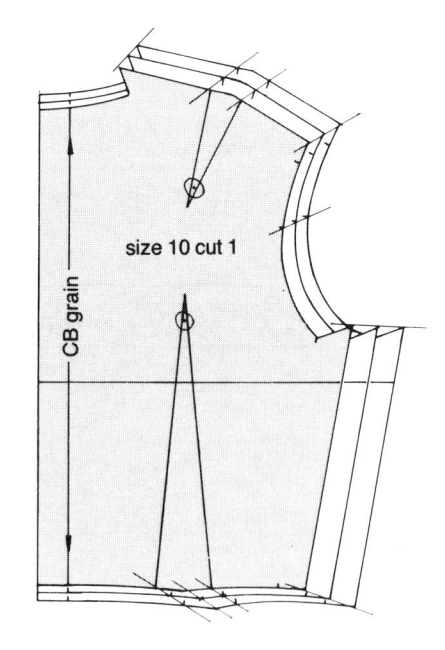

Figure 97 Checking the graded patterns

PART THREE

Women's Style Grading

CHAPTER 15

Introduction

USING THE INFORMATION IN THIS BOOK

It would be impossible for a book of this nature to include grades for every possible style permutation. The draft grades included in the style section have been selected because they **represent the major categories of garment and fully illustrate the most important grading principles for each category**. However, an intelligent approach to the use of this book will provide an almost unlimited source of information. For example, to grade French knickers, select the swimwear (Style 28) and the cami-knickers (Style 33) and combine them by:

1. Adjusting the zero points to accommodate both styles (refer to Chapter 11).
2. Recalculating the increments from the new zero point.

All the information contained in the style section will apply to all sections of the industry, whether it be tailoring or light clothing. So, for example, to grade a magyar jacket, use the techniques shown in the magyar grade (Style 21) and apply them to the appropriate silhouette which may be selected from the various silhouette examples in the book. Adjust the incremental intervals as necessary, for example, use a 6.0 cm grade instead of a 5.0 cm grade (see Chapter 2).

CAPES
The three-piece cape (Style 32) is one of the basic cape categories and has been fully illustrated. However, circular capes can be graded by studying circular skirts (Style 18). The same principles will apply. Fitted capes can be graded by studying the grown-on sleeves, especially the raglan style (Style 22) and the kimono style (Style 23).

BIFURCATED GARMENTS
Styles 28, 29, 30 and 33 and Figures 9 and 12 illustrate the increments and zero points for bifurcated garments. A whole range of grades can be developed by using the techniques illustrated in the above styles.

STYLE CHECKLIST
Style grades can be found under the following garment headings.

BIFURCATED TROUSERS CATEGORY
- Style 28 Swimsuit
- Style 29 Bikini. This is suitable for panties
- Style 30 Culottes. This is suitable for plus-fours and pyjamas
- Style 33 Cami-knickers. This is suitable for French knickers

COLLARS
- Style 1   Shawl
- Style 5   Laid-on – Peter Pan type
- Style 6   Convertible. This is suitable for all band and tie type collars
- Style 8   Sailor. This is suitable for all flat collars
- Style 9   Shirt – one-piece. This is suitable for a mandarin collar
- Style 32 Collar and rever

DRAPED STYLES
- Style 10 Cowls. This is suitable for sleeve and skirts and cowls
- Style 11 Side drape. This is suitable for skirts and sleeves
- Style 12 Centre drapes
- Style 19 Skirt with a side drape

FITTED BODICES
- Style 26 Halter neckline. This is suitable for all evening wear
- Style 27 Strapless blouse. This is suitable for evening wear
- Style 28 Swimsuit. The top section of the swimsuit is suitable for brassieres
- Style 29 Bikini. The top section of the bikini is suitable for brassieres

SILHOUETTES

Style	1	Fitted princess line
Style	2	Fitted
Style	4	Box blouse
Style	6	Shift
Style	9	Blouson
Style	12	Fitted
Style	13	Loose
Style	14	A-line
Style	16	Peg top
Style	17	Tiered
Style	18	Circles

SKIRTS

Style	1	Panelled principle. This is suitable for all princess styles
Style	6	Straight
Style	13	Pleated dirndl
Style	14	A-line
Style	15	Gores
Style	16	Peg top
Style	17	Tiered
Style	18	Circles: quarter, half, full. These will apply to sleeves, bodices and capes
Style	19	Draped
Style	20	Circle from a yoke. This will apply to a sleeve or bodice

All these skirts can be used to form part of a dress, jacket or coat.

SLEEVES

Style	1	Short sleeve. This is suitable for the bishop variety
Style	3	Short sleeve
Style	9	Short sleeve with tab on cuff
Style	21	Magyar
Style	22	Raglan. A cape grade may be formed using this style
Style	23	Kimono. This style may also be used to form a cap sleeve grade
Style	24	Batwing
Style	25	Dolman
Style	32	Two-piece. This is suitable for 50:50 sleeves

SUPPRESSION SEAMS

Style	2	Vertical – away from the bust point
Style	3	Horizontal and vertical – through the bust point
Style	5	Horizontal with gathers

This list of styles is endless. It is recommended that students and practitioners spend some time combining the various aspects of styles in order to gain proficiency in this important aspect of grading.

CHAPTER 16

Style Grades 1 to 33

GRADING – GENERAL PREPARATION

The following information is necessary before commencing a grade, and should be contained in a grading specification:

1. The correct size chart.
2. Specific instructions, i.e., 'height only' or 'girth only', etc.
3. How many sizes are required.
4. Special instructions, i.e., proportional features that need special discussion.

It is also essential to have the following before grading:

1. The correct sample garment.
2. The correct production pattern checked for accuracy and with the main block construction lines marked on each pattern section if possible.

Based on the grading specification information and the garment and pattern, the following decisions must be made:

1. Type of grade most suitable, i.e., two-dimensional, three-dimensional, etc.
2. The most suitable zero point or points.
3. Correct sectional increments.
4. Style and proportions of main features.

All the examples found in the following styles will be based on the above factors.

STYLE 1

THE GRADING OF A COMPLETE STYLE

This style has been specially selected as it contains a number of basic elements, i.e., collar, darts, seams, facings, etc., which commonly occur in style grading. The draft grade has been broken down into stages in order that the reader may follow more closely the thought processes that have gone into the pattern cutting and grading of a size range comprising seven sizes. This first style, Figure 98, has been treated in greater detail than subsequent styles.

	GRADING SPECIFICATION	
1	Size chart	Table 13
2	Size range	10·12·14·16·18·20·22
3	Height/girth/length	Height and girth
4	Proportioning	See notes
5	Type of grade	3 dim. Draft grade
6	Zero points front	Centre dart waist
7	Zero point back	Centre dart waist
8	Zero point sleeve	Bicep centre
9	Zero point front skirt	nil
10	Zero point back skirt	nil
11	Category of fit	Semi-fitting
Comments	Refer to text.	

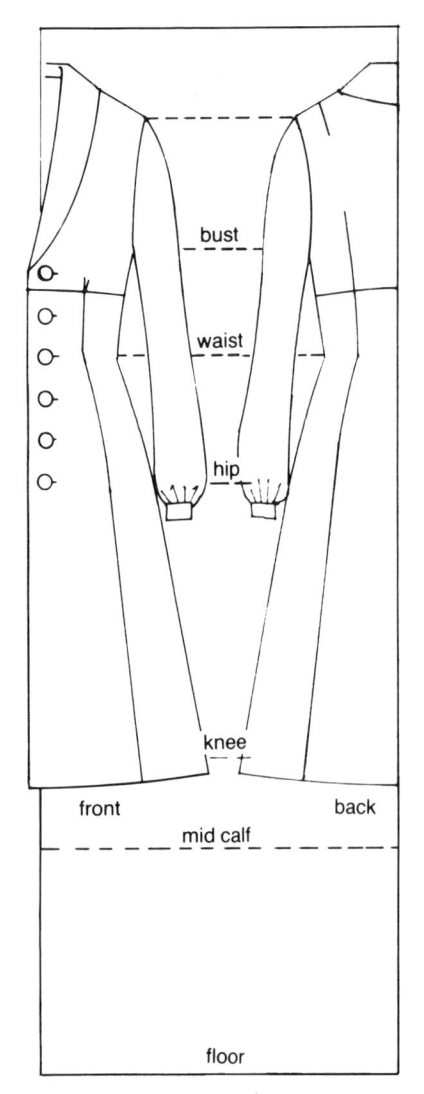

Figure 98 Style 1 – shawl collar, bishop sleeve with cuff button through

STAGE 1 Evaluation of style and choice of technique

Before commencing the grade, assess the style and the grading specification and evaluate all the areas that may need adjusting proportionally, for example:

1. The collar and the neckline. Should this deepen on the larger sizes? The answer to this is not straightforward as larger ladies may well prefer slimmer, proportionately narrower collars. This is a style decision to be discussed with the designer.
2. The underbust seam. The three-dimensional grade selected for this style advocates that the bust point should drop 0.4 cm per size. This automatically suggests that the underbust seam should drop with it. It could, however, be dropped more if it was thought necessary.

3 Vertical seam from underbust seam and panel widths. Moving the bust point away from the centre front by 0.6 cm takes care of this, and no extra proportioning should be necessary.

Style grading

Part One explained in detail the approach involved in grading the basic blocks. The next stage is grading a pattern that has been styled.

For the purpose of this book, styles have been divided into three broad categories:

1 Close-fitting
2 Semi-fitting
3 Loose-fitting

Each category has its own problems. This book sets out to highlight the best techniques for dealing with each type, and the following explanatory notes should be read carefully.

Close-fitting. Whenever possible, choose the three-dimensional draft system as it provides optimum results, conforming very closely to the survey.

Semi-fitting. The illustrated zeros for each specific exercise are the recommended ones, but it is suggested that other zeros are tried out for experience (refer to Chapter 11).

Loose-fitting. The grading specification with each style has been designed to list all the size requirements.

The grading specification for Style 1 should then be studied to determine the size range required and the grading technique to adopt. (The authors' recommended technique is contained in the grading specification and it is up to readers to decide whether they adopt this.) Also note that grade increments are given thus:

1 Figure 99a – the recommended optimum system for the specific style (three-dimensional).
2 Figure 99b – a simplified system (two-dimensional).

The choice of system is made mainly on the basis of the degree of fit. The closer the fit of the garment, the more significant the choice of grading technique becomes. As already mentioned, the three categories of fit are: close-, semi- and loose-fitting.

It is always recommended that the three-dimensional draft grade illustrated in this exercise is used for a tight-fitting garment. The reasons for this have been explained in previous chapters.

STAGE 2 Draft and graded cardinal points

1 Develop the pattern silhouette by manipulating the block patterns and then plan the style lines and panels. Alternatively, the production pattern can be returned to its original basic draft as shown in Figure 100. (See Style 3 for this technique.)
2 Study Figure 99a to determine the single size increase and then multiply all increments by the number of sizes required, in this case five sizes up. Grade out horizontally and vertically from original construction lines to establish the size 22 cardinal points.

Suppression

1 Back blade dart. See Chapter 10 on block grading.
2 Front bust dart. Establish the size 22 shoulder point and then describe an arc from the size 22 bust point through the new neck point.
3 Apply graded shoulder measurement from the new shoulder point to touch the arc. Connect up the points for the largest dart (see Figure 101).

Note. See Chapter 10 for a detailed discussion of this suppression technique.

STAGE 3 Completing the largest outline

Back dress (Figure 101)
1 Connect up all cardinal points to form the size 22 outline.
2 Mark any intermediary sizes required (see Figure 103).

Stylelines
1 Draw in the styled underbust line as in diagram.
2 Mark in back blade dart from graded size 22 dart end to shoulder.
3 Extend back skirt panels as in diagram.

Front dress
1 Connect up the cardinal points from the shoulder point around to the centre front break point.
2 Extend front skirt panels as in Figure 103.
3 Draw in styled underbust line.

Collar grade (Figure 102)
This shawl collar is graded directly on to the draft. The bust suppression is pivoted out at a later stage. Essentials such as the fish dart have been omitted due to the difficulties of illustration. See Figure 102 for a blow-up of the collar detail.

Line A–B = the size 12 half back neck measurement.
2 Point C = the size 22 neck point.

140 WOMEN'S STYLE GRADING

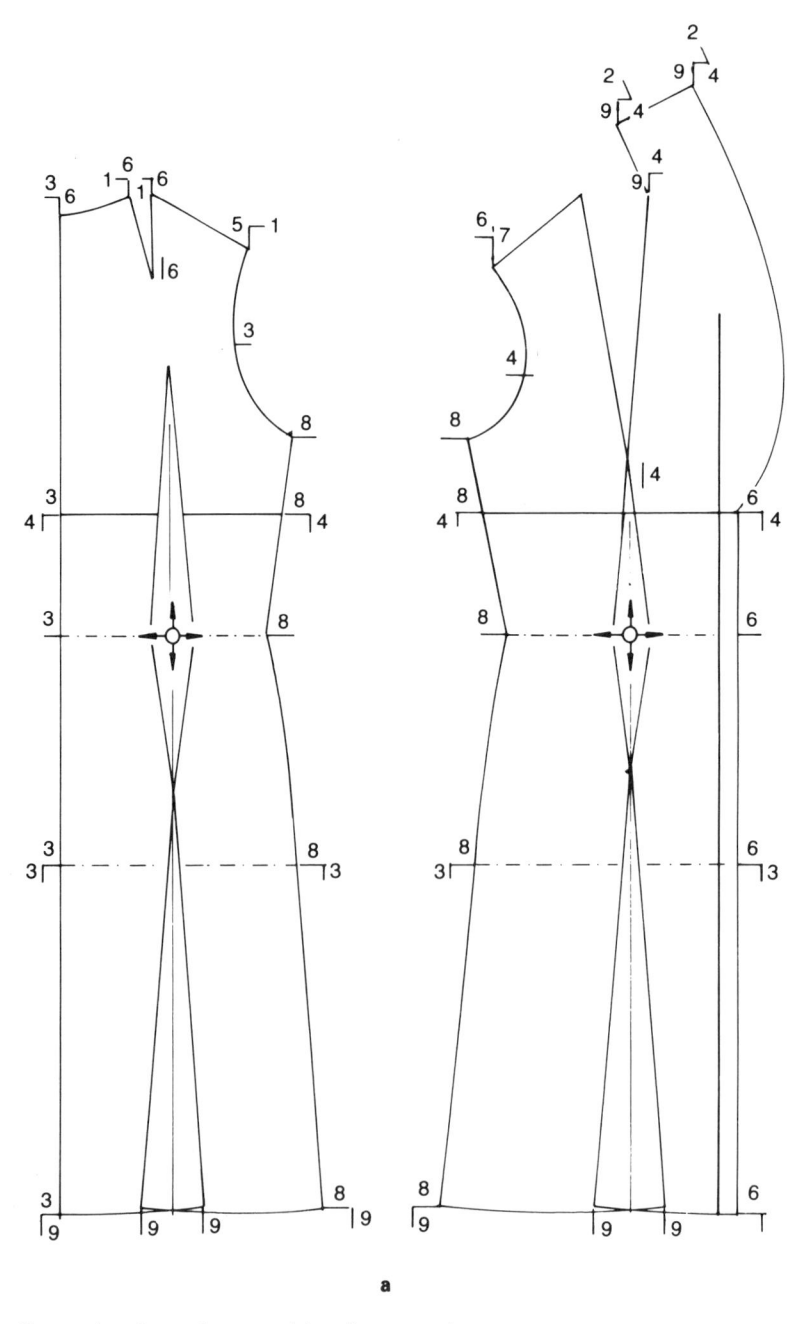

Figure 99 (a) Three-dimensional grade quantities for one size

STYLE GRADES 1 TO 33 141

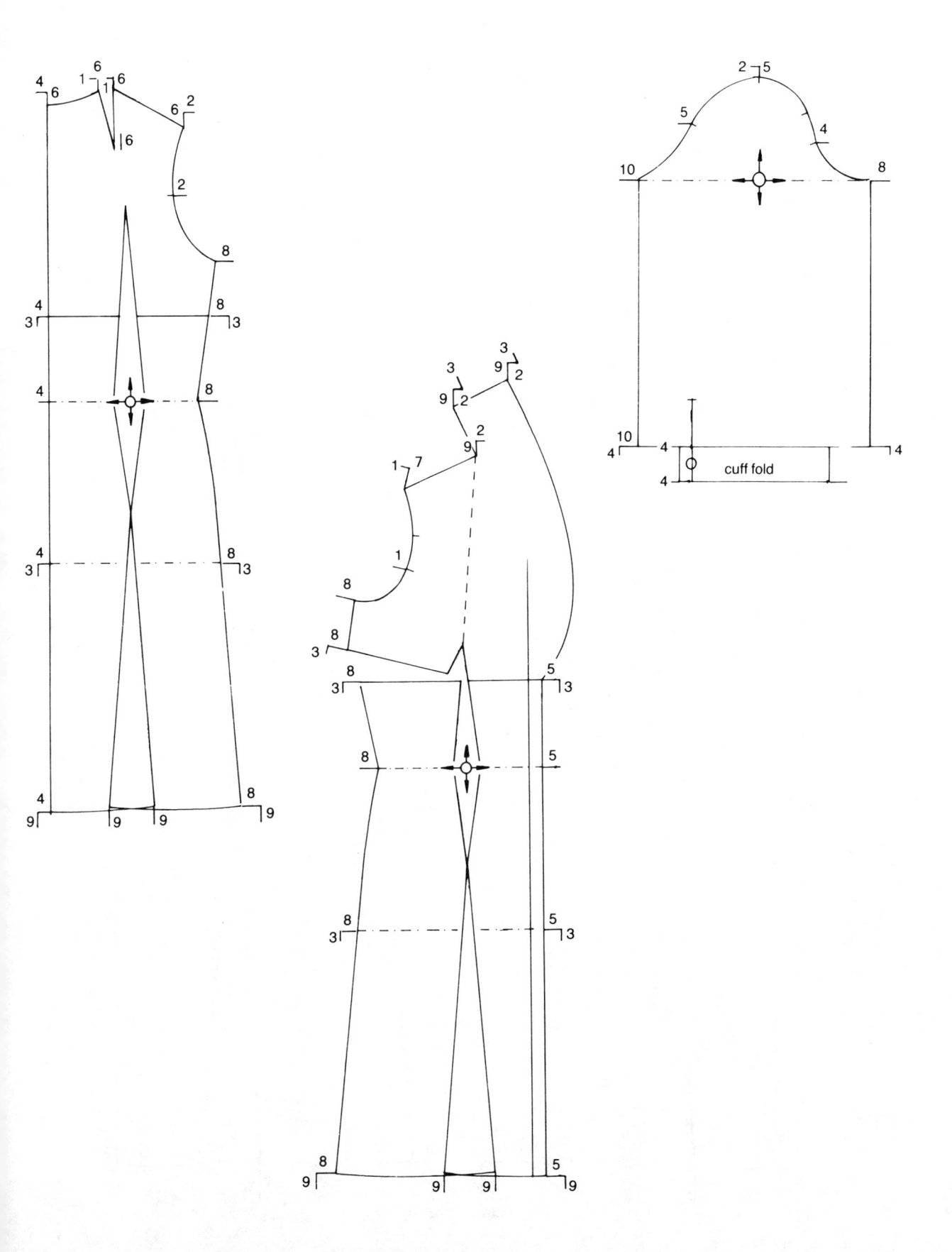

(b) Two-dimensional quantities for one size. This can be used for a draft or multi-track grade (see Chapter 13)

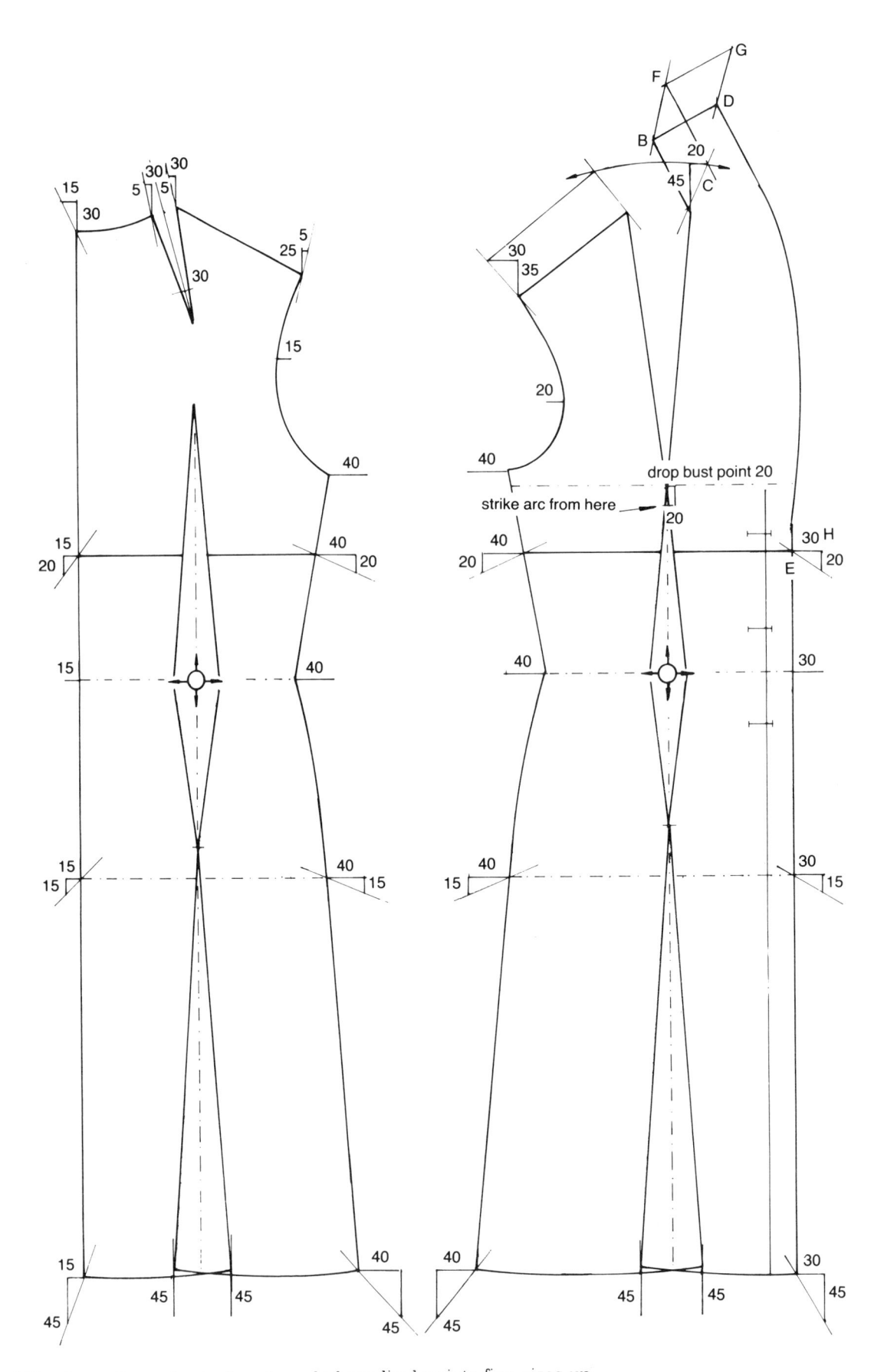

Figure 100 Stage 2 – style draft and graded cardinal points five sizes up

STYLE GRADES 1 TO 33　　　　　　　　　　　　　　　　　　　　　　　143

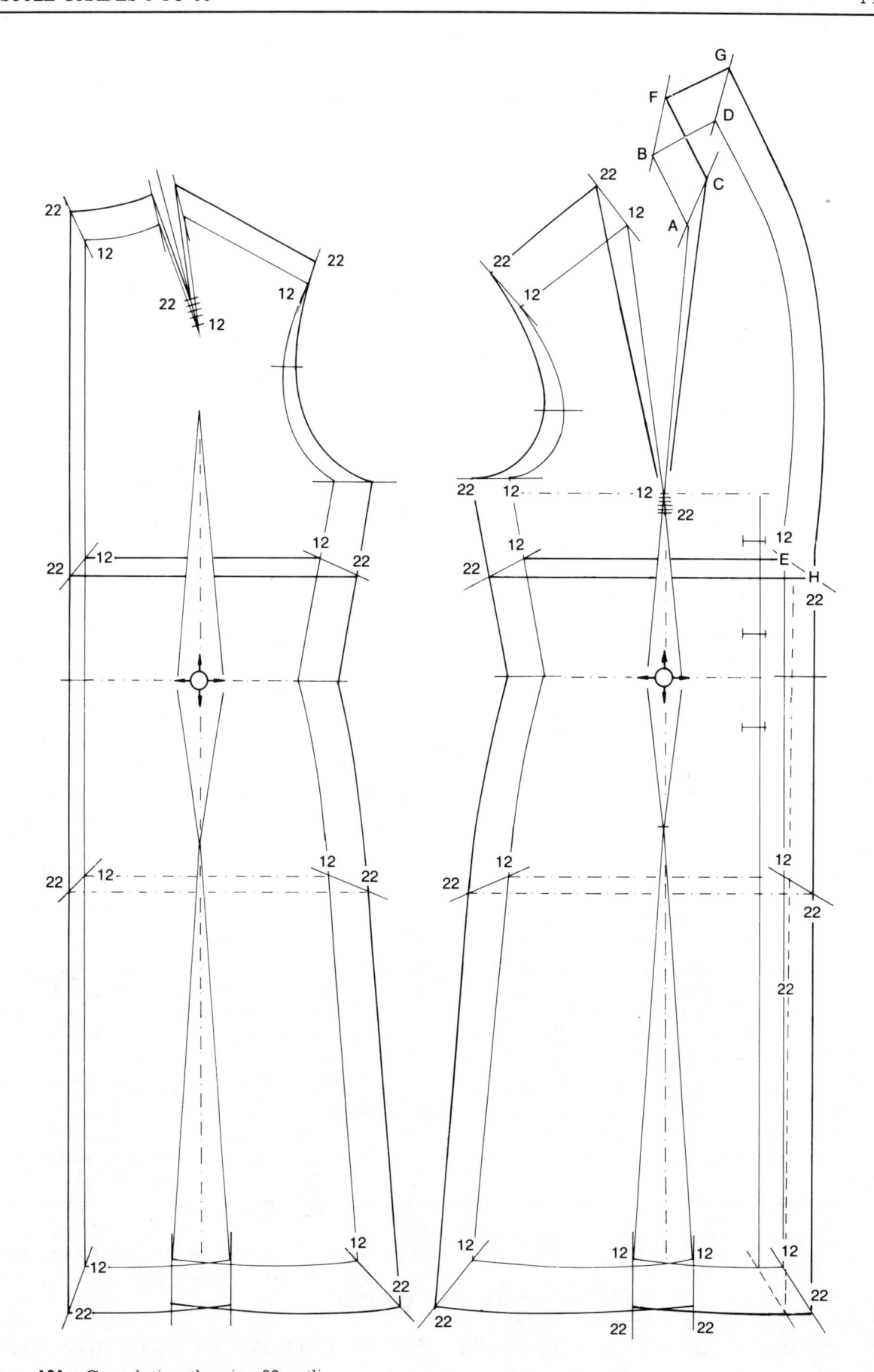

Figure 101　Completing the size 22 outline

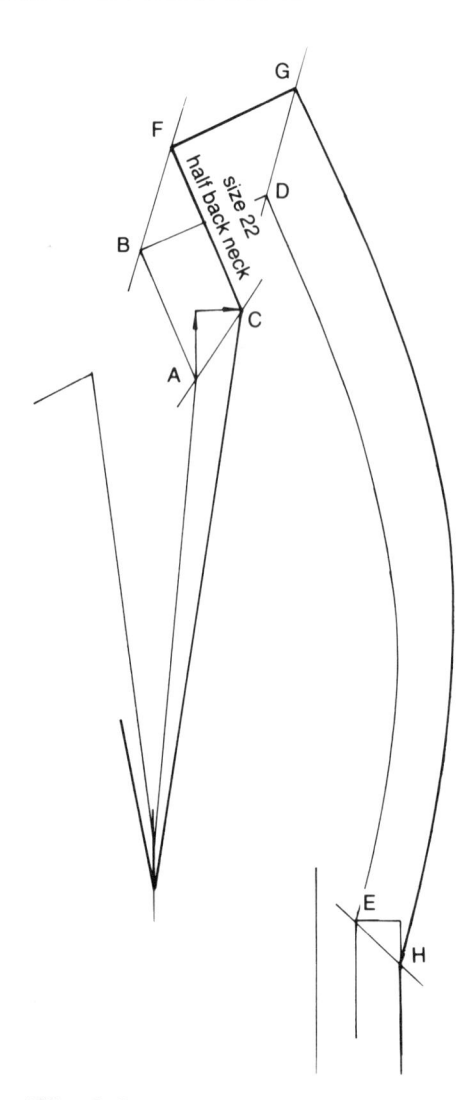

Figure 102 Collar grade

3 Line C–F = the size 22 half back measurement (to obtain this measurement simply measure the size 22 back neck on the draft).
F–C is parallel to B–A.
4 F–G is the collar centre back and is parallel to B–D. It should be noted that F–G can be increased if it is necessary to deepen the collar.
5 Connect G–H for the leaf edge (size 22).
6 Connect B–F and D–G for the diagonal grade lines.
7 Connect A–C for the front shoulder neck point.

Figure 103 illustrates the completed nested draft ready for spiking-off the required sizes.

Note that it is not essential to provide the complete draft as the required patterns can be spiked-off using the cardinal points as references, as in Figure 101.

STAGE 4 Spiking-off and checking graded patterns

Front and back bodice section
Trace-off or spike-off the front and back bodice sections, pivoting out the unwanted neck darts into their required positions (see Chapter 12 for techniques). Figures 104, 105 and 106 illustrate this. Check accuracy. Repeat for each size.

Skirt sections
Trace- or spike-off the required sizes of the side front and back and centre front and back skirt sections. Check for accuracy. Add seam allowances and mark up.

Facings
There are two basic methods of grading facings:

1 Use each size pattern to construct a facing in the conventional pattern cutting manner. This is safe, accurate and efficient.
2 Grade-up the size 12 facing according to the grade instructions (Figure 107), using A as the zero point. The procedure is as follows:
   a Using the size 12 facing continue line A–B to establish the size 22 half back neck measurement.
   b Divide the increase by five to establish the other intermediate sizes.
   c Blend leaf edge from C–D.

Note: Adjustments for underpressing made to the facing and collar leaf edges cannot be illustrated as they are too subtle. Buttonhole positions must also be graded appropriately to preserve proportion.

THE SLEEVE (Figure 108)
This sleeve is a separate set-in sleeve and, therefore, it may be dealt with as an entity after the main body of the garment. The five stages apply equally to the sleeve.

STAGE 1 Evaluation of style and choice of technique
The sleeve will lengthen according to the arm length increase. The cuff will probably remain the same width. The grade, therefore, will be applied to the sleeve but not the cuff. However this could be re-apportioned, i.e., 0.6 cm on to the sleeve and 0.3 cm on to the cuff width. See Figure 99 for the increments for one size. The zero point is as illustrated.

STAGE 2 Draft and graded cardinal points
1 Draft the sleeve and cuff as illustrated in Figure

STYLE GRADES 1 TO 33   145

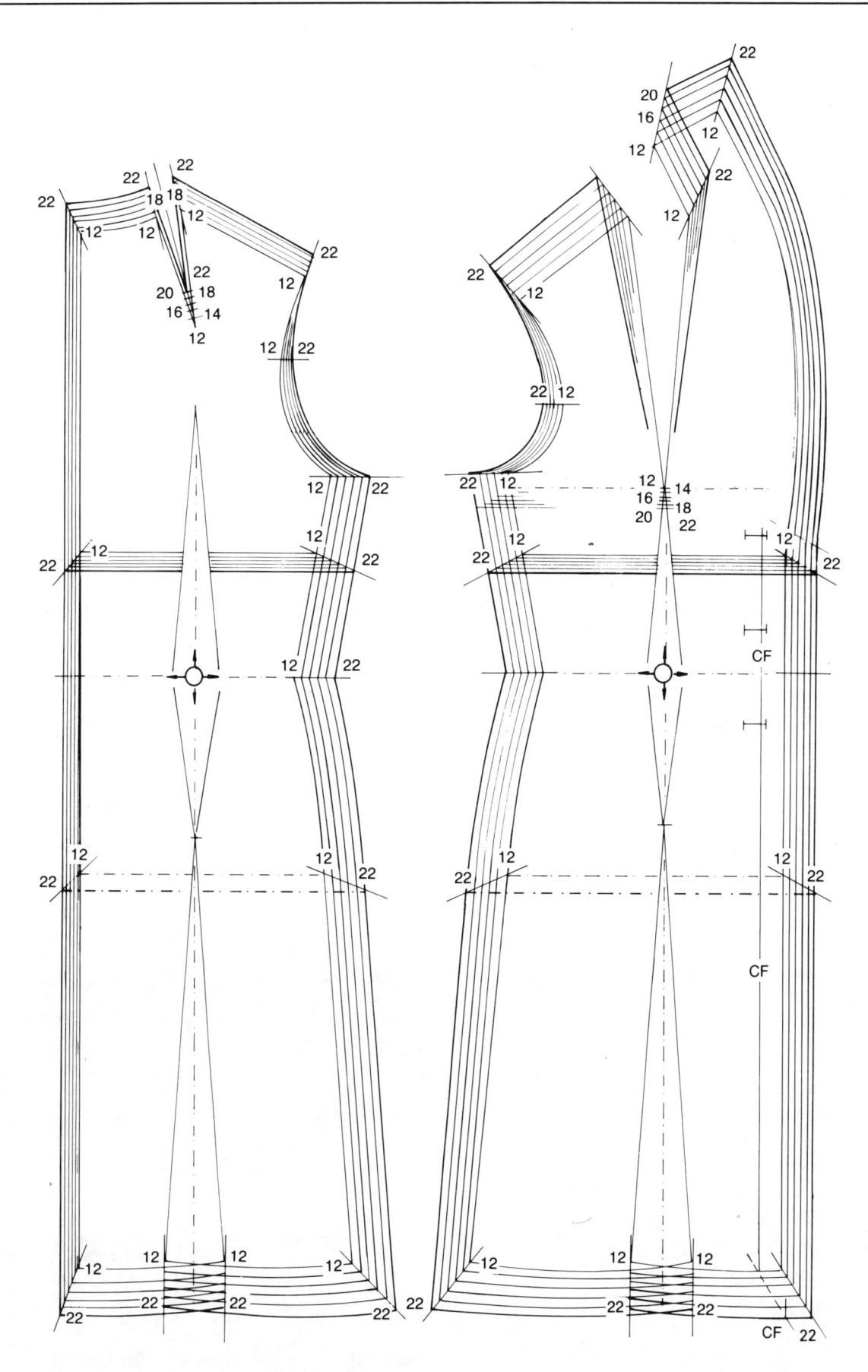

Figure 103 The completed nested draft

146　　　　　　　　　　　　　　　　　　　　　　　　　　　　WOMEN'S STYLE GRADING

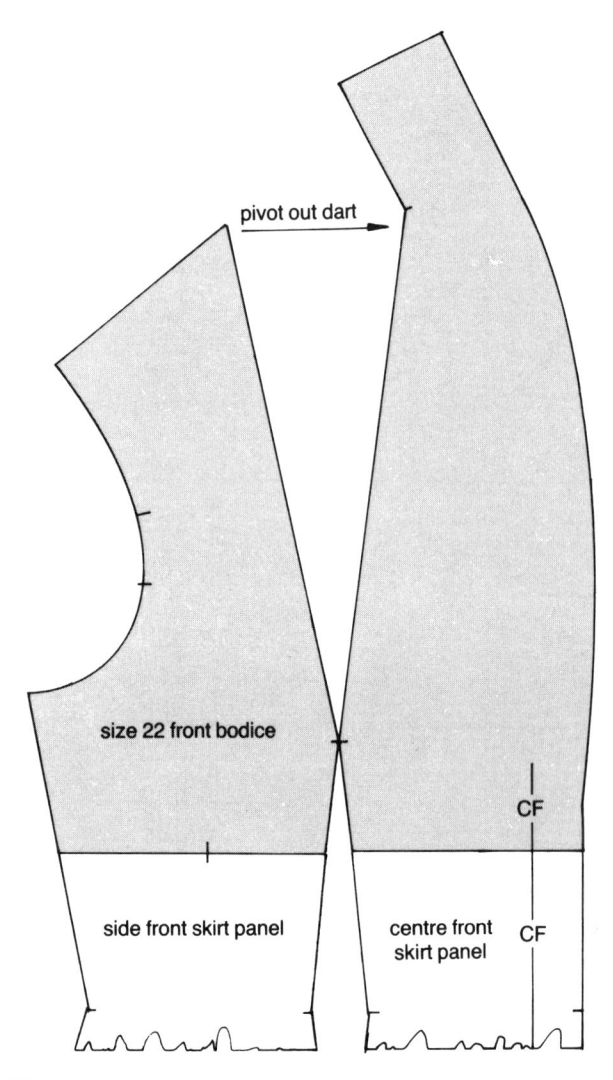

Figure 104　Trace-off front bodice

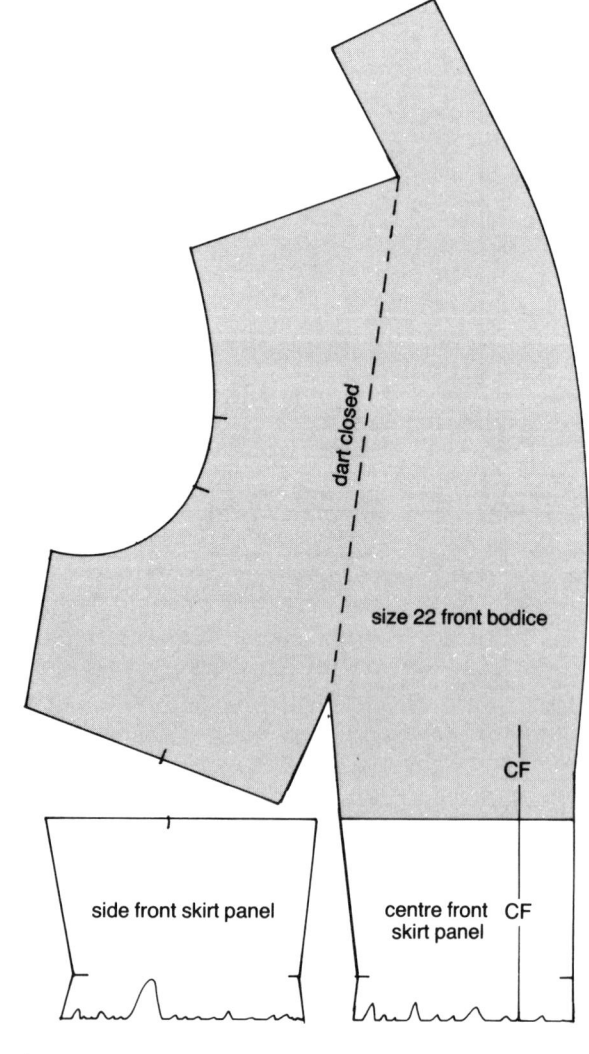

Figure 105　Pivot-out unwanted bust dart into underbust dart

STYLE GRADES 1 TO 33

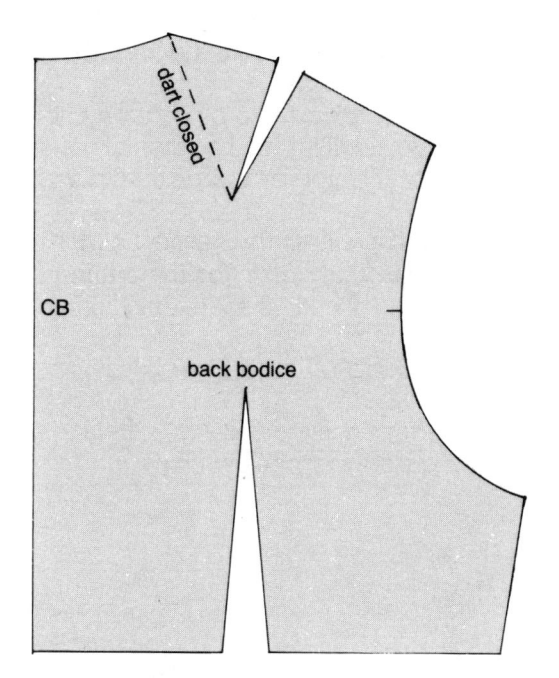

Figure 106 Blade dart transferred from neck to shoulder

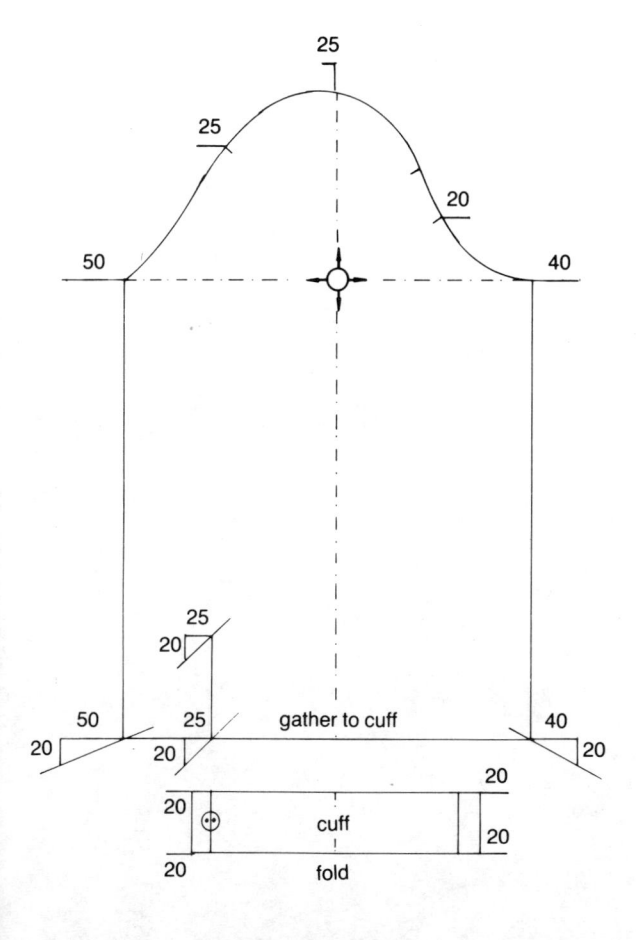

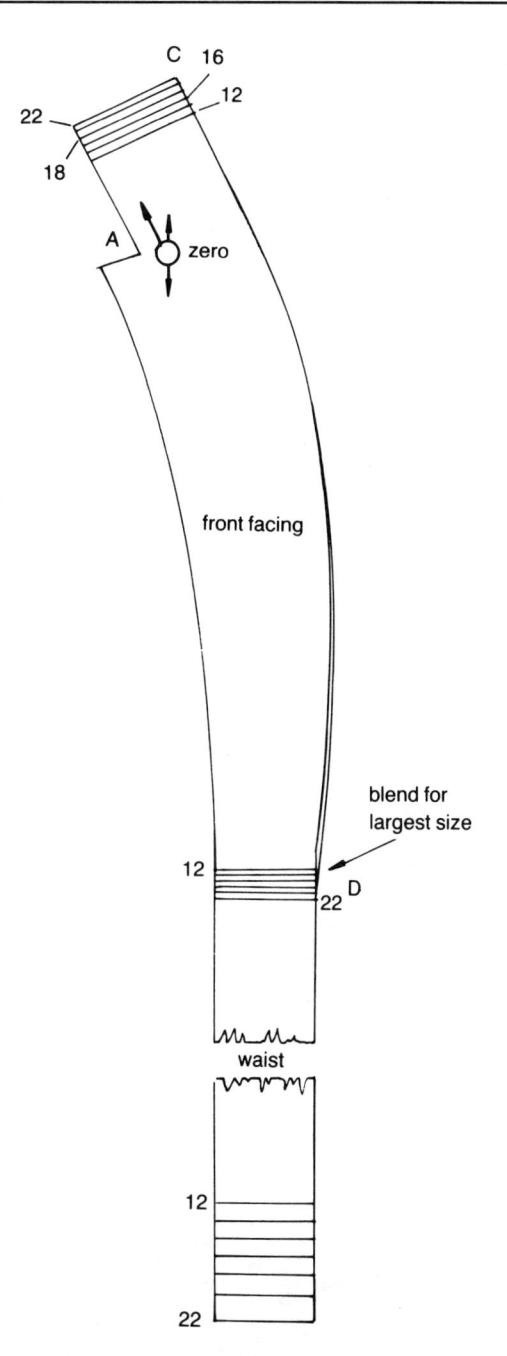

Figure 107 Draft grade of the front facing showing sizes 12 to 22 without seam allowances

Figure 108 Sleeve grade. Stage 1 – establish largest size

108. Leave enough room between cuff and sleeve for the grade.
2 Establish the largest size by squaring horizontally and vertically from the original construction lines at the upper arm girth and wrist.

STAGE 3   Completing the largest outline
Connect up cardinal points for the outline of the size 22 sleeve and cuff as shown in Figure 109.

STAGE 4   Spiking-off and checking graded pattern
Spike-off required sleeve sizes. Check against armhole and add seam allowances.

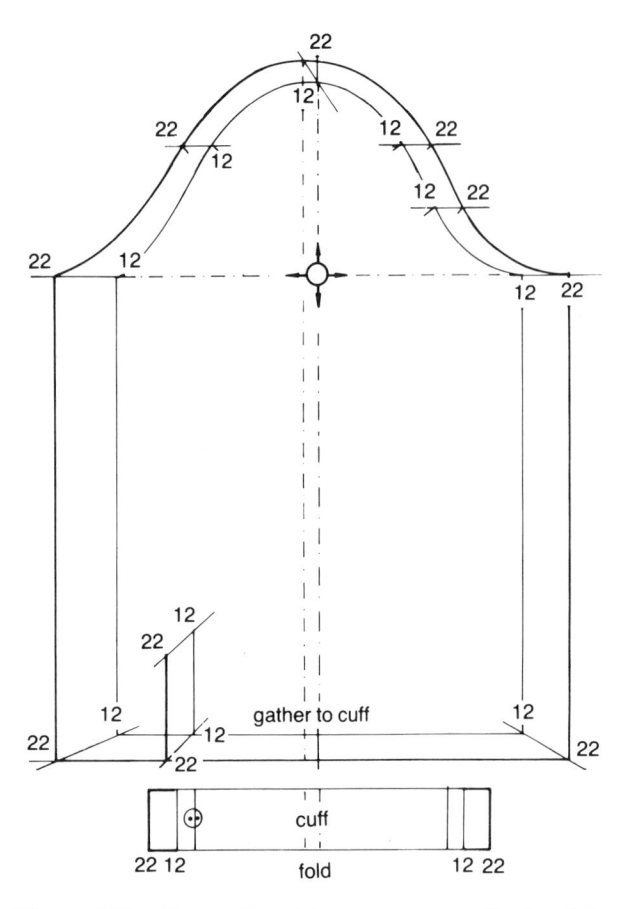

Figure 109   Stages 2 and 3 – connect cardinal points for outline

STYLE 2

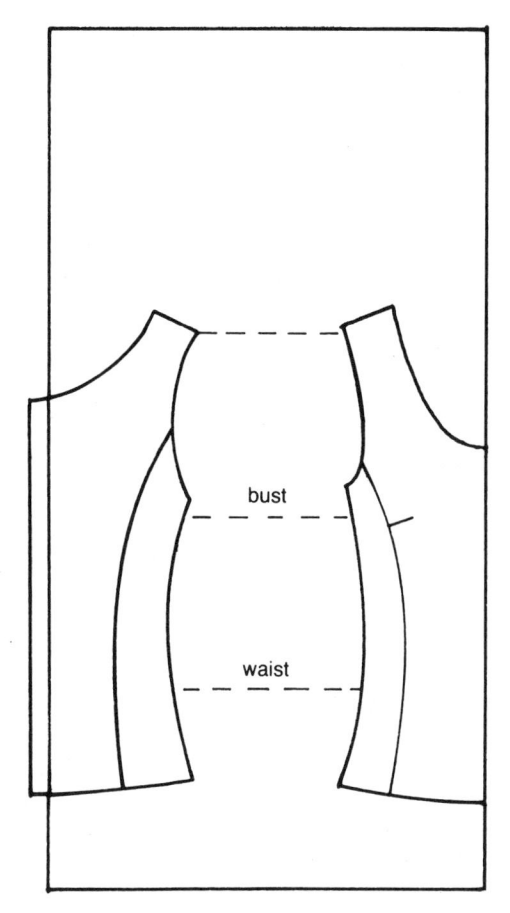

Figure 110 Style 2 – semi-fitting blouse with side-body and seam away from the bust point. The neckline back and front is scooped

	GRADING SPECIFICATION	
1	Size chart	Table 13
2	Size range	10·12·14·16·18·20·22
3	Height/girth/length	Height and girth all sizes
4	Proportioning	
5	Type of grade	3 dim. N.S.B.P.
6	Zero points front	C.F. waist dart position
7	Zero point back	C.B. waist dart position
8	Zero point sleeve	nil
9	Zero point front skirt	nil
10	Zero point back skirt	nil
11	Category of fit	Semi-fitting
Comments	NSBP = non static bust point. See text	

EVALUATION OF STYLE AND CHOICE OF TECHNIQUE AND ZERO

This semi-fitting blouse has a 'side body' and a low, scooped neckline. To obtain the best fit in the larger sizes it is important to ensure that the bust point and the dart connecting it to the vertical side body seam drops 0.4 cm per size. Therefore, the recommended method of grading this style is the three-dimensional draft with the non-static bust point.

STAGE 1   Style evaluation

The neckline
As the style increases in size it is recommended that the neckline is raised proportionately so that it does not become too revealing. (See Figures 111 and 112.) Alternatively, the neckline could be retained at the same level as the size 12 throughout the range. This, in effect, is dropping the neckline. **These alterations are style decisions.**

The vertical seam
The zero point selected for this draft allows the vertical seam to remain static. The proportioning of the side body is adjusted by the increases at the side seam. Alternatively, the side body vertical seam could be moved towards the side seam, 0.4 cm per size. This would increase the length of the small dart.

The shoulder width
In this particular style the shoulder width is based on the back shoulder of the size 12 continuing to the size 22. This is another style decision.

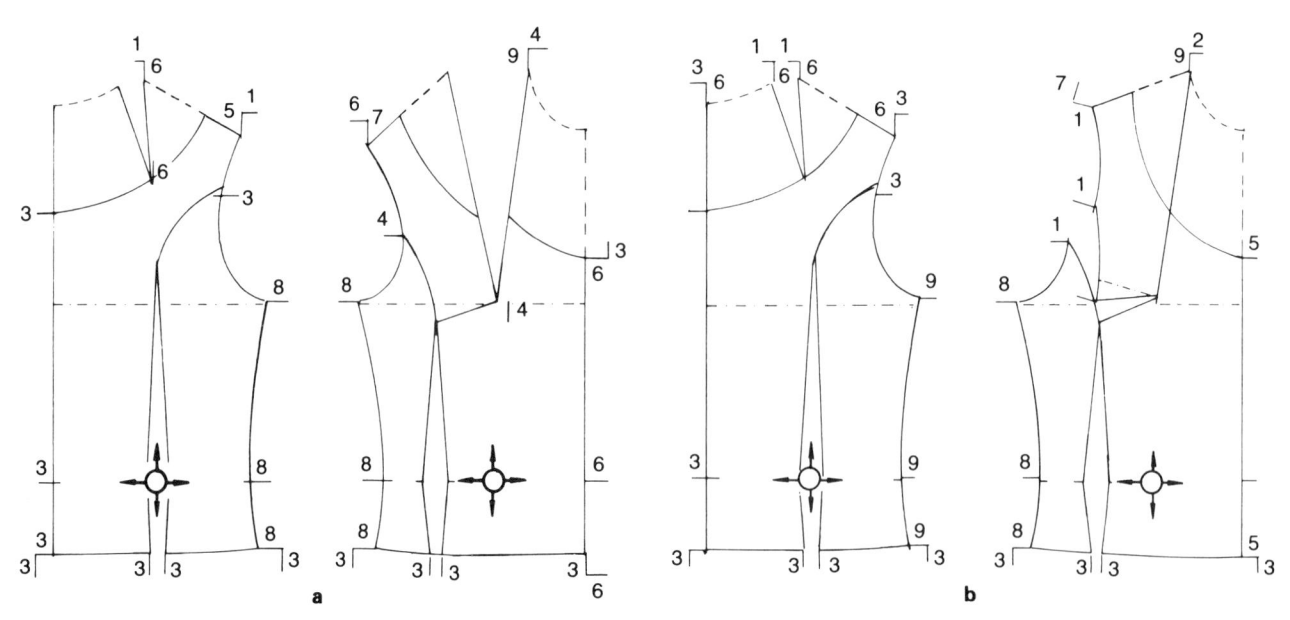

Figure 111 (a) Three-dimensional increments for one size
(b) Two-dimensional increments for one size. Suitable for draft grading or multi-track grading

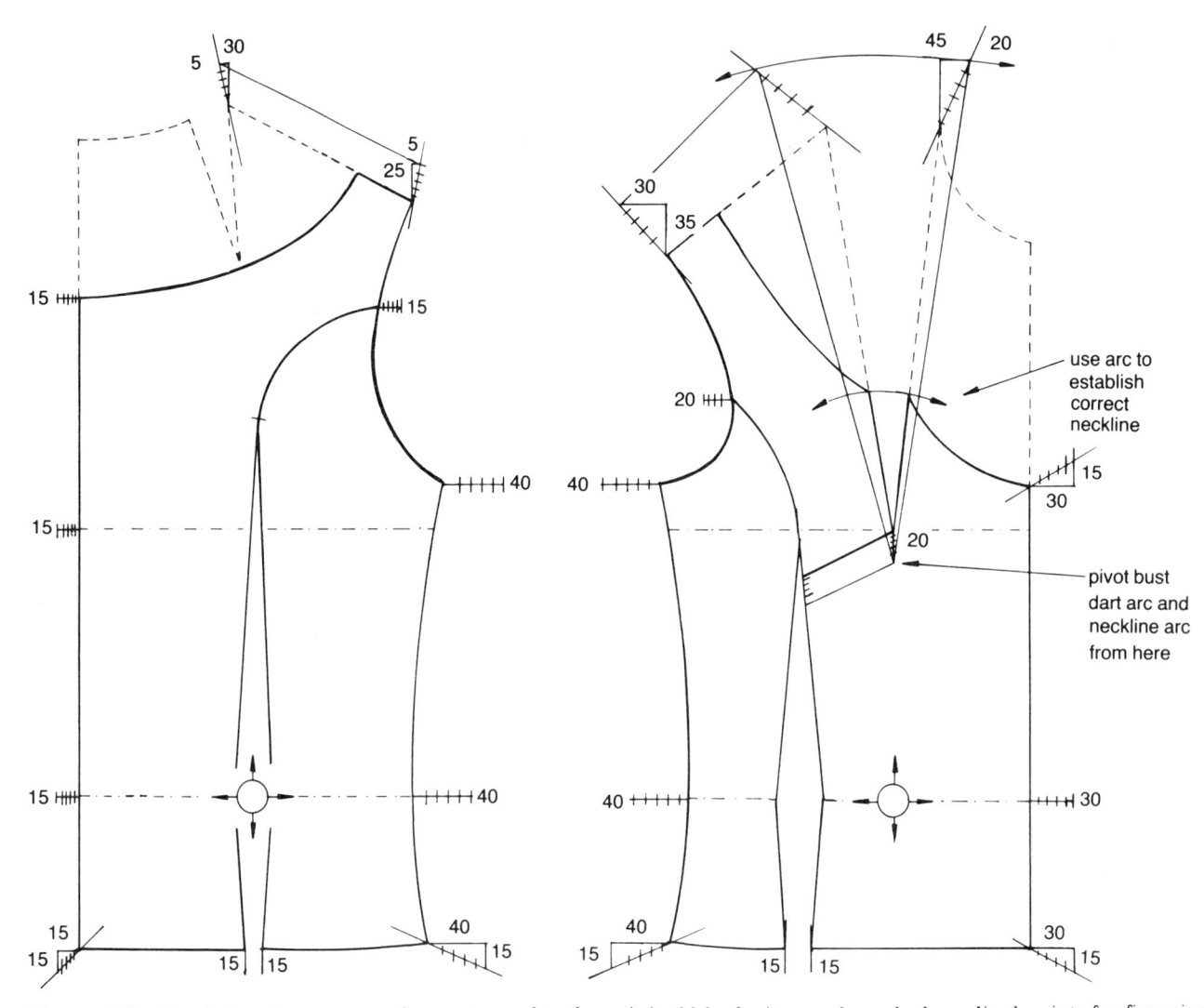

Figure 112 Draft showing suppressions returned to the original block sites and graded cardinal points for five sizes

STYLE GRADES 1 TO 33

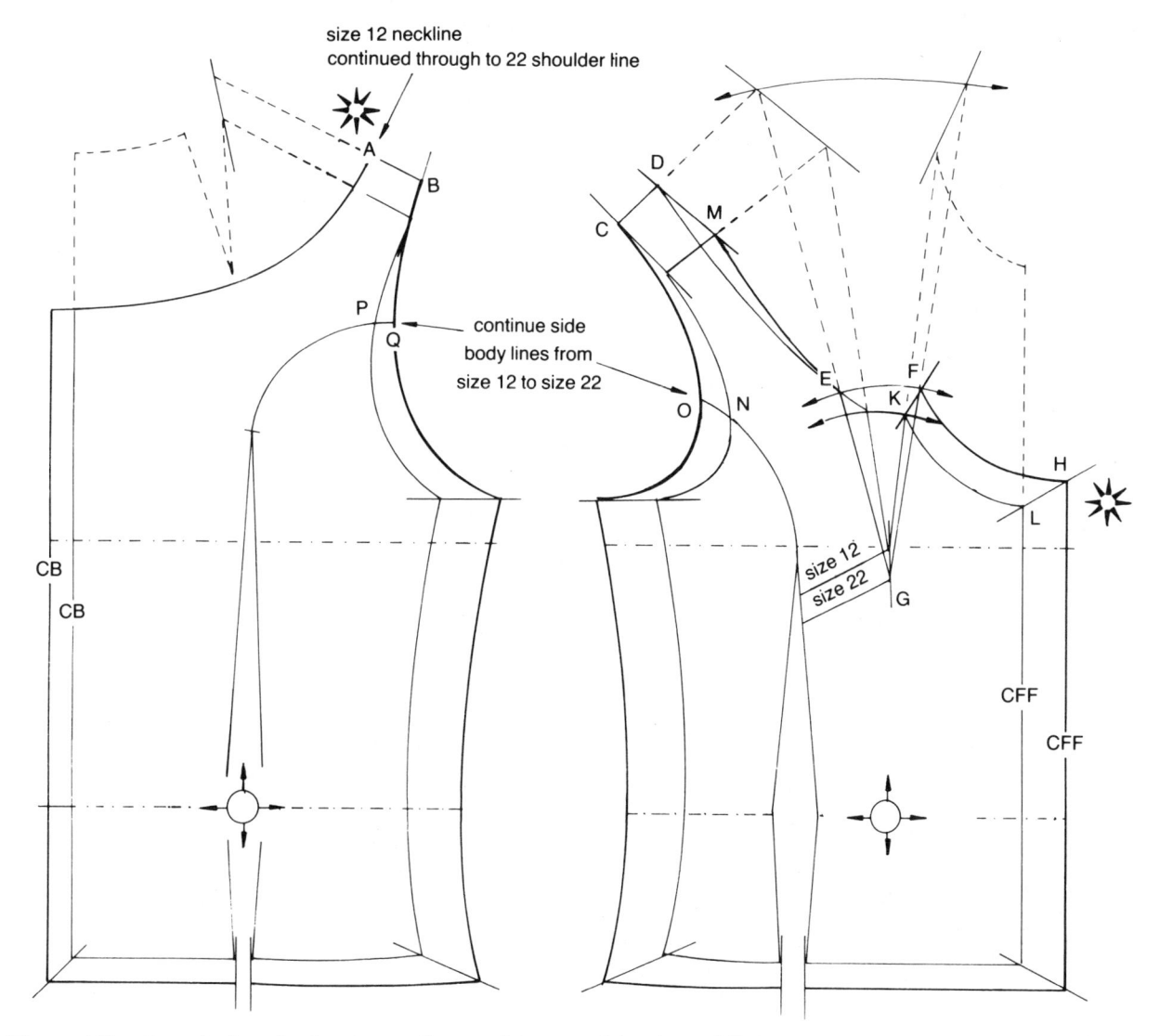

Figure 113 Completing the largest outline and front and back necklines

STAGE 2 Draft and graded cardinal points – three-dimensional grade

1. Draft the style and reposition the bust suppression back to its block form (see Figure 112).
2. Study the appropriate grade plan (Figure 111) and plan the increments on to the draft.
3. *Note that the grade and increment at centre front block neck point and back block neck are unnecessary for this style.*
4. Grade out from all the cardinal points according to the increments in Figure 111.

Front suppression

Plan the front suppression according to previous examples using arcs and drop the bust point by 0.4 cm. Connect each size bust point to the side body seam line.

Back blade dart

The back blade dart is unnecessary in this low necked style. However, it needs to be graded in order to obtain the correct shoulder angle. In order to simplify the back neckline grade, lengthen the blade dart (see Figures 110, 111 and 112) so that the neckline passes through the dart end.

STAGE 3 Completing the largest outline

1. Complete the size 22 outline as shown in Figure 113.
2. Connect up darts back and front.
3. Connect size 22 bust point with line parallel to size 12.

Neckline

1. Continue back neckline through to shoulder.

2 Measure A–B. Apply this measurement to C–D.
3 Blend line D–E.
4 Swing arc from G through E to F on largest dart.
5 Connect F–H for continuation of neckline.
6 Connect K–F and L–H and M–D for diagonal grade lines.
7 Side body front. Continue point N through to O.
8 Side body back. Continue point P through to Q.
9 Divide up 12–22 into required sizes.

STAGE 4 Spiking-off and checking graded patterns

Centre front panel (Figure 114)
1 Spike-off required sizes and pivot out bust dart into its new position.
2 Add seam allowances.
3 Repeat this with all sections.

STAGE 5 Facings
The recommended method of producing a set of facings for this style is to spike-off the completed pattern and then cut an 'all in one facing' from each size. Using the draft is complicated due to the pivoting out of the dart at neck.

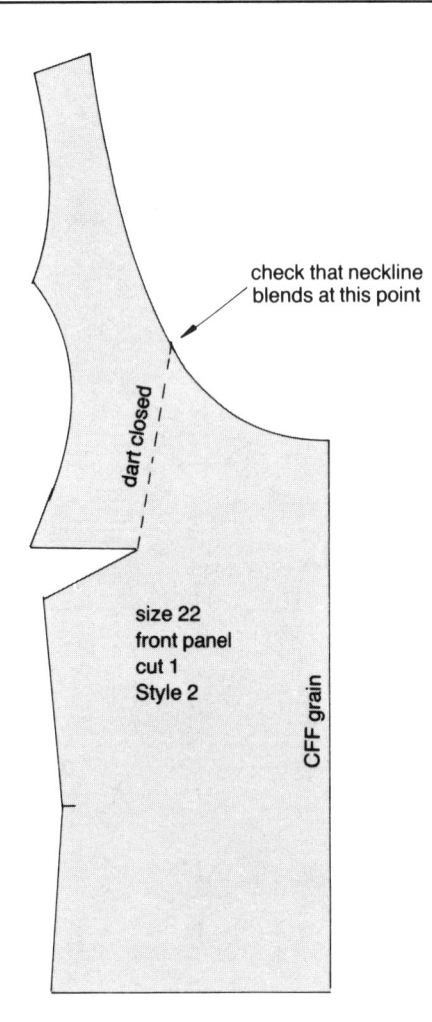

Figure 114 Trace-off required size front panel and close out bust dart into final position

STYLE 3

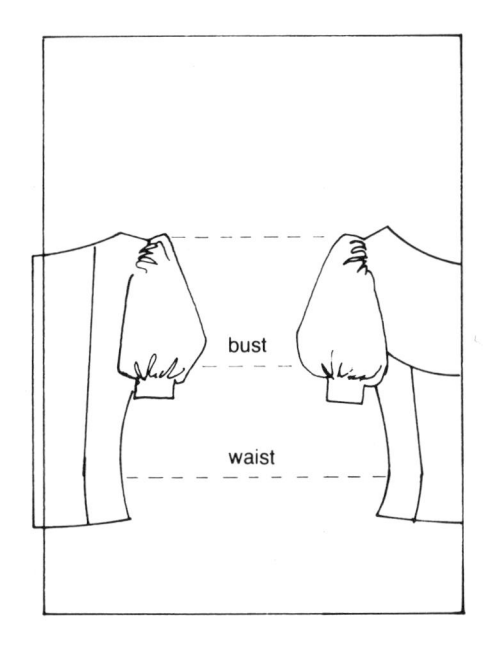

Figure 115 Style 3 – fitted blouse, boat neck, and vertical and horizontal seams, through the bust point

	GRADING SPECIFICATION	
1	Size chart	Table 13
2	Size range	10·12·14·16·18·20·22
3	Height/girth/length	Height and girth
4	Proportioning	
5	Type of grade	3 dim. N.S.B.P.
6	Zero points front	Bust point static waist moving upwards
7	Zero point back	Waist dart centre
8	Zero point sleeve	Centre bicep line
9	Zero point front skirt	nil
10	Zero point back skirt	nil
11	Category of fit	Tight

Comments

NSBP = non static bust point. See text below.

FITTED BLOUSE

STAGE 1 Style evaluation
This tight-fitting blouse (Figure 115) has a boat neck and a horizontal and vertical seam which both run through the bust point. It is recommended that the three-dimensional draft system with non-static bust point is used to grade this style as it is important that the neckline and seaming relate to the changing contours of the larger body (see Figure 116a).

Choice of zero
It has been established previously (see Chapter 11) that horizontal lines, such as the seam line positioned through the bust point, can be graded most effectively from the zero recommended. This is because the horizontal line remains virtually static and therefore the same for all sizes (see Figure 60). The back blouse, however, can be graded from the usual zero.

STAGE 2 Draft and graded cardinal points
1. Draft the pattern or use the production pattern to reposition the styled darts back in to their original block sites, back and front. (See Figure 117.)
2. Grade from all the cardinal points according to the increments in Figure 116. Multiply them by the number of sizes required.

   Note: To grade this type of neckline use the centre front neckline point and grade according to the increments stated (see Figure 117).
3. Obtain largest suppressions back and front according to previous examples.

STAGE 3 Completing the largest outline
Complete the largest outline. Connect up darts back and front.

154　　　　　　　　　　　　　　　　　　　　　　　　　　　　　　　　　　　WOMEN'S STYLE GRADING

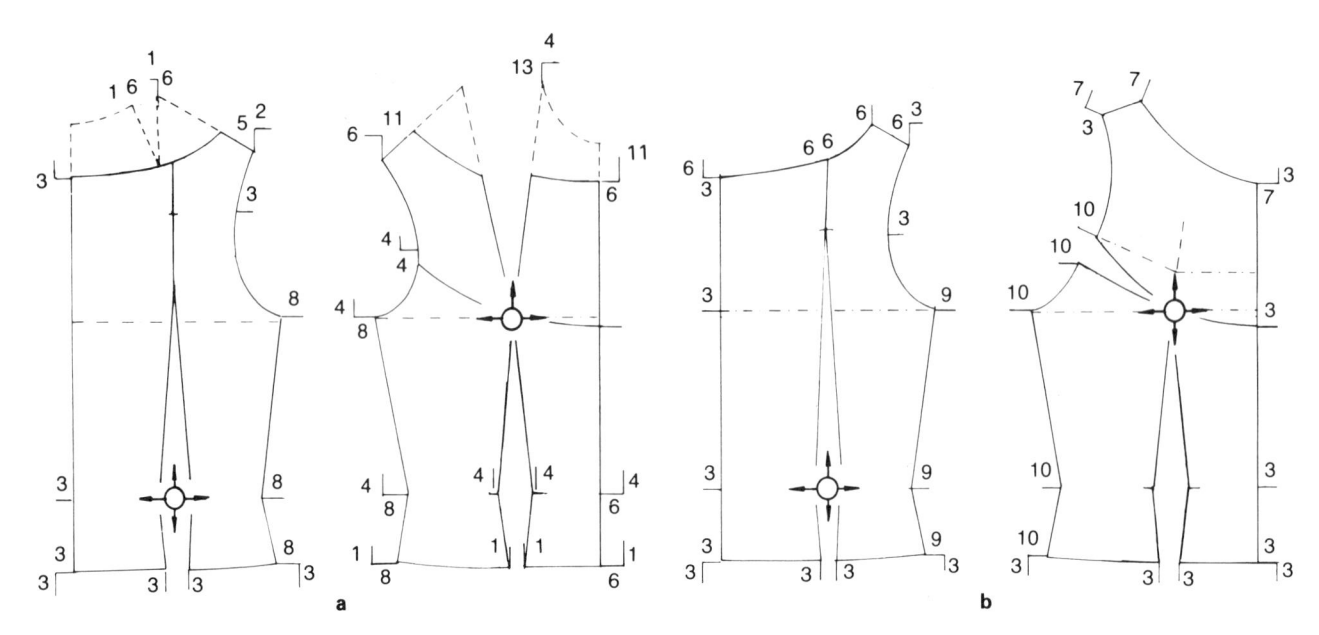

Figure 116　(a)　Three-dimensional quantities
　　　　　　　(b)　Two-dimensional quantities suitable for multi-track grading

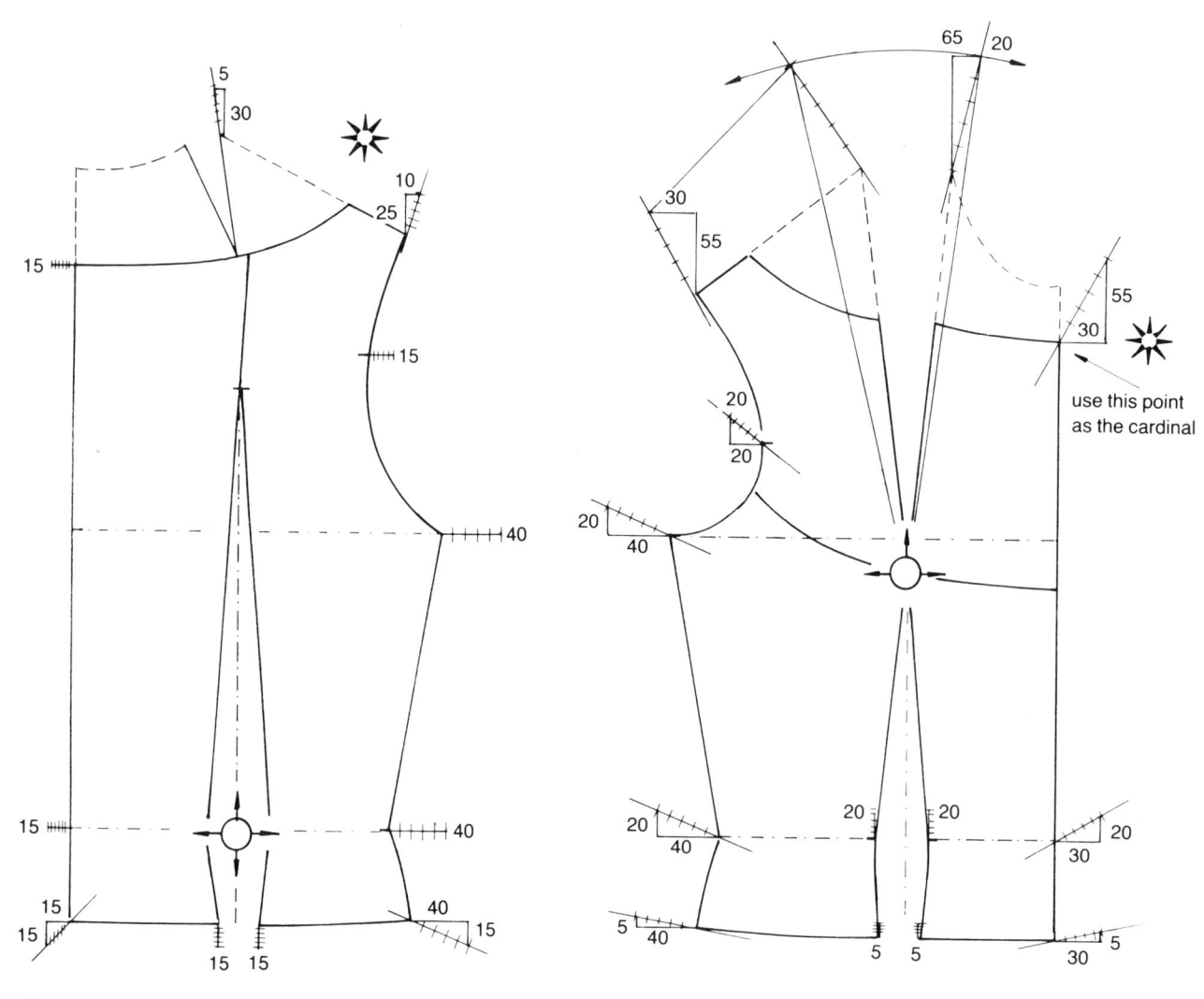

Figure 117　Establishing the graded cardinal points and largest darts. Increments for five sizes

STYLE GRADES 1 TO 33

The neckline (Figure 118)
Back:
1 Continue point A to point B.
2 Measure B–C and apply it to D–E on the front shoulder.

Front:
3 Mark point F. Establish line F–G (parallel to size 12 neckline).
4 Swing arc from bust point H through point G to establish point I.
5 Connect I–E.

Horizontal style line
Continue these style lines through to the size 22 outline.

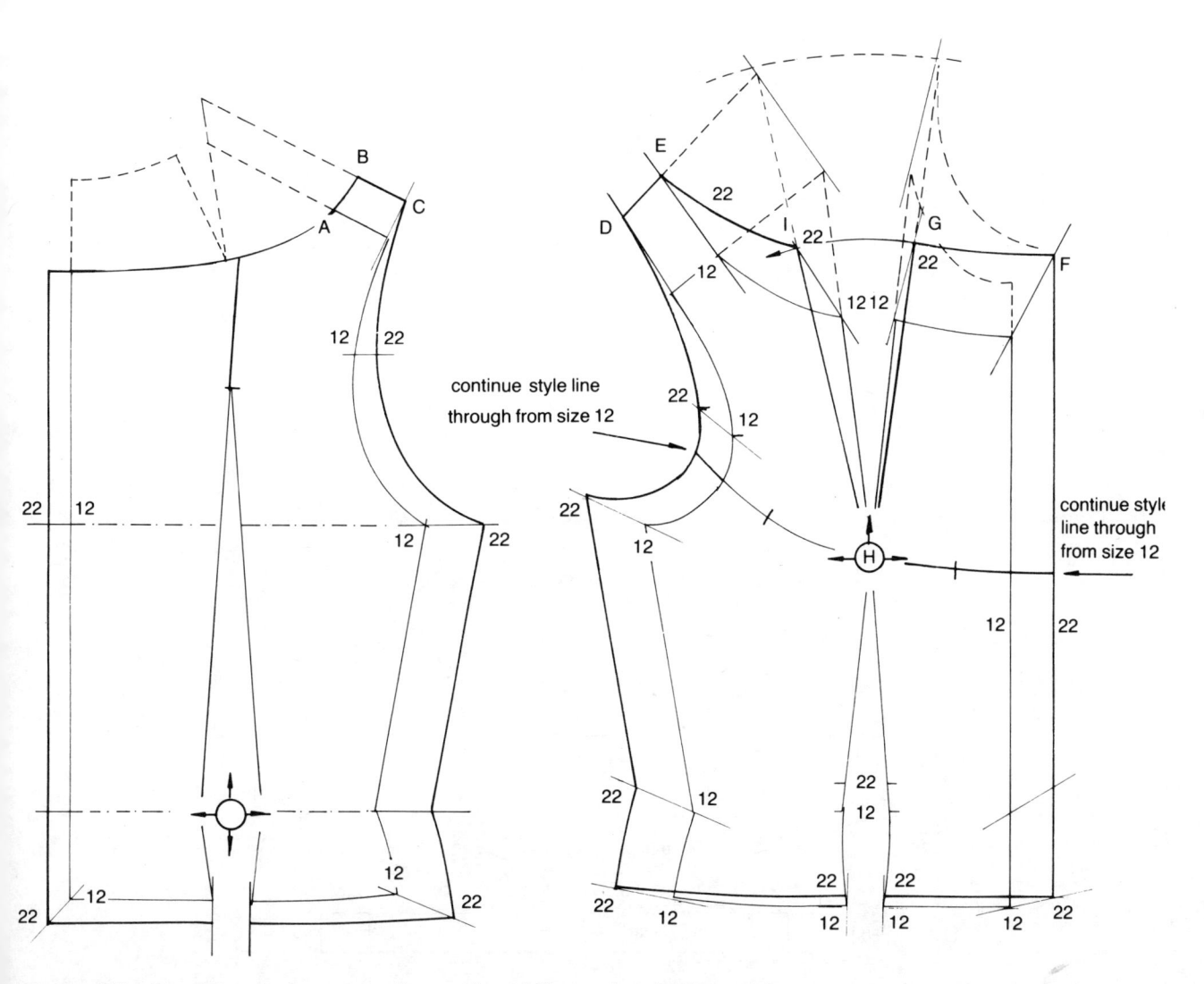

Figure 118 Stage 3 – the largest outline and neckline and style line grade

STAGE 4 Spiking-off and checking graded patterns

Divide up connecting lines and spike-off required sizes. Close out darts and return them to curved seam line. Check each section – particularly the neckline. Add seam allowances. (See Figure 119).

STAGE 5 Facings

Use the finished pattern to produce facings.

The sleeve (Figures 120 and 121)

Figure 120 illustrates the sleeve increments for one size. To grade this, follow the same stages as in previous examples.

Figure 121 shows the sleeve increments for five sizes.

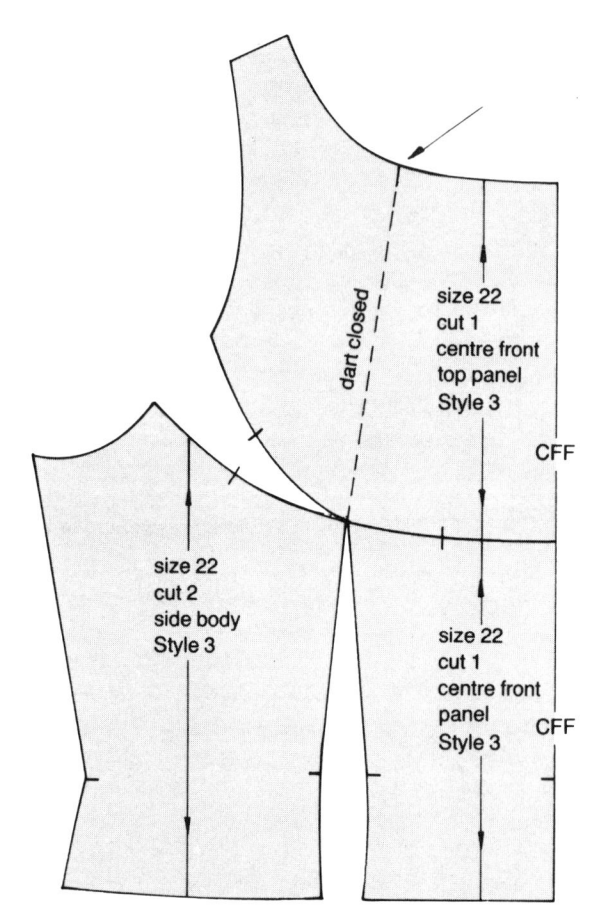

Figure 119 Stage 4 – trace-off largest size and close out unwanted darts and add seam allowances

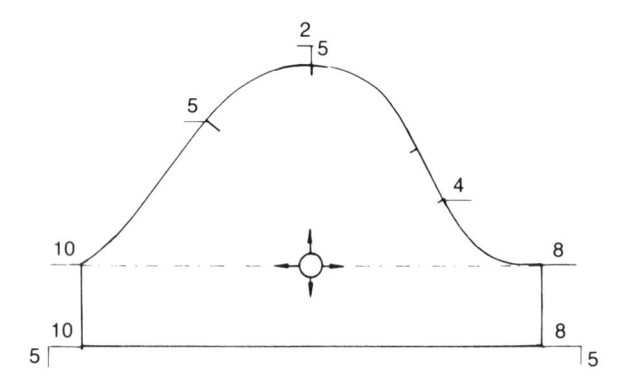

Figure 120 Sleeve grade suitable for two- and three-dimensional grade

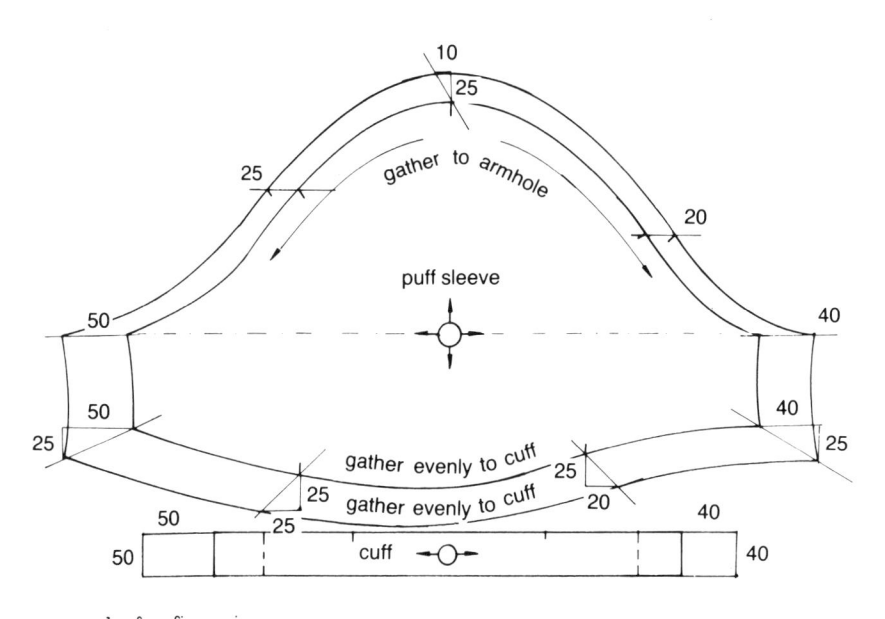

Figure 121 Sleeve grade for five sizes

STYLE GRADES 1 TO 33

GRADING A PATTERN WITH SEAM ALLOWANCES ADDED – GENERAL NOTES

There are many techniques of producing flat patterns suitable for industrial use. This book, therefore, has had to make some general assumptions about the most popular and well established methods in order that we may clearly present the selected grading examples. Figure 122 shows diagrammatically two ways of grading:

1. Direct from the style draft
2. From the production pattern

We assume that in method 1 the draft will probably be *without seam allowances*, and in method 2 *the production pattern will definitely have seam allowances added*, although sometimes some seam allowances may have been added to the draft. Most styles in this book are based on method 1, i.e., without seam allowances. This is because in book form it is easier to illustrate this clearly.

It is recognized that grading a pattern with seam allowances added is essential, especially if the set of grades is required in a hurry. Therefore, a method of accomplishing this is described below. Style 3 has been chosen as it has vertical and horizontal seamlines and is thus an ideal example to illustrate the principles of grading from seam allowances.

METHOD

There are two types of seamlines.

Figure 123 shows seamlines on each basic block section, which join it to another basic block section, for example, side, shoulder, armhole, neck, waist. These seamlines may have seam allowances added.

Figure 124 shows seamlines which are introduced into the basic block section for styling purposes. These are either decorative or suppression seamlines or a combination of both. Seam allowances are added to these seamlines after tracing-off from a draft.

When draft grading a pattern such as Figure 124 the aim is to eliminate the inner seam allowances so that the *finished seamline can be drawn on to the draft* and then graded in the normal way.

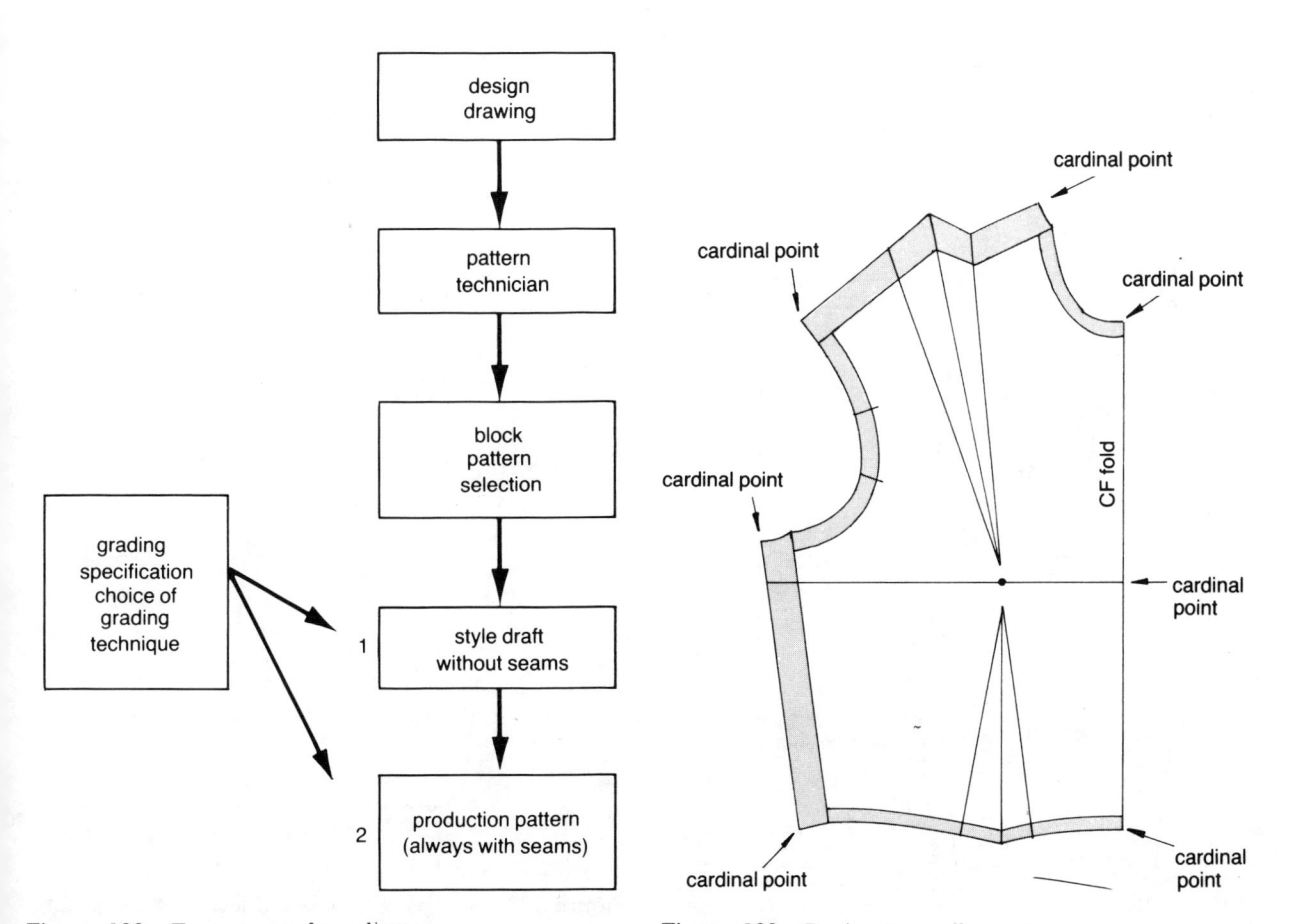

Figure 122 Two ways of grading

Figure 123 Basic seam allowances

158 WOMEN'S STYLE GRADING

The basic block seam allowances in Figure 123 provide the cardinal points and not the finished seamlines. Grading will then proceed as in all the other examples in this book. The only difference is that only seam allowances need to be added to the inner seamlines, thereby greatly speeding up the operation.

STYLE 3 WITH SEAM ALLOWANCES ADDED

METHOD

1. Study the pattern and mark in all the finished seamlines and basic construction lines (see Figure 124).
2. Lay the pattern back on to the draft, repositioning the darts back into their original sites by drawing a centre front line and a bust line at right angles to it (see Figure 125).

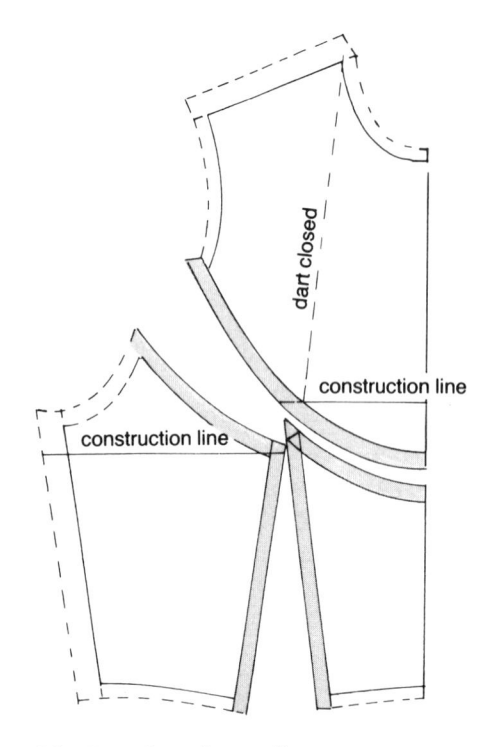

Figure 124 Introduced seamlines

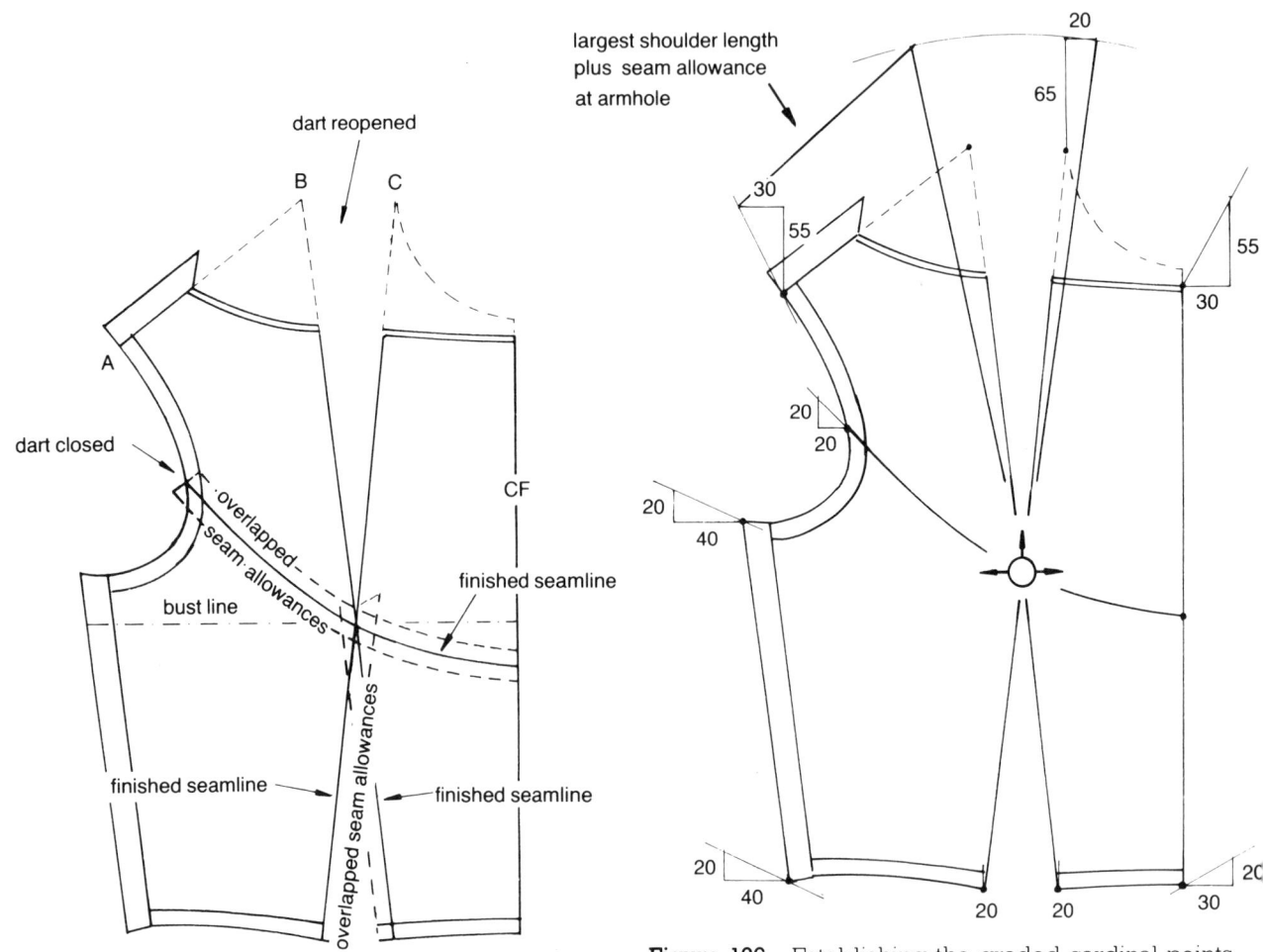

Figure 125 Showing overlap of inner seam allowances

Figure 126 Establishing the graded cardinal points and suppressions

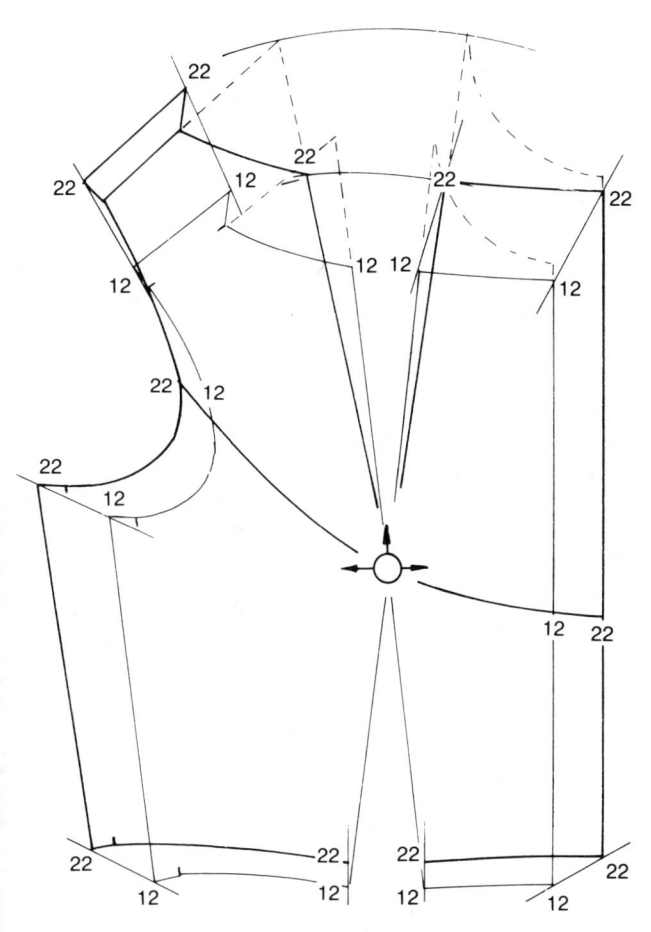

Figure 127 Illustrating sizes 12 and 22

Note: It is recommended that the original block pattern is drawn on to the draft and then the production pattern is superimposed on to it as in Figure 125.

3 Erase the overlapping seam allowances to leave the finished seamlines (Figure 126).

Commence the grade using the cardinal points indicated on the diagram.

Establish the largest size and the largest suppression (see previous examples). Note that the shoulder length grade and suppression quantities are calculated from the points marked A–B–C. See Figure 125. When applying shoulder and seam allowances use the finished size 12 pattern to draw outlines and seam ends.

To grade this neckline see Style 2.

Figure 127 illustrates the size 22 and size 12 patterns. Divide up the required number of intermediate sizes as in previous examples. Add seam allowances to the shoulder seam. Spike-off the required sizes and add seam allowances to the inner seamlines. Repeat this procedure with every pattern section that has inner styled seams.

STYLE 4

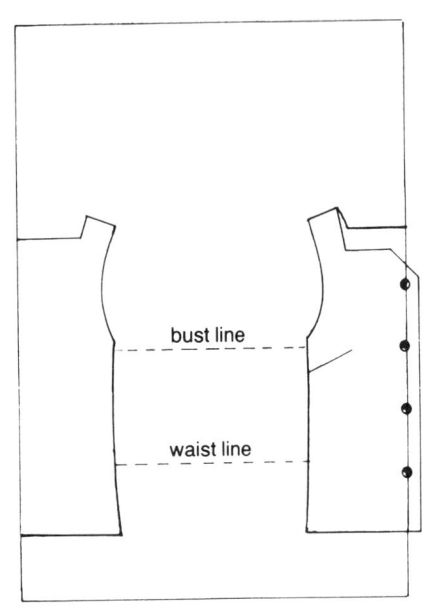

Figure 128 Style 4 – sleeveless box blouse with square neck

GRADING SPECIFICATION			
1	Size chart	Table 13	
2	Size range	10·12·14·16·18	
3	Height/girth/length	Height and girth increases all sizes	
4	Proportioning		
5	Type of grade	3 dim. N.S.B.P.	
6	Zero points front	Static bust point/ waist moving	
7	Zero point back	Centre waist dart	
8	Zero point sleeve	nil	
9	Zero point front skirt	nil	
10	Zero point back skirt	nil	
11	Category of fit	Loose	
Comments			
Size limited to one down and three up due to market requirements			

SLEEVELESS BOX BLOUSE WITH SQUARE NECK

STAGE 1 Style evaluation
This blouse (Figure 128) is box fitting and has a square neckline with a 'vee' at centre front. The three-dimensional draft system is recommended for this style.

Zero point
This zero enables the waist line to move up to the bust point and is the most suitable for the front blouse as it allows the front dart to remain virtually static. The back blouse is graded from the centre of the back waist dart.

STAGES 2 AND 3 Draft and graded cardinal points and largest outlines
Calculate the number of sizes required (Figure 130); in this case three up and one down, and multiply the quantities shown in Figure 129 by three. Mark the patterns on to a draft, returning the bust dart back to its block position. Calculate the increments for three sizes and complete the size 18 outline by grading from all cardinal points.

THE NECKLINE
The first step in grading this type of neckline is to establish the shoulder angle. This will depend on front and back suppressions. Once they have been established, proceed to plan the neckline grade.

Method
1. Grade the blade dart and bust dart and draw in the shoulder angles. Note that the back neckline can either be raised according to the back neck grade (this will maintain the proportion of the size 12) or alternatively the size 12 neckline can be left for all sizes. (This involves a lowering of the largest neckline).
2. Grade from A to B. For a size 18 neckline use the same grade as the nape. Mark point C parallel to the neckline.

STYLE GRADES 1 TO 33   161

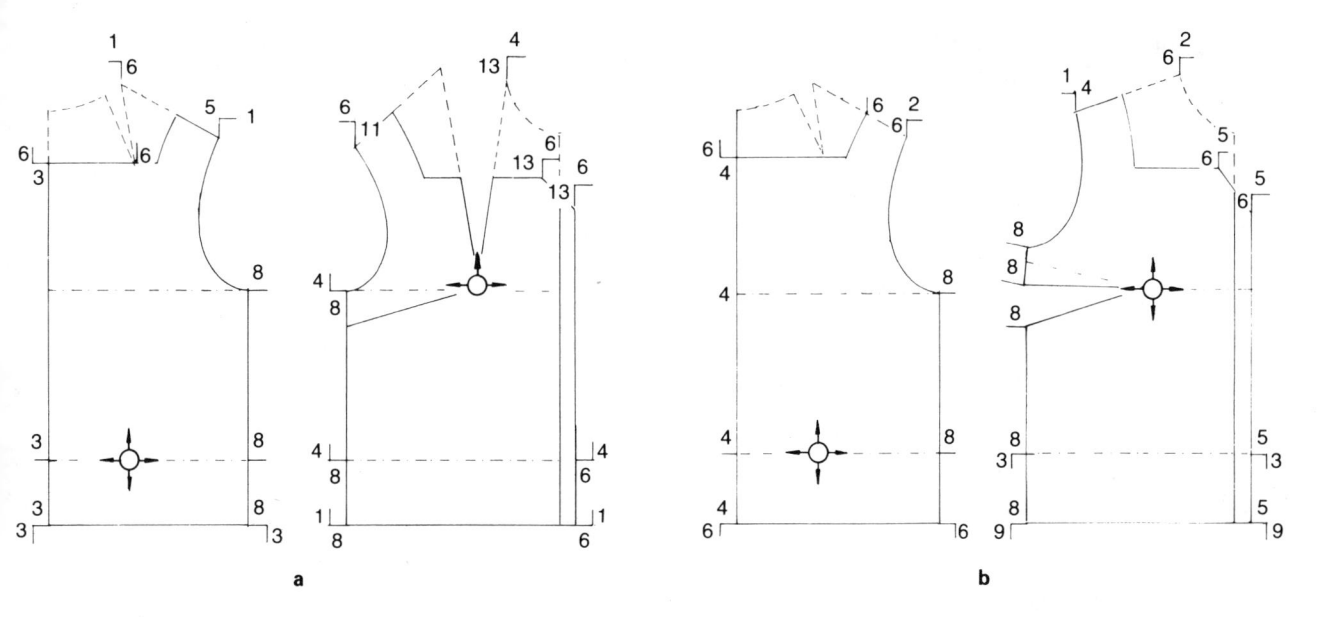

Figure 129 (a) Three-dimensional increments for one size only
(b) Two-dimensional increments suitable for a multi-track grade

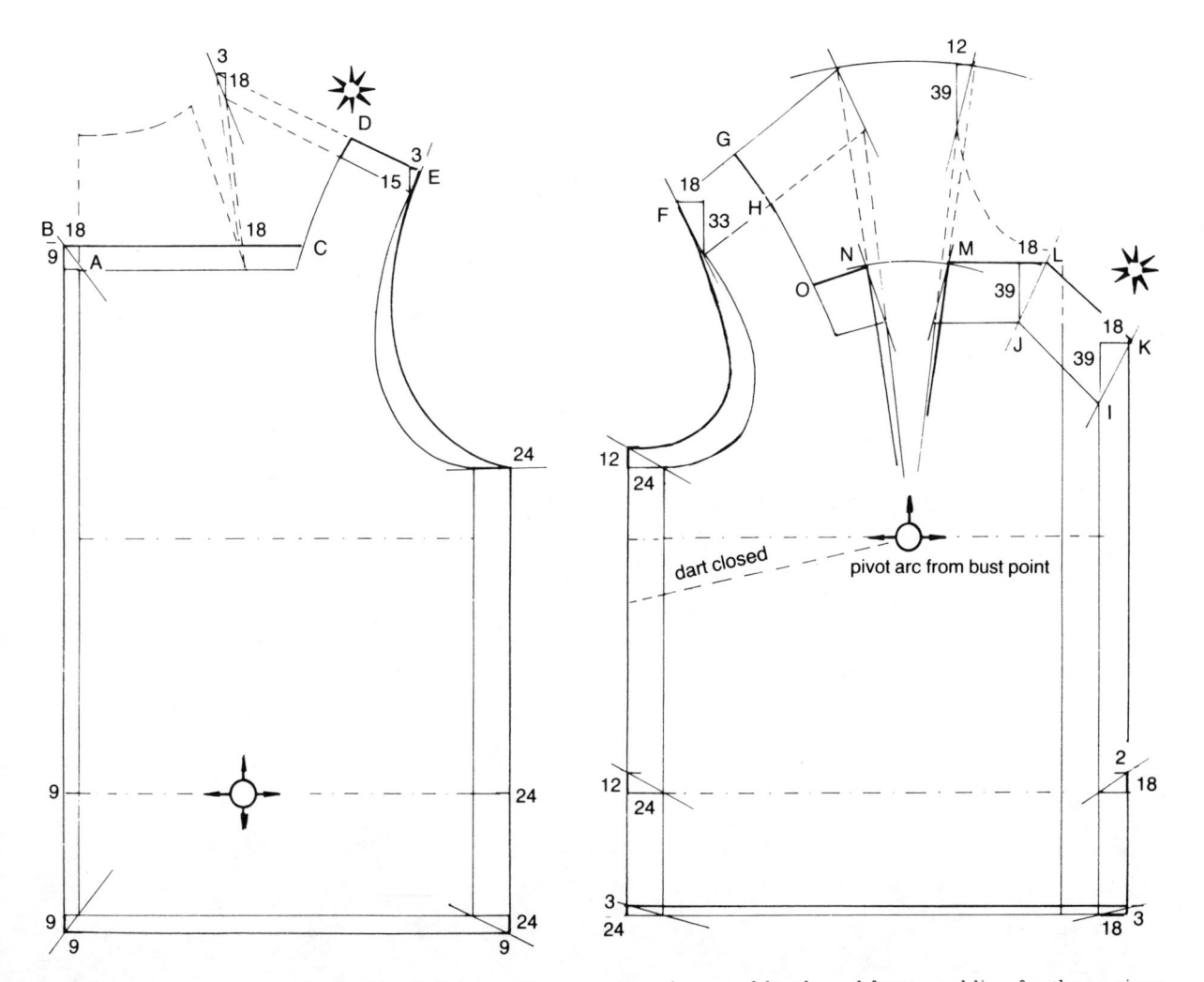

Figure 130 Stage 3 – completing the largest outline, suppressions and back and front neckline for three sizes

3. Continue C through to D.
4. Measure D–E and apply to the front shoulder, F–G.
5. Mark line G–H.
6. Mark points I–J. Grade these points according to front neck grade.
7. Mark points K–L–M.
8. Pivot arc from the bust point to establish N.
9. Connect N–O.
10. Line O–H–G = front neckline for all sizes.

Divide up all the connecting lines for intermediate sizes.

STAGE 4 Spiking-off
Spike-off the required sizes and add seam allowances.

STAGE 5 Facings
Grade facings as in previous examples.

STYLE 5

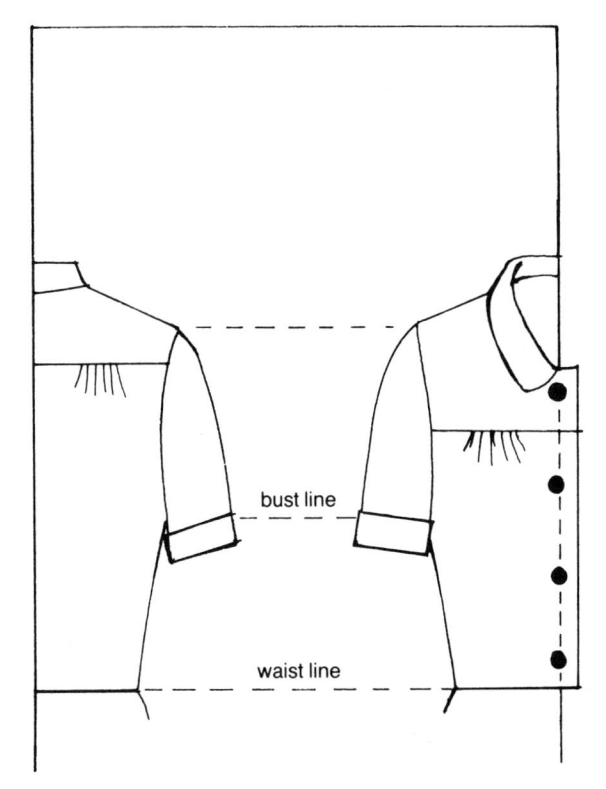

Figure 131 Style 5 – bodice with yoke, gathers and collar with slight stand

	GRADING SPECIFICATION	
1	Size chart	Table 13
2	Size range	10·12·14·16·18·20·22
3	Height/girth/length	Height and girth
4	Proportioning	Yoke 0.3 per size
5	Type of grade	3 dim. Static bust point
6	Zero points front	Centre yoke
7	Zero point back	Centre yoke
8	Zero point sleeve	Centre bicep line
9	Zero point front skirt	nil
10	Zero point back skirt	nil
11	Category of fit	Semi-fitting
Comments	This zero is calculated by using a seamline as the zero	

BODICE

STAGE 1 Evaluation of style and choice of technique and zero points

This style (Figure 131) has two areas of interest; the yokes at back and front and the laid-on collar.

The back and front yokes

1. Figure 132a and b shows that the style is graded from a zero point sited midway on the horizontal yoke line. The reason for choosing these zero points is that it enables the yoke line to remain static.
2. As the dart is manipulated into gathers it is sufficient to leave the bust point static.

Proportions

The depth of the yokes can be increased or left constant throughout the size range. This is a style decision. In this example the back and front yokes are increased by 0.3 cm per size.

The collar width, in this case, will be retained throughout the size range, although this is variable.

STAGE 2 Draft and graded cardinal points

Figure 132b shows the two-dimensional grade and the finished pattern shapes. To grade the front bodice three-dimensionally (Figure 132a) return the suppressions to their original block sites (see Figure 133). It should be noted that the back blade dart is manipulated into the back yoke seamline.

STAGE 3 Completing the largest outline

Complete the largest outline (see Figure 133) and the front suppression by describing an arc from the lowest bust point, A (Figure 134). For the method see previous examples.

In order to ensure a straight yoke line when the bust suppression is closed and to compensate

164　　　　　　　　　　　　　　　　　　　　　　　　　　　　　　　　　　　　　WOMEN'S STYLE GRADING

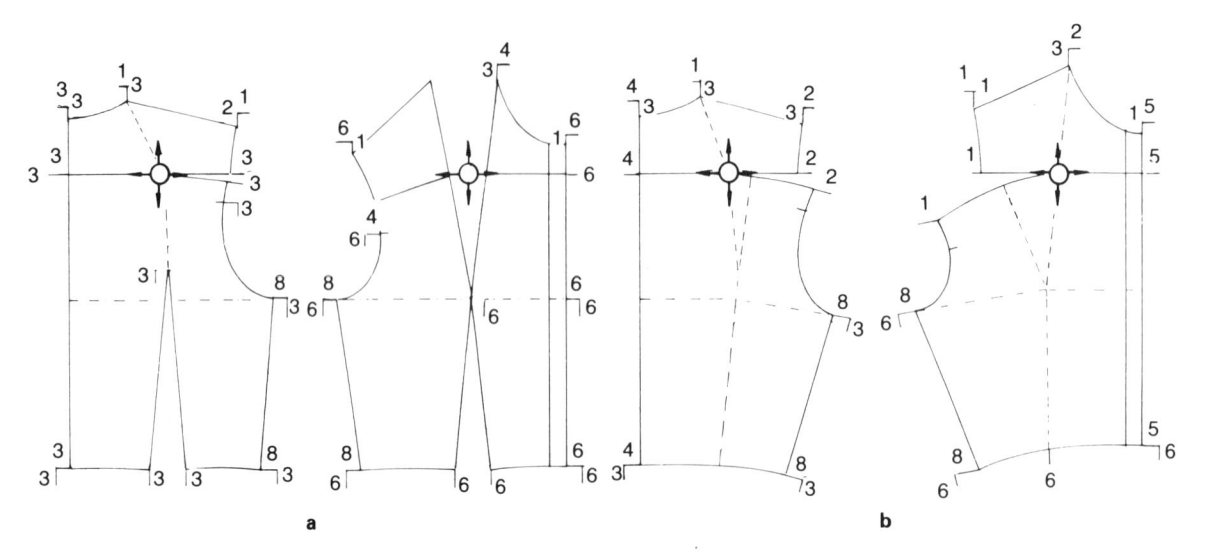

Figure 132 (a) Three-dimensional grade quantities for one size
(b) Two-dimensional quantities suitable for a multi-track grade

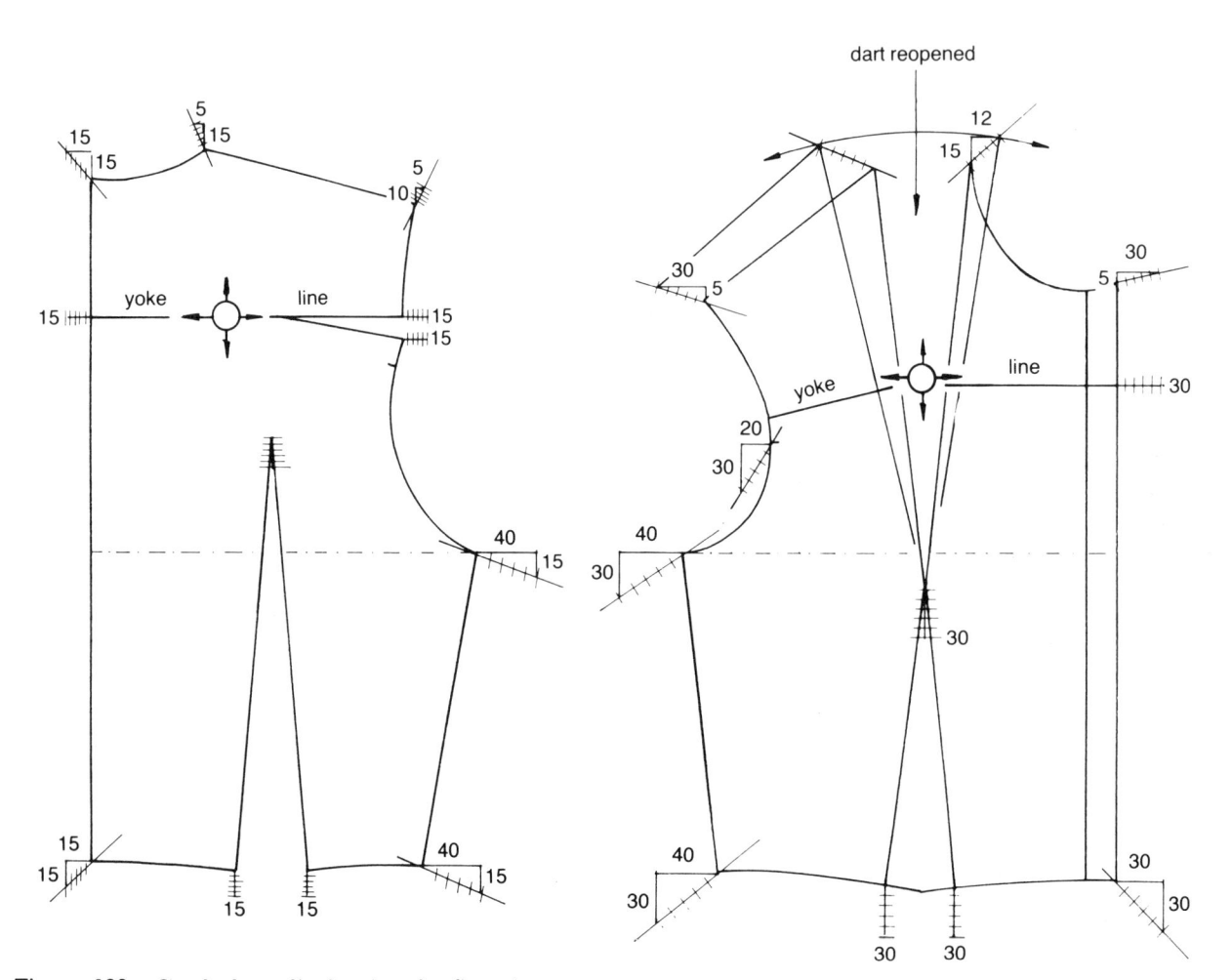

Figure 133 Graded cardinal points for five sizes

STYLE GRADES 1 TO 33

the side yoke line marked B–C–D (size 22) use the technique shown in Chapter 11. Divide up line C–D for the intermediate sizes as shown in Figure 134.

STAGE 4 Tracing-off
Trace-off the required sizes, close up unwanted darts and add seam allowances. Figure 135 shows the size 22 traced-off and the darts manipulated into the gathering areas.

THE COLLAR

Proportion
The proportion of this collar can either be altered, i.e., increased per size, or the same width of collar may be left throughout the size range. For this example the width of collar will not be altered. This will automatically adjust the proportion, i.e., it will provide a narrower collar on the larger sizes. The zero is as indicated in Figure 138.

Grading
When selecting a method for grading the collar, evaluate the collar shape and decide whether it is a flat collar, i.e., it lays exactly on to the draft bodice neckline (as in Figure 136), or whether it has had some stand introduced and will therefore not lie precisely on to the draft bodice neckline as in Figure 137. The flat collar can be graded on to the draft using the same grade angles as the neckline (see Style 8). The stand collar can be graded away from the neck on a separate draft (see Figure 138a, b and c).

Method
Calculate the front and back neck increases from the Style 5 grading specification apply them as in Figure 138a. The main point is to blend the graded front neck point into the leaf edge (see Figure 138b). To increase the collar width, decide on the increase and apply it as in Figure 138c.

SLEEVE GRADE
To grade the sleeve see Style 1.

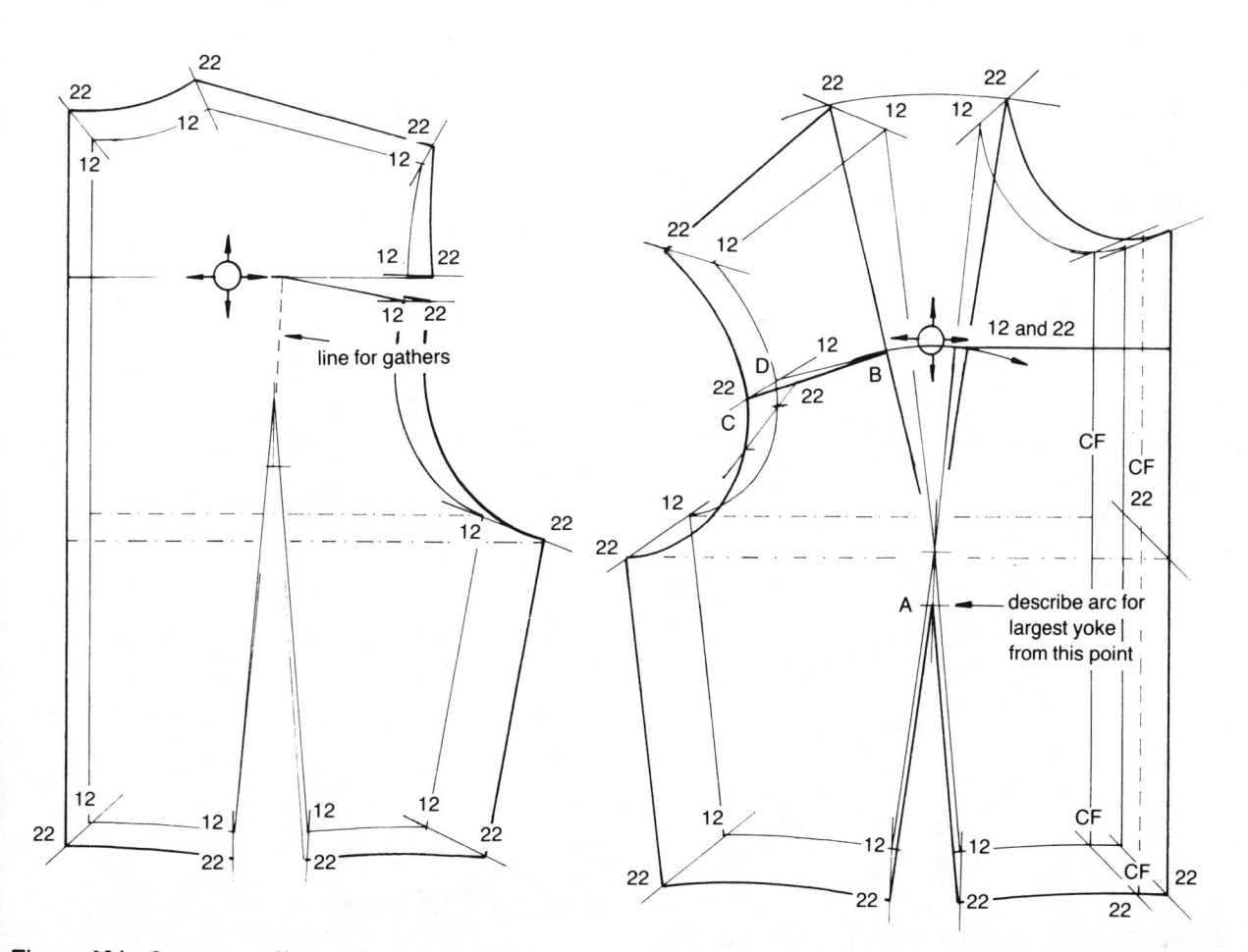

Figure 134 Largest outline and yoke continuation

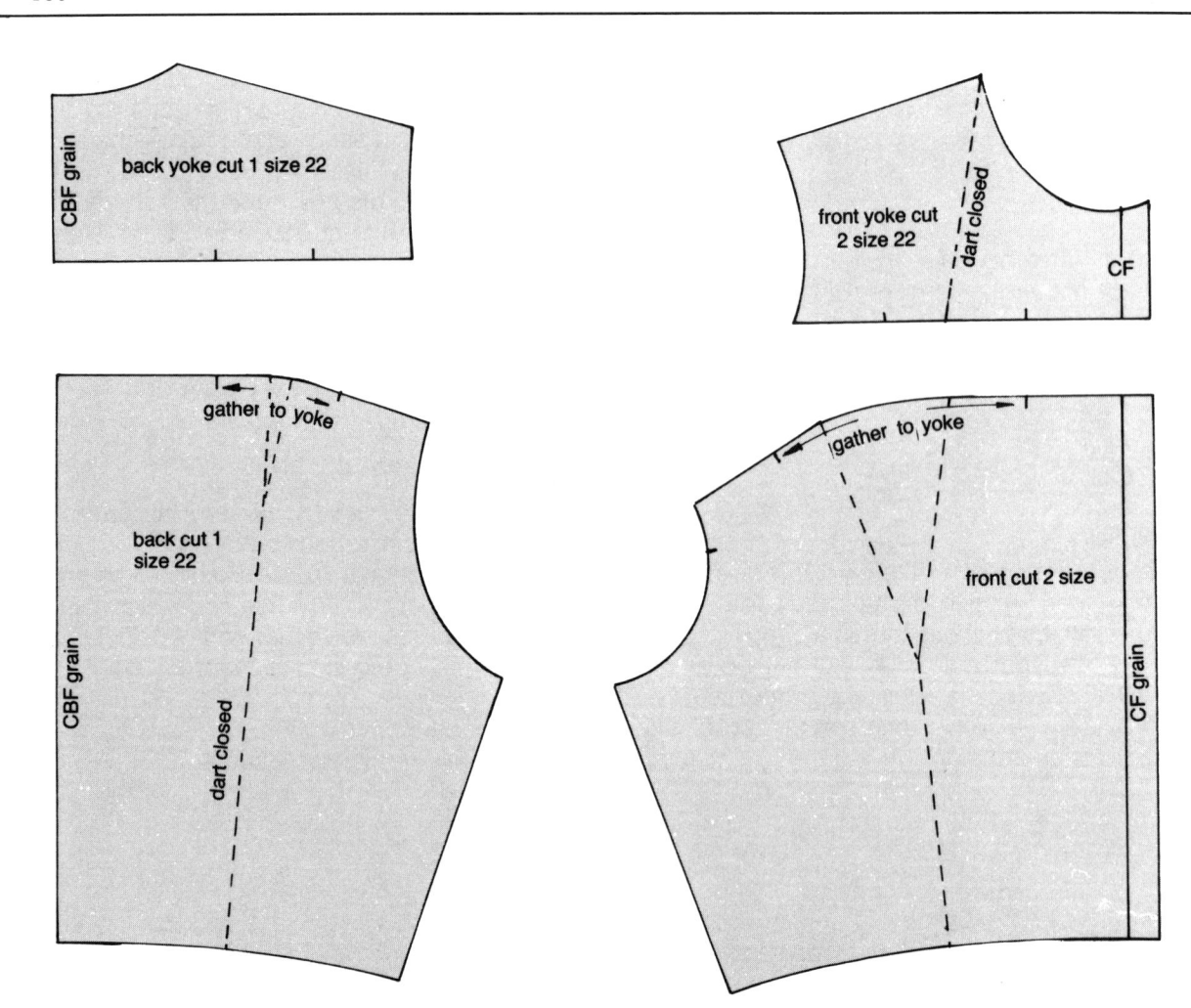

Figure 135 Traced-off pattern shapes for size 12

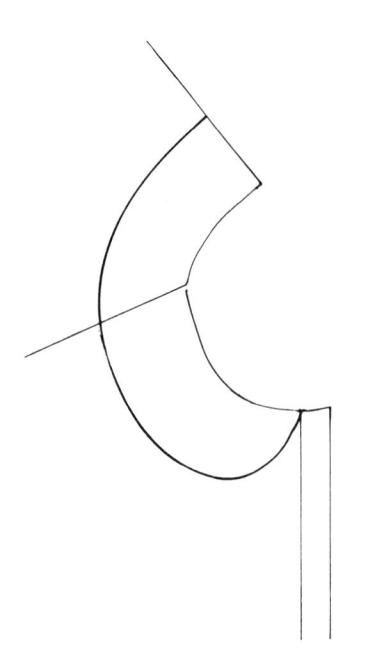

Figure 136 Flat collar developed directly on to the draft

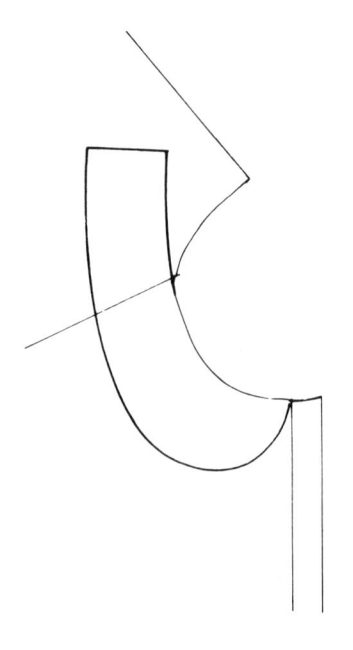

Figure 137 Collar with same stand. The collar neckline has been adjusted and straightened to introduce stand and fall

STYLE GRADES 1 TO 33

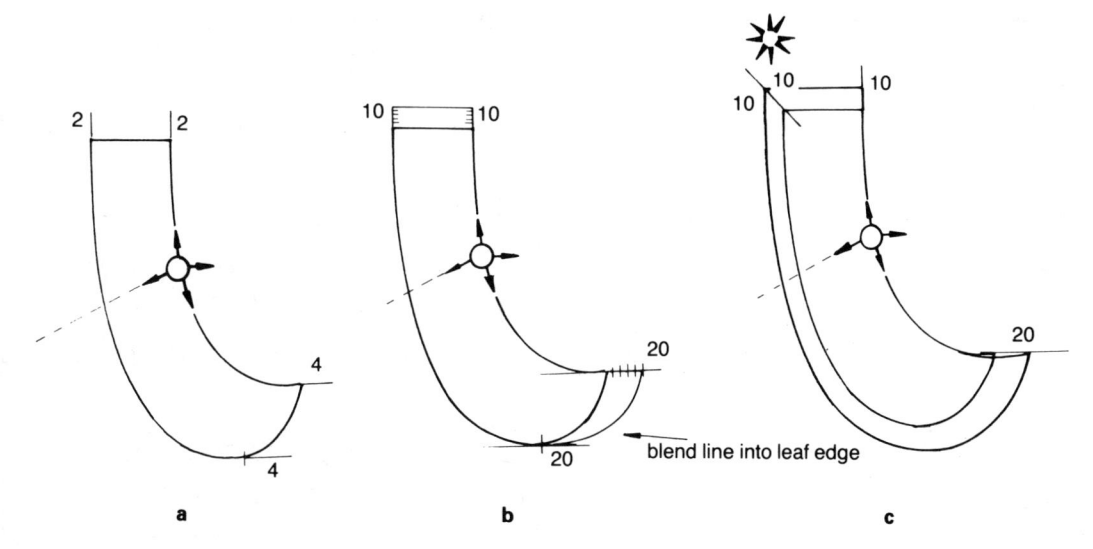

Figure 138 (a) Increments for one size girth only
(b) Increments for five sizes girth only
(c) Girth and width grade optional

STYLE 6

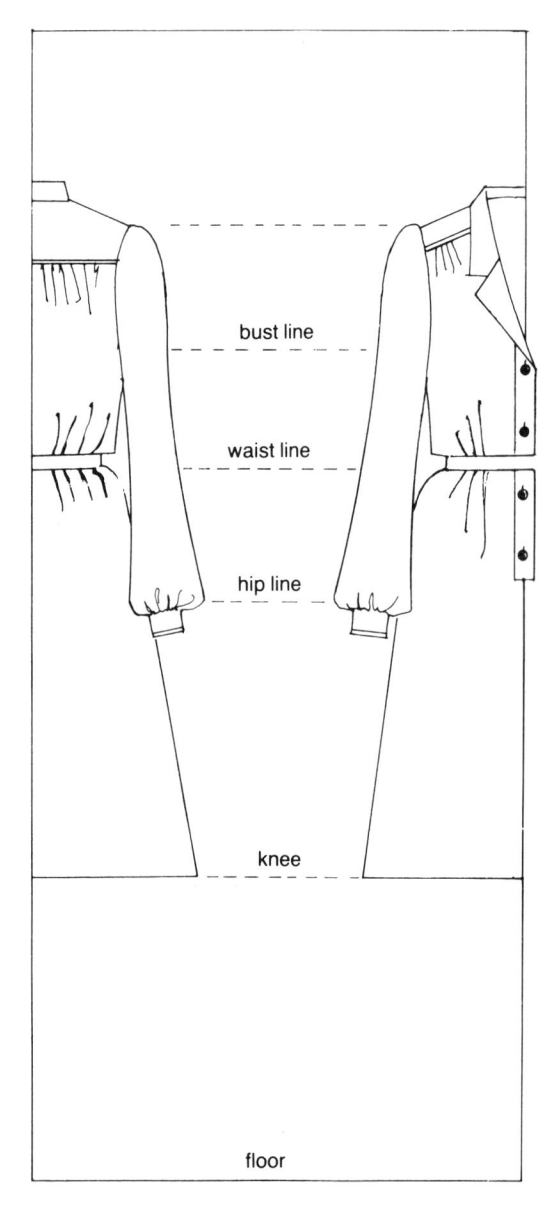

Figure 139 Style 6 – classical shirtwaister, convertible collar and tie belt

GRADING SPECIFICATION

1	Size chart	Table 13
2	Size range	10·12·14·16·18·20·22
3	Height/girth/length	Height/girth/length
4	Proportioning	Yoke increasing 0.6mm
5	Type of grade	3 dim. static bust point
6	Zero points front	Front yoke line
7	Zero point back	Back yoke line
8	Zero point sleeve	Centre bicep
9	Zero point front skirt	nil
10	Zero point back skirt	nil
11	Category of fit	Loose

Comments

Grade based on yoke proportions

CLASSICAL SHIRTWAISTER

This classical shirtwaister (Figure 139) will be graded from the centre of its yoke seam. See Figure 140 for increments. The yoke depth will increase by 0.6 cm per size. The centre front inset band will remain the same size throughout the range, as will the collar.

Figure 140b shows the finished pattern shapes minus seam allowances and the two-dimensional grade increments. There are zero points at the CB and CF bustline.

Return the front gathers into the neck dart and commence grading as in previous exercises (see Figure 141). On completion of the grading, trace-off separate pattern sections and return gathers to gathering positions.

STYLE GRADES 1 TO 33

Note: To establish a straight yoke line on all sizes, use the pivot paper technique described in Chapter 12.

THE SLEEVE (Figure 142)
The sleeve grade is shown in Style 1. Grade as for previous examples.

THE COLLAR (Figure 143)
This collar is based on a straight shape and can, therefore, be graded away from the bodice neckline. Use the increments shown in Figure 143a and b. Figure 143b shows a five size grade which includes a width adjustment of the collar.

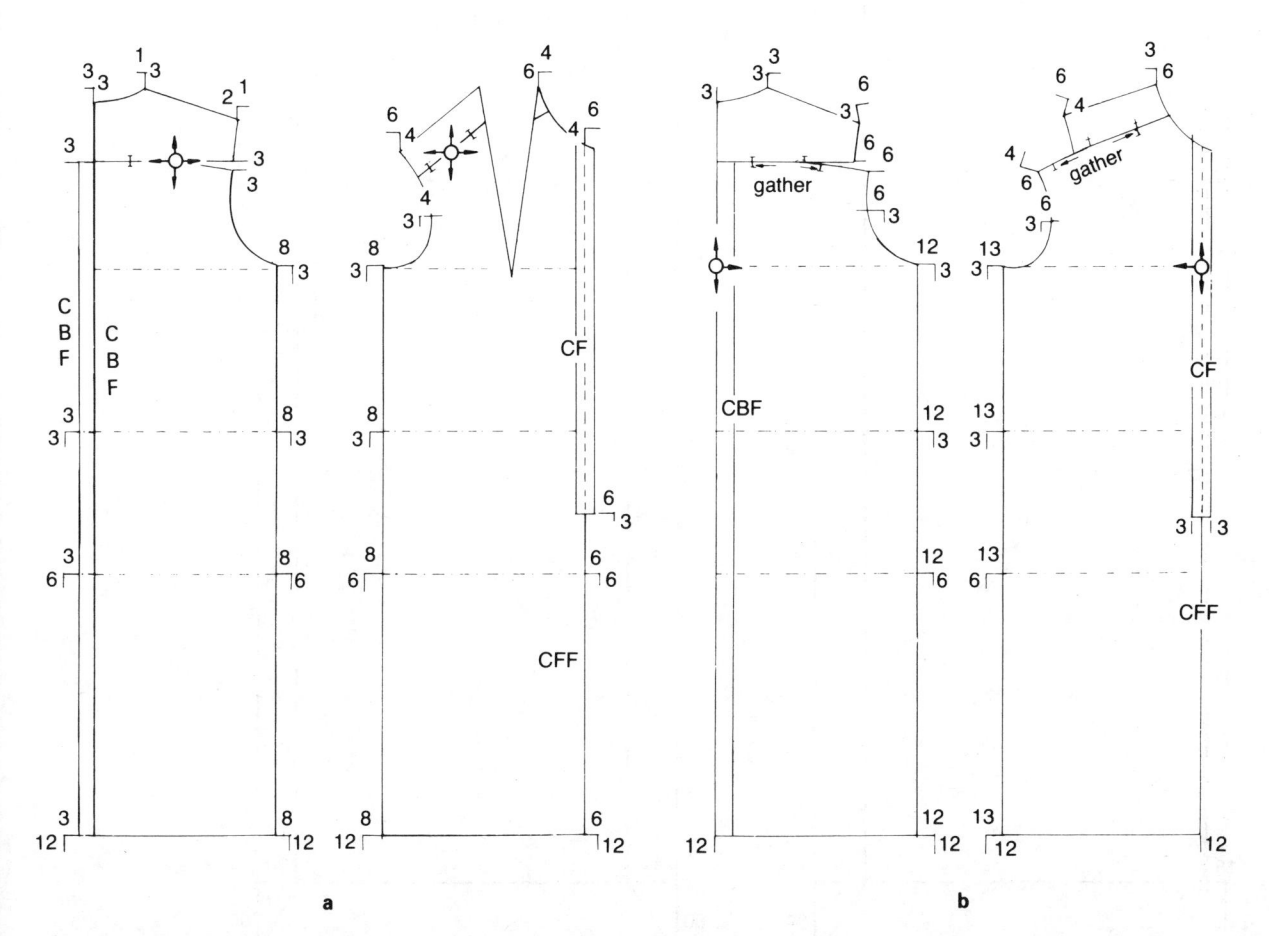

Figure 140 (a) Three-dimensional increments for one size only. The zero is based on yoke proportion. In this example half bodice height grade is positioned above the yoke and half the bodice height grade below the yoke

(b) Two-dimensional increments for one size only. Suitable for multi-track draft or track grading

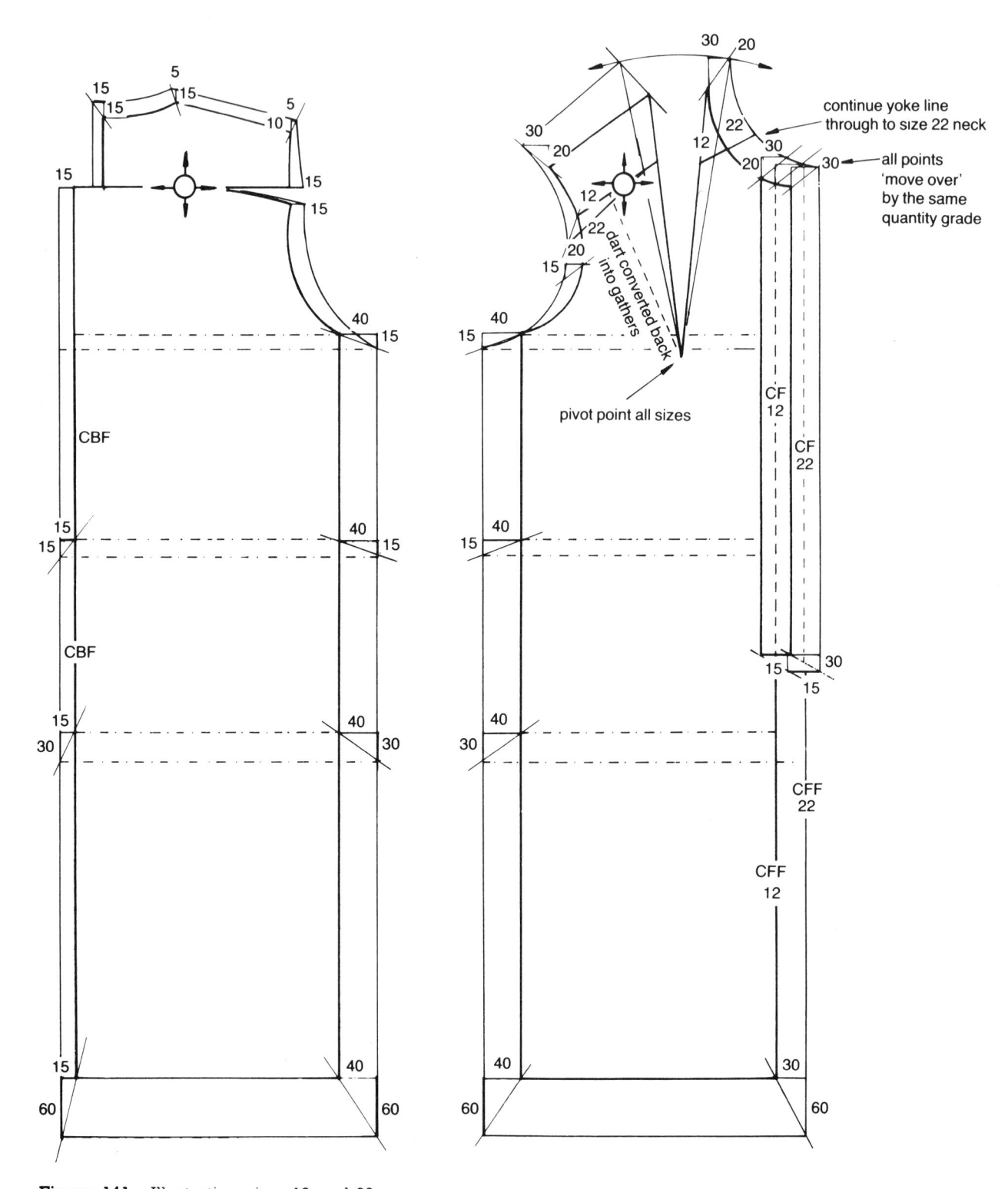

Figure 141 Illustrating sizes 12 and 22

STYLE GRADES 1 TO 33   171

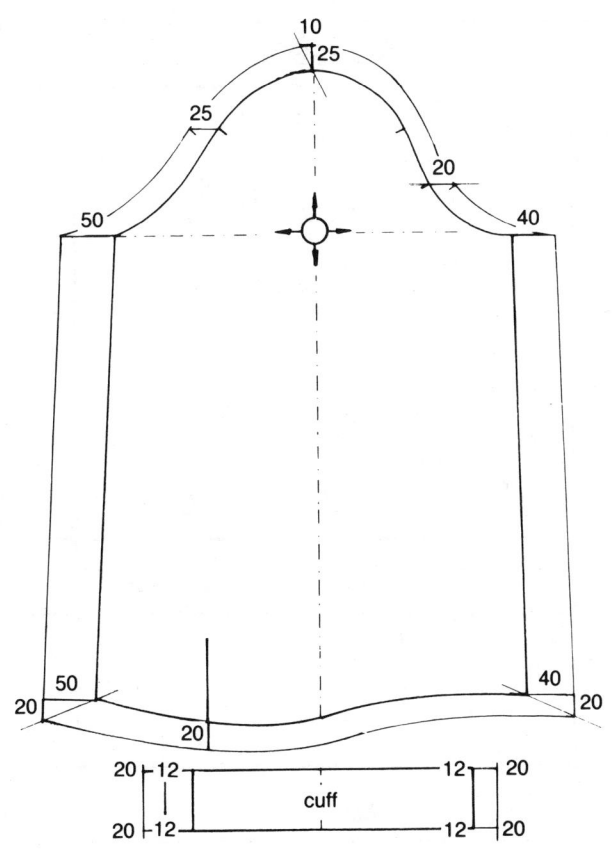

Figure 142 Sleeve grade for five sizes

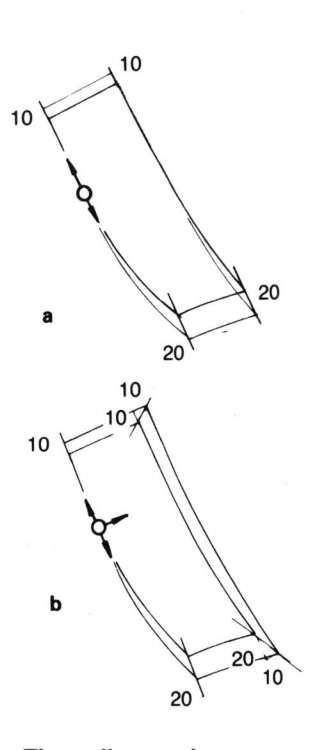

Figure 143 The collar grade
(a) Grade for five sizes – girth only
(b) Grade for five sizes – girth and width

STYLE 7

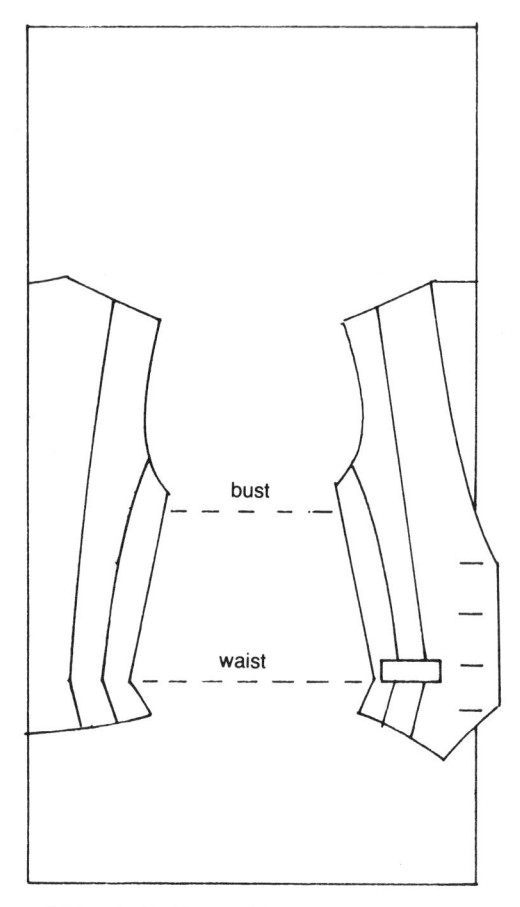

Figure 144 Style 7 – waistcoat

	GRADING SPECIFICATION	
1	Size chart	Table 13
2	Size range	Size 12 plus 3 height sizes = 7.2 cm
3	Height/girth/length	Height only
4	Proportioning	
5	Type of grade	Draft grade
6	Zero points front	Centre waist dart
7	Zero point back	Centre waist dart
8	Zero point sleeve	nil
9	Zero point front skirt	nil
10	Zero point back skirt	nil
11	Category of fit	Tight
Comments		
This style can also be efficiently track graded		

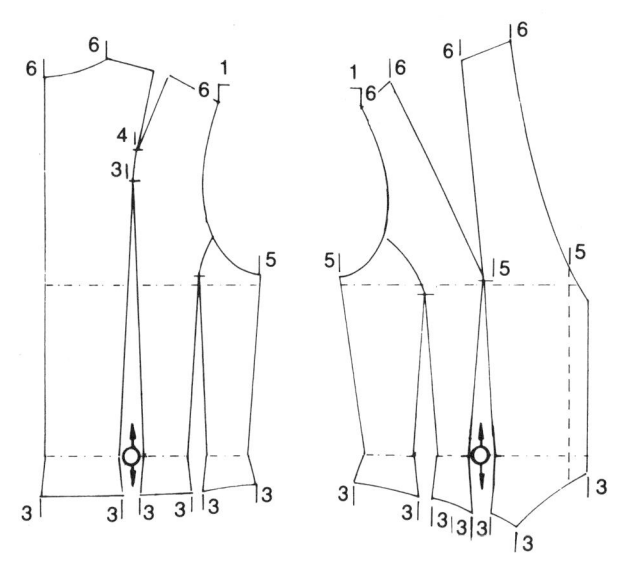

Figure 145 Height only increments

WAISTCOAT

This style (Figure 144) illustrates the technique of grading for height only. These increments represent an overall height grade of 2.4 cm and can be applied to any size pattern. In this case the waistcoat has been increased by 3 × 2.4 cm, equalling an overall height increase of 7.2 cm (see Figure 145). For a further discussion on height only grading, refer to Chapters 2 and 3, the section on *height increments* and Chapter 1 the section on *size chart construction*. Figure 146 shows the completed draft grades.

STYLE GRADES 1 TO 33   173

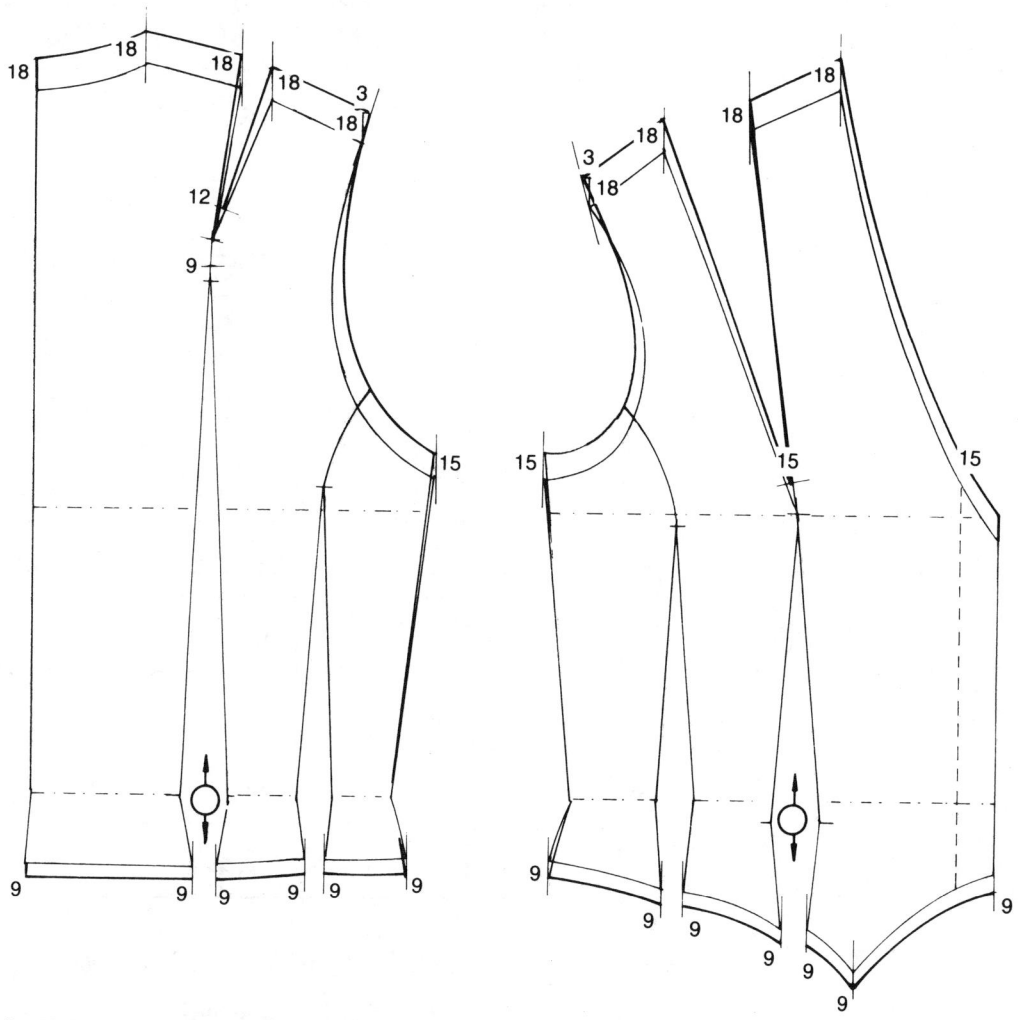

Figure 146   Height only grade, overall 2.4 cm

STYLE 8

	GRADING SPECIFICATION	
1	Size chart	Table 13
2	Size range	10·12·14·16·18
3	Height/girth/length	Height and girth
4	Proportioning	Increase collar as bodice grade
5	Type of grade	3 dim. N.S.B.P.
6	Zero points front	Centre waist dart
7	Zero point back	Centre waist dart
8	Zero point sleeve	nil
9	Zero point front skirt	nil
10	Zero point back skirt	nil
11	Category of fit	Tight

Comments

NSBP = non static bust point. See text below. Adjust collar width if necessary.

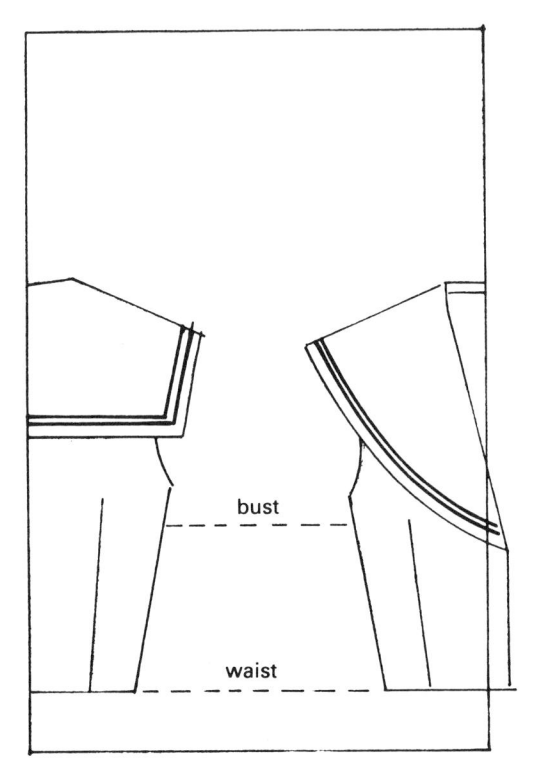

Figure 147 Style 8 – sleeveless blouse with flat sailor collar

SLEEVELESS BLOUSE WITH A FLAT SAILOR COLLAR

This style (Figure 147) has been selected in order to illustrate the grading technique for a flat collar. Figure 149 shows the basic method of creating this type of collar. As it is developed directly on to the bodice block neckline it is important to preserve the relationship between the collar and the bodice, **therefore the collar and bodice must be graded together**. It should also be noted that the back bodice does not have a blade dart. This style has been included because some industrial blocks are developed without blade suppression. The collar width will increase according to the bodice grade, although this is a style option.

METHOD
1. Separate the sailor collar at the shoulder and return the bust suppression back into the neck.
2. Commence grading using Figure 148a for three-dimensional increments, times the number of sizes required; in this case four.
3. Determine the bust suppression at neck by swinging an arc through the front neck point.
4. Spike-off the collar sizes required and rejoin the collar at shoulder (see Figure 149). Transfer the bust dart to the waist.

Note: Check that the 'collar run' at the points where it crosses the front dart is even, and reblend if required.

This collar grade should be adopted for all applied flat collars.

STYLE GRADES 1 TO 33   175

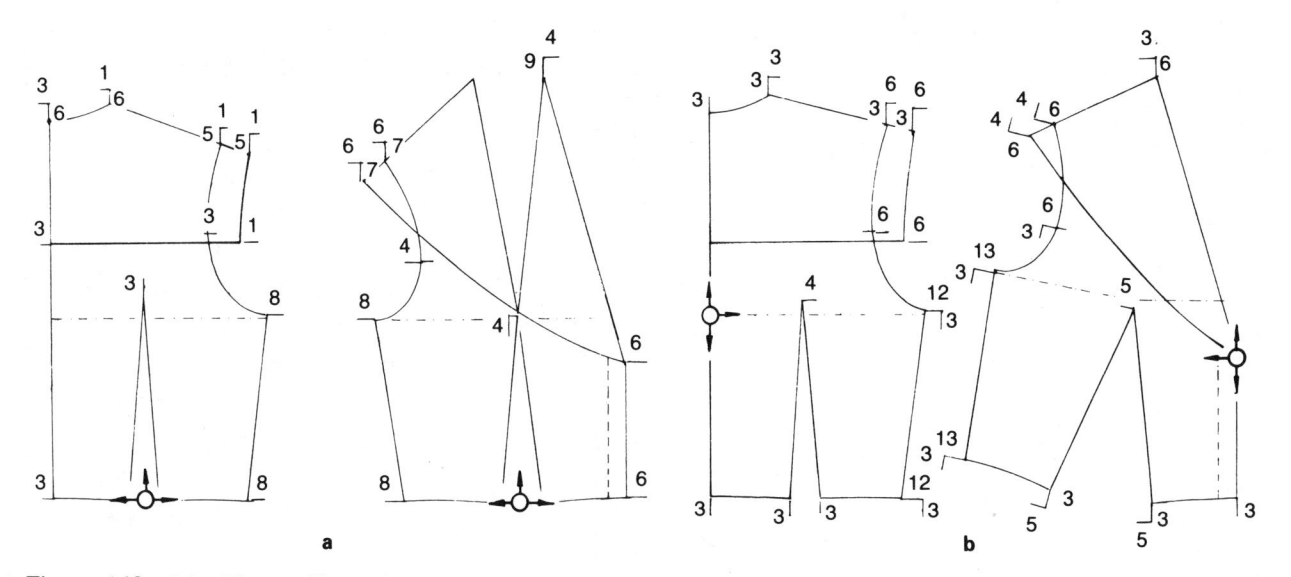

Figure 148 (a) Three-dimensional grade quantities for one size
(b) Two-dimensional grade quantities suitable for track or multi-track draft

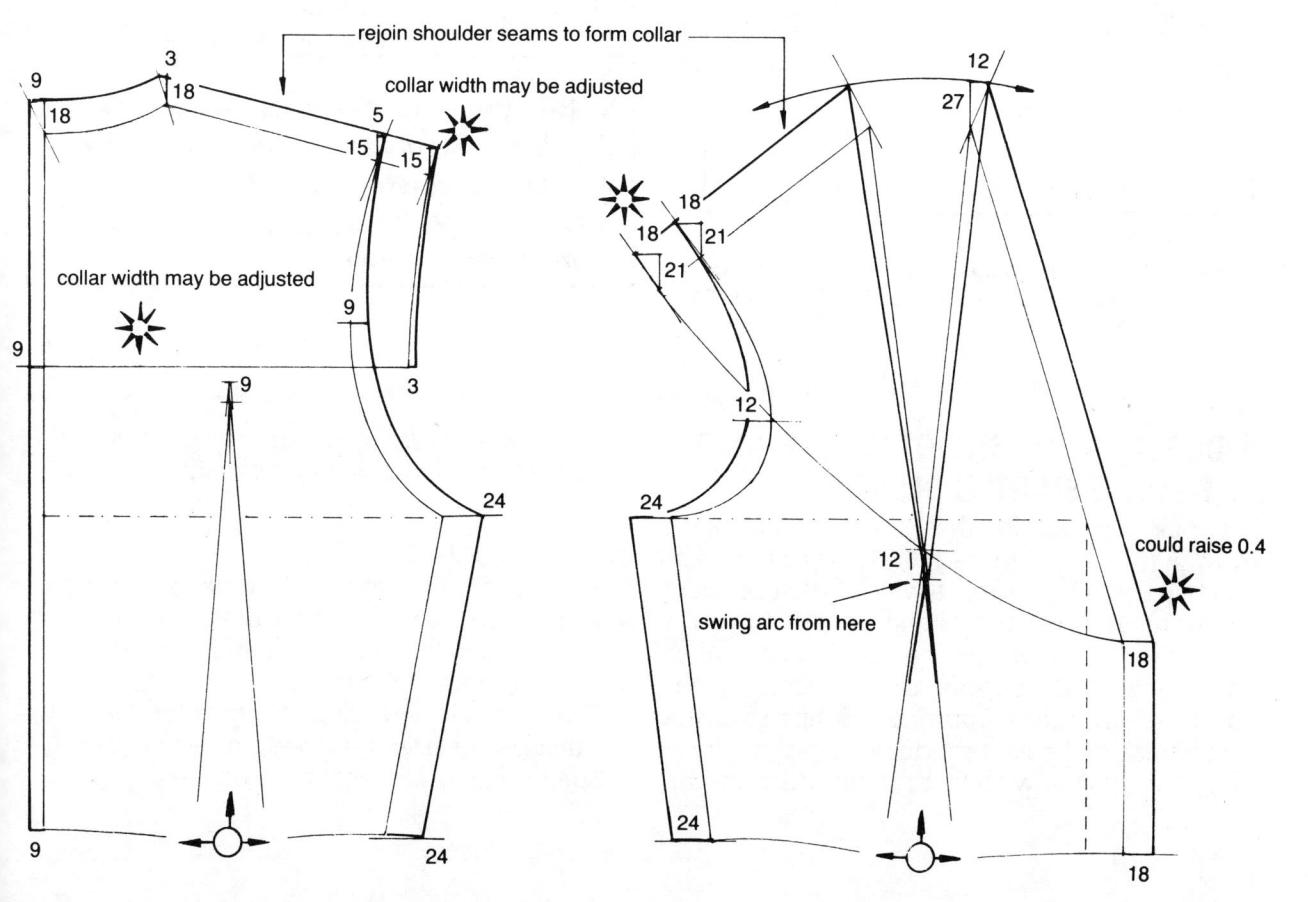

Figure 149 Completed grade for four sizes – 12, 14, 16 and 18

STYLE 9

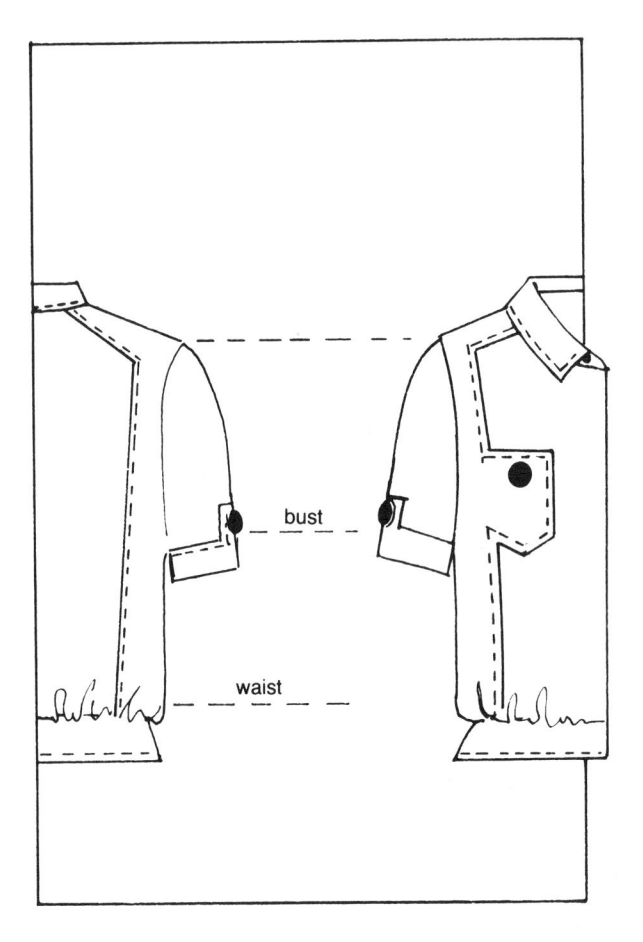

Figure 150 Style 9 – blouson with one-piece shirt collar, short sleeve and patch pockets

	GRADING SPECIFICATION	
1	Size chart	Table 13
2	Size range	10 · 12 · 14 · 16
3	Height/girth/length	Height and girth
4	Proportioning	Collar, constant size
5	Type of grade	2 dim. draft
6	Zero points front	C.F. Waist dart position
7	Zero point back	C.B. Waist dart position
8	Zero point sleeve	Centre bicep line
9	Zero point front skirt	nil
10	Zero point back skirt	nil
11	Category of fit	Loose – from dartless block
Comments		

In this the style the bust suppression has been dispersed and can ∴ be graded 2 dimensionally.
NB only to be used 2 sizes up and one down.

BLOUSON WITH SHORT SLEEVE AND ONE-PIECE SHIRT COLLAR

The bust suppression has been 'manipulated away' in this style (Figure 150). This is fairly common but it entails a practice which is theoretically not lawful. This situation is only acceptable for a very limited range of sizes, i.e., from 10 to 14, after which the bust suppression must be reintroduced, because from size 16 upwards the prominence of the bust produces unsightly dragging. Any blouse without bust suppression can only be two-dimensionally graded over sizes 10, 12 and 14 without undue complications.

STYLE EVALUATION

The shaped yoke and side body are proportionally increased. The pocket remains the same width, as does the collar, cuff and hip band. The zero is sited as in Figure 151.

Grade the blouse multiplying the increments by the number of sizes required; in this case two.

Spike-off and add seam allowances.

STYLE GRADES 1 TO 33   177

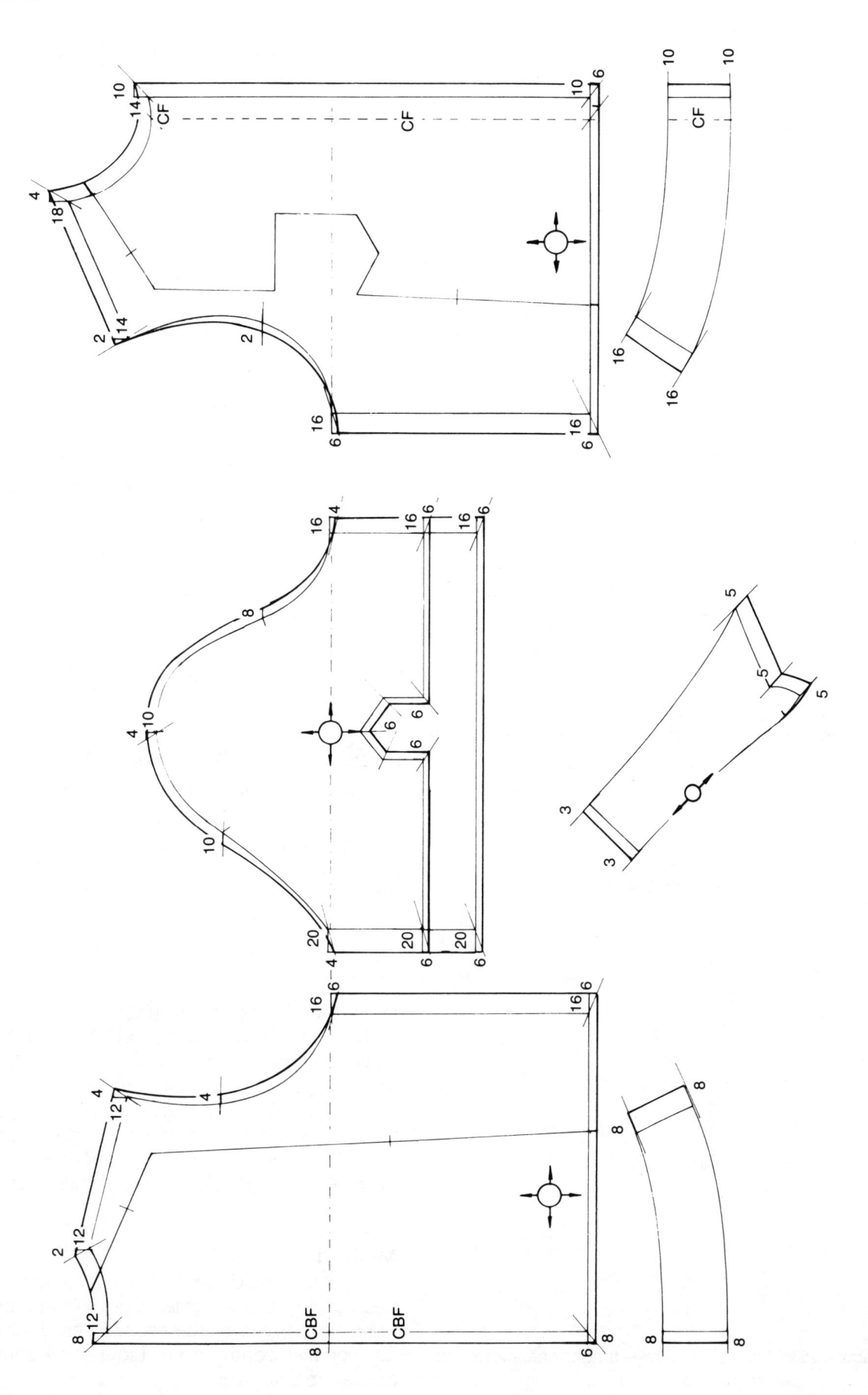

Figure 151 Two-dimensional increments and grade for two sizes up

STYLES 10A & B

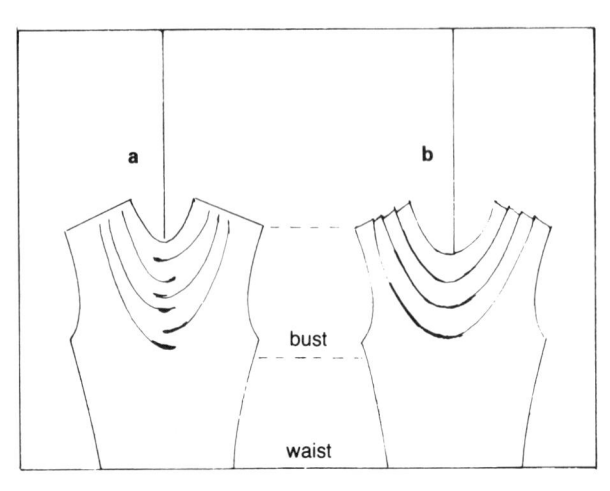

Figure 152 Style 10A – high cowl; Style 10B – pleated cowl

COWLS

These two cowl styles (Figures 152a and b) are dealt with in slightly different ways, but in each case the emphasis is on retaining the line of the drapes. The correct choice of zero is, therefore, essential.

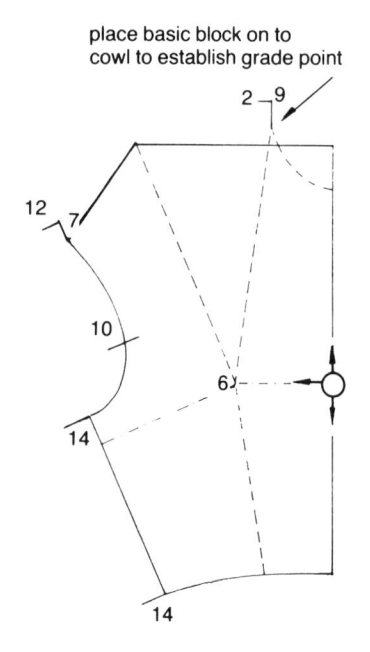

Figure 153 Style 10A – three-dimensional increments for one size

GRADING SPECIFICATION

1	Size chart	Table 13
2	Size range	10·12·14·16·18·20·22
3	Height/girth/length	Height and girth
4	Proportioning	
5	Type of grade	3 dim. static bust point (10A) 2 dim. (10B)
6	Zero points front	C.F. bust line (10A) F. shoulder neck point (10B)
7	Zero point back	nil
8	Zero point sleeve	nil
9	Zero point front skirt	nil
10	Zero point back skirt	nil
11	Category of fit	Tight fitting (10A) Loose fitting (10B)

Comments

<u>Note</u>: The grading specifications for styles 10A and 10B are the same except for 5, 6 and 11, where specifications for each style are given.

THE HIGH COWL (Style 10A)

Figure 152a shows a high cowl. The characteristic fullness has been developed by utilizing the entire front suppression, i.e., the waist and bust darts (see Figure 153). As this style is tight-fitting around the bust area it is necessary to grade suppression into it as is the normal practice in three-dimensional grading, but with a *static bust point*.

Method

The darts should be transferred back into the neck and grade as usual using increments from Figure 153. Spike-off the sizes required. Complete the cowl at centre front. Figure 154 shows the grade for five sizes.

STYLE GRADES 1 TO 33

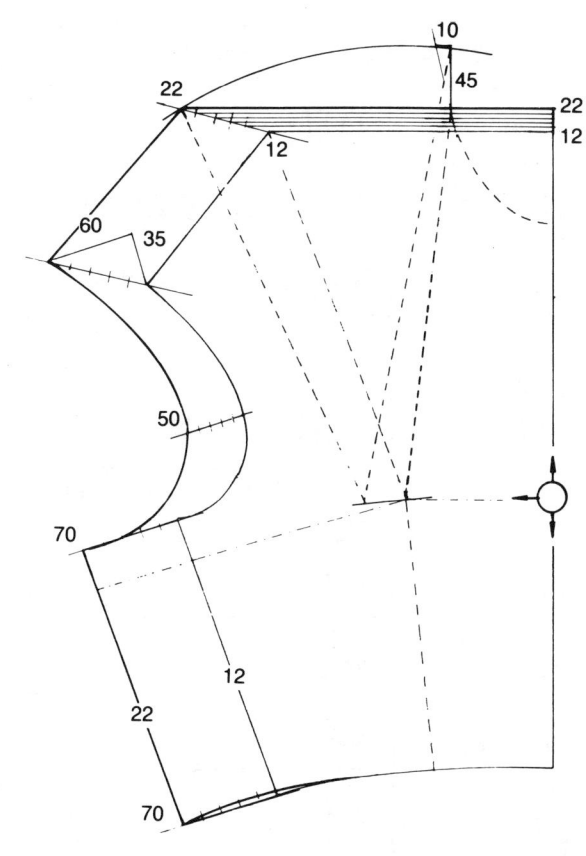

Figure 154 Grade for five sizes up

THE PLEATED COWL (Style 10B)

Figure 152b shows a pleated cowl. A two-dimensional draft or track grade is the most suitable method of grading this style. The zero selected enables the pleated shoulder to remain static (see Figure 156). Figure 155 indicates the appropriate increments.

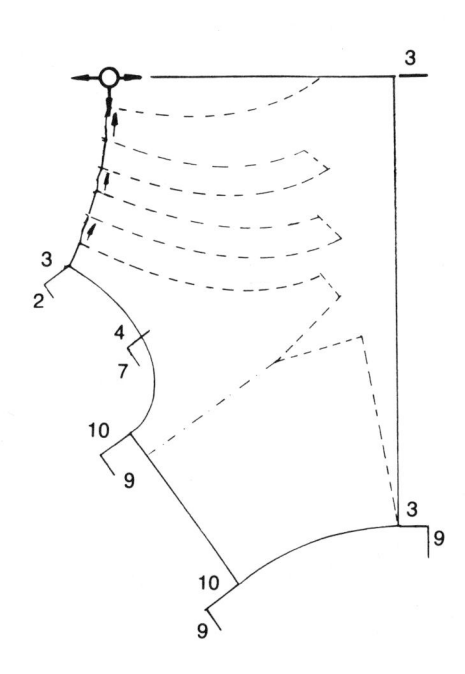

Figure 155 Style 10B – increments for one size

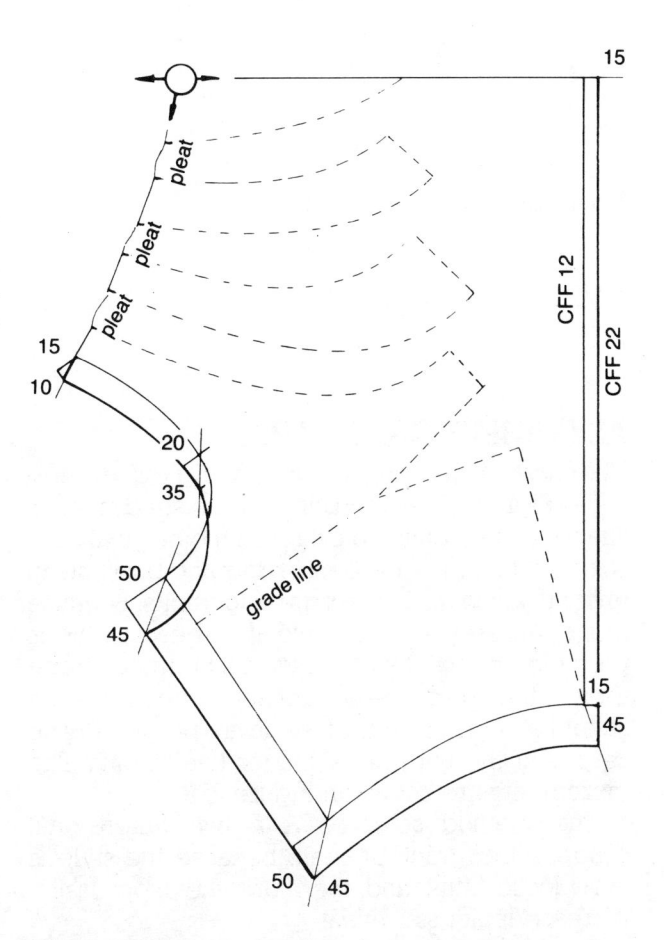

Figure 156 Illustrating five sizes

STYLE 11

GRADING SPECIFICATION		
1	Size chart	Table 13
2	Size range	10·12·14·16·18·20·22
3	Height/girth/length	Height and girth
4	Proportioning	
5	Type of grade	2 dim. draft
6	Zero points front	Left front shoulder neck point
7	Zero point back	nil
8	Zero point sleeve	nil
9	Zero point front skirt	nil
10	Zero point back skirt	nil
11	Category of fit	Loose

Comments: When using a multi-track grade and when grading down from the shoulder the zero is placed at shoulder neck point. Grade quantities are lost at the waist line due to overlapping tracks. In this case 0.2 cm per size on the total front waist. The pattern technician can compensate for this if required.

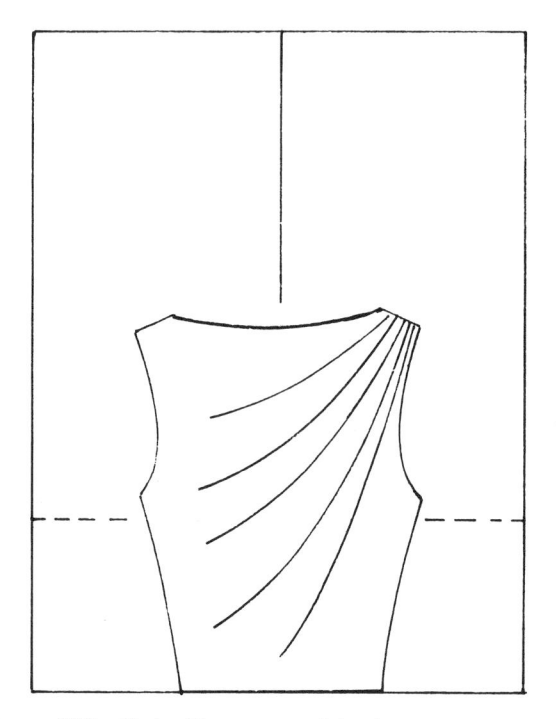

Figure 157 Style 11 – assymetric drape

ASYMMETRICAL DRAPE

The most satisfactory way of grading this draped style (Figure 157) is by using the finished pattern shape. It is essential to establish the original construction lines, i.e., the centre front and bust line, in order to know the correct grading tracks. Because this is an assymetrical style it is best, if this is possible, to establish the zero point in the drape area so that the drape control points, i.e., at the left shoulder, can remain as static as possible. The zero is at the left front shoulder neck point. The increments are shown in Figure 158.

The method selected is a two-dimensional grade, either track or draft, because the style is fairly loose-fitting and, therefore, the suppression increase is not so critical.

Grade the pattern as illustrated in Figure 159.

STYLE GRADES 1 TO 33

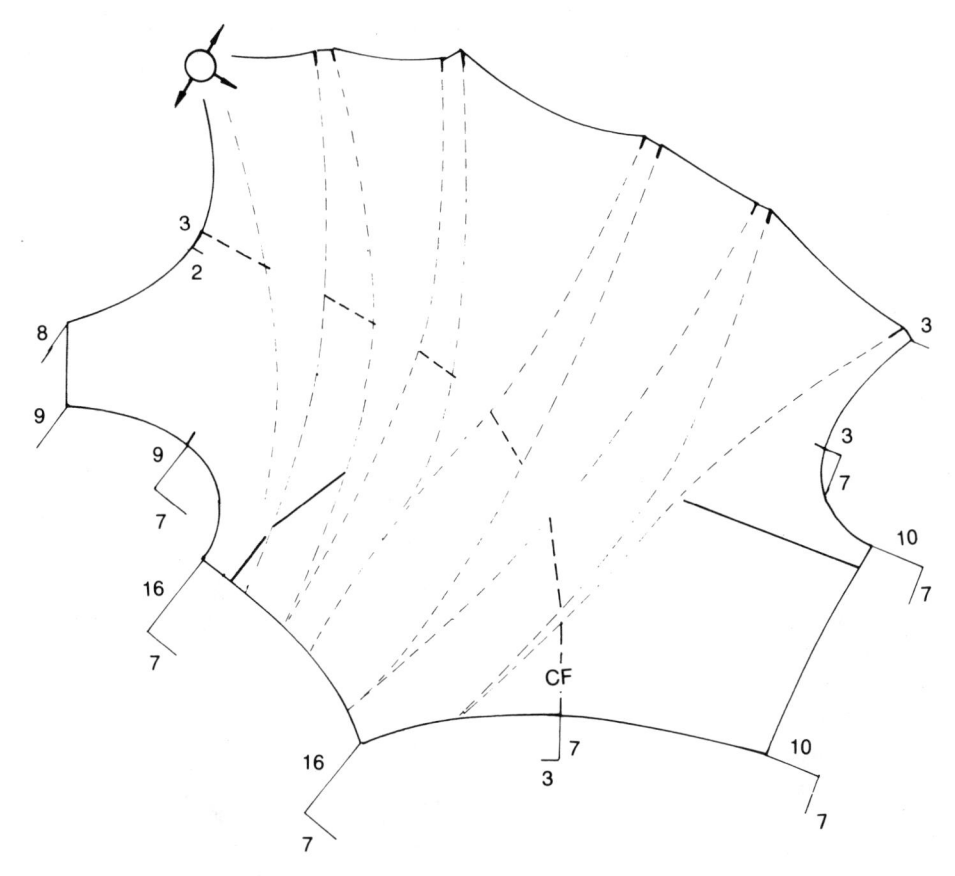

Figure 158 Two-dimensional increments for one size

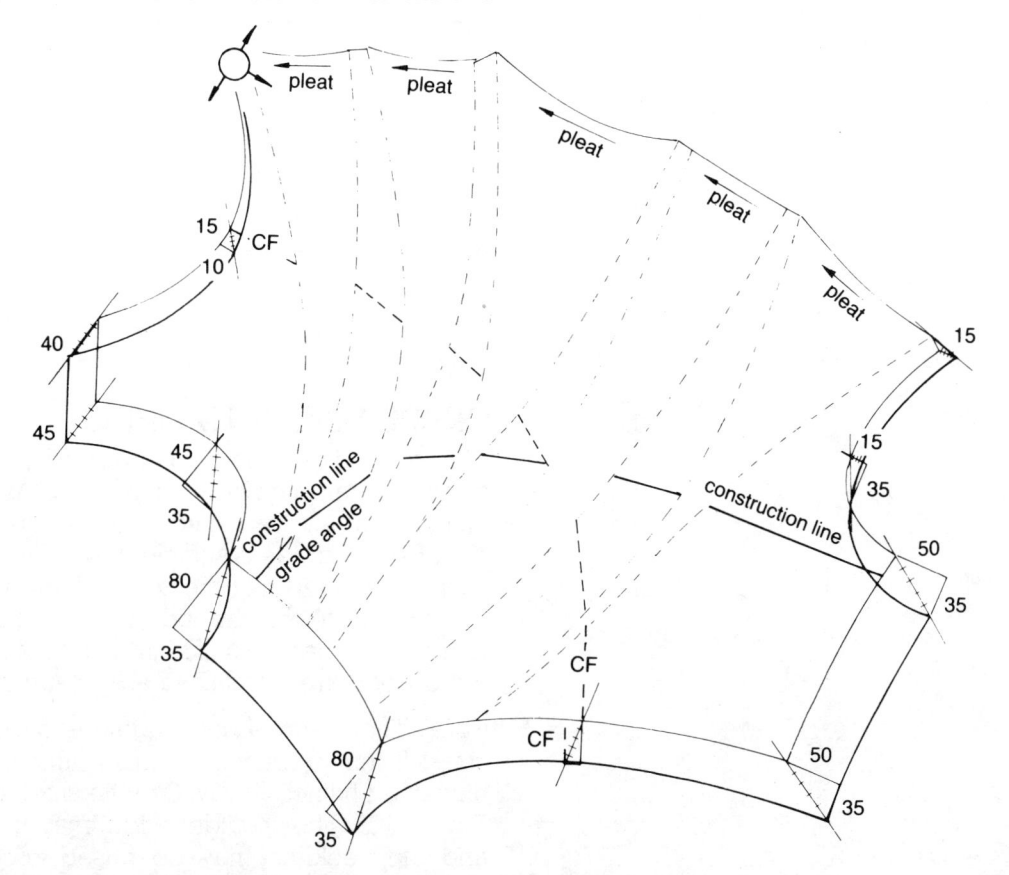

Figure 159 Two-dimensional grade, loose cowl drapes for five sizes up

STYLE 12

	GRADING SPECIFICATION		
1	Size chart	Table 13	
2	Size range	10·12·14·16·18·20·22	
3	Height/girth/length	Height and girth	
4	Proportioning		
5	Type of grade	2 dim. track or draft	
6	Zero points front	Side seam waist	
7	Zero point back	nil	
8	Zero point sleeve	nil	
9	Zero point front skirt	nil	
10	Zero point back skirt	nil	
11	Category of fit	Draped	
Comments			

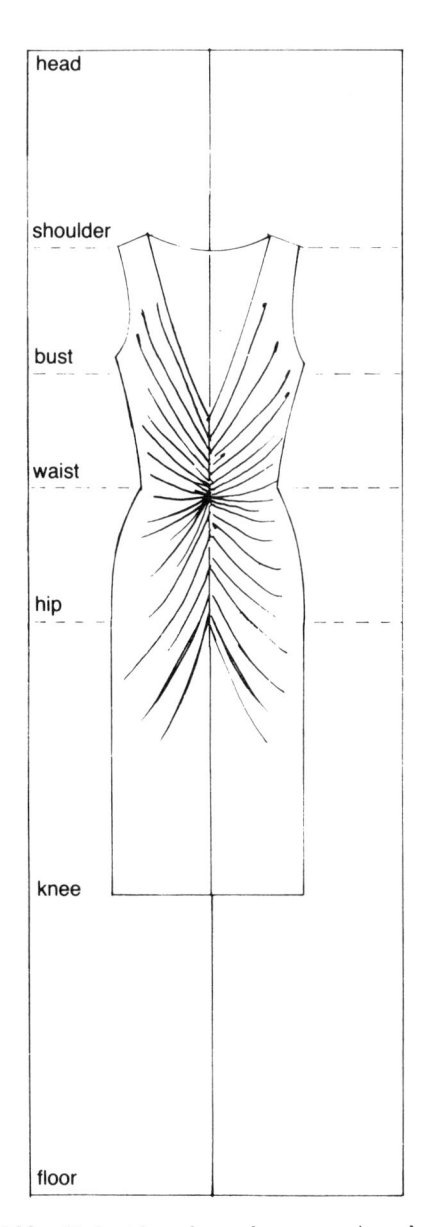

Figure 160 Style 12 – sleeveless evening dress

DRAPED EVENING DRESS

This draped style is best graded by either the track or draft method (Figure 160). As so much fullness is allowed into the pattern, a two-dimensional grade is sufficient (see Figure 161). It should be noted that the zero selected is, in this case, opposite the draped area. This is because there would be a loss of length at the side seam if the draped area was used as a static line.

Note: The centre front lengthens on the larger sizes. If this produces too much fullness, wedge unwanted fullness away. See the shaded areas in Figure 162. The shoulder width may be adjusted and the neckline may be raised according to design preference.

STYLE GRADES 1 TO 33

Figure 161 Two-dimensional grade for one size

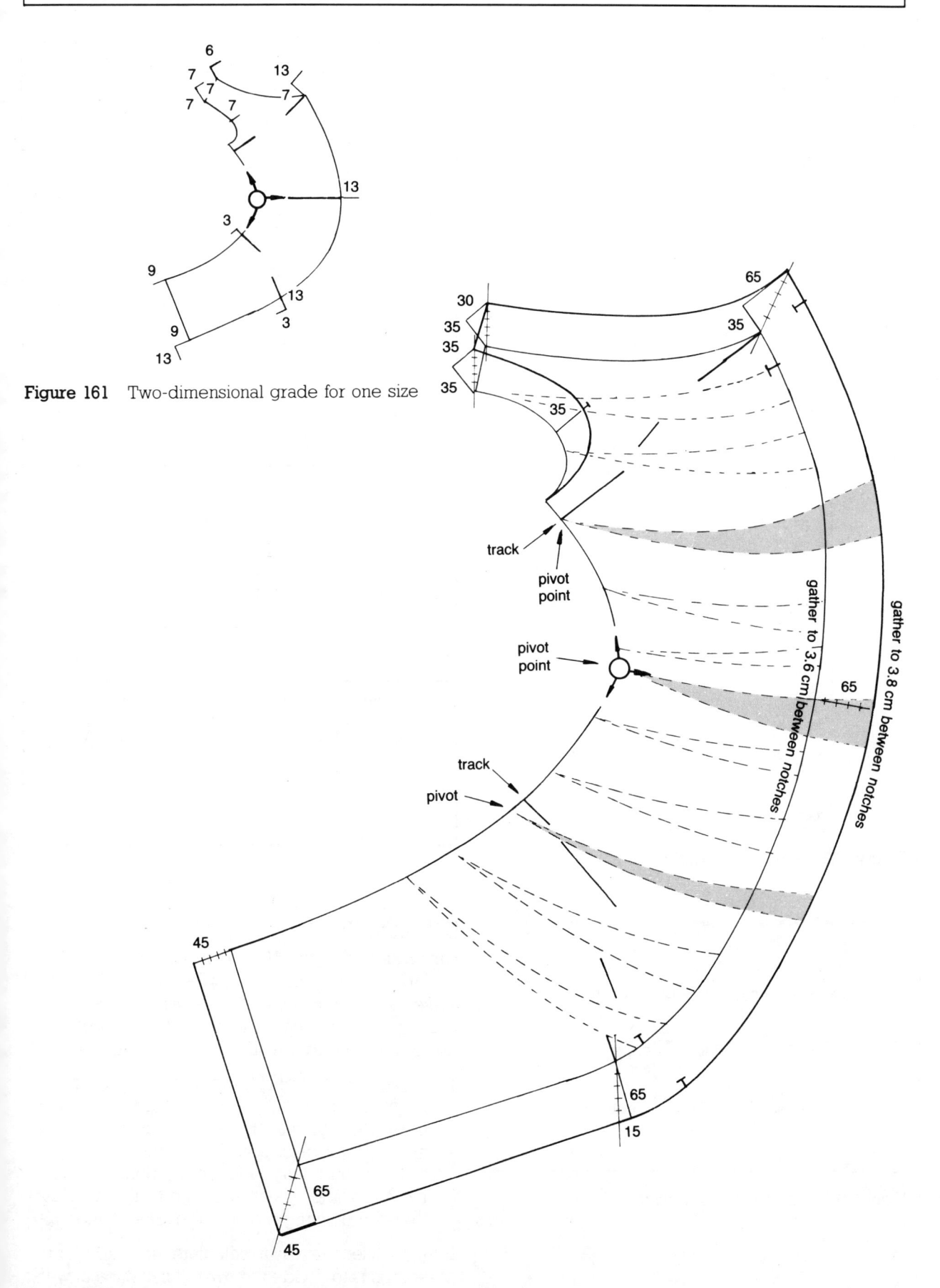

Figure 162 Grade and increments for five sizes up

STYLE 13

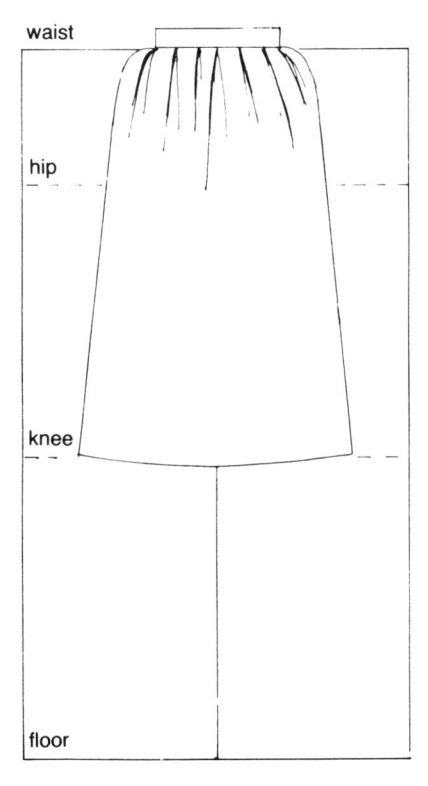

Figure 163 Style 13 – dirndl skirt

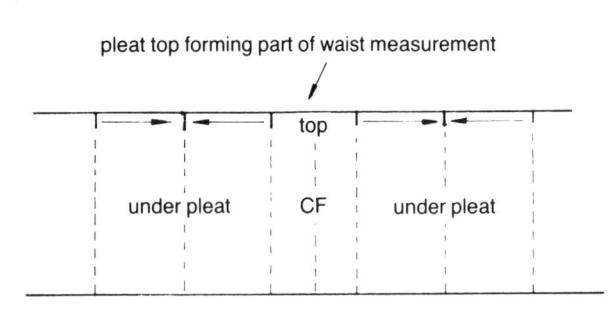

Figure 164 Section of dirndl skirt

GRADING SPECIFICATION

1	Size chart	Table 13	
2	Size range	10·12·14·16	
3	Height/girth/length	Height and girth	
4	Proportioning	Increase length by 0.6mm per size	
5	Type of grade	2 dim.	
6	Zero points front	nil	
7	Zero point back	nil	
8	Zero point sleeve	nil	
9	Zero point front skirt	nil	
10	Zero point back skirt	nil	
11	Category of fit	Loose	

Comments

Grade based on fabric costing.

DIRNDL SKIRTS

Dirndl skirts (Figure 163) are one example and can either be cut in one long piece, i.e., along the selvedge, or can be cut in several pieces comprising widths. The grading of these skirts will depend on the availability of fabric, for example:

1. A pleated dirndl (Figure 164) can be graded by increasing the pleat tops and decreasing the under pleats, thereby utilizing the same amount of fabric. See Figure 165.
2. The second way of grading this skirt is to increase the pleat tops and under pleats thereby utilizing more fabric. See Figure 166.

In both cases the way to calculate the grade for the pleat tops is to divide the overall increase at waist (in this book 5.0 cm) by the number of pleats and

STYLE GRADES 1 TO 33

re-adjust the notches. It is recommended that a new pattern be made for each size rather than grading from the stock size. For example, a skirt comprising ten pleats will be graded as follows:

Waist grade = 5.0 cm

Increase per pleat = 0.5 cm

So, re-adjust notches by 0.25 cm each side of the pleat. The skirt length may be increased by 0.6 cm per size.

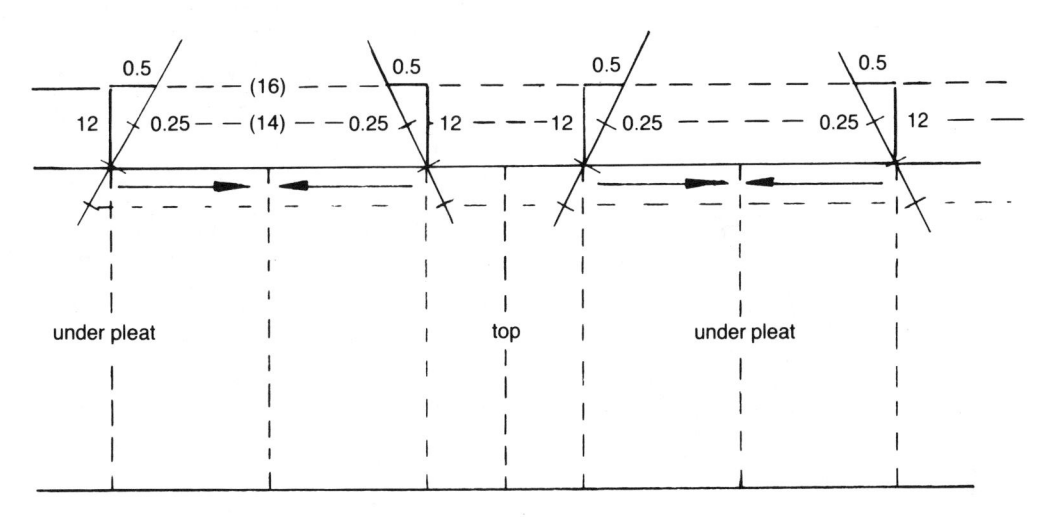

Figure 165 Two sizes up, one size down, utilizing the same fabric amount

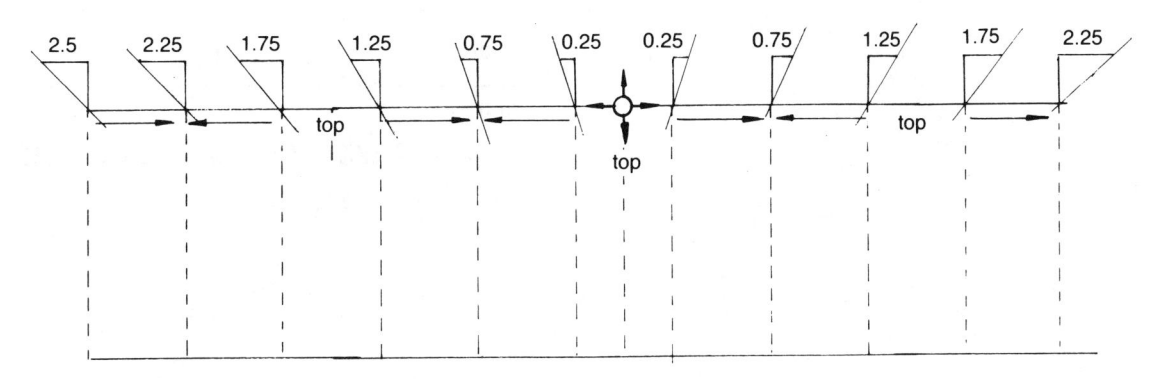

Figure 166 Increase for one size (not to scale) utilizing more fabric

STYLE 14

	GRADING SPECIFICATION	
1	Size chart	Table 13
2	Size range	10·12·14·16
3	Height/girth/length	Height and girth
4	Proportioning	
5	Type of grade	2 dim. draft or track
6	Zero points front	Pocket seam at waist
7	Zero point back	Waist centre
8	Zero point sleeve	nil
9	Zero point front skirt	nil
10	Zero point back skirt	nil
11	Category of fit	A-line
Comments		
3 dim. skirt grade could be used. See page 43.		

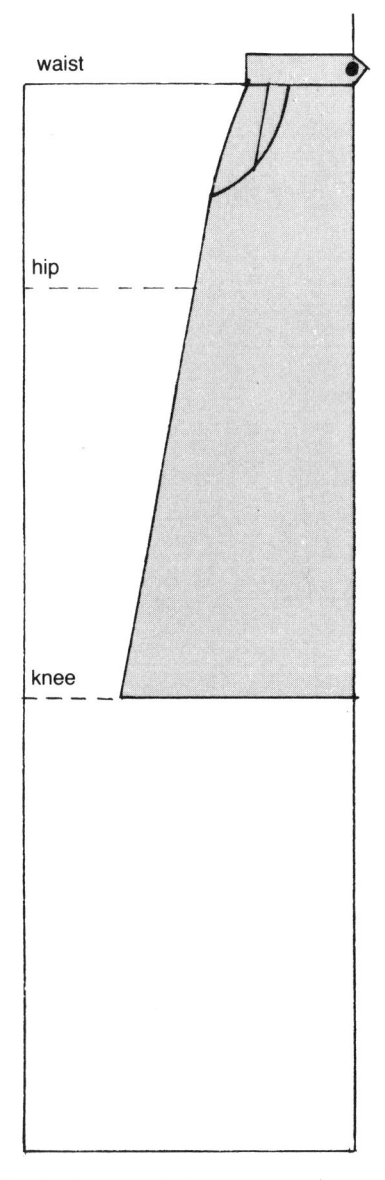

Figure 167 Style 14 – A-line skirt with pockets

A-LINE SKIRT WITH POCKET

This A-line skirt (Figure 167) can be graded using either a draft or a track system because a two-dimensional grade is sufficient for both its required size range and its specific style (see Figure 168).

The zero has been selected because it enables the pocket line to remain virtually static (see Figure 169 which illustrates the two-dimensional draft grade). This system is safer than a track system because the pocket bag and facing are graded together and therefore the sewing lines remain the same. If grading from a production pattern, relay on to a draft as in Figure 169. The waistband is graded according to the waist increments and adjusted as in Figure 169.

STYLE GRADES 1 TO 33 187

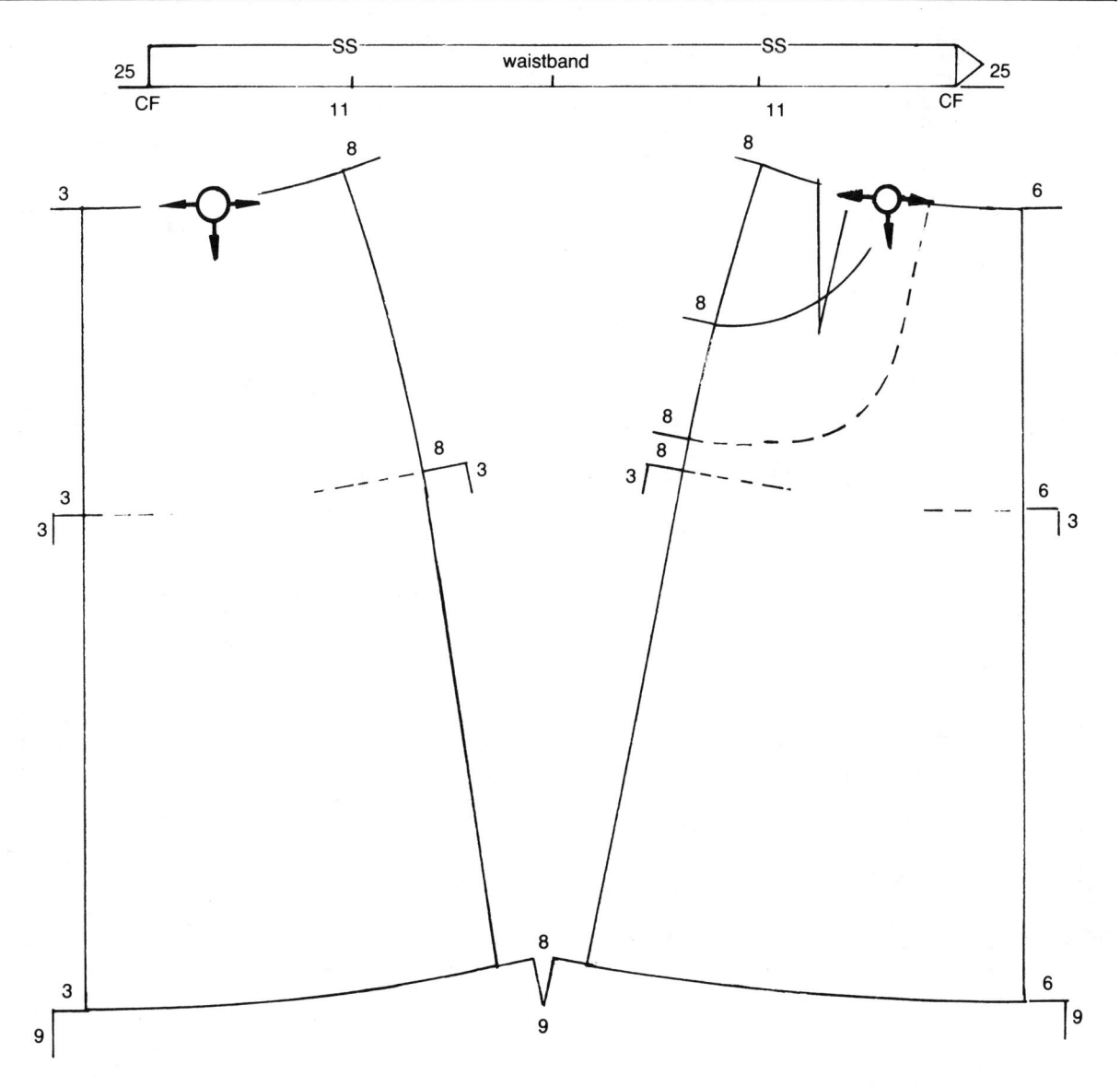

Figure 168 Two-dimensional grade for one size

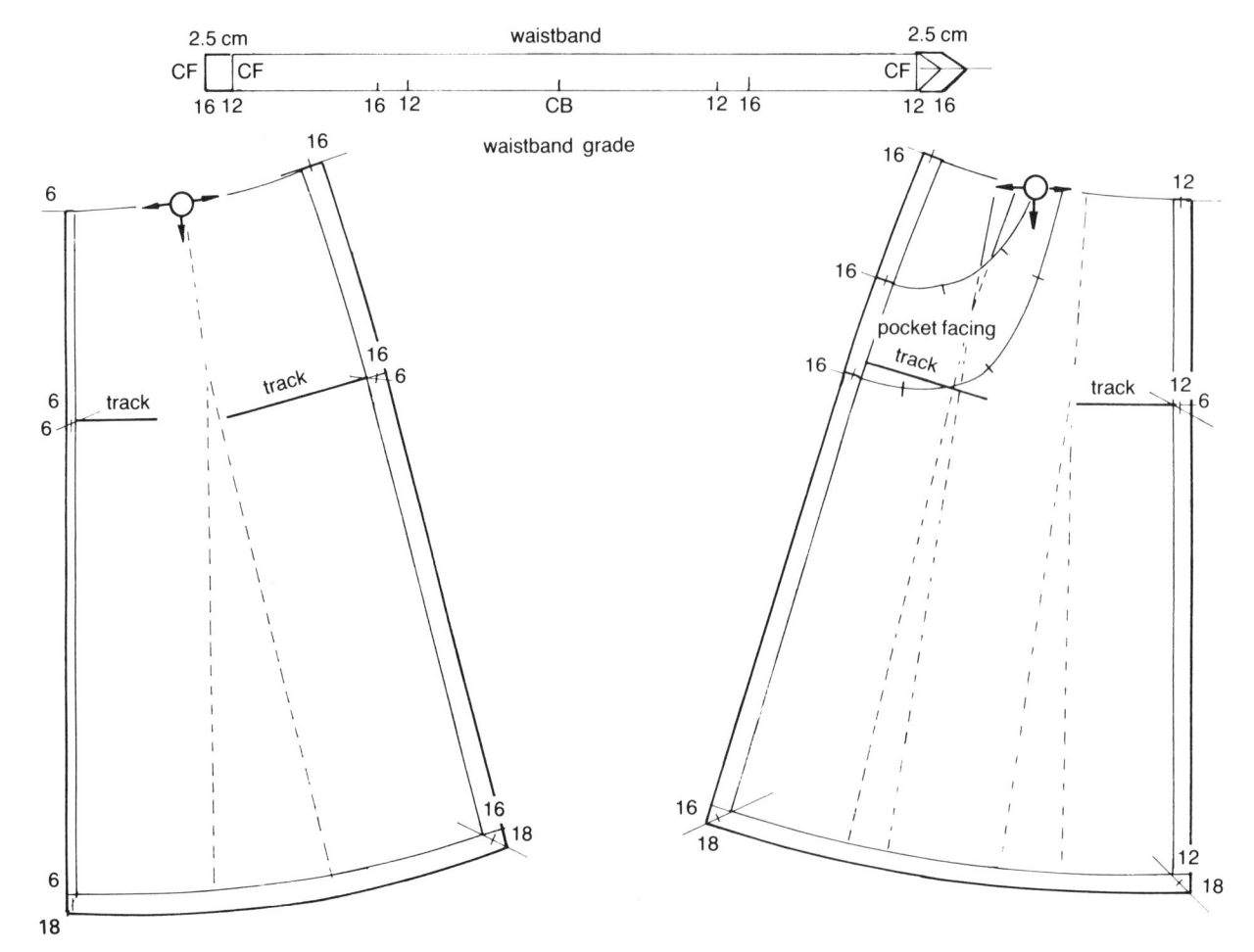

Figure 169 Two-dimensional grade for two sizes

STYLE 15

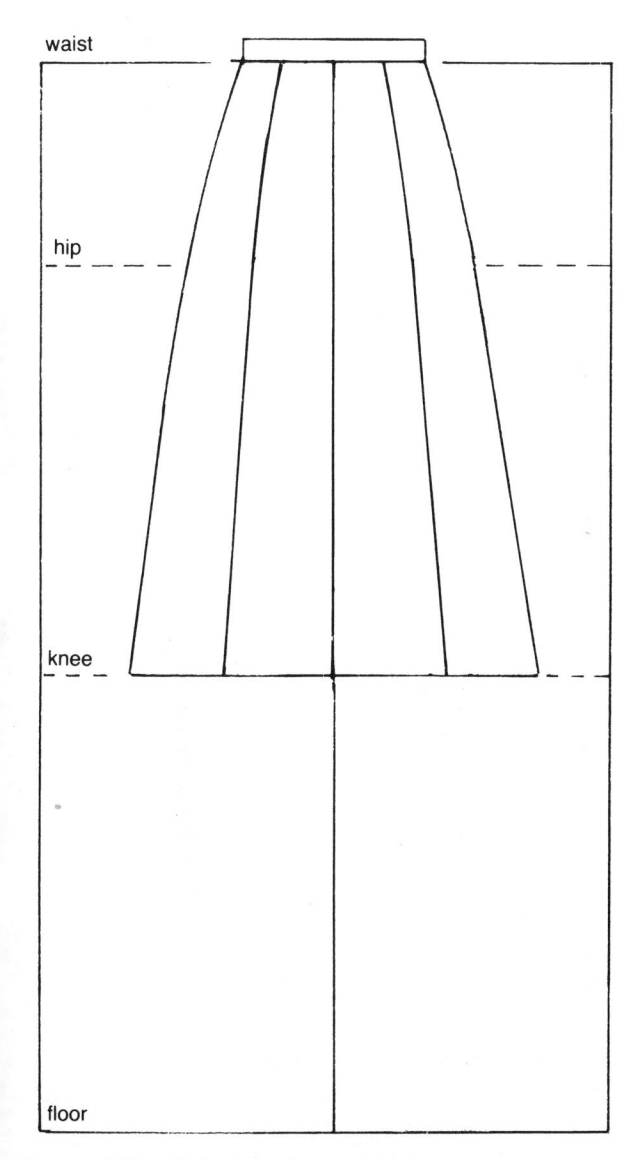

Figure 170 Style 15 – 8-gore skirt

	GRADING SPECIFICATION		
1	Size chart	Table 13	
2	Size range	10 · 12 · 14 · 16	
3	Height/girth/length	Height and girth	
4	Proportioning		
5	Type of grade	2 dim. track	
6	Zero points front	nil	
7	Zero point back	nil	
8	Zero point sleeve	nil	
9	Zero point front skirt	Hip	
10	Zero point back skirt	Hip	
11	Category of fit	Semi-fitting	
	Comments Length grade optional		

8-GORE SKIRT

As gored skirts (Figure 170) comprise sections that are all identical, it is sufficient to grade one section only. The method used is a two-dimensional track grade for two sizes up and one down. Simply divide the girth increase by the amount of gores, then halve the amount to grade half a section (Figure 171).

STAGE 1
Prepare the card and mark all the necessary increments and tracks. See Figures 172 and 173. Note that only half a pattern needs to be graded.

STAGE 2
Shift pattern around the tracks as indicated in Figure 173.

STAGE 3
Cut out the size 14 pattern. Use the size 12 pattern to grade up to size 16 by doubling the increments shown. For example:

Waist girth grade per size = 50 mm
Divide by amount of gores, i.e. 8, = 6.25 mm
To grade half a gore divide by 2 = 3.2 mm
(rounded up for ease of application)

Double 3.2 mm when grading from 12 to 16.

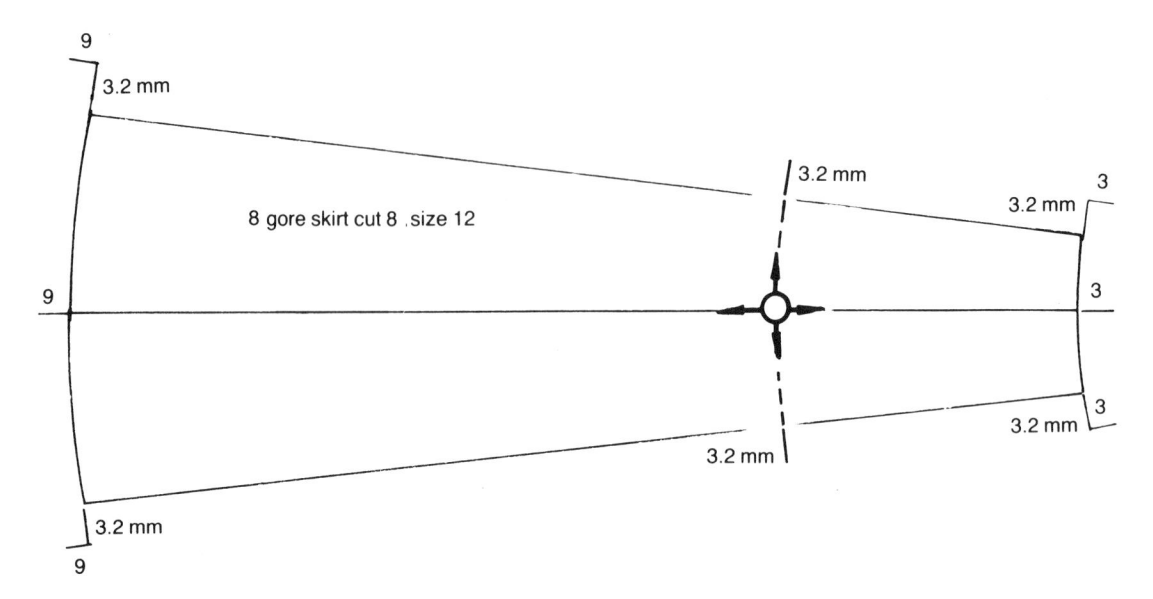

Figure 171 Increments for one size

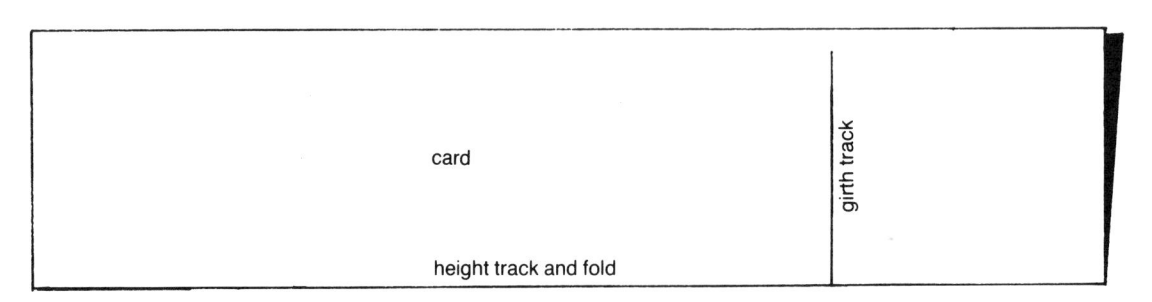

Figure 172 Prepare the card for the track grade

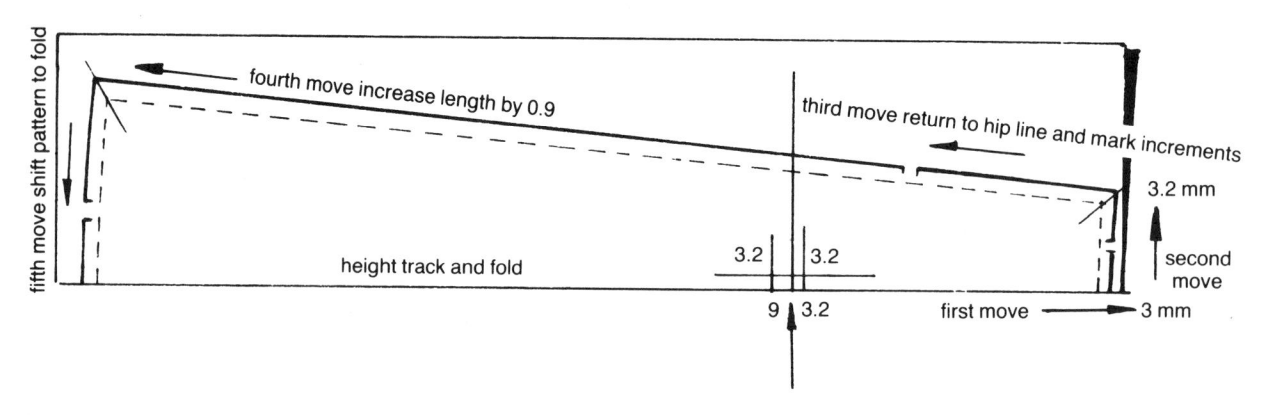

Figure 173 Track grade for one size

STYLE 16

GRADING SPECIFICATION		
1	Size chart	Table 13
2	Size range	10·12·14·16
3	Height/girth/length	Height and girth
4	Proportioning	Pleats move towards side seam
5	Type of grade	2 dim. track or draft
6	Zero points front	Hip at centre front
7	Zero point back	nil
8	Zero point sleeve	nil
9	Zero point front skirt	nil
10	Zero point back skirt	nil
11	Category of fit	Semi-fitting

Comments

Size of pleat retained. Back skirt as block (page 131)

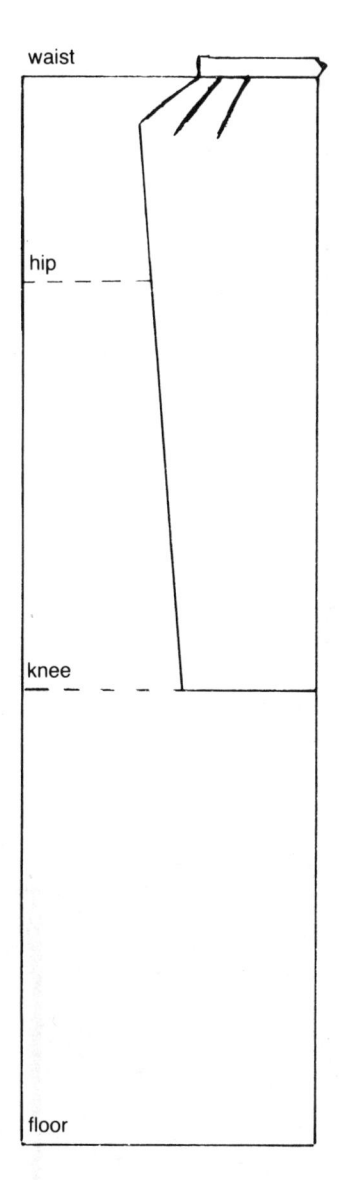

Figure 174 Style 16 – peg top skirt

PEG TOP SKIRT

This style (Figure 174) is very loose-fitting around the waist and therefore a two-dimensional track grade is adequate. Follow the procedure illustrated in Figures 175, 176 and 177.

Prepare the card and tracks (Figure 175).

Lay the pattern on to the tracks as shown in Figure 176. (See dotted outline for size 12.) Mark the pattern A, B, C, D, E, F, G as illustrated in Figure 175 and shift pattern around tracks to grade the next size up (Figure 177). Cut out skirt and repeat procedure.

A fuller discussion of track grading can be found in Chapter 14.

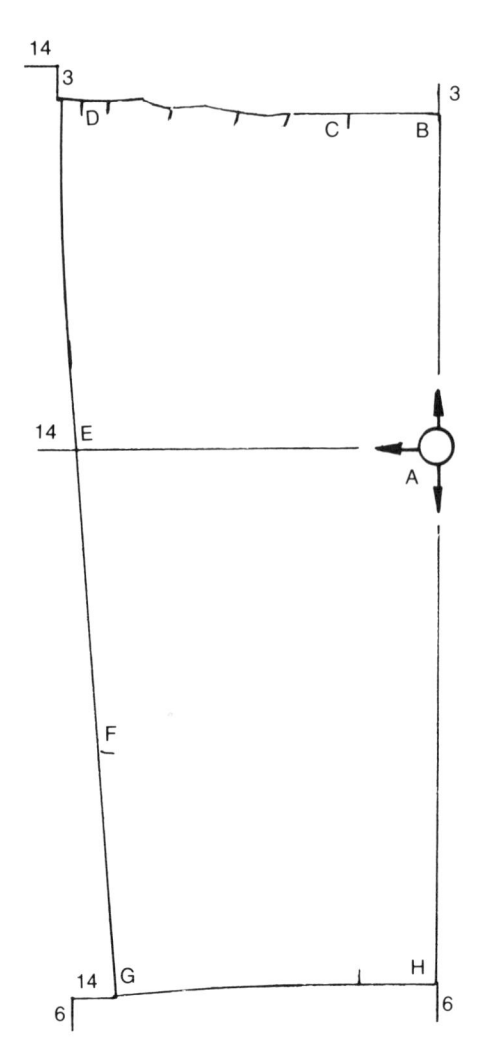

Figure 175 Increments for one size grade and lettering for track grading

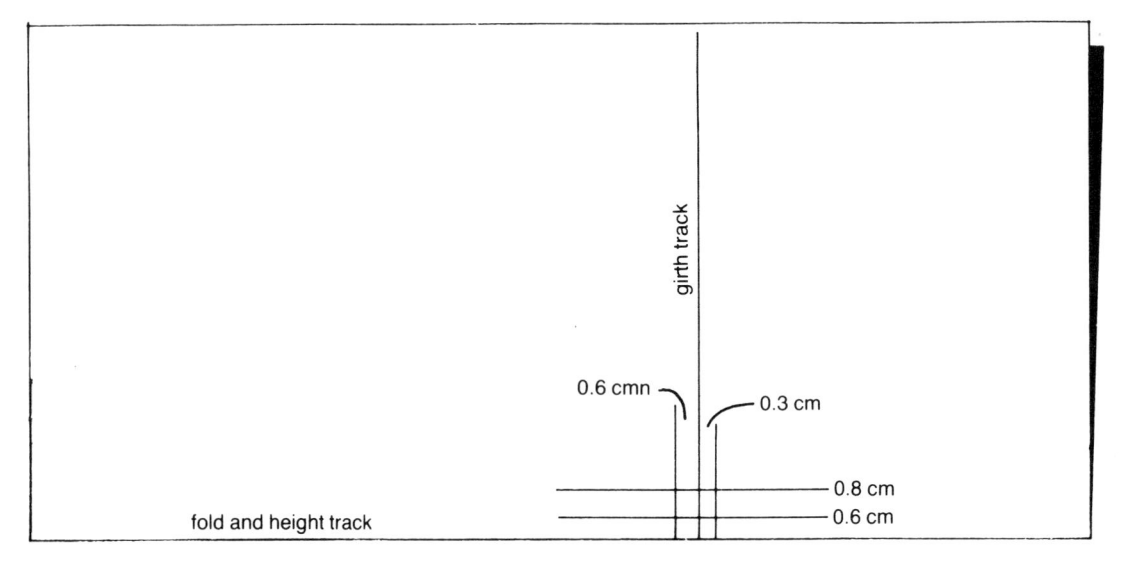

Figure 176 Prepare card and mark tracks

STYLE GRADES 1 TO 33

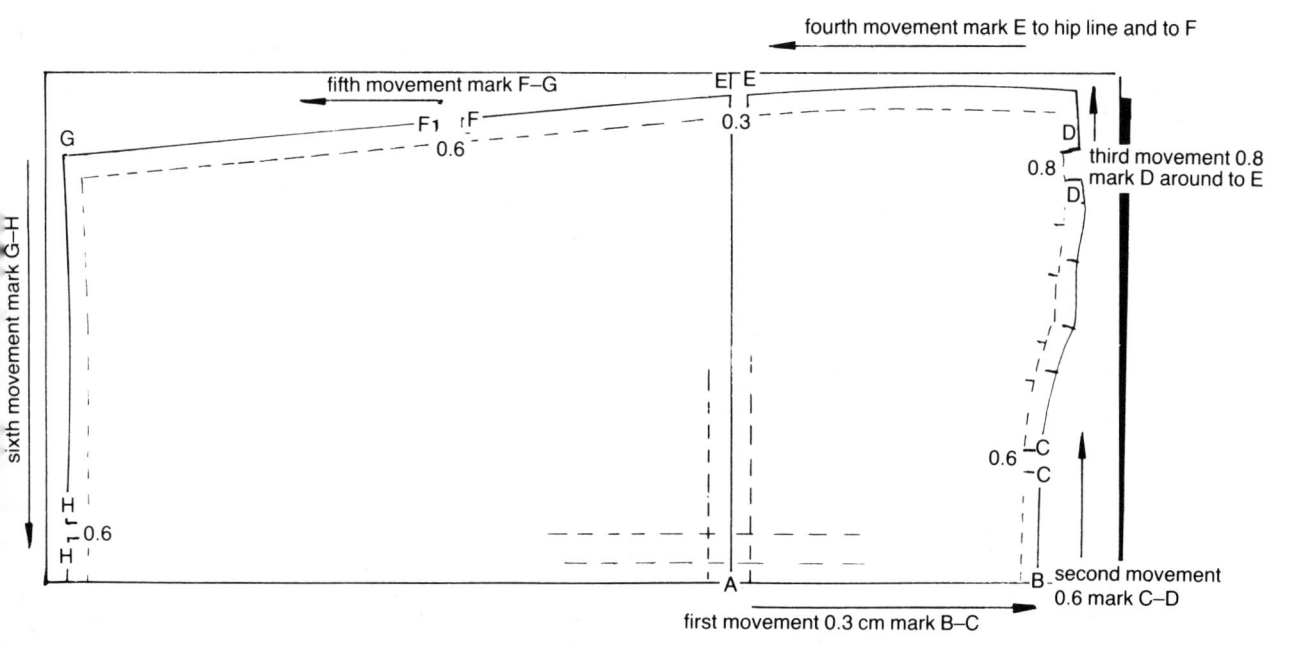

Figure 177 Shift pattern around tracks and blend lines

STYLE 17

	GRADING SPECIFICATION	
1	Size chart	Table 13
2	Size range	10·12·14·16
3	Height/girth/length	Height and girth
4	Proportioning	Equally into tiers
5	Type of grade	2 dim. draft or track
6	Zero points front	nil
7	Zero point back	nil
8	Zero point sleeve	nil
9	Zero point front skirt	Side seam at dart base
10	Zero point back skirt	Side seam at dart base
11	Category of fit	Semi-fitting
Comments		
Adjust proportions as length increases. 3 dim. grade could be applied.		

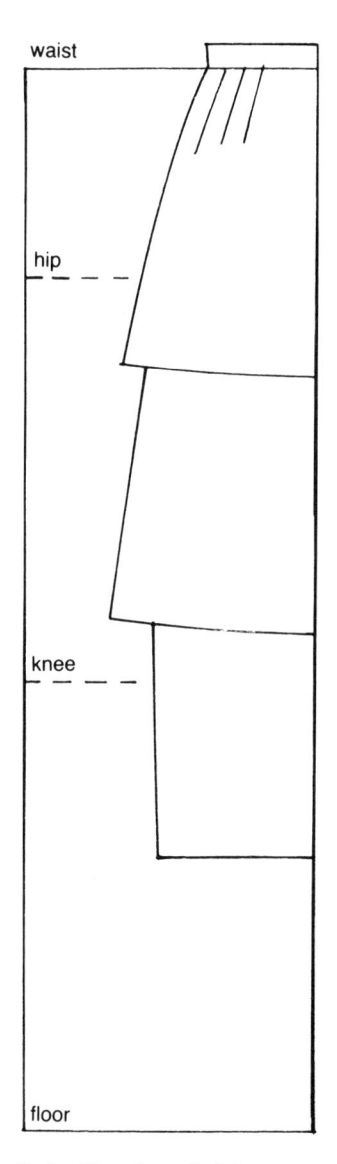

Figure 178 Style 17 – tiered skirt

TIERED SKIRT

The principle of grading a tiered garment (Figure 178) is to ensure that increments are planned in such a way as to retain the proportions of the original garment. In this skirt the overall height increase is 0.9 cm per size. This must be added to the hem. The tiers must also be re-proportioned: in this case 0.3 cm and 0.6 cm respectively (see Figures 179 and 180, and the grading specifications for Style 17).

STYLE GRADES 1 TO 33   195

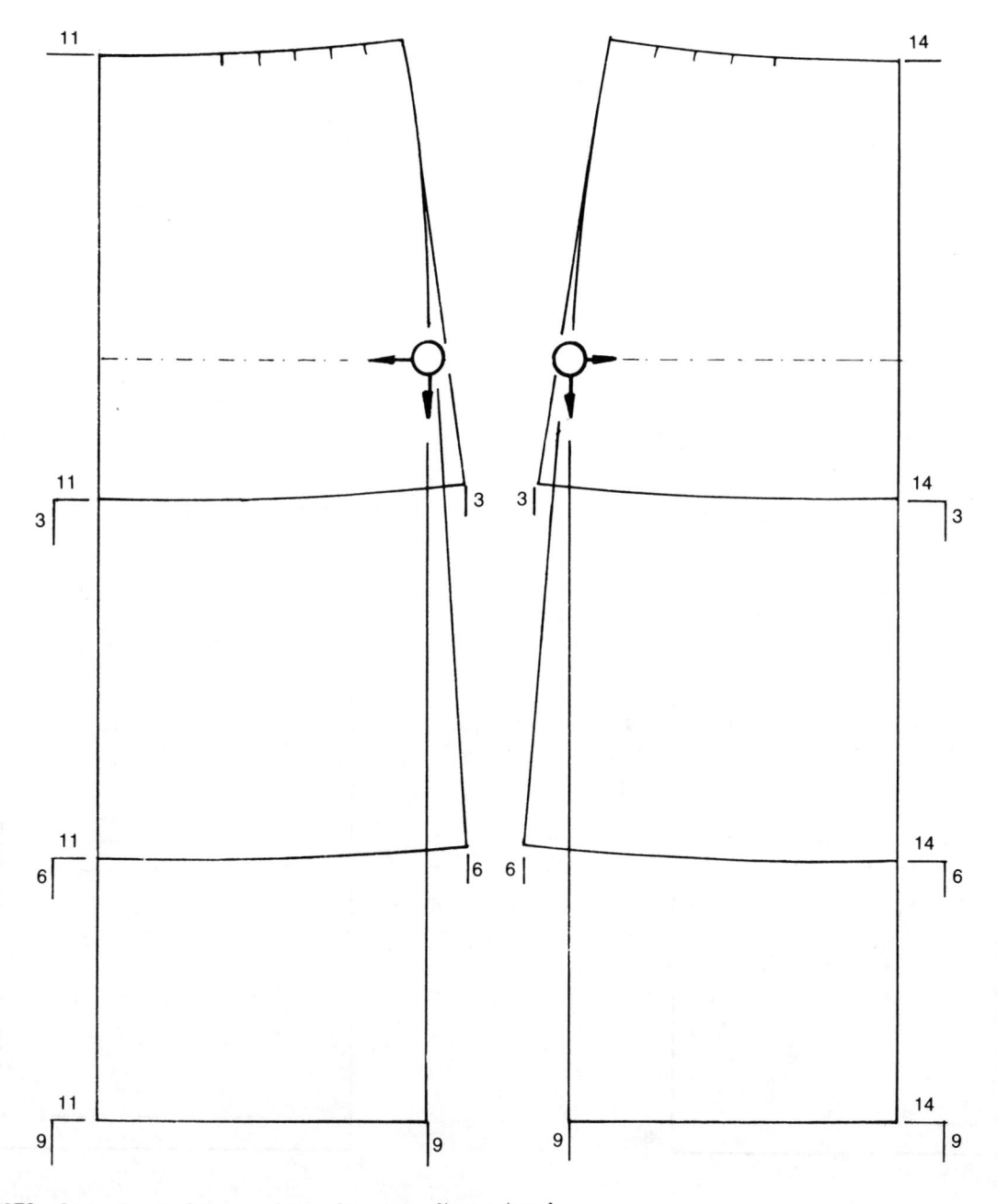

Figure 179 Increments for one size only – two-dimensional

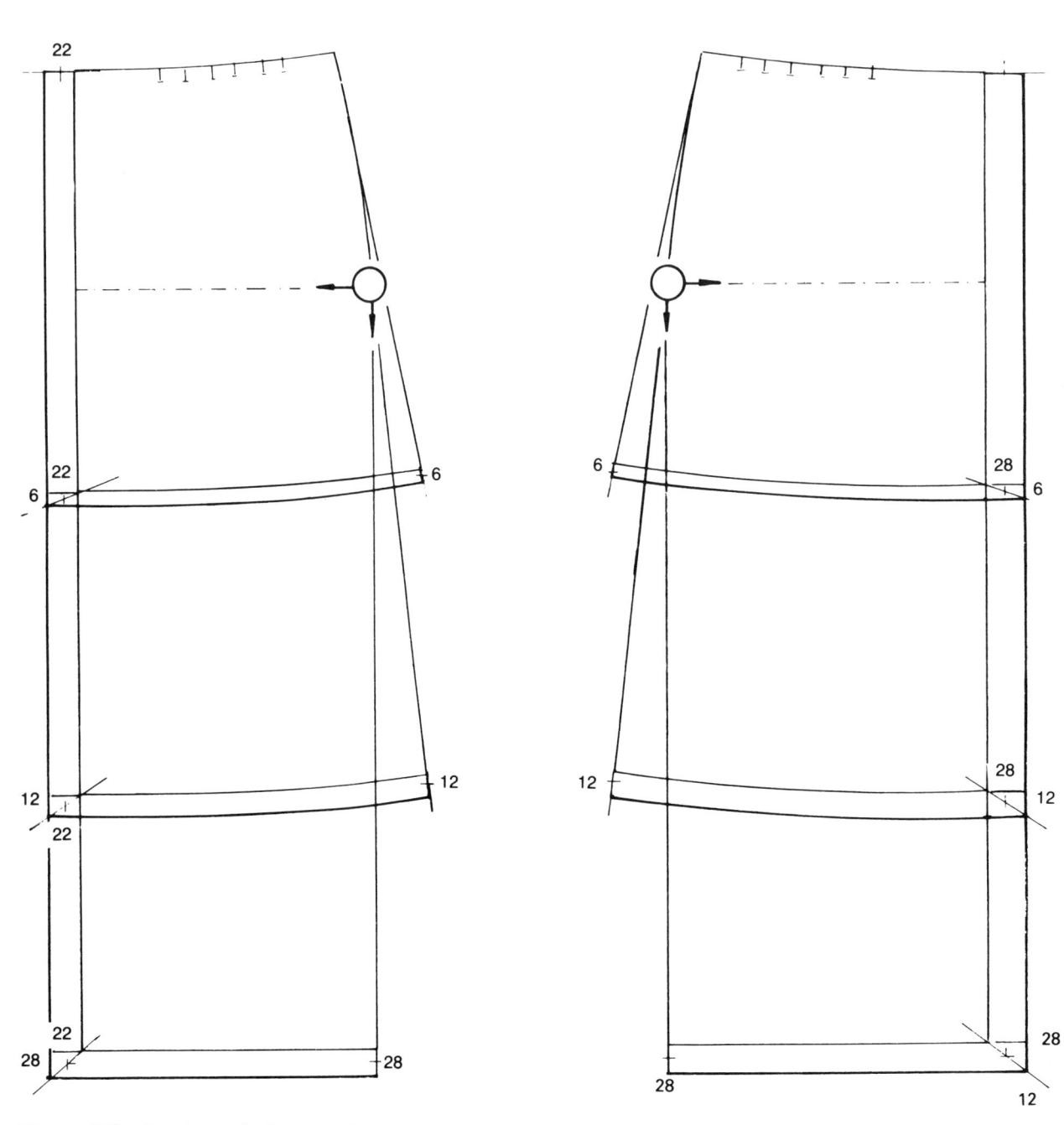

Figure 180 Track grade for one size

STYLES 18A, B & C

CIRCLE GRADING
The information given below applies to the construction and grading of all forms of circular pattern shapes, for example skirts, frills, sleeves and collars.

CONSTRUCTION
The examples shown are of the full circle, half circle and quarter circle skirt (see Figure 181). The most effective method of drafting circular skirts is by using π (π = 3.142 or $\frac{22}{7}$), which is $\frac{\text{circumference}}{\text{diameter}}$. The formulae are:

Full circle (Figure 182)

$$\frac{\text{circumference}}{2\pi} = \text{radius of a full circle.}$$

This results in an increase of 8 mm per size on a 5.0 cm grade.

Half circle (Figure 183)

$$\frac{\text{circumference}}{\pi} = \text{radius of a half circle.}$$

This results in an increase of 16 mm per size.

Quarter circle (Figure 184)

$$\frac{2 \text{ circumference}}{\pi} = \text{radius of a quarter circle.}$$

The length of the circle will depend on fashion requirements.

The inner circumference of the circle controls the hang of the garment, or the part of the garment. It is therefore crucial to preserve the correct curve. The best method of grading these garments is to *reconstruct a different size circumference each time*. However, for grading one size up or down it is common practice to add the increment to the side seam.

GRADING SPECIFICATION

1	Size chart	Table 13
2	Size range	10·12·14·16
3	Height/girth/length	Height and girth
4	Proportioning	
5	Type of grade	2 dim.
6	Zero points front	nil
7	Zero point back	nil
8	Zero point sleeve	nil
9	Zero point front skirt	Centre of circle
10	Zero point back skirt	nil
11	Category of fit	

Comments

System could be used for all forms of circular styling.

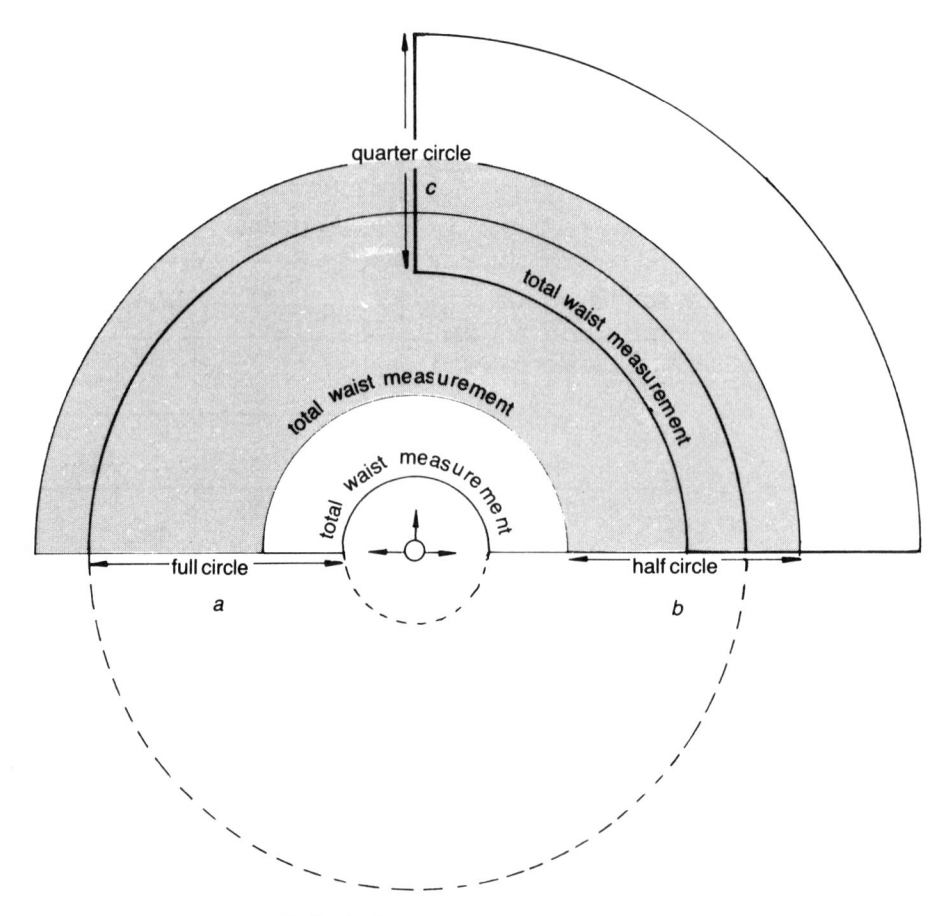

Figure 181 Style 18 – circle grading   (a) Full circle;   (b) Half circle;   (c) Quarter circle

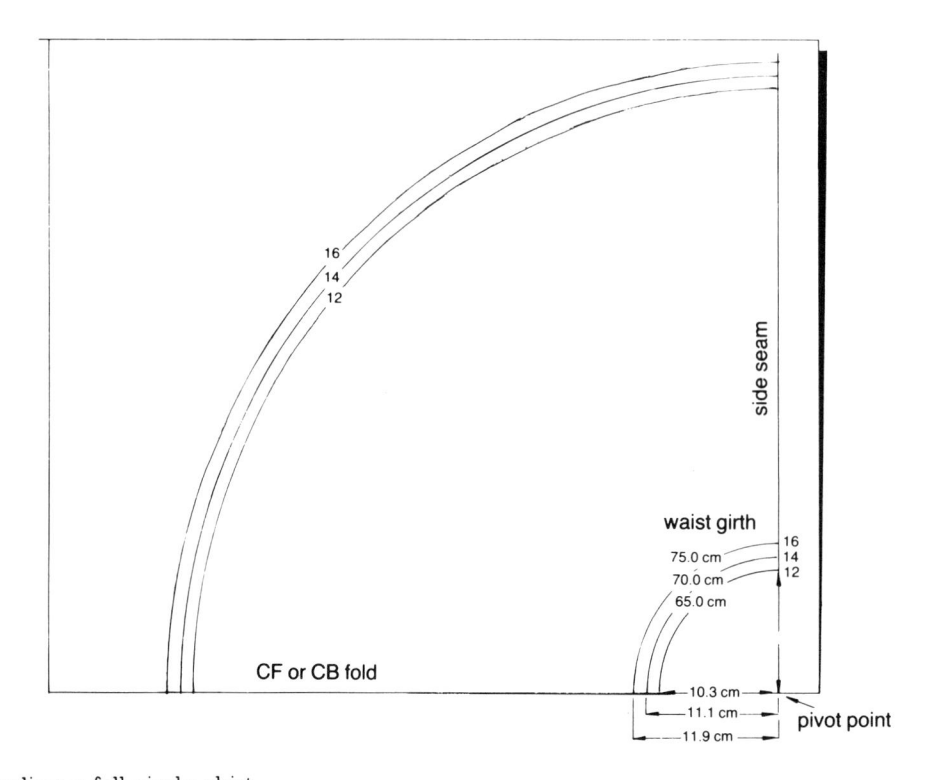

Figure 182 Grading a full circle skirt

STYLE GRADES 1 TO 33

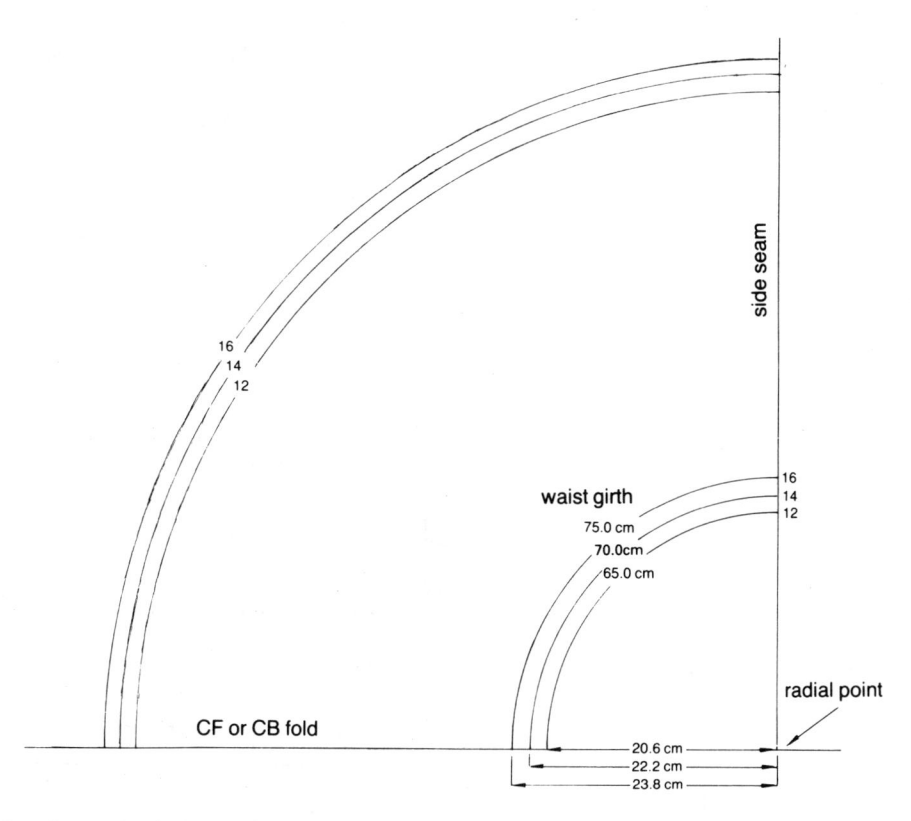

Figure 183 Grading a half circle skirt

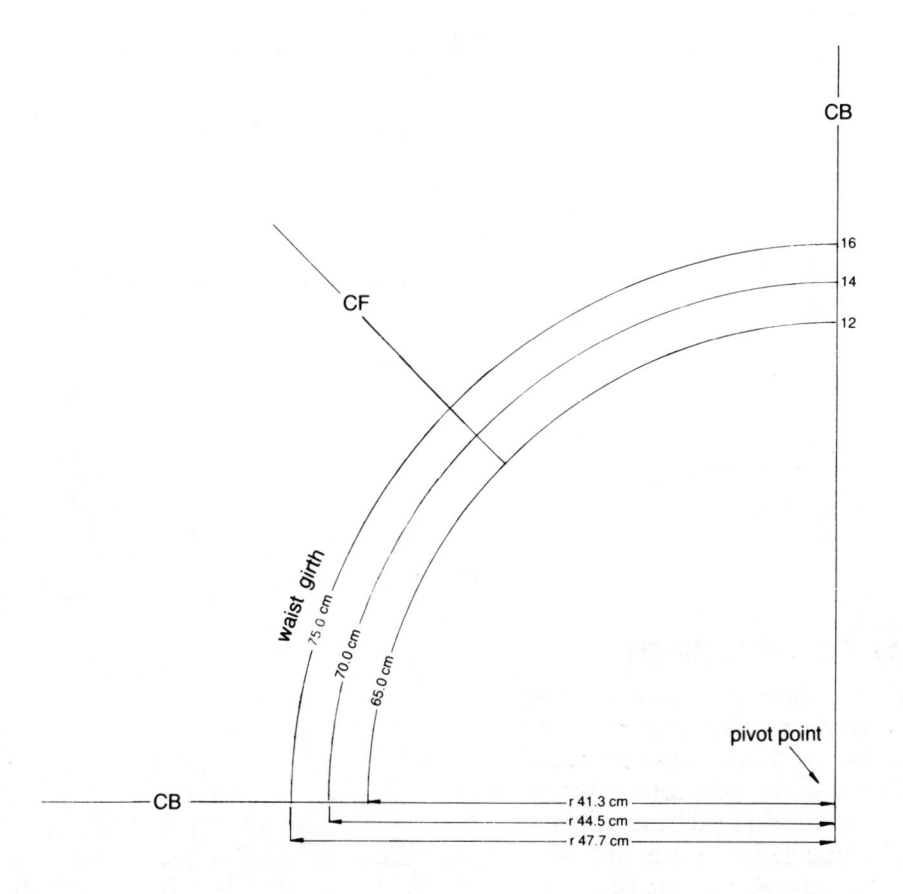

Figure 184 Grading a quarter circle

200   WOMEN'S STYLE GRADING

STYLE 19

GRADING SPECIFICATION

1	Size chart	Table 13
2	Size range	10·12·14·16
3	Height/girth/length	Height and girth
4	Proportioning	Drape lengthened
5	Type of grade	2 dim. draft
6	Zero points front	nil
7	Zero point back	nil
8	Zero point sleeve	nil
9	Zero point front skirt	Centre front waist
10	Zero point back skirt	
11	Category of fit	

Comments

Grade on length of drape optional.

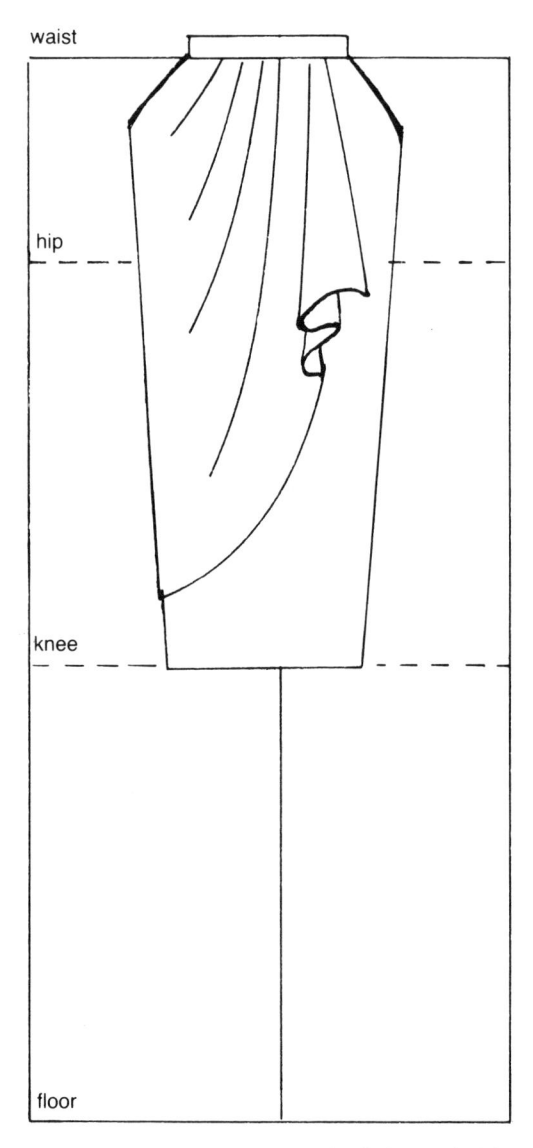

Figure 185 Style 19 – assymetrical draped skirt

ASYMMETRICAL DRAPED SKIRT

This draped skirt (Figure 185) is best graded using a two-dimensional draft system (Figure 186) because it enables the grader to have an overview of the style. To retain the proportions of the draped overskirt it is increased by 0.6 cm per size (see Figure 186). Figures 187 and 188 are self-explanatory. The zero selected enables the pleated section of the waistline to remain static.

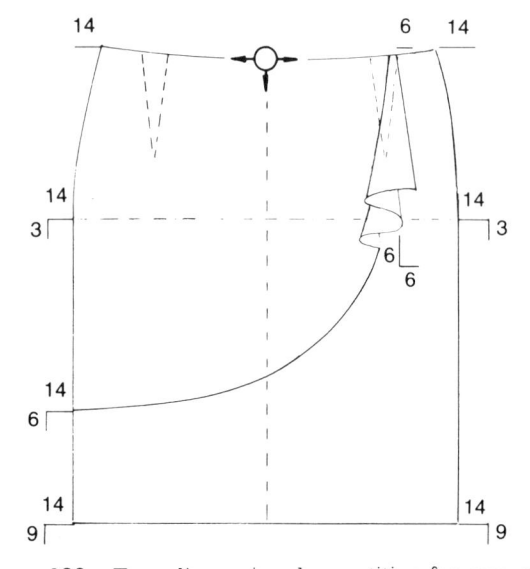

Figure 186 Two-dimensional quantities for one size

STYLE GRADES 1 TO 33

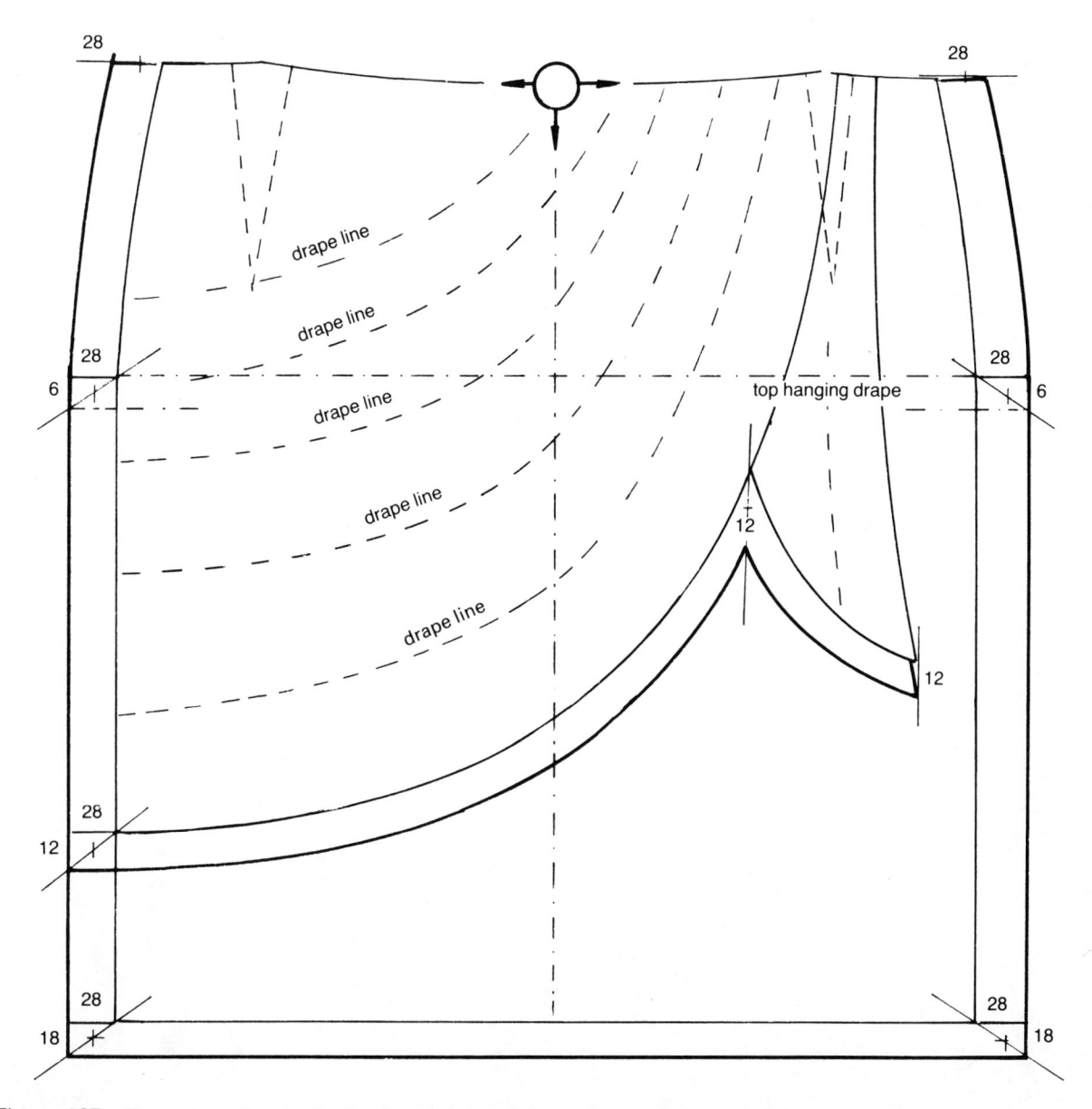

Figure 187 Illustrating the draft of a draped overskirt and two sizes up grade

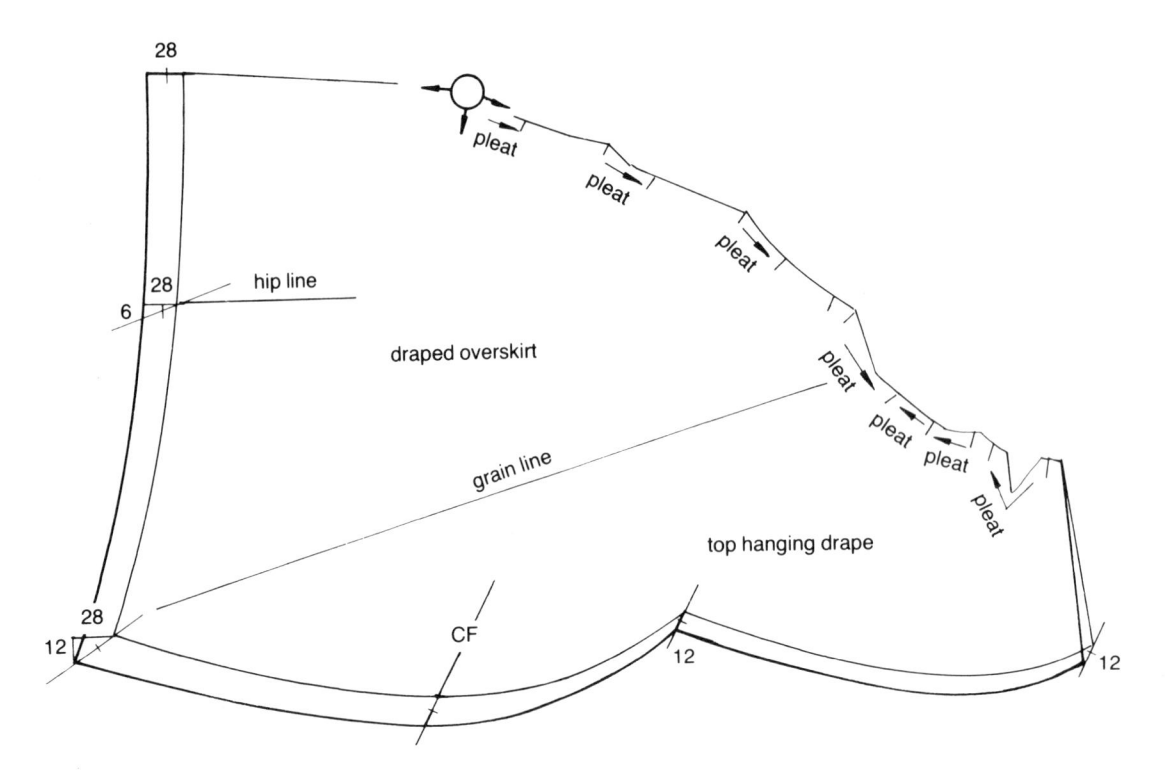

Figure 188 Graded draped overskirt two sizes up. This illustrates the pattern section traced-off from the draft (Figure 187) and split and opened up forming the final pattern.

STYLE GRADES 1 TO 33   203

STYLE 20

	GRADING SPECIFICATION	
1	Size chart	Table 13
2	Size range	10.12.14.16
3	Height/girth/length	Height and girth
4	Proportioning	Hip yoke same all sizes
5	Type of grade	2 dim. track
6	Zero points front	nil
7	Zero point back	nil
8	Zero point sleeve	nil
9	Zero point front skirt	Centre front
10	Zero point back skirt	nil
11	Category of fit	Hip yoke tight
Comments	3 dim. skirt grade could be applied. (see page 43).	

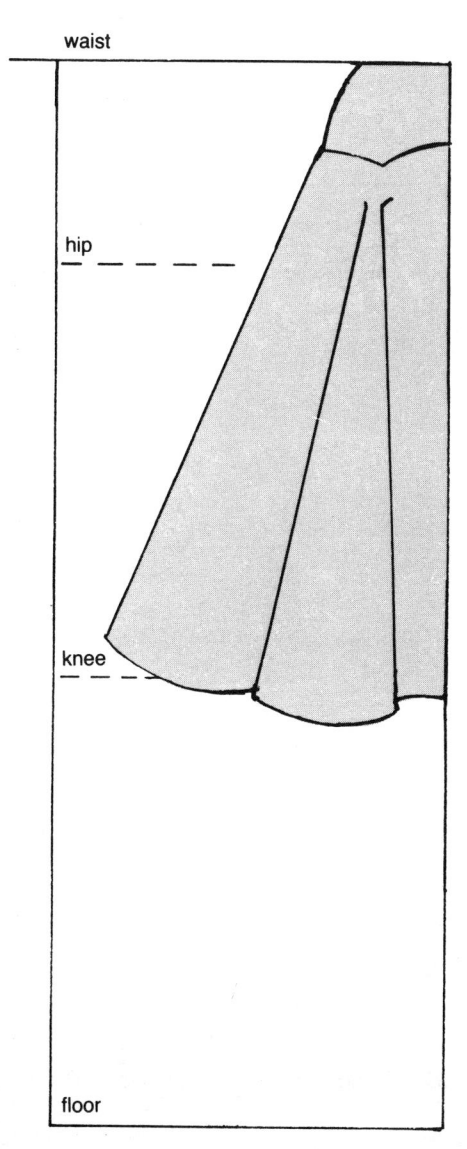

Figure 189 Style 20 – circular skirt suspended from a hip yoke

CIRCULAR SKIRT SUSPENDED FROM A HIP YOKE

A two-dimensional track grade has been selected as the best method of grading this style (see Figures 189 and 190).

The front yoke and front skirt have been developed from the basic skirt block by manipulating the darts and adding fullness to the pattern. The correct way to track grade this style is, therefore, to use multi-tracks. This will ensure that the skirt seam at the hipline retains its proper relationship with the hip yoke and consequently will hang properly on subsequent sizes. See Tables 20 and 21.

The girth tracks are established by defining the construction lines on each pattern section, in this case the hipline (see Figure 191). The procedure is illustrated in Figures 192 and 193 and there is a fuller discussion in Chapter 13.

204 WOMEN'S STYLE GRADING

Table 20

		PATTERN SECTION – HIP YOKE		
	Zero	Centre front midpoint of yoke		
	Required size	12→14 up grade		
Sequence	Pattern section	Pattern movement	Increment	Section to mark
	To increase:	*Position pattern on to tracks (Figure 192)*		
		Mark A–B and D–E		
1	Waist girth	Shift pattern along first track	0.6	B–C and E–F
2	Waist girth	Shift pattern along second track	0.8	C around to F

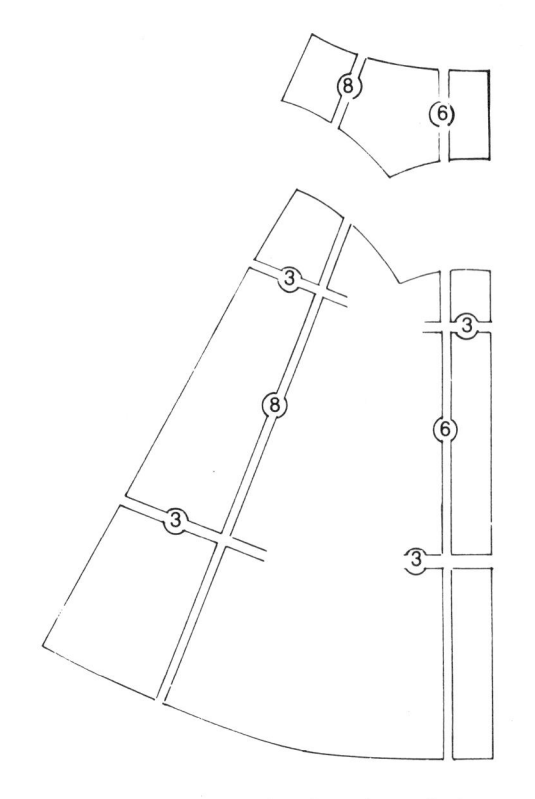

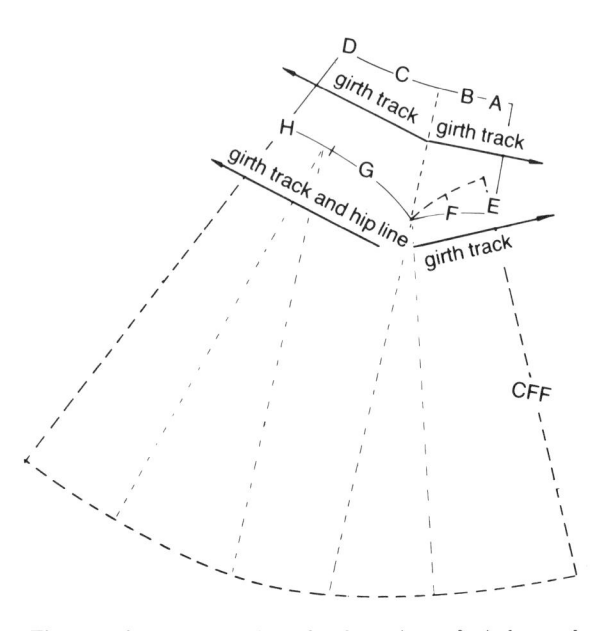

Figure 190 Two-dimensional track grade increments for one size

Figure 191 Illustrating the location of girth tracks

STYLE GRADES 1 TO 33

Table 21

PATTERN SECTION – FRONT SKIRT

	Zero	Centre front hipline		
	Required size	12→14 up grade		
Sequence	Pattern section	Pattern movement	Increment	Section to mark
	To increase:	*Position pattern on to tracks. Mark A–B*		
1	Hip girth	Shift pattern out along first track	0.6	B–C
2	Side hip	Shift pattern out along second track	0.8	C–D
3		*Return to zero*		
4	Length	Shift pattern down height track	0.6	E–F
5	Hem girth	Shift pattern out along first height track	0.6	F–G
6	Hem girth	Shift pattern along second track to connect with previously graded side seam	0.8	G–D
		Repeat with other required sizes		

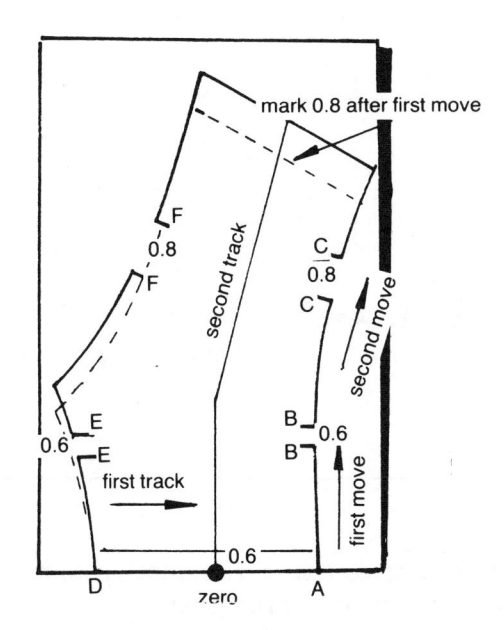

Figure 192 Graded yoke for one size

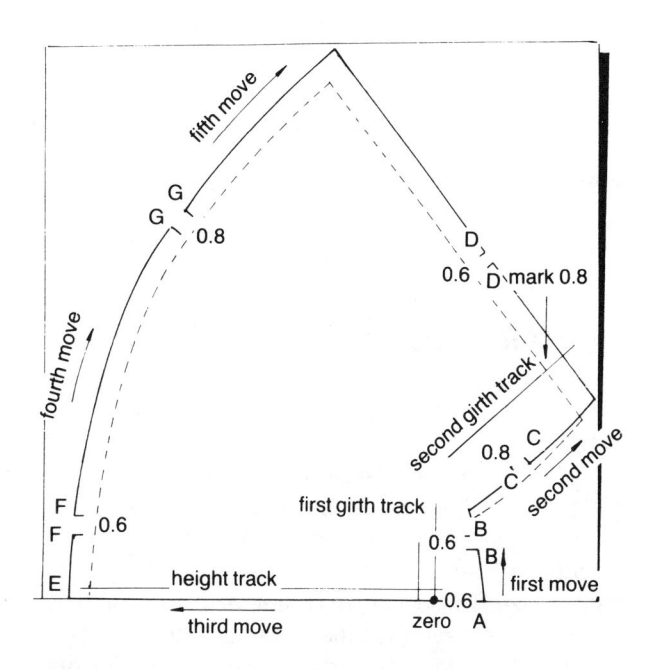

Figure 193 Graded skirt for one size

STYLE 21

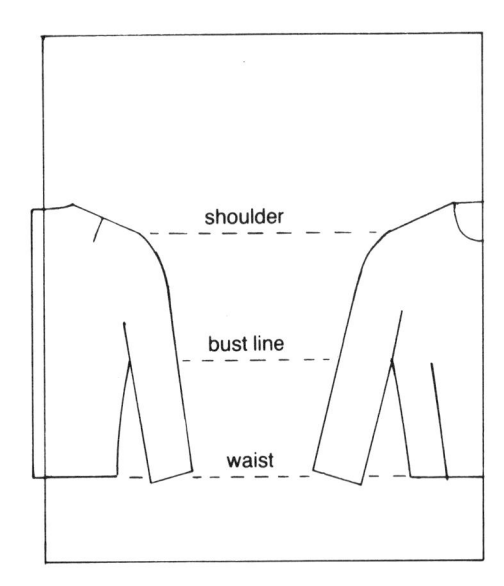

Figure 194 Style 21 – magyar sleeve with diamond gusset

GRADING SPECIFICATION			
1	Size chart	Table 13	
2	Size range	10·12·14·16·18·20·22	
3	Height/girth/length	Height and girth	
4	Proportioning	nil	
5	Type of grade	3 dim. draft	
6	Zero points front	Centre waist dart	
7	Zero point back	Centre waist dart	
8	Zero point sleeve	nil	
9	Zero point front skirt	nil	
10	Zero point back skirt	nil	
11	Category of fit	Fitted	
Comments			
2 dim. quantities could be applied over a limited range 10–16			

MAGYAR WITH DIAMOND GUSSET

The grading of the magyar sleeve (Figure 194) is based on its construction. It is not possible to calculate the necessary increments purely on size differences, as the sleeve angle, i.e., the pitch of both the front and back sleeves, changes as the size increases. The method used to calculate the following three-dimensional grade was to construct a size 12 bodice and sleeve and a size 22 bodice and sleeve and then manipulate both patterns to produce a magyar for each size (Figure 195). They were then superimposed on to one another. Grade angles and increments were then calculated on a single track system, i.e., parallel and vertical to the centre front and centre back lines.

CONSTRUCTION NOTES

Magyar construction is not the concern of this book. However, it is important that the side seams are centralized back and front in order to produce seams that are the same length.

The bust dart indicated in Figure 196 is small because half of the normal suppression quantity has been transferred into the armhole in order to achieve the correct sleeve angle. The remaining suppression at neck would be transferred into any subsequent styling suppression.

GRADING

Grade this style using either the three-dimensional draft or the three-dimensional track method. The three-dimensional factor, i.e., the bust dart increase, has been included in the increments shown (see Figure 195). The grade angles are based on the centre front and centre back lines. Note that this system is suitable for use on a computer grade because it is based on horizontal and vertical co-ordinates. This is discussed further in Chapters 6 and 7.

Figure 197 shows the size 12 and 22 outlines. The change in sleeve angle should be noted.

Trace-off the required sizes and check for length.

STYLE GRADES 1 TO 33

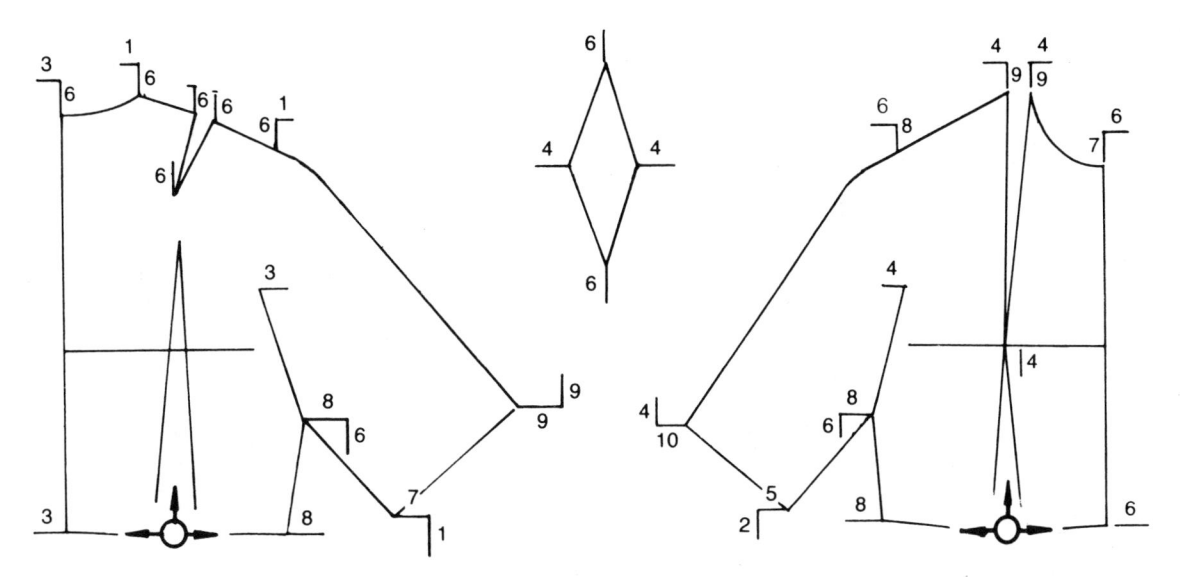

Figure 195 Increments for one size (including suppression factor)

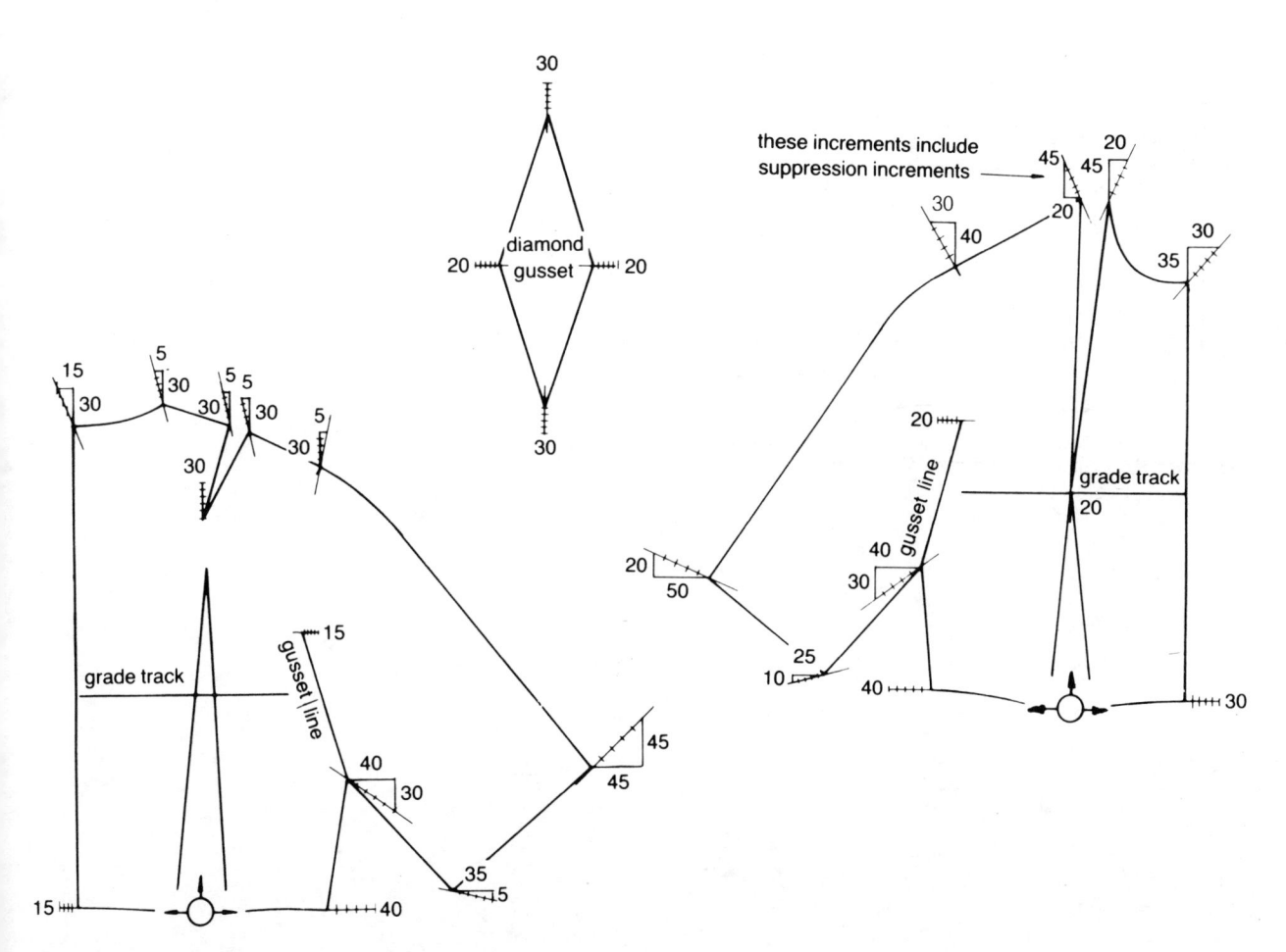

Figure 196 Increments for five sizes and grade angles

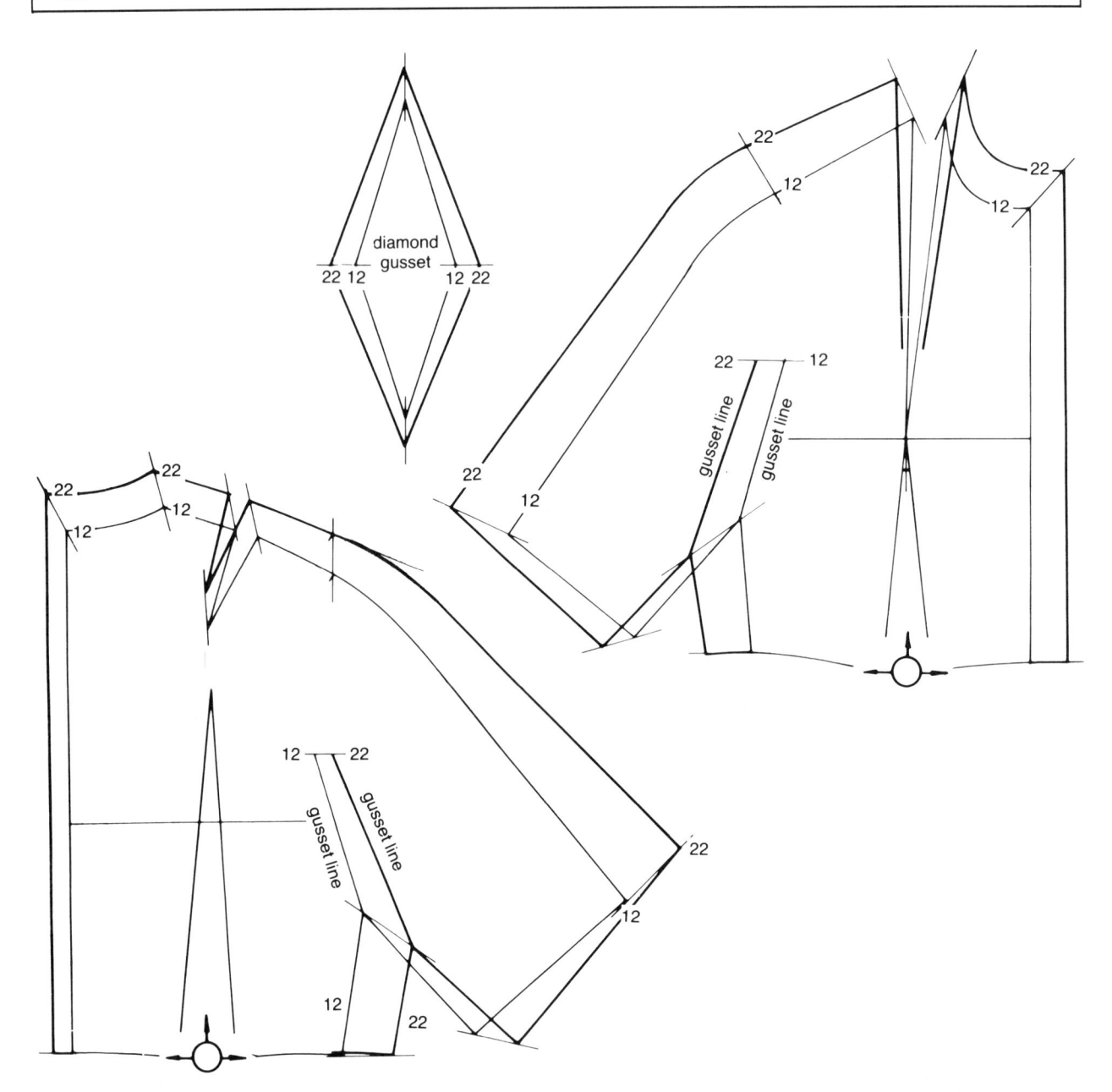

Figure 197 Size 12 and size 22 outlines

STYLE 22

	GRADING SPECIFICATION		
1	Size chart	Table 13	
2	Size range	10·12·14·16·18·20·22	
3	Height/girth/length	Height and girth	
4	Proportioning		
5	Type of grade	3 dim. draft N.S.B.P.	
6	Zero points front	Front pitch	
7	Zero point back	Back pitch	
8	Zero point sleeve	nil	
9	Zero point front skirt	nil	
10	Zero point back skirt	nil	
11	Category of fit	Fitted	

Comments
Non static bust point essential for this style.

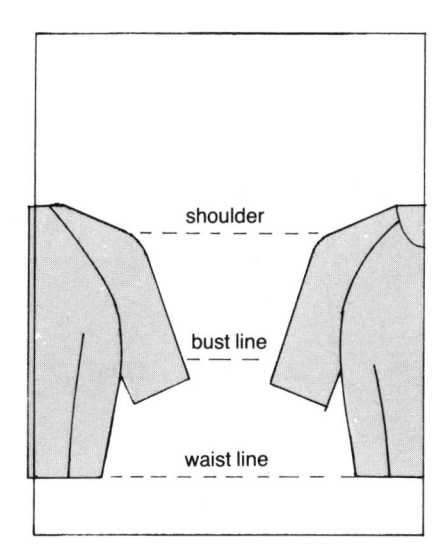

Figure 198 Style 22 – raglan sleeve

RAGLAN SLEEVE

This semi-grown-on sleeve is shown in its basic form, i.e., as a raglan sleeve (Figure 198). The style line which connects the pitch points to the neck can be varied according to design. The increments shown in Figure 199 will remain virtually the same, depending on the zero selected. The zero selected for this draft is positioned at the front and back pitch points. This enables the style lines to remain virtually static.

METHOD
Construct a raglan sleeve draft or reposition the production pattern back to its basic block form, with the dart at the neck.

Figure 199 shows the increments for one size. Multiply these by the number of sizes required and apply them to the draft (see Figure 200).

Front suppression and style line (Figures 201 and 202)
1. To establish the front suppression quantity swing and arc from the size 22 bust point A through B.
2. C is the size 22 shoulder point.
3. C–D is the size 22 shoulder length, where it touches the arc from B.
4. Mark points A, B, C, D, E, F and G.
5. Continue line F–G through to point H.
6. Swing an arc centre A through point J (located on size 22 dart line).
7. Mark point K.
8. Blend K through to point L (the front pitch point and zero).
9. Divide line E–K up into the required sizes. Divide M–B and N–A into required sizes and repivot style lines F–H back to the other side of the dart (see Figure 202).

Back dart and style line
1. Continue line A–C through to point D.
2. Trace-off A–B–C and apply to point D.
3. Mark points E–F.
4. Connect E–D through to A for back style line.

210　　　　　　　　　　　　　　　　　　　　　　　　　　WOMEN'S STYLE GRADING

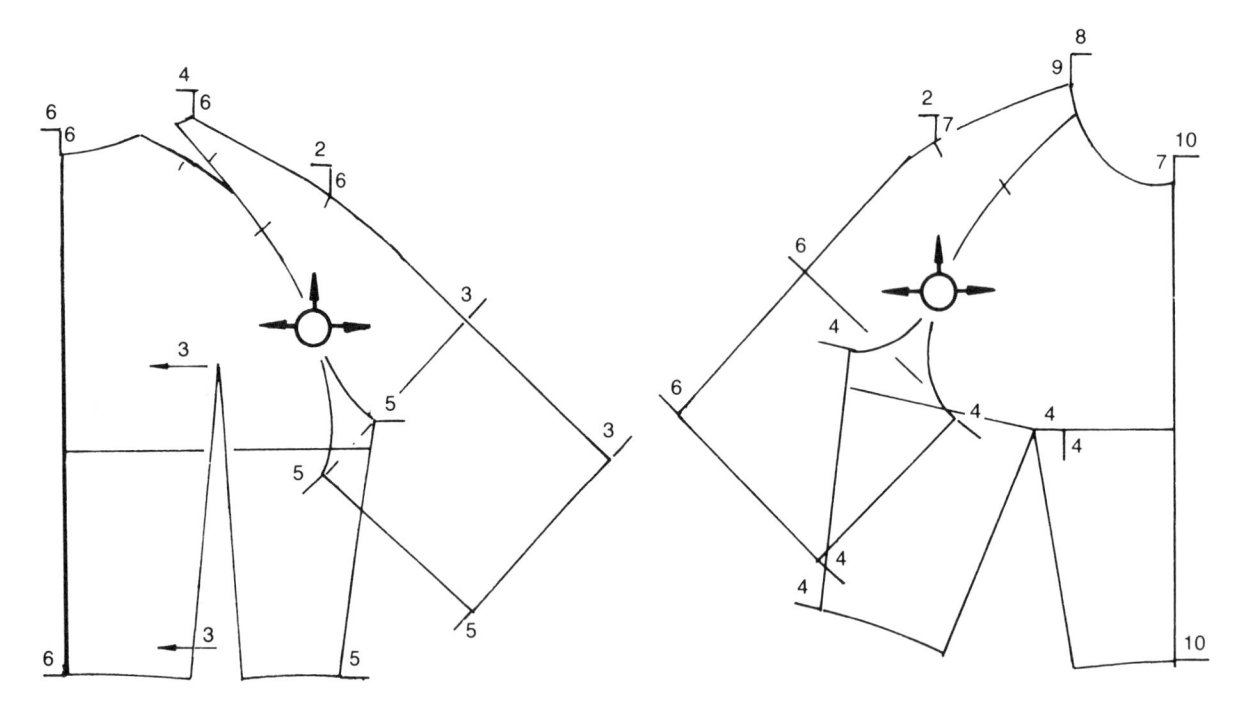

Figure 199　Increments for one size

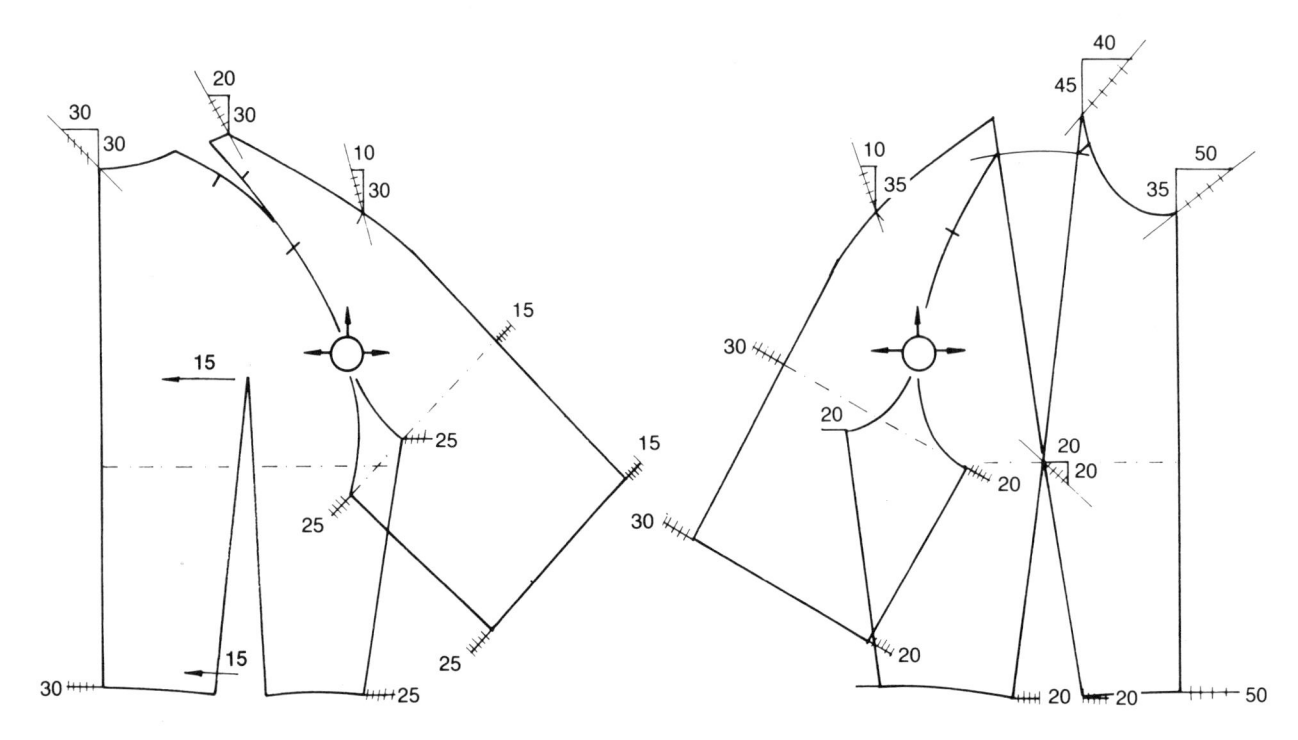

Figure 200　Increments for five sizes

STYLE GRADES 1 TO 33   211

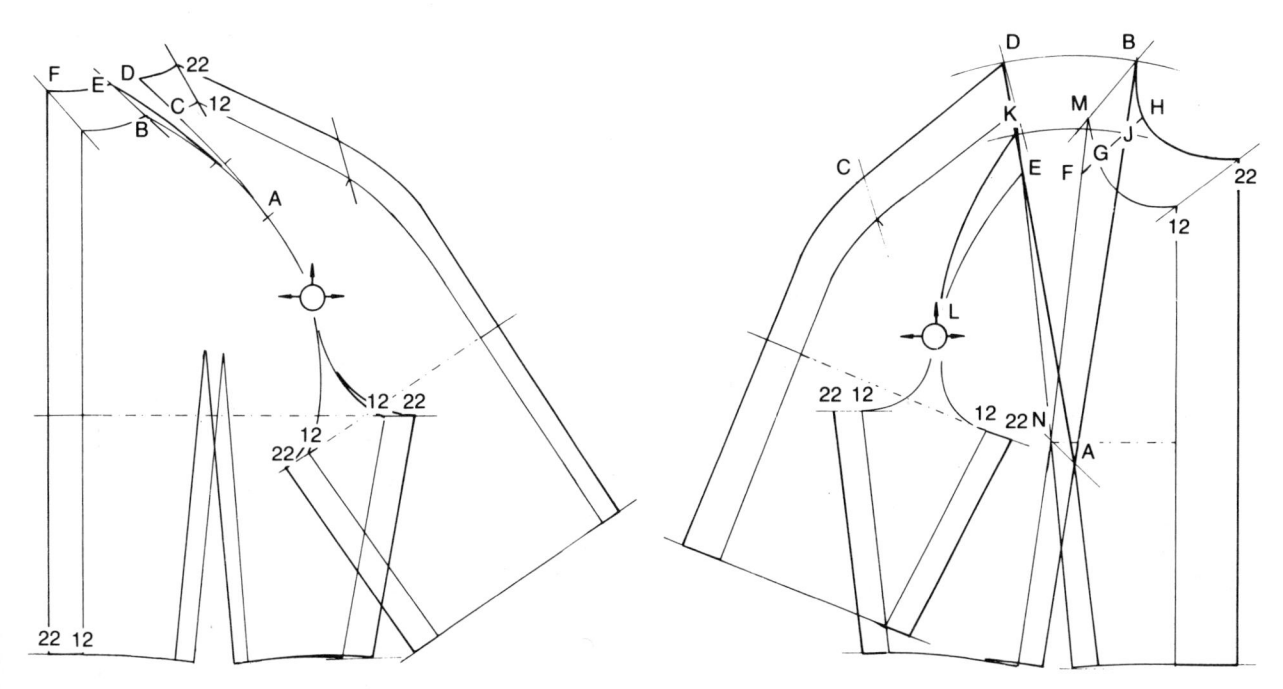

Figure 201 Five size grade

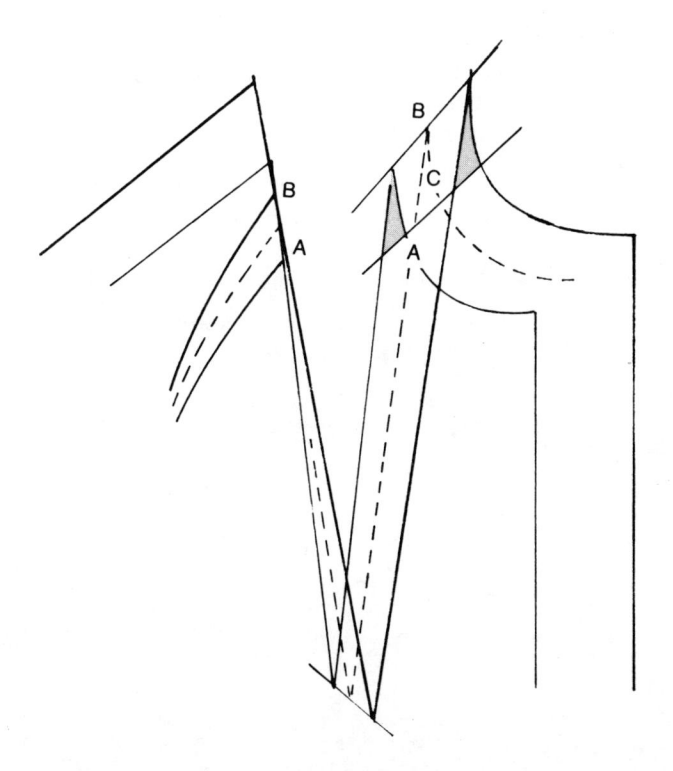

Figure 202 Illustrating the division of the gorge side of the style line. Trace-off section A–B–C and connect to points A–B. For size 16 raglan sleeve section

STYLE 23

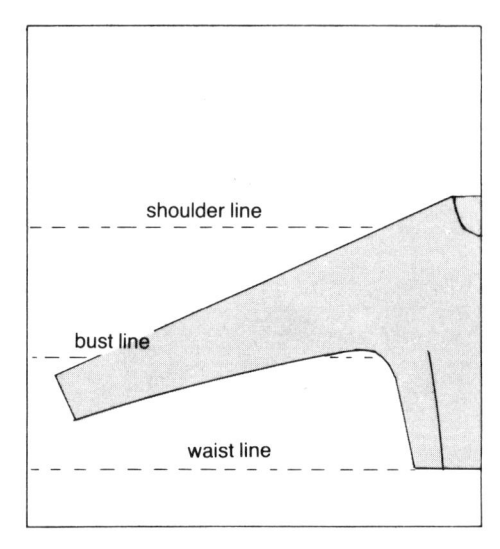

Figure 203 Style 23 – basic kimono

THE BASIC KIMONO

ZERO SELECTION

The kimono (Figure 203) is probably the most common variety of grown-on sleeve. When grading this sleeve, the zero point, shown in Figure 204a, is probably the best one as it presents a slight advantage because the side seam remains virtually static for each size.

GRADING SPECIFICATION

1	Size chart	Table 13
2	Size range	10·12·14·16·18·20·22
3	Height/girth/length	Height and girth
4	Proportioning	
5	Type of grade	2 dim. draft or track
6	Zero points front	Side seam at waist
7	Zero point back	Side seam at waist
8	Zero point sleeve	nil
9	Zero point front skirt	nil
10	Zero point back skirt	nil
11	Category of fit	Fitted
Comments		
Check underarm length on completion.		

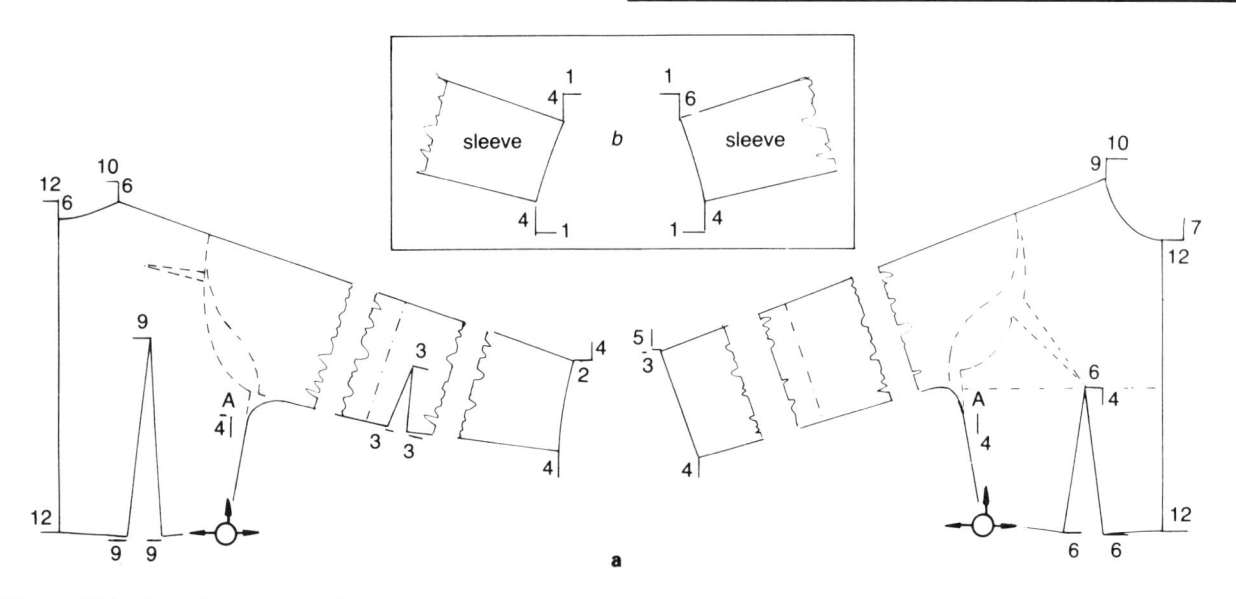

Figure 204 (a) Increments for one size
(b) Alternative grading for the sleeve ends

STYLE GRADES 1 TO 33

SLEEVE ANGLE
Unlike the magyar, the sleeve angle does not have to change for each size because this type of sleeve is fairly loose-fitting and the angle, once established for the size 12, can be retained throughout the size range.

BUST SUPPRESSION
A two-dimensional grade is suitable for this style because an increase in suppression is not considered significant on a loose-fitting garment.

THE GRADING SYSTEM
The system illustrated for this grade is a single track system and is based on vertical and horizontal angles to the centre front and back. These grade quantities are applied using either a draft or track grade. Also note that the girth grade is simplified, i.e., an increase of 12.0 cm front and back.

Note: The increments for the sleeve ends shown in Figure 204a are only applicable where the front shoulder angle is approximately 25° from the

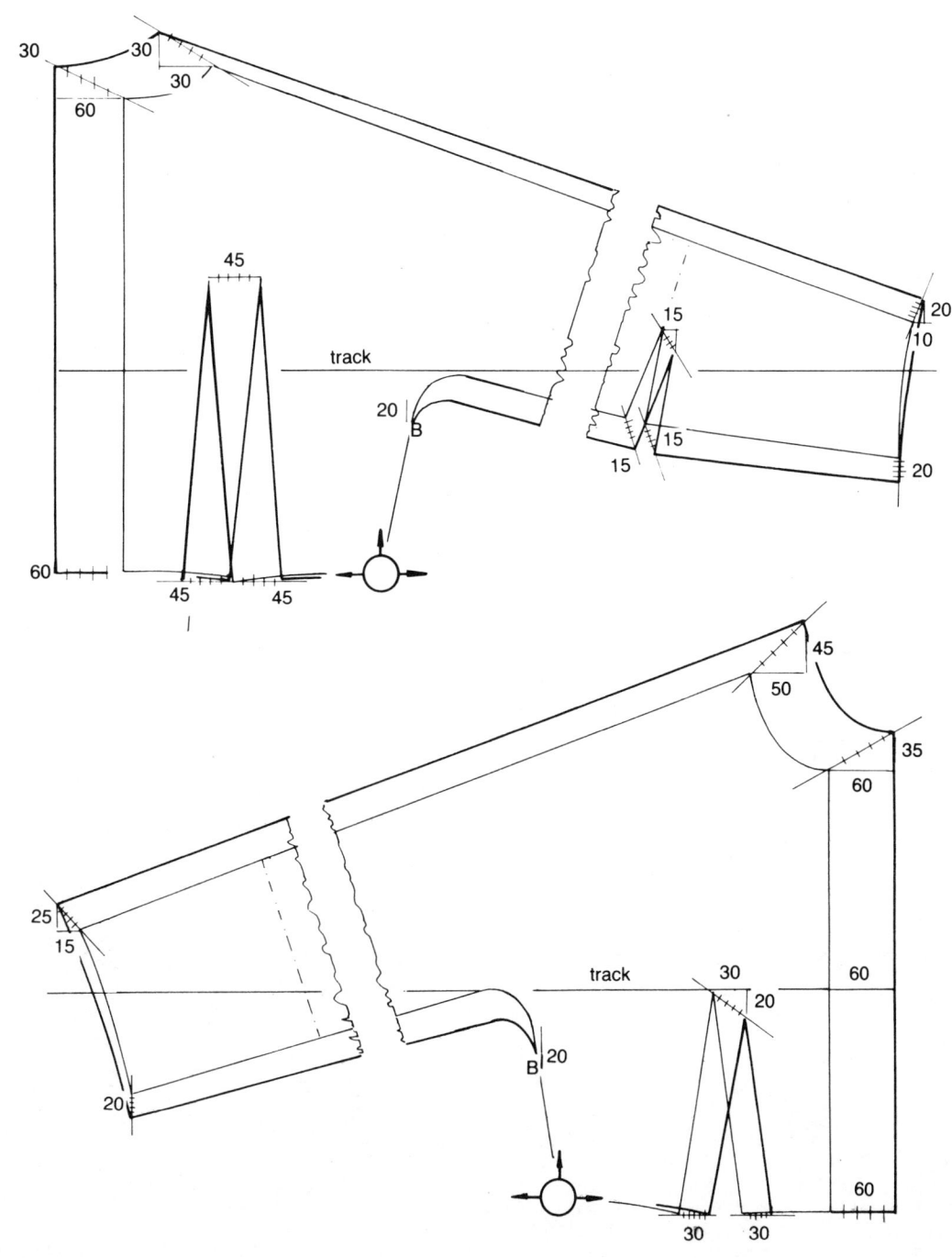

Figure 205 Grade for five sizes

centre front and the back shoulder angle approximately 22° from the centre back. If a sleeve differs greatly from these angles then grade the sleeve ends as in Figure 204b.

METHOD
1. Mark around the kimono pattern or construct directly from the basic blocks.
2. Figure 204a shows the increments for one size. Multiply these by the number of sizes required and apply them to the cardinal points as illustrated in Figure 205.
3. Point A is where the curve of the underarm sleeve seam meets the side seam of the bodice. Point B is a guide to aid the shaping of the size 22 underarm seam and is located 0.4 cm down from B.
4. Divide up intermediate sizes and spike-off.

STYLE GRADES 1 TO 33

STYLE 24

	GRADING SPECIFICATION		
1	Size chart	Table 13	
2	Size range	10·12·14·16·18·20·22	
3	Height/girth/length	Height and girth	
4	Proportioning	Neck band and style line retained	
5	Type of grade	2 dim. track or draft	
6	Zero points front	Side seam at waist	
7	Zero point back	Side seam at waist	
8	Zero point sleeve	nil	
9	Zero point front skirt	nil	
10	Zero point back skirt	nil	
11	Category of fit	Loose	
Comments			
Loose style only requiring elementary grade.			

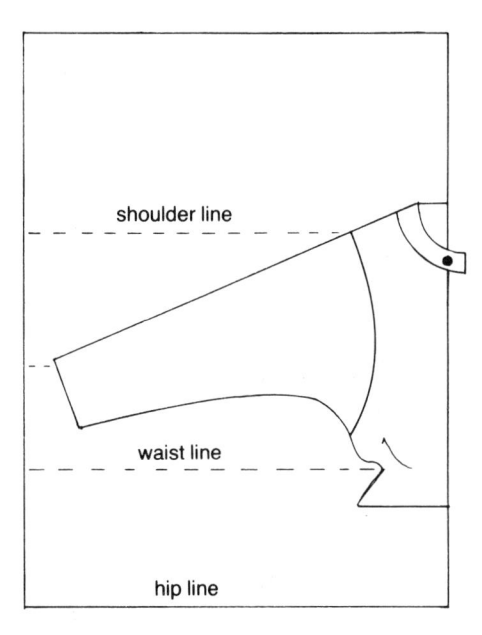

Figure 206 Style 24 – batwing blouse with inset front tab opening

BATWING BLOUSE WITH INSET NECK BAND

This style (Figure 206) is graded by the same method as the kimono sleeve. It should be noted that the style line moves over by the same amount as the shoulder, i.e., 2 mm per size. The simplest method of grading the neck band is to:

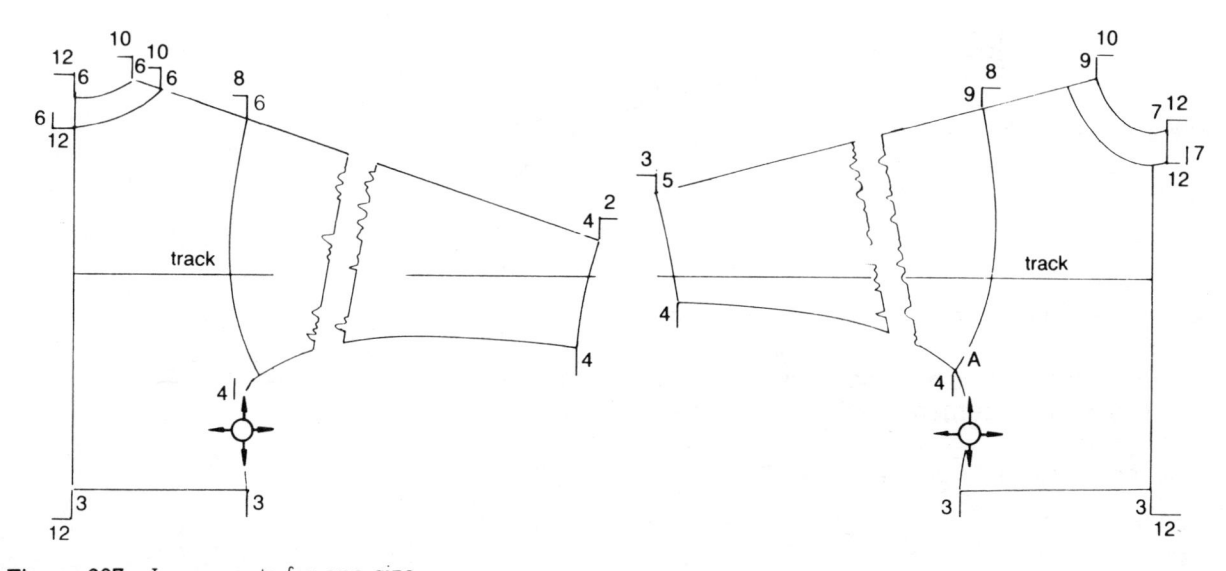

Figure 207 Increments for one size

Figure 208 Grade for five size

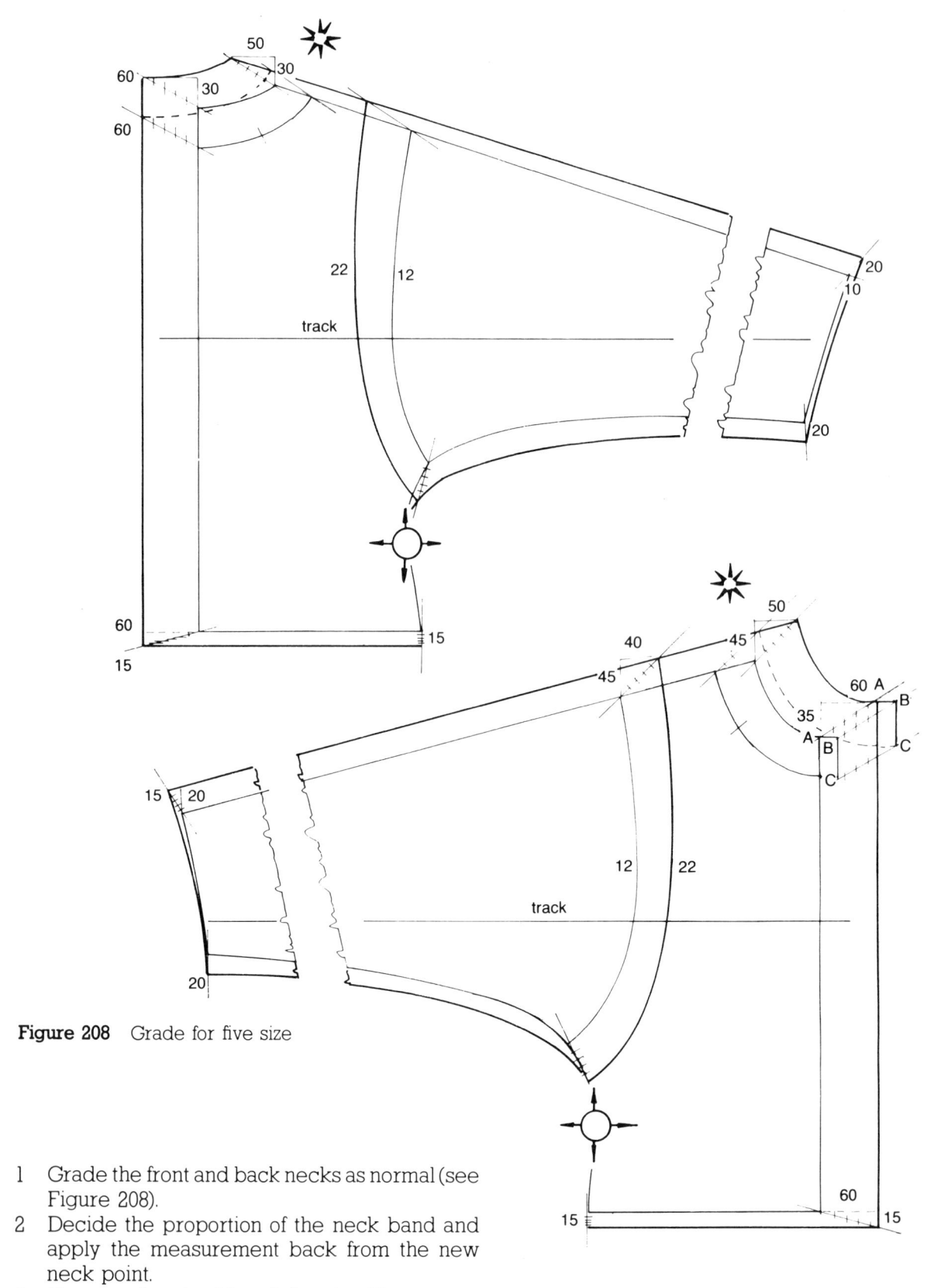

1. Grade the front and back necks as normal (see Figure 208).
2. Decide the proportion of the neck band and apply the measurement back from the new neck point.
3. Connect the size 12 and the size 22.

The neck band is a style option because it could change size if required. Mark the intermediate sizes, spike-off and check seam lengths.

STYLE GRADES 1 TO 33   217

STYLE 25

	GRADING SPECIFICATION	
1	Size chart	Table 13
2	Size range	10·12·14·16·18·20·22
3	Height/girth/length	Height and girth
4	Proportioning	
5	Type of grade	3 dim. N.S.B.P.
6	Zero points front	Pitch points B.+ F.
7	Zero point back	nil
8	Zero point sleeve	nil
9	Zero point front skirt	nil
10	Zero point back skirt	nil
11	Category of fit	Tight
	Comments	
	See raglan grade	

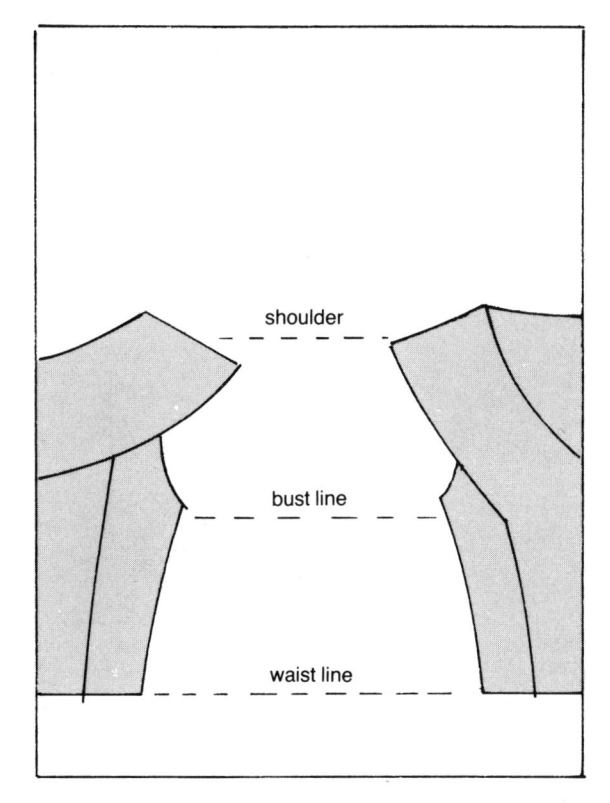

Figure 209 Style 25 – cap sleeve running into a styled suppression seam

CAP SLEEVE

The grade for the cap sleeve (Figure 209) is based on the raglan grade. The zero is sited at the front and back scye pitch points.

Figure 210 shows the increments and grade angles for one size. It should be noted that to obtain the correct suppression increase, grade the front neck point and shoulder point as the block neck grade (see Figure 211 and also previous examples).

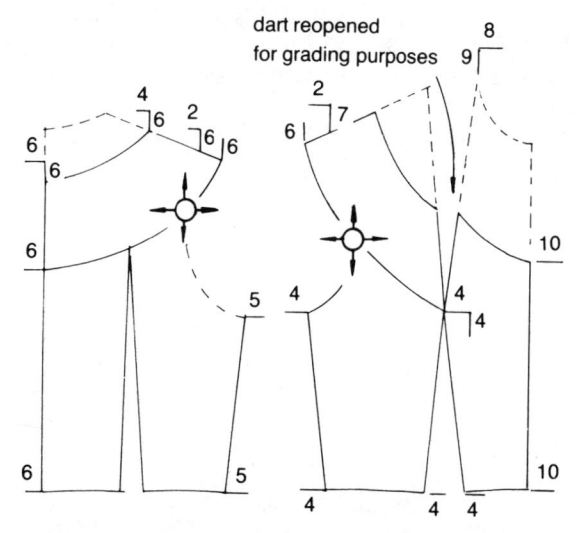

Figure 210 Increments for one size and grade angles

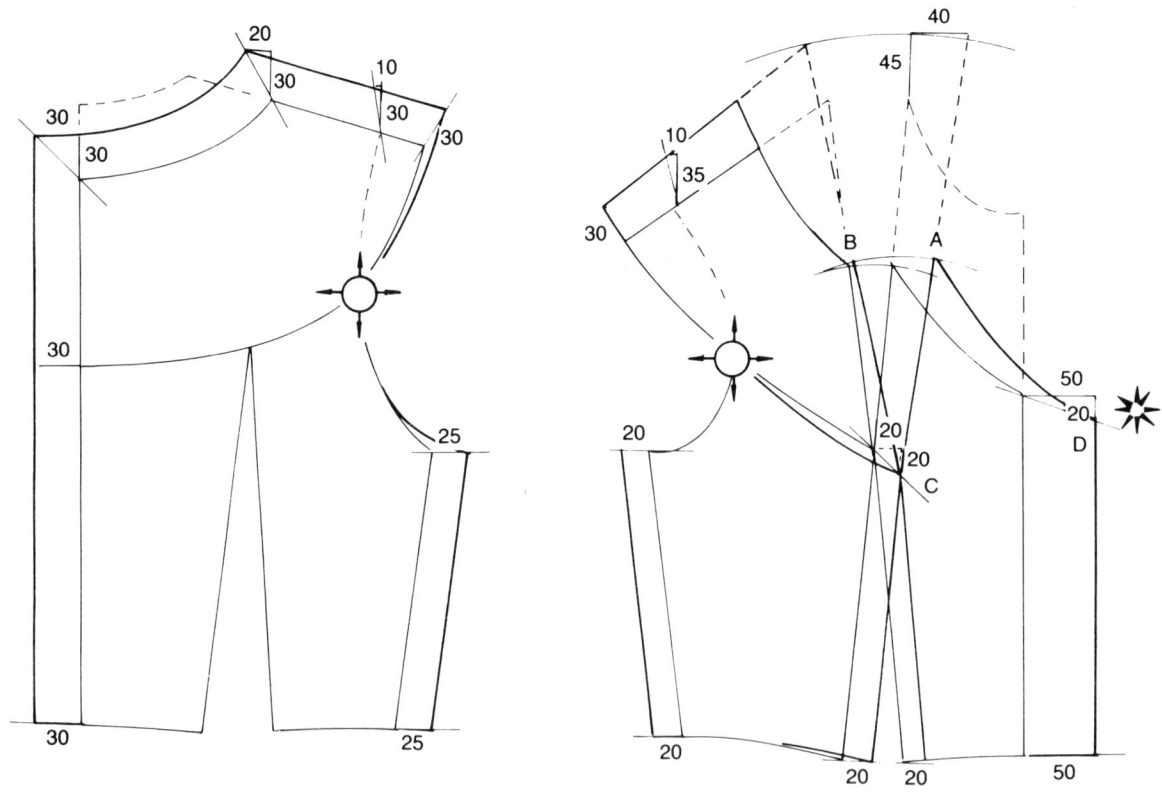

Figure 211 Grade for five sizes

NECKLINE
Continue neckline through to the size 22 shoulder. Swing an arc centre C through B to establish A. Then continue line down to the new centre front. Point D is graded downwards. However, this is a style decision.

SHOULDER LINE
Blend the line from zero to the new bust point, C. Alternatively raise the bust point so that the line from the zero can be continued without adjustment.

Spike-off required sizes and close out unwanted neck dart into waist dart.

STYLE GRADES 1 TO 33   219

STYLE 26

	GRADING SPECIFICATION	
1	Size chart	Table 13
2	Size range	10·12·14·16·18·20·22
3	Height/girth/length	Height and girth
4	Proportioning	
5	Type of grade	3 dim. draft
6	Zero points front	Centre waist dart
7	Zero point back	Centre waist dart
8	Zero point sleeve	Midway bicep line
9	Zero point front skirt	nil
10	Zero point back skirt	nil
11	Category of fit	Tight
Comments		
Could be 2 dim. graded over a limited size range.		

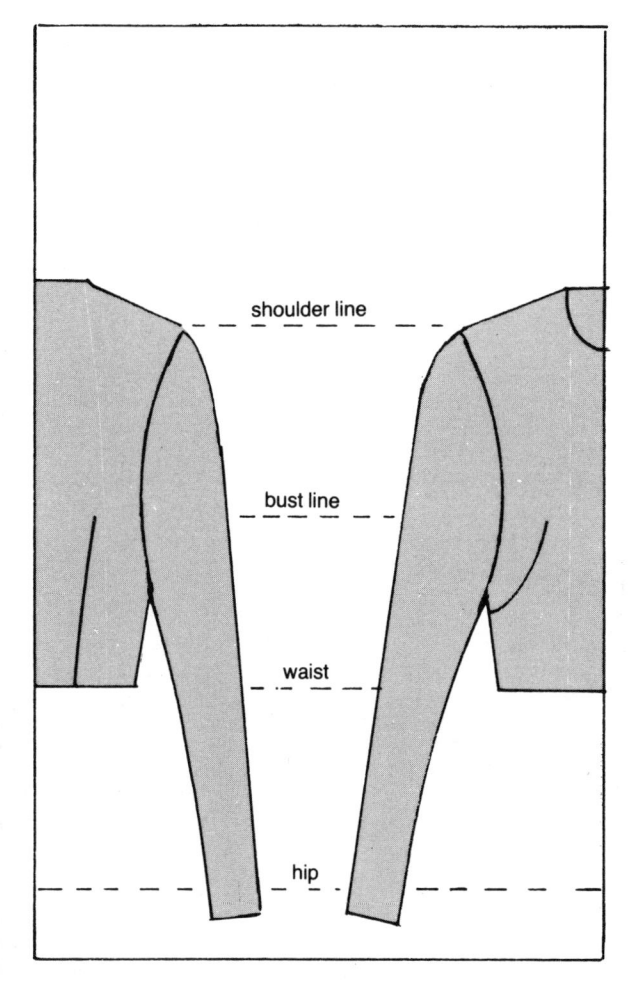

Figure 212 Style 26 – split dolman sleeve with curved dart

DOLMAN OR DEEP SCYE SLEEVE

The dolman or deep scye sleeve (Figure 212) is an adaptation of the basic set-in sleeve and bodice.

1. To grade this bodice and sleeve, follow the instructions shown in Figures 213 and 214.
2. Note that to obtain the largest size suppression, describe an arc from A through B. Apply largest shoulder measurement, i.e., 13.5 cm from C to touch arc. See Chapter 10 for a fuller explanation.
3. To obtain the back dart, grade points D and E. Then apply back bodice to point D and mark around dart. Connect to point E.

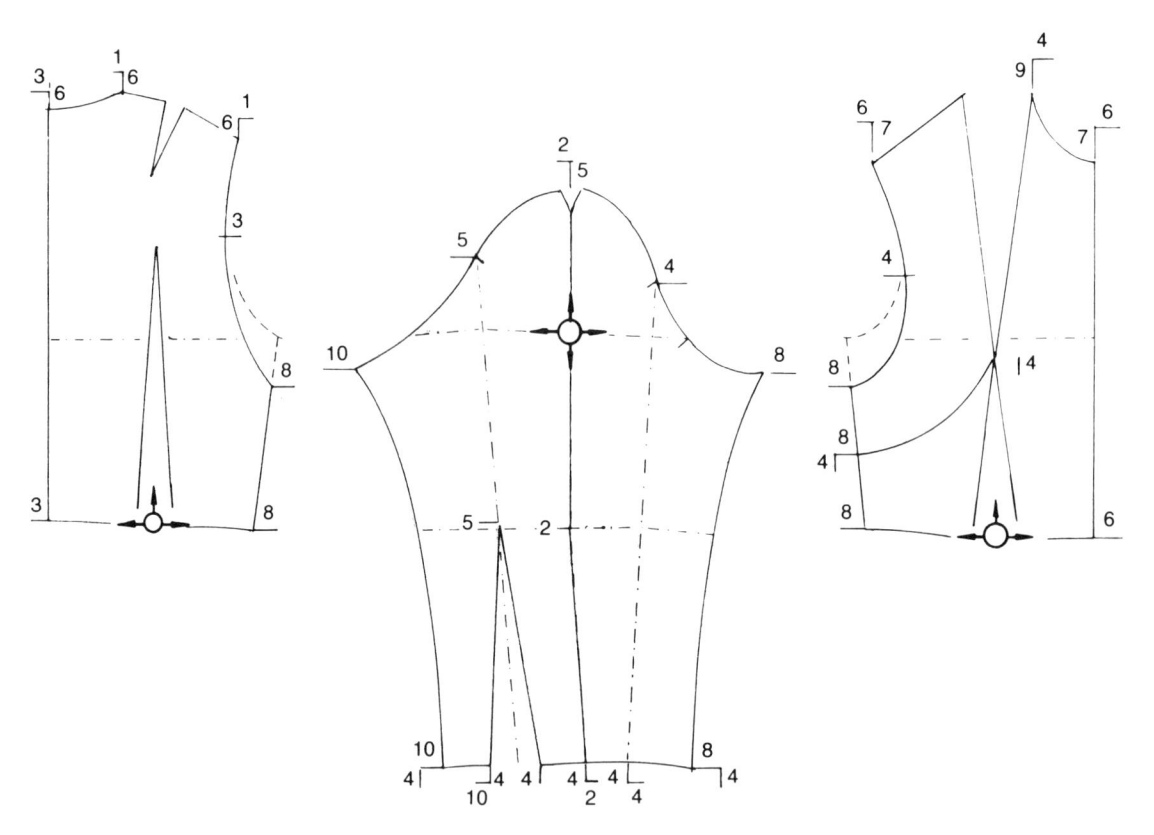

Figure 213 Increments for one size

STYLE GRADES 1 TO 33

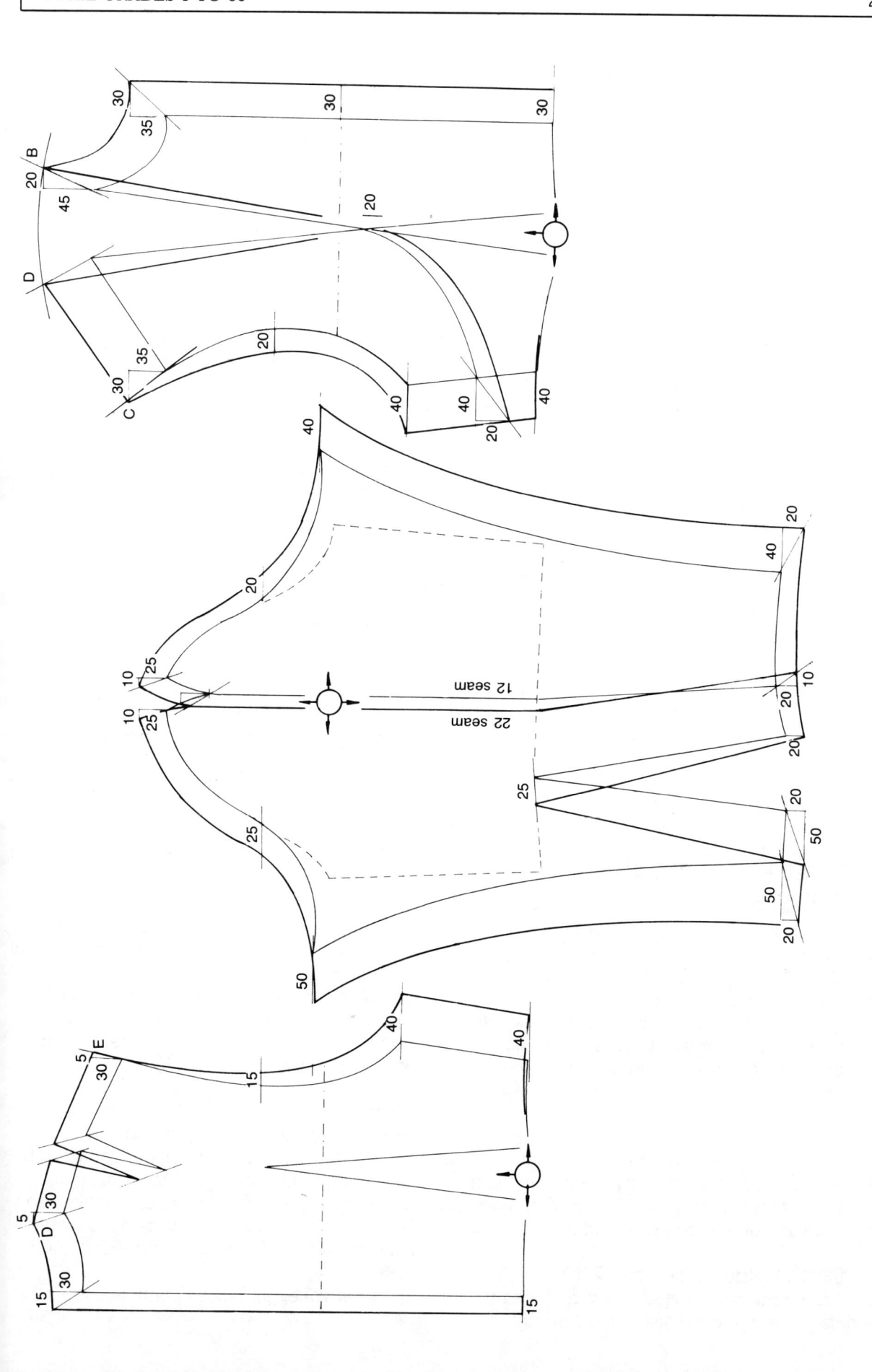

Figure 214 Grade for five sizes

STYLE 27

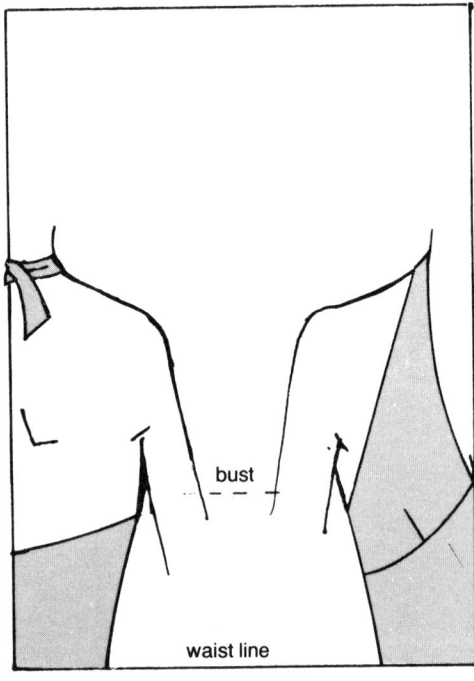

Figure 215 Style 27 – halter neck

GRADING SPECIFICATION		
1	Size chart	Table 13
2	Size range	10·12·14·16
3	Height/girth/length	Height and girth
4	Proportioning	
5	Type of grade	3 dim. draft N.S.B.P.
6	Zero points front	Waist at dart. Static bust point
7	Zero point back	Waist
8	Zero point sleeve	nil
9	Zero point front skirt	nil
10	Zero point back skirt	nil
11	Category of fit	Tight
Comments		
If stretch fabric, a 2 dim. grade could be used.		

FITTED HALTER NECK WITH UNDERBUST SEAM

To grade this style (Figure 215) return the pattern to its draft form, i.e., with all its darts sited as in Figure 216. This will enable the bust suppression to increase per size, an essential prerequisite of this very fitted contour style. It is also essential to drop the bust point per size in order to retain the necessary fit on the important underbust seam. To achieve this, the special zero has been selected.

THE ZERO

This front zero point enables the bust point to stay static and the waist moves up by the amount that the bust point should drop, i.e., 0.4 cm. The back zero is midway on the centre waistline.

SUPPRESSION (Figures 217 and 218)

Most of this grade is self-explanatory, however the suppression needs to be discussed further.

1. Establish the shoulder neck point grade (point C, Figure 217).
2. Establish the shoulder end grade (point D).
3. Swing an arc centre bust point E through C.
4. Apply largest shoulder measurement from point D to touch arc (point F).
5. Connect F and C to the bust point.
6. Continue E through F to G. (The grade of the back neck extension will depend on its fastening, for example if it is a tie, it may possibly be long enough to accommodate all sizes.)
7. Connect A–C and A–F to establish other sizes.
8. Spike-off largest size and close out unwanted bust dart into the lower part of the dart (Figure 218).
9. Spike-off yokes and close out unwanted waist dart.

STYLE GRADES 1 TO 33   223

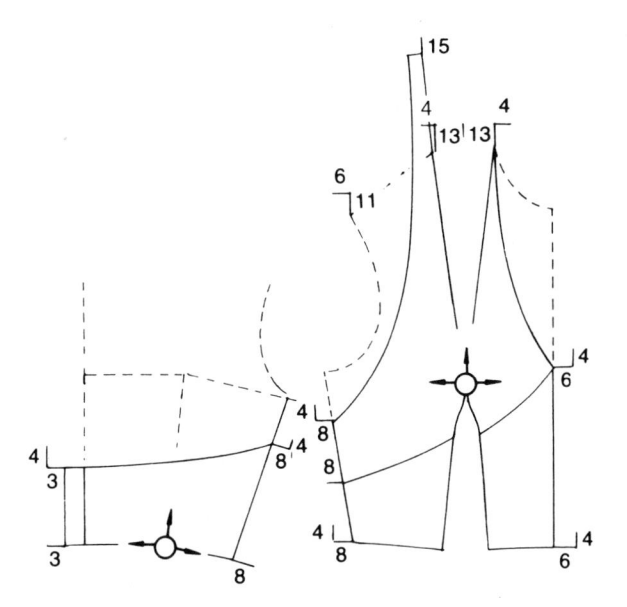

Figure 216 Grade angles and increments for one size

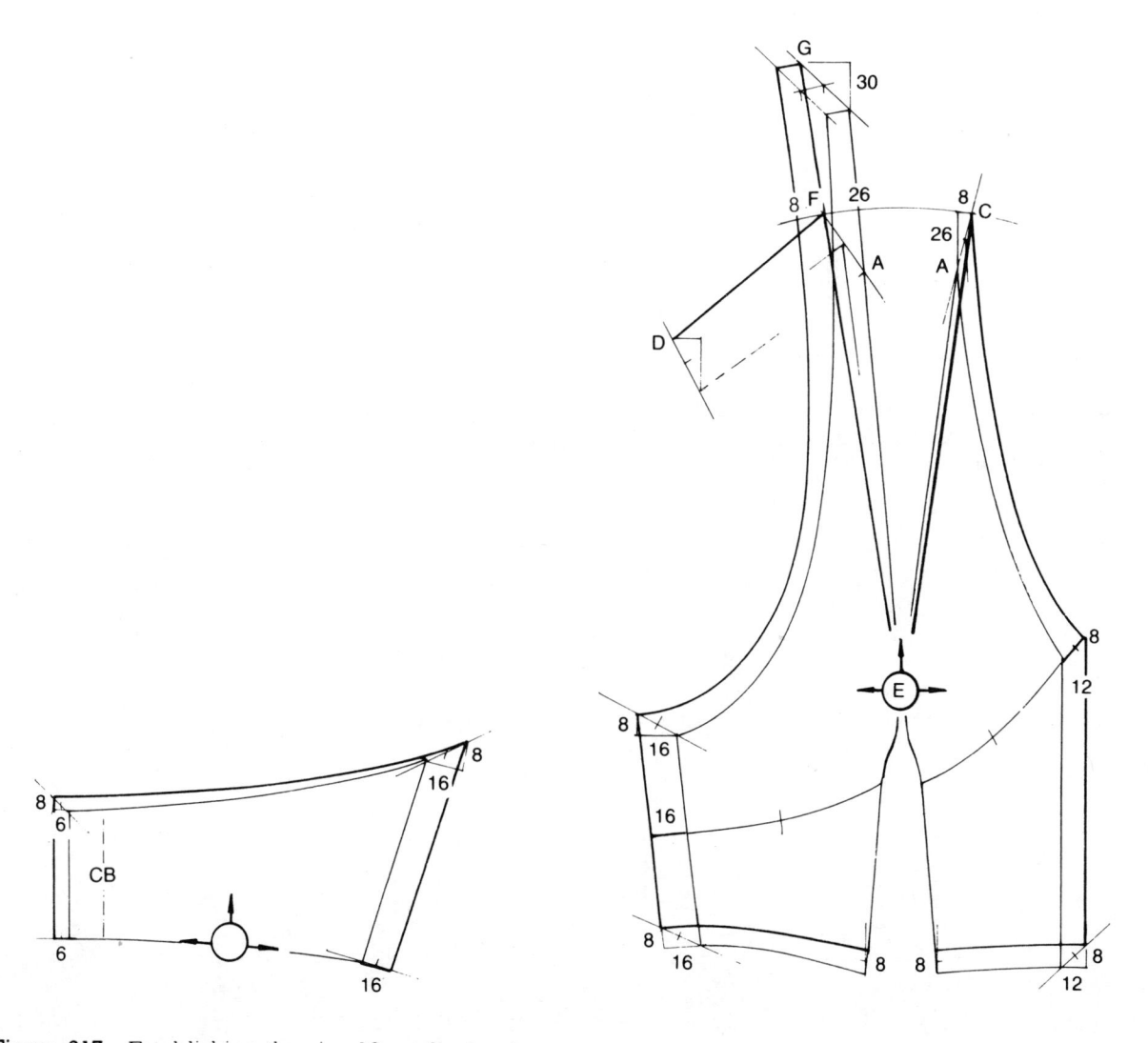

Figure 217 Establishing the size 16 cardinal points

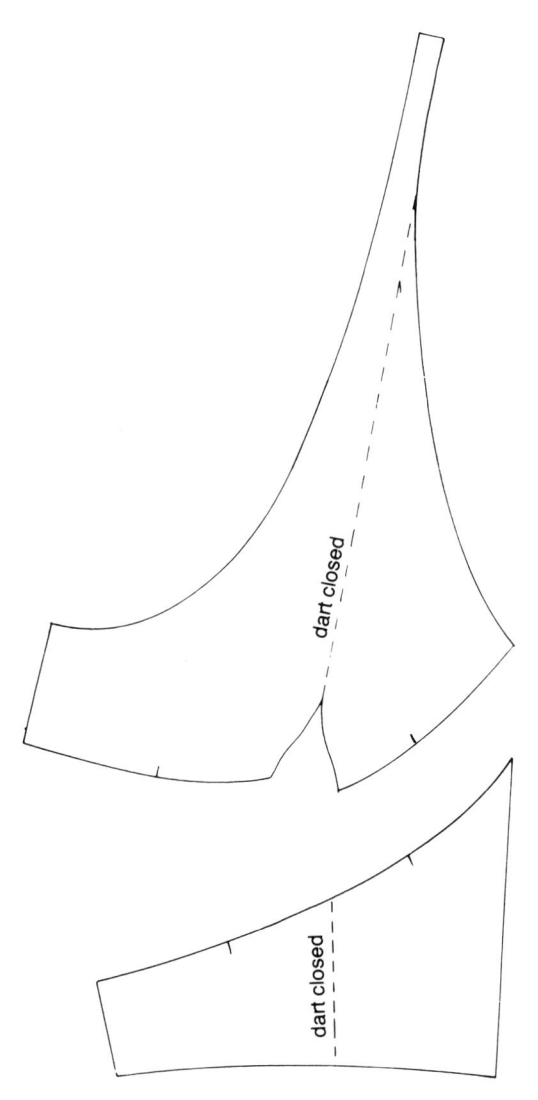

Figure 218 Size 16 spiked-off from the draft and suppressions returned to finished positions

STYLE 28

	GRADING SPECIFICATION	
1	Size chart	Table 13
2	Size range	10·12·14·16
3	Height/girth/length	Height and girth
4	Proportioning	
5	Type of grade	3 dim. draft N.S.B.P.
6	Zero points front	Waist
7	Zero point back	Waist
8	Zero point sleeve	nil
9	Zero point front skirt	nil
10	Zero point back skirt	nil
11	Category of fit	Tight
Comments		
If stretch fabric, a 2 dim. grade could be used.		

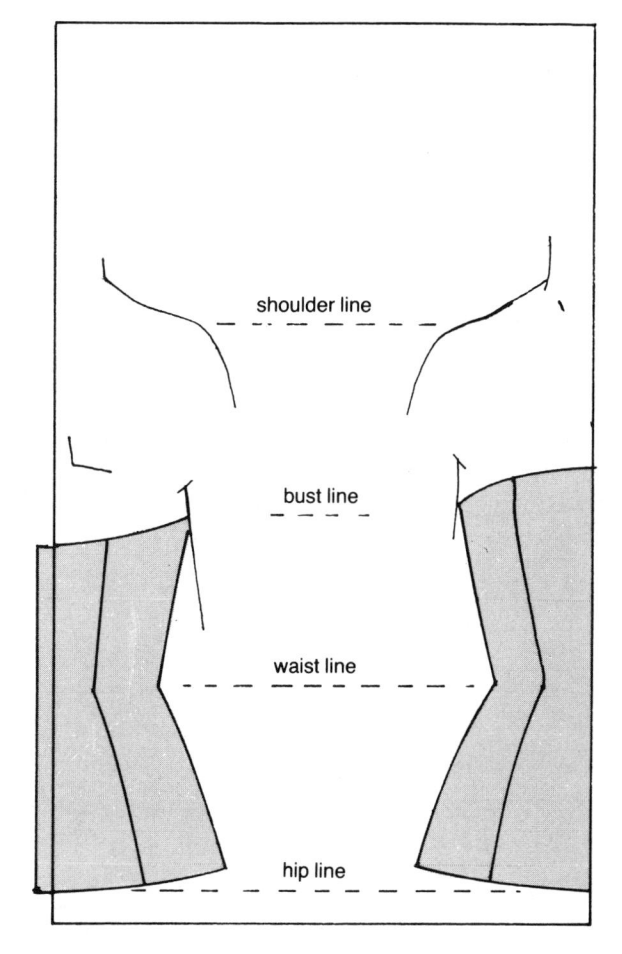

Figure 219 Style 28 – fitted evening top

FITTED STRAPLESS EVENING TOP

The bodice part of this garment (Figure 219) follows the contours of the body and the hip section is slightly flared from the waist.

SUPPRESSION

The grading of this style is self-explanatory except for the front suppression. As this is a very fitted top, the suppression must be adjusted for each size (see Figure 221). It is unnecessary to use the arc system as illustrated in the previous style (27). Simply follow the grade directions and increments shown in Figure 220. These increments are based on a chest grade which is 0.9 cm per size. For example, across the bust,

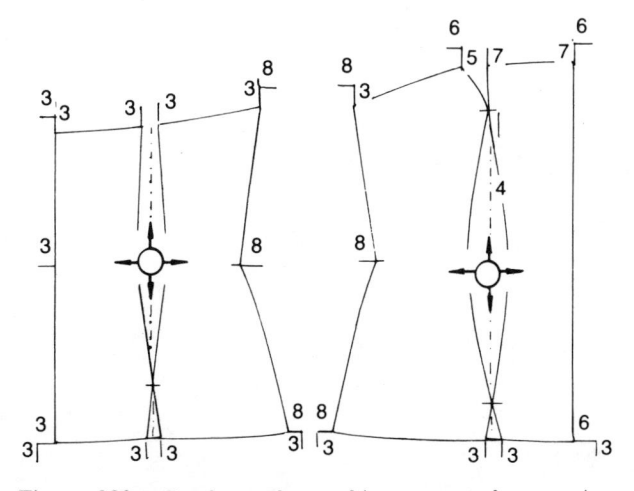

Figure 220 Grade angles and increments for one size

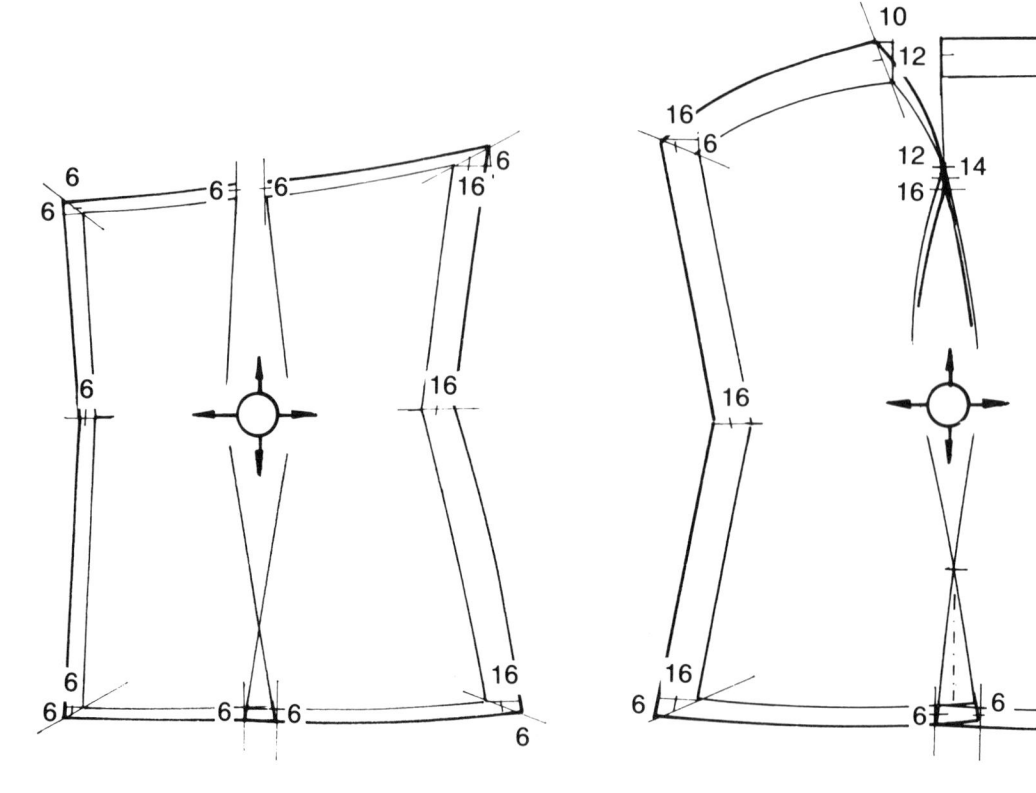

Figure 221 Grade for two sizes

increases on the draft by 14 mm. The chest should increase according to the survey by 9 mm. Therefore the difference is used to increase the front suppression, i.e., 5 mm. Use this technique for all strapless garments.

STYLE GRADES 1 TO 33

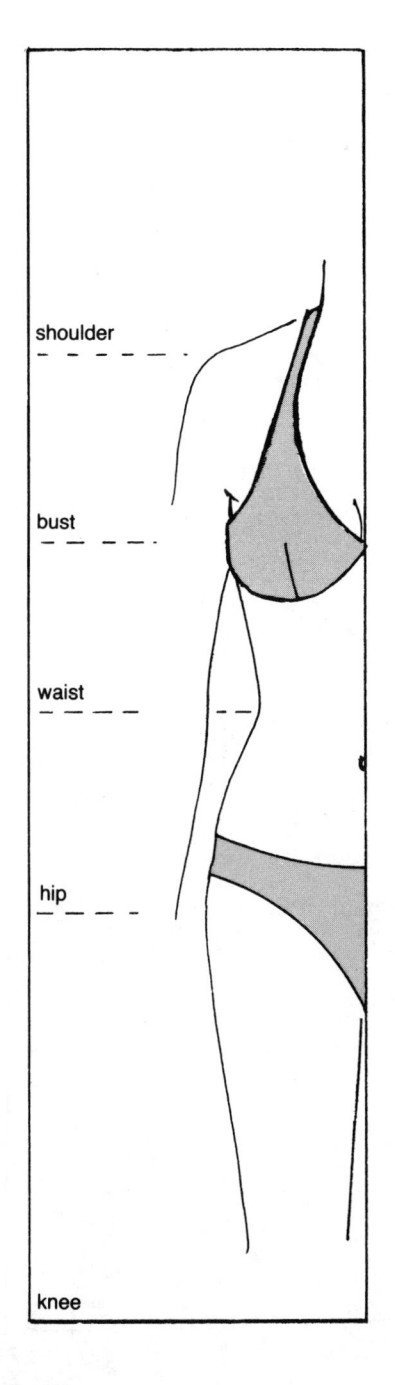

STYLE 29

	GRADING SPECIFICATION	
1	Size chart	Table 13
2	Size range	10·12·14·16
3	Height/girth/length	Height and girth
4	Proportioning	Cup increased per size
5	Type of grade	3 dim. draft N.S.B.P.
6	Zero points front	Bust point
7	Zero point back	nil
8	Zero point sleeve	nil
9	Zero point front skirt	Midway hip seam
10	Zero point back skirt	Midway hip seam
11	Category of fit	Tight
Comments		
Based on 3 dim. block grade, also compare with brassiere grade.		

BIKINI

This style (Figure 222) can be graded three-dimensionally by opening the dart by 0.5 cm per size at point A. This dart can then be repositioned into its final underbust position (see Figures 223 and 224).

Figure 222 Style 29 – bikini

228　　　　　　　　　　　　　　　　　　　　　　　　　　　　　　　　　　　　　　WOMEN'S STYLE GRADING

Figure 223 Three-dimensional increments for one size

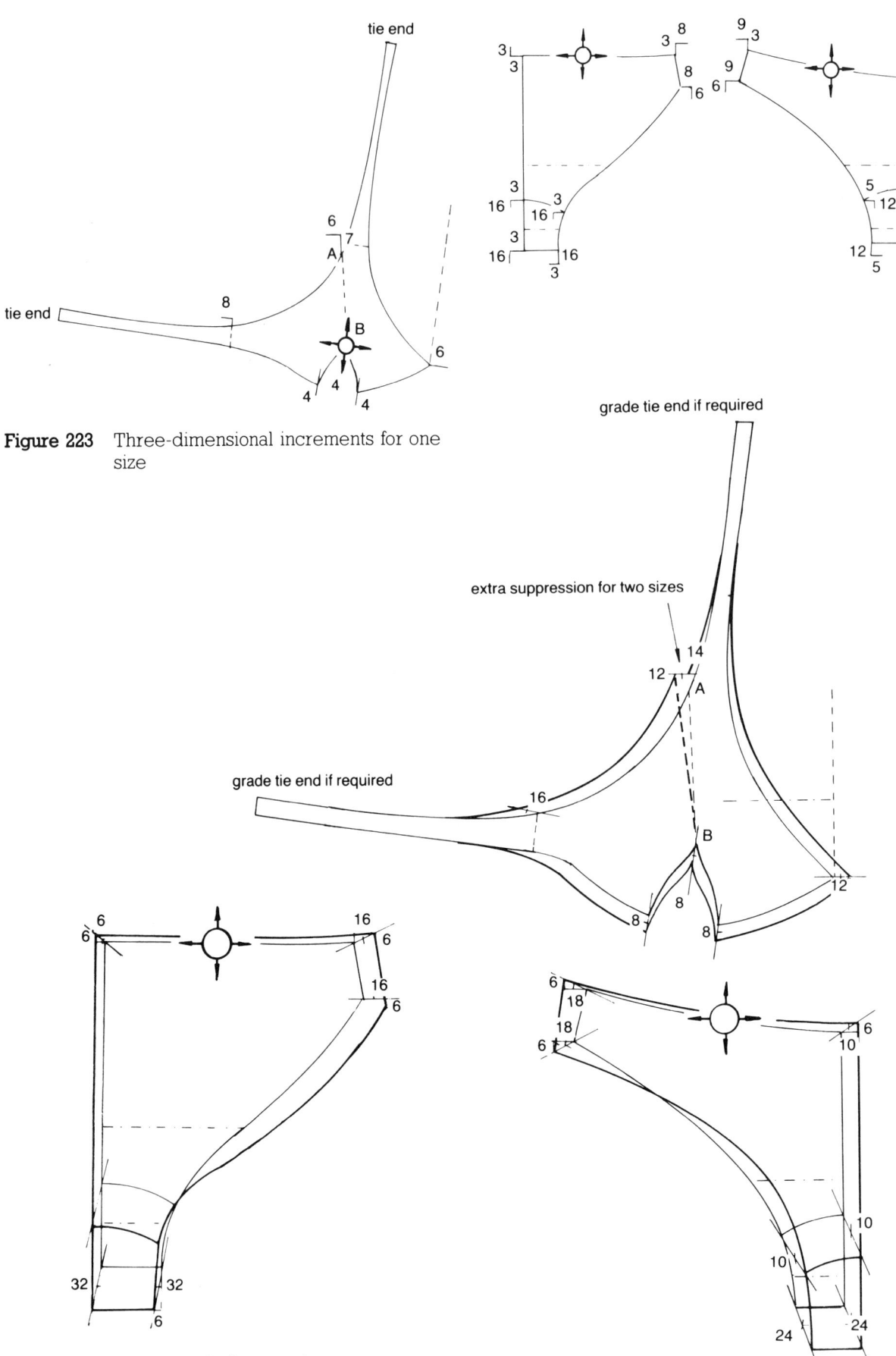

Figure 224 Bikini grade for two sizes

STYLE 30

	GRADING SPECIFICATION	
1	Size chart	Table 13
2	Size range	10·12·14·16·18
3	Height/girth/length	5.0 girth 2.4 height
4	Proportioning	
5	Type of grade	3 dim. draft
6	Zero points front	nil
7	Zero point back	nil
8	Zero point sleeve	nil
9	Zero point front skirt	Midway hip line
10	Zero point back skirt	Midway hip line
11	Category of fit	Semi-fitting
Comments	Could be a 2 dim. grade.	

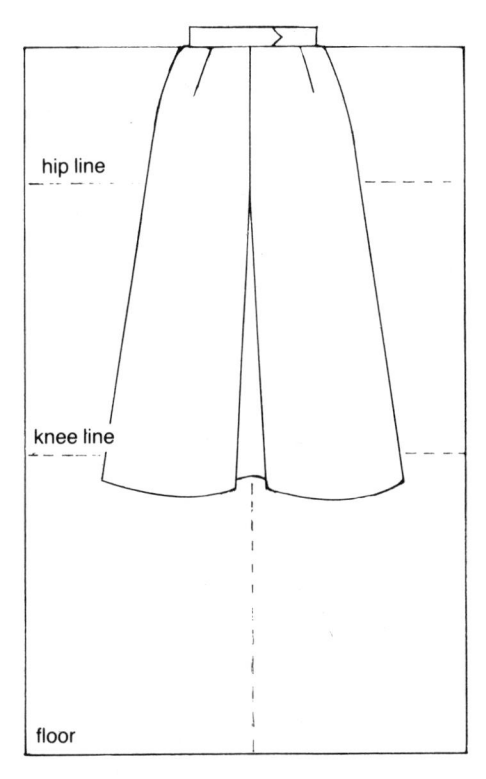

Figure 225 Style 30 – culottes

CULOTTES

This divided skirt style (Figure 225) is graded as a bifurcated garment and, therefore, the increments shown in the trouser grade, Chapter 2, and Figure 10 are used. Figure 226 shows the method of grading for one size only and Figure 227 shows the method of grading for three sizes.

230　　　　　　　　　　　　　　　　　　　　　　　　　　　　　　　　　WOMEN'S STYLE GRADING

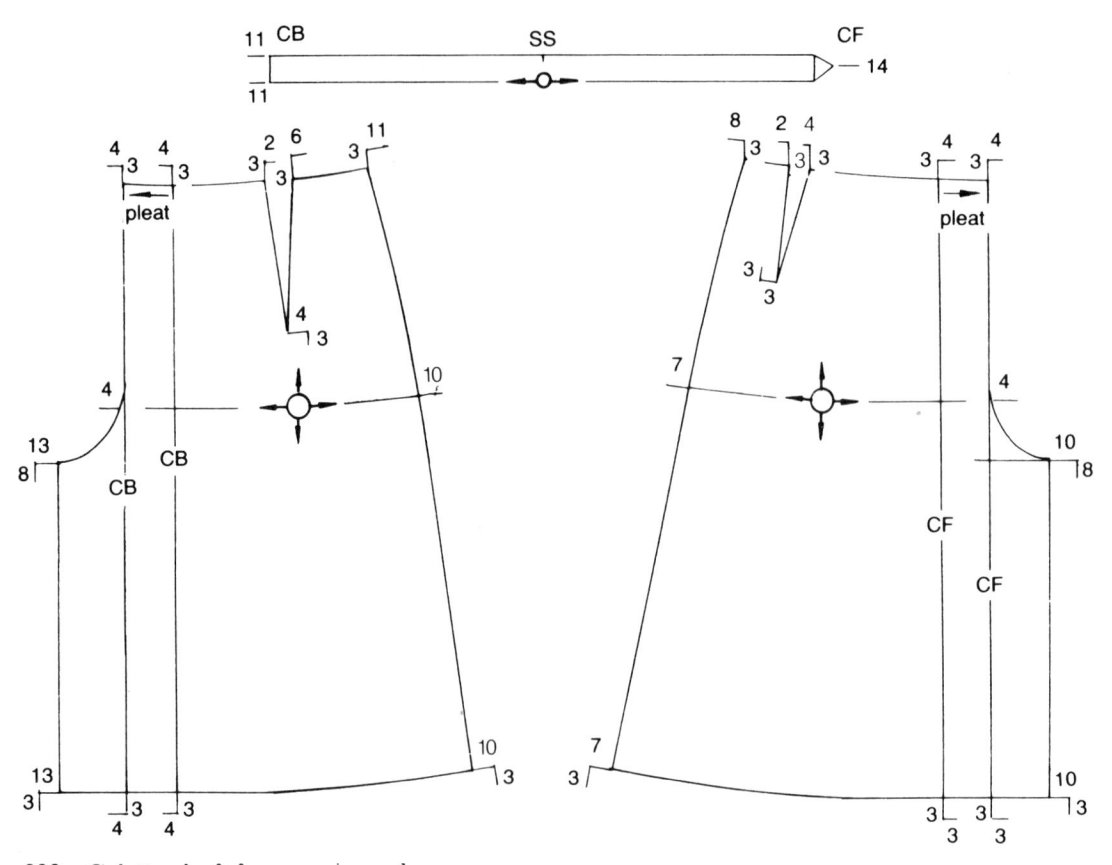

Figure 226　Culotte draft for one size only

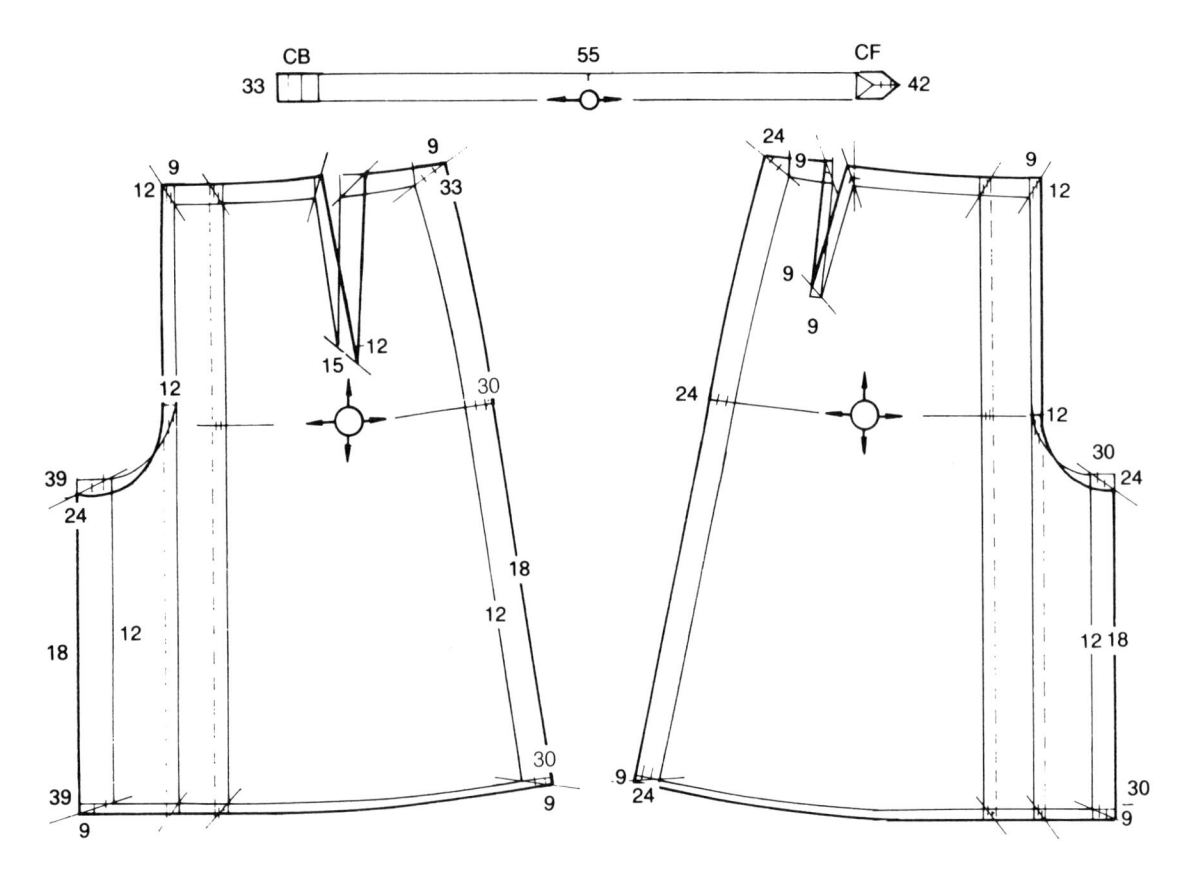

Figure 227　Grade for three sizes

STYLE GRADES 1 TO 33

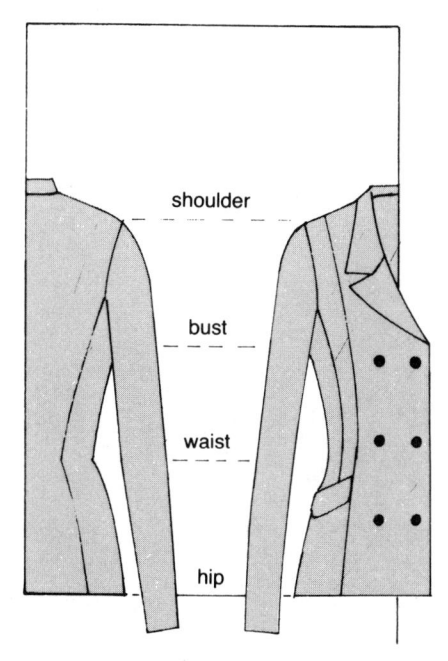

STYLE 31

Figure 228 Style 31 – double-breasted jacket and two-piece sleeve

DOUBLE-BREASTED JACKET WITH A TWO-PIECE SLEEVE

This classical jacket (Figure 228) is graded three-dimensionally using the increments shown in Figure 229. It is usual in the outerwear section of

	GRADING SPECIFICATION	
1	Size chart	Table 15
2	Size range	10·12·14·16·18·20·22
3	Height/girth/length	Height and girth
4	Proportioning	
5	Type of grade	3 dim. N.S.B.P.
6	Zero points front	Waist
7	Zero point back	Waist
8	Zero point sleeve	Centre bicep line
9	Zero point front skirt	nil
10	Zero point back skirt	nil
11	Category of fit	Tight
Comments	2 dim. grade not recommended.	

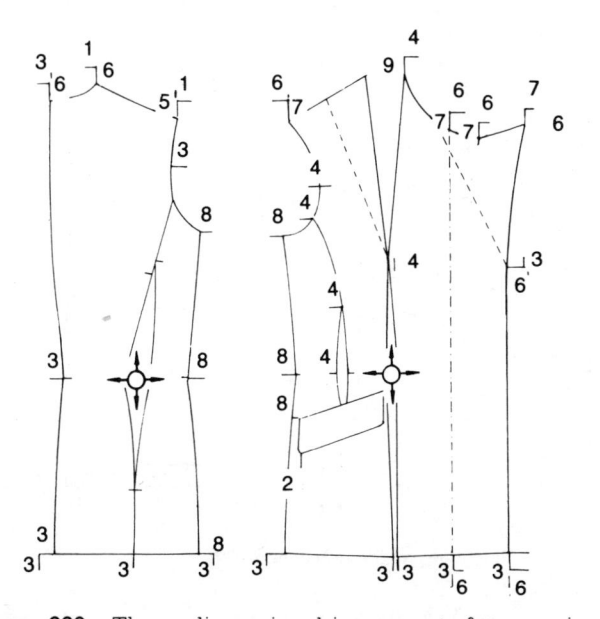

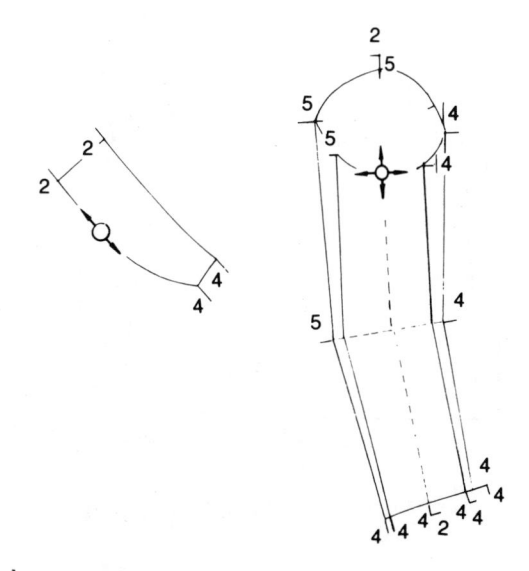

Figure 229 Three-dimensional increments for one size only

232 WOMEN'S STYLE GRADING

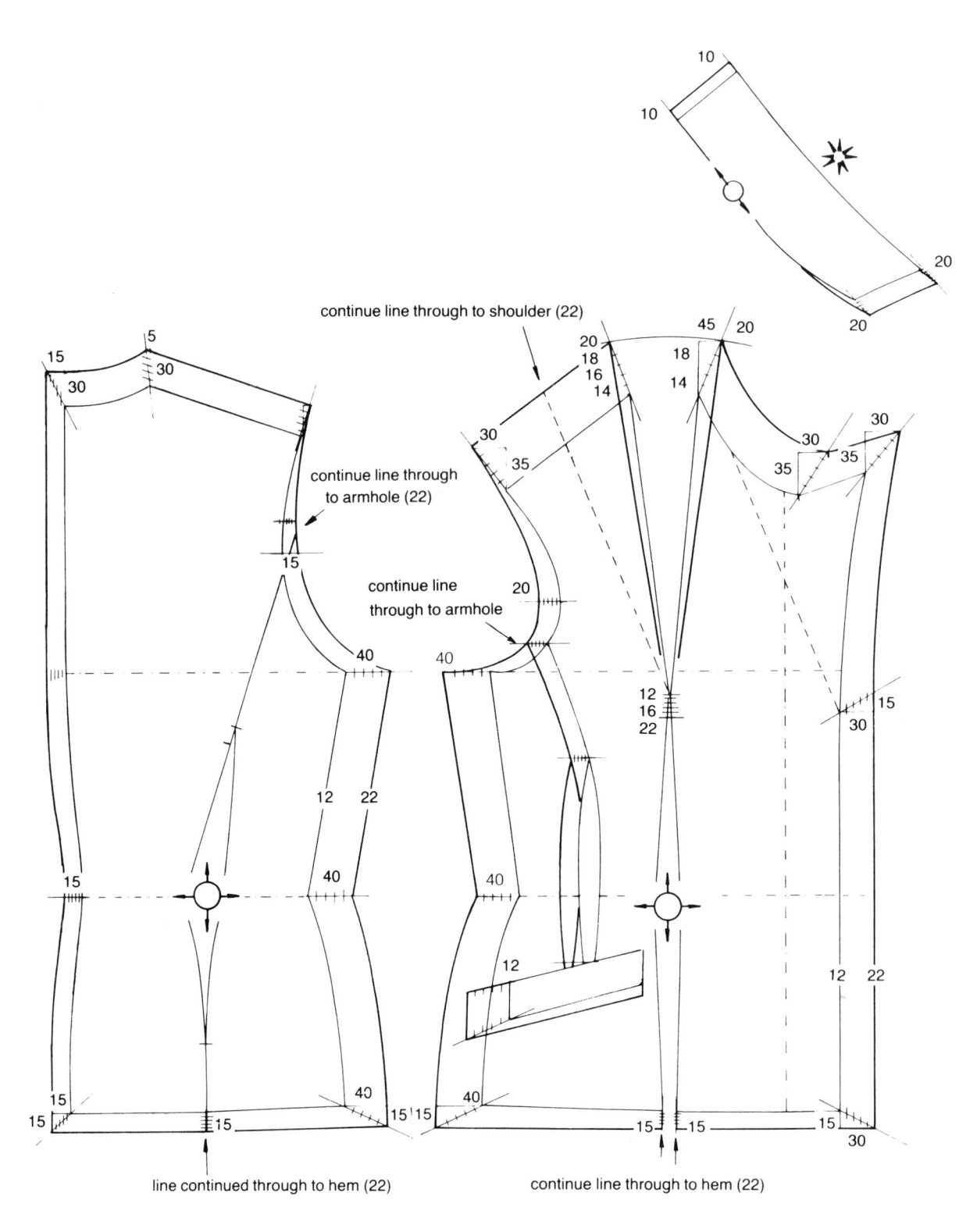

Figure 230 Increments for five sizes

STYLE GRADES 1 TO 33

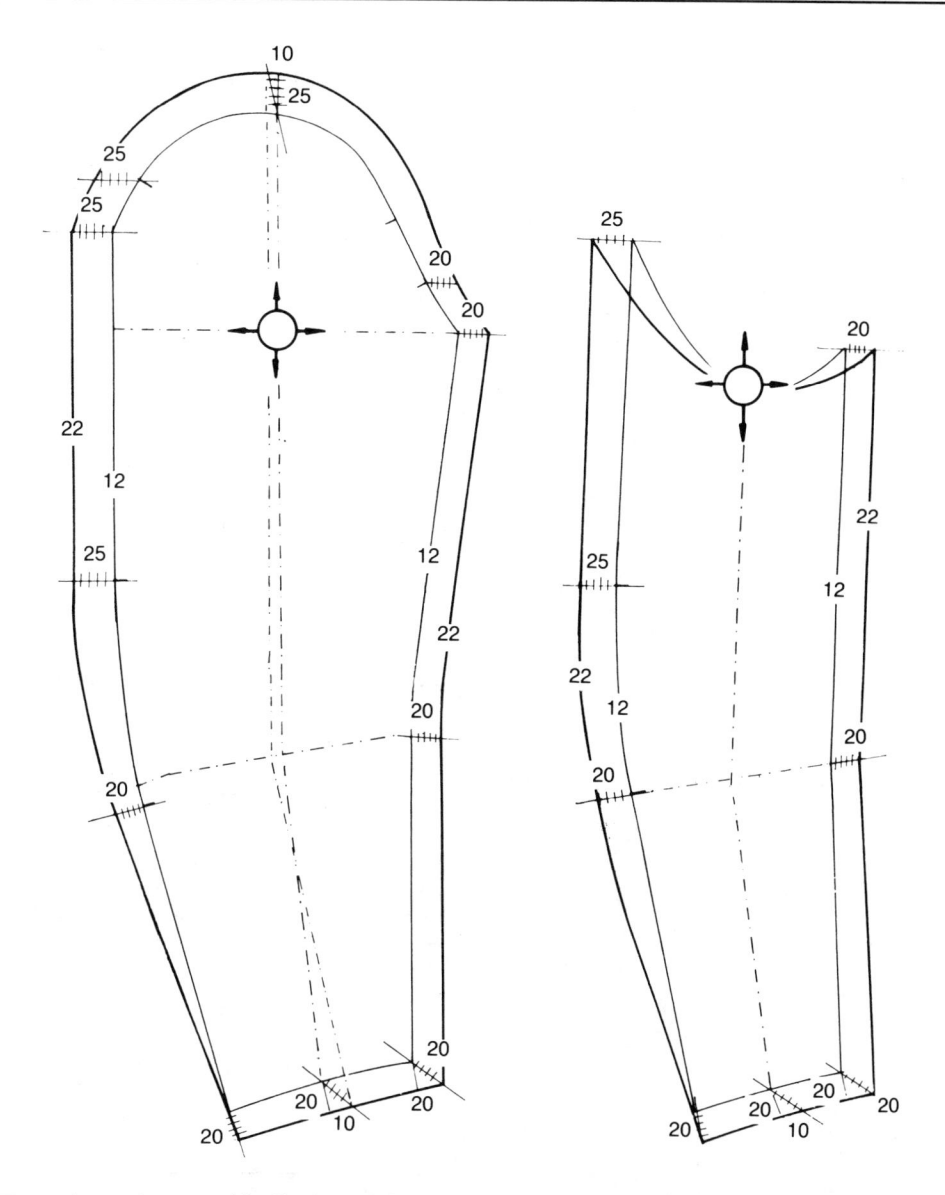

Figure 231 Two-piece sleeve with displaced forearm and hindarm. Grade for five sizes

the industry to use a 4.0 cm grade rather than a 5.0 cm grade. Refer to increments in Chapter 2 for a 4.0 cm grade plan. Note that the style line from the front shoulder to the bust point has been manipulated temporarily into the neck position to facilitate grading. It will subsequently be returned to its final position after the grades have been spiked-off (see Figure 230). It should also be noted that in the two-piece sleeve grade (Figure 231) all the wrist increase is located at forearm. It is important to ensure that the 'run' between top and undersleeve at the crown be checked and maintained. For sleeve grade tracks refer to the block grade in Chapter 10.

STYLE 32

	GRADING SPECIFICATION	
1	Size chart	Table 13
2	Size range	10.12.14.16.18.20.22
3	Height/girth/length	Height and girth
4	Proportioning	
5	Type of grade	3 dim. N.S.B.P.
6	Zero points front	Waist
7	Zero point back	Waist
8	Zero point sleeve	Bicep line centre
9	Zero point front skirt	nil
10	Zero point back skirt	nil
11	Category of fit	Semi-fitting
Comments	2 dim. grade could be used over a limited size range.	

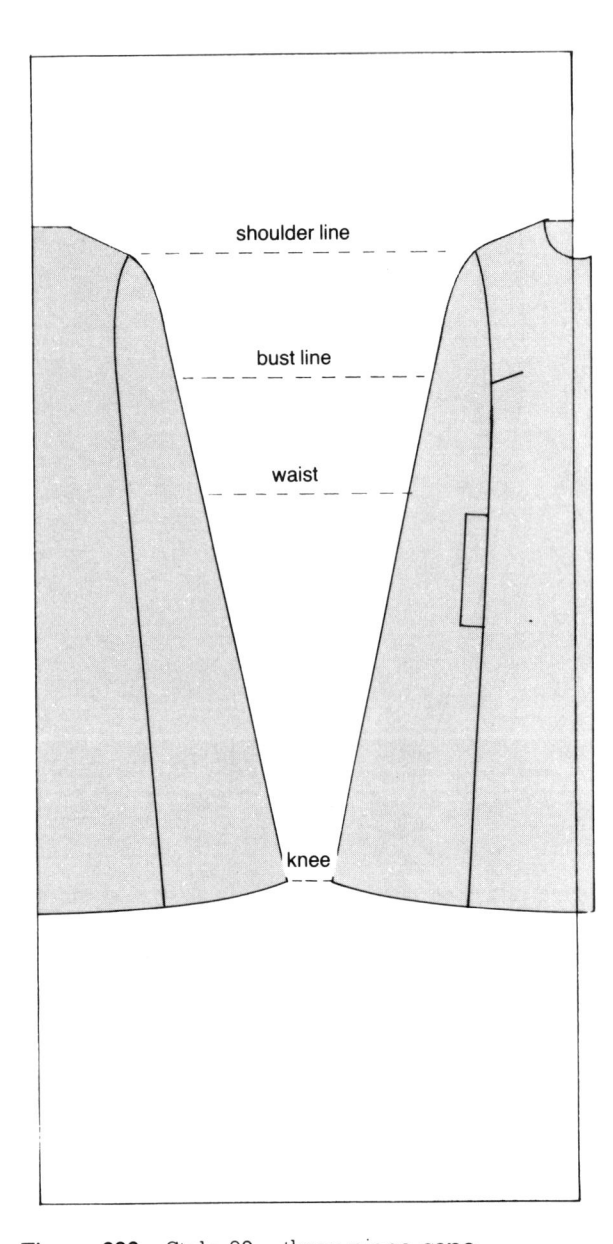

Figure 232 Style 32 – three-piece cape

THREE PIECE CAPE

This knee length cape (Figure 232) is graded three-dimensionally because it fits fairly snugly around the bust before flaring out at the hem. Grade this style in the same manner as other three-dimensional styles (Figure 233). Note that the dart from the style line to the bust point is transferred into the bust position for grading and then transferred back to its final position when the necessary sizes have been spiked-off. See Figure 234 for the method.

STYLE GRADES 1 TO 33   235

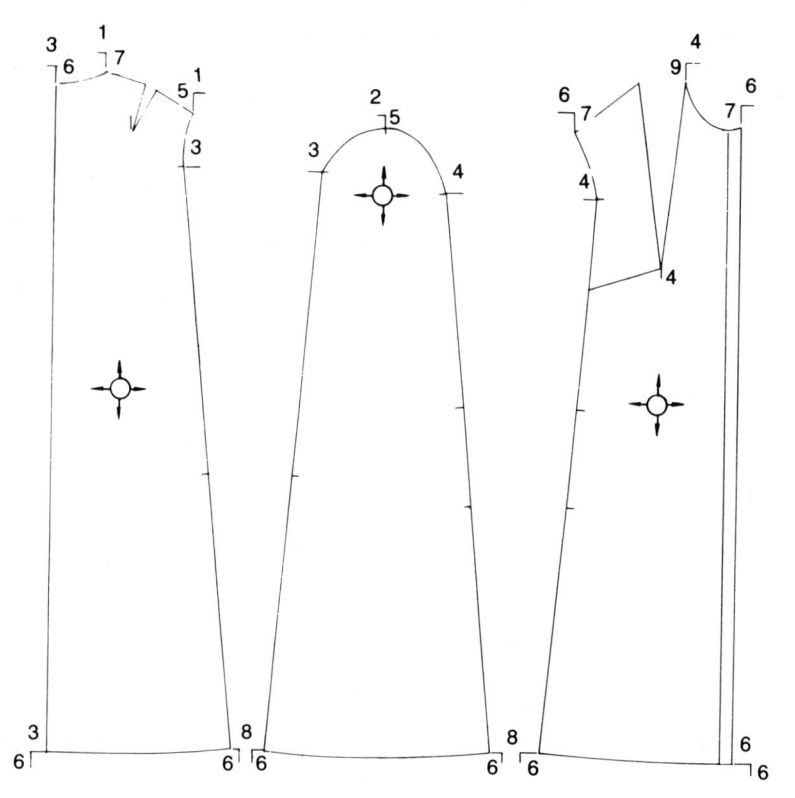

Figure 233 Three-dimensional increments for one size only

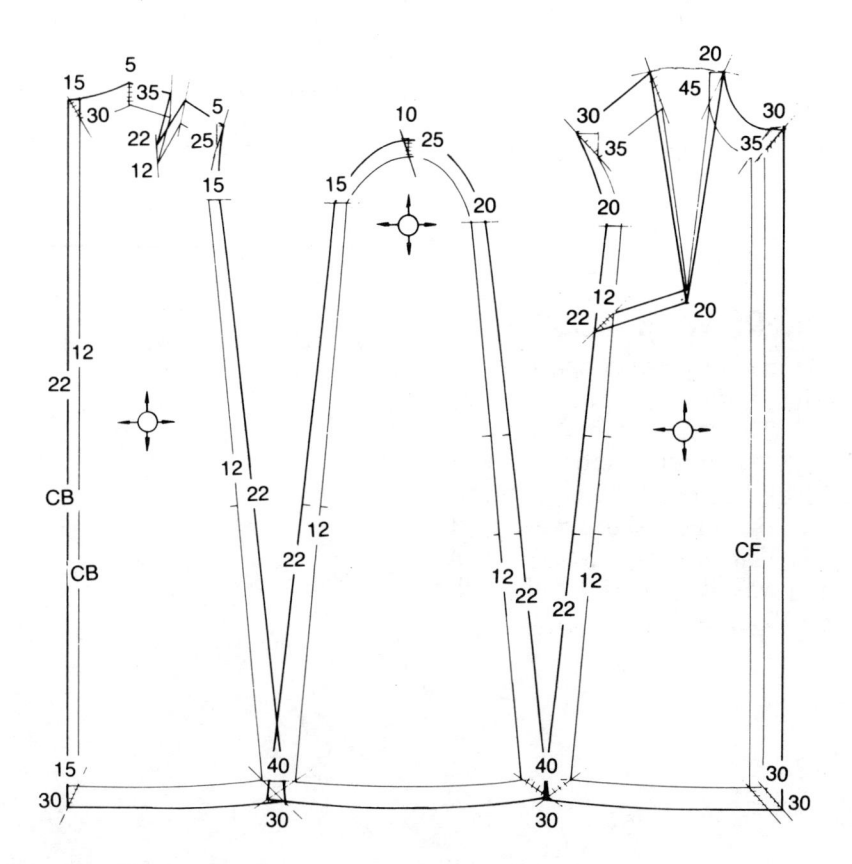

Figure 234 Grade for five sizes

STYLE 33

	GRADING SPECIFICATION	
1	Size chart	Table 13
2	Size range	10.12.14.16.18.20.22
3	Height/girth/length	Height and girth
4	Proportioning	
5	Type of grade	2 dim. track or draft
6	Zero points front	nil
7	Zero point back	nil
8	Zero point sleeve	nil
9	Zero point front skirt	Mid waist
10	Zero point back skirt	Mid waist
11	Category of fit	Loose
Comments		
Grade based on trouser quantities.		

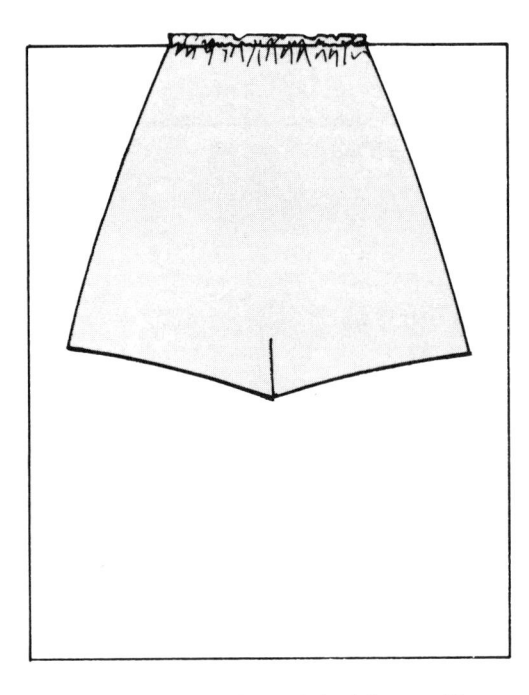

Figure 235 Style 33 – French knickers with gusset

FRENCH KNICKERS WITH GUSSET

French knickers (Figure 235) are constructed by inserting a gusset into a slit located at the centre front and back line. The insertion of the gusset provides the 'through leg fitting' which is based on the basic trouser block. The grade increments are taken from the two-dimensional trouser grade plan (see Chapter 2). Flare can be introduced into the pattern from the waist but does not affect the basic grading. See Figures 236 and 237.

STYLE GRADES 1 TO 33   237

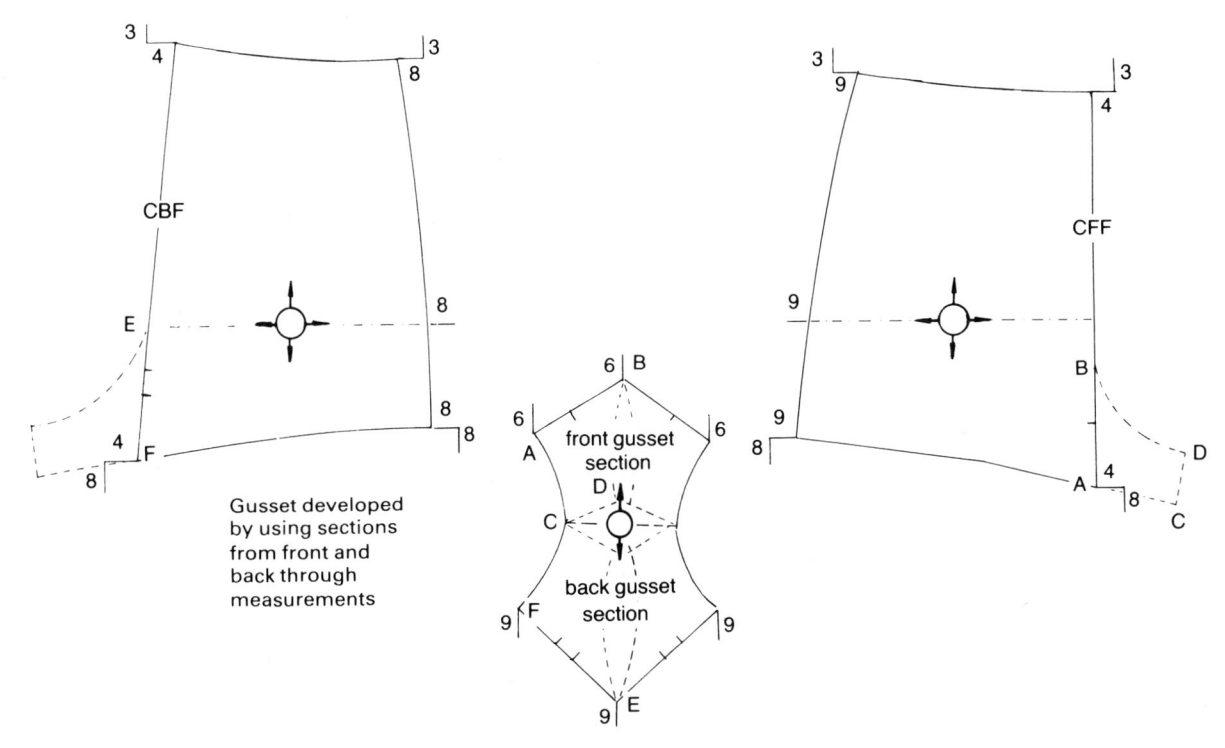

Figure 236 Two-dimensional grade for one size

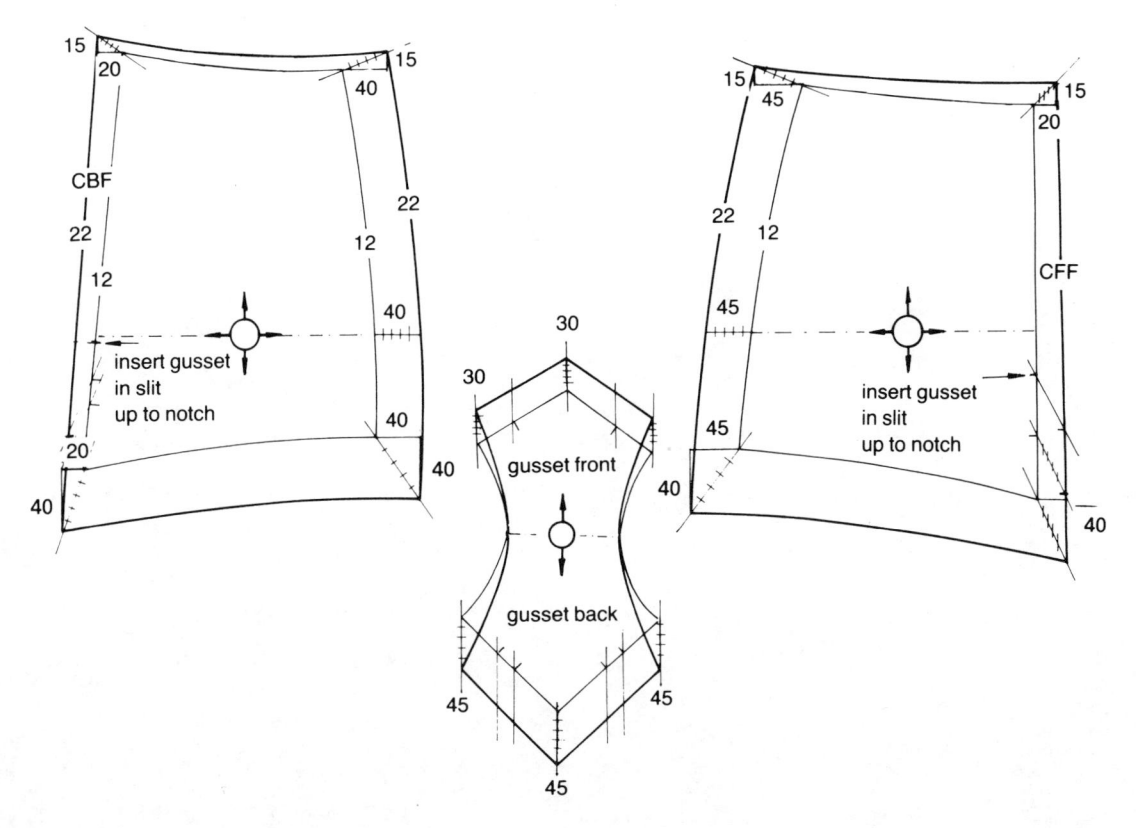

Figure 237 Grade for five sizes

PART FOUR

Men's Grading

CHAPTER 17

Men's classical and fashion wear grading

SIZE CHARTS

Men's size charts are mostly made up of garment rather than body measurements but classified by a **main body measurement** such as the chest for a jacket or the waist and inside leg for trousers. This is because classical men's clothing has little variation in cut and fit and therefore wholesale tailoring size charts have tended to concentrate on garment measurements which are easier to establish. This makes garment measurement quality control easier to achieve. The fit of a man's tailored suit is more critical than, for example, that of a dress, due to the difference in cost and the emphasis on the classical appearance of a suit as opposed to the many style variations and garment types found in women's clothing. Traditional men's clothing is therefore offered in more size categories than women's. Major girth measurements are related to three height categories; short, regular and long. The three height categories, when combined with seven chest girths for a jacket or waist girths for trousers, provide a comprehensive size range to fit a large section of the male population. The extra short or extra long man must go to specialist shops to buy his clothes.

HEIGHT CLASSIFICATION

Height range

Short   160–173
Regular 174–180
Long   181–184

These classifications will mainly affect the vertical garment measurements such as jacket and sleeve length, body rise and outside leg measurements.

CHEST CLASSIFICATION FOR MAN OF REGULAR STATURE

Regular stature is defined by the ratio between the chest and waist. Regular or medium stature reveals a body measurement difference of 12.0 cm in the slimmer male which decreases as the male puts on weight. In other words the waist gets larger in relation to the chest to form the portly or semi-stout figure.

Table 22 Close body measurements for men of medium stature (cm)

Chest girth	86.0	91.0	96.0	101.0	106.0	111.0	116.0
Waist girth	74.0	80.0	86.0	92.0	98.0	104.0	110.0
Difference	12.0	11.0	10.0	9.0	8.0	7.0	6.0

This decreasing difference means that when grading a man's jacket the waist girth is increased more than the seat and the chest.

The following body measurement size chart is for men of regular height and medium stature (as compiled by Philip Kunick FCFI and used with his permission). It is a source chart for a wide variety of classical and fashion clothing. (See Table 23.)

Table 23 Close body measurements for men of medium stature and regular height (cm)

	Horizontal measurements								Size increment
1	Chest	86.0	91.0	96.0	101.0	106.0	111.0	116.0	5.0
		(34")	(36")	(38")	(40")	(42")	(44")	(46")	(2")
2	Waist	74.0	80.0	86.0	92.0	98.0	104.0	110.0	6.0
3	Seat	91.0	96.0	101.0	106.0	111.0	116.0	121.0	5.0
4	Across back	37.6	38.8	40.0	41.2	42.4	43.6	44.8	1.2
5	Across chest	36.4	38.2	40.0	41.8	43.6	45.4	47.2	1.8
6	Scye width	12.0	13.0	14.0	15.0	16.0	17.0	18.0	1.0
7	Armscye	41.0	43.0	45.0	47.0	49.0	51.0	53.0	2.0
8	Neck base	38.8	40.0	41.2	42.4	43.6	44.8	46.0	1.2
		(15")	(15½")	(16")	(16½")	(17")	(17½")	(18")	(½")
9	Shoulder	12.7	13.0	13.3	13.6	13.9	14.2	14.5	0.3
10	Upper arm	26.0	28.0	30.0	32.0	34.0	36.0	38.0	2.0
11	Wrist	16.6	17.2	17.8	18.4	19.0	19.6	20.2	0.6
12	Maximum thigh	49.6	52.8	56.0	59.2	62.4	65.6	68.8	3.2
13	Knee	35.4	36.7	38.0	39.3	40.6	41.9	43.2	1.3
14	Small girth	31.0	32.5	34.0	35.5	37.0	38.5	40.0	1.5
15	Calf	33.4	35.0	36.6	38.2	39.8	41.4	43.0	1.6
16	Minimum ankle	21.0	22.0	23.0	24.0	25.0	26.0	27.0	1.0
	Vertical measurements								
17	Stature	174.0	175.0	176.0	177.0	178.0	179.0	180.0	1.0
18	Cervical height	149.4	150.2	151.0	151.8	152.6	153.4	154.2	0.8
19	Depth of scye	19.8	20.4	21.0	21.6	22.2	22.8	23.4	0.6
20	Nape to waist	41.8	42.4	43.0	43.6	44.2	44.8	45.4	0.6
21	Waist to hip	20.8	20.9	21.0	21.1	21.2	21.3	21.4	0.1
22	Hip height	89.2	89.6	90.0	90.4	90.8	91.2	91.6	0.4
23	Knee height	47.8	47.9	48.0	48.1	48.2	48.3	48.4	0.1
24	Outside leg	110.0	110.5	111.0	111.5	112.0	112.5	113.0	0.5
25	Inside leg	81.0	81.0	81.0	81.0	81.0	81.0	81.0	0.0
26	Body rise	29.0	29.5	30.0	30.5	31.0	31.5	32.0	0.5
27	Arm length	62.4	62.7	63.0	63.3	63.6	63.9	64.2	0.3
28	Crotch length	68.6	70.8	73.0	75.2	77.4	79.6	82.0	2.2

For men aged 18 to 30 reduce waist girth by 3.0 cm.

CHAPTER 18

Trouser grading

Sizing men's trousers is usually based on the following three factors:

1. The waist girth measurement
2. The inside leg measurement
3. The trouser bottom width.

The waist girth and the inside leg are body measurements. The trouser bottom width is an important style factor, subject to fashion change.

Six waist sizes are often offered with three length choices, i.e. short, regular and long. The inside leg measurement is normally identified on the ticket with the waist measurement.

A typical trouser size chart will offer a 5.0 cm waist grade and a 5.0 cm inside leg grade and look as follows:

Waist	75.0	80.0	85.0	90.0	95.0	100.0
Inside leg, regular	81.0	81.0	81.0	81.0	81.0	81.0
Inside leg, short	76.0	76.0	76.0	76.0	76.0	76.0
Inside leg, long	86.0	86.0	86.0	86.0	86.0	86.0

Trouser bottom width   Fashion variable

Note that with more expensive trousers, the current trend is to cut the trouser length generously and turn up the hem at the point of sale.

Figure 238 shows a split diagram with girth and

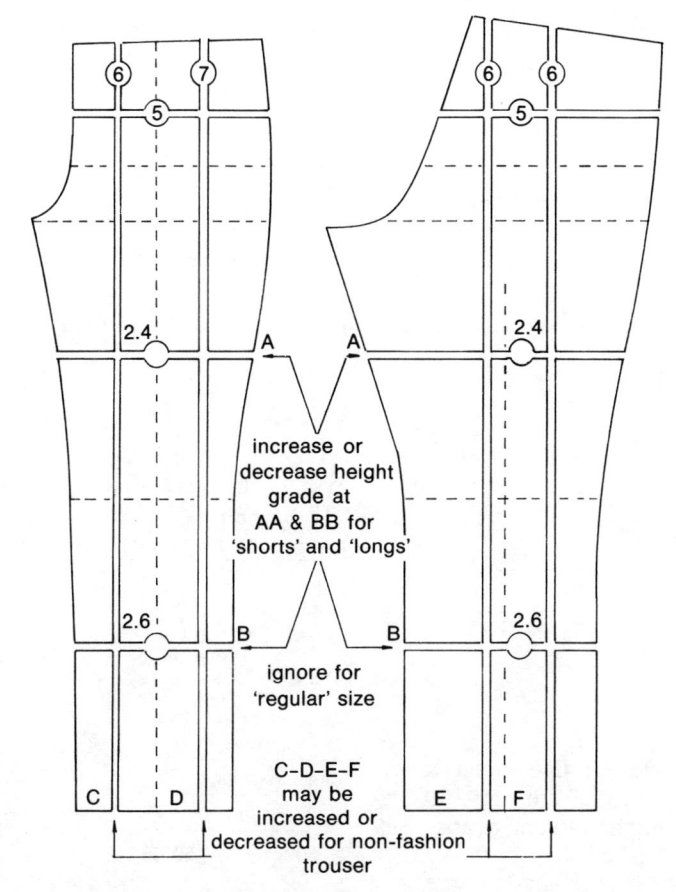

Figure 238
Trouser split diagram

height combined, i.e. 5.0 cm height and 5.0 cm girth. When grading 'Shorts' and 'Longs' the grade is positioned above and below the knee. Also note that the body rise is graded 0.5 cm per size.

Figure 239 shows a grade and grade directions for one size only, using a zero located on the junction of the seat and crease line. In this grade the trouser bottom width remains a constant measurement throughout the size range. As a style option the trouser bottom width can be increased by 0.5 cm every other size to retain the leg shape.

Figure 240 shows the completed five size grade with three leg lengths.

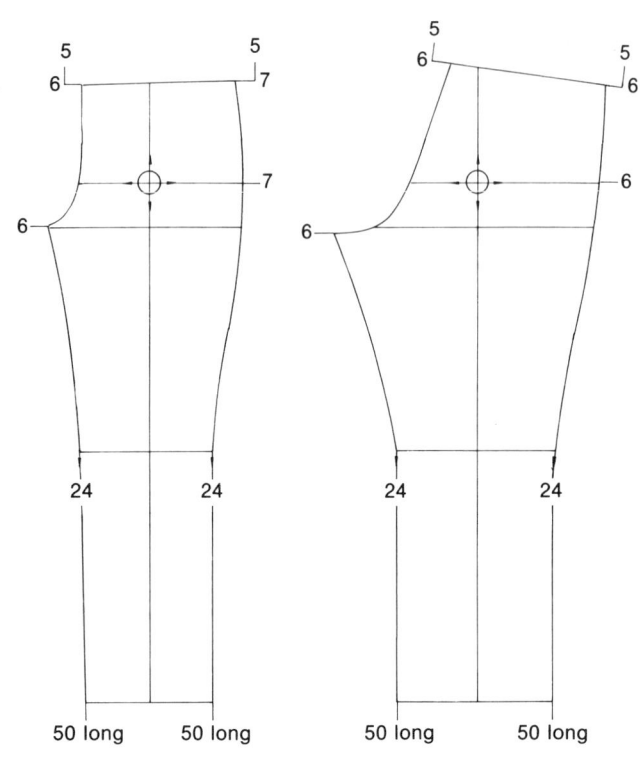

Figure 239 Grade plan for fashion trouser. Static trouser bottom width

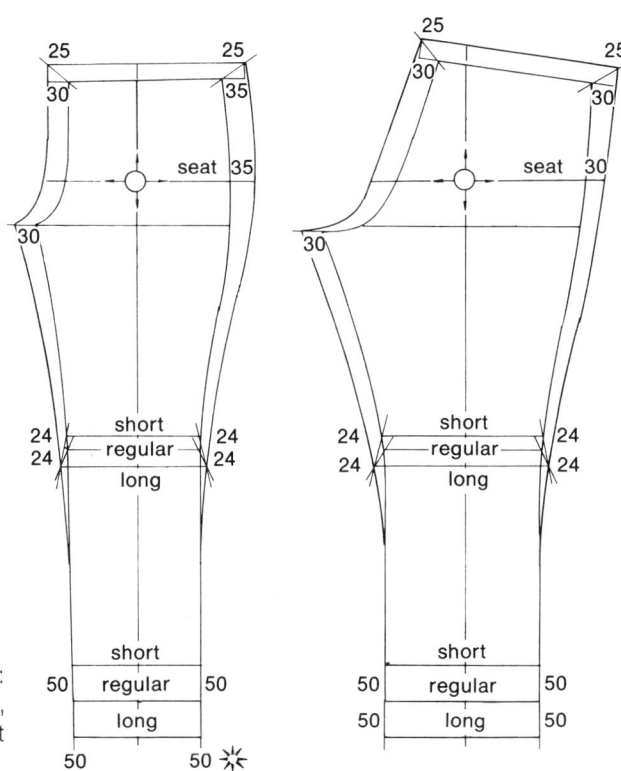

Figure 240 Completed grade for five waist sizes: 80 cm, 85 cm, 90 cm, 95 cm and 100 cm, and two leg lengths 5.0 cm grade. Set bottom width

CHAPTER 19

Jacket grading

Men's jacket grading can be divided into two main categories:

1 Lapel garments
2 Fitted and semi-fitted throat garments.

LAPEL GARMENTS

Lapel garments, e.g. single and double breasted collar and reverse jackets and coats, are the most common of this category. When grading these tailored classical garments two factors must be observed:

1 The front neck line retains the same dimensions throughout the size range; the grade is positioned at the back neck only. This is because the garment is not cut to button up to the neck so a vertical neck grade is unnecessary, and the front lapel retains the same shape changing the angle of the collar break line. This changing of angle is due to the positioning of more fullness across the man's waist.
2 To retain the look of the sleeve and front scye the dimensions and shape of the stock size pattern remains unchanged throughout the size range.

FITTED AND SEMI-FITTED THROAT GARMENTS

The semi-fitted throat garment, e.g. a safari jacket which can either be worn open or buttoned up the neck, must be graded through the front and back neck for it to fit the larger sizes. The same applies to fitted throat garments such as the coat in Figure 249, and all shirts.

A typical man's jacket size chart will look as follows:

Table 24

								Grade
Chest	86.0	91.0	96.0	101.0	106.0	111.0	116.0	5.0
Regular								
Jacket length	73.6	74.8	76.0	77.2	78.4	79.6	80.8	1.2
Sleeve length	62.4	63.0	63.6	64.2	64.8	65.4	66.0	0.6
Short: minus 3.0 cm jacket length and 1.2 cm sleeve length.
Jacket length	70.6	71.8	73.0	74.2	75.4	76.6	77.8	1.2
Sleeve length	61.2	61.8	62.4	63.0	63.6	64.2	64.8	0.6
Long: plus 3.0 cm jacket length and 1.2 cm sleeve length.
Jacket length	76.6	77.8	79.0	80.2	81.4	82.6	83.8	1.2
Sleeve length	63.6	64.2	64.8	65.4	66.0	66.6	67.2	0.6

The following grades are height and girth grades and are based on the regular fit chart above.

Figure 241 shows a single breasted jacket.

Figure 242 and Figure 243 show a one size grade and the grade angles for the jacket back and forepart and the sleeve. Note that the front scye on both the body and the sleeve are 'held' to retain the sleeve appearance throughout the range. To achieve this a zero point is selected at the front armscye position.

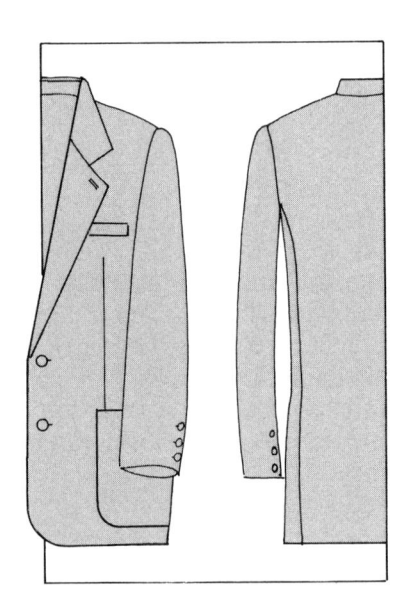

Figure 241 Single breasted jacket

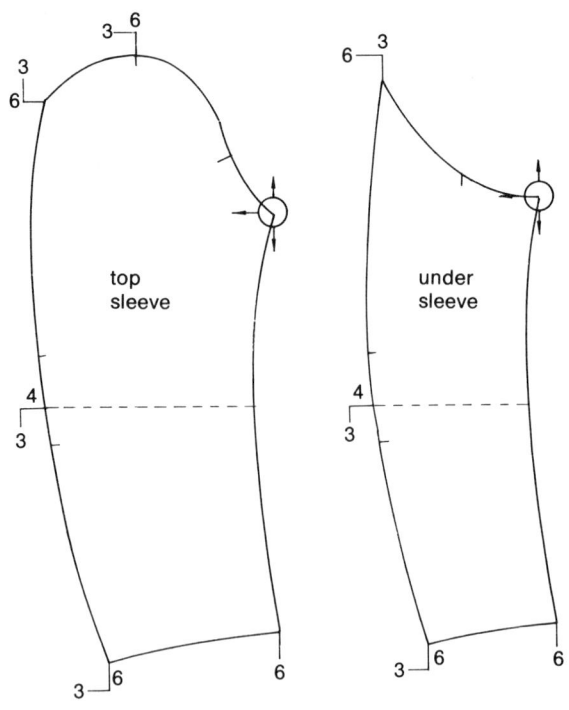

Figure 243 One size grade for two piece sleeve girth and height

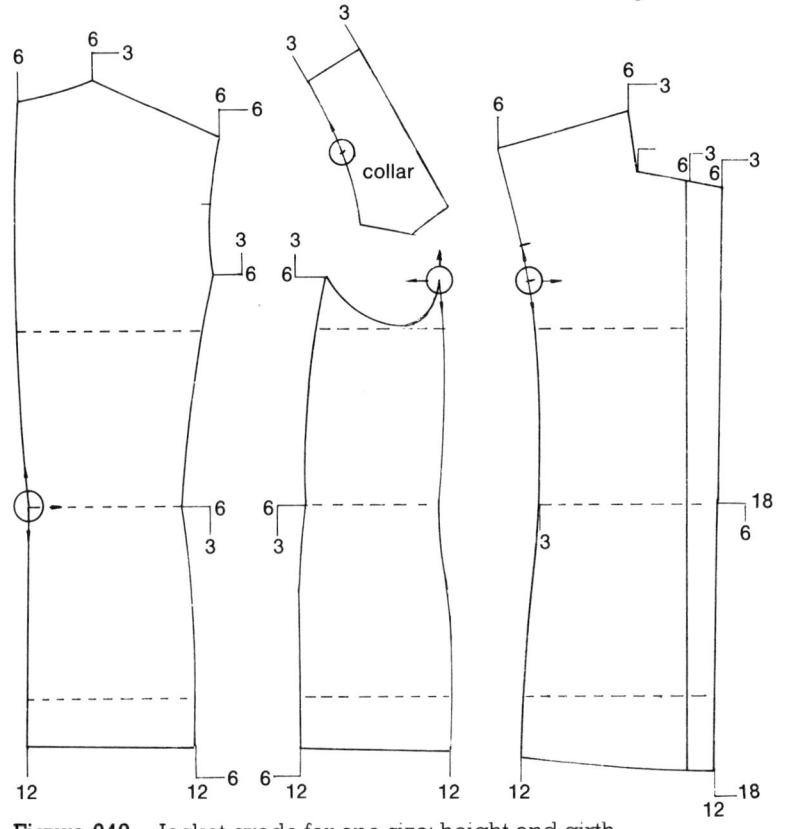

Figure 242 Jacket grade for one size: height and girth

JACKET GRADING

Figure 244 and Figure 245 illustrate the five size grade.

Figure 246 shows a safari jacket. This casual style is a semi-throat fitting jacket and requires a grade plan that takes into account the growth of the front neck if the garment is to be worn buttoned up.

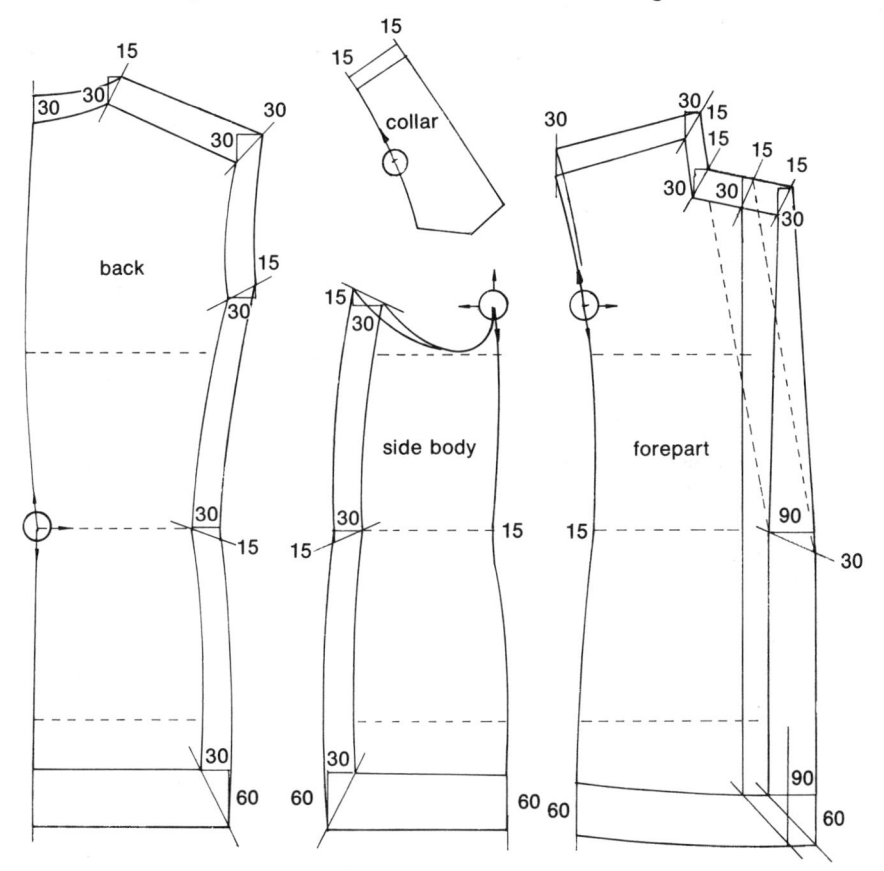

Figure 244 Five size height and girth grade

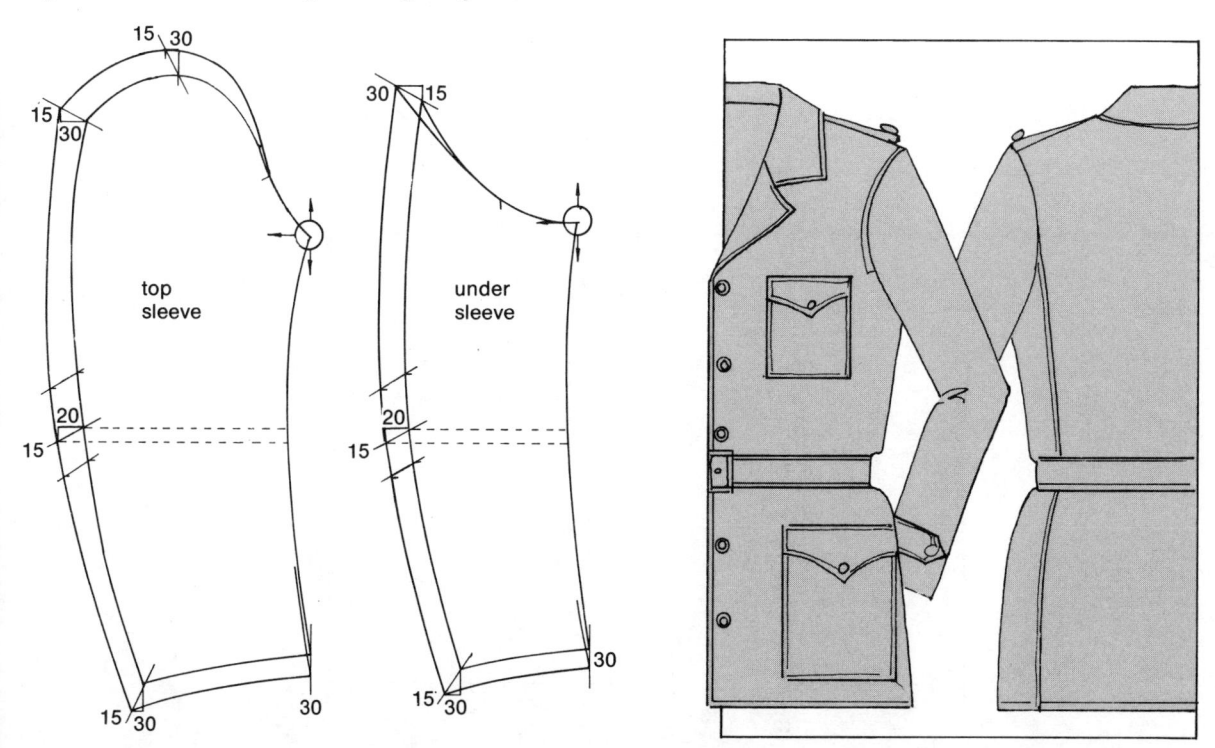

Figure 245 Sleeve grade – height and girth five sizes

Figure 246 Safari jacket

Figure 247 is a split diagram showing the positions of the girth and height increments. Note that the height increments are included in the 'regular' grade. The grade for 'shorts and longs' are located in areas A and B both on the jacket and sleeve. See Figures 247 and 248.

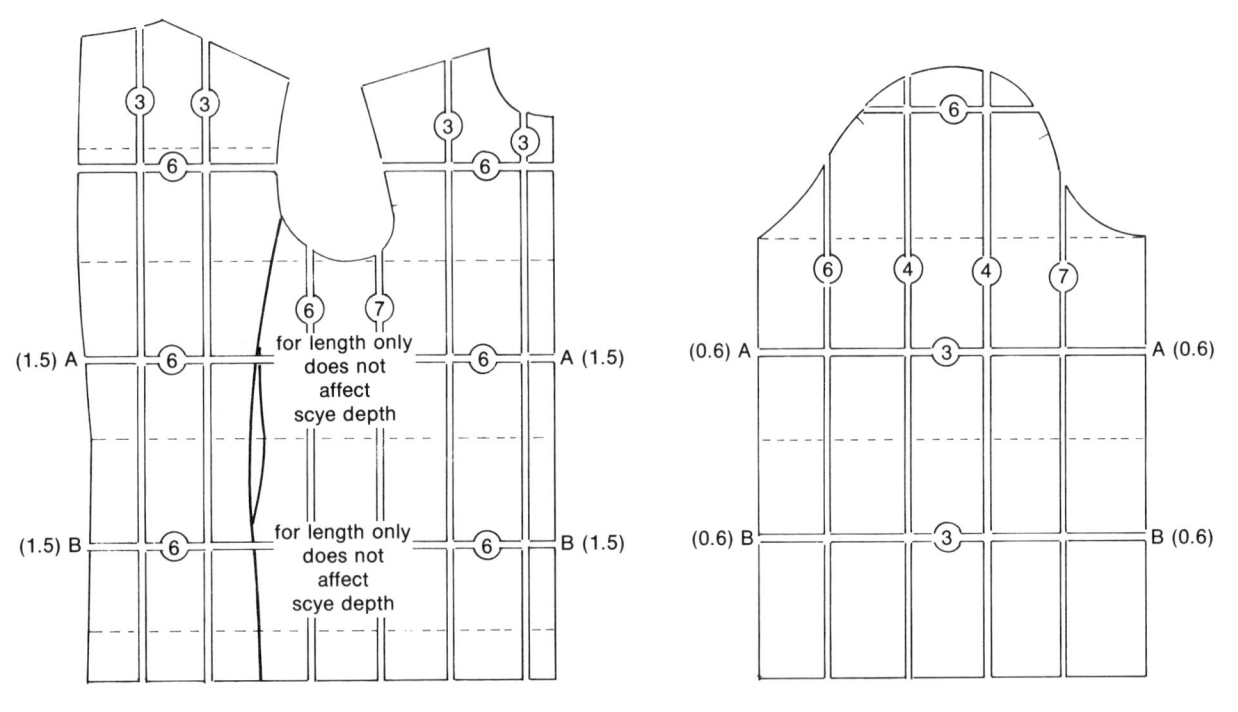

Figure 247 Split diagram for throat garments

Figure 248 Split diagram – straight sleeve

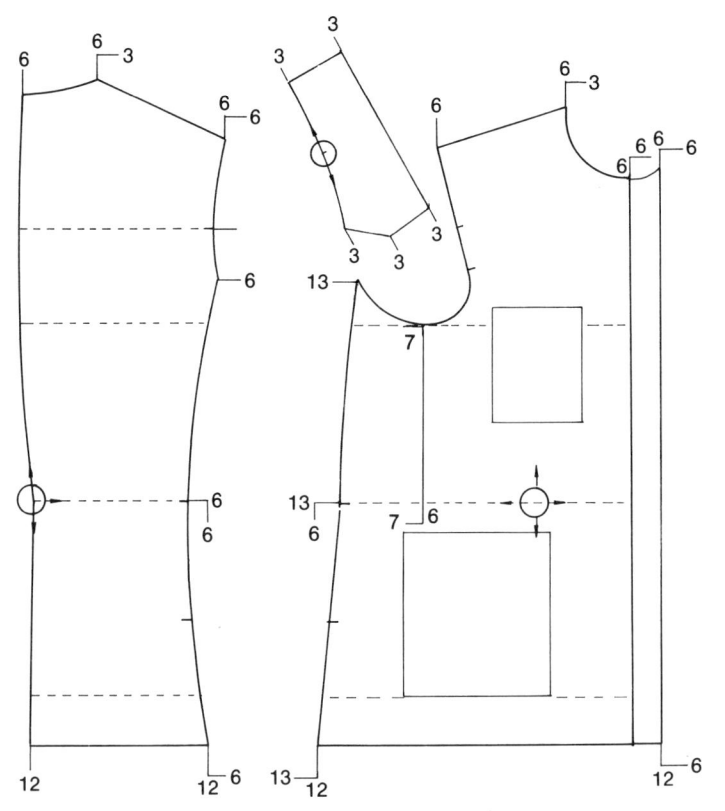

Figure 249 One size grade height and girth

JACKET GRADING

249

Figure 249 and Figure 250 show the one-size grade plan and grade angles for a regular fitting.

Figure 251 shows a safari jacket regular grade for five sizes. The grade angles are as indicated. Note that the 'star symbol' indicates style grade options at the pockets, which can be graded up or down as required.

Figure 252 shows a coat with high buttoned collar and raglan sleeve. This regular coat grade is based on the split diagram shown in Figure 247 and Figure 248.

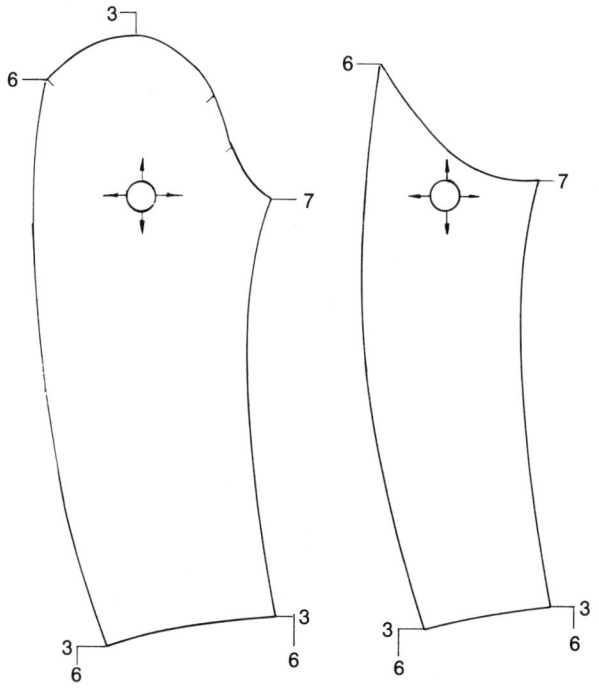

Figure 250 Two piece sleeve – increments for one size height and girth

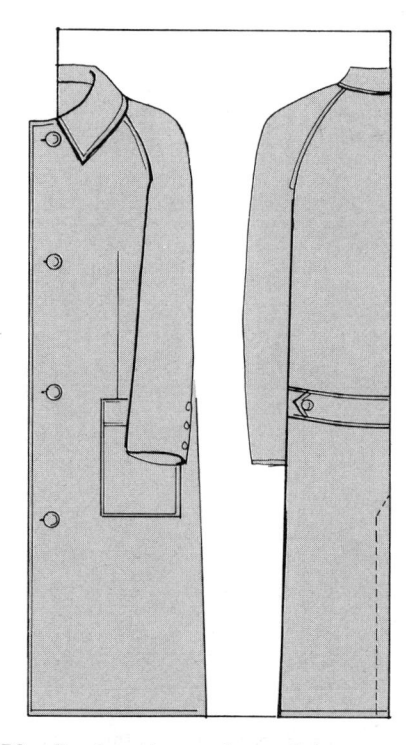

Figure 252 Raglan sleeve throat fitting coat

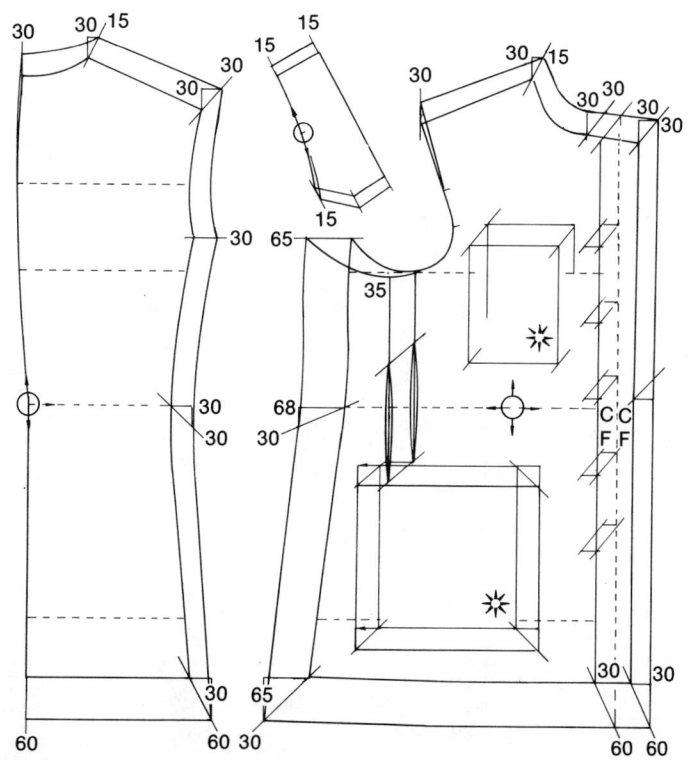

Figure 251 Safari jacket grade (semi-throat fitting) five sizes

Figure 253 is one size grade plan and grade angles. Note that the wrist has only been graded by 0.8 cm per size but this can be increased if a looser fit is required.

Figure 254 is a five size regular coat grade.

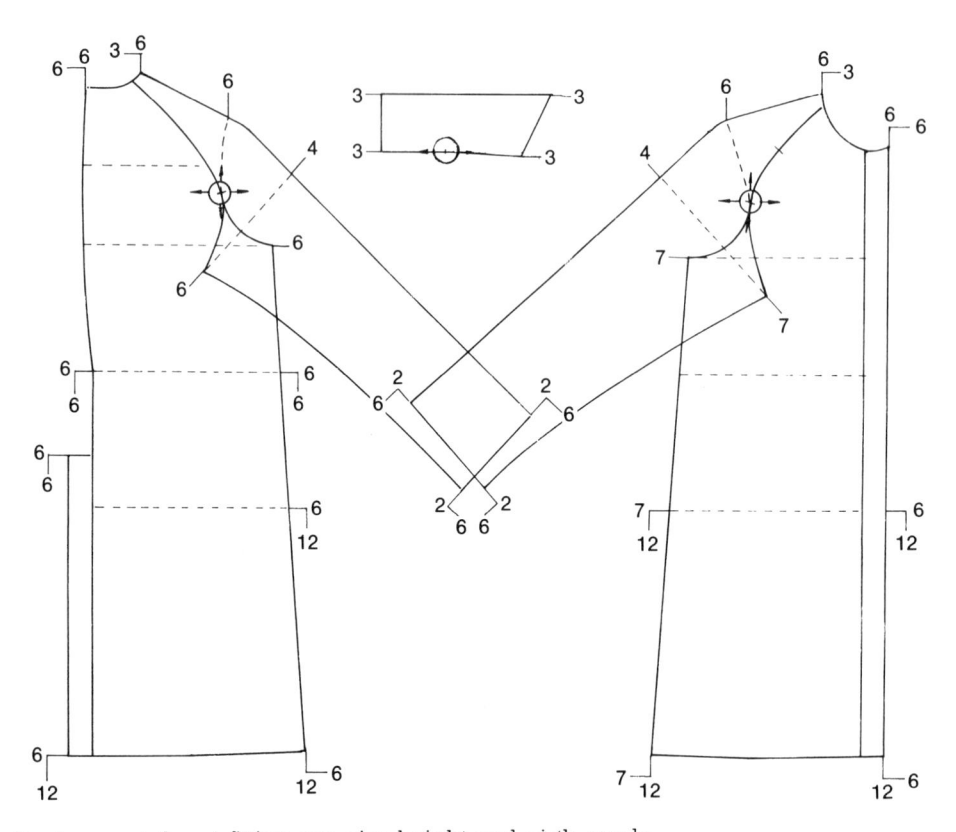

Figure 253 Raglan coat throat fitting one size height and girth grade

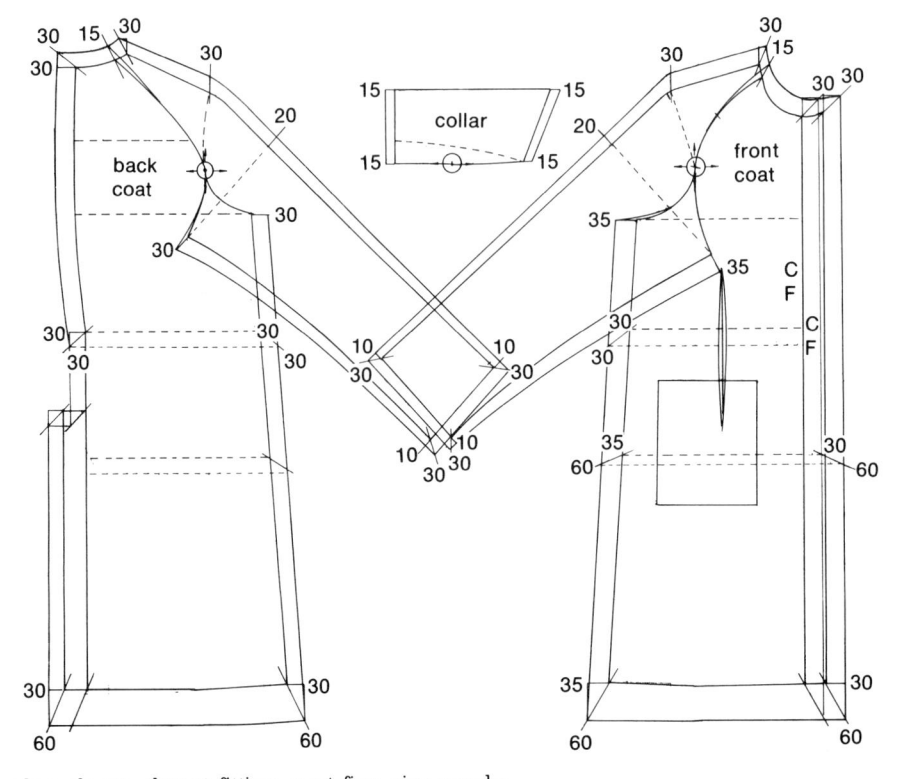

Figure 254 Raglan sleeve throat fitting coat five size grade

CHAPTER 20

Shirt sizing and grading

Men's shirts are classified by two main measurements:

1. The neck, which is a **body measurement** and
2. The chest, which is a **loose garment measurement** and will vary according to style.

The shirt style obviously has an effect on the manner in which the shirt is graded. For example, a classically fitting dress shirt or a close fitting shirt for the younger man will need a much more sophisticated grade than a sports shirt which has not been cut to button up at the neck and may be classified simply as Small, Medium or Large.

MAN'S SHIRT (Figure 255)

The usual neck increase is 1.2 cm per size and the customer is offered a size range from 35.6 cm (14″) to 46.2 cm (18″) – a range of eight sizes. The chest is based on a half size grade of 2.5 cm per size. All other body measurements are halved to establish a consistent grade. An alternative to the half size grade is to grade up the shirt by a full 0.5 cm every other size, i.e. retaining one chest size per two neck sizes.

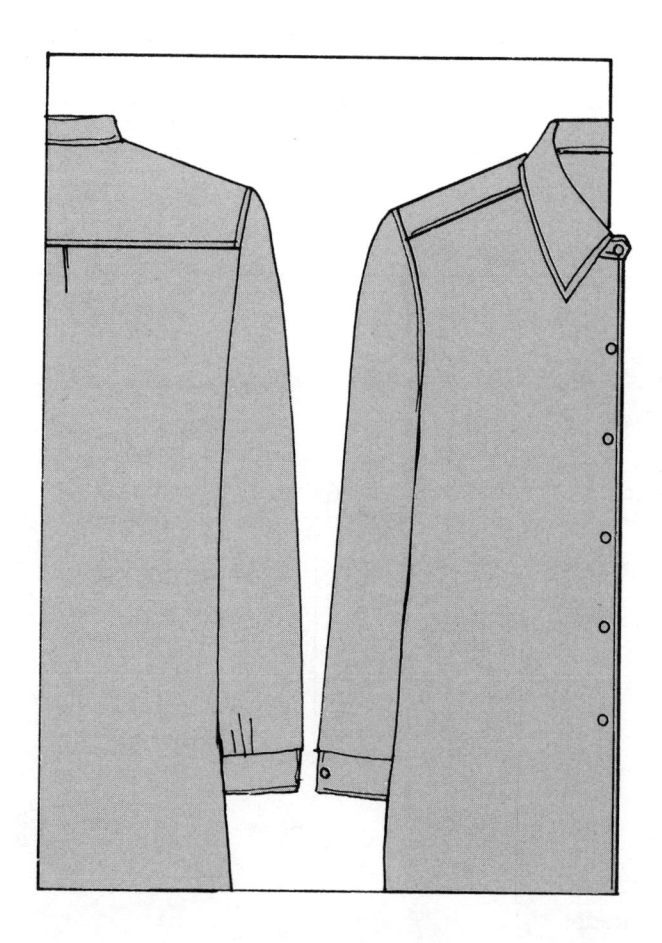

Figure 255 Man's shirt

SIZE CHART (Table 25)

This size chart covers a range of fourteen neck sizes and is based on a 1.2 cm neck grade and a 2.5 cm chest grade. Comparisons with the main men's size chart (Table 25) will be difficult due to the inclusion of the half sizes.

Figure 256 shows the one size grade plan. It is important to note that increments are rounded to the nearest whole millimetre. The one piece and the two piece collar grades are shown.

The grade angles are based on the centre front and the centre back and chest construction lines.

Table 25

Body measurements															Half increment
Neck	$12\frac{1}{2}''$ 31.0	13'' 33.2	$13\frac{1}{2}''$ 34.4	14'' 35.6	$14\frac{1}{2}''$ 36.8	15'' 38.0	$15\frac{1}{2}''$ 39.2	16'' 40.4	$16\frac{1}{2}''$ 41.6	17'' 43.8	$17\frac{1}{2}''$ 45.0	18'' 46.2	$18\frac{1}{2}''$ 47.4	19'' 48.6	$\frac{1}{2}''$ 1.2 cm
Chest	83.5	86.0	88.5	91.0	93.5	96.0	98.5	101.0	103.5	106.0	108.5	111.0	113.5	116.0	2.5 cm
Half across chest	17.75	18.2	18.65	19.1	19.55	20.0	20.45	20.9	21.35	21.8	22.25	22.7	23.15	23.6	0.45
Half across back	18.5	18.8	19.1	19.4	19.7	20.0	20.3	20.6	20.9	21.2	21.5	21.8	22.1	22.4	0.3 cm
Shoulder	12.55	12.7	12.85	13.0	13.15	13.3	13.45	13.6	13.75	13.9	14.05	14.1	14.25	14.4	0.15 cm
Arm length	62.25	62.4	62.55	62.7	62.85	63.0	63.15	63.3	63.45	63.6	63.75	63.9	64.05	64.2	0.15 cm
Depth of scye	19.5	19.8	20.1	20.4	20.7	21.0	21.3	21.6	21.9	22.2	22.5	22.8	23.1	23.4	0.3 cm
Wrist girth	16.3	16.6	16.9	17.2	17.5	17.8	18.1	18.4	18.7	19.0	19.3	19.6	19.9	20.2	0.3 cm

Garment measurements	
Centre back length	88.0 cm Constant
Centre front length	88.0 cm Constant
Back and front line	Constant on classical shirt

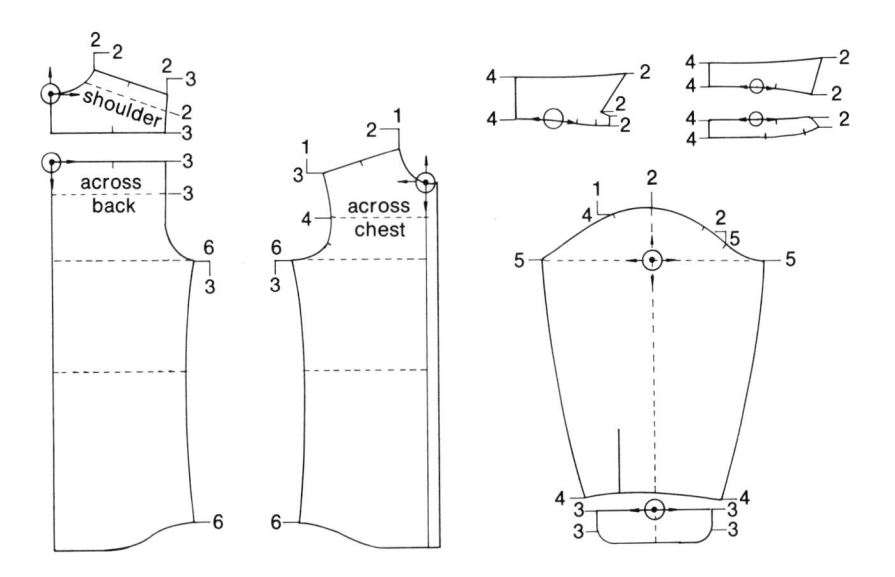

Figure 256 One size shirt grade

SHIRT SIZING AND GRADING

Note that the back and front yoke depths are not normally graded, and that the shirt length remains constant.

Figure 257 illustrates the whole graded nest of eight sizes. Divide up the diagonal connecting lines to establish the intermediate sizes.

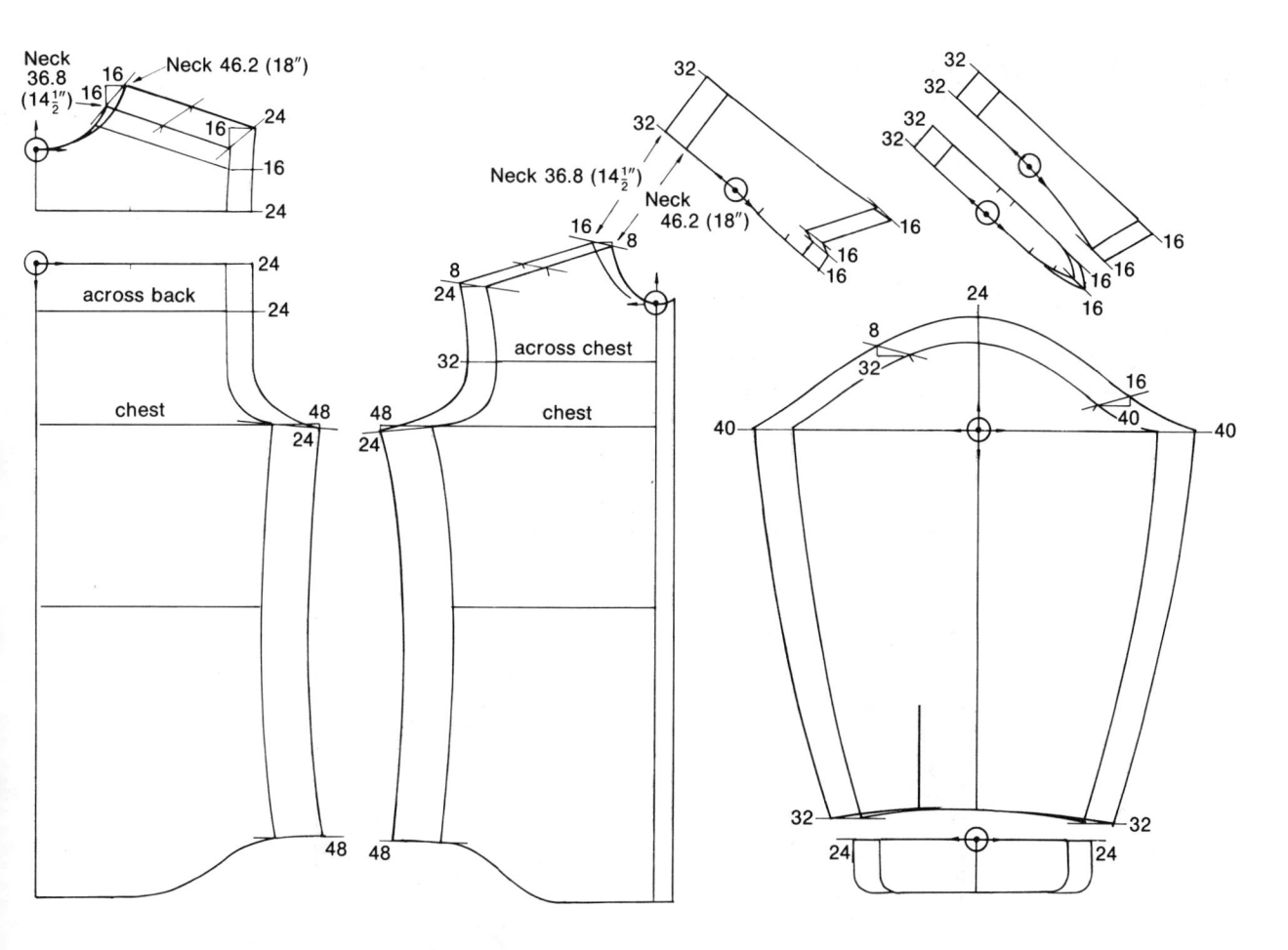

Figure 257 Eight neck size shirt grade from 36.8 cm ($14\frac{1}{2}''$) to 46.2 cm (18'')

CHAPTER 21

Man's waistcoat

The man's waistcoat (Figure 258) is graded as the jacket with a lapel, i.e. the armhole is 'held' and the main bulk of the grade is positioned into the chest. This causes a change in the front neck angle.

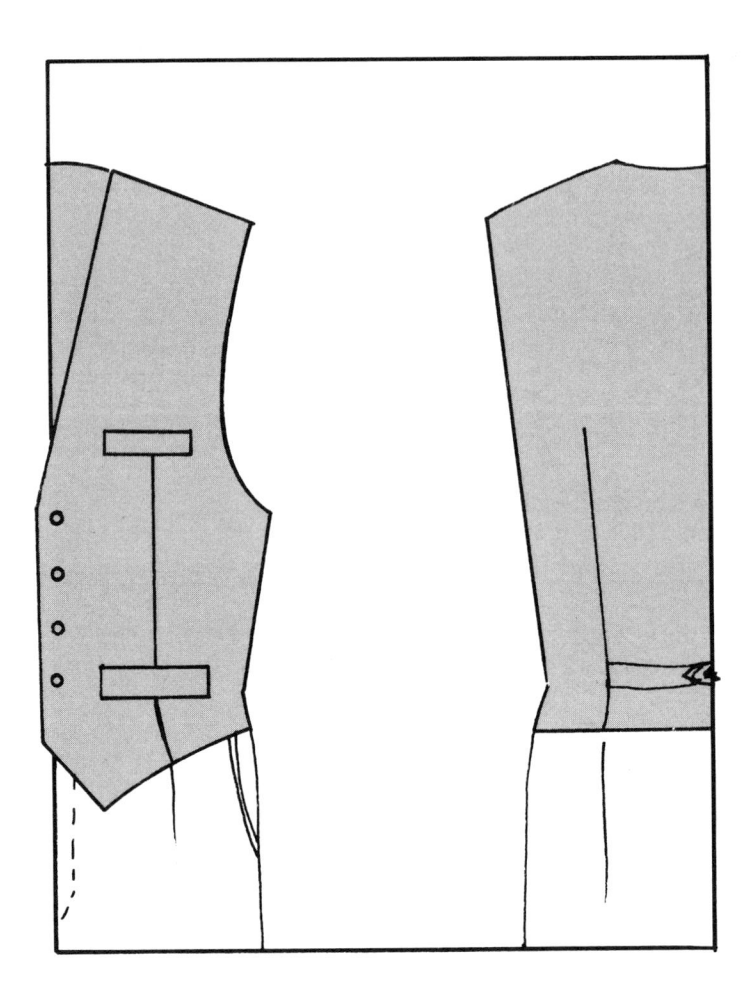

Figure 258 Man's waistcoat

WAISTCOAT

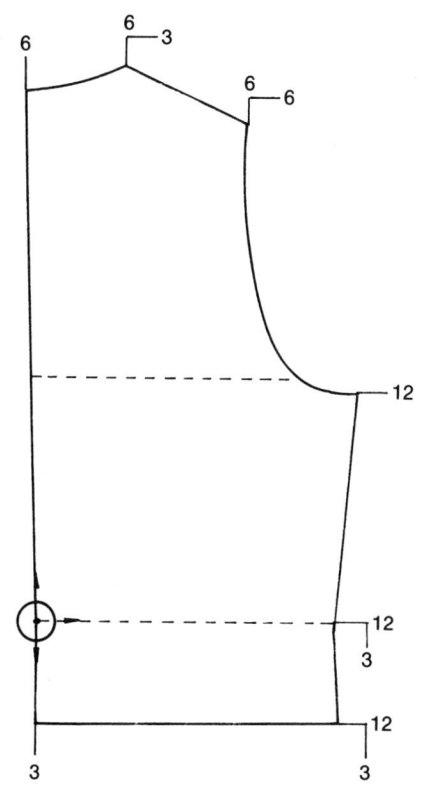

Figure 259 One size height and girth grade waistcoat

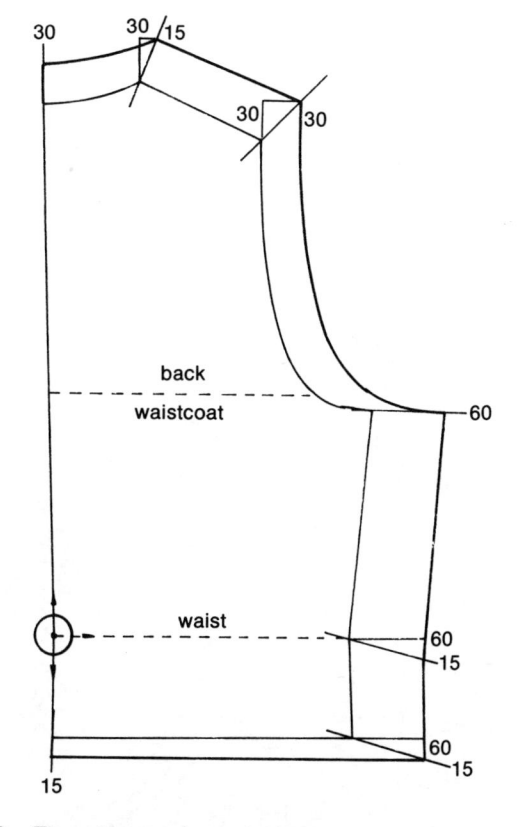

Figure 260 Five size grade waistcoat

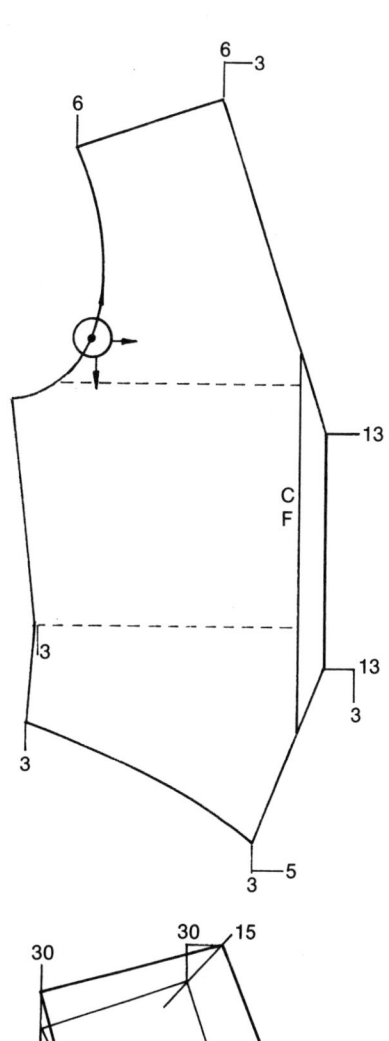

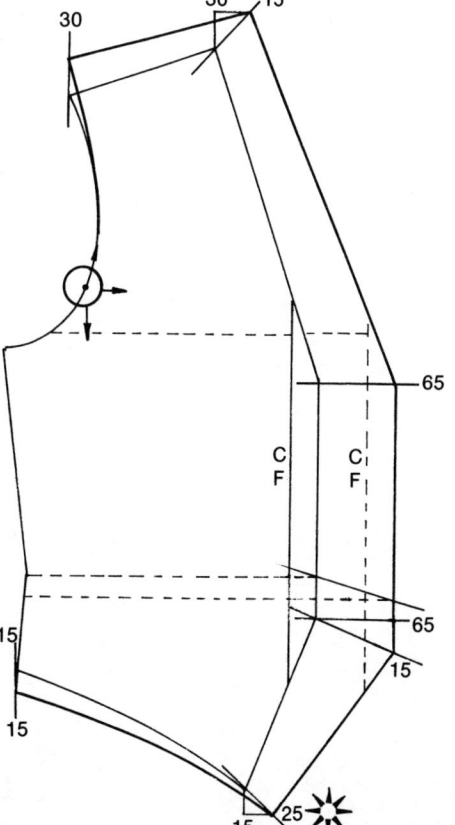

PART FIVE

Children's Wear

CHAPTER 22

Children's grading and size charts

The main difficulty in manufacturing 'off the peg' children's clothing lies in the fact that it is an area of growth, which brings a range of variables that are sometimes difficult to cater for. Since height is the dimension that increases at a greater rate than all the others, it must therefore form the basis of any sizing system. Weight should also come into the equation since it is theoretically possible to calculate the major girths by combining the height and weight. But this has to be disregarded. Children's retailers have found from experience that parents do not know their children's weight or height: all they know is their age. The age of a child is not an accurate indication of their size. But because of parents' ignorance of the basic dimensions of their infants it has become necessary to base the sizing on age, and sometimes height is loosely quoted for a given age group. Of course the age is related to the height, but the wide variation between these two dimensions makes it unreliable.

Children's clothing is roughly divided into three categories. The first is from nil years to approximately two years, which represents infant clothing. The second is children's clothing from three years to approximately twelve years, and the last is teenage clothing from thirteen to sixteen.

Up to twelve years old the two sexes can be treated as one with regard to shape and size, but not, of course, for style. After twelve the shapes obviously diverge. There are differences in the sexes up to the age of twelve but they are small enough to be disregarded.

After sixteen it is safe to assume that growth has more or less finished, that is skeletal growth, but muscle will continue to develop in the male for some time after.

If a sizing system were to accurately follow the growth patterns of the child it would be so complex that no manufacturer or retailer would be able to cope with it, therefore a very simplified version has to be employed in order to have any chance of mass producing growth clothing at all.

Ideally a sizing system would consist of height increases of about 5 or 6 centimetres between each size and each height category would have at least three girth options; small, medium and large. Six centimetres roughly corresponds to the average growth in one year so that the age is quoted with each height category.

This would produce approximately 42 sizes between the age of three and sixteen years. If this were possible then the designer could design any type of garment, regardless of the need to build into it excess tolerance and waist girth flexibility. By definition it would entail three dimensional grading throughout the range and this would be unacceptable as well as almost impossible.

The only way to overcome these obstacles is to design clothes that have inbuilt flexibility and sufficient tolerances. If this is done well then a single girth option in each height category is just about adequate to cope with the situation. Most companies construct their sizes to fit the largest girth in a given height category.

It means that the tall thin child will have the worst deal, looking a bit swamped in the garment of correct height. In fact what happens is that companies offer sizes with 6 cm height increments coupled to the age and one girth option in each height category.

But companies are always trying to economise and the height increment these days is usually 10 cm coupled to the age at one and a half year intervals. This gives about twelve sizes for a 6 cm increment and nine sizes using a 10 cm height increment.

In the grade plans offered in this chapter the waist grade is taken as the same as the chest above the waist, and the same as the hip for trouser and skirt. This is done to make life easier and it gives extra tolerance in the waist girth. This is not done for the teen sizes where a proper three dimensional grade is used for the female and a two dimensional for the male.

No style examples are given for the children's grading because they are the same as the adult examples, but using the children's grade plans.

IMPORTANT

It is suggested that a block be constructed for each of the size categories.

FOR THE 6.0 cm HEIGHT GRADES

A *one year old block*, for the infants, which would be graded down three sizes and up two sizes.

A *five year old block*, for the next category, which would be graded two sizes down and two sizes up.

A *nine year old block*, for the next category, which would be graded one size down and two sizes up.

An *eleven year old block*, for the boys' category, which would be graded three sizes down and four sizes up.

A *thirteen year old block*, for the girl teens, which would be graded one size down and two sizes up. *Or use an adult size 12 block and grade down three sizes.*

FOR THE 10 cm GRADES

A *one year old block*, for the infants, which would grade two sizes down and one size up.

A *six/seven year block*, for the next category, which would grade two sizes down and two sizes up.

An *eleven/twelve year old block*, for the boys' sizes, which would grade one size down and two sizes up.

A *thirteen/fourteen year old block*, for the girl teens category, which would grade one size up and one size down. *Or use an adult size 12 block and grade three sizes down.*

CHILDREN'S STANDS

To construct these blocks accurately would entail buying five children's stands and constructing a block for each of them. It would be inadvisable to use any less than this as it would give rise to too much error.

1. A one year old unisex
2. A five year old unisex
3. A nine year old unisex
4. An eleven year old boy
5. A thirteen year old girl

When constructing the blocks take note of minimum tolerances indicated in the size charts.

REFERENCE LIST

Each of the following pages contains a size chart, a head/height ratio diagram and a complete set of grade plans for the age ranges set out in each size chart. For easy reference they are listed as follows:

(A) 6.0 cm HEIGHT GRADE

Children's grade plan 1: Infant's sizes from three months to two years: unisex.
Children's grade plan 2: Children's sizes from three years to seven years: unisex.
Children's grade plan 3: Girls' sizes from eight years to eleven years.
Children's grade plan 4: Boys' sizes from eight years to fifteen years.
Children's grade plan 5: Teenage girls from twelve years to fifteen years.

(B) 10.0 cm HEIGHT GRADE

Children's grade plan 6: Infants' sizes from three months to two years: unisex.
Children's grade plan 7: Children's sizes from two/three years to ten/eleven years.
Children's grade plan 8: Boys' sizes from nine/ten years to fifteen/sixteen years.
Children's grade plan 9: Teenage girls from twelve to fifteen years.
Composite size chart: 6.0 cm grade.
Composite size chart: 10.0 cm grade.

CHILDREN'S GRADING AND SIZE CHARTS

(A) 6.0 cm HEIGHT GRADE

Children's grade plan 1

Infants' sizes from three months to two years: unisex.

Table 26 Sectional size chart

Age (months)		3	6	9	12	18	24	Increment
Height (cm)		62	68	74	80	86	92	6.0
Weight (kg)		7	8	9	10	12	14	1.2
Chest	Body	43	45	47	49	51	53	2.0
	Block	51	53	55	57	59	61	2.0
Waist	Body	45.4	46.6	47.8	49	50.2	51.4	1.2
	Block	52.4	53.6	54.8	56	57.2	58.4	1.2
Hips	Body	46	48	50	52	54	56	2.0
	Block	54	56	58	60	62	64	2.0
X back	Body	19	19.6	20.2	20.8	21.4	22	0.6
	Block	20	20.6	21.2	21.8	22.4	23	0.6
X chest		19	19.5	20	20.5	21	21.5	0.5
Scye depth	Body	8	8.5	9	9.5	10	10.5	0.5
	Block	9.5	10	10.5	11	11.5	12	0.5
Nape to waist		17	17.8	18.6	19.4	20.3	21.2	0.8
Shoulder		6.2	6.5	6.8	7.1	7.4	7.7	0.3
Sleeve length		23	24.5	26	27.5	29	30.5	1.5
Body rise		12	13	14	15	16	17	1.0
Thigh		24.6	25.8	27	28.2	29.4	30.6	1.2
Neck	Body	22.4	23	23.6	24.2	24.8	25.4	0.6
	Block	23.4	24	24.6	25.2	25.8	26.4	0.6
Bicep	Body	14.2	14.8	15.4	16	16.6	17.2	0.6
	Block	18.2	19.8	19.4	20	20.6	21.2	0.6
Wrist		10.4	10.6	10.8	11	11.2	11.4	0.2

General note: 6.0 cm height grade and 2.0 cm chest grade. The waist increases in line with the chest instead of 1.2 cm as illustrated in the size chart.

262　　　　　　　　　　　　　　　　　　　　　　　　　　　　　　　　　　　　　　　CHILDREN'S WEAR

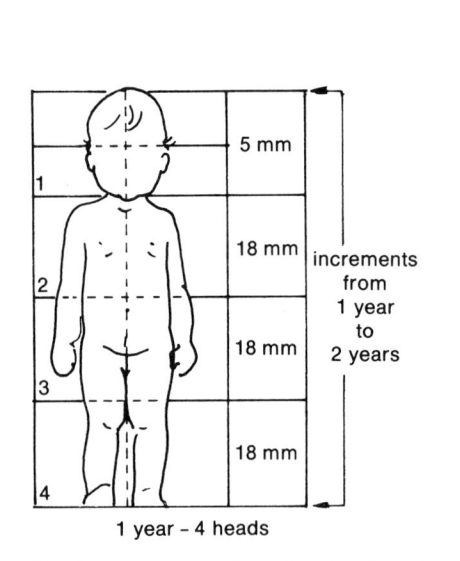

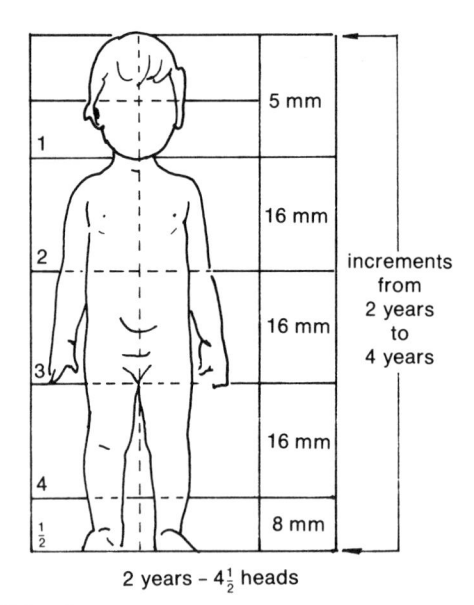

Figure 261 Grade increments/head ratio. Age 1 to 2 years

Figure 262 Grade increments/head ratio. Age 2 to 4 years

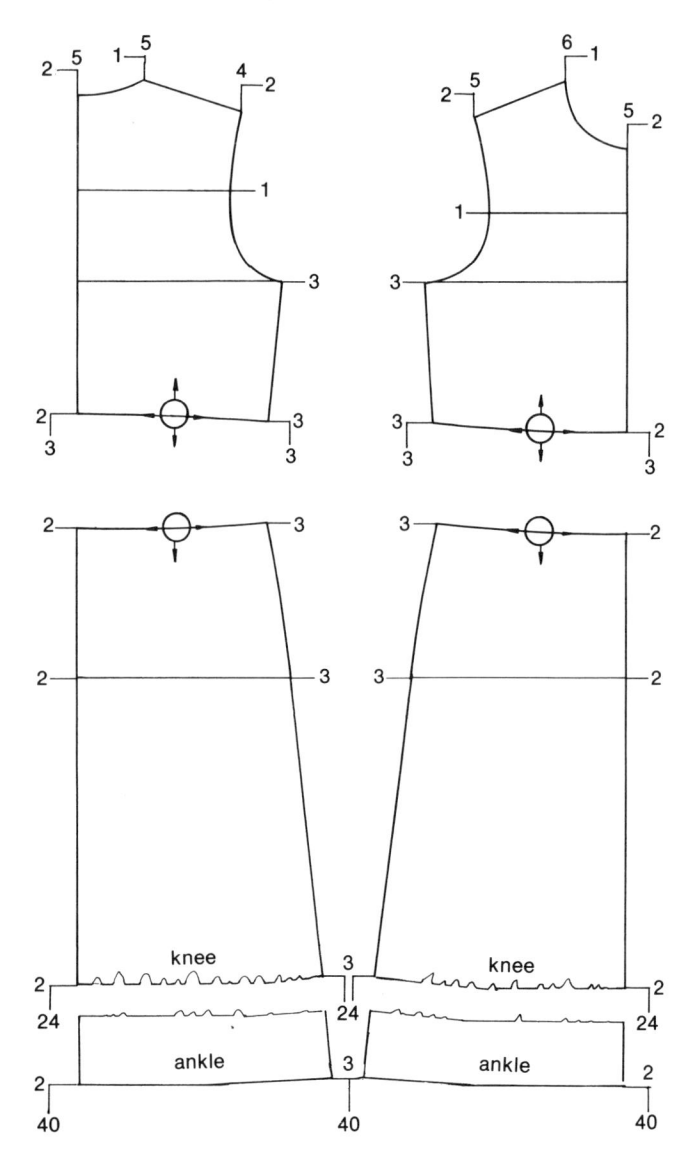

Figure 263 Bodice and skirt grade for infants from 3 months to 2 years. 6.0 cm height grade and 2.0 cm chest. (Waist increases in line with chest instead of 1.2 cm.) Unisex

CHILDREN'S GRADING AND SIZE CHARTS

Figure 264 Sleeve grade. 6.0 cm height grade for infants from 3 months to 2 years. Unisex

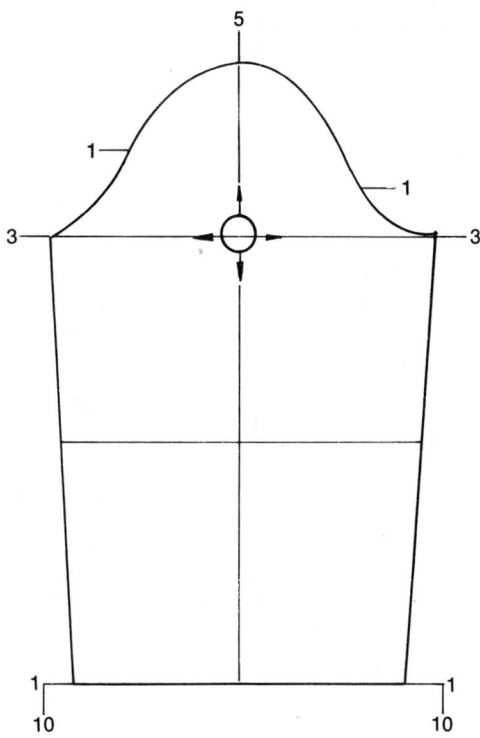

Figure 265 Trouser grades. Unisex infants, 3 months to 2 years, 6.0 cm height grade. (Waist as chest instead of 1.2 cm)

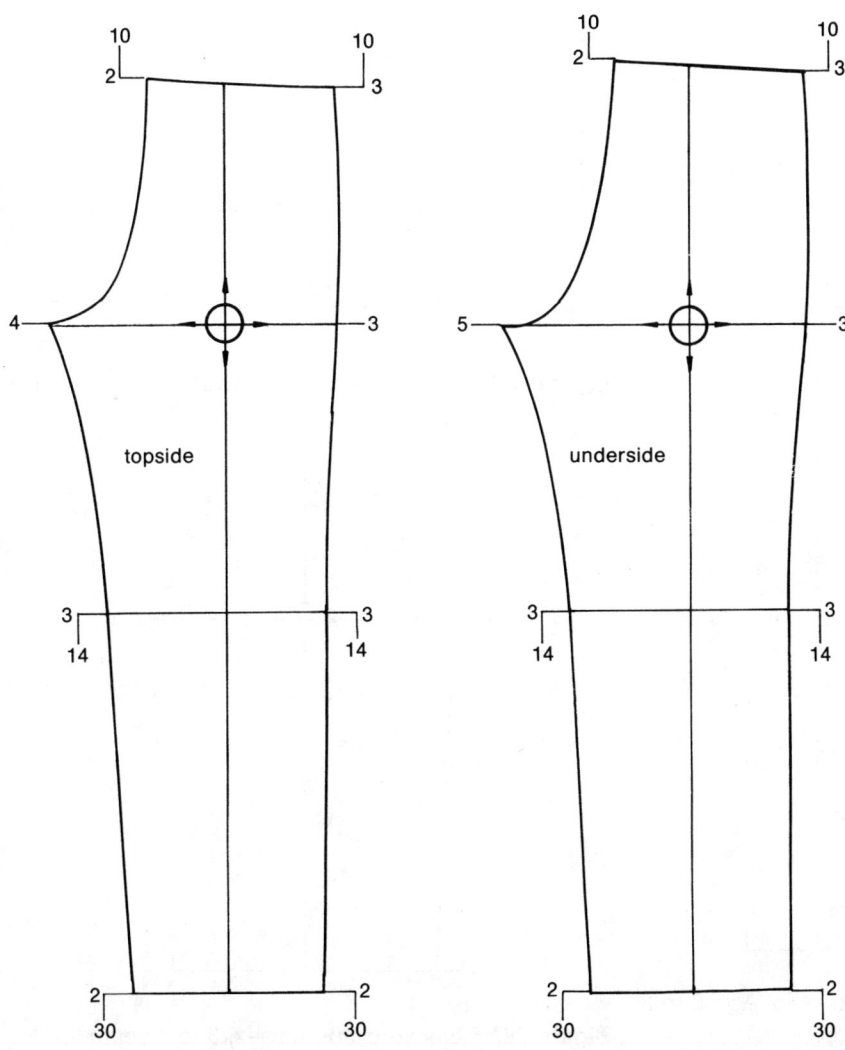

Children's grade plan 2

Children's sizes from three years to seven years: unisex.

General note: 6.0 cm height grade and 2.0 cm chest grade.

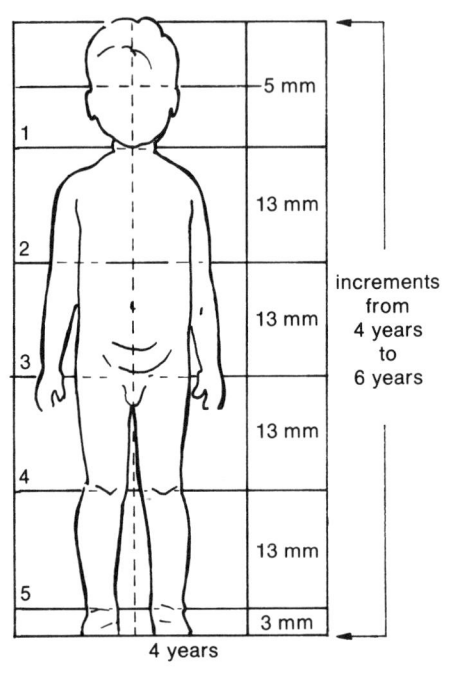

Figure 266 Grade increments/head ratio. Age 4 to 6 years. (4 years: $5\frac{1}{4}$ heads.)

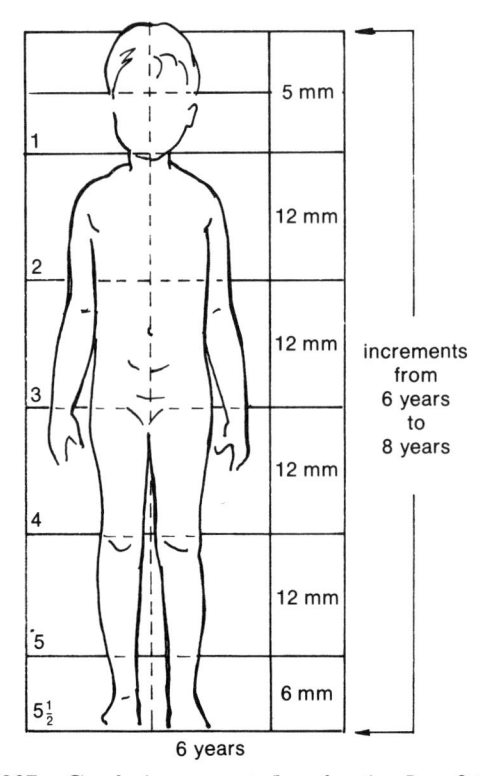

Figure 267 Grade increments/head ratio. Age 6 to 8 years. (6 years: $5\frac{1}{2}$ heads.)

Figure 268 Bodice and skirt grade unisex, 3 to 7 years

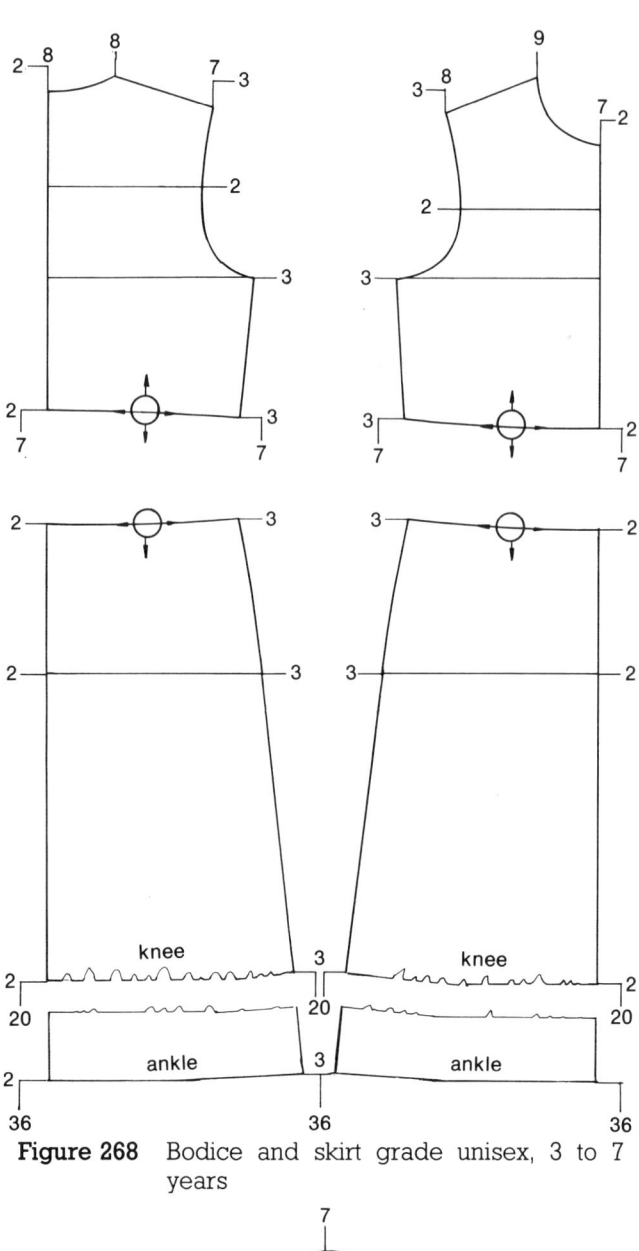

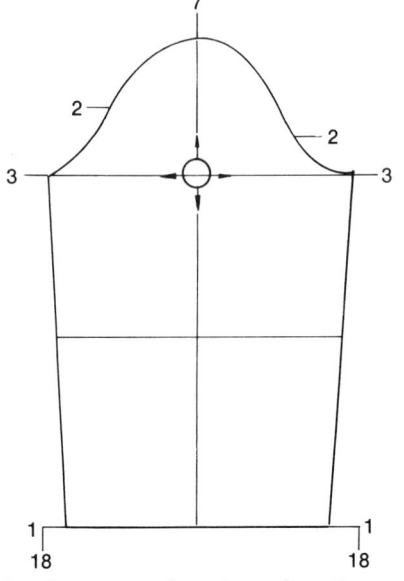

Figure 269 Sleeve grade unisex, 3 to 7 years

CHILDREN'S GRADING AND SIZE CHARTS

Figure 270 Trouser grade. 3 to 7 years. Unisex 6.0 cm height grade and 2.0 cm chest. (Waist increases in line with chest instead of 1.2 cm. Hip increases 2.4 cm.)

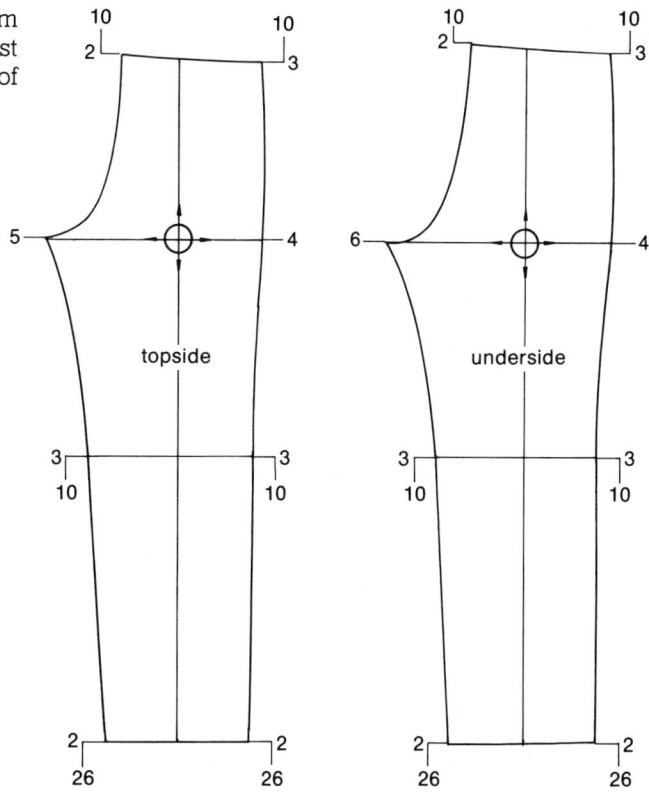

Table 27 Sectional size chart

		Unisex					
Age (years)		3	4	5	6	7	Increment
Height (cm)		98	104	110	116	122	6.0
Weight (kg)		16	17	19	21	23	2
Chest	Body	55	57	59	61	63	2.0
	Block	62	64	66	68	70	2.0
Waist	Body	52.6	53.8	55	56.2	57.4	1.2
	Block	58.6	59.8	61	62.2	64.4	1.2
Hips	Body	58.6	61	63.4	65.8	68.2	2.4
	Block	63.6	66	68.4	70.8	73.2	2.4
X back	Body	22.8	23.6	24.4	25.2	26	0.8
	Block	24.8	25.6	26.4	27.2	28	0.8
X chest		23	23.8	24.6	25.4	26.2	0.8
Scye depth	Body	11.2	12	12.8	13.6	14.4	0.8
	Block	13.2	14	14.8	15.6	16.4	0.8
Nape to waist		23	24.5	26	27.5	29	1.5
Shoulder		7.9	8.2	8.5	8.8	9.1	0.3
Sleeve length		32	34.5	37	39.5	42	2.5
Body rise		18	19	20	21	22	1.0
Thigh		31.5	33	34.5	36	37.5	1.5
Neck	Body	25	26	27	28	29	1.0
	Block	26	27	28	29	30	1.0
Bicep	Body	17.4	18	18.6	19.2	19.8	0.6
	Block	22.4	23	23.6	24.2	24.8	0.6
Wrist		11.5	11.8	12.1	12.4	12.7	0.3

The waist increases in line with the chest instead of 1.2 cm as illustrated in the size chart.

Children's grade plan 3

Girls' sizes from eight years to eleven years.

General note: 6.0 cm height grade and 3.2 cm chest grade. The waist increases in line with the chest grade instead of 1.2 cm as shown in the size chart.

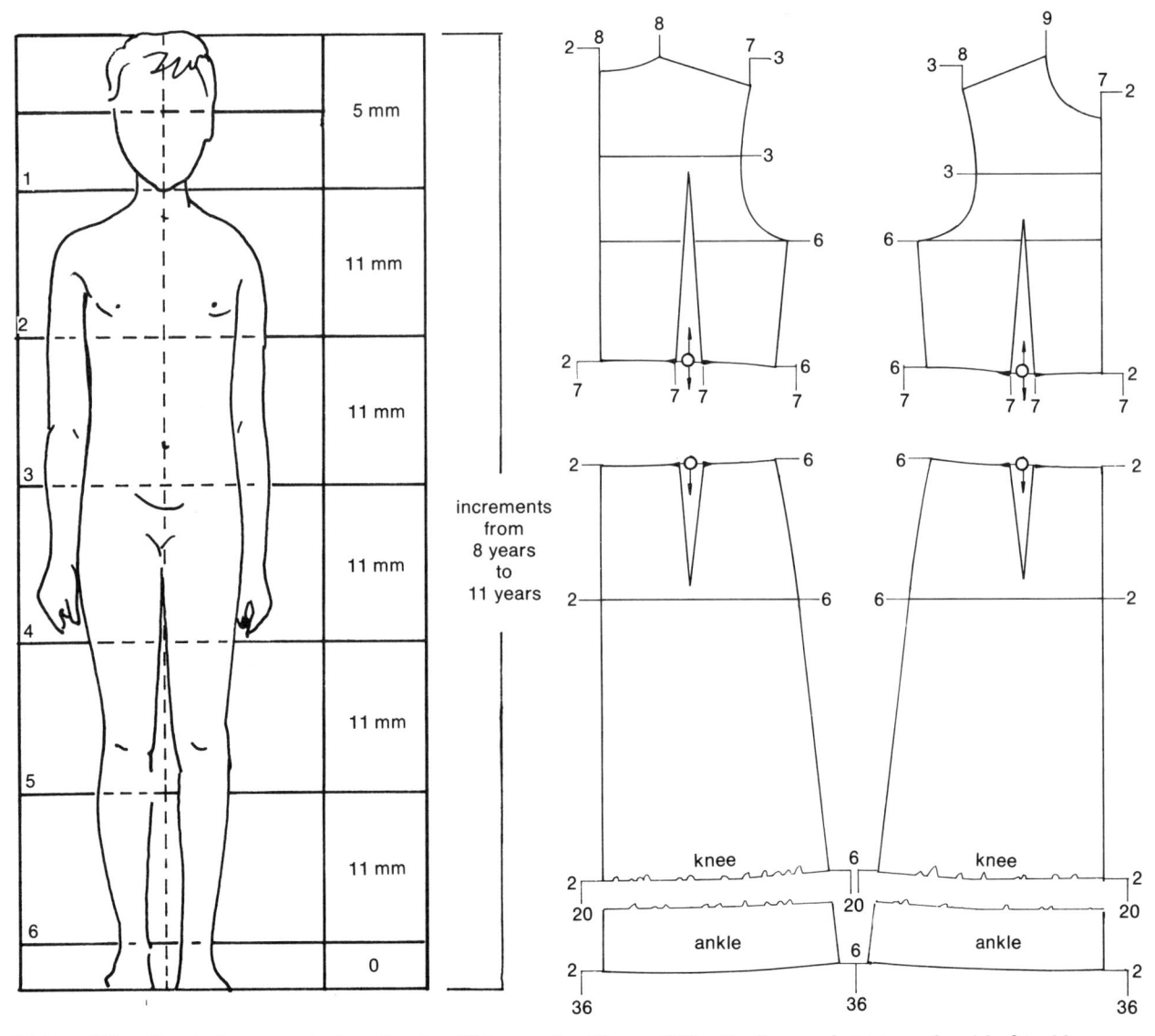

Figure 271 Grade increments/head ratio. Girls aged 8 to 11 years. (8 years: $6\frac{1}{3}$ heads.)

Figure 272 Bodice and skirt grade girls 8 to 11 years. 6.0 cm height and 3.2 cm chest. Waist follows chest for convenience. Hip 3.6 cm

CHILDREN'S GRADING AND SIZE CHARTS

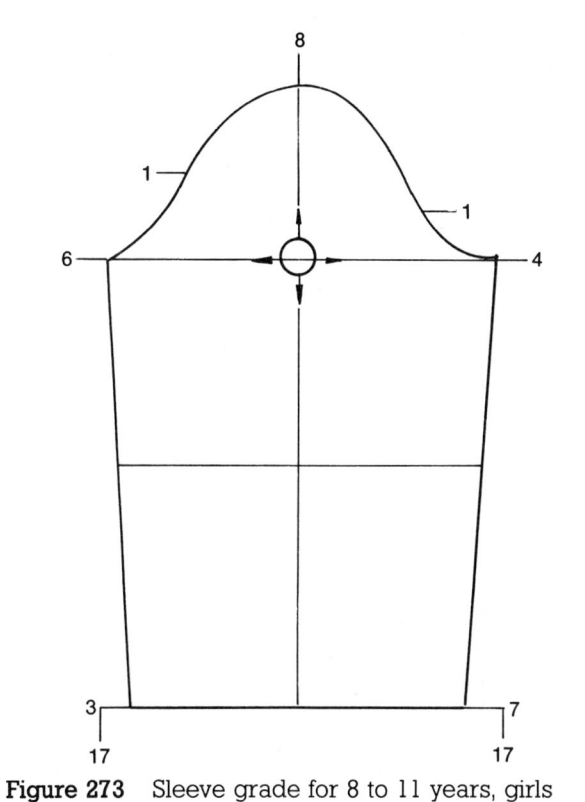

Figure 273 Sleeve grade for 8 to 11 years, girls

Figure 274 Trouser grade. 6.0 cm height grade. Girls 8 to 11 years

Table 28 Sectional size chart

		Unisex				
Age (years)		8	9	10	11	Increment
Height (cm)		128	134	140	146	6.0
Weight (kg)		25	29	33	37	4
Chest	Body	66.2	69.4	72.6	75.8	3.2
	Block	74.2	77.4	80.6	83.8	3.2
Waist	Body	59	60.6	62.2	63.8	1.6
	Block	64	65.6	67.2	68.8	1.6
Hips	Body	71.8	75.4	79	82.6	3.6
	Block	76.8	80.4	84	87.6	3.6
X back	Body	27	28	29	30	1.0
	Block	29	30	31	32	1.0
X chest		27	28	29	30	1.0
Scye depth	Body	15.2	16	16.8	17.6	0.8
	Block	17.7	18.5	19.3	20.1	0.8
Nape to waist		30.5	32	33.5	35	1.5
Shoulder		9.4	9.7	10	10.3	0.3
Sleeve length		44.5	47	49.5	52	2.5
Body rise		23	24	25	26	1.0
Thigh		39	40.5	42	43.5	1.5
Neck	Body	30	31	32	33	1.0
	Block	31	32	33	34	1.0
Bicep	Body	20	21	22	23	1.0
	Block	26	27	28	29	1.0
Wrist		13	13.3	13.6	13.9	0.3

Children's grade plan 4

Boys' sizes from eight years to fifteen years.

General note: 6.9 cm height grade and 3.2 cm chest grade. The hip section (Figure 275) may be grown onto the bodice by re-arranging the zero point for styling purposes.

Figure 275 Grade increments/head ratio. Boys aged 8 to 15 years

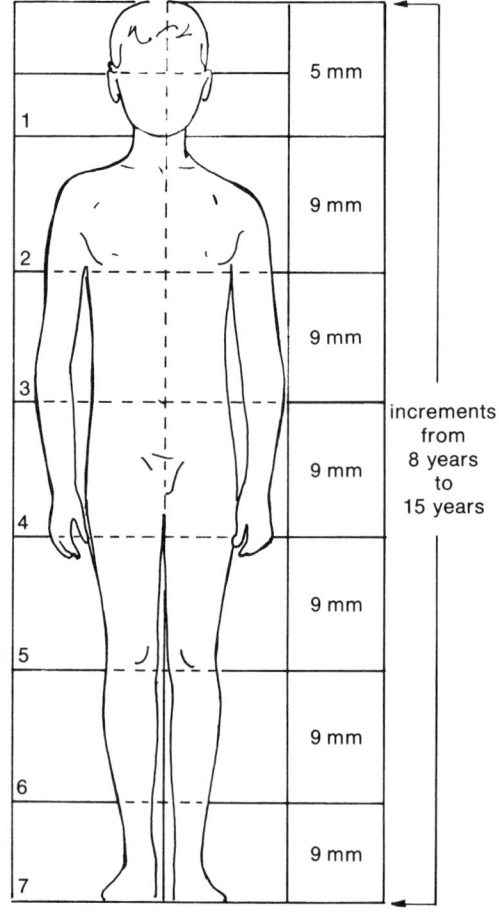

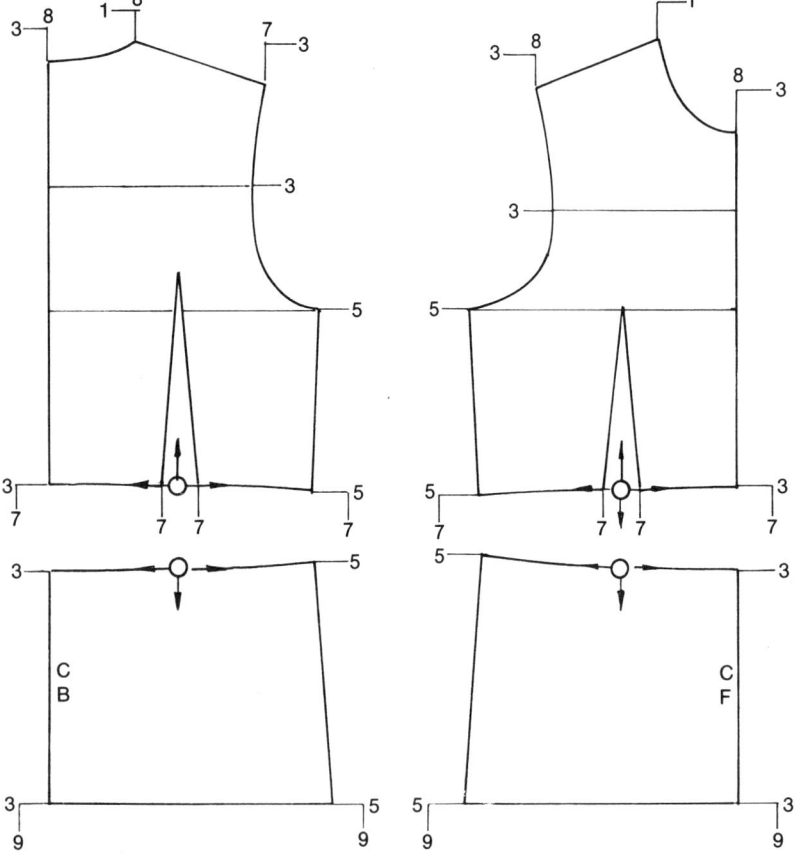

Figure 276 Boys' bodice 6.0 cm grade. Boys aged 8 to 15 years

CHILDREN'S GRADING AND SIZE CHARTS

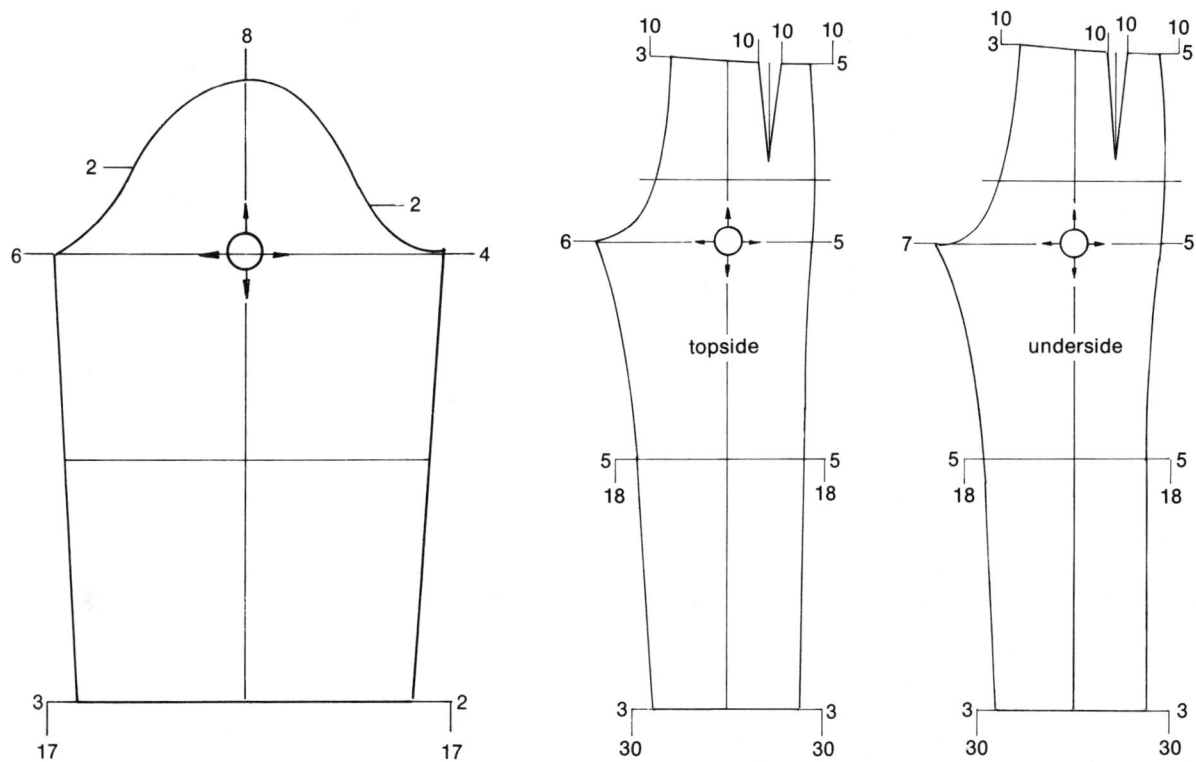

Figure 277 Sleeve grade. Boys aged 8 to 15 years

Figure 278 Trouser grade. 6.0 cm height grade. Boys aged 8 to 15 years. 3.2 cm chest: waist follows chest. 3.2 cm hip

Table 29 Sectional size chart

Age (years)		8	9	10	11	12	13	14	15	Increment
Height (cm)		128	134	140	146	152	158	164	170	6.0
Weight (kg)		24	29	34	39	44	49	54	59	5
Chest	Body	67	70.2	73.4	76.6	79.8	83	86.2	89.4	3.2
	Block	77	80.2	83.4	86.6	89.8	93	96.2	99.4	3.2
Waist	Body	61	63	65	67	69	71	73	75	2.0
	Block	65	67	69	71	73	75	77	79	2.0
Hips	Body	70	73.2	76.4	79.6	82.8	86	89.2	92.4	3.2
	Block	75	78.2	81.4	84.6	87.8	91	94.2	97.4	3.2
X back	Body	28	29.2	30.4	31.6	32.8	34	35.2	36.4	1.2
	Block	30	31.2	32.4	33.6	34.8	36	37.2	38.4	1.2
X chest		27.2	28.4	29.6	30.8	32	33.2	34.4	35.6	1.2
Scye depth	Body	16.6	17.4	18.2	19	19.8	20.6	21.4	22	0.8
	Block	19.6	20.4	21.2	22	22.8	23.6	24.4	25	0.8
Nape to waist		31	32.5	34	35.5	37	38.5	40	41.5	1.5
Shoulder		11	11.4	11.8	12.2	12.6	13	13.4	13.8	0.4
Sleeve length		45.5	48	50.5	53	55.5	58	60.5	63	2.5
Body rise		21	22	23	24	25	26	27	28	1.0
Thigh		38	40	42	44	46	48	50	52	2.0
Neck	Body	30	31.2	32.4	33.6	34.8	36	37.2	38.4	1.2
	Block	31	32.2	33.4	34.6	35.8	37	38.2	39.4	1.2
Bicep	Body	21	22	23	24	25	26	27	28	1.0
	Block	27	28	29	30	31	32	33	34	1.0
Wrist		13.5	14	14.5	15	15.5	16	16.5	17	0.5

Children's grade plan 5

Teenage girls from twelve years to fifteen years.

The easiest option is to take an adult size 12 block and grade down using these grade rules (reversing the plan shown on this page).

General note: 6.0 cm height grade, 3.2 cm chest, 2.4 cm hip and 1.0 cm waist.

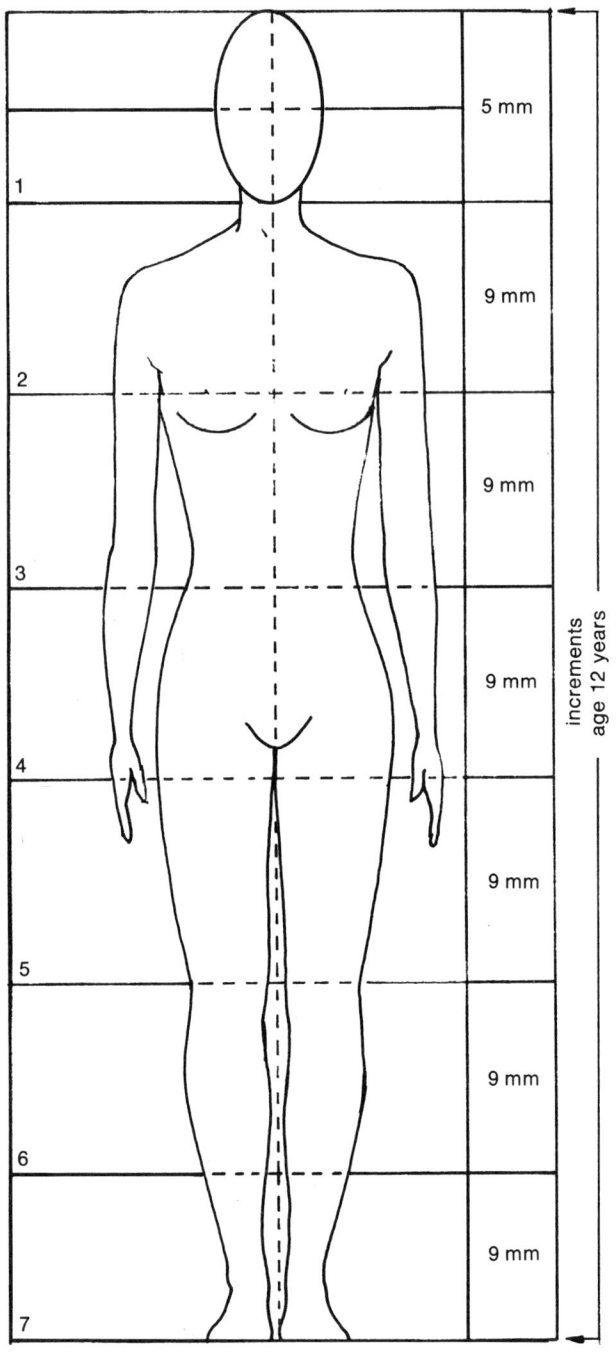

Figure 279 Grade increments/head ratio. Teenage girls 12 to 15 years

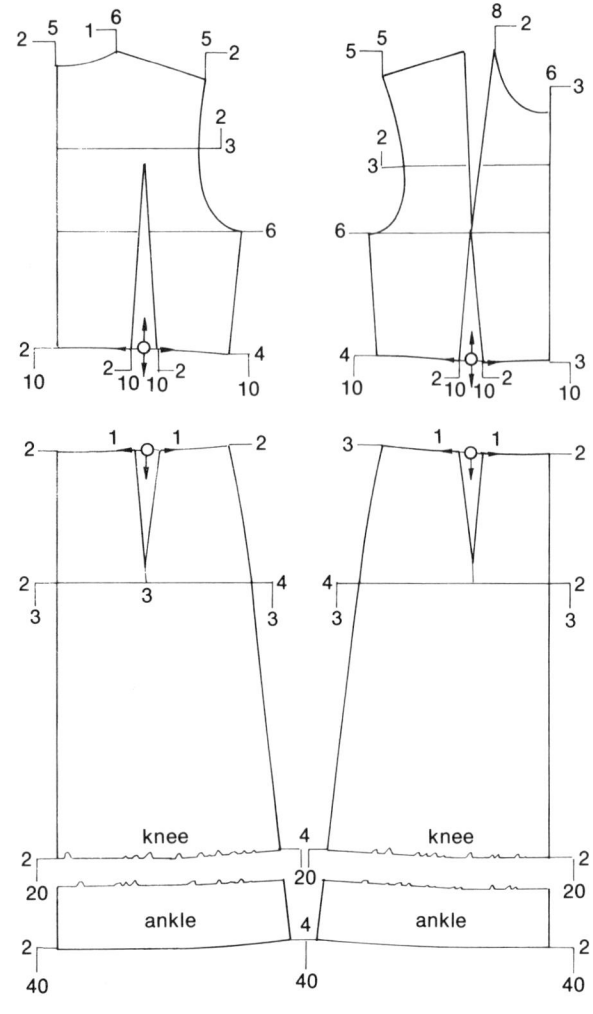

Figure 280 Bodice and skirt grade. 6.0 cm height grade. Teenage girls 12 to 15 years. Chest 3.2 cm, hips 2.4 cm

shoulder grade = A–B plus shoulder grade of 0.3 cm per size.

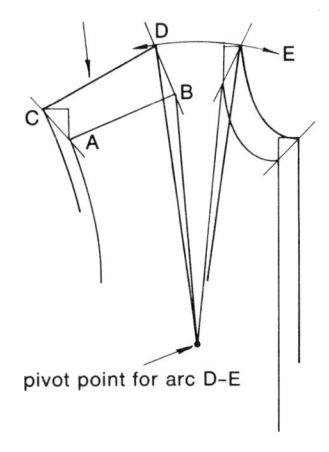

Figure 281 Illustrates how to increase the bust dart by pivoting from the bust point. For more detailed information see Chapter 15

CHILDREN'S GRADING AND SIZE CHARTS

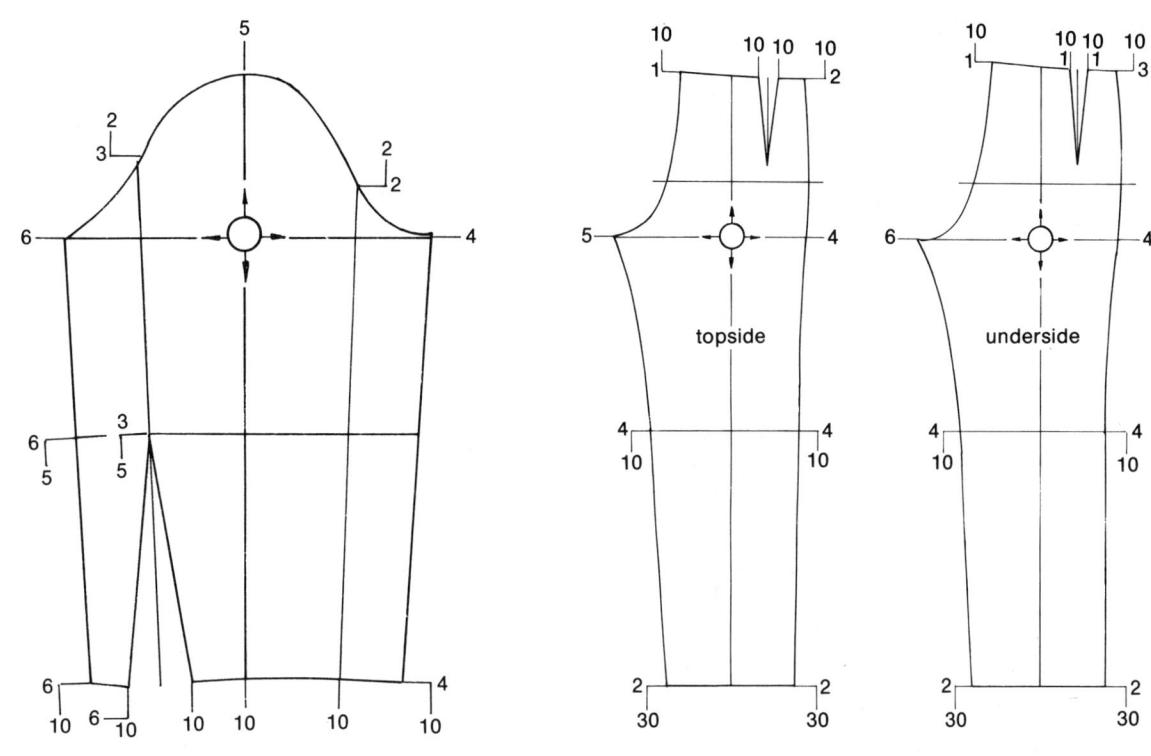

Figure 282 Sleeve grade. Teenage girls aged 12 to 15 years

Figure 283 Trouser grade. Teenage girls aged 12 to 15 years

Table 30 Sectional size chart

		Teenage girls				
Age (years)		12	13	14	15	Increment
Height (cm)		150	154	158	162	4.0
Weight (kg)		43	47	50	52	4-2
Chest	Body	76.4	79.6	82.8	86	3.2
	Block	75.4	78.6	91.8	95	3.2
Waist	Body	64	65	66	67	1.0
	Block	68	69	70	71	1.0
Hips	Body	84.8	87.2	89.6	92	2.4
	Block	89.8	92.2	94.6	97	2.4
X back	Body	31	32	33	34	1.0
	Block	33	34	35	36	1.0
X chest		31	32	33	34	1.0
Scye depth	Body	18	18.4	18.8	19.2	0.4
	Block	21	21.4	21.8	22.2	0.4
Nape to waist		35.5	37	38.5	40 0	1.5
Shoulder		10.6	10.9	11.2	11.5	0.3
Sleeve length		53.5	55	56.5	58	1.5
Body rise		27	28	29	30	1.0
Thigh		46	49	52	55	3.0
Neck	Body	34	35	36	37	1.0
	Block	35	36	37	38	1.0
Bicep	Body	24	25	26	27	1.0
	Block	30	31	32	33	1.0
Wrist		14.4	14.8	15.2		0.4

10.0cm HEIGHT GRADE

Children's grade plan 6

Infants' sizes from three months to two years: unisex.

General note: 10.0 cm height grade, 2.0 cm chest, 3.0 cm hip. The waist increases in line with the chest grade (3.0 cm) instead of the 2.0 cm illustrated in the size chart.

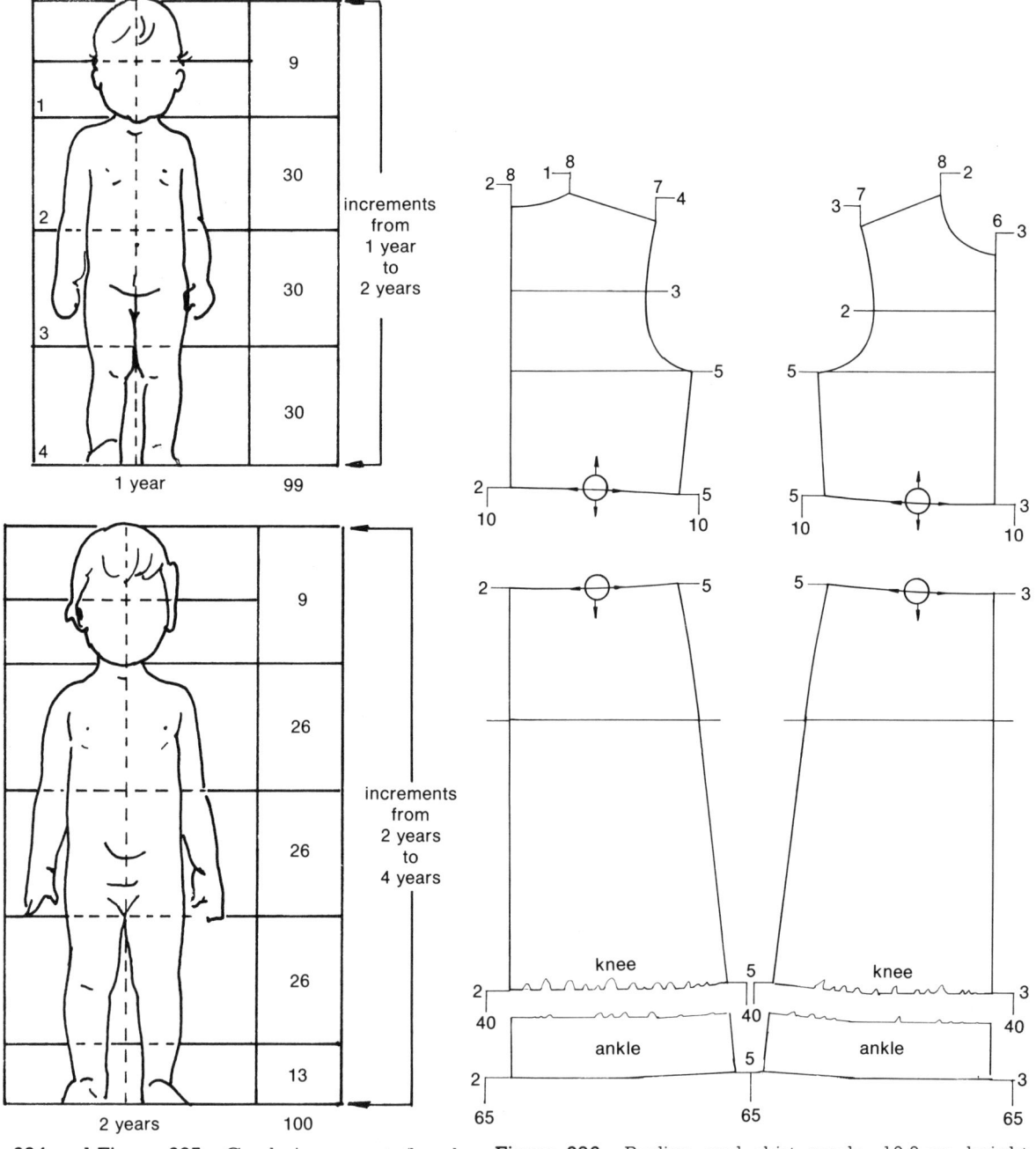

Figure 284 and Figure 285 Grade increments/head ratio. Age 1 to 2 years

Figure 286 Bodice and skirt grade. 10.0 cm height infants' unisex grade – 3 months to 2 years

CHILDREN'S GRADING AND SIZE CHARTS

Figure 287 Sleeve grade 3 months to 2 years unisex grade

Figure 288 Trouser grade – 3 months to 2 years unisex

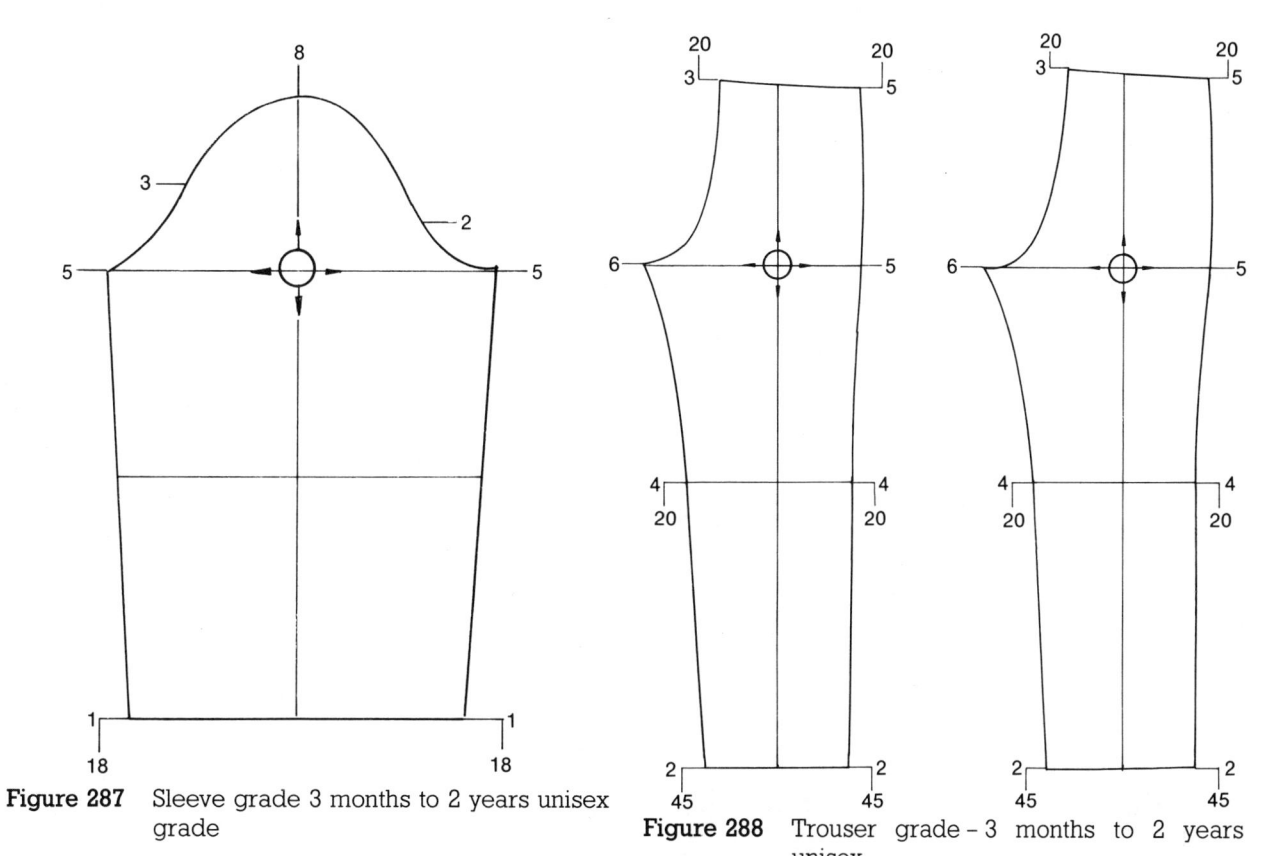

Table 31 Sectional size chart

		Infants				
Age		3 months	6 months	12 months	2 years	Increment
Height (cm)		60	70	80	90	10.0
Weight (kg)		7	9	11	14	2-3
Chest	Body	43	46	49	52	3.0
	Block	51	52	57	60	3.0
Waist	Body	46	48	50	52	2.0
	Block	53	55	57	59	2.0
Hips	Body	46	49	52	55	3.0
	Block	54	57	60	63	3.0
X back	Body	19	20	21	22	1.0
	Block	20	21	22	23	1.0
X chest		19	20	21	22	1.0
Scye depth	Body	8	8.8	9.6	10.4	0.8
	Block	9.5	10.3	11.1	11.9	0.8
Nape to waist		17	18.8	20.6	22.4	1.8
Shoulder		6.2	6.7	7.2	7.7	0.5
Sleeve length		23	25.5	28	30.5	2.5
Body rise		11	13	15	17	2.0
Thigh		24	26	28	30	2.0
Neck	Body	22.5	23.3	24.1	24.9	0.8
	Block	23.5	24.3	25.1	25.9	0.8
Bicep	Body	14	15	16	17	1.0
	Block	18	19	20	21	1.0
Wrist		10.4	10.8	11.2	11.6	0.4

Children's grade plan 7

Children's sizes, two/three years to ten/eleven years: unisex.

General note: 10.0 cm height grade and 5.0 cm chest grade and 6.0 cm hip grade. The waist grade increases in line with the chest grade (5.0 cm) instead of the 3.0 cm illustrated in the size chart.

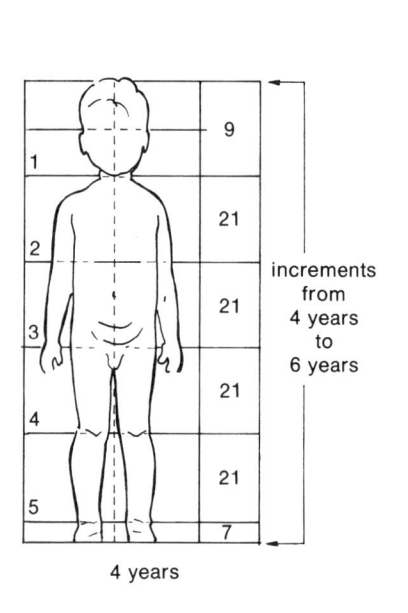

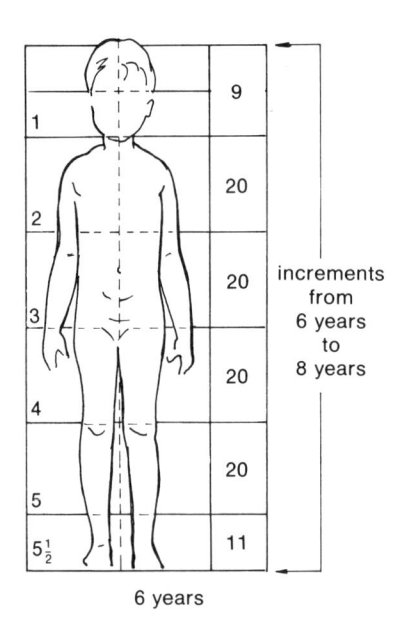

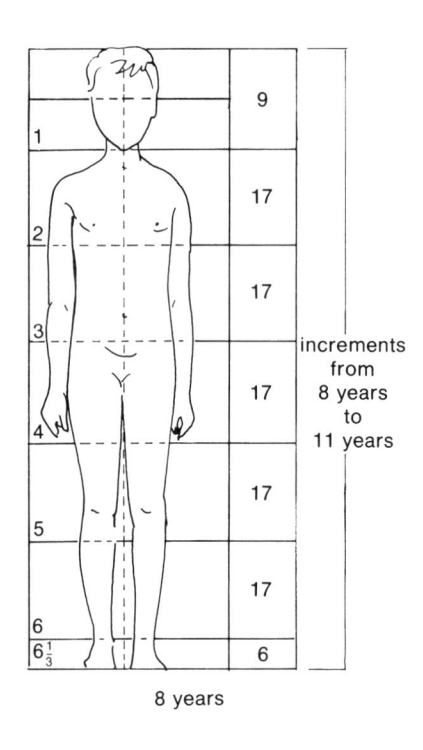

Figure 289/Figure 290/Figure 291
Grade increments/head ratio. From 2 to 11 years

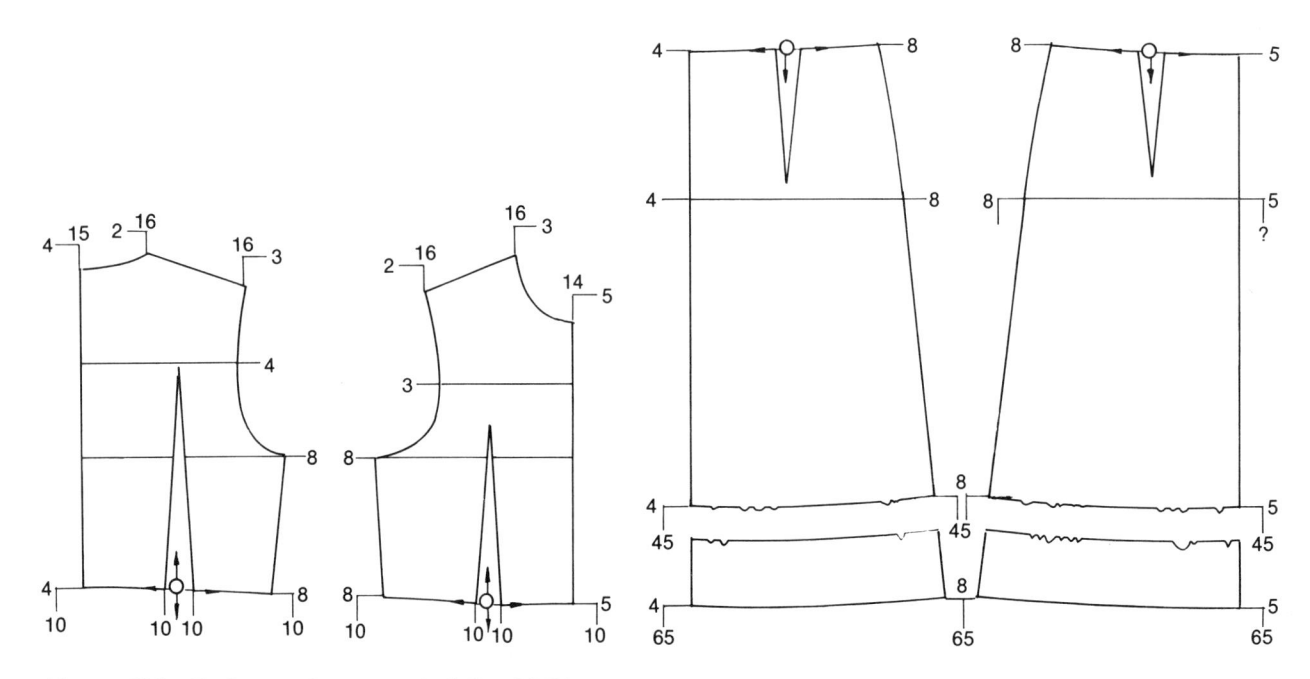

Figure 292 Bodice and skirt grade 2/3 to 10/11 years. Unisex

CHILDREN'S GRADING AND SIZE CHARTS

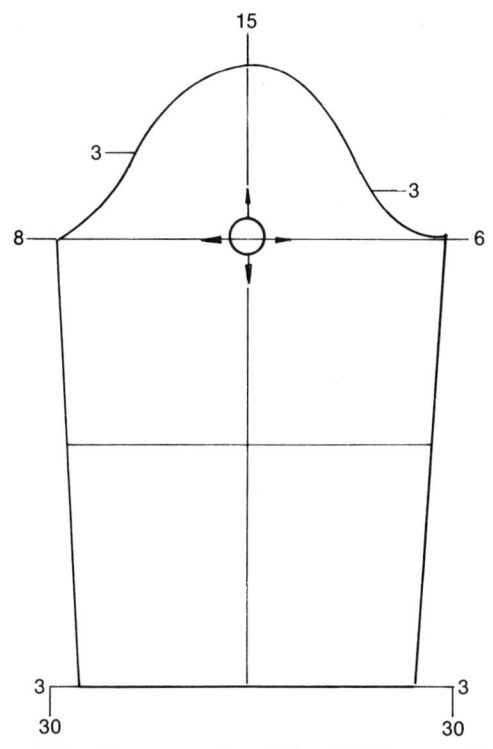

Figure 293 Sleeve grade – 2/3 to 10/11 years. Unisex

Figure 294 Trouser grade – 2/3 to 10/11 years. Unisex

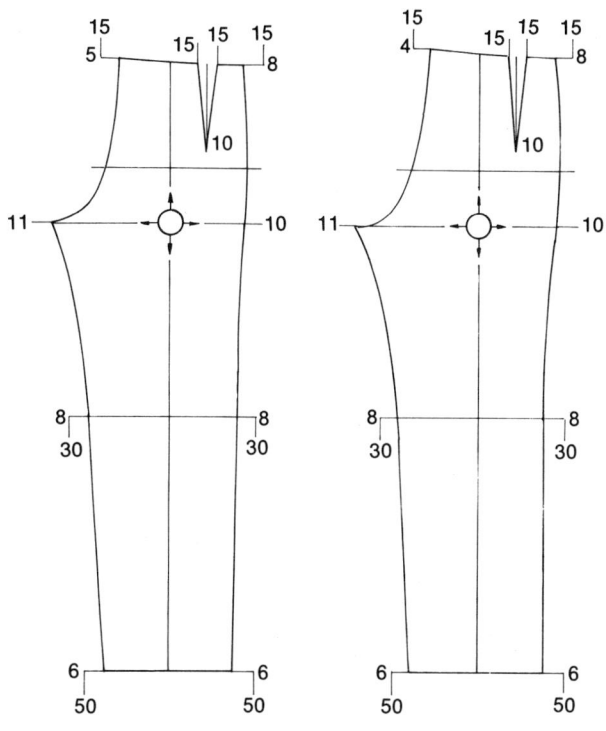

Table 32 Sectional size chart

		\multicolumn{5}{c}{Children unisex}	
Age (years)		2/3	4/5	5/7	8/9	10/11	Increment
Height (cm)		100	110	120	130	140	10.0
Weight (kg)		16	19	23	29	37	3-8
Chest	Body	55	60	65	70	75	5.0
	Block	63	68	73	78	83	5.0
Waist	Body	53	56	59	62	65	3.0
	Block	58	61	64	67	70	3.0
Hips	Body	58	64	70	76	82	6.0
	Block	63	69	75	81	87	6.0
X back	Body	23	24.6	26.2	27.8	29.4	1.6
	Block	24	25.6	27.2	28.8	30.4	1.6
X chest		23	24.6	26.2	27.8	29.4	1.6
Scye depth	Body	11	12.5	14	15.5	17	1.5
	Block	13	14.5	16	17.5	19	1.5
Nape to waist		23	25.5	28	30.5	33	2.5
Shoulder		8	8.6	9.4	10	10.6	0.6
Sleeve length		33	37.5	42	46.5	51	4.5
Body rise		18	19.5	21	22.5	24	1.5
Thigh		32	34.5	37	39.5	42	2.5
Neck	Body	26	27.6	29.2	30.8	32.4	1.6
	Block	27	28.6	30.2	31.8	33.4	1.6
Bicep	Body	17.5	18.7	19.9	21.1	22.3	1.2
	Block	22.5	23.7	24.9	26.1	27.3	1.2
Wrist		11.8	12.3	12.8	13.3	13.8	0.5

Children's grade plan 8

Boys' sizes from nine/ten years to fifteen/sixteen years.

General note: 10.0 cm height grade: 5.0 cm chest grade: 5.0 cm hip grade. The waist grade increases in line with the chest grade (5.0 cm) instead of the 4.0 cm illustrated in the size chart.

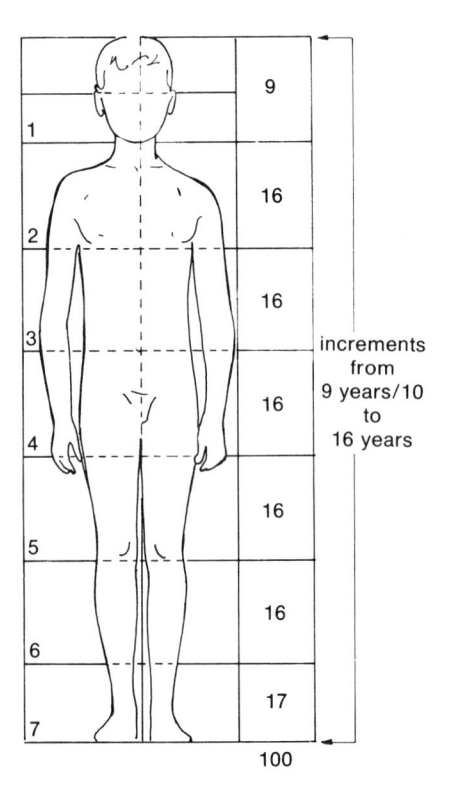

Figure 295 Grade increments/head ratio – 9/10 to 15/16 years. Boys

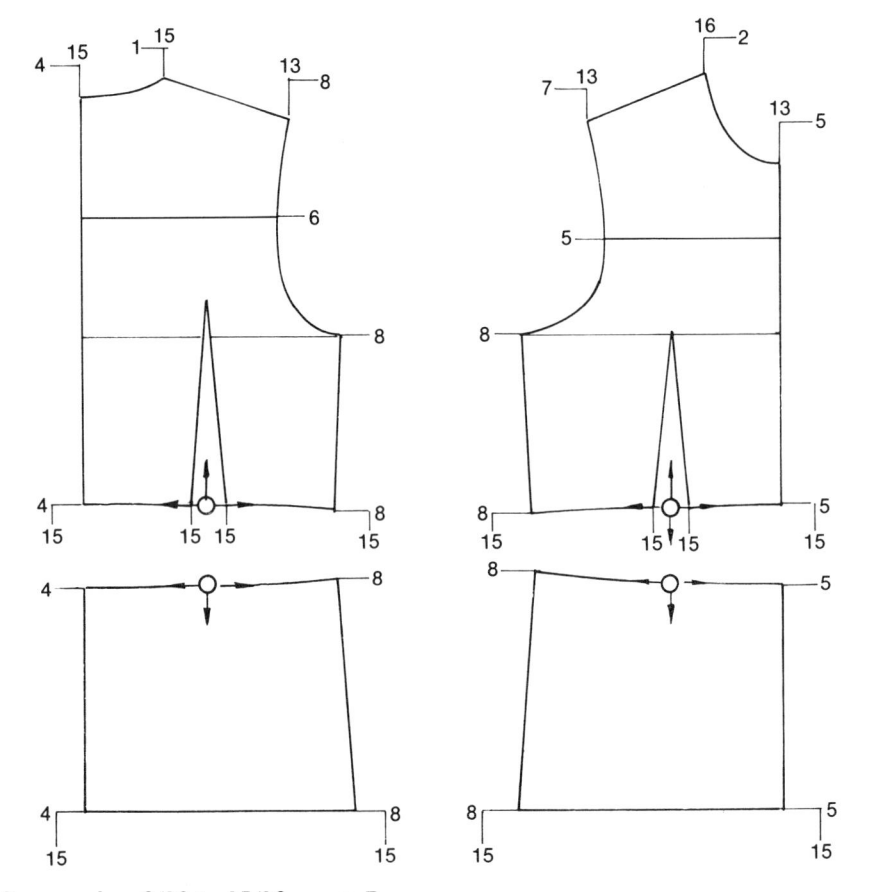

Figure 296 Bodice grade – 9/10 to 15/16 years. Boys

CHILDREN'S GRADING AND SIZE CHARTS

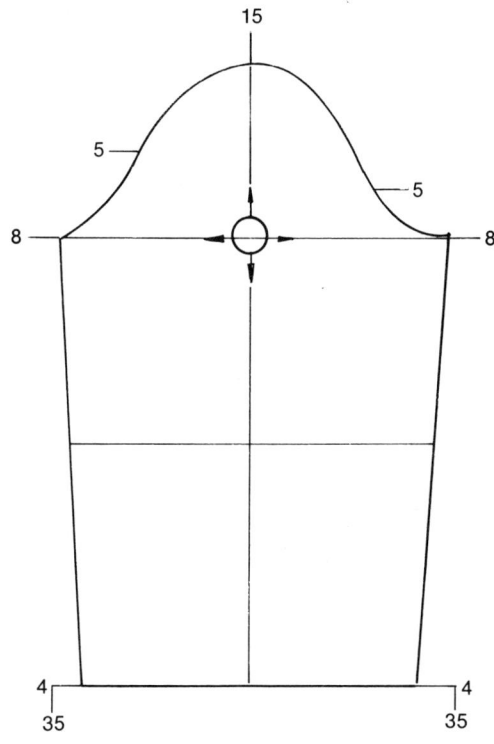

Figure 297 Sleeve grade 9/10 and 15/16. Boys

Figure 298 Trouser grade – 9/10 to 15/16 years. Boys

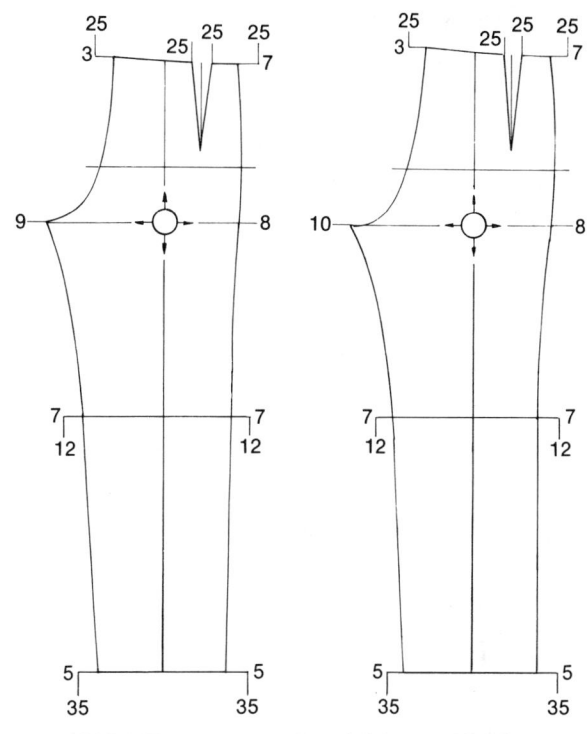

Table 33 Sectional size chart

		Boys				
Age		9/10	11/12	13/14	15/16	Increment
Height (cm)		140	150	160	170	10.0
Weight (kg)		34	44	54	64	10
Chest	Body	73	78	83	88	5.0
	Block	83	88	93	98	5.0
Waist	Body	65	69	73	77	4.0
	Block	69	73	77	81	4.0
Hips	Body	76	81	86	91	5.0
	Block	81	86	91	96	5.0
X back	Body	32	34	36	38	2.0
	Block	34	36	38	40	2.0
X chest		32	34	36	38	2.0
Scye depth	Body	17.5	19	20.5	22	1.5
	Block	20.5	22	23.5	25	1.5
Nape to waist		33	36	39	42	3.0
Shoulder		11	12	13	14	1.0
Sleeve length		47	52	57	62	5.0
Body rise		21	23.5	26	28.5	2.5
Thigh		42	45.5	49	52.5	3.5
Neck	Body	32	34	36	38	2.0
	Block	33	35	37	39	2.0
Bicep	Body	22.5	24.5	26.5	28.5	2.0
	Block	28.5	30.5	32.5	34.5	2.0
Wrist		14	15	16	17	1.0

278   CHILDREN'S WEAR

Children's grade plan 9

Teenage girls from eleven/twelve to fifteen/sixteen years.

The easiest option is to take an adult size 12 block and grade down using these grade rules (reversing the plan shown on this page).

General note: 10.0 cm height grade, hip and bust both increase by 5.0 cm. Waist grade 2.0 cm.

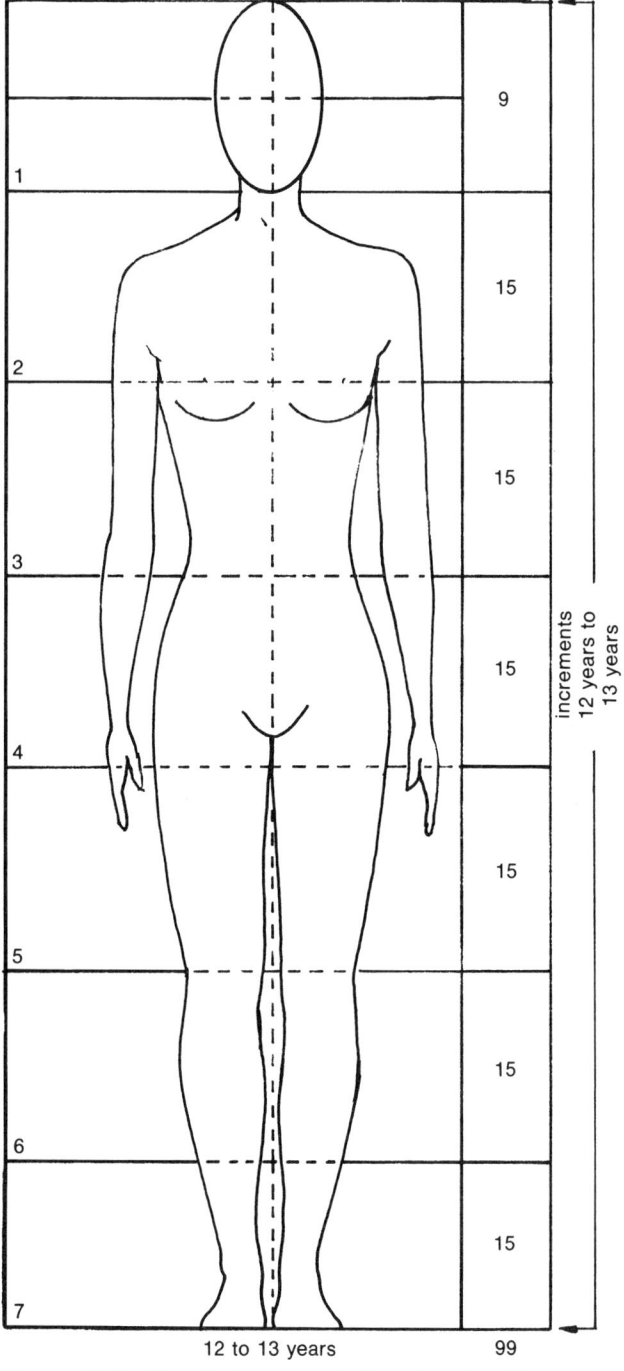

Figure 299 Grade increments/head ratio. Teenage girls from 11/12 years to 15/16 years

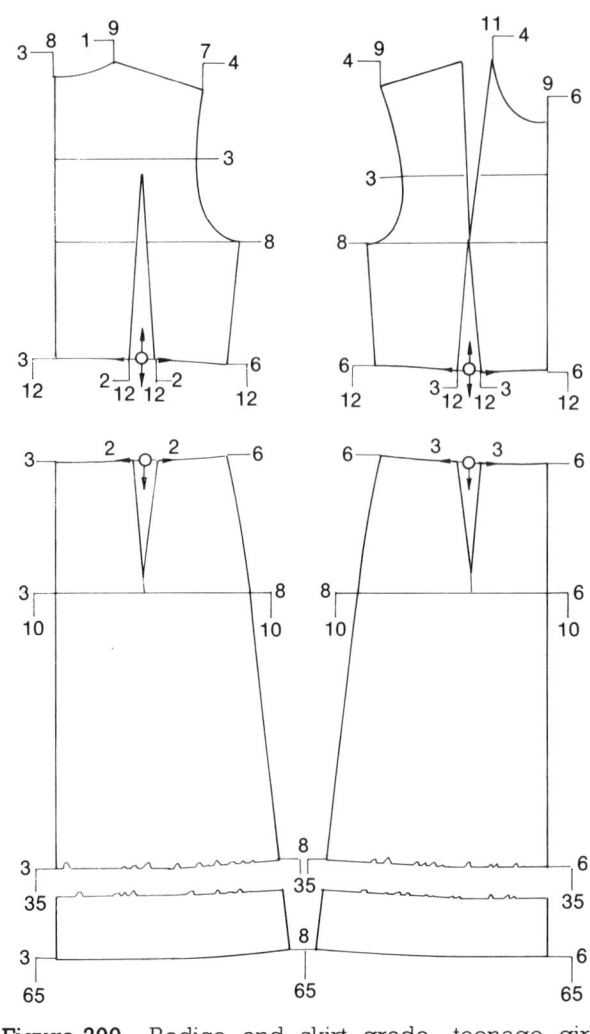

Figure 300 Bodice and skirt grade – teenage girls 11/12 to 15/16 years

shoulder grade = A − B plus shoulder grade of 0.3 cm per size

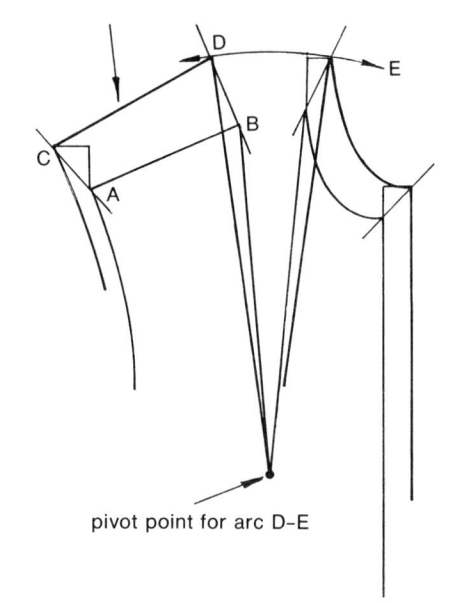

pivot point for arc D−E

Figure 301 Technique illustrating bust dart increase

CHILDREN'S GRADING AND SIZE CHARTS

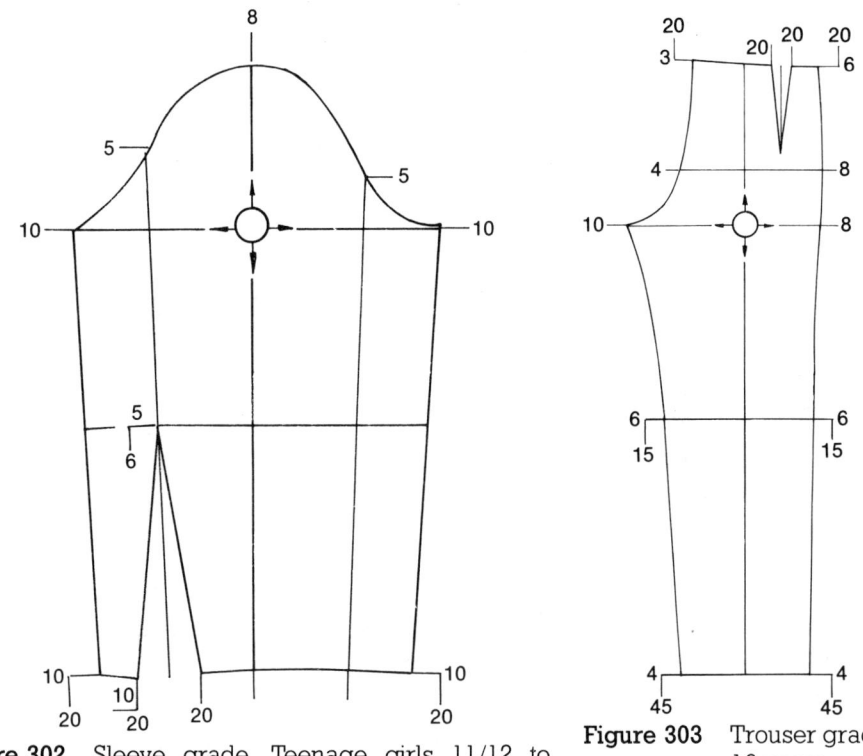

Figure 302 Sleeve grade. Teenage girls 11/12 to 15/16 years

Figure 303 Trouser grade. Teenage girls 11/12 to 15/16 years

Table 34 Sectional size chart

		Girls			
Age		11/12	13/14	15/16	Increment
Height (cm)		150	160	170	10.0
Weight (kg)		43	50	58	7-8
Chest	Body	76	81	86	5.0
	Block	85	90	95	5.0
Waist	Body	64	66	68	2.0
	Block	67	69	71	2.0
Hips	Body	84	89	94	5.0
	Block	89	94	99	5.0
X back	Body	31.6	32.8	34	1.2
	Block	33.6	34.8	36	1.2
X chest		31.6	32.8	34	1.2
Scye depth	Body	17.5	18.3	19.1	0.8
	Block	20.5	21.3	22.1	0.8
Nape to waist		35	37	39	2.0
Shoulder		11	11.5	12	0.5
Sleeve length		53	56	59	3.0
Body rise		25	27	29	2.0
Thigh		44	49	54	5.0
Neck	Body	33	34.5	36	1.5
	Block	33	35.5	37	1.5
Bicep	Body	23	25	27	2.0
	Block	29	31	33	2.0
Wrist		14.5	15	15.5	0.5

Table 35 Composite size chart. 6.0 cm grade

Infant and children unisex

Age (months)		3	6	9	12	18	24	Increment
Height (cm)		62	68	74	80	86	92	6.0
Weight (kg)		7	8	9	10	12	14	1/2
Chest	Body	43	45	47	49	51	53	2.0
	Block	51	53	55	57	59	61	2.0
Waist	Body	45.4	46.6	47.8	49	50.2	51.4	1.2
	Block	52.4	53.6	54.8	56	57.2	58.4	1.2
Hips	Body	46	48	50	52	54	56	2.0
	Block	54	56	58	60	62	64	2.0
X back	Body	19	19.6	20.2	20.8	21.4	22	0.6
	Block	20	20.6	21.2	21.8	22.4	23	0.6
X chest		19	19.5	20	20.5	21	21.5	0.5
Scye depth	Body	8	8.5	9	9.5	10	10.5	0.5
	Block	9.5	10	10.5	11	11.5	12	0.5
Nape to waist		17	17.8	18.6	19.4	20.3	21.2	0.8
Shoulder		6.2	6.5	6.8	7.1	7.4	7.7	0.3
Sleeve length		23	24.5	26	27.5	29	30.5	1.5
Body rise		12	13	14	15	16	17	1.0
Thigh		24.6	25.8	27	28.2	29.4	30.6	1.2
Neck	Body	22.4	23	23.6	24.2	24.8	25.4	0.6
	Block	23.4	24	24.6	25.2	25.8	26.4	0.6
Bicep	Body	14.2	14.8	15.4	16	16.6	17.2	0.6
	Block	18.2	19.8	19.4	20	20.6	21.2	0.6
Wrist		10.4	10.6	10.8	11	11.2	11.4	0.2

Children unisex

Age (years)		3	4	5	6	7	Increment
Height (cm)		98	104	110	116	122	6.0
Weight (kg)		16	17	19	21	23	2
Chest	Body	55	57	59	61	63	2.0
	Block	62	64	66	68	70	2.0
Waist	Body	52.6	53.8	55	56.2	57.4	1.2
	Block	58.6	59.8	61	62.2	64.4	1.2
Hips	Body	58.6	61	63.4	65.8	68.2	2.4
	Block	63.6	66	68.4	70.8	73.2	2.4
X back	Body	22.8	23.6	24.4	25.2	26	0.8
	Block	24.8	25.6	26.4	27.2	28	0.8
X chest		23	23.8	24.6	25.4	26.2	0.8
Scye depth	Body	11.2	12	12.8	13.6	14.4	0.8
	Block	13.2	14	14.8	15.6	16.4	0.8
Nape to waist		23	24.5	26	27.5	29	1.5
Shoulder		7.9	8.2	8.5	8.8	9.1	0.3
Sleeve length		32	34.5	37	39.5	42	2.5
Body rise		18	19	20	21	22	1.0
Thigh		31.5	33	34.5	36	37.5	1.5
Neck	Body	25	26	27	28	29	1.0
	Block	26	27	28	29	30	1.0
Bicep	Body	17.4	18	18.6	19.2	19.8	0.6
	Block	22.4	23	23.6	24.2	24.8	0.6
Wrist		11.5	11.8	12.1	12.4	12.7	0.3

CHILDREN'S GRADING AND SIZE CHARTS

Table 35—cont.

Girls

Age (years)		8	9	10	11	Increment
Height (cm)		128	134	140	146	6.0
Weight (kg)		25	29	33	37	4
Chest	Body	66.2	69.4	72.6	75.8	3.2
	Block	74.2	77.4	80.6	83.8	3.2
Waist	Body	59	60.6	62.2	63.8	1.6
	Block	64	65.6	67.2	68.8	1.6
Hips	Body	71.8	75.4	79	82.6	3.6
	Block	76.8	80.4	84	87.6	3.6
X back	Body	27	28	29	30	1.0
	Block	29	30	31	32	1.0
X chest		27	28	29	30	1.0
Scye depth	Body	15.2	16	16.8	17.6	0.8
	Block	17.7	18.5	19.3	20.1	0.8
Nape to waist		30.5	32	33.5	35	1.5
Shoulder		9.4	9.7	10	10.3	0.3
Sleeve length		44.5	47	49.5	52	2.5
Body rise		23	24	25	26	1.0
Thigh		39	40.5	42	43.5	1.5
Neck	Body	30	31	32	33	1.0
	Block	31	32	33	34	1.0
Bicep	Body	20	21	22	23	1.0
	Block	26	27	28	29	1.0
Wrist		13	13.3	13.6	13.9	0.3

Teenage girls

Age (years)		12	13	14	15	Increment
Height (cm)		150	154	158	162	4.0
Weight (kg)		43	47	50	52	4-2
Chest	Body	76.4	79.6	82.8	86	3.2
	Block	75.4	78.6	91.8	95	3.2
Waist	Body	64	65	66	67	1.0
	Block	68	69	70	71	1.0
Hips	Body	84.8	87.2	89.6	92	2.4
	Block	89.8	92.2	94.6	97	2.4
X back	Body	31	32	33	34	1.0
	Block	33	34	35	36	1.0
X chest		31	32	33	34	1.0
Scye depth	Body	18	18.4	18.8	19.2	0.4
	Block	21	21.4	21.8	22.2	0.4
Nape to waist		35.5	37	38.5	40	1.5
Shoulder		10.6	10.9	11.2	11.5	0.3
Sleeve length		53.5	55	56.5	58	1.5
Body rise		27	28	29	30	1.0
Thigh		46	49	52	55	3.0
Neck	Body	34	35	36	37	1.0
	Block	35	36	37	38	1.0
Bicep	Body	24	25	26	27	1.0
	Block	30	31	32	33	1.0
Wrist		14.4	14.8	15.2		0.4

Table 35—cont.

		Boys								
Age (years)		8	9	10	11	12	13	14	15	Increment
Height (cm)		128	134	140	146	152	158	164	170	6.0
Weight (kg)		24	29	34	39	44	49	54	59	5
Chest	Body	67	70.2	73.4	76.6	79.8	83	86.2	89.4	3.2
	Block	77	80.2	83.4	86.6	89.8	93	96.2	99.4	3.2
Waist	Body	61	63	65	67	69	71	73	75	2.0
	Block	65	67	69	71	73	75	77	79	2.0
Hips	Body	70	73.2	76.4	79.6	82.8	86	89.2	92.4	3.2
	Block	75	78.2	81.4	84.6	87.8	91	94.2	97.4	3.2
X back	Body	28	29.2	30.4	31.6	32.8	34	35.2	36.4	1.2
	Block	30	31.2	32.4	33.6	34.8	36	37.2	38.4	1.2
X chest		27.2	28.4	29.6	30.8	32	33.2	34.4	35.6	1.2
Scye depth	Body	16.6	17.4	18.2	19	19.8	20.6	21.4	22	0.8
	Block	19.6	20.4	21.2	22	22.8	23.6	24.4	25	0.8
Nape to waist		31	32.5	34	35.5	37	38.5	40	41.5	1.5
Shoulder		11	11.4	11.8	12.2	12.6	13	13.4	13.8	0.4
Sleeve length		45.5	48	50.5	53	55.5	58	60.5	63	2.5
Body rise		21	22	23	24	25	26	27	28	1.0
Thigh		38	40	42	44	46	48	50	52	2.0
Neck	Body	30	31.2	32.4	33.6	34.8	36	37.2	38.4	1.2
	Block	31	32.2	33.4	34.6	35.8	37	38.2	39.4	1.2
Bicep	Body	21	22	23	24	25	26	27	28	1.0
	Block	27	28	29	30	31	32	33	34	1.0
Wrist		13.5	14	14.5	15	15.5	16	16.5	17	0.5

CHILDREN'S GRADING AND SIZE CHARTS

Table 36 Composite size chart. 10.0 cm grade

		Infants unisex				
Age		3 months	6 months	12 months	2 years	Increment
Height (cm)		60	70	80	90	10.0
Weight (kg)		7	9	11	14	2-3
Chest	Body	43	46	49	52	3.0
	Block	51	52	57	60	3.0
Waist	Body	46	48	50	52	2.0
	Block	53	55	57	59	2.0
Hips	Body	46	49	52	55	3.0
	Block	54	57	60	63	3.0
X back	Body	19	20	21	22	1.0
	Block	20	21	22	23	1.0
X chest		19	20	21	22	1.0
Scye depth	Body	8	8.8	9.6	10.4	0.8
	Block	9.5	10.3	11.1	11.9	0.8
Nape to waist		17	18.8	20.6	22.4	1.8
Shoulder		6.2	6.7	7.2	7.7	0.5
Sleeve length		23	25.5	28	30.5	2.5
Body rise		11	13	15	17	2.0
Thigh		24	26	28	30	2.0
Neck	Body	22.5	23.3	24.1	24.9	0.8
	Block	23.5	24.3	25.1	25.9	0.8
Bicep	Body	14	15	16	17	1.0
	Block	18	19	20	21	1.0
Wrist		10.4	10.8	11.2	11.6	0.4

		Children unisex					
Age		2/3	4/5	5/7	8/9	10/11	Increment
Height (cm)		100	110	120	130	140	10.0
Weight (kg)		16	19	23	29	37	3-8
Chest	Body	55	60	65	70	75	5.0
	Block	63	68	73	78	83	5.0
Waist	Body	53	56	59	62	65	3.0
	Block	58	61	64	67	70	3.0
Hips	Body	58	64	70	76	82	6.0
	Block	63	69	75	81	87	6.0
X back	Body	23	24.6	26.2	27.8	29.4	1.6
	Block	24	25.6	27.2	28.8	30.4	1.6
X chest		23	24.6	26.2	27.8	29.4	1.6
Scye depth	Body	11	12.5	14	15.5	17	1.5
	Block	13	14.5	16	17.5	19	1.5
Nape to waist		23	25.5	28	30.5	33	2.5
Shoulder		8	8.6	9.4	10	10.6	0.6
Sleeve length		33	37.5	42	46.5	51	4.5
Body rise		18	19.5	21	22.5	24	1.5
Thigh		32	34.5	37	39.5	42	2.5
Neck	Body	26	27.6	29.2	30.8	32.4	1.6
	Block	27	28.6	30.2	31.8	33.4	1.6
Bicep	Body	17.5	18.7	19.9	21.1	22.3	1.2
	Block	22.5	23.7	24.9	26.1	27.3	1.2
Wrist		11.8	12.3	12.8	13.3	13.8	0.5

Table 36—cont.

		Boys				
Age		9/10	11/12	13/14	15/16	Increment
Height (cm)		140	150	160	170	10.0
Weight (kg)		34	44	54	64	10
Chest	Body	73	78	83	88	5.0
	Block	83	88	93	98	5.0
Waist	Body	65	69	73	77	4.0
	Block	69	73	77	81	4.0
Hips	Body	76	81	86	91	5.0
	Block	81	86	91	96	5.0
X back	Body	32	34	36	38	2.0
	Block	34	36	38	40	2.0
X chest		32	32	36	38	2.0
Scye depth	Body	17.5	19	20.5	22	1.5
	Block	20.5	22	23.5	25	1.5
Nape to waist		33	36	39	42	3.0
Shoulder		11	12	13	14	1.0
Sleeve length		47	52	57	62	5.0
Body rise		21	23.5	26	28.5	2.5
Thigh		42	45.5	49	52.5	3.5
Neck	Body	32	34	36	38	2.0
	Block	33	35	37	39	2.0
Bicep	Body	22.5	24.5	26.5	28.5	2.0
	Block	28.5	30.5	32.5	34.5	2.0
Wrist		14	15	16	17	1.0

		Girls			
Age		11/12	13/14	15/16	Increment
Height (cm)		150	160	170	10.0
Weight (kg)		43	50	58	7-8
Chest	Body	76	81	86	5.0
	Block	85	90	95	5.0
Waist	Body	64	66	68	2.0
	Block	67	69	71	2.0
Hips	Body	84	89	94	5.0
	Block	89	94	99	5.0
X back	Body	31.6	32.8	34	1.2
	Block	33.6	34.8	36	1.2
X chest		31.6	32.8	34	1.2
Scye depth	Body	17.5	18.3	19.1	0.8
	Block	20.5	21.3	22.1	0.8
Nape to waist		35	37	39	2.0
Shoulder		11	11.5	12	0.5
Sleeve length		53	56	59	3.0
Body rise		25	27	29	2.0
Thigh		44	49	54	5.0
Neck	Body	33	34.5	36	1.5
	Block	33	35.5	37	1.5
Bicep	Body	23	25	27	2.0
	Block	29	31	33	2.0
Wrist		14.5	15	15.5	0.5

CHILDREN'S GRADING AND SIZE CHARTS

Table 37 Head size chart

Age	Girls A	B	C	Circ.	Boys A	B	C	Circ.
1	19.5	16.7	13.7	47.4	20.9	17.2	14.2	48.9
2	20	16.9	13.8	48.0	21	17.4	14.3	49.5
3	20.5	17.1	13.9	48.6	21.5	17.6	14.4	50.1
4	21	17.3	14	49.2	22	17.8	14.5	50.7
5	21.5	17.5	14.1	49.8	22.5	18.0	14.6	51.3
6	22	17.7	14.2	50.4	23	18.2	14.7	51.9
7	22.5	17.9	14.3	51	23.5	18.4	14.8	52.5
8	23	18.1	14.4	51.6	24	18.6	14.9	53.1
9	23.5	18.3	14.5	52.2	24.5	18.8	15.0	53.7
10	24	18.5	14.6	52.8	25	19.0	15.1	55.3
11	24.5	18.7	14.7	53.4	25.5	19.2	15.2	55.9
12	25	18.9	14.8	54	26	19.4	15.3	56.5
13	25.5	19.1	14.9	54.6	26.5	19.6	15.4	57.1
14	26	19.3	15.0	55.2	27	19.8	15.4	57.8
15	26.5	19.5	15.0	56	27.5	20	15.4	57.8
Adult	27	19.7	15.0	57	28	20	15.5	59

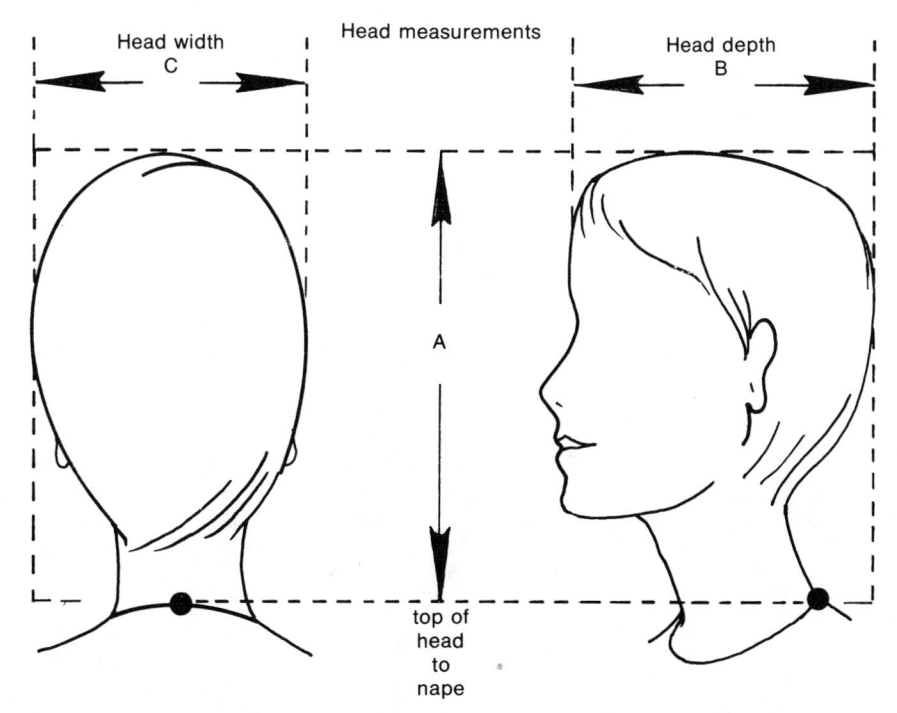

Figure 304 Illustrates the measurements needed to grade heads and other headwear

Index

abdominal seat diameter, 49, 55, 81-3
age, children's, 259
age factor, 12
A-line skirt, 186-9
alpha-numeric keyboard, 70-1
ankle, 53, 82, 242
area increments table, 18-19
armhole, 53, 67-9; see also scye
armpit, 54
asymmetrical drape, 180-1, 200-2

back bodice, 126
back pitch, 54
back scye, 54-5
back skirt grade (track), 130-1
back neck width, 56
balance, 26
base size, 60
batwing sleeves, 215-16
bicep, 52
bifurcated garments, 135; culottes, 229-30; grading, 81-3
bikini, 227-8
bitrochanteric width, 48
blade dart, 89
blouses: fitted, 153; semi-fitting, 149
blouson, 176-7
boat neck, 153
body contours, 58
body rise, 55, 82-3
body sections, 50-1, 61-5, 82
boy's grade, 276-7
brassieres, 53, 76-81
British Standards, 13, 21-5
bust, 17, 49
bust height relationship, 12-13
bust hip relationship, 11
bust point, 54, 57, 59, 98, 116-17
bust width, 54

calf, 53
cap sleeve, 217-18
capes, 135, 234-6
card preparation, 125-8, 130
cardinal points, 26, 65, 148
central processing unit (CPU), 71
checking, track grades, 132
chest, 51
chest classification, men's, 242
circle grading, 197-9
collars, 135, 139, 144, 163, 165-7; convertible, 168; sailor, 174-5
computer grading, 71-5
constant lines, 125-6
contour block, 81-3
cowl necklines, 178-9
crease line, 82-3
crotch, 82

crown, sleeve, 56
cuff, 147-8
culottes, 229-30
cup grade, 75-80
curvature of spine, 63-4

deep scye, 219-21
digitiser, 70
dirndl skirts, 184-5
disc drive, 71
disc memory, 74
dolman sleeve, 219-21
draft grade, 58, 87-97
draped styles, 135, 180-3, 200-2

elbow, 52
evaluation of style, 138
evening dress, draped, 182-3
evening top, strapless, 225-6

fabric characteristics, 58
facings, 143, 145, 150
fitted bodices, 135
fitted categories, 139
fitted sleeve grade, 129-30
french knickers, 236-7
front balance, 55
front bodice, 127-8; block grade, 191
front pitch, 54
front scye, 54
front skirt grade (track), 131-2
full circle skirt, 197-8

garment categories, 57; see also grade options
gathers, 163-9
girth and height grade, 18-22
girth only grade, 18-19
gored skirt, 189-90
gorge, 211
grade options, 58
grade plans, 29-47; see also style grades
grade specification, 138
grade techniques, 58
graphic display, 71
growth, children, 259
grown-on sleeves; batwing, 215-16; kimono, 212-14; magyar, 206-8; raglan, 209-11
gusset knickers, 236-7
gusset sleeve, 207-8

half circle skirt, 197-9
halter neck, 222-4
head size chart, 285
height, 13-24, 48; men, 242; children, 259
height only grade, 18; style grade, 172-3
hems, 14
hip, 49
hip sizes, 13

hip width, 55
hip yoke, 203-5

imperial measurements, 16, 18
increments options, 14
inner sleeve length, 55
input-output, 70-4
inside leg, 82; men's, 243
interactive graphic display, 71

jacket, double-breasted, 231-33; men's, 245; safari, 249; single-breasted, 246
kimono, 212-14
knee, 53
knickers, french, 236-7
Kunic, Philip, 241

lapel garment, men's, 245

magyar jacket, 133; with diamond gusset, 206-8
major girths, 27
market selection, 13
multi-tracks, 65-9, 117-19

nape measurements: to bust point, 54-5; to knee, 55; to waist, 55
neck, 52; men's 251
neckband, 215-16
neckline, 139, 144, 149-52, 155
neck width, 122
nested grading, 26, 58

off-line functions, 76
off-the-peg garments, 11
outer sleeve length, 56

patch pockets, 176
pattern design systems (PDS), 71-4
peg-top skirt, 191-3
pivot paper, 114-16
pleated skirts, 184-5
plotter, 71
pockets, 186-8
preparation for grading, 137
production pattern grading, 117
proportions, 163
puff sleeve, 153, 156

quarter circle, 197-9

raglan sleeve, 209-11; men's, 249-51
ready-made garments, 13
rib cage, 52

scye depth, 54, 122; width, 53-4
seams: style lines, 149-53, 155; allowances, grading with, 156-9
sectional girth increases, 60-4
shirt collar, men's, 251
shirt, men's, 251
shirtwaister, 168-71
shoulder angle, 56, 66-7
shoulder blade complex, 64
shoulder grading, 122
shoulder length, 53
side-body blouse, 149

silhouette, 136
simplified two-dimensional system, 124
size charts, 11-14, 16, 18-20
size indicator, 12
skirt block grade, 96-7
skirts: A-line, 186-8; circular, 197-9; circular from yoke, 203-5; dirndl, 184-5; gores, 189-90; peg-top, 191-3; tiered, 194-6
sleeve angles: kimono, 211; magyar, 204-6
sleeve crown, 56
sleeve grades: block, 91-3; fitted, 127-8
sleeveless box blouse, 158
sleeves, 136, 144, 148, 153; batwing, 215-16; cap, 217-18; dolman, 219-21; kimono, 212-14; magyar, 206-8; puff, 121; raglan, 209-11; shirt, 71; short, 176-7; two-piece, 231-3
source file, grading, 73
spiking-off, 61, 87-90, 113-14, 156
spine, 60-4
split diagrams, 28-46, 98
square neckline, 160
stack grade, 59
stacked grading, 26
stance, 60-4
stands, 60
static point, 27
statistically average figure, 13, 16-17
strapless evening top, 225-6
style decisions, 136
style evaluation, 149, 160, 176
style grades, 135-8
style grading, 136
suppression grading, 26
suppression seams, 136
survey book, 48
surveys, 11
systems printer, 71

terminology, 26
thigh, 53
three-dimensional draft grade, 26, 58
throat garment, 245
tiered skirt, 194-6
tolerances, 13
top hip, 51
track grade, 65-9, 124-33
tracks, 115-19, 124
trouser, men's, 243
truing a line, 114-16
two-dimensional grade draft, 27
two-piece collar, men's, 252; teenager's, 259
two-piece sleeve, women's, 231-3; men's, 246

underbust (rib cage), 52

waist, 50
waistband, 187-8
waistcoat, women's, 172-3; men's, 243
weight, 48; children's 259
wrist, 53

X-back, 53
X-chest, 53

yoke, 163, 168, 176

zero points, 29, 98-112